THE REAL METAPHYSICAL CLUB

SUNY Series in American Philosophy and Cultural Thought
RANDALL E. AUXIER AND JOHN R. SHOOK, EDITORS

THE REAL METAPHYSICAL CLUB

The Philosophers, their Debates,
and Selected Writings
from 1870 to 1885

Edited by Frank X. Ryan, Brian E. Butler, and James A. Good
with a Narrative History of the Metaphysical Club by John R. Shook

Map of the city of Cambridge, Mass., 1877. Map reproduction courtesy of the Norman B. Leventhal Map Center at the Boston Public Library.

Published by State University of New York Press, Albany

© 2019 State University of New York

For information, contact State University of New York Press, Albany, NY
www.sunypress.edu

Library of Congress Cataloging-in-Publication Data

Names: Ryan, Frank X., editor. | Butler, Brian E. (Professor), editor. | Good, James A. (James Allan), editor. | Shook, John R., writer of introduction.
Title: The real Metaphysical Club : the philosophers, their debates, and selected writings from 1870 to 1885 / edited by Frank X. Ryan, Brian E. Butler, and James A. Good ; with a narrative history of the Metaphysical Club by John R. Shook.
Description: Albany : State University of New York, [2019] | Series: SUNY series in American philosophy and cultural thought | Includes bibliographical references and index. Identifiers: LCCN 2018017083| ISBN 9781438473253 (hardcover) | ISBN 9781438473260 (e-book) | ISBN 9781438473246 (paperback)
Subjects: LCSH: Philosophy, American—19th century.
Classification: LCC B936 .R38 2019 | DDC 191—dc23 LC record available at https://lccn.loc.gov/2018017083

10 9 8 7 6 5 4 3 2 1

CONTENTS

Part Two: Law and Pragmatism

Part Three: Varieties of Idealism

A NOTE ON THE TEXTS

Typographical errors and obvious misspellings in the original texts have been corrected. Quotations in the texts from other writings have been checked and corrected where necessary. This publication retains alternative spellings and grammatical phrasings common from the time period of their first publication. A few adjustments of punctuation have been made to standardize the text for contemporary readability. Gratitude is extended to Houghton Library at Harvard University for its assistance with Chauncey Wright's Notes on Nihilism in the William James Papers.

A Narrative History of the Metaphysical Club

John R. Shook

IN THE SUMMER OF 1891, EARLY IN AUGUST TO BE SPECIFIC, THE TWO GREATEST MINDS of American education were cabin neighbors, camping on farmland owned by Thomas Davidson high in the Adirondack Mountains of eastern New York, and comparing views on the philosophical logic of G. W. F. Hegel. One of these men was the professor of philosophy of the University of Michigan, who could look across the rugged landscape to glimpse Lake Champlain, where his home town of Burlington lay only twenty-five miles to the northeast in Vermont. He was thirty-one years old, and his name was John Dewey. The other man was fifty-five years old, his name was William T. Harris, and he was the United States Commissioner of Education. Although Davidson and his Glenmore Summer School for the Culture Sciences was fondly remembered by attendees for its rustic accommodations nestled below the peak of Mt. Hurricane, this vacationing escape for professors and their audiences was no mere picnic. Seeds of America's intellectual future were being sown in fertile mental soil.

History remembers those two thinkers as educational giants, important philosophers, and discriminating scholars of German idealism. Devotees of American philosophy's heritage may note that Dewey and Harris had delivered lectures during June 1890 at Davidson's earlier summer school in Farmington, Connecticut. (That school had been a spinoff from the Concord School of Philosophy, founded by Amos Bronson Alcott and led by Harris and Davidson, which had closed in 1888.) William T. Harris and John Dewey also had this obscure fact in common: neither of them was a member of the Metaphysical Club.

The real Metaphysical Club was always small and fairly exclusive, and its members had intricate personal and professional relationships with each other. The time was the 1870s, and the locale was Cambridge, Massachusetts. Some academics can recall how pragmatism originated there.[1] However, historians have generally overlooked the involvement of more philosophers besides pragmatists, and other philosophical movements were initiated among Metaphysical Club members than just pragmatism. To comprehend what the Metaphysical Club really meant, one must understand the many relationships bonding its members and impelling them toward their distinctive philosophical achievements.

Their collaborative and competitive productivity made the Metaphysical Club real, as real as anything could be. Its existence was made all the more real as its influence spread far beyond the close-quarters of sitting rooms of one or another Cambridge resident. A web of entangled connections extending back decades into the past, and forward decades into the future, link otherwise coincidental events left inexplicable without the Metaphysical Club. That most curious web, the astounding proliferation of philosophy woven into America's fabric after the devastation of the Civil War, demands sufficient explanation. If the Metaphysical Club had gone unremarked without a lasting trace, it would be useful to postulate its existence.

Take the relationship between those two camping neighbors as an example. After Dewey graduated from the University of Vermont in 1879, he was teaching in a high school in Oil City, Pennsylvania, and contemplating how to enter an academic career. The only philosophy journal in America, the one he had avidly read in his college's library, was *The Journal of Speculative Philosophy*. He had written an article about "The Metaphysical Assumptions of Materialism" that gathered up idealistic arguments gleaned from its pages and the tutelage of his philosophy professor at Vermont, H. A. P. Torrey. The letter accompanying his submission to *The Journal of Speculative Philosophy* asked its editor, who was William T. Harris, for a sign of approval that Dewey should pursue philosophy further. Harris did accept that paper, and a second paper about Spinoza too, so Dewey applied to Johns Hopkins University in 1882, the only university in America offering a graduate program in philosophy at that time. He later confided to Harris that "in one sense you are the progenitor."[2] To have the good fortune, as Dewey did, of having two scholars of German idealism as mentors before reaching graduate school can also be taken as a sign of the tight circles enclosing intellectual life during those times, for his mentors were related to each other: William Torrey Harris's great-grandfather was H. A. P. Torrey's great-great-grandfather, Reverend Joseph Torrey of the Connecticut Torreys.

This brief narrative about Dewey does relate to the Metaphysical Club. It relates in a genealogical sense because Joseph Torrey's father-in-law, Reverend John Fiske, was descended from the Massachusetts Fiskes who were also the ancestors of one of the Metaphysical Club members, John Fiske. But there are also academic connections to recount. Harris founded the *Journal of Speculative Philosophy*, the first journal devoted to philosophy in the English-speaking world, in 1867, the year after he helped to inaugurate the St. Louis Philosophical Society. When some of its members came east in the mid-1870s, they naturally chose Cambridge and the Boston area for its hospitality to idealism, setting the stage for the second phase of the Metaphysical Club after the first stage had abruptly ended with the unexpected death of Chauncey Wright in 1875. William James warmly welcomed the arriving idealists, and he published his first formulations of pragmatism in 1878 in a *Journal of Speculative Philosophy* article titled "Remarks on Spencer's Definition of Mind as Correspondence." Harris himself arrived in 1881, invigorating the next philosophical society, the Hegel Club, as he was nearing the height of his prestige as the editor of America's philosophy journal. But that journal might never had existed at all save for a singular event that altered the course of America's intellectual life. Harris founded his journal in 1867 after his essay criticizing Herbert Spencer was rejected by the *North American Review*. Only one philosopher had been consulted, and that single evaluation, as negatively dismissive as a single paragraph could be, was rendered by Chauncey Wright.

We have only just begun to trace some of the innumerable strands weaving together the lives of our main characters, and many more are awaiting their introduction. Let us return to young John Dewey. At Johns Hopkins, he took philosophy courses with George Sylvester Morris and psychology courses with G. Stanley Hall. Hall had received his own PhD in psychology in 1878, as the first person to receive a graduate degree in psychology in America, from William James at Harvard University. Hall had found philosophy and then psychology as a career only after abandoning his theological studies at Union Theological Seminary in New York in order to go to Germany for advanced studies in philosophy, inspired by the prior example set by a fellow seminary student, who was none other than George S. Morris.[3] Hall attended some meetings of the Metaphysical Club, and the later Hegel Club as well, and his 1879 article describing "Philosophy in the United States" drew heavily upon his acquaintances with their members. Dewey was a member of a Metaphysical Club, the philosophy club at Johns Hopkins University, which was founded and led by his third professor, Charles Sanders Peirce. This namesake echo of the Cambridge Metaphysical Club was perhaps its most significant organizational spinoff, where Peirce, Dewey, and several other Johns Hopkins graduate students read promising papers on philosophy, psychology, and logic which became valuable publications. Like Dewey, Peirce and Hall had both published their early philosophical work in *The Journal of Speculative Philosophy*.

Although a philosopher could reach an audience of intellectual peers in a journal's pages, philosophers were few in number and there were fewer opportunities for direct interactions. In the 1860s and 1870s, a philosopher's dialogue partners were, of necessity, local residents with connections to the area. For the real Metaphysical Club, the locale was Cambridge, and the preeminent connection for everyone was Harvard University. This club was a nine-years-long episode within a much broader pattern of informal philosophical discussion, which had enlivened Cambridge and the Boston area from the 1840s to the 1880s.

Small clubs for convivial discussions of literary and intellectual matters were commonplace in Cambridge, going back to the previous generation of Ralph Waldo Emerson, Oliver Wendell Holmes Sr., and Henry James Sr. By the 1860s and 1870s, the elder transcendentalists had their Saturday Club dinners in Boston, while the next generation of freethinkers had their Radical Club (founded in 1867 and later called the Chestnut Street Club). What they all had in common was Harvard University. To graduate from Harvard or teach at Harvard meant a lifetime of opportunities to dine and discourse with alumni, if one resided anywhere in the vicinity. It was an opportunity for classmates to maintain social ties, pursue professional connections, and promote civic interests. Small gatherings were held in private homes after the dinner hour in Cambridge; larger gatherings could be scheduled as dinners at any of Boston's genteel restaurants. To have an upcoming "club" meeting on one's calendar might be a reminder about an evening at a friend's house, an afternoon to spend with admirers of literature, or a group dinner at one of Boston's eating establishments, such as Parker's Hotel or the Union Club.

Our narrative has, so far, mentioned philosophical organizations, among several, where professors of philosophy, their students, and intellectual enthusiasts could regularly gather:

St. Louis Philosophical Society (1866–mid-1880s)
The Radical Club, or Chestnut St. Club, in Boston (1867–1880)
The Metaphysical Club in Cambridge (1872–79)
The Metaphysical Club at Johns Hopkins University (1879–1885)
The Concord School of Philosophy (1879–1888)
The Hegel Club in Boston (1880–88)
Farmington Summer School for the Culture Sciences (1888–1890)
Berkeley Philosophical Union at the University of California (1889–1910s)
Glenmore Summer School for the Culture Sciences (1891–1900)

These organizations, large and small, played an indispensable role for the profession, since there was no other obvious opportunity for philosophical minds to gather. The first meetings of the Western Philosophical Association and the Eastern Philosophical Association were not inaugurated until 1900–01. During the nineteenth century, smaller groups at regional levels fulfilled that academic need. The hundreds of speakers and lecturers who offered their talks and their time to those organizations read like a "Who's Who" of American collegiate and literary life during that era.

Chauncey Wright, Harvard class of 1852, seems central to any important intellectual gathering around the Cambridge area. He was renowned in town for his social demeanor and amiable intelligence. He had been a central participant in intellectual groups, such as the "Septem" club consisting of college friends, and literary gatherings such as the Shakespeare club, since in the mid-1850s. Thanks largely to Wright, the core of the Metaphysical Club had known each other for more than a decade before its first official assembly. After Wright met Charles Peirce (Harvard 1859) in 1857, they struck up a philosophical comradeship that drew in John Fiske (Harvard 1863) and William James (Harvard MD 1869) during in the early 1860s, and James brought along Oliver Wendell Holmes Jr. (Harvard 1861). Their letters and reminiscences are sprinkled with references to encounters on the occasion of a philosophical lecture they attended, or evening visits to each other's homes for conversation, throughout the 1860s. Writing home from Brazil in 1865 while a member of the Agassiz expedition, James admits his homesickness: "Would I might hear Chauncey Wright philosophize for one evening, or see La Farge, or Perry, or Holmes."[4]

After 1866, their interactions deepened and accelerated. Holmes was a regular visitor at the James house, Wright and Fiske were frequent interlocutors, Wright was corresponding with a classmate of Peirce's, Frank Abbot (Harvard 1859), about space and time, and Peirce and Wright were debating over Mill and Kant on a practically daily basis.[5] While traveling in Europe, James wrote to Holmes in January 1868 to again confess his longing for deep conversation, and he proposed a plan of action:

> When I get home let's establish a philosophical society to have regular meetings and discuss none but the very tallest and broadest questions to be composed of none but the very topmost cream of Boston manhood. It will give each one a chance to air his own opinion in a grammatical form, and to sneer and chuckle when he goes home at what damned fools all the other members are—and may grow into something very important after a sufficient number of years.[6]

After James returned to Cambridge in November 1868, a dinner club was waiting for him, but no philosophical society was formed. Nevertheless, Peirce and James grew to appreciate each other's acumen as much as they both esteemed Wright's brilliance. In 1869, James remarked in a letter to Henry P. Bowditch, "I have just been quit by Chas. S. Peirce, with whom I have been talking about a couple of articles in the St. Louis 'Journal of Speculative Philosophy' by him, which I have just read. They are exceedingly bold, subtle and incomprehensible, and I can't say that his vocal elucidations helped me a great deal to their understanding, but they nevertheless interest me strangely."[7] Peirce's articles were "Questions Concerning Certain Faculties Claimed for Man" and "Some Consequences of Four Incapacities" from 1867, in which intuited and a priori certainties are overthrown by the inferential and fallible nature of all thinking and belief.

James also heard some of Peirce's 1869 Harvard lectures on British logicians, and despite James's episodes of depression during 1868–1871, the ongoing life of Harvard was a welcome distraction. Harvard's new president, Charles William Eliot, reoriented the university lectures in philosophy toward graduate-level instruction. Francis Bowen accordingly delivered the first graduate lectures given in America, on the subject of "Seventeenth-Century Philosophy," in the early fall of 1869. John Fiske also gave philosophy lectures during 1869–70, and Nicholas St. John Green (Harvard 1851) was an instructor lecturing on mental philosophy, metaphysics, and logic during 1869–70. In the Medical School, Bowditch opened a new physiology laboratory in 1871, where James spent much time. James also saw Harvard friends such as Holmes, Fiske, William Dean Howells, Thomas Sergeant Perry, and John Chipman Gray at a monthly dinner club that started in 1868 and met on occasion during the early 1870s.

Wright, like James, was suffering from depression, but worsened by alcoholism, during the late 1860s. His friends took action, surrounding him with social activities and securing a lecturing opportunity at Harvard. His lectures on psychology based on Alexander Bain during the fall of 1870 and spring of 1871 were visited by Peirce and James, and lawyer Joseph Bangs Warner (Harvard 1869). Wright and Green, who had known each other from their college days, reinvigorated their intellectual bonds in Harvard's halls, becoming the closest of friends by 1870. Peirce was in the company of Wright and Green then, where he heard Green expound his admiration for Alexander Bain's definition of belief as "that upon which a man is prepared to act." Peirce was also guiding Warner and Francis G. Peabody through Kant's *Critique of Pure Reason* during the winter of 1870–71, and during that time

Peirce was composing his review of Fraser's edition of *The Works of George Berkeley*, in which he declares, "A better rule for avoiding the deceits of language is this: Do things fulfil the same function practically? Then let them be signified by the same word. Do they not? Then let them be distinguished." In his 1908 article "A Neglected Argument for the Reality of God," Peirce recollects the significance of that insight: "In 1871, in a Metaphysical Club in Cambridge, Mass., I used to preach this principle as a sort of logical gospel, representing the unformulated method followed by Berkeley, and in conversation about it I called it 'Pragmatism.' "[8] Peirce was in Cambridge during March–October 1871, between Coast Survey assignments to Europe and Washington, D.C., so pragmatism's introduction to the world was likely to have taken place in 1871. Although Fiske was probably among their company during those months, James was not circulating socially in Cambridge that season, so neither he nor Holmes were present for Peirce's preaching, and the Metaphysical Club was not yet assembled for this birthing of pragmatism.

Everything required for the congealing of the real Metaphysical Club, both socially and intellectually, came together at the start of 1872. The original set of members were Chauncey Wright, Charles Sanders Peirce, William James, Oliver Wendell Holmes Jr., Nicholas St. John Green, John Fiske, and Joseph Bangs Warner. Francis Ellingwood Abbot joined them in 1873. Peirce identified all eight members in this detailed account in 1907:

> It was in the earliest seventies that a knot of us young men in Old Cambridge, calling ourselves, half-ironically, half-defiantly, "The Metaphysical Club,"—for agnosticism was then riding its high horse, and was frowning superbly upon all metaphysics— used to meet, sometimes in my study, sometimes in that of William James. It may be that some of our old-time confederates would today not care to have such wild-oats-sowings made public, though there was nothing but boiled oats, milk, and sugar in the mess. Mr. Justice Holmes, however, will not, I believe, take it ill that we are proud to remember his membership; nor will Joseph Warner, Esq. Nicholas St. John Green was one of the most interested fellows, a skillful lawyer and a learned one, a disciple of Jeremy Bentham. His extraordinary power of disrobing warm and breathing truth of the draperies of long worn formulas, was what attracted attention to him everywhere. In particular, he often urged the importance of applying Bain's definition of belief, as "that upon which a man is prepared to act." From this definition, pragmatism is scarce more than a corollary; so that I am disposed to think of him as the grandfather of pragmatism. Chauncey Wright, something of a philosophical celebrity in those days, was never absent from our meetings. I was about to call him our corypheus; but he will better be described as our boxing-master whom we—I particularly—used to face to be severely pummelled. He had abandoned a former attachment to Hamiltonianism to take up with the doctrines of Mill, to which and to its cognate agnosticism he was trying to weld the really incongruous ideas of Darwin. John Fiske and, more rarely, Francis Ellingwood Abbot, were sometimes present, lending their countenances to the spirit of our endeavours, while holding aloof from any assent to their success.[9]

That same list of eight members is indirectly confirmed by James, whose letters in 1876 mention Francis Abbot, Nicholas St. John Green, Oliver Wendell Holmes Jr., John Fiske, and Joseph Warner as participants in the second phase of the Metaphysical Club. Their biographical highlights at Harvard are as follows:

> Chauncey Wright (1830–1875, Harvard AB 1852). Lecturer in psychology (1870–71), Instructor of physics (1874–75)
>
> Charles Sanders Peirce (1839–1914, Harvard AB 1859, ScB 1863). Lecturer in logic of science (1865), Lecturer in philosophy (1869–71)
>
> William James (1842–1910, Harvard MD 1869). Instructor of anatomy and physiology (1872–76), Assistant Professor of physiology (1876–1880), Assistant Professor of philosophy (1880–85), Professor of psychology (1889–1897), Professor of philosophy (1885–89, 1897–1910)
>
> Oliver Wendell Holmes Jr. (1841–1935, Harvard AB 1861, LLB 1866). Lecturer in the Law School (1871–73), Overseer (1876–82)
>
> Nicholas St. John Green (1830–1876, Harvard 1851). Lecturer in political economy (1869–70), Lecturer in the Law School (1870–73)
>
> John Fiske (1842–1901, Harvard AB 1863, LLB 1865). Lecturer in history and philosophy (1869–71), Assistant Librarian (1872–1879), Overseer (1879–91, 1899–1901)
>
> Joseph Bangs Warner (1848–1923, Harvard AB 1869, LLB 1873). Instructor of history (1872–73), Lecturer in the Law School (1886–87)
>
> Francis Ellingwood Abbot (1836–1903, Harvard AB 1859, PhD 1881). Instructor of philosophy (1887–88)

It deserves to be said again that by 1872, the original members had known each other for around ten or fifteen years, or even longer. Wright and Green were classmates in preparatory school in the late 1840s, and then at Harvard. Wright and Peirce met in 1857 and often discussed philosophy during the 1860s. James met Peirce in 1861 at Harvard's Lawrence Scientific School, and he was introduced to Wright soon after. Fiske met Wright in 1862, and they remained very close friends. James met Holmes at Harvard in 1864 (their fathers were close friends), and they met Warner by 1868 while he was a student at Harvard Law School. Wright had begun an active correspondence with Abbot in 1864, and welcomed Abbot to the Metaphysical Club upon his relocation to Cambridge in 1873. There is ample evidence in their correspondence, journals, and later reminiscences to illustrate their fondness for visiting each other's homes for literary and philosophical conversations. By the time that the Metaphysical Club in Cambridge had received its baptism, all of its members could look back on many years of discussion and debate together.

They were also aware of the leading lights involved with London's Metaphysical Club, which was founded in 1869 and lasted until 1880. Papers from its meetings were published in a serial review available in Boston, and Peirce had been in London in 1870 and again in 1871 to hear of its fame. An experiment in intellectual debate as audacious as any, this Metaphysical Club brought together leading scientific, philosophical, and theological minds of England to forge an alliance against unbelief. James Martineau was among its founders; in November 1869 he recounted the basis for that alliance.

> A project, suggested I believe by Mr. Tennyson, has been started here, of a Metaphysical Society for the thorough discussion of the ultimate grounds of intellectual, moral, and religious belief. The scheme originated in a desire to bring together from different sides the scattered representatives of a theistical philosophy, and present a strong front of resistance to the advance of Positivism and the dogmatic Materialism of the newer science. On being asked to join, I urged the absolute reciprocity of inviting the heads of the negative party into the Society from the very first, and making the Society unreservedly one of philosophical search, for patient and impartial comparison of ideas among differing equals. This principle has been adopted, and Mill, Bain, and Tyndall have been asked to join—with what result I have not yet heard.[10]

Science was indeed well represented, and papers by Alexander Bain, Thomas Huxley, and W. K. Clifford about science, morality, and religion were closely read back in Cambridge. In January 1872, Peirce returned from Washington to find James equally eager to collect the full complement of Harvard intellectuals into a single club. The name of their own club was easily settled.

The month of the Metaphysical Club's founding can be determined: January 1872. Peirce's later recollections sent his mind back to the club's start after his return from travels—he returned to Cambridge from a European trip in March 1871, and returned to Cambridge after a residency in Washington, D.C., in January 1872. An inauguration for the club in 1871 is improbable because James was still recovering from health breakdowns, he spent the summer in Maine, and his letters from that year only mention personal visits from individuals, such as Holmes. By mid-January 1872, James was telling his brother about the newly founded metaphysical club. Henry James reports to a friend on January 24, 1872, how his brother William "has just helped to found a metaphysical club, in Cambridge (consisting of Chauncey Wright, C. Pierce etc.)."[11] Henry's letter to Charles Norton on February 4, 1872, relates this news: "He [Holmes], my brother, and various other long-headed youths have combined to form a metaphysical club, where they wrangle grimly and stick to the question. It gives me a headache merely to know of it."[12] Peirce can help confirm this year of 1872. He gave the late 1860s, 1871, and 1872 as dates for the club's founding in some scattered reminiscences after 1900. But his most specific memory was about "a paper I read—it must have been in 1872—to a group of young men who used, at that time, to meet once a fortnight in Cambridge, Mass., under the name of 'The Metaphysical Club' "[13]

The other member besides Peirce on record labelling this club as the Metaphysical Club was James. The evidence was published in Perry's *Thought and Character of William James* in 1935. James's letter on February 10, 1876, informs his brother Robertson that "we have reorganized a metaphysical club here, and contains some very acute heads."[14] Not only does James speak of an active metaphysical club in 1876, but he clearly understood its predecessor as the "metaphysical club" as well. One of James's invitation letters, to Frank Abbot on January 23, 1876, shows how much continuity this reorganized club possessed: "You are invited to join a Club for reading and discussing philosophical authors, which meets once a week at present and is composed of C. C. Everett, N. St. John Green, O. W. Holmes, Jr., John Fiske, Thos. Davidson. J. B. Warner, Prof. Bowen, and one or two others."[15] This second phase did not disperse until 1879, so the entire duration of the real Metaphysical Club is 1872 to 1879. This club therefore had two phases, distinguished by the most active participants and the main topics pursued: empiricism and pragmatism (1872–75), followed by idealism (1876–79). Six members were able to attend meetings of both phases of the Metaphysical Club: William James, Francis Abbot, Nicholas St. John Green, Oliver Wendell Holmes Jr., John Fiske, and Joseph Warner. Two members of the first "pragmatist" phase were absent for the second "idealist" phase: Chauncey Wright had died in September 1875; and Peirce was in Europe until September 1876, stayed in Cambridge for a few weeks, and moved to New York City in October 1876.

The "pragmatist" Metaphysical Club was intended to meet twice a month, but it was able to meet only on irregular occasions, even during its most active periods. They usually met in the home of Peirce or James in Cambridge during the spring of 1872. Peirce departed for Washington, D.C., in April, but club members continued to see each other. In late May, James mentions a visit from Wright,[16] and then Wright left for a European trip in July 1872. The entire club was briefly reunited in November 1872, when Wright returned and Peirce was also in Cambridge. James wrote to his brother Henry on November 24, 1872: "He [Peirce] read us an admirable introductory chapter to his book on logic the other day."[17]

What paper did Peirce deliver to the Metaphysical Club in November 1872? Peirce was working on drafts of chapters for a book on logic during 1871 and 1872, and he knew that he was due to return to Washington in December 1872 for an extended residency. Years later, Peirce offered this reminiscence: "Our metaphysical proceedings had all been in winged words (and swift ones, at that, for the most part) until at length, lest the club should be dissolved, without leaving any material souvenir behind, I drew up a little paper expressing some of the opinions that I had been urging all along under the name of pragmatism. This paper was received with such unlooked-for kindness, that I was encouraged, some half dozen years later, on the invitation of the great publisher, Mr. W. H. Appleton, to insert it, somewhat expanded, in the *Popular Science Monthly* for November, 1877 and January, 1878."[18] In another recollection, Peirce says that central portions of "The Fixation of Belief" and "How to Make Our Ideas Clear" were in a paper read to the Metaphysical Club in 1872.[19]

Material in hand from Peirce's logic manuscript served his purpose of outlining pragmatism for the club. Many of the chapter drafts from mid-1872 were preserved, and the first three were titled "Of the Difference between Doubt & Belief," "Of Inquiry," and "Four Methods of Settling Opinions," dated to May and June 1872 while Peirce was in Washington.[20] In these drafts Peirce states: "Our beliefs guide our desires and shape our actions"; "Doubt is an uneasy and dissatisfied state from which we struggle to free ourselves and pass into the state of belief"; and "It is certainly best for us that our beliefs should be such as may truly guide our actions so as to satisfy our desires."[21] Peirce defines scientific method: "There are real things, whose characters are entirely independent of our opinions about them; those realities affect our senses, according to regular laws, and though our sensations are as different as our relations to the objects, yet by taking advantage of the laws which subsist we can ascertain by reasoning how the things really are, and any man if he have sufficient experience and reason enough about it, will be led to the one true conclusion."[22] The principal tenets of Peirce's pragmatism in "The Fixation of Belief" (1878) are heard here, but the "pragmatic maxim" presented in "How to Make Our Ideas Clear" (1878) nowhere appears in those 1872 drafts. That maxim is:

> Consider what effects, which might conceivably have practical bearings, we conceive the object of our conception to have. Then, our conception of these effects is the whole of our conception of the object.[23]

However, by 1871 Peirce had already formulated his criterion for the meaning of a word, specifying that the function of the word distinguishes its meaning. We have James's corroboration in "Philosophical Conceptions and Practical Results" (1898) that the core ideas of pragmatism were discussed among Metaphysical Club members:

> Years ago this direction was given to me by an American philosopher whose home is in the East, and whose published works, few as they are and scattered in periodicals, are no fit expression of his powers. I refer to Mr. Charles S. Peirce, with whose very existence as a philosopher I dare say many of you are unacquainted. He is one of the most original of contemporary thinkers; and the principle of practicalism or pragmatism, as he called it, when I first heard him enunciate it at Cambridge in the early '70's is the clue or compass by following which I find myself more and more confirmed in believing we may keep our feet upon the proper trail. Peirce's principle, as we may call it, may be expressed in a variety of ways, all of them very simple. . . . Beliefs, in short, are really rules for action; and the whole function of thinking is but one step in the production of habits of action. If there were any part of a thought that made no difference in the thought's practical consequences, then that part would be no proper element of the thought's significance. Thus the same thought may be clad in different words; but if the different words suggest no different conduct, they are mere outer accretions, and have no part in the thought's meaning.[24]

Although no member's writings during the early 1870s use the word *pragmatism,* the term and what it stood for was thoroughly discussed among the Metaphysical Club's members back then, with both Peirce and James affirming that pragmatism labeled Peirce's theory about the psychological function and empirical confirmation of belief. Pragmatism had a birth, and the birthplace was Cambridge, Massachusetts, during 1871–72.

Other members of the Metaphysical Club published important writings during its formative years, about scientific, legal, or psychological topics for group discussion that related to pragmatism. Among the philosophers, Wright published his influential defense of Darwin's *The Origin of Species* in 1872, and his 1873 essay "The Evolution of Self-Consciousness" reached a climactic midway point by claiming that phenomena are not initially experienced as external objects in the world nor as internal sensations for self-consciousness, which is a thesis anticipating James's radical empiricism by decades. As for James, his review of *The Unseen Universe* in 1875 urges a practical justification for religious faith that he would later elaborate as the "will to believe."

The lawyers in this club—Holmes, Green, and Warner—were deeply interested in evolution and empiricism, and they knew James Stephen's *A General View of the Criminal Law in England*, which averred that people believe because they must act. During the 1870s, Green and Holmes dealt with difficulties to determining responsibility, culpability, and criminal states of mind, along with broader issues about the nature of law from a culturally developmental perspective. Both lawyers made important advances in the theory of negligence, which relied on a pragmatic approach to belief, and they formulated important justifications for the "reasonable person" standard in juridical deliberations. Green had published "Proximate and Remote Cause" in 1870, followed by "Insanity in Criminal Law" in 1871, in the *American Law Review*. Holmes's early articles for that law review during 1872–73 explore pragmatic definitions of law that work out his "prediction theory" prioritizing future judicial consequences rather than past legislative acts. Holmes had few remembrances of the Metaphysical Club to share. He later recalled that "in those days I was studying law and I soon dropped out of the band, although I should have liked to rejoin it when it was too late. I think I learned more from Chauncey Wright and St. John Green, as I saw Peirce very little."[25]

The reason that Holmes saw little of Peirce is due to Coast Survey responsibilities keeping Peirce away from Cambridge after 1872. The entire Metaphysical Club met only irregularly after the year of its founding. As its core consisted of Wright, Peirce, and James, then there were only seven months during 1872–75 in which all three were simultaneously residing in Cambridge: January–June 1872, and November 1872. Peirce later stated that Wright was present for all meetings; Wright traveled in Europe from July 1872 to early November 1872. In December 1872, Peirce relocated to Washington, D.C., and took charge of U.S. Coast Survey pendulum research and related projects, which kept him on the move across several Eastern states and some European countries for scientific experiments and conferences over the next few years.

Peirce did visit Cambridge on occasion during 1873 and 1874, and two Metaphysical Club meetings are confirmable during those years. Because Peirce later recalled Abbot's attendance at only a single meeting, and Abbot moved to Cambridge in April 1873, then Peirce remembered a Metaphysical Club meeting in either 1873 or 1874. James was in Europe from October 1873 to March 1874, and Peirce was then occupied in Washington, so presumably no meetings were held during that period. The other confirmable meeting was in the fall of 1874, as James recalled an evening with Peirce and Wright (but not Abbot) to discuss Fiske's new book *Outlines of Cosmic Philosophy*. There may have been meetings during the winter months of 1874–75. By spring 1875, their career demands, travels, and a death had dispersed them. Holmes was busy with his new law partnership. Peirce went to Europe in April. James taught Harvard courses in the spring and took his usual summer holiday in the Adirondacks. And then Wright died on September 12.

The Metaphysical Club needed new life, literally. That vitality soon arrived from St. Louis. Our narrative must return to 1866, the year when William Torrey Harris, at the prodding of fellow "Kant Club" member Henry C. Brokmeyer, closely studied Hegel's "larger" *Logic* and composed his article about Hegel that so disappointed Wright. Harris brought Ralph Waldo Emerson and Amos Bronson Alcott to meet the St. Louis philosophers that year, and the group made a favorable impression on the two transcendentalists. At Emerson's suggestion, Thomas Davidson, who was enjoying the intellectual company of the Radical Club in Boston, moved to St. Louis in 1868 for a teaching job arranged by Harris. His Aristotelian individualism was a marked contrast to St. Louis Hegelianism, and he promptly started an Aristotle society. But better academic opportunities were still back east, as George Holmes Howison showed by departing from St. Louis and then becoming Massachusetts Institute of Technology's philosophy professor in 1872.

After Emerson's literary executor, James Elliot Cabot, joined Harvard's board of overseers in 1874 and recruited Howison as an overseer in 1875, they next plotted an idealist transformation of Harvard by trying to secure a philosophy position for Howison and then adding Davidson. Davidson duly arrived in Cambridge in the fall of 1875 in the hopes of joining the Greek faculty. Although both newcomers gave public lectures at Boston's Lowell Institute, their hopes for joining Harvard were disappointed. Davidson's scathing criticisms of Greek instruction at Harvard, published in 1877 in *The Atlantic Monthly*, turned the Harvard community against him. As for Howison, President Charles William Eliot permitted him to lecture on ethics at the Divinity School, but not the philosophy department. Eliot instead decided to appoint James to teach psychology in 1876 and philosophy as well by 1878.

Davidson's only connection to Harvard was to be through the Metaphysical Club. Although Davidson promptly got reacquainted with the Radical Club, he was soon writing to Harris in September 1875 that an Aristotle society was what Cambridge needed. Cabot helpfully suggested a broader theme, empiricism versus idealism, and pointed out how several local philosophers were already accustomed to vigorous debate. T. H. Green's edition of Hume's *Treatise of Human Nature* had recently been published, complete with Green's lengthy Introduction offering a refutation of Hume using Kantian and Hegelian arguments. Having heard Cabot's high praise of Davidson, James assented to their plan to discuss Hume and Green, and brought along the available members of the Metaphysical Club. If they held any meetings in December 1875, that has gone unrecorded; the earliest information about a full meeting is in Davidson's letter to Harris on January 17, 1876:

Last night our new philosophical society, to which I have given shape and direction at least, met at Mr. James's—present Bowen, C. C. Everett, Dr. James, Messrs. Green, Warner, Holmes (Wendell jun'.), Fenollosa, and myself; absent John Fiske, whose children were ill. We are reading Hume on Human Nature, and, I doubt not, we shall have a most interesting time.[26]

Abbot was added next; he, Cabot, and Howison were present at the meeting at James's house on January 30. In one of James's later recollections, his philosophy colleague George Herbert Palmer appears amid the others. James's new psychology graduate student G. Stanley Hall also attended some meetings. Joining original members, the new members and their relevant activities were:

Thomas Davidson (1840–1900). Lecturer at Concord School of Philosophy (1879, 1884–87), Leader of Farmington Summer School for the Culture Sciences (1888–90), Leader of Glenmore Summer School for the Culture Sciences (1891–1900).

James Eliot Cabot (1821–1903, Harvard AB 1840, LLB 1845). Lecturer in philosophy (1869–71), Lecturer in logic (1874–75), Overseer (1874–1883).

Charles Carroll Everett (1829–1900, Harvard STB 1859). Bussey Professor of theology (1869–1878), Dean of Harvard Divinity School (1878–1900).

George Holmes Howison (1834–1916). Professor of logic and philosophy of science at Massachusetts Institute of Technology (1871–79), Lecturer in the Harvard Divinity School (1879–80), Overseer (1875–1880).

Ernest Francisco Fenollosa (1853–1908, Harvard AB 1874). Professor of philosophy and political economy (1878–80) and Professor of philosophy and logic (1880–86) at Tokyo University.

Francis Bowen (1811–1890, Harvard AB 1833). Instructor in natural, intellectual, and moral philosophy (1836–39), Alford Professor of natural religion, moral philosophy, and civil polity (1853–1889).

George Herbert Palmer (1842–1933, Harvard AB 1864). Instructor in philosophy (1872–73), Assistant Professor of philosophy (1873–1883), Professor of philosophy (1883–89), Alford Professor of philosophy (1889–1913).

Granville Stanley Hall (1846–1924, Harvard PhD 1878). Instructor in English (1876–77), Lecturer in philosophy (1880–83). Lecturer in psychology (1881–83) and Professor of philosophy and pedagogy at Johns Hopkins University (1884–88).

Bowen attended one or two meetings in February 1876, but to the others' apparent relief, he made no further appearance. Another arrival in Boston quickly found his way into the club: Borden Parker Bowne (1847–1910), who had become Boston University's professor of philosophy in 1877.

The members of the club's first phase were not unfamiliar to the new members. Everyone knew James, but Fiske among all of them was the most prominent philosopher at that time. He had precociously defended his "Cosmic Theism" in his 1874 book *Outlines of Cosmic Philosophy*, identifying the unknowable supreme power behind the observable world, an ultimate acknowledged by Herbert Spencer, with a purposive yet impersonal God. Everett, who was combining Hegelian views with insights from East Asian philosophy, responded to Spencer and Fiske with review articles titled "The Known and the Unknowable in Religion" in 1875 and "Cosmic Philosophy" in 1876. For Everett, the immanent teleology and love of God could not be unknowable, even if our own souls are largely a mystery even to ourselves. Fiske accused Hegel of pantheism, but Everett had a more nuanced interpretation of Hegel on the relationality of spirit. Although Fiske and Everett disagreed about humanity's capacity to comprehend the underlying Power responsible for nature's ways, they agreed that life evolves toward higher forms, anthropomorphic religion is just myth, and that pantheism must be rejected. Bowne also composed a lengthy response to Fiske's book in a review article titled "The Cosmic Philosophy" in 1876. He similarly rejected the "unknowable" as scientifically useless and philosophically empty, and added his view that a primal energetic ordering, rather than chaos or mechanism, is a better explanatory postulate for the universe's basis. For Bowne, that fundamental ordering is God's intelligent activity responsible for all phenomenal processes, which our minds in turn process into knowledge.

Nicholas St. John Green died on September 8, 1876, but another voice for the empiricist side soon arrived. G. Stanley Hall came to Cambridge from Antioch College as an instructor in English in the fall of 1876, and he took this opportunity to study physiology and psychology under Bowditch and James. His graduate thesis on "The Muscular Perception of Space," for which he received the first American PhD degree in psychology in June 1878, offered a resolution to a key question dividing empiricists and idealists: Must the rational mind supply the relations permitting one's experience of an external world extended in space? Since our perceptions of phenomena are fused with our feelings of movement, Hall reasoned, and feelings of our own motions are intrinsically extended, therefore a person's immediate sensations are already spatial before higher mental operations are engaged. Hall attended some meetings of the Metaphysical Club during the spring and fall semesters of 1877. Cabot's idealist stance is presented in his article "Considerations on the Notion of Space" in *The Journal of Speculative Philosophy* in 1878. James responded to Cabot in "The Spatial Quale" in that journal in January 1879, with Cabot's rejoinder, "The Spatial Quale: An Answer," appearing in the April issue.

James's memories of that time largely revolved around his other friend and ally, Thomas Davidson:

> At that time I saw most of him at a little philosophical club which used to meet (often at his rooms in Temple Street) every fortnight. . . . Davidson used to crack the whip of Aristotle over us; and I remember that whatever topic was formally appointed for the day, we almost invariably wound up with a quarrel about space perception.[27]

After receiving his doctorate, Hall departed for additional study in Europe, and James was again heavily outnumbered by the idealists of the Metaphysical Club. While in Germany,

Hall fulfilled a request from the editors of *Mind* in England (James had recommended him) to compose an account of "Philosophy in the United States" for publication in 1879. This account included lengthy passages about members of the Metaphysical Club and the St. Louis Hegelian movement.

James was then teaching psychology as a physiology professor. His scheme to situate psychology with the philosophy department had to begin with his accumulation of publications in philosophy. By the end of 1877 he completed his "Remarks on Spencer's Definition of Mind as Correspondence" for publication in *The Journal of Speculative Philosophy* in 1878. He followed that piece with two papers in *Mind* in 1879. "Are We Automata?" posed the question in order to deliver the negative answer, and "The Sentiment of Rationality" developed a recognizably pragmatist approach to the human mind. James was also flirting with the new graduate university in Baltimore, Johns Hopkins University, by agreeing to deliver lectures there while President Daniel Coit Gilman was delaying a decision about appointing a full-time professor of philosophy. James lectured on "The Senses and the Brain and their Relation to Thought" during February 1878, with graduate student Josiah Royce in attendance. Before James arrived, the first graduate course offered in philosophy there, indeed the very first graduate course in philosophy leading to a doctorate in philosophy given anywhere in America, was the Spring 1877 course on Schopenhauer, taught by Royce.[28] George Morris began lecturing at Johns Hopkins in January 1878, Peirce arrived to teach logic in late 1879, and Hall began lecturing in psychology in 1882, when he met John Dewey among his students. Back at Harvard, President Eliot was unwilling to lose James, so his position in the philosophy department became permanent in 1878, and James became influential enough to recommend the next philosophy hire, the appointment of Royce in 1882.

During the academic year of 1877–78, Howison was busy with invited lectures and Davidson went to Italy, but the club's monthly meetings carried on, revolving around Kant and idealism and fixated on refuting sensationalism and materialistic agnosticism. In a September 1878 letter to William T. Harris about *The Journal of Speculative Philosophy*, James listed the Boston-area thinkers of his closest acquaintance:

> I fancy you could get more original contributions, if the journal aimed at a more modern cachet. There are five or six people here who I should think would send you then at least an article a year—Howison, Everett (C.C.) Cabot, Bowne, possibly Bowen, a man named Dunbar, Fennollosa, Hall, and perchance others. Many of these are non-hegelian however, and I am not sure whether you wd. consider so much infidel matter to be again.[29]

Quoting more from James's later reminiscence of Davidson, a similar list had come to his mind:

> At that time I saw most of him at a little philosophical club which used to meet (often at his rooms in Temple Street) every fortnight. Other members were W. T.

Harris, G. H. Howison, J. E. Cabot, C. C. Everett, B. P. Bowne, and sometimes G. H. Palmer.[30]

Regarding the second list, James was mistaken about Harris, who did not reside in the Boston area until 1881, and James understandably failed to mention Frederic Henry Hedge, then Harvard's professor of German, who was attending occasional meetings by then. On the first list, the man "Dunbar" that James mentioned to Harris was Josiah Newell Dunbar, a recent graduate of Harvard Divinity School, who was teaching at a preparatory school near Boston. In such recollections, Peirce is never mentioned as a visitor to the club's meetings, although he was invited to speak in the Boston area on occasion. For example, Peirce read a paper on "The Relations of Logic to Philosophy" to students in the new Harvard Philosophical Club on May 21, 1879.

The confluence of James, Davidson, Alcott, Howison, and Bowne in the Boston area during 1875–1885 engendered the second and third seminal developments in American thought sponsored by the Metaphysical Club, both of them on the side of pluralism over monism: process philosophy and personalism.[31] James strongly encouraged these developments. One of Davidson's talks made a great impression on James, from a paper titled "Individuality," of which only an abstract survives. Davidson gave this talk at the Radical Club on October 21, 1878, and then again to the Metaphysical Club's meeting at Howison's house soon after. Thereafter, meetings were held at Davidson's new residence in Boston on Temple Street, and scheduled for twice a month by 1879. It was a surprise to everyone, perhaps even to the combatants, that Davidson and Howison erupted into an angry dispute over Aristotle at the meeting on April 26, 1879. James tried to patch things up, but no more meetings appear to have happened after that, and later letters from James to Hall and Royce sadly confess that the club had expired.[32]

The philosophical energy easily passed on to nourish other idealist projects. In the summer of 1879 three St. Louis Hegelians made their way to Concord. Harris, Samuel Emery, and Edward McClure participated in Alcott's first Concord School of Philosophy during July and August. Harris had to go back to St. Louis, but Emery and McClure entered Harvard Law School. Having brought a manuscript of Hegel's larger *Logic*, they soon started a club for studying Hegel and joined George Herbert Palmer's philosophy course on Hegel in 1880. Harris took over as this club's leader at the start of 1882 after moving permanently to Concord.

Although the Metaphysical Club ended in 1879, its philosophical debates lived on. How is knowledge of the world possible? Should biological facts or transcendental principles reconcile humanity with nature? Is ultimately reality a unified whole, or a system of individuals? Could science be compatible with religion?

Several Metaphysical Club members published their fuller answers after the club's demise. Bowne's revolutionary achievement in *Metaphysics* (1882) renounced substance for process, denounced pantheism, and pointed the way toward personalism. Abbott's *Scientific Theism* (1885) defended a type of pantheism while affirming that God is personal. (Peirce reviewed this book in 1886 in *The Nation*.) Howison and Harris read papers for a symposium on science and pantheism held at the 1885 Concord School of Philosophy. Howison's paper appeared in *The Journal of Speculative Philosophy*, asking "Is Modern Science Pantheistic?" He denied that science could support any cosmic worldview, whether supernatural, pantheist, or atheist. Harris published his paper "Is Modern Science Pantheistic?" in the same issue to counterargue that both the scientific intellect and the scientific worldview presumes an absolute universal intelligence.

As the 1880s passed into the 1890s and then the 1900s, Peirce was only seen in Cambridge when James could arrange some lecturing opportunities, but James ensured that his old friend's philosophy would be visible to the world. James's "Philosophical Conceptions and Practical Results" of 1898, presented at Howison's spinoff club the Philosophical Union at the University of California, credited Peirce with pragmatism's birth and the Metaphysical Club for supplying its cradle. The second chapter of James's book *Pragmatism* from 1907 again credits Peirce for pragmatism's reality—past, present, and future:

> A glance at the history of the idea will show you still better what pragmatism means. The term is derived from the same Greek word πράγμα, meaning action, from which our words "practice" and "practical" come. It was first introduced into philosophy by Mr. Charles Peirce in 1878. In an article entitled "How to Make Our Ideas Clear," in the *Popular Science Monthly* for January of that year Mr. Peirce, after pointing out that our beliefs are really rules for action, said that to develop a thought's meaning, we need only determine what conduct it is fitted to produce: that conduct is for us its sole significance. And the tangible fact at the root of all our thought-distinctions, however subtle, is that there is no one of them so fine as to consist in anything but a possible difference of practice. To attain perfect clearness in our thoughts of an object, then, we need only consider what conceivable effects of a practical kind the object may involve—what sensations we are to expect from it, and what reactions we must prepare. Our conception of these effects, whether immediate or remote, is then for us the whole of our conception of the object, so far as that conception has positive significance at all.
>
> This is the principle of Peirce, the principle of pragmatism. It lay entirely unnoticed by anyone for twenty years, until I, in an address before Professor Howison's philosophical union at the university of California, brought it forward again and made a special application of it to religion. By that date (1898) the times seemed ripe for its reception. The word "pragmatism" spread, and at present it fairly spots the pages of the philosophic journals. On all hands we find the "pragmatic movement" spoken of, sometimes with respect, sometimes with contumely, seldom with clear understanding. It is evident that the term applies itself conveniently to a number of tendencies that hitherto have lacked a collective name, and that it has "come to stay."[33]

James's concluding prophecy, that pragmatism's place in philosophy is permanent, can practically convey the meaning of the Metaphysical Club's reality.

NOTES

1. Louis Menand, *The Metaphysical Club: A Story of Ideas in America* (New York: Farrar, Straus and Giroux, 2001), ch. 9.

2. Jay Martin, *The Education of John Dewey: A Biography* (New York: Columbia University Press, 2002), 53.

3. Steven Rockefeller, *John Dewey: Religious Faith and Democratic Humanism* (New York: Columbia University Press, 1991), 17.

4. Ralph Barton Perry, *The Thought and Character of William James* (Boston: Little, Brown, 1935), vol. 1, 221.

5. Philip P. Wiener, *Evolution and the Founders of Pragmatism* (Cambridge: Harvard University Press, 1949), 43.

6. Perry, *The Thought and Character of William James*, vol.1, 508.

7. William James, *The Correspondence of William James, Volume 4: 1856–1877*, ed. Ignas K. Skrupskelis, Elizabeth M. Berkeley et al. (Charlottesville: University Press of Virginia, 1995), 363.

8. *Collected Papers of Charles S. Peirce*, ed. Charles Hartshorne, Paul Weiss, and Arthur Burks (Cambridge: Harvard University Press, 1931–1958), vol. 6, 882.

9. Ibid., vol. 5, 12.

10. Abraham Willard Jackson, *James Martineau: A Biography and Study* (Boston: Little, Brown, 1900), 98.

11. Henry James, *Henry James: Selected Letters*, ed. Leon Edel (Cambridge: Harvard University Press, 1987), vol. 1, 269.

12. Ibid., 273.

13. Peirce, *Collected Papers*, vol. 7, 313, note.

14. Perry, *The Thought and Character of William James*, vol. 1, 713.

15. James, *Correspondence*, vol. 4, 531.

16. Ibid., 422.

17. Ibid., vol. 1, 177.

18. Peirce, *Collected Papers*, vol. 5, 13.

19. Ibid., vol. 7, 313, note.

20. *Writings of Charles Sanders Peirce, Volume 3, 1872–1878*, ed. Max Fisch et al. (Bloomington: Indiana University Press, 1986), 22–23.

21. Ibid.

22. Ibid., 27.

23. Peirce, *Collected Papers*, vol. 5, 402.

24. William James, "Philosophical Conceptions and Practical Results," *University Chronicle* 1 (September 1898): 290.

25. Max H. Fisch, *Peirce, Semeiotic, and Pragmatism*, ed Kenneth L. Ketner and Christian J. W. Kloesel (Bloomington: Indiana University Press, 1986), 102, note 5.

26. Quoted in ibid., 141.

27. William Knight, ed. *Memorials of Thomas Davidson: The Wandering Scholar* (Boston: Ginn, 1907), 111.

28. John Clendenning, *The Life and Thought of Josiah Royce* (Madison: University of Wisconsin Press, 1985), 66–67.

29. James, *Correspondence*, vol. 5, 22.

30. Knight, *Memorials*, 111.

31. Randall E. Auxier, *Time, Will, and Purpose: Living Ideas from the Philosophy of Josiah Royce* (Chicago: Open Court, 2013), ch. 7.

32. Fisch, *Peirce, Semeiotic, and Pragmatism*, 153–54.

33. William James, *Pragmatism, a New Name for Some Old Ways of Thinking* (New York: Longmans, Green, 1907), 46–47.

BIBLIOGRAPHY

Auxier, Randall E. *Time, Will, and Purpose: Living Ideas from the Philosophy of Josiah Royce.* Chicago: Open Court, 2013.

Behrens, Peter J. "The Metaphysical Club at the Johns Hopkins University (1879–1885)." *History of Psychology* 8 (2005): 331–46.

Blau, Joseph. *Men and Movements in American Philosophy.* Englewood Cliffs, NJ: Prentice-Hall, 1952.

Bridgman, Raymond L., ed. *Concord Lectures on Philosophy, Comprising Outlines of all the Lectures at the Concord Summer School of Philosophy in 1882, with an Historical Sketch.* Cambridge, MA: Moses King, 1883.

Burke, F. Thomas. *What Pragmatism Was.* Bloomington: Indiana University Press, 2013.

Clendenning, John. *The Life and Thought of Josiah Royce.* Madison: University of Wisconsin Press, 1985.

Good, James A. *A Search for Unity in Diversity: The "Permanent Hegelian Deposit" in the Philosophy of John Dewey.* Lanham, MD: Rowman and Littlefield, 2006.

Fisch, Max. "Introduction." In *Writings of Charles S. Peirce, Volume 3, 1872–78,* edited by Christian J. W. Kloesel, xxix–xxxvi. Bloomington: Indiana University Press, 1986.

Fisch, Max H. *Peirce, Semeiotic, and Pragmatism.* Edited by Kenneth L. Ketner and Christian J. W. Kloesel (Bloomington: Indiana University Press, 1986); see these chapters: "Justice Holmes, the Prediction Theory of Law, and Pragmatism," 6–18; "Alexander Bain and the Genealogy of Pragmatism," 79–109; "A Chronicle of Pragmaticism, 1865–1879," 114–36; "Philosophical Clubs in Cambridge and Boston," 137–70; "Peirce's Progress from Nominalism toward Realism," 184–200.

———. "Was There a Metaphysical Club in Cambridge?" In *Studies in the Philosophy of Charles Sanders Peirce,* edited by Edward C. Moore and Richard S. Robin, 3–32. Amherst: University of Massachusetts Press, 1964.

Flower, Elizabeth, and Murray G. Murphy. *A History of Philosophy in America,* 2 vols. New York: G. P. Putnam's Sons, 1977.

Kuklick, Bruce. *The Rise of American Philosophy: Cambridge, Massachusetts, 1860–1930.* New Haven: Yale University Press, 1977.

Goetzmann, William H., ed. *The American Hegelians: an Intellectual Episode in the History of Western America.* New York: Alfred A. Knopf, 1973.

Gould, James A. "R. B. Perry on the Origin of American and European Pragmatism." *Journal of the History of Philosophy* 8 (1970): 431–50.

Harvard University. *Quinquennial Catalogue of the Officers and Graduates of Harvard University, 1636–1900.* Cambridge: Published by the University, 1900.

Jackson, Abraham Willard. *James Martineau: A Biography and Study.* Boston: Little, Brown, 1900.

James, William. *The Correspondence of William James, Volume 4: 1856–1877.* Edited by Ignas K. Skrupskelis, Elizabeth M. Berkeley et al. Charlottesville: University Press of Virginia, 1995.

Knight, William, ed. *Memorials of Thomas Davidson: The Wandering Scholar.* Boston: Ginn, 1907.

Kuklick, Bruce. *The Rise of American Philosophy: Cambridge, Massachusetts, 1860–1930.* New Haven and London: Yale University Press. 1977.

Leidecker, Kurt F. *Yankee Teacher: The Life of William Torrey Harris.* New York: Philosophic Library, 1946.

———, ed. *The Record Book of the St. Louis Philosophical Society founded February 1866.* Lewiston, NY: Edwin Mellen Press, 1990.

Martin, Jay. *The Education of John Dewey: A Biography.* New York: Columbia University Press, 2002.

Menand, Louis. *The Metaphysical Club: A Story of Ideas in America.* New York: Farrar, Straus and Giroux, 2001.

Misak, Cheryl. *The American Pragmatists.* Oxford: Oxford University Press, 2013.

Murphey, Murray G. "Kant's Children the Cambridge Pragmatists." *Transactions of the Charles S. Peirce Society* 4 (1968): 3–33.

Murray, J. Clarke. "A Summer School of Philosophy." *Scottish Review* 19 (1892): 98–113.

Pearce, Trevor. " 'Science Organized': Positivism and the Metaphysical Club, 1865–1875." *Journal of the History of Ideas* 76 (2015): 441–65.

Perry, Ralph Barton. *The Thought and Character of William James,* 2 vols. Boston: Little, Brown, 1935.

Pochmann, Henry A. *New England Transcendentalism and St. Louis Hegelianism: Phases in the History of American Idealism.* New York: Haskell House, 1970.

Riedl, John O. "The Hegelians of St. Louis, Missouri, and their Influence in the United States." In *The Legacy of Hegel,* edited by J. J. O'Malley et al., 268–87. The Hague: Martinus Nijhoff, 1973.

Rockefeller, Steven. *John Dewey: Religious Faith and Democratic Humanism.* New York: Columbia University Press, 1991.

Ronda, Bruce. "The Concord School of Philosophy and the Legacy of Transcendentalism." *New England Quarterly* 82 (2009): 575–607.

Rosenblatt, Rand. "Holmes, Peirce, and Legal Pragmatism." *Yale Law Journal* 84 (1975): 1123–40.

Sargent, Mary Elizabeth Fiske, ed. *Sketches and Reminiscences of the Radical Club of Chestnut Street*. Boston: J. R. Osgood, 1880.

Schaub, Edward L., ed. *William Torrey Harris, 1835–1935*. Chicago: Open Court, 1936.

Schneider, Herbert W. *A History of American Philosophy*. New York: Columbia University Press, 1946.

Skrupskelis, Ignas K. "Evolution and Pragmatism: An Unpublished Letter of William James." *Transactions of the Charles S. Peirce Society* 43 (2007):745–52.

Smith, Harriette Knight. *The History of the Lowell Institute*. Boston: Lamson, Wolffe, 1898.

Snider, Denton J. *The St. Louis Movement in Philosophy, Literature, Education, Psychology, with Chapters of Autobiography*. St. Louis: Sigma, 1920.

Thayer, H. Standish. *Meaning and Action: A Critical History of Pragmatism*. New York: Bobbs-Merrill, 1968.

Warren, Austin. "The Concord School of Philosophy." *New England Quarterly* 2 (1929): 199–233.

Watson, David. "The Neo-Hegelian Tradition in America." *Journal of American Studies* 14 (1980): 219–34.

White, Morton. *Science and Sentiment in America*. Oxford: Oxford University Press, 1972.

Wiener, Philip P. *Evolution and the Founders of Pragmatism*. Cambridge: Harvard University Press, 1949.

CHAUNCEY WRIGHT

Selected Writings

"A Physical Theory of the Universe." Review of Herbert Spencer, *Essays: Scientific, Political, and Speculative. North American Review* 99 (July 1864): 1–34. In *Philosophical Discussions*, 1–34.

"Bowen's Logic." Review of Francis Bowen, *A Treatise on Logic. North American Review* 99 (October 1865): 592–605.

"The Philosophy of Herbert Spencer." Review of Eight of Herbert Spencer's books. *North American Review* 100 (April 1865): 423–76. In *Philosophical Discussions*, 43–96.

"Mill on Hamilton." Review of John Stuart Mill, *An Examination of Sir William Hamilton's Philosophy. North American Review* 103 (July 1866): 250–60.

"The Reign of Law." Review of the Duke of Argyll, *The Reign of Law. The Nation* 4 (June 13, 1867): 470.

"Peabody's Positive Philosophy." Review of A. P. Peabody, *The Positive Philosophy. North American Review* 106 (January 1868): 285–94.

"The Genesis of Species." Review essay of Charles Darwin's *The Descent of Man* and *The Origin of Species*, 5th ed.; George Mivart's *On the Genesis of Species*; and Alfred Wallace's *Contributions to the Theory of Natural Selection*. *North American Review* 113 (July 1871): 63–104. In *Philosophical Discussions*, 126–67.

"C. S. Peirce's Review of Berkeley." Note about Charles S. Peirce's review of A. C. Fraser, *The Works of George Berkeley*. *The Nation* 13 (November 30, 1871): 355–56.

"Evolution by Natural Selection." Review essay on Charles Darwin's *The Origin of Species*, 6th ed.; and George Mivart's "Evolution and its Consequences," and "Specific Genesis." *North American Review* 115 (July 1872): 1–31. In *Philosophical Discussions*, 168–98.

"Cause and Effect." (1873). In *Philosophical Discussions*, 406–13. From a manuscript that Wright never published.

"Evolution of Self-Consciousness." *North American Review* 116 (April 1873): 245–310. In *Philosophical Discussions*, 199–266.

"John Stuart Mill." Commemorative notice. *Proceedings of the American Academy of Arts and Sciences* n.s. 1 (1873–74): 285–97. In *Philosophical Discussions*, 414–28.

"Lewes's 'Problems of Life and Mind.'" Review of George H. Lewes, *Problems of Life and Mind*, first series, *The Foundations of a Creed*. *The Nation* 18 (June 11, 1874): 381–82. In *Philosophical Discussions*, 360–74.

Philosophical Discussions by Chauncey Wright with a Biographical Sketch of the Author. Edited by Charles Eliot Norton. New York: Henry Holt, 1877. Reprint as volume 1 of *The Evolutionary Philosophy of Chauncey Wright*. Edited by Frank X. Ryan. Bristol, UK: Thoemmes Press, 2000.

Letters of Chauncey Wright with some Account of His Life. Edited by James Bradley Thayer. Cambridge, MA: John Wilson and Son, 1878. Reprint as volume 2 of *The Evolutionary Philosophy of Chauncey Wright*. Edited by Frank X. Ryan. Bristol, UK: Thoemmes Press, 2000.

The Philosophical Writings of Chauncey Wright: Representative Selections. Edited by Edward H. Madden. New York, Liberal Arts Press, 1958.

Writings about Wright

Blau, Joseph L. "Chauncey Wright: Radical Empiricist." *New England Quarterly* 19 (December 1946): 495–517.

Bowne, Borden Parker. "Chauncey Wright as a Philosopher." *New Englander* 146 (1878): 585–603.

Fiske, John. "Chauncey Wright." In *Darwinism, and Other Essays*, 79–110. Boston: Houghton Mifflin, 1892.

Giuffrida, Robert. "Chauncey Wright and the Problem of Relations." *Transactions of the Charles S. Peirce Society* 16 (Fall 1980): 293–308.

———. "The Philosophical Thought of Chauncey Wright." *Transactions of the Charles S. Peirce Society* 24 (1988): 33–64.

Grigoriev, Serge. "Chauncey Wright: Theoretical Reason in a Naturalist Account of Human Consciousness." *Journal of the History of Ideas* 73 (October 2012): 559–82.

James, William. "Chauncey Wright." *The Nation* 21.534 (September 23, 1875), 194.

Kennedy, Gail. "The Pragmatic Naturalism of Chauncey Wright." In *Studies in the History of Ideas*, vol. 3. New York: Columbia University Press, 1935.

Madden, Edward H. *Chauncey Wright and the Foundations of Pragmatism*. Seattle: University of Washington Press, 1963.

Marcell, David W. "John Fiske, Chauncey Wright, and William James: A Dialogue on Progress." *Journal of American History* 56 (March 1970): 802–18.

Norton, Charles Eliot. "Biographical Sketch of Chauncey Wright." In Chauncey Wright, *Philosophical Discussions*, edited by C. E. Norton, vii–xxiii. New York, Henry Holt, 1878.

Perry, Ralph Barton. "Chauncey Wright." In *The Thought and Character of William James, edited by* Ralph Barton Perry, vol. 1, 520–32. Boston: Little, Brown, 1935.

Ryan, Frank X., ed. *The Evolutionary Philosophy of Chauncey Wright*, vol. 3: *Influence and Legacy*. Bristol, UK: Thoemmes Press, 2000. Collects 18 articles about Wright, including the pieces by Bowne, James, and Fiske referenced here.

Wiener, Philip P. "Chauncey Wright, Defender of Darwin and Precursor of Pragmatism." In *Evolution and the Founders of Pragmatism*, 31–69, 207–12. Cambridge: Harvard University Press, 1949.

———. "Biographical Notes on Chauncey Wright (1830–1875)." In *Evolution and the Founders of Pragmatism*, 207–12. Cambridge: Harvard University Press, 1949.

———. "The Chauncey Wright Papers at Northampton, Massachusetts." In *Evolution and the Founders of Pragmatism*, 213–20 (Cambridge: Harvard University Press, 1949).

CHARLES SANDERS PEIRCE

Selected Writings

"Nominalism versus Realism." *The Journal of Speculative Philosophy* 2, no.1 (1868): 57–61.

"Questions Concerning Certain Faculties Claimed for Man." *Journal of Speculative Philosophy* 2, no.2 (1868): 103–14.

"Some Consequences of Four Incapacities." *Journal of Speculative Philosophy* 2, no. 3 (1868): 140–57.

"Grounds of Validity of the Laws of Logic: Further Consequences of Four Incapacities." *Journal of Speculative Philosophy* 2, no.4 (1869): 193–208.

"Professor Porter's *Human Intellect*." *The Nation* 8 (March 18, 1869): 211–13.

"The English Doctrine of Ideas." *The Nation* 9 (November 25, 1869): 461–62.

"Fraser's *The Works of George Berkeley*." *North American Review* 113 (October 1871): 449–72.

"Mr. Peirce and the Realists." Letter to the Editor, about Chauncey Wright's note on Peirce's review of Fraser's Works of Berkeley. *The Nation* 13 (December 14, 1871): 386.

Toward a Logic Book. Manuscript written during 1872–73. In *Writings of Charles S. Peirce*, vol. 3, 14–108.

"Nicholas St. John Green." *Proceedings of the American Academy of Arts and Sciences* n.s. 4 (1876–77): 289–91.

"The Fixation of Belief." *Popular Science Monthly* 12 (November 1877): 1–15.

"How to Make Our Ideas Clear." *Popular Science Monthly* 12 (January 1878): 286–302.

"The Doctrine of Chances." *Popular Science Monthly* 12 (March 1878): 604–15.

"The Probability of Induction." *Popular Science Monthly* 12 (April 1878): 705–18.

"The Order of Nature." *Popular Science Monthly* 13 (June 1878): 203–17.

"Deduction, Induction, and Hypothesis." *Popular Science Monthly* 13 (August 1878): 470–82.

Studies in Logic by Members of the Johns Hopkins University. Boston, 1883; Amsterdam, 1983. Peirce contributed the "Preface," iii–vi; "A Theory of Probable Inference," 126–81; "Note A (On a Limited Universe of Marks)," 182–86; and "Note B (The Logic of Relatives)," 187–203.

Collected Papers of Charles S. Peirce, 8 volumes. Edited by Charles Hartshorne, Paul Weiss, and Arthur Burks. Cambridge: Harvard University Press, 1931–1958.

Writings of Charles Sanders Peirce, Volume 3, 1872–1878. Edited by Max Fisch et al. Bloomington: Indiana University Press, 1986.

Writings about Peirce

Agler, David W. "W. T. Harris, Peirce, and the Charge of Nominalism." *Hegel Bulletin* 36 (2015): 135–58.

Altshuler, Bruce. "Peirce's Theory of Truth and His Early Idealism." *Transactions of the Charles S. Peirce Society* 16 (1980): 118–40.

Behrens, Peter J. "The Metaphysical Club at the Johns Hopkins University (1879–1885)." *History of Psychology* 8 (2005): 331–46.

Boler, John. *Charles Peirce and Scholastic Realism.* Seattle: University of Washington Press, 1963.

Brent, Joseph. *Charles Sanders Peirce: A Life*, 2nd edition. Bloomington: Indiana University Press. 1998.

Cadwallader, Thomas C. "Charles S. Peirce (1839–1914): The First American Experimental Psychologist." *Journal of the History of the Behavioral Sciences* 10 (1974): 291–98.

———. "Peirce as an Experimental Psychologist." *Transactions of the Charles S. Peirce Society* 11 (1975): 167–86.

Girel, Mathias. "The Metaphysics and Logic of Psychology: Peirce's Reading of James's *Principles.*" *Transactions of the Charles S. Peirce Society* 39 (2003): 163–203.

Hookway, Christopher. *The Pragmatic Maxim: Essays on Peirce and Pragmatism.* Oxford: Oxford University Press, 2012.

Ladd-Franklin, Christine. "Charles S. Peirce at the Johns Hopkins." *Journal of Philosophy* 13 (1916): 715–22.

Murphey, Murray G. *The Development of Peirce's Philosophy*, rev. edition. Indianapolis: Hackett, 1993.

O'Connor, Daniel D. "Peirce's Debt to F. E. Abbot." *Journal of the History of Ideas* 25 (1964): 543–64.

Peterson, Sven R. "Benjamin Peirce: Mathematician and Philosopher." *Journal of the History of Ideas* 16 (1955): 89–112.

WILLIAM JAMES

Selected Writings

"Review of H. Maudsley, *Responsibility in Mental Disease*." *Atlantic Monthly* 34 (September 1874): 364–65.

"Review of G. H. Lewes's *Problems of Life and Mind*." *Atlantic Monthly* 36 (September 1875): 361–63.

"Remarks on Spencer's Definition of Mind as Correspondence." *Journal of Speculative Philosophy* 12 (January 1878): 1–18.

"Brute and Human Intellect." *Journal of Speculative Philosophy* 12 (July 1878): 236–76.

"The Spatial Quale." *Journal of Speculative Philosophy* 13 (January 1879): 64–87.

"Are We Automata?" *Mind* o.s. 4 (January 1879): 1–22.

"The Sentiment of Rationality." *Mind* o.s. 4 (July 1879): 317–46.

"Reflex Action and Theism." *The Unitarian Review and Religious Magazine* 16 (November 1881): 389–416.

"Rationality, Activity, and Faith." *Princeton Review* 2 (July 1882): 58–86.

"On the Function of Cognition." *Mind* o.s. 10 (January 1885): 27–44.

"Philosophical Conceptions and Practical Results." *University Chronicle* 1 (September 1898): 287–310.

Pragmatism, a New Name for Some Old Ways of Thinking. New York: Longmans, Green, 1907.

Writings about James

Bordogna, Francesca. *William James at the Boundaries: Philosophy, Science, and the Geography of Knowledge*. Chicago: University of Chicago Press, 2008.

Croce, Paul Jerome. *Eclipse of Certainty: Science and Religion in the Era of William James*. Chapel Hill: University of North Carolina Press, 1995.

Greenwood, John D. "Mechanism, Purpose and Progress: Darwin and Early American Psychology." *History of the Human Sciences* 21 (2008): 103–26.

James, Henry. *Henry James: Selected Letters*. Edited by Leon Edel. Cambridge: Harvard University Press, 1987.

Judd. Charles H. "Radical Empiricism and Wundt's Philosophy." *Journal of Philosophy* 2 (1905): 169–76.

Klein, Alexander. "On Hume on Space: Green's Attack, James' Empirical Response." *Journal of the History of Philosophy* 47 (2009): 415–49.

Kraushaar, Otto F. "Lotze as a Factor in the Development of James's Radical Empiricism and Pluralism." *Philosophical Review* 48 (1939): 455–71.

Madden, Marian C., and Edward H. Madden. "William James and the Problem of Relations." *Transactions of the Charles S. Peirce Society* 14 (1978): 227–46.

Perry, Ralph Barton, ed. *The Thought and Character of William James*, 2 vols. Boston: Little, Brown, 1935.

Richardson, Robert D. *William James: In the Maelstrom of American Modernism*. New York: Houghton Mifflin Harcourt, 2007.

GRANVILLE STANLEY HALL

Selected Writings

"Notes on Hegel and His Critics." *Journal of Speculative Philosophy* 12 (January 1878): 93–103.

"Color Perception." *Proceedings of the American Academy of Arts and Sciences* n.s. 3 (1877–78): 402–13.

"The Muscular Perception of Space." *Mind* 3 (October 1878): 433–50.

"Democritus and Heraclitus." *Unitarian Review and Religious Magazine* 10 (December 1878): 611–21.

"Philosophy in the United States." *Mind* o.s. 4 (January 1879): 89–105.

"Laura Bridgman." *Mind* o.s. 4 (April 1879): 149–72.

"Recent Researches on Hypnotism." *Mind* o.s. 6 (January 1881): 98–104.

"The Education of the Will." *Princeton Review* 2 (July-December 1882): 306–25.

"Experimental Psychology." *Mind* o.s. 10 (April 1895): 245–49.

Founders of Modern Psychology. New York: D. Appleton, 1912.

Life and Confessions of a Psychologist. New York: D. Appleton, 1923.

Writings about Hall

Green, Christopher D. "Johns Hopkins's First Professorship in Philosophy: a Critical Pivot Point in the History of American Psychology." *American Journal of Psychology* 120 (2007): 303–23.

Hogan, John D. "G. Stanley Hall: Educator, Organizer, and Pioneer Developmental Psychologist." In *Portraits of Pioneers in Psychology*, vol. 5, edited by G. A. Kimble and M. Wertheimer, 19–36. Washington, DC: American Psychological Association, 2003.

Hulse, Stewart H., and Bert F. Green Jr., eds. *One Hundred Years of Psychological Research in America: G. Stanley Hall and the Johns Hopkins Tradition.* Baltimore: Johns Hopkins University Press, 1986.

Leary, David E. "Between Peirce (1878) and James (1898): G. Stanley Hall, the Origins of Pragmatism, and the History of Psychology." *Journal of the History of the Behavioral Sciences* 45 (2009): 5–20.

Ross, Dorothy. *G. Stanley Hall: The Psychologist as Prophet.* Chicago: University of Chicago Press, 1972.

NICHOLAS ST. JOHN GREEN

Selected Writings

"Proximate and Remote Cause." *American Law Review* 4 (January 1870): 201–16. In *Essays and Notes on the Law of Tort and Crime*, 1–17.

"Contributory Negligence on the Part of an Infant." *American Law Review* 4 (April 1870): 405–16. In *Essays and Notes on the Law of Tort and Crime*, 18–30.

"Insanity in Criminal Law." Review of I. Ray, *A Treatise on the Medical Jurisprudence of Insanity*, 5th ed. *American Law Review* 5 (July 1871): 704–709. In *Essays and Notes on the Law of Tort and Crime*, 161–67.

"Some Results of Reform in Indictments." Review of Francis Wharton, *Precedents of Indictments and Pleas. American Law Review* 5 (July 1871): 732–35. In *Essays and Notes on the Law of Tort and Crime*, 151–54.

"Married Women." Review of J. P. Bishop, *Commentaries on the Law of Married Women under the Statutes of the Several States and at Common Law and in Equity. American Law Review* 6 (October 1872): 57–74. In *Essays and Notes on the Law of Tort and Crime*, 31–48.

"Slander and Libel." Review of John Townsend, *A Treatise on the Wrongs called Slander and Libel*, 2nd edn. *American Law Review* 6 (July 1872): 593–613. In *Essays and Notes on the Law of Tort and Crime*, 49–70.

"Torts Under the French Law." Review of M. A. Sourdat, *Traité Général de la Responsabilité ou de l'Action en Dommages-in-térêts en dehors des Contracts. American Law Review* 8 (April 1874): 508–29. In *Essays and Notes on the Law of Tort and Crime*, 71–92.

"The Three Degrees of Negligence." *American Law Review* 8 (July 1874): 649–68. In *Essays and Notes on the Law of Tort and Crime*, 93–111.

In Story, Joseph. *Commentaries on the Law of Agency as a Branch of Commercial and Maritime Jurisprudence.* 8th edition revised with additions by Nicholas St. John Green. Boston: Little, Brown, 1874. Short notes by Green are on pp.: 7, 14, 21, 34, 35, 77–78, 92–93, 106, 117, 118, 118–19, 121, 124, 127, 140, 149, 156, 166, 167, 172, 172–73, 174, 208, 242, 248, 260, 262, 298–99, 305, 306, 316, 330, 380, 385, 389, 478–79, 504–505, 519, 548–49, 551, 610, 611, 634, 640, 641, 648, 657, 660.

Longer significant notes by Green are on pp.: 23–32 ("The Powers and Duties of Attorneys at Law," *Essays and Notes*, 115–26); 78–80; 157–59; 233; 298 ("Sale in the Roman Law," *Essays and Notes*, 114); 299–301; 334; 543–45 ("The Liability of a Principal to Third Persons for the Torts of his Agents and Servants," *Essays and Notes*, 127–30); 546–47; 559–66 (559–64 as "The Liability of a Master to his Servants," *Essays and Notes*, 131–37); 638–39 ("Mandate in the Roman Law," *Essays and Notes*, 112–13).

Criminal Law Reports, 2 volumes. New York: Hurd and Houghton, 1874–75. Significant notes by Green are:

vol. 1, 180 ("The Effect of a Pardon," *Essays and Notes*, 198); 317–18 ("Rape under the Statutes of Westminster," *Essays and Notes*, 199–204); 343–44 ("The Locus of Larceny," *Essays and Notes*, 195–97); 294 ("Indictments for Statutory Offences," *Essays and Notes*, 160); 390 ("The Power of the Will over Conduct," *Essays and Notes*, 168–69); 392; 399–405 ("The Punishability of Children," *Essays and Notes*, 170–80);405–406 ("Retrial after Partial Acquittal as Double Jeopardy," *Essays and Notes*, 148–50); 490–91 ("The Right to Repel Attack on the Dwelling-House," *Essays and Notes*, 206–11).

vol. 2, 101–102; 215–26; 244–46 ("The Maxim that a Man Is Presumed to Intend the Natural Consequences of His Acts," 191–94); 271–75 ("Threat of Violence as Criminal Assault," *Essays and Notes*, 138–47); 208–10 ("The Distinction between Mistake of Fact and Mistake of Law," *Essays and Notes*, 181–90); 286–89; 381–82 ("The Requisites of an Indictment for Murder," *Essays and Notes*, 155–58); 392–94; 437 ("Reasonable Doubt," *Essays and Notes*, 205); 574 ("Failure to Prove a Descriptive Allegation as a Variance," *Essays and Notes*, 159).

Essays and Notes on the Law of Tort and Crime. Edited by Frederick Green. Menasha, WI: George Banta, 1933.

Writings about Green

Anon. "Mr. Nicholas St. John Green." Memorial notice. *American Law Review* 11 (October 1876): 173–74. Probably written by John Chipman Gray.

Fisch, Max. "Was There a Metaphysical Club in Cambridge?" In *Studies in the Philosophy of Charles Sanders Peirce,* edited by Moore and Robin, 3–32. Amherst: University of Massachusetts Press, 1964.

Hackney, James. "The Intellectual Origins of American Strict Products Liability: A Case Study in American Pragmatic Instrumentalism." *American Journal of Legal History* 39 (1995): 443–509.

Peirce, Charles S. "Nicholas St. John Green." *Proceedings of the American Academy of Arts and Sciences* n.s. 4 (1877): 289–91.

Wiener, Philip P. "The Pragmatic Legal Philosophy of Nicholas St. John Green." In *Evolution and the Founders of Pragmatism,* 152–71. Cambridge: Harvard University Press, 1949.

———. "Biographical Notes on Nicholas St. John Green (1835–1876)." In *Evolution and the Founders of Pragmatism,* 231–34. Cambridge: Harvard University Press, 1949.

OLIVER WENDELL HOLMES JR.

Selected Writings

"Codes, and the Arrangement of Law." *American Law Review* 5 (October 1870): 1–13.

"Review of *Law Magazine and Review*, April 1872." *American Law Review* 6 (July 1872): 723–25.

"The Arrangement of the Law. Privity." *American Law Review* 7 (October 1872): 46–66.

"The Theory of Torts." *American Law Review* 7 (July 1873): 652–63.

"Primitive Notions in Modern Law. I." *American Law Review* 10 (April 1876): 422–39.

"Primitive Notions in Modern Law. II." *American Law Review* 11 (July 1877): 641–60.

"The Path of the Law." *Harvard Law Review* 10 (March 1897): 457–78.

The Common Law. Boston: Little, Brown, 1881.

Collected Legal Papers. New York: Harcourt, Brace and Howe, 1920.

Justice Oliver Wendell Holmes: His Book Notices and Uncollected Letters and Papers. Edited by Harry C. Shriver. New York: Central Book, 1936.

The Formative Essays of Justice Holmes: The Making of an American Legal Philosophy. Edited by Frederic Rogers Kellogg. Westport, CT: Greenwood, 1984.

Writings about Holmes

Bloustein, Edward J. "Holmes: His First Amendment Theory and His Pragmatist Bent." *Rutgers Law Review* 40 (1988): 283–302.

Fisch, Max. "Justice Holmes, the Prediction Theory of Law, and Pragmatism." *Journal of Philosophy* 39 (1942): 85–97.

Frank, Jerome. "A Conflict with Oblivion: Some Observations on the Founders of Legal Pragmatism." *Rutgers Law Review* 9 (1954): 425–63.

Gregg, Paul L. "The Pragmatism of Mr. Justice Holmes." *Georgetown Law Journal* 31 (1943): 262–95.

White, G. Edward. *Justice Oliver Wendell Holmes: Law and the Inner Self.* Oxford: Oxford University Press, 1993.

———. *Tort Law in America: An Intellectual History.* Oxford: Oxford University Press, 2003.

Tamanaha, Brian Z. "Pragmatism in U.S. Legal Theory: Its Application to Normative Jurisprudence, Sociolegal Studies, and the Fact-Value Distinction." *American Journal of Jurisprudence* 41 (1996): 315–55.

JOSEPH BANGS WARNER

Selected Writings

"Review of Holmes, *The Common Law*." *American Law Review* 2 (May 1881): 331–38.

"The Responsibilities of the Lawyer." *International Journal of Ethics* 7 (January 1897): 204–26.

Writings about Warner

Anon. "Joseph Bangs Warner." In *The Class of 1869 of Harvard College*, 97. Boston: Houghton Mifflin, 1908.

Anon. "Obituary." *Boston Transcript*, January 2, 1923.

Wiener, Philip P. "Biographical Notes on Joseph B. Warner (1848–1923)." In *Evolution and the Founders of Pragmatism*, 235–42. Cambridge: Harvard University Press, 1949.

The Letters of John Fiske. Edited by Ethel Fisk. New York: Macmillan, 1940.

JOHN FISKE

Selected Writings

Outlines of Cosmic Philosophy Based on the Doctrine of Evolution, with Criticisms on the Positive Philosophy, 2 vol. Boston: Houghton, Mifflin, 1874.

"The Triumph of Darwinism." *North American Review* 124 (January 1877): 90–106.

Darwinism and Other Essays. Boston: Houghton, Mifflin, 1879.

The Idea of God as Affected by Modern Knowledge. Boston: Houghton, Mifflin, 1885.

Through Nature to God. Boston: Houghton, Mifflin, 1899.

The Life and Letters of John Fiske, 2 vol. Edited by Joseph Spencer Clark. Boston: Houghton, Mifflin, 1917.

The Letters of John Fiske. Edited by Ethel Fisk. New York: Macmillan, 1940.

Writings about Fiske

Davis, Andrew M. "John Fiske." *Proceedings of the American Academy of Arts and Sciences* 17 (1901–02): 31–44.

Pannill, H. Burnell. *The Religious Faith of John Fiske.* Durham: Duke University Press, 1957.

Perry, Thomas S. *John Fiske.* Boston: Small, Maynard, 1906.

Roberts, Jon H. *Darwinism and the Divine in America.* Notre Dame: University of Notre Dame Press, 2001.

CHARLES CARROLL EVERETT

Selected Writings

The Science of Thought: A System of Logic. Boston: Hall and Whiting, 1869. 2nd ed. 1882. Reprinted in *The Early American Reception of German Idealism*, vol. 5, edited by James A. Good. Bristol, UK: Thoemmes Press, 2002.

"The Data of Ethics." *The Unitarian Review and Religious Magazine* 13 (January 1880): 43–59.

"Supernatural Religion." *Old and New* 11 (May 1875): 593–98.

"The Known and the Unknowable in Religion." *The Unitarian Review and Religious Magazine* 3 (May 1875): 445–456.

"The Scottish Philosophy." *The Unitarian Review and Religious Magazine* 3 (July 1875): 24–38.

"Cosmic Philosophy." *The Unitarian Review and Religious Magazine* 5 (May 1876): 482–96.

"The Relation of Modern Philosophy to Liberalism." *The Unitarian Review and Religious Magazine* 12 (December 1879): 602–24.

"The Theistic Argument as Affected by Recent Theories." *The Unitarian Review and Religious Magazine* 16 (November 1881): 447–57.

Fichte's Science of Knowledge: A Critical Exposition. Chicago: S. C. Griggs, 1884.

Essays, Theological and Literary. Boston: Houghton, Mifflin, 1901.

Immortality and Other Essays. Boston: Houghton, Mifflin, 1902.

Writings about Everett

Fenn, William W. "The Theology of Charles Carroll Everett." *Harvard Theological Review* 3 (1910): 1–23.

Gilman, Nicholas Paine. "Charles Carroll Everett." *The New World: A Quarterly Review of Religion, Ethics, and Theology* 9 (December 1900): 724–26.

Royce, Josiah. "Professor Everett as a Metaphysician." *The New World: A Quarterly Review of Religion, Ethics, and Theology* 9 (December 1900): 726–41.

Toy, Crawford H. "Charles Carroll Everett." *The New World* 9 (December 1900): 714–24.

JAMES ELLIOT CABOT

Selected Writings

"Hegel." *The North American Review* 106 (April 1868): 447–83.

"Some Considerations on the Notion of Space." *The Journal of Speculative Philosophy* 12 (July 1878): 225–36.

"The Spatial Quale." *The Journal of Speculative Philosophy* 13 (April 1879): 199–204.

A Memoir of Ralph Waldo Emerson, 2 vols. Boston: Houghton Mifflin, 1888.

Writings about Cabot

Higginson, Thomas Wentworth. "James Elliot Cabot." *Proceedings of the American Academy of Arts and Sciences* 39 (1903–04): 649–55.

THOMAS DAVIDSON

Selected Writings

"Parmenides." *The Journal of Speculative Philosophy* 4, no. 1 (1870): 1–16.

"On Professor Tyndall's Recent Address." *The Journal of Speculative Philosophy* 8 (October 1874): 361–70.

"Education." *The Atlantic Monthly* 39 (January 1877), 123–28. Davidson replies to criticisms in the March issue, 386–88.

"The Philosophy of Thomas Aquinas." *The Journal of Speculative Philosophy* 13 (January 1879): 87–107.

"Perception." *Mind* o.s. 7 (October 1882): 496–513.

"The Concord Philosophical School." *Town Topics* (August 22, 1885), 7.

"Noism." *The Index* (April 29, 1886), 522–25.

"The Soul's Progress in God." *The Journal of Speculative Philosophy* 21 (July 1887): 288–324.

Writings about Davidson

DeArmey, Michael H. "Thomas Davidson's Apeirotheism and Its Influence on William James and John Dewey." *Journal of the History of Ideas* 48 (1987): 691–708.

Good, James A. "The Value of Thomas Davidson." *Transactions of the Charles S. Peirce Society* 40 (2004): 289–318.

James, William. "Thomas Davidson: A Knight-Errant of the Intellectual Life." In *Memories and Studies*, 75–103. New York: Longmans, Green, 1911.

Knight, William, ed. *Memorials of Thomas Davidson: The Wandering Scholar*. Boston: Ginn, 1907.

Snider, Denton J. *The St. Louis Movement in Philosophy, Literature, Education, Psychology, with Chapters of Autobiography*. St. Louis: Sigma, 1920.

BORDEN PARKER BOWNE

Selected Writings

The Philosophy of Herbert Spencer. New York: Nelson and Phillips, 1874.

"Some Difficulties of Modern Materialism." *The Princeton Review* n.s. 14 (November 1881): 344–72.

Studies in Theism. New York: Phillips and Hunt, 1882.

Metaphysics: A Study in First Principles. New York: Harper and Brothers, 1882.

Philosophy of Theism. New York: Harper and Brothers, 1887.

Writings about Bowne

Burrow Jr., Rufus. "The Personalism of George Holmes Howison and Borden Parker Bowne." *The Personalist Forum* 13 (Fall 1997): 287–303.

Dorrien, Gary J. *The Making of American Liberal Theology: Imagining Progressive Religion, 1805–1900* (Louisville: Westminster John Knox Press, 2001), ch. 6.

Flewelling, Ralph Tyler. *Personalism and the Problems of Philosophy: An Appreciation of the Work of Borden Parker Bowne.* New York and Cincinnati: The Methodist Book Concern, 1915.

Knudson, Albert C. *The Philosophy of Personalism: A Study in the Metaphysics of Religion.* New York: The Abingdon Press, 1927.

Marshall, Mason "The Role of Reason for Borden Parker Bowne." *Transactions of the Charles S. Peirce Society* 38 (2002): 649–71.

Robinson, Daniel S., ed. "Borden Parker Bowne's Letters to William T. Harris." *Philosophical Forum* 13 (1955): 89–95.

FRANCIS ELLINGWOOD ABBOT

Selected Writings

Scientific Theism. Boston: Little, Brown, 1885.

The Way Out of Agnosticism: Or The Philosophy of Free Religion. Boston: Little, Brown, 1890.

The Collected Essays of Francis Ellingwood Abbot (1836–1903): American Philosopher and Free Religionist, 4 vols. Edited by W. Creighton Peden and Everett J. Tarbox Jr. Lewiston, NY: Edwin Mellon Press, 1996.

Writings about Abbot

Ahlstrom, Sydney E., and Robert B. Mullin. *The Scientific Theist: A Life of Francis Ellingwood Abbot.* Macon, GA: Mercer University Press, 1987.

Peden, W. Creighton. *The Philosopher of Free Religion: Francis Ellingwood Abbot, 1836–1903.* New York: Peter Lang, 1992.

Royce, Josiah. "Dr. Abbot's *Way Out of Agnosticism.*" *International Journal of Ethics* 1 (1890): 98–113.

GEORGE HOLMES HOWISON

Selected Writings

"Some Aspects of Recent German Philosophy." *The Journal of Speculative Philosophy* 17 (January 1883): 1–44.

"Hume and Kant." *The Journal of Speculative Philosophy* 19 (January 1885): 85–89.

"Is Modern Science Pantheistic?" *Journal of Speculative Philosophy* 19 (October 1885): 363–84.

The Conception of God, with Josiah Royce et al. Berkeley: Executive Council of the Union, 1895. 2nd edition, New York: Macmillan, 1897.

The Limits of Evolution and Other Essays Illustrating the Metaphysical Theory of Personal Idealism. New York: Macmillan, 1901. 2nd edition, New York: Macmillan, 1904.

George Holmes Howison, Philosopher and Teacher: A Selection from His Writings, with a Biographical Sketch. Edited by John Wright Buckham and George Malcolm Stratton. Berkeley: University of California Press, 1934.

Writings about Howison

Burrow, Rufus Jr. "Authorship: The Personalism of George Homes Howison and Borden Parker Bowne." *The Personalist Forum* 13 (1997): 287–303.

———. "Teleological or Ethical Personalism: George Holmes Howison." In *Personalism: A Critical Introduction*, 53–66. St. Louis: Chalice Press, 1999.

Flewelling, Ralph Tyler. "George Holmes Howison: Prophet of Freedom." *The Personalist* 38 (1957): 5–19.

Hanley, Thomas O. "George Holmes Howison." *Pacific Historical Review* 30 (1961): 271–78.

McDermott, John J. "The Confrontation between Royce and Howison." *Transactions of the Charles S. Peirce Society* 30 (1994): 779–90.

McLachlan, James. "George Holmes Howison: The Conception of God Debate and the Beginnings of Personal Idealism." *The Personalist Forum* 11 (1995): 1–16.

———. "The Idealist Critique of Idealism: Bowne's Theistic Personalism and Howison's City of God." *The Personalist Forum* 13 (1997): 89–106.

Perry, Ralph Barton. "George Howison." In *The Thought and Character of William James* vol. 1, 763–77. Boston: Little, Brown, 1935.

Part One

Science and Pragmatism

Science and Pragmatism

AN INTRODUCTION

Frank X. Ryan

CHAUNCEY WRIGHT, CHARLES S. PEIRCE, AND WILLIAM JAMES WERE THE HEARTH and heart of the original Metaphysical Club. Their philosophical agility shaped the legacy that would solidify pragmatism as America's most significant contribution to philosophy. The essays and reviews anthologized here not only unearth the foundation of this revolutionary worldview, but also offer a personal glimpse of three lifelong friends whose disagreements are as insightful as their shared commitment to a philosophy of action, problem solving, and experimentalism.

CHAUNCEY WRIGHT AND THE EVOLUTION OF CONSCIOUSNESS

Chauncey Wright (1830–1875) was a popular fixture at the many informal discussion groups that sprang up in Cambridge in the 1850s and 1860s. Wright's writings are often ponderous, and his few attempts at academic teaching ended in failure. He struggled to support himself as a computer tallying lengthily figures. Awkward and shy in most public settings, among close friends he blossomed into the "Local Socrates" who "lived for conversation."[1]

Wright met Charles Sanders Peirce (1839–1914) at one such group in 1857, the first of "a thousand close disputations" preceding the formation of the Metaphysical Club.[2] Wright was one of the few interlocutors Peirce considered his intellectual equal—a "boxing master" whom the younger philosopher frequently faced "to be severely pummeled."[3]

Wright's enthusiasm for Peirce's emerging philosophy is evident in a published comment about the latter's 1871 review of A. C. Fraser's *The Works of George Berkeley*. Peirce had been teasing an eclectic reading of scholastic realism and Kant into a rebuke of rationalism and nominalistic realism. Wright praises Peirce for challenging the popular misconception that scholastic realism endorses Platonic forms or inscrutable things-in-themselves:

The realistic schoolmen were not such dolts as to contend for an incognizable reality beyond any powers we have for apprehending it, nor of the existence of universals as the objects of general conceptions existing outside the mind.[4]

To assert that "the reality of the [scholastic] realists was the final upshot of experience"[5] is not, however, a nominalism admitting only the subjective content of individual minds that Berkeley pushed to the bizarre yet inevitable conclusion that all reality is in the mind of some perceiver—be it human or Divine.

But where Peirce sides wholly with scholastic realism, decrying the nominalists' "veil of perception," which fosters skepticism and nihilism, Wright urges a more balanced view. Even in exposing its own limitations, skepticism remains "the source of most of the impulses which the spirit of enquiry has received in the history of philosophy."[6] And where Peirce lauds the faith that sustained scholastic realism's arduous sojourn into the anatomy of universals, Wright suspects a "conservatism and dogmatism" anathema to an experimental outlook.

Though we'll return to the loftier aspirations of Peirce's scholastic realism shortly, exploring Wright's own goals may help us determine the extent to which he shared them. Wright aligned himself with "positive" philosophy, though in the tradition of J. S. Mill's analysis of induction rather than the social utopianism of Auguste Comte. With Mill, all talk about reality beyond confirmable empirical hypotheses is forbidden. Metaphysics, whether cast in the mold of materialism, organism, or spiritualism, may be a permissible pump for the imagination, but it's bogus when masquerading as factual description.

For Wright, the epitome of scientific philosophy is Darwin's *On the Origin of Species*. In 1872, Wright both wrote an enthusiastic review of the sixth edition for the *North American Review* and traveled to England to meet Darwin at Down House in Kent. The two corresponded frequently thereafter until Wright's untimely death in 1875.

In an era when American universities were still dominated by clergy, Wright was among a handful of intellectuals on his side of the Atlantic who fully understood, let alone endorsed, Darwin's momentous idea. His review opens with the observation that Darwin's greatest achievement lies not in advocating evolution, which dates from Empedocles in Ancient Greece and whose nineteenth-century champions include John Tyndall and Charles Lyell, but rather in a scrupulous devotion to observation and evidence. Indeed, Darwin's methodology is as important as his findings: though the facts will take decades to fully process and fathom, from the outset it's clear that the cautious positing of hypotheses—framed in abundant data from multiple perspectives—minimizes bias and promotes stable results. Respect for this approach also sets an appropriate bar for future discussion and debate.[7]

Darwin's thesis is that evolution occurs by variation and natural selection. Lacking a proper understanding of genetics, he had no adequate explanation for variation by mutation. But selection was a different matter, for there are many examples of both planned and accidental variations in creatures that survive to pass the trait to their offspring in an altered environment where those without it perish.

Wright's views were sharpened by a debate in print with the prominent Jesuit naturalist St. George Mivart. In 1871 Wright reviewed Mivart's book *On the Genesis of Species*
and compared it unfavorably to Darwin's superior *On the Origin of Species*. Mivart, though
initially a supporter of Darwin's theory, was bothered by the vagaries of variation, and
ultimately rejected it on the ground that there are no *accidents* in nature. He published
a response to Wright in early 1872. Mivart likened the notion of accidental or random
variation to the atheism of the Ancient atomists. Nature, said Mivart, is orderly, rather
than chaotic. Environmental conditions do evolve species by natural selection, but only by
actualizing latent traits already within them by divine design.[8] Wright replied to Mivart
by pointing out how Mivart's speculations are both ad hoc and slipshod about meaning.
Accidents, as Darwin intends the word, are neither uncaused nor random. Instead, they
merely denote events we can't fully anticipate from our current fund of knowledge, and
thus challenge us to investigate their underlying causes. In natural selection, as well as
everywhere else, "accidents" are relative to our knowledge of causes.[9]

In his reviews of Darwin, and in an unpublished "Fragment on Cause and Effect"
penned five years later, Wright clarifies the broader question of "causality" itself.
Metaphysicians are fond of forcing reality into universal chains of causation bound by
notions such as "quiddity," "similarity," or "dependence." But, notes Wright:

> Scientific doctrines and investigations are exclusively concerned with connections
> in phenomena which are susceptible of demonstration by inductive observation,
> and independent of diversities or resemblances in their hidden natures, or of any
> question about their metaphysical derivation, or dependence.[10]

As such, causality signifies relations *we* select and hope to associate by inductive inference.
It is *not* the underbelly of existence, be this mechanistic materialism or, with Mivart, the
lawful ordering of a divine intellect. Our tenuous search for meaning is insignificant in a
vast and indifferent cosmos which, like the weather, is subject to change but oblivious to
notions such as progress or improvement.

Impressed with Wright's review, Darwin asked the Socrates of Cambridge to help
him tackle the ultimate frontier of evolution theory—how variation and natural selection
might explain the miracle of *human* consciousness and will:

> As your mind is so clear, and as you consider so carefully the meaning of words, I
> wish you would take some incidental occasion to consider when a thing may prop-
> erly be said to be effected by the will of man.[11]

Having published *The Descent of Man* the previous year, Darwin was battered by critics on three fronts: (1) unscientific souls who rejected evolution in any form; (2) those
who accepted evolution for all species except *homo sapiens;* and (3) a more learned
group that admitted human physiological evolution but exempted the mental realm.[12]
In contemplating a response to the third group, Darwin wondered whether cognitive
evolution might be a kind of "unconscious selection" patterned on the "unconscious

thoughts" manifest in hypnosis. But the idea wasn't even clearly formed, let alone worth advocating.

Wright meets Darwin's challenge in his signature work, "Evolution of Self-Consciousness." Though he agrees with Locke's claim that all knowledge arises from percepts or representations, he finds the mere "association" of such "simple ideas" both imprecise and too limiting. Instead, following Berkeley, he insists that (1) a representation is a *sign* whose function is to point to an objective existence beyond itself, and joins Peirce in noting that (2) each sign is tied to a *general* or *universal* significance we're typically unaware of yet functions as a disposition to a predictable range of responses.

Imagine, for example, being startled by the sudden charge of a lion. For animals with brains sufficiently advanced to have a capacity for learning, previous encounters with predators have established a connection between the current percept and a general disposition to fear and flight. Moreover, in its capacity as a sign the attribution of the representation is transferred from itself to the external object. It is the lion we fear, not the representation.[13]

One of the classical pragmatists' grandest insights—what, respectively, Peirce, James, and Dewey call "firstness," "pure experience," and "nonreflective having"—is that in its "integral unity" experience is not divided between subject and object, self and other, thing and thought.[14] Since we're typically not aware of either signs or general dispositions, Darwin's intuition about "unconscious thoughts" is confirmed, though in a form that anticipates pragmatism's dynamic problem solving rather than the id or unconscious of psychoanalysis. According to Wright, nonhuman animals are strictly limited to this reactive and noncognitive response. However, due to enhanced functions of memory and discrimination, human brains have evolved the additional ability to separate the representation from its intended object—that is, to recognize representations *as* representations of events that are external yet imminent. According to Wright, the "miracle" of human self-consciousness consists of two consequences of this capacity: (1) the gap between the representation and its object opens options for deliberation and choice not previously possible, which in turn (2) permits the initial recognition of *myself* as the author and agent of such deliberation.[15]

According to Wright, self-consciousness is greatly magnified when, in addition to the representation, the object itself is a sign. Beginning with simple gestures and vocal cues that later develop into speech, these "outward signs" connect to "inward signs or the representative mental images."[16] Anticipating Mead and Dewey, Wright affirms that social communication prefigures even so-called categories of human understanding.[17] Such advances, however, portend no "cognitive utopia" of complete rational control. Natural selection permeates the social realm as thoroughly as it does the biological: we create meanings, but meanings direct our motives, values, and very behaviors—often in ways that are, "in fact, unconscious, if not unintended."[18]

Wright aligns human will and emotion with this agency view of self-consciousness. If cognition is intrinsically the capacity for deliberation in pursuit of some external end, then *will* means simply the ability to pursue this end with focus and tenacity. A will is "free" insofar as it can deflect impulses and distractions. As with consciousness itself, will is a function of directed behaviors, not an occult force or power.

Wright's contribution to a scientific naturalism and pragmatism is a mixed bag of clear affinities and suggestive gaps. His credentials in science are impeccable—he was both a philosopher of science and a practicing scientist whose interests ranged from evolution to calculating leaf distributions optimal for the absorption of sunlight. And around the same time that Peirce was formulating pragmatism, Wright incorporated its central tenets of real generals, sign-indices, and noncognitive habits into his essay on self-consciousness.

Wright's early death prevented his work from coalescing into anything like Peirce's pragmatic *Weltanschauung* grounded in a systematic analysis of phenomenological categories. Although Wright's positivism prefigures James's radical empiricism in its preference for method over metaphysics, Wright would have rejected any suggestion that truth is the "cash value" of an idea. Among the classical pragmatists, Wright's scientific empiricism most clearly anticipates Dewey's experimental pragmatism, where truth lies in the physical confirmation of hypotheses, though even here Wright's "cosmic weather" precludes the meliorism of his successor's normative and social aspirations.

CHARLES S. PEIRCE AND THE CIRCUIT OF BELIEF-DOUBT-INQUIRY

As we've seen, Wright's enthusiasm for Peirce's scholastic realism is tempered by worries about a dogmatic conservatism at odds with the fallibilism and experimentalism they both share. This did not escape Peirce's notice, whose published reply wryly thanks Wright for a "too glittering notice of my remarks" that "attributed to me a degree of originality which is not my due."[19] Peirce's point is that his version of scholastic realism renounces all ties to the dogmatic and the absolute, and that, to the contrary, his intent was to expose the nominalist weakness for "absolutely external causes" that precludes seeing universals in actual realities "present to us."[20]

A closer look at Peirce's review of Fraser's *Works of Berkeley* both further exonerates him from any flirtation with absolutism and, more significantly, locates the opening move in a bold new philosophical gambit. Peirce insists that the greatest of the schoolmen, Duns Scotus, rejected the nominalist notion that what we call "realities" consist merely of "thought-signs" cut off from their purported external causes, holding instead the "more natural and obvious" view that objects have "an existence independent of your mind or mine or that of any number of persons."[21]

Peirce is quick to jump on the misconception that "independent existence" denotes a thing-in-itself or even "mind-independence" per se. In a bold stroke toward pragmatism, he holds that reality is not some self-contained state or condition, but a function of a *drift* or *gravitation* from error toward truth:

> To assert that there are external things which can be known only as exerting a power on our sense, is nothing different from asserting that there is a general *drift* in the

history of human thought which will lead to one general agreement. . . . And any truth more perfect than this destined conclusion, any reality more absolute than what is thought in it, is a fiction of metaphysics.[22]

We usually think of realism as differentiating an inherent "fact of the matter" from the human task of confirming it, but Peirce vigorously rejects this notion of "mind-independence," offering instead a

theory of reality instantly fatal to the idea of a thing in itself—a thing existing independently of all relation to the mind's conception of it. . . . [My] theory involves a phenomenalism. But it is the phenomenalism of Kant, and not that of Hume. Indeed, what Kant called his Copernican step was precisely the passage from the nominalistic to the realistic view of reality. It was the essence of his philosophy to regard the real object as determined by the mind. That was nothing else than to consider every conception and intuition which enters necessarily into the experience of an object, and which is not transitory and accidental, as having objective validity. In short, it was to regard the reality as the normal product of mental action, and not as the incognizable cause of it.[23]

While defending Kant's Copernican revolution, wherein the nominalist doctrine that the mind conforms to its object is reversed such that objects conform to mind, Peirce has nonetheless outgrown Kant's formal conception of mind consisting of sensible conditions of time and space plus intellectual categories. Following Hegel, mind is now organic—manifest in what Peirce proclaims as "the fountain of the current of human thought."[24] The reality of universals is thus demonstrated in the role they play in the gravitation from error to truth:

General conceptions enter into all judgments, and therefore into true opinions. Consequently a thing in the general is as real as in the concrete. . . . It is a real which only exists by virtue of an act of thought knowing it, but that thought is not an arbitrary or accidental one dependent on any idiosyncrasies, but one which will hold in the final opinion.[25]

Peirce is acutely aware that appealing to "opinion" risks the charge of subjectivism, especially insofar as it seems to downplay the role of perception as *representing* objects in the external world. This concern is unfounded, however, for he fully grants that sensations alert us to objects. However, they do so as sign functions *in* inferences—a shrill sound alerts us to a ceiling alarm that directs our attention to smoke as a sign of a hidden fire. In such functions, moreover, we distinguish signs with overtly external referents from thoughts and dreams without them, and thus come to differentiate objective from subjective. Sign functions are "mind-dependent" in the sense that the full series from sensation to articulated conception is, as Dewey might say, "open and above board" in the play of signs, and not the mere end-product of a thing-in-itself lurking behind a veil of perception.[26]

If Peirce's first great step toward pragmatism is recasting Kant's Copernican revolution as a dynamic framework of rectified error, his second step is recognizing that the function of universals in this process is predominantly *nonreflective*. Where virtually all philosophies—Platonism, rationalism, nominalism, direct realism—hold that universals are bright cognitive beacons collecting likenesses from perceived particulars as the basis for recognizing other things of that kind, Scotus ingeniously hit upon the notion "that a conception exists which is in the mind *habituliter,* not *actualiter.*"[27] For example, we recognize a particular horse not by cognitively consulting a concept, but rather through a tacit understanding of horses coalesced in experiences that concur with the consensus of the community. Scotus's *habituliter,* recast by Peirce as habituated belief, becomes a cornerstone of pragmatism.

Peirce admits that scholastic realism was all but obliterated by the nominalism that flourished with Ockham, Hobbes, Locke, Berkeley, Hume, and Mill. In contemporary times, nominalism has even co-opted the word *realism,* and its propensity for materialism and individualism has penetrated the very sinews of science and culture. However,

> the question whether the *genus homo* has any existence except as individuals, is the question whether there is anything of any more dignity, worth, and importance than individual happiness, individual aspirations, and individual life.[28]

Peirce thought there was, and, unlike Wright, set out to create a systematic and fully integrated alternative. He knew that Kant had already begun to loosen the formal tethers of the first *Critique*, where categories of the intellect impose ready-made concepts upon sense, by suggesting that concepts are often constructed by observation and hypothesis— we learn about organisms by learning how they flourish within their environments. This practical and experimental approach to knowledge, which Kant called the *pragmatische,* inspired Peirce to a worldview he dubbed *pragmatism.*[29]

Although there are suggestive discussions in earlier writings, what became known as the "pragmatic method" debuts in Peirce's "The Fixation of Belief" (1877). One of the few works known to be presented in draft form to the original Metaphysical Club, Peirce's expansion of Alexander Bain's notion that belief is a "bet" we're willing to act upon would have appealed to the legal minds Oliver Wendell Holmes and Nicholas St. John Green, as well as the empiricism of Wright and James.

For Peirce, the various ways we "fix" beliefs are "Illustrations of the Science of Logic"— where logic is a "habit of mind" useful in drawing sound inferences. Taking a page from Scotus's *habituliter,* he notes that such habits, or guiding principles, are seldom noticed in tasks that are routine or familiar. It is when something goes wrong—our ship becomes lost in a storm—that deliberate attention to a skill such as navigation is required.[30]

In the broader art of navigating life we internalize countless guiding principles—social, cultural, normative, and scientific. In building a worldview, however, we look for principles that are "absolutely essential" for inference. Peirce identifies the relation of *belief* and *doubt* as "subject to some rules which all minds are alike bound by." We must presuppose belief and doubt "before we can have any clear conception of reasoning at all," for these are "rules of reasoning which are deduced from the very idea of the process."[31]

Peirce casts belief as a "calm and satisfactory state" marked by an established "habit which will determine our actions." Belief evokes neither conscious thought nor action. Instead, it sets up a disposition to "behave in a certain way, when the occasion arises." Doubt, to the contrary, "is an uneasy and dissatisfied state from which we struggle to free ourselves and pass into the state of belief"; it "stimulates us to action until it is destroyed."[32]

The passage from doubt to renewed belief constitutes *inquiry,* the third essential guiding principle. Inquiry emerges from "the irritation of doubt" in a concerted effort to identify and resolve what's wrong so as to restore the serenity of nonreflective belief. For those who assert that reflective thought begins in wonder or for the sheer love of truth, Peirce's dissention is stark: we think primarily to get ourselves out of trouble:

> With the doubt, therefore, the struggle begins, and with the cessation of doubt it ends. Hence, the sole object of inquiry is the settlement of opinion. We may fancy that this is not enough for us, and that we seek, not merely an opinion, but a true opinion. But put this fancy to the test, and it proves groundless; for as soon as a firm belief is reached, we are entirely satisfied, whether the belief be true or false.[33]

Here Peirce stops short of James's later pronouncement that truth *is* such settled opinion, and Dewey's claim that any object is an attained *objective* of inquiry. Nonetheless, it's clear that for Peirce the circuit of belief-doubt-inquiry reconfigures the Kantian account of objectivity, and does not merely describe a subjective state or process used to access a mind-independent world:

> It is clear that nothing out of the sphere of our knowledge can be our object, for nothing which does not affect the mind can be the motive for a mental effort.[34]

Despite its nascent form, Peirce's circuit clearly foreshadows James's characterization of the stream of consciousness as a series of "perchings and flights" and Dewey's famous pattern of inquiry from nonreflective experience to problematic situation, diagnosis, hypothesis, test, and final attained objective. As such, the "Fixation of Belief" is justly regarded as pragmatism's *opus primum.*

In the breezier second half of the essay, Peirce considers historically significant ways of "fixing" or achieving belief: (1) the method of tenacity, where I cling to a belief *because* it is mine; (2) the method of authority, where tenacity expands to embrace socially approved truths; and (3) the a priori method, where agreement by appeal to "reason" actually masks aesthetic preferences. While each has its merits, Peirce unsurprisingly stumps for (4) the method of scientific investigation, due to its objectivity, fairness, and capacity for producing verifiable results.[35]

In characterizing the method of science, Peirce makes an oft-quoted claim:

> There are real things, whose characters are entirely independent of our opinions about them; those realities affect our senses according to regular laws, and, though our sensations are as different as our relations to the objects, yet, by taking advantage of the laws of perception, we can ascertain by reasoning how things really are.[36]

Unlike the codicil in "The Works of Berkeley," on this occasion Peirce does not repeat Kant's warning that "real things" are nonetheless perceiver-dependent—an omission many cite as evidence of a swing toward a realism more conventionally externalist than the modified scholastic realism we've tracked. Though such an interpretation is plausible, it's worth noting that Peirce's allusion to "existence independent of your mind or mine or that of any number of persons" is virtually identical the earlier phrase where he insists that reality independent of "any number of persons" is *not* independent of the eventual agreement of the *community* of observers, and that *sensation* is an originating event in a play of signs, not the causal imprint of some mind-independent realm.

This observation, of course, does not counter the possibility that Peirce changed his mind about realism somewhere between 1871 and 1877. To assess this possibility, let's consult the 1878 sequel to "The Fixation of Belief." Peirce opens "How to Make Our Ideas Clear" with a scathing indictment of the rationalists' foundation of clear and distinct ideas. For Descartes, a clear idea is one "recognized whenever it is met with." But, chides Peirce, this just amounts to "familiarity," which cannot distinguish ideas that *are* clear from those that merely *seem* clear.[37] A *distinct* idea fares no better, since it merely "contains nothing which is not clear." Anticipating Quine's critique of analyticity, Peirce also mocks Leibniz's aligning an idea with its definition, inasmuch as "nothing new can ever be learned by analyzing definitions." Accordingly, "that much-admired 'ornament of logic'—the doctrine of clearness and distinctness—may be pretty enough, but it is high time to relegate [it] to our cabinet of curiosities."[38]

Unsurprisingly, Peirce's counterproposal for conceptual clarity counsels the attentive cultivation of the method of belief-doubt-inquiry. After all, the full course of our lives is permeated with the ebb and flow of security and disruption: from mundane annoyances such as searching for cab fare to full-scale emergencies, belief is beset by challenges "slight or energetic, calm or turbulent."[39] As the *immediate* locus of disruption, sensation protrudes from the background of *mediate* guiding principles to initiate the inferential sign-sequence of inquiry; thought then supervenes as "a thread of melody running through the succession of our sensations" until belief returns as "the demi-cadence which closes a musical phrase in the symphony of our intellectual life."[40]

Practically speaking, ideas are clearer when we minimize distinctions among beliefs that differ only in their grammatical construction or mode of expression. But the highest grade of clarity is achieved by acknowledging the inseparable bond between our idea of a thing and its observed sensible effects:

Consider what effects, which might conceivably have practical bearings, we conceive the object of our conception to have. Then the whole of our conception of those effects is the whole of our conception of the object.[41]

To illustrate this, Peirce asserts that something may be called *hard* only when "it will not be scratched by many other substances."[42] In other words, and coordinate with belief itself, meaning is a *disposition* for something to behave in observable and predictable ways when put to the test of inquiry. According to Peirce, both science and philosophy would greatly benefit by adhering to this maxim—for example, to define "mass" as a capacity for sustained movement in the absence of an opposing force, or even "force" itself as regularities observed in various changes of motion, removes all traces of occult "powers" from scientific explanation and metaphysical essences from philosophy.[43]

Peirce anticipates the externalist complaint that his dispositional criterion confuses the human *observation* of effects with properties things themselves possess regardless of such tests. Isn't it ludicrous, after all, to say a diamond that's never tested isn't really hard, or becomes hard only to the extent to which it's tested? Similarly, aren't we slighting the meaning of force in reducing it to mere observations of acceleration when we should be looking for it as the *cause* of acceleration?[44]

Peirce's analysis of "properties things possess of their own accord" echoes his attack on "in-itself reality" in "The Works of Berkeley." While it's logically possible to speculate on the status of untested diamonds, for all practical purposes it's completely idle to do so—a diamond that becomes hard only when tested is empirically indistinguishable from another that's hard all along; hence, the difference exists only at the level of language. The same argument extends to deciding whether force *is* or is the *cause* of acceleration—if the alternatives are unobservable in principle, there's no factual dispute, though in this case the tendency to lapse into thinking of force as a mysterious power is sufficient to avoid such speculation.[45]

Combined with the habituated belief of real generals and the circuit of belief-doubt-inquiry, Peirce's pragmatic maxim yields a principle sound enough to support further approaches to inquiry developed by James and Dewey. We have not yet resolved, however, the lingering question of Peirce's realism, which he takes up at the end of his essay. Here, we're reminded that insofar as we generally have no problem distinguishing thoughts and dreams from perceived externalities, we "define the real as that whose characters are independent of what anybody may think them to be." However, we've no clear idea of "reality" on the basis of this definition alone:

> Here, then, let us apply our rules. According to them, reality, like every other quality, consists in the peculiar sensible effects which things partaking in it produce. The only effect which real things have is to cause belief, for all the sensations which they excite emerge into consciousness in the form of beliefs.[46]

In other words, as late as 1878 Peirce still insists that reality is not a mind-independent cause or antecedent condition of our awareness of things, but an effect, or *realization,* forged in the problem-solving function of belief-doubt-inquiry. And if reality is optimally the "settled opinion" of competent observers, the same holds for "the ideas of truth and falsehood, [which] in their full development, appertain exclusively to the scientific method of settling opinion."[47] Together, truth as *experimental* and reality as *realization* renders "How to Make Our Ideas Clear" wholly consonant with his earlier pronouncement:

> Reality is independent, not necessarily of thought in general, but only of what you or I or any finite number of men may think about it.... The opinion which is fated to be ultimately agreed to by all who investigate, is what we mean by the truth, and the object represented in this opinion is the real. That is the way I would explain reality.[48]

Though Peirce's view of reality after 1878 is beyond this volume's purview,[49] let's recall his debt to Kant in (1) deriving pragmatism from the *pragmatische,* thus (2) preserving the Copernican Revolution's dictum that objects conform to mind—where (3) "mind" is the dispositional matrix of habituated guiding principles and (4) whose "essential" categories comprise the circuit of belief-doubt-inquiry. These tenets establish Peirce's pragmatism as a new and—dare we say?—"systematic" worldview that outpaces Wright's protean positivism, or for that matter the aspirations of any other member of the original Metaphysical Club.[50]

WILLIAM JAMES AND THE WILL TO RECOVER

Four years Peirce's junior, and twelve years Wright's, William James (1843–1910) was still gaining his philosophical legs when the Metaphysical Club first met in 1872; as such, the bulk of the pieces collected here are reviews and commentaries that predate by a decade his first seminal contributions to psychology and pragmatism. James met Peirce upon enrolling in Harvard's Lawrence Scientific School in 1861, and shortly thereafter was introduced to Wright. Youth was not the only factor that delayed his development. In the late 1860s James fell into a "vastation" he described as "a horrible fear of my own existence."[51] The core of his spiritual and philosophical views surfaced in his arduous recovery from this affliction.

If Wright was Peirce's boxing master, James must have felt like a sorcerer's apprentice under the mercurial Peirce. Lacking his mentor's expertise in logic and mathematics, the young medical student was alternately mesmerized and confused by his "exceedingly bold subtle & incomprehensible" arguments.[52] James gradually earned Peirce's respect, after James refused to "be overawed by his sententious manner and his paradoxical & obscure statements," and began to "grasp firmly, contradict, push hard, make fun of him."[53]

James's relationship with Wright was even more complex. His natural amiability easily cut through the older philosopher's social unease and inertia. Their friendship was deep and abiding, with Wright a fixture at the James family home in Cambridge.[54] And while it would take years for James to assimilate Peirce's systematic pragmatism, Wright's lean antimetaphysical empiricism meshed well with his yen for psychology.

Wright's influence on James is evident in an 1872 review of Hippolyte Taine's *On Intelligence*. Despite sound credentials as a literary theorist and historicist, James suggests that Taine is out of his league when dabbling in speculative philosophy. Indeed, *On Intelligence* is an ungainly pairing of a famished nominalism that pulverizes concepts into particular acts of naming with a gluttonous metaphysics that elevates general qualities to the status of ultimate reality.[55] Taine's theory of perception is similarly askew: he effectively undercuts his own endorsement of Mill's restriction of reality to "permanent possibilities of sensation" by oddly insisting that such "hallucinations" become "veridical" in correspondence with genuine external qualities.

Wright's antipathy toward metaphysics, extreme nominalism, and correspondence realism are all evident in this review. Nonetheless, and as we've touched on earlier, Wright and James came to loggerheads over a dispute that ultimately rattled their friendship. The source of James's dissent goes back to his vastation struggles. Grasping for hope, he was buoyed by Charles Renouvier's deft defense of free will: if all beliefs are determined, then my very affirmation of this is also determined, in which case I have no way to tell whether it's actually true. To avoid this conundrum, I affirm free will on the observable grounds that I can *choose* to do so when I might have other thoughts.[56]

Renouvier's avowal of free will marked the turning point in James's recovery. He next embraced pioneering psychiatrist Henry Maudsley's hope that mental afflictions can be overcome by acts of sheer will. In *The Prevention of Insanity*, Maudsley tags inheritance and intemperance as the two chief causes of mental illness. But even these, it so happens, are remediable. The key, as James quotes Maudsley in an 1874 review, is the insight that each of us "has a power over himself to prevent insanity." For, indeed, "Not many persons need go mad, perhaps—at any rate from moral causes—if they only knew the resources of their nature, and how to develop them systematically."[57]

The *systematic* development of the resourceful mind led James to the work of the prominent English philosopher, actor, and scientist George Henry Lewes. James found Lewes thoroughly versed in, and somewhat sympathetic to, the positivistic empiricism of the mid-nineteenth century. Such philosophers deny all continuity in nature itself: "The syntheses of data we think necessary are only so to *us*, from habit."[58] However, even Mill, the arch-positivist, must concede that the only world *for us* is the world *as we can come to know it*—thus, to subtract the human framework through which we investigate the world is to leave us with no world at all. James applauds Lewes for his willingness to embrace such a world—a world inherently relational and continuous; in short, a *uni*-verse.[59]

If Mill is the king of positivism, Wright is lord executioner who wields the scythe of cosmic randomness against any suggestion of ultimate order or purpose. James's discontent eventually swelled to the point of challenging his mentor directly. "Against Nihilism," an unpublished 1874 essay likely circulated within the Metaphysical Club, opens with a blunt attack: "My complaint against Wright's Nihilism after all amounts to this: that he denies this to be a Universe, and makes it out a 'Nulliverse.'" For Wright, existence is sheer happenstance without rhyme or reason. But this "contradicts the vague but deep notion of common sense" that each thing "has a *meaning,* serves a purpose, is a cause, or an end."[60] Even more tellingly, Wright ignores Peirce's dictum that the real is *relational*—according to which nature itself is real only insofar as it exhibits connectedness or continuity. In denying any such continuity, Wright effectively "denies that there is any universe."[61] But, as Lewes and Peirce insist, perception of things is no mere sequence of unrelated sensations, but inferential sign-activity where part of the past is preserved in a present that opens into a *directed* future. Such continuous transition is not sheer happenstance, but normative and teleological: a

> "relation of reality which implies not only that we feel so & so, but that we *should* feel so, that we are meant to feel so, that there *is* something outside of the feeling itself as an instant conscious existence." Metaphysical speculation aside, this minimally asserts "the *continuity* of the real world," thus rebuffing the sheer particularism of nihilism.[62]

A year later James was emboldened enough to make his attack public, and indulge in a bit of cosmic speculation of his own.

In 1852, William Thomson had published a theory, later known as the second law of thermodynamics, about the "universal tendency in nature to the dissipation of mechanical energy."[63] The alarming thought that the entire universe was unraveling from complex to simpler forms soon captured the imagination of scientists and the literate public alike. Two Scottish physicists, Balfour Stewart and Peter Guthrie Tait, capitalized on this frenzy in *The Unseen Universe.* Their theory, as reviewed by James, accepts the disintegration of complex physical orders, but argues that their "memory" is preserved in an ether, cosmic backdrop, or "hidden world." Indeed, they argue, the true nature of the universe is the reverse of what we've supposed: in this hidden realm is the cognitive blueprint of the physical universe—the latter, having run its course, is now being called home. For Steward and Tait, it's but a short step to identify this cosmic mind with God, whose beloved Son is immanent in the physical world.[64]

For James, *The Hidden Universe* offers an inviting account of how the continuity of mind extends into the realm of the physical—the thesis of "Against Nihilism." At the same time, he deems the overall project so speculative that its tactics are "identical with those of the most primitive, 'unscientific,' and short-winded theologians." In fact, believing in a divine blueprint would call for an act of faith as indulgent as that "of the most narrow minded old woman [who] so quickly embraces her briefly-recited cosmogony."[65]

Just as we think James is about to consign the theory to an ash pile, he conjures a burning bush:

> We, for our part, not only hold that such an act of trust is licit, but we think, further, that *any one to whom it makes a practical difference* (whether of motive to action of mental peace) is duty bound to make it. If "scientific" scruples withhold him from making it, this proves his intellect to have been simply sicklied o'er and paralyzed by scientific pursuits.[66]

For Wright, this was the proverbial last straw. He'd been acutely aware of his protégé's "rebellious" attacks, both private and public. Giving as good as got, Wright excoriated James's appeal to faith as puerile and gutless. Confronting James to his face on the outrageous claim of being *duty bound* to faith, Wright managed to wring a retraction of the "duty" to believe.

Some themes explored in these early reviews, such as the continuity of thought and the will—if not the duty—to believe, became hallmarks of James's later philosophy.[67] Overall, however, Wright's criticism seems fair insofar as James's indulgences reveal not just immaturity, but a lingering cloud of spiritual angst.[68]

Sadly, Wright did not live long enough to reconcile their dispute, or to witness James's slow delivery from metaphysical mysticism into what he had once dismissed as the "sicklied" science. Nonetheless, the sky was brightening. James soon abandoned Maudsley's suggestion that a disciplined mind is sufficient to ward off insanity: Most individuals so incapacitated require help, and only the occasional genius can transform cognitive affliction into productive and creative acts.[69] Even more significantly, though still decades away from espousing pragmatism as an experimental methodology that supplants metaphysics, James was now inclined to tether such speculation to the natural sciences.

This is evident in an 1875 review of Wilhelm Wundt's *Grundzüze der physiologischen Psychologie.*[70] James praises Wundt's years of laboratory work under the guidance of the German physician and physicist Hermann von Helmholtz. Grounded in physics and physiology, the *Grundzüze* marks Wundt's groundbreaking foray into psychology. For James, Wundt leads a vanguard committed to revitalizing philosophy through science.

Ever since Descartes, philosophers had assumed that perception is a mechanical process of stimulus and response. Upon receiving a percept, sense organs transmit a signal to the brain that produces a direct motor response. The mind becomes aware of this reflex arc, but plays no role in its transmission. While noting such invariant physiological elements, Wundt's experiments determined that response time also depends upon psychological factors, including the perceiver's *selection* of sensations and her *expectations* about the perceptual experience. Indeed, given these factors, Wundt surprisingly showed that motor response often begins *before* the stimulus is received.[71]

Wundt's findings convinced James of the folly of both the mechanical Cartesian arc and empiricism's isolated sense impressions merely bundled into complex ideas by the mind. It confirmed his intuition that matter and mind, the physical and the psychological, are thoroughly entwined and reciprocally interdependent—themes that figure prominently both in James's mature psychology and Dewey's ventures beyond the reflex arc to an *organic circuit* of mind, body, and environment.

Further evidence of James's retreat from metaphysics is evident in an 1878 critique of Herbert Spencer's metaphysics. Spencer's cosmic evolution had been a favorite target of Wright, whom he accused of substituting his own pet theories for physical evidence in an especially egregious example of metaphysical whimsy. James presses this charge: the "correspondence" Spencer expostulates between "inner and outer relations" in the process of mental evolution (1) is pure intellect with no acknowledgment of emotional, aesthetic, or normative content, (2) assumes a wholly materialistic basis without argument or justification, and (3) holds that all evolution is merely the inevitable unfolding of traits fully defined in an embryonic state.[72] Moreover, this obscure "correspondence" is cashed out in equally vague synonyms such as fit, adjustment, and conformity. And though Spencer ultimately characterizes fitness as "survival at any price," as a *summum bonum,* this shamefully eschews values such as caring, cooperation, and sacrifice that "make survival worthwhile."[73]

James's loudest complaint is that Spencer's universe of unfolding latent traits precludes human agency empowered to shape a novel future. Yet *survival* itself is an anticipated outcome of how we *should* act. Indeed, and more generally, what we call an outer existence is the projection of a hypothesis successfully realized. Thus,

> the knower is not simply a mirror floating with no foot hold anywhere and passively reflecting an order that he comes upon and finds simply existing. The knower is an actor, and co-efficient of the truth on one side, whilst on the other he registers the truth which he helps to create. Mental interests, hypotheses, postulates, so far as they are bases for human action—action which to a great extent transforms the world—help to *make* the truth which they declare.[74]

James's pilgrimage toward Peirce and pragmatism takes another significant step forward in "The Sentiment of Rationality," the only fully original published essay (not a review or critique) included in this set. His commitment to the continuity of mind and nature has not wavered, but now his analysis is wholly psychological rather than metaphysical. The basic idea is that "rationality," hailed by others as certitude delivered on a blinding light of insight or intuition, actually expresses a *sentiment*—a "strong feeling of ease, peace, rest":

> This feeling of the sufficiency of the present moment, of its absoluteness—this absence of all need to explain it, account for it or justify it—is what I call the Sentiment of Rationality.[75]

In other words, rationality is akin to what Peirce calls *belief,* or perhaps that brief moment of conceptual resolution on the verge of fading into habit.

James also shares Peirce's insight that *doubt* is thought's constant companion, which he expresses in psycho-physiological terms:

> All feeling whatever, in the light of certain psychological speculations, seems to depend for its physical condition not on simple discharge of nerve-currents, but on their discharge under arrest, impediment or resistance. . . . When the movement is inhibited or when the thought meets with difficulties, we experience a distress which yields to an opposite feeling as fast as the obstacle is overcome.[76]

Also like Peirce, for whom the circuit of belief-doubt-inquiry is a nonmystical way to explain the "ingression" of universals upon particulars, James regards the sentiment of rationality as middle position between nominalists content with the *clarity* of particular experiences and the *unity* longed for by metaphysicians.[77]

James's compromise between clarity and unity acknowledges, with nominalism, that sensation consists of distinct qualities. Yet, says James, our ability to recognize the *same quality* of white in a cloud and in snow is a visceral continuity nominalists ignore at their peril. In assembling the contents of its world, experience tacitly sifts through multiple levels of affinities and differences guided by needs and interests. Though clearly no longer the unity of Maudsley's utopian metaphysics, the continuity of human thought is remarkable. Indeed, constructing a world through such selections is a profound source of satisfaction and well-being: "The gratification of the sentiment of rationality depends hardly at all on the worth of the attribute which strings things together but almost exclusively on the mere fact of their being strung at all."[78]

James thus proposes an interface of mind and world that explains the connectedness of things without the metaphysical extravagance of Maudsley and Lewes. The mind, says James, is quantitatively limited to grasping one fact at a time; what it must connect is the qualitative diversity of its functions—sensational, volitional, normative, aesthetic. The physical universe, on the other hand, is just the opposite: though reducible to a single quality, for instance, force or matter, its sheer quantity of facts remains inexhaustible. Hence, we are compelled to accept the Kantian compromise that what the mind connects is merely the phenomenal—how things appear to us rather than as they actually are.

On its face, this seems a "most miserable and inadequate substitute for the fullness of truth." Yet perhaps this limitation is also its strength, or at least a consolation. If knowledge could be complete and final, if all limitation and doubt could be eliminated, then so too would be the sentiment of rationality itself—forged as it is in the restless swing between disruptive doubt and restored continuity.[79]

Despite its palpable advance toward pragmatism, "The Rationality of Belief" remains a transitional work. James later explicitly rejects the identity of simple sensations: "*There is no proof that the same bodily sensation is ever got by us twice. . . . What is got twice is the same OBJECT*," meaning the social artifact constructed in contexts of use.[80] And the "miserable" compromise of the phenomenal later contrasts to a "noumenal" only in the sense of experiences yet to be traversed by the serpent's trail, rather than any inkling of an inaccessible in-itself—themes that emerge a decade later in *The Principles of Psychology* and James's subsequent writings on pragmatism.

HALL'S AMERICA OF YOUTH AND CURIOSITY

Granville Stanley Hall (1846–1924) attended Williams College and taught at Antioch College before enrolling at Harvard in 1876. Arriving a year after the death of Wright and the dissolution of the original Metaphysical Club, he befriended William James, who shared his passion for Wilhelm Wundt. Hall did participate in the "Idealist" Metaphysical Club, and in 1879 received the first doctorate in psychology granted by

Harvard. After a whirlwind tour of Europe meeting luminaries such as Wundt and Helmholtz, the future world-renowned psychologist and president of Clark College returned to Cambridge to participate in a lecture series on education which inspired "Philosophy in the United States."

Hall's thesis is that "if philosophers in America are as rare as snakes in Norway, it is because the country is yet too young."[81] He notes that all but a handful of the several hundred colleges in the United States are controlled by clergy who censor or suppress the free pursuit of ideas, especially those lurking in "an abyss of skepticism and materialism."[82] A course in philosophy is a slop-bucket of religion, history, ethics, aesthetics, and syllogistic logic typically thrown together by the institution's president. In the rare instances when teachers trained in philosophy are lucky enough to find work, they must teach an onerous course load in other disciplines, and labor in departments that are unappreciated and underfunded.[83]

Fortunately, however, the very philistinism that compels trustees and donors to support only profitable disciplines is countered by "the enterprise and individuality which are characteristic of American life, and which have shown themselves in all sorts of independent speculation." Thus, the slack created by narrow-minded colleges has been taken up by informal clubs and debating societies.[84]

Though buoyed by philosophical enclaves such as the St. Louis Hegelians and emerging journals such as *The Journal of Speculative Philosophy* and *Popular Science Monthly*, Hall is most enthusiastic about the original Metaphysical Club. James is hailed for his advances in physiological psychology, Wright for his penetrating grasp of the evolution of self-consciousness, and Peirce for his forward-looking circuit of belief, doubt, and inquiry.[85] These three philosophers, in particular, resonate with an American sentiment that is broadly scientific, experimental, interdisciplinary, and hopeful:

> It is philanthropic, full of faith in human nature and in the future. And if, according to a leading canon of the new psychology, the active part of our nature is the essential element in cognition and all possible truth is practical, then may we not rationally hope that even those materialisms of faith and of business which we now deplore, are yet laying the foundations for a maturity of philosophical insight deep enough at some time to intellectualize and thus harmonise all the diverse strands in our national life.[86]

The need to harmonize strands of divisiveness is as pressing today as it was a century and a half ago. Fanaticism and religious zeal are again denying the legitimacy of science, and higher education is under the heavy thumb of the boardroom and business model: the humanities in general, and philosophy in particular, are increasingly regarded as dispensable luxuries. But if problem solving extends to the heart of our nature and the horizons of our world, if truth is revisable, if the ultimate philosophical idea is the social, the vision of the original leaders of the Metaphysical Club may yet guide us toward an identity of innovation, enfranchisement, diversity, and pursuit of the common good.

NOTES

1. Louis Menand, *The Metaphysical Club: A Story of Ideas in America* (New York: Farrar, Sraus and Giroux, 2001), 205–206.

2. Charles S. Peirce, "Essays Toward the Interpretation of Our Thoughts" (1909). MS 620, Charles S. Peirce Papers, Houghton Library, Harvard University, Cambridge, MA.

3. Charles S. Peirce, "Pragmatism," in *Collected Papers of Charles Sanders Peirce*, ed. Charles Hartshorne, Paul Weiss, and Arthur Burks (Cambridge: Harvard University Press, 1931–1966), vol. 1, §269. Hereafter references to the *Collected Papers* (*CP*) are given by volume and paragraph numbers.

4. Chauncey Wright, "C. S. Peirce's Review of Berkeley." Note about Charles S. Peirce's review of A. C. Fraser, *The Works of George Berkeley* in *The Nation* 13 (November 30, 1971): 355.

5. Ibid.

6. Ibid., 356.

7. Chauncey Wright, "Review of Charles Darwin's *The Origin of Species*, 6th Ed., and George Mivart's "Evolution and its Consequences" and "Specific Genesis," *North American Review* 115 (July 1872): 3–4.

8. St. George Mivart, "Specific Genesis." *North American Review* 115 (April 1872): 465–66.

9. Wright, "Review of Charles Darwin's *The Origin of Species*," 7.

10. Chauncey Wright, "A Fragment on Cause and Effect," in *Philosophical Discussions by Chauncey Wright,* ed. Charles E. Norton (New York: Henry Holt, 1877), 408.

11. Charles Darwin to Chauncey Wright, 1872, in *The Life and Letters of Charles Darwin*, vol. 3, ed. Francis Darwin (London: John Murray, 1888), 164.

12. Among the latter was Alfred Russel Wallace, whose expertise in natural selection was second only to Darwin's.

13. Chauncey Wright, "The Evolution of Self-Consciousness," *North American Review* 116 (April 1873): 253.

14. John Dewey, *Experience and Nature*, vol. 1 of *The Later Works of John Dewey*, ed. Jo Ann Boydston (Carbondale: Southern Illinois University Press, 1988), 18–19.

15. Wright, "The Evolution of Self-Consciousness," 254.

16. Ibid., 269.

17. Ibid., 264.

18. Ibid., 306.

19. Charles S. Peirce,"Mr. Peirce and the Realists." *The Nation* 13 (December 14, 1871): 386.

20. Ibid.

21. Ibid., 454–55.

22. Ibid., 456.

23. Ibid., 456–57.

24. Ibid., 458.

25. Ibid., 457.

26. Ibid., 456.

27. Ibid., 459.

28. Ibid., 472.

29. *CP* 5, 412.

30. Charles S. Peirce, "The Fixation of Belief," *Popular Science Monthly* 12 (November 1877): 4.

31. Ibid., 4–5.

32. Ibid., 5–6.

33. Ibid., 6.

34. Ibid.

35. Ibid., 7–15.

36. Ibid., 13.

37. Charles S. Peirce, "How to Make Our Ideas Clear," *Popular Science Monthly* 12 (January 1878): 286.

38. Ibid., 288.

39. Ibid., 290.

40. Ibid., 290–91.

41. Ibid., 293.

42. Ibid., 294.

43. Ibid., 295–97.

44. Ibid., 294, 297.

45. Ibid., 297.

46. Ibid., 298.

47. Ibid.

48. Ibid., 300.

49. For a discussion of the complexities of Peirce's realism, see Frank Ryan, "Scholastic Realism and Pragmatic Contextualism," in *The Future of Realism in the American Tradition of Pragmatic Realism,* ed. John R. Shook (Amherst, NY: Prometheus Books, 2003), 321–50.

50. Excepting, perhaps, John Fisk, though metaphysical aspirations were at best tangential to pragmatism.

51. William James, *The Varieties of Religious Experience* (Cambridge: Harvard University Press, 1985), 134.

52. William James, *The Correspondence of William James*, vol. 1, ed. Ignas K. Skrupskelis and Elizabeth M. Berkeley (Charlottesville: University Press of Virginia, 1995), 361.

53. Ibid., 246.

54. Menand, *The Metaphysical Club*, 218.

55. William James, "Review of H. Taine, *On Intelligence*," *The Nation* 15 (August 29, 1872): 140. James remarks that it is little consolation that Taine limits such general qualities to predicates and adjectives—white, cold, hard—and denies them of "essences" such as mind, matter, or ego.

56. Menand, *The Metaphysical Club*, 218–19.

57. Henry Maudsley, quoted by William James in "Review of Maudsley, *Responsibility in Mental Disease*," *Atlantic Monthly* 34 (September 1874): 365.

58. William James, "Review of G. H. Lewes's *Problems of Life and Mind*," *Atlantic Monthly* 36 (September 1875): 361.

59. Ibid., 362.

60. William James, "Against Nihilism" (1874), in *The Works of William James: Manuscript Essays and* Notes, ed. Frederick Burkhardt et al. (Cambridge: Harvard University Press, 1988), 150.

61. Ibid., 151–52.

62. Ibid., 153–54.

63. William Thomson, "On a Universal Tendency in Nature to the Dissipation of Mechanical Energy" (communicated on April 19, 1852), printed in *Proceedings of the Royal Society of Edinburgh* 3 (1858): 139–42.

64. William James, "Review of B. Stewart and P. G. Tait, *The Hidden Universe*," *The Nation* 20 (May 27, 1875): 367.

65. Ibid.

66. Ibid.

67. Menand, *The Metaphysical Club*, 220–21. James recast this argument two decades later, and it remains one of his most influential yet controversial ideas. In its mature form, an optional "*will* to believe" supplants the "*duty* to believe." Moreover, "sicklied" science is softened to the notion that when confronted with choices that are live, momentous, forced, and *cannot be adjudicated by scientific or intellectual inquiry,* spiritual beliefs that fortify our resolve and steady our moral compass are justified. Though still contentious among secular pragmatists, the will to believe is far more palatable than any permission to ride off on meta-physical banshees masquerading as responsible science.

68. This recovery was never fully complete, and James wrestled with depression and insomnia throughout his life. See Menand, *The Metaphysical Club*, 219.

69. William James, "Notes on Insanity and Genius," in *Manuscript Lectures*, 59 ff.

70. William James, "Review of Wilhelm Wundt's *Grundzüze der physiologischen Psychologie*," *North American Review* 121 (July 1875): 195.

71. Ibid.

72. William James, "Remarks on Spencer's Definition of Mind as Correspondence," *Journal of Speculative Philosophy* 12 (January 1878): 1–3.

73. Ibid., 7.

74. Ibid., 18.

75. William James, "The Sentiment of Rationality," *Mind* 4 (July 1879): 318.

76. Ibid., 317. James does not identify Peirce in this passage.

77. Ibid., 321–23.

78. Ibid., 328.

79. Ibid., 334–42.

80. William James, *The Principles of Psychology* (New York: Henry Holt, 1890), vol. 1, 231.

81. G. Stanley Hall, "Philosophy in the United States," *Mind* 4 (January 1879): 95.

82. Ibid., 91.

83. Ibid., 89–92.

84. Ibid., 93, 95.

85. Ibid., 97–103.

86. Ibid., 105.

Chauncey Wright

CHARLES PEIRCE'S BERKELEY REVIEW

The Nation 13 (30 November 1871): 355–356

Response to Charles Peirce, Fraser's *The Works of George Berkeley* (October 1871)

Mr. Charles S. Peirce, in his review of Berkeley in the last *North American*, to which we promised to return, takes the occasion to trace out in the history of philosophical thought in Great Britain the sources of Berkeley's doctrines and of later developments in English philosophy. These he traces back to the famous disputes of the later schoolmen on the question of realism and nominalism—that question on which each new-fledged masculine intellect likes to try its powers of disputation. But the motive of the schoolmen who started this question or gave it prominence, was not in any sense egotistical, however pugilistic it may have been, but was profoundly religious—more religious, in fact, than anything modern, and, perhaps, more fitly to be compared to the devotion that produced the Gothic architecture than to anything else. The most remarkable thing in the essay is Mr. Peirce's interpretation of the actual question so earnestly agitated. This, it should seem, is not at all what has become the universally accepted account of this voluminous dispute—an account derived, it appears, from Bayle's *Dictionary*. The realistic schoolmen were not such dolts as to contend for an incognizable reality beyond any powers we have for apprehending it, nor for the existence of universals as the objects of general conceptions existing outside of the mind. They only contended (against the sceptical or nominalistic tendency) that reality, or the truth of things, depends on something besides the actual courses of experience in individual minds, or is independent of differences and accidents in these; and that truth is not determined by the conventions of language, or by what men choose to mean by their words. So far from being the reality commonly supposed—that is to say, the vivid, actual, present contact with things—the reality of the realists was the final upshot of experience, the general agreement in all experience, as far removed as possible from any particular body's sight, or hearing, or touch, or from the accidents which are inseparable from these.

Yet it is essentially intelligible, and, in fact, is the very most intelligible, and is quite independent of conventions in language. The faith of the realists (for theirs was a philosophy of faith) was that this result of all men's experience would contain agreements not dependent on the laws and usages of language, but on truths which determine these laws and usages. Modern science affords ample evidence of the justness of this position.

That this truly was the position of the realistic schoolmen, Mr. Peirce contends; and he bases his opinion and belief on an original examination of their works, such as has not, we venture to say, been undertaken, outside of Germany, for a very long time. In spite of the confirmation of this position which modern science gives, the course of the development of modern science has, nevertheless, as Mr. Peirce points out, been closely associated with the opposite doctrine—nominalism, the representative of the sceptical spirit. This appears in Berkeley's philosophy, who is a nominalist, notwithstanding his *penchant* for Platonic ideas or spiritual archetypes. Hume, a complete representative of the nominalistic and sceptical spirit, is an historical product of Berkeley's nominalism; and, though commonly regarded as the author of modern philosophical movements, was not, historically considered, so different from Berkeley but that Mr. Peirce regards the latter as entitled to "a far more important place in the history of philosophy than has usually been assigned to him." So far as Berkeley was a link in the chain, this is undoubtedly true. So far as Hume (in common with all independent thinkers of the sceptical type) was not such a link, he was, we think, a starting-point in the movement of thought which has resulted in English empiricism, or the so-called "Positivism" of modern science, which Mr. Peirce seems inclined to attribute to a regular development of philosophical thought. Scepticism, though perhaps never original, as we are taught by orthodoxy, and only a revival of old and the oft-exploded errors, is, nevertheless, by its criticism, the source of most of the impulses which the spirit of enquiry has received in the history of philosophy. The results of modern science, the establishment of a great body of undisputed truths, the questions settled beyond debate, may be testimony in favor of the realistic schoolmen; but this settlement was the work, so far as it depended on the impulse of philosophy, of the nominalistic or sceptical tendencies of modern thought, which has put itself in opposition, not to the faith of the realists, as Mr. Peirce understands them, but to their conservatism and dogmatism, to their desire to agree with authority—that admirable devotion of theirs. It is curious that these things, the most certain of all on which the actual arts of life are now dependent, should be the results equally of the faith of the realists and the sceptical enquiries of the nominalists. But this is enough to account for the gratitude and the indifference which we owe to both of them, especially as the confirmation which science has afforded is not of the sort which the realists anticipated. It is the empirical conjectures of the visionary, not the inspired teachings of the wise, that have established realities for themselves and for truth in general. There are many other curious points of history and criticism in this article which will engage the scrutiny of the student of metaphysics, and doubtless afford him great delight. We are afraid to recommend it to other readers, as Mr. Peirce's style reflects the difficulties of the subject, and is better adapted for persons who have mastered these than for such as would rather avoid them.

Evolution by Natural Selection

North American Review 115.1 (July 1872): 1–31.

Review of Charles Darwin, *The Origin of Species, Sixth Edition* (1872); George Mivart, "Evolution and its Consequences: A Reply to Professor Huxley," *Contemporary Review* (January 1872); and George Mivart, "Specific Genesis," *North American Review* (April 1872).

The physical problem, proposed independently and almost simultaneously near the beginning of this century by three eminent men of genius—by Goethe, Geoffroy St. Hilaire, and the elder Darwin—the question *how* animals and plants came to have the structures and habits that characterize them as distinct species, which was proposed in place of the teleological inquiry, *why* they were so produced, has now fairly become a direct question for scientific investigation. There is no longer any doubt that this effect was by some natural process, and was not by a formless creative fiat. Moreover, there scarcely remains any doubt that this natural process connects the living forms of the present with very different forms in the past; and that this connection is properly described in general terms as "descent with modification." The question has thus become narrowed down to the inquiry, What is the nature of this modification, or what are the causes and the modes of action by which such modifications have been effected?

This is a great step in scientific progress. So long as a doubt remained about the fact that such modifications have been effected, and that present living forms are the results of them, the inquiry, how they were effected, belonged to the region of profitless speculation—profitless except for this, that speculative minds, boldly laying aside doubts which perplex and impede others, and anticipating their solution, have often in the history of science, by preparing a way for further progress, greatly facilitated their actual solution. Difficulties and questions lying beyond such doubts—walls to scale after outworks and ditches are passed—do not inspire the cautious with courage. And so the scientific world waited, though prepared with ample force of evidence, and hesitated to take the step which would bring it face to face with the questions of the present and the future. Darwin's "Origin of Species," by marshaling and largely reinforcing the evidences of evolution, and by candidly estimating the opposing evidence, and still more by pointing out a way to the solution of the greatest difficulty, gave the signal and the word of encouragement which effected a movement that had long been impending.

The "that," the fact of evolution, may be regarded as established. The "how," the theory or explanation of it, is the problem immediately before us. Many years of patient investigation may be needed. Much discussion, which will doubtless be disturbed by acrimonious disputes, as well as helped by more generous rivalries, may be expected, more especially in the immediate future; while what may be called the dialectics of the subject are being developed, or while the bearings and the limits of views and questions, and conceptions and definitions and kinds of arguments appropriate to the discussion, are the subjects on which it is necessary to come to a common understanding. It is highly desirable that this discussion should be as free as possible from mere personalities, and there is strong hope that it may be kept so through the experience which the history of modern science affords, or through the manners and methods of procedure which this experience has established. That it is impossible, however, to avoid errors of this sort altogether, is evident from the provocations experienced and keenly felt by some of the noblest of modern students of science in their establishment of theories in modern astronomy, and of theories in geology, to which may now be added the theory of evolution. That the further discussion of rival hypotheses on the causes and modes of evolution will profit by these older examples may be hoped, since there have grown up general methods of investigation and discussion, which prescribe limits and precautions for hypothesis and inference; and, more than all, for the conduct of debate on scientific subjects, that have been of the greatest value to the progress of science, and will, if faithfully observed, doubtless direct the present discussion to a successful issue.

These methods are analogous in their purposes to the general rules in courts of law, and constitute the principles of method in experimental philosophy, or in philosophy founded on the sciences of observation. They serve to protect an investigation from prejudice, by demanding that it shall be allowed on certain pretty strict conditions (in the conduct of experiments and observations, and in the formation and verification of hypotheses) to proceed without hindrance from prejudice for any existing doctrine or opinion. An investigation may thus start from the simplest basis of experience, and, for this purpose, may waive, yet without denying, any presumption or conclusion held in existing theories or doctrines. Again, these rules protect an investigation from a one-sided criticism or *ex parte* judgment, since they demand of the criticism or judgment the same judicial attitude that is demanded of the investigation. Advocacy, and especially the sort that is of essential value in courts of law, where two advocates are set against each other, each with the duty of presenting only what can be said for his own side, and where the same judge and jury are bound to hear both, is singularly out of place in a scientific discussion, unless in oral debate before the tribunal of a scientific society. Moreover, there are no burdens of proof in science. Such advocacy in a published work claiming scientific consideration is almost an offence against the proprieties of such discussions. To collect together in one place all that can be said for an hypothesis, and in another all that can be said against it, is at best a clumsy and inconvenient method of discussion, the natural results of which may best be seen in the present condition of theological and religious doctrines. These practical considerations are of the utmost importance for the attainment of the end of scientific pursuit; which is not to arrive at decisions or judgments that are probably true only on the whole and in the long run, but is the discovery of the real truths of nature, for which science can afford to wait, and for which suspended judgments are the soundest substitutes.

No work of science, ancient or modern, dealing with problematic views and doctrines, has more completely conformed to these principles or justified them by its success than the "Origin of Species." For its real or principal success has been in convincing nearly all naturalists, a majority of whom, at least, were still unconvinced, of the truth of the theory of evolution; and this depended on its obvious fairness and spirit of caution almost as much as on the preponderance of the evidences for the theory when thus presented. But the very same qualities of spirit and method governed the leading and more strictly original design of the work, which cannot yet be said to be a complete success, namely, the *explanation* of evolution by natural selection. That Mr. Darwin himself is fully convinced of the truth of this explanation is sufficiently evident. By this, however, must be understood that he holds, as he has done from the first publication of his work, that natural selection is the principal or leading cause in determining the changes and diversities of species, though not the only cause of the development of their characters. Conspicuously at the close of the Introduction in the first edition of the work, and in all subsequent editions, occur these words: "I am convinced that Natural Selection has been the most important, but not the exclusive, means of modification." That the work is not a merely dialectical performance is clear; and it is equally clear that in proportion to the strength of the author's conviction is his solicitude to give full and just weight to all valid objections to it. In this respect the work stands in marked contrast to much that has been written on the subject and in reply to it.

Once to leave the vantage-ground of scientific method and adopt the advocate's *ex parte* mode of discussion almost necessitates a continuance of the discussion under this most inconvenient form. Mr. Mivart's "Genesis of Species," which we examined in this Review last July, though a conspicuous example of such a one-sided treatment of a proper scientific question, was by a writer so distinguished for his attainments in science that his criticism could not well be passed by without notice; and, having also the character of a popular treatise, it came within a wider province of criticism that that of strictly scientific reviews. This notice was chiefly devoted to supplying something of what could be and had been said in favor of the theory thus criticized, both by way of defining and defending it. We also followed the author to some extent into the consideration of a subject, namely, the general philosophical and theological bearings of this theory, which does not, we endeavored to show, belong properly to the discussion, and ought to be kept in abeyance, in accordance with the laws of experimental philosophy, so long, at least, as these laws are observed in the conduct of the inquiry. One of the first questions asked in past times in regard to physical hypotheses, which have now become established theories or doctrines of science, was, whether they were orthodox, or at least theistic, or atheistical; and the adverse decision of this question by what was deemed competent authority determined temporarily and in a measure the fate of the hypothesis and the standing of those who held to it. It was to be hoped that, in the light of such a history, this discussion could be spared the question, at least till the hypothesis could be fairly tried, when, if it should be found wanting in scientific validity, its banishment to the limbo of exploded errors might, without much harm, be changed to a severer sentence; and, if it should withstand the tests of purely scientific criticism, the same means of reconciling it to orthodoxy would doubtless be found as in the case of older physical hypotheses. Mr. Mivart himself claimed and argued a similar exemption for the general theory of evolution, or rather attempted the later office of recon-ciliation, or of proving its conformity to the most venerable and authoritative decisions of orthodoxy. But he appeared unwilling to allow either such an exemption or the possibil-ity of an accordance with orthodoxy to the theory of natural selection, for he quoted and applied to the discussion of this theory the saying and supposed opinions of an old hereti-cal heathen philosopher, Democritus, in several passages of his book.

In his reply to our criticisms (see the April number of this Review), he wonders who could have so misled us as to make us suppose that his was a "theological education" and a "schooling against Democritus"; the fact being just the reverse of this, his education being in that philosophy of "nescience," out of the evils and fallacies of which he had at length struggled. Clearly we were misled by the author himself. Our error, slight except as a biographical one, would have been amended if we had referred the character of his criticism to his theological *studies*. This would have left the period in his life in which he acquired his mode of thought and discussion as undetermined, as it was unimportant to the point of our criticism; since, through the influence of these studies, or similar dialec-tical pursuits, his unquestionable abilities appeared to us to have been developed, and, as we believe, misapplied. It was the bringing in of "the fortuitous concourse of atoms," and "blind chance," "accidents," and "hap-hazard results," in a discussion with which they had no more to do, and no less, than they have to do with geology, meteorology, politics, phil-osophical history, or political economy;—it was this irrelevancy in his criticism which we regarded as oblivious of the age in which we live and for which he wrote—the age of experimental philosophy. Mr. Mivart thinks he is clear of all blame for speaking of the theory of natural selection as liable "to lead men to regard the present organic world as formed, so to speak, *accidentally*, beautiful and wonderful as is confessedly the hap-haz-ard result," since he qualified the word "accidentally" by the phrase "so to speak." The real fault was in speaking so at all.

Accidents in the ordinary every-day sense are causes in every concrete course of events—in the weather, in history, in politics, in the market—and no theory of these events can leave them out. Explanation of the events consists in showing how they will result, or have resulted, through certain fixed principles or laws of action from the occa-sions or opportunities, which such accidents present. Given the state of the atmosphere over a large district in respect to temperature, moisture, pressure and motion—none of which could have been anticipated without similar data for a short time before, all in fact being accidents—and the physical principles of meteorology might enable us to explain the weather that immediately follows. So with the events of history, etc. In no other sense are accidents supposed as causes in the theory of natural selection. Accidental variations and surrounding conditions of existence, and the previous condition of the organic world, (none of which could have been anticipated from anything we actually know, all in fact being "accidents")—these are the causes which present the occasions or opportunities through which principles of utility and advantage are brought to bear in changing structures and habits, and improving their adaptations. If this is like the philosophy of Democritus, or any other excommunicated philosopher of antiquity, and is, therefore, to be condemned for the heresy, then all the sciences with which we have compared it, and many others, the conquests of human intelligence, must share the condemnation.

We dwelt in our review, perhaps unnecessarily, on the fact that accidents in this sense, and in the theory of natural selection, as well as elsewhere, are relative to our knowledge of causes; that the same event, like an eclipse of the sun, might be an accident to one mind, and an anticipated event to another. We did so because we could not understand otherwise why our author should single out the theory of natural selection from analogous theories and sciences for a special criticism of this sort; or except on the idea that the accidents in natural selection were supposed by him to be exceptional, and of the type which Democritus is reputed to have put in the place of intelligent design, or on the throne of Nous. We did not, as Mr. Mivart imagines, think him "ignorant that the various phenomena which we observe in nature have their respective phenomenal antecedents," nor suppose that he "held the opinion that phenomena of variation, etc., are not determined by definite, invariable, physical antecedents." We only thought that, knowing better—knowing that "natural selection," like every other physical theory, dealt with physical causes and their laws—he was unjust and inconsistent in condemning the employment of it, as a leading or prominent cause, in explanation of the phenomena of the organic world, in the manner in which he did; except on the hypothesis, which we repudiated in behalf of experimental philosophy, but without positively attributing it to him—the hypothesis of absolute accidents. It was inconsistency and irrelevancy which we meant to attribute to him.

That he supposed absolute accidents to be meant in the ancient atheistically philosophy appeared from a passage in his chapter on theology and evolution (p. 276), in which he speaks of the kind of action we might expect in physical nature from a theistic point of view, as an action "which is orderly, which *disaccords* with the action of blind chance and with the 'fortuitous concourse of atoms' of Democritus." But in his reply to us he repudiates the idea that this old philosophy held events to be accidental in the strict sense; and he further says of us that we "know very well that Democritus and Empedocles and their school no more held phenomena to be undetermined or unpreceded by other phenomena than do their successors at the present day." We are far from being so well informed, or willing to accept this as a statement of our views. For, in the first place, the terms "undetermined" and "unpreceded" are not quite synonymous. Moreover, so far as phenomena are determined, they are "orderly," "harmonize with man's reason" (p. 275), though in their complexity they may be quite beyond the power of any man's imagination to represent or disentangle; and, as our author has said, they are what we might expect "from a theistic point of view."

Whether Democritus believed in absolute accidents or not we do not know. Little is really known of his opinions in this respect. The question has been disputed, but not decided. All his works are lost, except a few quoted sentences and maxims. He is in a peculiarly exposed condition for an attack from any one disposed to be his opponent. His teachings, probably already sufficiently garbled, are unprotected by contexts, or by the scruples an opponent might feel about them in assigning to him his place in the history of speculation. It is very likely that he did not hold to such accidents as occurring in the course of nature; though it is very doubtful whether he was so thoroughly convinced as his "successors of the present day" are of the universality of the "law of causation," or that *every* event must have determinant antecedents. The conception of cause, as based by experimental science on the elementary invariable orders of phenomenal successions, is altogether too precise and abstract for the apprehension of a mind untrained by scientific studies, even at the present day. How much more so must it have been when among the old Ionian philosophers the first crude conceptions of science were being fashioned by attempts at discovering the physical bond of union and the inchoate form of nature, regarded as a universe. It is an anachronism to speak of these philosophers as materialists and atheists, since the distinctions and questions which could make such a classification intelligible had not yet been proposed. And it is equally an anachronism to attribute even to later thinkers like Democritus such a conception of physical causation as only the latest and maturest products of scientific thought have rendered definite.

There can be no antithesis in the problem of the beginning of the world between accident and law, or accident and the orderly movements which imply determinant antecedents. The real antithesis is between accident and miracle, or accident and the extraordinary action of pre-existent designing intelligence; and in this relation Accident can only have an absolute meaning, equivalent in fact to Destiny or Fate, when unintelligible. Unintelligible Destiny or "blind chance" is directly opposed to the intelligible Destiny which is the principle of "law" in nature; though these have often been confounded as equally fatalistic and atheistical. Our author, however, does not confound them; for he has said that the latter is what we might expect from a theistic point of view. It is altogether likely, however, that the Democritus to whom the former meaning could be attributed as a characteristic one is not the real thinker, but is a myth; or is rather the orthodox lay-figure of atheism of the theological studio.

The reputation for atheism which the real Democritus doubtless had, may have come from a cause which has often produced it in the history of physical science. He invented a theory of atoms, with which he attempted physical explanations quite in advance of previous speculations. And the invention of physical hypotheses has often been regarded as an invasion of the province and jurisdiction of divine power and a first cause. For men rarely allow the explanation of any important effect in nature to remain an open question. If observed or inferred physical causes do not suffice, invisible or even spiritual ones are invented; and thus the ground is preoccupied and closed against the inquiries of the physical philosopher. It is probably the general direction or tendency of these inquiries, rather than any positive positions or results at which they may arrive, which puts the physical philosopher in an apparently irreligious attitude. For in following out the consequences of physical hypotheses into the details of natural phenomena, reasoning from supposed causes to their effects, his interests and his modes of thought are the reverse of those of mankind in general, and of the religious mind. He appears to turn his back on divinity, and though seeking to approach nearer the first cause, or the total order of nature, his aspect of looking downward from a proximate principle through a natural order appears to the popular view to be darkened by a somber shadow. The theory of universal gravitation was condemned on this account for impiety by even so liberal and enlightened a thinker as Leibnitz. This seems very strange to us now, since the law of gravitation is almost as familiar as fire, or even gravity itself. When in ancient times any one had burned his fingers, or been bruised by a fall, one did not, except perhaps in early childhood, attribute the harm to a person, a spirit, or a god, but to the qualities of fire or gravity; yet the sounds of the thunder were still referred by him directly to Zeus. We all remember how in the "Clouds" of Aristophanes the comic poet puts impiety in the mouth of Socrates, or the doctrine that Zeus does not exist, and that it is ethereal Vortex, reigning in his stead, which drives the clouds and makes them rain and thunder. Such a view of physical inquiries is not confined to comic poets or their audiences. The meteorological sophists of that day were in very much the same position as the Darwinian evolutionists of the present time.

However important it may be to bear these considerations in mind, there is, as we have said, no more occasion for it with reference to the theory of natural selection than with reference to many other analogous theories, not only in physical science, like those of meteorology and geology (including the theory of evolution), but also in sociological science, like theories of political economy, and those theories of history which explain the growth of institutions, governments, and national characteristics. The comparison of the continuous order in time, and the total aspect of the organic world at any period, to the progressive changes and the particular aspect at any time of the weather, will, doubtless, strike many minds as inapt, since the latter phenomena are the type to us of indetermination and chance, while the former present to us the most conspicuous evidences of orderly determination and design. This contrast, though conspicuous, is, nevertheless, incidental to the point of view, and is not essential to the contrasted orders themselves. The movements in one are almost infinitely slower than in the other. We see a single phase and certain orderly details in one. We see only confused and rapid combinations and successions in the other. One is seen in fine, the other in gross form. Looked at from the same point of view, regarding each as an *ensemble* of details in time and space, they are equally without definite order or intelligible plan; "beautiful and wonderful as is," according to our author, "the hap-hazard result." It is in the intimate and comparatively minute parts of the organic world, in individual structures or organisms, that the beautiful and wonderful order is seen. When we look at great groups, like the floras and faunas of various regions, or at past geological groupings—the shifting clouds, as it were, of organic life—this order disappears or is hidden for the most part. There remains enough of apparent order to indicate continuity in time and space, but hardly anything more. Perfectly as the individual organism may exhibit adaptations or the applications of principles of utility, there is no definite clue in it to the cause of the particular combination of uses which it embodies, or the existence of it in a particular region, or at a particular period in the history of the world, or to its co-existence with many other quite independent particular forms. But in precise analogy with what is conspicuously regular and indicative of simple laws in the organic world, correspond the intimate elementary changes of the atmosphere, some of which, like the fall and even the formation of rain and snow, the development and disappearance of clouds, are almost as precisely simple exhibitions of natural laws as experiments in the laboratory. What, even in the laboratory, can exceed the beauty, simplicity, and completeness of that exemplification of definite physical laws which the fall of dew on clear, calm nights demonstrates? Moreover, there are in the successions of changes in the weather sufficient traces of order to indicate a continuity in space and time corresponding to the geographical distributions and geological successions of the organic world. The elementary orders, which exhibit ultimate physical laws in simple isolation, are, in their aggregate and complex combination, the causes of the successions of changes in the weather and the source of whatever traces of order appear in them, and are thus analogous to what the theory of natural selection supposes in the organic world, namely, that the adaptations, or the exhibitions of simple principles of utility in structures, are in their aggregate and complex combinations the causes of successive and continuous changes in forms of life.

Far more important, however, than such analogies in the doctrine of evolution is the clear understanding of what the theory of natural selection undertakes to explain, and what is the precise and essential nature of its supposed action. There appears to be much confusion on this subject, arising probably from the influence of preconceived opinions concerning the nature both of the matters explained and the mode of explanation, or on the nature of the changes which take place in species and the relations of them to this cause. These would seem, at first sight, very simple matters for conception, and difficult only in the evidences and the adequacy of the explanation. Such appeared, and still appears, to be the opinion of our author. Perhaps the best way to make a difficult theory plain is the negative one of correcting the misconceptions of it as they arise. This is what we attempted in our review with reference to the character of the variations from which nature normally and for the most part selects. But new difficulties have emerged in Mr. Mivart's later writings which deserve consideration. In his answer to Professor Huxley, in the January number of the "Contemporary Review" (p. 170), he says of the theory of natural selection, "That the benefit of the individual in the struggle for life was announced as the one determining agent, fixing slight beneficial variations into enduring characters," for which he thinks it quite incompetent. And again, in reply to us (p. 453), he speaks of "*The* origin, not, of course, of slight variations, but of the fixing of these in definite lines and grooves"; and this origin, he believes, cannot be natural selection. And we believe that his conclusions are right! That is, if the more obvious meaning of these expressions are their real ones. They appear to mean that natural selection will not account for the unvarying continuance in succeeding generations of *simple* changes made accidentally in individual structures (whether the change be large or small), or will not account for the direct conversion of a *simple* change in a parent into a permanent alteration of its offspring. Such is the apparent meaning of these expressions, but they might possibly be taken as loose expressions of the opinion that this cause will not account for permanent changes in the *average* characters, or mid-points, about which variations oscillate; and, in this case, we believe that he is wrong. This permanency must not be understood, however, as meaning that changes cease, but only that they are not reversed. The same cause, natural selection, prevents such reversion, on the whole, and except in individual cases, which it exterminates.

The first and obviously intended meaning of these expressions has let in light upon the author's own theory and his general difficulty about the theory of natural selection, which we did not have before. They show how fundamentally the matter has been misconceived, either by him or by us. That we did not more fully perceive this fundamental difference doubtless arose from a tacit assumption in his earlier criticisms of the principle of "specific stability," which was explicitly treated of in a later chapter and as a subordinate topic. This, as we shall find, is the source of the most serious misunderstanding. We were not aware that it was anywhere supposed that particular variations ever became *fixed* and heritable changes in the characters of organisms by the direct agency of natural selection, or, indeed, by any other known cause. The proper effect of this cause is not to fix variations, though it must *determine their averages and limit their range*, and must act indirectly to increase the useful ones and diminish the injurious; or rather to permit the one and forbid the other, and when these are directly opposed to each other, it must act to shift the average or normal character, instead of fixing it. Variation as a constant and normal phenomenon of organization, exhibited chiefly in the ranges of individual differences, is, as it were, the agitation or irregular oscillation that keeps the characters of species from getting too closely *fixed* in "definite lines and grooves," through the too rigid inheritance of ancestral traits; or it is a principle of alertness that keeps them ever ready for movement and change in conformity to changing conditions of existence. What fixes species (when they are fixed) is the continuance of the same advantages in their structures and habits, or the same conditions for the action of selection, together with the force of long-continued inheritance.

This, though almost trite from frequent repetition, appears a very difficult conception for many minds, probably on account of their retaining the old stand-point. It would appear that our author is really speaking of the *fixed* species of the old and still prevalent philosophy, or about *real* species, as they are commonly called. Natural selection cannot, of course, account for these figments. Their true explanation is in the fact that naturalists formerly assumed, without proper evidence, that a change too slow for them to perceive directly could not exist, and that characters widely prevalent and so far advanced as to become permanently adapted to very general and unchanging conditions of existence, like vertebral and articulate structures, the numbers and positions of the organs of locomotion in various animals, the whorl and the spiral arrangement of leaves in plants, and similar homological resemblances, could never have been vacillating and uncertain ones. It was not many years ago that a distinguished writer in criticizing the views of Lamarck affirmed that "the majority of naturalists agree with Linnaeus in supposing that all the individuals propagated from one stock have certain distinguishing characters in common, which never vary, and which have remained the same since the creation of each species." The influence of this opinion still remains, even with naturalists who would hesitate to assert categorically the opinion itself. This comes, doubtless, from the fact that long-prevalent doctrines often get stamped into the very meanings of words, and thus acquire the character of axioms. The word "species" became synonymous with *real* or *fixed* species, or these adjectives became pleonastic. And this was from the mere force of repetition, and without valid foundation, in fact, or confirmation from proper inductive evidence.

Natural selection does not, of course, account for a fixity that does not exist, but only for the adaptations and the diversities in species, which may or may not be changing at any time. They are fixed only as the "fixed" stars are fixed, of which very many are now known to be slowly moving. Their fixity, when they are fixed, is temporary and through the accident of unchanging external conditions. Such is at least the assumption of the theory of natural selection. Mr. Mivart's theory seems to assume, on the other hand, that unless a species or a character is tied to something it will run away; that there is a necessity for some internal bond to hold it, at least temporarily, or so long as it remains the *same* species. He is entitled, it is true, to challenge the theory of natural selection for proofs of its assumption, that "fixity" is not an essential feature of natural species; for, in fact, so far as direct evidence is concerned, this is an open question. Its decision must depend chiefly on the preponderance of indirect and probable evidences in the interpretation of the "geological record," a subject to which much space is devoted, in accordance with its importance, in the "Origin of Species." Technical questions on the classification and description of species afford other evidences, and it is asserted by naturalists that a very large number of specimens, say ten thousand, is sufficient, in some departments of natural history, to break down any definition or discrimination even of living species. Other evidences are afforded by the phenomena of variation under domestication. Mr. Mivart had the right, and may still have it, to resist all this evidence, as not conclusive; but he is not entitled to call upon the theory of natural selection for an explanation of a feature in organic structures which the theory denies in its very elements, the *fixity* of species. This is what he has done—implicitly, as it now appears, in his book, and explicitly in his later writings.

The question of zoological philosophy, "Whether species have a real existence in nature," in the decision of which naturalists have so generally agreed with Linnaeus, refers directly and explicitly to this question or the fixity of essential characters, and to the assumption that species must remain unaltered in these respects so long as they continue to exist, or until they give birth to new species; or, as was formerly believed, give place in perishing to new independent creations. The distinction involved in this question should not be confounded, as it might easily be, with the distinction in Logic of "real kinds" from other class-names. Logic recognizes a principal division in class-names, according as these are the names of objects which agree with each other and differ from other objects in a very large and indefinite number of particulars or attributes, or are the names of objects which agree only in a few and a definite number of attributes. The former are the names of "real kinds," and include the names of natural species, as man, horse, etc., and of natural genera, as whale, oak, etc. These classes are "real kinds," not because the innumerable particulars in which the individual members of them agree with each other and differ from the members of other classes, are themselves fixed or invariable in time, but because this sort of agreement and difference is fixed or continues to appear. An individual hipparion resembled its immediate parents and the other offspring of them as closely as, or, at least, in the same intimate manner in which one horse resembles another, namely, in innumerable details. But this is not opposed to the conception that the horse is descended from the hipparion by insensible steps of gradation or continuously. For examples of names that are not the names of "real kinds," we may instance such as objects that are an inch in length, or in breadth, or are colored black, or are square, or (combining these particulars) that are as black square inches. These objects may be made of paper, or wood, or ivory, or differ in all other respects except the enumerated and definite particulars. They are not "real" or natural "kinds," but factitious ones.

The confusion which, as we have said, might arise between the "real kinds" of Logic, and the *real* species of biological speculation, would depend on a vagueness in the significance of the word "real," which in common usage combines in uncertain proportions two elementary and more precise ideas, that of fixedness and that of breadth of relationship. Both these marks of reality are applied habitually as tests of it. Thus if an object attests its existence to several of my senses, is seen, heard, touched, and is varied in its relations to these senses, and moreover is similarly related to the senses of another person, as evinced by his testimony, then I know that the object is real, and not a mere hallucination or invention of my fantasy; though it may disappear immediately afterwards in an unexplained manner, or be removed by some unknown but supposable agency. Here the judgment of reality depends on breadth of relationship to my experience and sources of knowledge. Or again I may only *see* the object and consult no other eyes than my own; but seeing it often, day after day, in the same place, I shall judge it to be a real object, provided its existence is conformable to the general possibilities of experience, or to the test of "breadth." Here the test of reality is "fixity" or continuance in time. That natural species are real in one of these senses, that individuals of a species are alike in an indefinite number of particulars, or resemble each other intimately, is unquestionable as a fact, and is not an invention of the understanding or classifying faculty, and is moreover the direct natural consequence of the principles of inheritance. In this sense species are equivalent to large natural stocks or races existing for a limited but indeterminate number of generations. That they are real in the other sense, or fixed in time absolutely in respect to any of the particulars of their resemblance, whether these are essential (that is, useful for discrimination and classification) or are not, is far from being the axiom it has seemed to be. It is, on the contrary, highly improbable, though tacitly assumed, as we have seen, in criticisms of the theory of natural selection; and in that significance often attached to the word "species" in which the notions of fixedness and distinctiveness have coalesced. It is true that without this significance in the word "species" the names and descriptions of organic forms could not be permanently applicable. No system of classification, however natural or real, could be final. Classification would, indeed, be wholly inadequate as a representation of the organic world on the whole, or as a sketch of the "plan of creation," and would be falsely conceived as revealing the categories and thoughts of creative intelligence—a consequence by no means welcome to the devout naturalist, since it seems to degrade the value of his work. But this may be because he has misconceived its true value, and dedicated to the science of divinity what is really the rightful inheritance of natural or physical science.

If instead of implicitly assuming the principle of specific stability in the criticisms of the earlier chapters of his book, and deferring the explicit consideration of it to a later chapter and as a special topic, our author had undertaken the establishment of it as the essential basis of his theory (as indeed it really is), he would have attacked the theory of natural selection in a most vital point; and if he had succeeded, all further criticism of the theory would have been superfluous. But without success in establishing this essential basis, he leaves his own theory and his general difficulties concerning the theory of natural selection without adequate foundation. The importance of natural selection in the evolution of organic species (its predominant influence) depends entirely on the truth of the opposite assumption, the *instability* of species. The evidences for and against this position are various, and are not adequately considered in the author's chapter on this subject. Moreover, some of the evidences may be expected to be greatly affected by what will doubtless be the discoveries of the immediate future. Already the difficulties of discrimination and classification in dealing with large collections have become very great in some departments of natural history, and even in paleontology the gradations of fossil forms are becoming finer and finer with almost every new discovery; and this in spite of the fact that nothing at all approaching to evidence of continuity can rationally be expected anywhere from the fragmentary geological record. To this evidence must be added the phenomena of variation under domestication. The apparent limits of the changes which can be effected by artificial selection are not, as they have been thought, proofs of the doctrine of "specific stability," or of the opinion of Linnaeus, but only indications of the dependence of variation on physiological causes, and on laws of inheritance; and also of the fact that the laws of variation and the action of natural selection are not suspended by domestication, but may oppose the aims and efforts of artificial selection. The real point of the proof afforded by these phenomena is that permanent changes may be effected in species by insensible degrees. They are permanent, however, only in the sense that no tendency to reversion will restore the original form, except by the action of similar causes.

Against the conclusions of such inductive evidences the vague analogies of the organic to the inorganic world would avail little or nothing, even if they were true. They avail little or nothing, consequently, in confirmation of them in being proved false; as we showed one analogy to be in the illustration given by our author, namely, the supposed analogy of specific characters in crystals to those of organisms; and his inference of abrupt changes in organic species, corresponding by this analogy to changes in the mode or species of crystallization, which the same substance undergoes, in some cases with a change of surrounding conditions, such as certain other substances may introduce by their presence. A complete illustration of the chemical phenomenon is afforded by the crystals of sulfur. Crystals produced in the wet way, or from solution in the bisulphide of carbon, are of a species entirely distinct from those formed in the dry way, or from the fused mineral; and there are many other cases of these phenomena of *dimorphism* and *polymorphism,* as they are called. We recur to this topic, not on account of its importance to the discussion, but because Mr. Mivart accuses us of changing a quotation from Mr. J. J. Murphy, so that he "is unlucky enough to be blamed for what he never said, or apparently thought of saying." We have looked with true solicitude for the evidences of the truth of this charge, and find them to be as follows: We transcribed from Mr. Mivart's book these sentences, as quoted by him (p. 185), from Mr. Murphy: "It needs no proof that in the case of spheres and crystals, the forms and *the* structures are the effect, and not the cause, of the formative principle*s*. Attraction, whether gravitative or capillary, produces the spherical form; the spherical form does not produce attraction. And crystalline polarities produce crystalline structure and form; crystalline structure and form do not produce *crystalline* polarities." The superfluous letter and words, which we have put in italics, were omitted in the printing, we do not know how, but it looks like an unwarrantable attempt in a final revision of proofs to improve the English of the quotation. Certainly the changes were of no advantage to our criticism, especially as they only have the effect to render the antithesis, which was the object of the criticism, slightly weaker. Even less advantage, we believe, will come to the author of such an accusation, made without specifications or proofs. It is impossible to see how these changes have exposed Mr. Murphy to undeserved censure. We blamed him and our author, not for the use of abstractions as causes—a use which, as our author says, we ourselves make whenever it is convenient—but for asserting the antithesis of cause and effect between abstractions, both of which are descriptive of effects, namely, the character of the attractions, gravitative and capillary, which produce spherical forms *vs.* the spherical form itself; and the polar character of the forces that produce crystals *vs.* the crystalline form and structure. Each of these effects (both in the case of the sphere and of the crystal) is doubtless a concause or condition that goes to the determination of the other. The spherical form arranges and determines the consultants of the elementary forces, and thus indirectly determines itself, or determines that action of the elementary forces thus combined, which results in the maintenance or stable equilibrium of the spherical form. Again, in crystallization the already formed bodies, with the particular directions of their faces and axes, determine in part how the resultants of elementary polar forces will act in the further growth of the crystal, or in the repair of a broken one; and the elementary forces, thus determined and combined, result in the crystalline form and structure. Both of the effects which are put in the antithesis of cause and effect in the above quotation are also partial agents. They act and react on each other in the production of actual crystals.

But this point was of importance to the discussion only as exhibiting a kind of "realism" by which scientific discussion is very liable to be confused. In this case, the wordy profundity was not quite so bald and conspicuous as the ordinary putting of a single-worded abstract description of an effect for its cause, since it consisted in putting one of two such abstractions as the cause of the other. More important, as affecting the truth of the supposed analogy of *species* in crystals to those of organisms, was the statement which our author confesses is utterly beyond him, and as he certainly has misinterpreted it, we may be pardoned for repeating and explaining it. We said, "Moreover, in the case of crystals, neither these forces [the elementary] nor the abstract law of their action in producing definite *angles* reside in the finished bodies, but in the properties of the surrounding media, portions of whose constituents are changed into crystals, according to these properties and other conditioning circumstances." Our author has made us say "crystals" where we said "angles," though the unintelligible character of the sentence ought to have made him the more cautious in copying it. We said "angles," because these are prominent marks of the *species* of the crystal; and this species we referred to the nature of the fluid material out of which the crystal is formed, and to the modifying influences of the presence of other substances, when the crystallization takes place from solutions, or in the wet way. The fact that the determination of the *species* of a crystal is not in any germ or nucleus or anything belonging in a special way to the particular crystal itself, but is in the molecular forces of the fluid solution, makes the analogy of species in crystals to those of organisms not only vague but false. What is really effected by the introduction of a foreign substance, acid or alkali, in the solution, is a change, not in such accidents as the surrounding conditions are to an organism, but in the essential forces, which *ought* to change the character or species of the crystal suddenly, *per saltum*, or discontinuously; and it has not, therefore, the remotest likeness to such suppositions as that a duck might be hatched from a goose's egg, or a goose from a duck's; or that a horse might have been the foal of an hipparion.

Notwithstanding that our statement was "utterly beyond" our author, he has ventured the following confident comments (p. 460): "If this is so," he says, "then when a broken crystal completes itself, the determining forces reside exclusively in the media, and not at all in the crystal with its broken surface! The first atoms of a crystal deposited arrange themselves entirely according to the forces of the surrounding media, and their own properties are utterly without influence or effect in the result!" The marks of exclamation appended to these statements ought to have been ours, since nothing in the statements themselves has the remotest dependence on anything we said; but on the contrary these statements are directly opposed to the objections we made to Mr. Murphy's antitheses. They might be deducible, perhaps, from our proposition, in the form to which it was altered through the substitution of the word "crystals" for "angles," by supposing the concrete actual crystals to be referred to, instead of their *species,* of which these angles are prominent marks. But we had insisted that neither the resulting form, nor the resultants of elementary forces, are exclusively effects, or exclusively causes in the formation or in the mending of actual crystals; yet the *species* of the crystal is fully determined by what is outside of it, or by causes that may be abruptly changed by a change in the medium. Hence the phenomena of *dimorphism* and *polymorphism,* and similar chemical phenomena, have nothing in common with the hypothesis of "specific genesis."

Several similar misunderstandings of more special criticisms in our review tempt us (chiefly from personal considerations) to undertake their rectification; but our object in this article is only to further the discussion, so far as it can be done under the inconvenient form of polemical discussion, by removing, as far as we are able, confusions and misunderstandings in essential matters. Hence we shall not dwell upon the discussion of what may be called hypotheses of the second degree, or hypothetical illustrations of the action of natural selection. It was a part of Mr. Mivart's plan, in attacking the hypothesis of the predominant agency of natural selection in the origination of species, to discredit a number of subordinate hypotheses, as well as to challenge the theory to offer any adequate ones for the explanation of certain extraordinary structures. We considered in detail several objections of this sort, though we might have been content with simply pointing out a sufficient answer in the logical weakness of such a mode of attack. The illustrations of the theory which have been proposed have in general not at all the force of arguments, or except where the utility of a structure is simple and obvious and can be shown by direct evidence to be effective in developing it out of accidental beginnings, and even in perfecting it, as in cases of the mimicry of certain insects by others for a protection, which is thus really acquired. In general, such illustrations serve only to show the mode of action supposed in the theory, without pretending to reconstruct the past history of an animal, even by the roughest sketch; or to determine all the uses, or the relative importance of them, of any structure. To discredit these particular secondary hypotheses has no more weight as an argument against the theory than the hypotheses themselves have in confirmation of it. To be convinced on general grounds that such a structure as that of the giraffe's neck was developed by insensible steps from a more common form of the neck in Ungulates, through the oscillations of individual differences, and by the special utilities of the variations which have made the neck longer in some individuals than in others, or through the utilities of these to the animals under the special conditions of their past existence, is very different from believing that this or that particular use in the structure was *the* utility (to adopt our author's favorite form of definiteness) which governed the selection or determined the survival of the fittest. *The* use which may be presumed in general to govern selection is a combination, with various degrees of importance, of all the actual uses in a structure. There can be no more propriety in demanding of the theory of natural selection that it should define this use, or trace out the history hypothetically of any particular structure in its relations to past conditions of existence, than there would be in demanding of political economy that it should justify the correctness of its general principles by success in explaining the record of past prices in detail, or accounting in particular for a given financial anomaly. In either case, the proper evidence is wanting. Any instance of a structure which could be conclusively shown (a very difficult kind of proof) to exist, or to be developed in any way, without reference in the process of development to any utility whatever, past or present, or to any past forms of the structure, would be an instance in point, and would go far towards qualifying the evidence, otherwise mostly affirmative, of the predominant agency of natural selection.

We may remark by the way that Mr. Mivart's definite thesis, "that natural selection is not *the* origin of species," is really not *the* question. No more was ever claimed for it than that it is the most influential of the agencies through which species have been modified.

Lamarck's principle of the direct effect of habit, or actual use and disuse, has never been abandoned by later evolutionists; and Mr. Darwin has given much more space to its proof and illustration in his work on "Variation under Domestication" than any other writer. Moreover the physiological causes which produce reversions and correlations of growth, and which, so far as they are known, are quite independent of natural selection, are also recognized as causes of change. But all these are subordinated in the theory to the advantage and consequent survival of the fittest in the struggle for life, or to natural selection. Upon this point we must refer our readers to the "Additions and Corrections" in the lately published sixth edition of the "Origin of Species"; in which also all the objections brought forward by Mr. Mivart, which had not previously been examined in the work, are fully considered; and, we need hardly add, far more thoroughly and adequately than could be possible for us, or in the pages of this Review.

We will, nevertheless, give in sheer self-defense the correction of one perversion of our criticism. Mr. Mivart had argued in his book that the use of the giraffe's long neck for browsing on the foliage of trees, and the advantage of it in times of drought, could not be the cause of its gradual increase by selection; since this advantage, if a real one, would be equally an advantage to all Ungulates inhabiting the country of the giraffe, or similar regions; and that the other Ungulates, at least in such regions, ought to have been similarly modified. We allowed that there was force in the objection, but we were mistaken. The very conditions of the selection must have been a competition which would have soon put a large majority of the competitors out of the lists, and have narrowed the contest to a few races, and finally to the individuals of a single race. All the rest must have early given up the struggle for life in this direction; since a slight increase in the length of the neck could have been of no advantage if the reach of it still fell far short of the unconsumed foliage. The success of the survivors among them must have been won in some other direction, like the power of rapid and wide ranging, or organs better adapted to close grazing. For a fuller development and illustration of this reply we must refer to Chapter VII in the new edition of the "Origin of Species" in which most of Mr. Mivart's objections are considered. We attempted a reply to this objection in a direction in which his own remarks led us. Granting that the advantage of a long neck would have been equally an advantage to all Ungulates in South Africa; that there was no alternative or substitute for it; and that the use of the neck for high reaching in times of drought could not *therefore* have been *the* efficient cause of its preservation and increase through selection; still there were other and very important uses in such a neck, to which these objections do not apply, and through which there would be advantages in the struggle for life, that would determine competition only among the individuals of a single race; while those of other races would compete with each other on other grounds. Our author admitted that there might be several lines of advantage in means of *protection* or *defense;* and cited instances from Mr. Wallace, showing, for example, that a dull color, useful for concealing an animal, would not be an advantage to those animals which are otherwise sufficiently protected, and do not need concealment. The use of the giraffe's neck, then, as a means of defense and offense, for which there was ample evidence, its use as a watch-tower and as a weapon of offense, would be raised by the author's objection to greater prominence, and might be the principal ground of advantage and competition between giraffe and giraffe, or one herd of them and another, with reference to protection from the larger beasts of prey; an advantage which would be incessant instead of occasional, like the high-reaching advantage in times of drought. *The* use, as we have said, means, with reference to the advantage in the struggle for life, the combination of all the uses that are of importance to the preservation of life. Accordingly we demanded whether our author, having made a special objection to the *importance* of *one* use, as affording advantages and grounds for selection (an objection which we allowed, though unwarrantably), we demanded whether he could possibly suppose that this exhausted the matter, or that the supposed small importance of this use precluded the existence of uses more important which *would* afford grounds of advantage and competition in the struggle for life.

As with one having the true "philosophical habit of mind," and distinguished from the "scientific," our author's notice was attracted to the *form* in which we made this inquiry, rather than to the material import of it, and "as we might *a priori* expect to be the case," he showed "that breadth of view, freedom of handling, and flexibility of mind" which he believes to characterize the true philosopher, as contrasted with the mere physicist; but in a manner which appears to us to characterize rather the mere dialectician. With great fertility of invention he attempts the interpretation of our inquiry (which we grant was not sufficiently explicit for the "philosophical habit of mind"). The first interpretation is playful, and too delicate a jest to be transplanted to our pages. The next is, on the other hand, altogether too serious. He asks in return (p. 463), whether we can suppose "that he ever dreamed that the structures of animals are not useful to them, or that his position is an altogether anti-teleological one." No, we certainly do not. We only suppose that his position is not sufficiently teleological to interest him in the inquiry, and that he has overlooked many uses in the structures of animals, to which his special objections do not apply, and has vainly imagined, that by making those he felt called upon to examine as few and as faint as possible (except for the purpose of inspiring the agreeable emotion of admiration), he has reduced them to mere luxuries, having little or no value as grounds of advantage in the actual, incessant, and severe struggle to which all life is subject. "Nothing is easier than to admit in words the truth of the universal struggle for life, or more difficult"—even Mr. Darwin finds it so—"than constantly to bear this conclusion in mind. Yet unless it is thoroughly engrained in the mind, the whole economy of nature, with every fact on distribution, rarity, abundance, extinction, and variation, will be dimly seen or quite misunderstood."

Supposing us possessed by some such idea as that his "position is an altogether anti-teleological one," Mr. Mivart observes that we proceed "to exhibit the giraffe's neck in the character of a 'watch-tower.' But," he adds, "this leaves the question just where it was before. Of course I concede most readily and fully that it *is* a most admirable watch-tower, as it also *is* a most admirable high-reaching organ, but this tells us nothing of its *origin*. In both cases the long neck is most useful *when you have got it*; but the question is how it *arose*, and in this species *alone*. And similar and as convincing arguments could be brought against the watch-tower theory of origin as against the high-reaching theory, and not only this, but also against every other theory which could possibly be adduced." It appears that Mr. Mivart is prepared, *a priori,* to meet any number of foes of this sort that may present themselves singly. But *the* use, that is, all the essential uses of a structure, do not thus present themselves to our consideration and criticism. To deal adequately with the problem, we need the power to conceive how closely the uses lie to the actual necessities of life; how, while we may be admiring in imagination the almost superfluous bounties of nature, this admirable watch-tower and high-reaching organ may just be failing to save the poor animal, so highly endowed, from a miserable death. A lion whose stealthy approach it would have detected, if a few inches more in the length of its neck, or in those of its companions, had enabled it, or them, to see a few rods further, or over some intervening obstacle, has meantime sprung upon the wretched beast, and is drawing its life-blood. This, if we were aware of it, would be the proper occasion to turn our admiration upon the fine endowments of the lion. Or, continuing our contemplation of the giraffe, it may be that its admirable high-reaching organ has just failed to reach the few remaining leaves near the tops of trees, which might have served to keep up its strength against the attacks of its enemies, or enabled it to deal more effective blows with its short horns, so admirably placed as weapons of offense; or might have served to sustain it through the famine and drought, till the returning rains would have given it more cause for gratitude (and us more occasion for admiration), for a few additional inches of its neck than for all the rest. Meantime for the lack of these inches our giraffe may have sickened and perished miserably, failing in the competition and struggle for life. This need not stagger the optimist. The bounty of nature is not exhausted in giraffes. We can still admire the providential structure of the tree, which by its high-reaching branches has preserved some of its foliage from destruction by these beasts, and perhaps thereby saved not only its own life, but that of its kind. The occasions of destruction, even in the best guarded, most highly endowed lives, are all of the nature of accidents, and are generally as slight as the individual advantages are, for which so much influence is claimed in the theory of natural selection. Even death from old age is not a termination preordained in the original powers of any life, but is the effect of accumulated causes of this sort. Much of the destruction to which life is subject[1] is *strictly fortuitous so far as* either the general powers or individual advantages in structures and habits are concerned; and is, therefore, quite independent of the effects of these advantages. Hence these effects are not thereby limited; for though a form of life presses, and is pressed upon, in all directions, yet it presses forward no less in the directions of its advantages.

The "philosophical habit of mind," which Mr. Mivart admires for its "breadth of view, freedom of handling, and flexibility of mind," is sometimes optimistic, sometimes pessimistic in its views of providence in nature, according as this flexible mind has its attention bent by a genial or morose disposition to a bright or dark aspect in things. But, whichever it is, it is generally extreme or absolute in its judgments. The "scientific" mind, which Mr. Mivart contrasts with it, and believes to be characterized by "a certain rigidity and narrowness," is held *rigidly* to the truth of things, whether good or bad, agreeable or disagreeable, admirable or despicable, and is *narrowed* to the closest, most uncompromising study of facts, and to a training which enables it to render in imagination the truest account of nature as it actually exists. The "scientific" imagination is fashioned by physical studies after the patterns of nature itself. The "philosophical habit of mind," trained in the school of human life, is the habit of viewing and interpreting nature according to its own dispositions, and defending its interpretations and attacking others with the skill and weapons of forensic and dialectical discussions. The earlier physical philosophers, the "physicists" of the ancient school, were "philosophers" in our author's sense of the term. They had not the "scientific" mind, since to them nature was a chaos hardly less confused than human affairs, and was studied with the same "breadth of view, freedom of handling, and flexibility of mind" which are fitted for and disciplined by such affairs. They were wise rather than well-informed. Their observation was guided by tact and subtlety, or fine powers of discrimination, instead of by that machinery of knowledge and the arts which now fashions and guides the "scientific" mind. Thus the theory of atoms of Democritus has little resemblance to the chemical theory of atoms, since "the modern theory is the law of definite proportions; the ancient theory is merely the affirmation of indefinite combinations." Indefinite, or at least inexplicable, combinations meet the modern student of science, both physical and social, at every step of his researches; and in all the sciences with which we have compared the theory of natural selection. He does not stop to lay hold upon these *a priori,* with the loose though flexible grasp of the "philosophical habit of mind," but studies the intimate and elementary orders in them, and presumes them to be made up of such orders, though woven in infinite and inexplicable complexity of pattern.

The division which Mr. Mivart makes in kinds of intellectual ability, the "philosophical" and "scientific," and regards as a more real distinction than the threefold division we proposed, is really determined by a broad distinction in the object-matter of thought and study, and is not in any way inconsistent with what we still regard as an equally real but more elementary one, which is equivalent in fact to the logical division of "hypothesis," "simple induction," and "deduction." These are not, indeed, co-ordinate as logical elements, since induction and deduction exhaust the simple elements of understanding when unaided by trained powers of perception and imagination. But practically, as habits of thought and disciplined skill in the study of nature and human affairs, they are distinct and divergent modes of investigation, partly determined by the character of the problem—whether it is to explain, to properly name and classify, or to prove a fact from assumed or admitted premises. Skill in the formation and verification of hypothesis, dependent on a power of imagination, which physical studies discipline peculiarly, belongs peculiarly to the student of physical science; and though, perhaps, "a poor monster," as our author says, when without an adequate basis in more strictly inductive studies, yet in that division of labors and abilities, on which the economy and efficiency of scientific investigation so largely depend, there is no propriety in thus regarding it, so long as co-operation in the pursuit of truth mends the monster with its counterpart and produces a symmetrical whole in that solid general progress of science which such co-operation promotes.

NOTES

1. The fortuity or chance is here, as in all other cases, a relative fact. The *strictest* use of the word applies to events which could not be anticipated except by Omniscience. To speak, therefore, of an event as *strictly accidental* is not equivalent to regarding it as undetermined, but only as determined in a manner which cannot be anticipated by a finite intelligence (see Mr. Mivart's reply, p. 458). There are degrees in the intelligibility of things, according to human means and standards. Events like eclipses, which are the most normal and predictable of all events to the astronomer, are to the savage pure accidents; and with still lower forms of intelligence events are unforeseen which are familiar anticipations in the intelligence of the savage. To believe events to be *designed* or not, according as they are or are not predictable by us, is to assume for ourselves a complete and absolute knowledge of nature which we do not possess. Hence faith in a *designing* intelligence, supreme in nature, is not the result of any capacity in our own intelligence to comprehend the design, and is quite independent of any distinctions we may make, relative to our own powers of prediction, between orderly and accidental events.

* Editor's note: See Wright, "The Genesis of Species" (1871), reprinted in *Philosophical Discussions*, ed. C. E. Norton (New York: Henry Holt, 1877), p. 141. The reader may compare that passage, and this page, with Peirce's early views on the fixation of belief and scientific inference.

Cause and Effect

Philosophical Discussions, ed. C. E. Norton (New York: Henry Holt, 1877), pp. 406–413.

Norton made this selection from a manuscript dated to 1873 that Wright never published.

"Thought is a secretion of the brain" was the announcement of a distinguished naturalist and physiologist, which excited strong aversion to those studies and views of nature which could thus degrade, as it appeared to do, the dignity of so important a function of life. What was, probably, meant, however, by the saying, is the physiological truth that the brain is the organ of thought in a manner analogous to that in which a gland is the organ of secretions, or a muscle of contractions, or the heart and vascular system of circulations. Thought no more resembles a secretion, however, than this resembles a contraction, or than either of these resembles the movements and effects of circulation; not so much, indeed, as these three resemble each other; yet, like all these three kinds of action, it is dependent, as physiological investigations show, on the intimate structure and vital activity of a special tissue, and its living arrangements and special changes in the brain. It is altogether likely that this is what was meant, and all that was meant, by the somewhat sinister and disagreeable observation that "thought is a secretion of the brain." Men of science sometimes resort to paradoxes, figures of speech, concrete ways of stating truths in science, which those who are ignorant of the science and its real ground of evidence, but imagine that they can judge of its conclusions, are almost sure to misunderstand. Irony is not a more dangerous figure than such a use of comparisons and illustrative figures of speech. Men of science are supposed, except by other men of science, to be literal and exact, and unlike poets, in all their utterances, and when, as Professor Carl Vogt did in the present instance, they seek to impress the imagination by a comparison or figure which is made at the expense of sentiment, their expositions are almost sure to be misconceived, not only by those who are ignorant of their science and its grounds of inference, but even by the more sentimental and unreflective student of the science. What these persons seem to have supposed to be meant is not that thought and its expression are allotted to the brain as a secretion is to a gland, but that thought is a function in life which, as function, is of no more worth or dignity than the functions of the kidneys or of a cutaneous gland. It is altogether probable, however, that a certain feeling of impatience or contempt for the sentimental shallowness which could so misinterpret a scientific comparison, and confound it with moral or practical considerations is a real motive prompting to the utterance of shocking paradoxes, in disregard alike of the practical effect and of scientific clearness and discrimination in the communications of truth. Native common sense is too apt to be coarse and barbarous in its manners, and too inconsiderate of weakness.

We will not venture to say that this was the case with the distinguished biologist whose words have been the cause of so much scandal. The metaphysical doctrine of materialism so often charged against or imputed to such scientific thinkers, is, in fact, a doctrine quite foreign to science, quite out of its range. It belongs, so far as it is intelligible, to the sphere of sentiment, moral feeling and practical principles. A thinker is properly called a materialist when he concludes that his appetites and passions and actions, having material objects and results for their motives, are those most worthy of serious consideration. This does not imply that he believes that natures so different as thoughts, sensations, bodies liquid and solid and their movements, are all fundamentally of the same nature, or are natures some of which are derived from certain other more fundamental ones among them: the spiritual from the material ones. It does not imply the opinion that thought is constituted of motions or liquids, does not even imply that the materialist thinker believes in, or knows anything about, the truth that actual thinking depends, phenomenally, on the tissues, structures and conditions of an organ, as intimately as the liquid secretions and the internal and external movements of a living body do. Scientific doctrines and investigations are exclusively concerned with connections in phenomena which are susceptible of demonstration by inductive observation, and independent of diversities or resemblances in their hidden natures, or of any question about their metaphysical derivation, or dependence.

That like produces like, and that an effect must resemble its cause are shallow scholastic conceptions, hasty blunders of generalization, which science repudiates: and with them it repudiates the scholastic classification or distinction of material and spiritual which depended on these conceptions, or supposed that a cause conferred its nature on its effect, or that the conditions of a cause by the combination of their natures constituted the nature of the effect. This, in a sense—in an identical or tautological sense—is indeed true; but from this true, though identical, sense a false and mischievous one was generalized, and still continues to corrupt and misinterpret the results of scientific observation.

In discovering anything to be the cause of something else we have added to our knowledge of the nature of the first thing. We have included in our conception of this thing the attribute of its producing, or being the cause of, the second. If now this attribute of it be the most prominent quality of it in our regard, as it is in contemplating a cause *qua* cause, the effect may, in an identical sense, be said to be constituted by its cause. In this view all the other attributes of the cause are subordinated to the attribute of producing a defined effect, or are regarded as accidental or non-essential attributes, and this is the view of the elementary relations in geometry and mathematics generally which abstraction produces, and is the source of the semblance of demonstrative certainty, and objective necessity which mathematical theorems have. But when science discovers, by induction or empirically, a new cause, the thing previously known by other attributes, to which is now added the attribute of producing a given or defined effect, has nothing in its essential or previously defining attributes at all resembling, implying or constituting its effect, and its newly discovered attribute of producing this effect remains among the added, subordinate or accidental attributes of such a cause. In its essence it does not imply, suggest or resemble its effect, and in this case the assertion that the nature of the cause determines or defines the nature of its effect, is clearly seen, so far as it is true, to be an identical proposition, meaning only that the production of the defined effect is a part, and a subordinate part, of the nature of a thing. The definition of the effect is added to that of the thing which is its cause, at least while we are contemplating this as the cause of the defined effect, and it is only by refunding to the effect what we have thus borrowed from it that we arrive at the metaphysician's mathematical conception of causation, the transference of the nature of one thing, that is, the cause, to another thing, its effect. In mathematics the elements of demonstration are so selected, by abstraction, and their definition so determined that this transference of nature is what is ostensibly done; though it is no more really done than in inferring consequents from antecedents, or effects from causes in so-called empirical science. In all cases where this appears to be the character of the connection of antecedent and consequent, or cause and effect, the transference of the nature of the cause to its effect, is only a restoration to the effect of natures borrowed from it, or into which it is resolvable by analysis. This fact is observed especially in mathematical inference, since such inference is always from a complex antecedent, or from the combination of a number of conditions, of which the aggregate is not known, named or defined by any attributes other than those which by the analysis and recombinations of mathematical demonstrations are shown to depend on the most obvious and elementary truths of our experience of measured quantities. The protasis of a geometrical theorem by the aid of geometrical constructions previously shown, or, when ultimate, simply assumed to be legitimate, is resolved into conditions which, recombined, are the apodosis or conclusion of the proposition. These conditions may be used to define the natures of both the antecedent or reason, and the consequent, and by this means their natures become identical. And both are analyzed ultimately in the course of a series of demonstrations into a few axioms, and these axiomatic truths implied in a few definitions. But not only in the mathematical, but also in the so-called empirical discovery of the connections of antecedent and consequent, or cause and effect, the antecedent or cause is almost always a combination of conditions, or a concurrence of things, relations and events, the definition of which in their aggregate, in merely logical consideration, my as well be the effect which follows, provided this is sufficient for defining it, as be anything else; since this aggregate of conditions is not usually denoted by a single name, the connotation of which would define its nature. Yet for practical and scientific purposes this aggregate is best defined by the enumeration of the conditions that compose it, to which observation adds the fact, or nature, that it will whenever it exists be followed by a given or defined effect. In this case the conditions which constitute the cause do not constitute the effect. They are simply followed by the effect, whose nature is wholly unlike that of its cause, or is like and is implied in its cause only so far as the capacity of producing it may be thought of identically as a part of the nature of its cause. Thus a stone, or any body denser (1) than the air, left unsupported (2) above (3) the surface of the earth, will fall (4) to it, is a proposition in so-called empirical science, in which the conditions (1) (2) (3) form an aggregate to which if we add as a part of its nature the result (4), that is, add the unconditional *tendency* to fall inferred from facts of observation, then the fall is a necessary consequence of the nature of its antecedent conditions, and it is like or is implied in this nature, quite as truly as any mathematical consequence is necessary, or is implied in mathematical protases of causes or antecedents. But ordinarily physical philosophers are not so anxious to make a scholastic show of demonstration as to surreptitiously add (4) to the group of conditions (1) (2) and (3) so as to make out their proof on the maxims that like produces like, or that effects resemble or partake of the nature of their causes. These maxims are really no more true of abstract reasonings in the elementary demonstrations of geometry; but the aim of these elementary reasonings justifies the procedures which give apparent countenance to their maxims.

Other and real illustrations vaguely related to these apparent ones are given in the organic world, in the phenomena of assimilation and reproduction. Tissues turn nutriment into substances of the same kind as their own. Offspring resemble their parents. These facts, together with the geometrical principle of Sufficient Reason appeared to be sufficient grounds with scholastic philosophers for generalizing the identity of natures in real causes and effects. But, in fact, the very opposite is true. Elementary relations of antecedence and consequence are always those of unlikeness. A simple nature or phenomenon A is invariably followed by, or joined with, another different one B. Weight in a body manifested to us primarily by pressure, or in the tension of our muscles through the statical muscular sense, is a simple nature not resembling or implying at all the downward movement which always follows it when isolated or freed from other forces or conditions that are of a nature to produce an opposite effect, namely, an elastic movement, or bearing upward, and are as unlike this effect as weight is unlike the movement of falling. So in the elements of geometry the quality straightness and that of minimum length—duration or effort in traversing a line—are antecedent and consequent, or else concomitant qualities which are essentially different in their natures, but so intimately joined in all experience and in our conceptive powers, that they seem to be different aspects of one and the same nature. Yet the fully adequate and constructive definition of straight lines as a sort, of which only one can be drawn between two given points, does not imply that this is the shortest that can be drawn, or the one soonest and easiest traversed. This constructive definition joined to the meaning of the word inclosure gives what is often regarded as an axiom, the more complex proposition, that two straight lines cannot inclose a space. Starting with these and other constructive definitions, with the most general axioms of quantity, and with postulates of construction, and combining them into more and more complex relations of magnitudes in extension, we arrive at geometrical theorems in which the protasis states the least possible that is essential as the cause, or reason, and the apodosis, or conclusion, defines succinctly the consequent, or effect; theorems in which the connections of these two terms is far from obvious, but is nevertheless necessary, at least in the abstract, or on the supposition of precise, real definition and construction. Reason and consequent imply one the other, or the nature of a cause determines that of its effect, because one is analyzed into relations already determined from fundamental propositions, and these relations serve to define, or constitute the other. It is not true in general that the effect is like its cause, or has a nature determined by that of its cause, but it is true that like causes produce like effects. Parents may be said with tolerable correctness to be the causes of their offspring resembling them, and hence in this case causes produce effects like themselves; yet it is more correct to say that the offspring resemble their parents, because both are products, though successive ones, of similar real causes and processes, some of which in no-wise resemble or transfer their natures to their effects. Some implements and agents of the useful arts likewise are used to make precisely similar implements and agents, as a blacksmith's hammer to produce a similar hammer, or fire to kindle another one, or to reproduce the easily ignited substances with which fires are kindled; yet in these cases the agent that produces its like is not the whole of the cause of production. The blacksmith's forge and anvil and his arm and sight are concauses or conditions of this reproduction: and the nature of these does not re-appear in the effect, unless, as we have said, there is added to the conception of the aggregate of conditions, namely, to the conception of the iron, forge, welding-hammer, arm and sight combined, also the fact that these will produce an effect resembling one of its conditions. So in organic reproduction, the plant produces seed similar not to itself but to the seed from which it grew, and the new seed grows into a similar plant: and in this alternation in which the immediate cause really produces effects unlike itself there are many subordinate conditions and processes the similarity of which in the parent and offspring makes them similar through successive effects of similar causes, which are not of the same nature as their effect. It is only because one condition or element of the cause (the one which resembles its effect) is singled out and, in accordance with the practical usage of common language, is called the cause, on account of its prominence or conspicuousness, that it is at all proper to speak of the parent organism as the cause of the production of its offspring. The existence of the parent organism is a condition *sine qua non* of the production of its offspring, but there are other conditions equally indispensable, the natures of which in themselves are in no wise reproduced in the effects.

The Evolution of Self-Consciousness

North American Review 116 (April 1873): 245–310.

It has come to be understood, and very generally allowed, that the conception of the origin of man as an animal race, as well as of the origin of individual men within it, in accordance with the continuity of organic development maintained in the theory of evolution, does not involve any very serious difficulties, or difficulties so great as are presented by any other hypothesis of this origin would have, not excepting that of "special creation"—if that can be properly called a hypothesis, which is, in fact, a resumption of all the difficulties of natural explanation, assuming them to be insuperable and summarized under a single positive name. Yet in this evolution, as in that of embryonic and infantile life, the birth of self-consciousness is still thought by many to be a step not following from antecedent conditions in "nature," except in an incidental manner, or in so far only as "natural" antecedents have prepared the way for the "supernatural" advent of the self-conscious soul.

Independently of the form of expression, and of the false sentiment which is the motive of the antithesis in this familiar conception, or independently of its mystical interest, which has given to the words "natural" and "supernatural" their commonly accepted meanings, there is a foundation of scientific truth in the conception. For the word "evolution" conveys a false impression to the imagination, not really intended in the scientific use of it. It misleads by suggesting a continuity in the *kinds* of powers and functions in living beings, that is, by suggesting transition by insensible steps from one *kind* to another, as well as in the *degrees* of their importance and exercise at different stages of development. The truth is, on the contrary, that according to the theory of evolution, new uses of old powers arise discontinuously both in the bodily and mental natures of the animal, and in its individual developments, as well as in the development of its race, although, at their rise, these uses are small and of the smallest importance to life. They seem merged in the powers to which they are incident, and seem also merged in the special purposes or functions in which, however, they really have no part, and which are no parts of them. Their services or functions in life, though realized only incidentally at first, and in the feeblest degree, are just as distinct as they afterwards come to appear in their fullest development. The new uses are related to older powers only as *accidents*, so far as the special services of the older powers are concerned, although, from the more general point of view of natural law, their relations to older uses have not the character of accidents, since these relations are, for the most part, determined by universal properties and laws, which are not specially related to the needs and conditions of living beings. Thus the uses of limbs for swimming, crawling, walking, leaping, climbing, and flying are distinct uses, and are related to each other only through the general mechanical principles of locomotion, through which some one, in its first exercise, may be incident to some other, though, in its full exercise and perfection of special service, it is independent of the other, or has only a common dependence with the other on more general conditions.

Many mental as well as bodily powers thus have mixed natures, or independent uses; as, for example, the powers of the voice to call and allure, to warn and repel, and its uses in music and language; or the numerous uses of the human hand in services of strength and dexterity. And, on the contrary, the same uses are, in some cases, realized by independent organs as, for example, respiration in water and in the air by gills and lungs, or flight by means of fins, feathers, and webs. The appearance of a really new power in *nature* (using this word in the wide meaning attached to it in science), the power of flight in the first birds, for example, is only involved potentially in previous phenomena. In the same way, no act of self-consciousness, however elementary, may have been realized before man's first self-conscious act in the animal world; yet the act may have been involved potentially in pre-existing powers or causes. The derivation of this power, supposing it to have been observed by a finite angelic (not animal) intelligence, could not have been foreseen to be involved in the mental causes, on the conjunction of which it might, nevertheless, have been seen to depend. The angelic observation would have been a purely empirical one. The possibility of a subsequent analysis of these causes by the self-conscious animal himself, which would afford an explanation of their agency, by referring it to a rational combination of simpler elements in them, does not alter the case to the angelic intelligence, just as a rational explanation of flight could not be reached by such an intelligence as a consequence of known mechanical laws; since these laws are also animal conditions, or rather are more general and material ones, of which our angelic, spherical[1] intelligence is not supposed to have had any experience. Its observation of the conditions of animal flight would thus also be empirical; for an unembodied spirit cannot be supposed to analyze out of its general experiences the mechanical conditions of movement in animal bodies, nor, on the other hand, to be any more able than the mystic appears to be to analyze the conditions of its own intelligence out of its experiences of animal minds.

The forces and laws of molecular physics are similarly related to actual human intelligence. Sub-sensible properties and powers can only be empirically known, though they are "visualized" in the *hypotheses* of molecular movements and forces. Experimental science, as in chemistry, is full of examples of the discovery of new properties or new powers, which, so far as the conditions of their appearance were previously known, did not follow from antecedent conditions, except in an incidental manner—that is, in a manner *not then fore-seen* to be involved in them; and these effects became afterwards predictable from what had become known to be their antecedent conditions only by the empirical laws or rules which inductive experimentation had established. Nevertheless, the phenomena of the physical or chemical laboratory, however new or unprecedented, are very far from having the character of miracles, in the sense of supernatural events. They are still *natural* events; for, to the scientific imagination, *nature* means more than the continuance or actual repetition of the properties and productions involved in the course of ordinary events, or more than the *inheritance* and reappearance of that which appears in consequence of powers which have made it appear before. It means, in general, those kinds of effects which, though they may have appeared but once in the whole history of the world, yet appear dependent on conjunctions of causes which *would always* be followed by them. One experiment is sometimes, in some branches of science, (as a wide induction has found it to be in chemistry, for example,) sufficient to determine such a dependence, though the particular law so determined is a wholly empirical one; and the history of science has examples of such single experiments, or short series of experiments, made on general principles of experimentation, for the purpose of ascertaining empirical facts or laws, qualities, or relations, which are, nevertheless, generalized as universal ones. Certain "physical constants," so called, were so determined, and are applied in scientific inference with the same unhesitating confidence as that inspired by the familiarly exemplified and more elementary "laws of nature," or even by axioms. Scientific research implies the *potential* existence of the natures, classes, or kinds of effects which experiment brings to light through instances, and for which it also determines, in accordance with inductive methods, the previously unknown conditions of their appearance. This research implies the *latent* kinds or natures which mystical research contemplates (erroneously, in some, at least, of its meditations) under the name of "the supernatural."

To make any event or power supernatural in the mystic's regard requires, however, not merely that it shall be isolated and unparalleled in nature, but that it shall have more than an ordinary, or merely scientific, interest to the mystic's or to the *human* mind. The distinctively human or self-conscious interest, or sentiment, of self-consciousness gives an emphasis to the contrast named "natural and supernatural," through which mysticism is led to its speculations or assumptions of correspondingly emphatic contrasts in real existences. For mysticism is a speculation interpreting as matters of fact, or real existences outside of consciousness, impressions which are only determined within it by emphasis of attention or feeling. It is for the purpose of deepening still more, or to the utmost that its interest suggests, the really profound distinction between human and animal consciousness, or for the purpose of making the distinction *absolute*, of deepening this gulf into an unfathomable and impassable one, that mysticism appears to be moved to its speculations, and has imbued most philosophy and polite learning with its conceptions. Mental philosophy, or metaphysics, has, consequently, come down to us from ancient times least affected by the speculative interests and methods of modern science. Mysticism still reigns over the science of the mind, and it is *felt* to be true even where it is not comprehended in its systems. The *theory* of mysticism in general, or what is common to all theories called mystical, is very vague, and obscure even in the exclusively religious applications of the term; this vagueness has given rise to the more extended use and understanding of the term as it is here employed, which indicates little else than the generally apprehended *motive* of its speculations, or the feelings allied to all its forms of conception. These centre in the feeling of absolute worthiness in self-consciousness, as the source, and at the same time the perfection of existence and power. The naturalist's observations on the minds of men and animals are impertinences of the least possible interest to this sense of worth, very much as the geologist's observations are generally to the speculator who seeks in the earth for hidden mineral treasures.

Mysticism in mental philosophy has apparently gained, so far as it has been materially affected by such observations, a relative external strength, dependent on the real feebleness of the opposition it has generally met with from lovers of animals and from empirical observers and thinkers, in whom generous sympathy with the manifestations of mind in animals and a disposition to do justice to them have been more conspicuous than the qualities of clearness or consistency. For, in the comparisons which they have attempted they have generally sought to break down the really well-founded distinctions of human and animal intelligence, and have sought to discredit the theory of them in this way, rather than by substituting for it a rational, scientific account of what is real in them. The ultimate metaphysical mystery which denies all comparison, and pronounces man a paragon in the kinds, as well the degrees, of his mental faculties, is, as a solution, certainly *simpler*, whatever other scientific excellence it may lack, than any solution that the difficulties of a true scientific comparison are likely to receive. It is not in a strictly empirical way that this comparison can be clearly and effectively made, but rather by a critical re-examination of the phenomena of self-consciousness in themselves, with reference to their possible evolution from powers obviously common to all animal intelligences, or with reference to their potential, though not less natural, existence in mental causes, which could not have been known to involve them before their actual manifestation, but may, nevertheless, be found to do so by an analysis of these causes into the more general conditions of mental phenomena. Mystical metaphysics should be met by scientific inquiries on its own ground, that is, dogmatically, or by theory, since it despises the facts of empirical observation, or attributes them to shallowness, misinterpretation, or errors of observation, and contents itself with its strength as a system, or its impregnable self-consistency, Only an explanation of the phenomena of human consciousness, equally clear and self-consistent with its own, and one which, though not so simple, is yet more in accordance with the facts of a wider induction, could equal it in strength. But this might still be expected as the result of an examination of mental phenomena from the wider interests of true science; since many modern sciences afford examples of this in their triumphs over equally ancient, simple, and apparently impregnable doctrines. The history of science is full, indeed, of illustrations of the impotence, on one hand, of exceptional and isolated facts against established theory, and of the power, on the other hand, of their organization in new theories to revolutionize beliefs. The physical doctrine of a *plenum*, the doctrine of epicycles and vortices in astronomy, the corpuscular theory of optics, that of cataclysms in geology, and that of special creations in biology, each gave way, not absolutely through its intrinsic weakness, but through the greater success of a rival theory which superseded it. A sketch only is attempted in this essay of some of the results of such an examination into the psychological conditions, or antecedents, of the phenomena of self-consciousness; an examination which does not aim at diminishing, on the one hand, the real contrasts of mental powers in men and animals, nor at avoiding difficulties, on the other, by magnifying them beyond the reach of comparison.

The terms "science" and "scientific" have come, in modem times, to have so wide a range of application, and so vague a meaning, that (like many other terms, not only in common speech, but also in philosophy and in various branches of learning, which have come down to us through varying usages) they would oppose great difficulties to any attempts at defining them by *genus* and difference, or otherwise than by enumerating the branches of knowledge and the facts, or relations of the facts, to which usage has affixed them as names. Precision in proper definition being then impossible, it is yet possible to give to these terms so general a meaning as to cover all the knowledge to which they are usually applied, and still to exclude much besides. As the terms thus defined coincide with what I propose to show as the character of the knowledge peculiar to men, or which distinguishes the minds of men from those of other animals, I will begin with this definition. In science and in scientific facts there is implied a conscious purpose of including particular facts under general facts, and the less general under the more general ones. Science, in the modern use of the term, consists, essentially, of a knowledge of things and events either as effects of general causes, or as instances of general classes, rules, or laws; or even as isolated facts of which the class, law, rule, or cause is sought. The conscious purpose of arriving at general facts and at an adequate statement of them in language, or of bringing particular facts under explicit general ones, determines for any knowledge a scientific character.

Many of our knowledges and judgments from experience in practical matters are not so reduced, or sought to be reduced, to explicit principles, or have not a theoretical form, since the major premises, or general principles, of our judgments are not consciously generalized by us in forms of speech. Even matters not strictly practical, or which would be merely theoretical in their bearing on conduct, if reduced to a scientific form, like many of the judgments of common-sense, for example, are not consciously referred by us to explicit principles, though derived, like science, from experience, and even from special kinds of experience, like that of a man of business, or that of a professional adept. We are often led by being conscious of a sign of anything to believe in the existence of the thing itself, either past, present, or prospective, without having any distinct and general apprehension of the connection of the sign and thing, or any recognition of the sign under the general character of a sign. Not only are the judgments of common-sense in men, both the inherited and acquired ones, devoid of heads, or major premises (such as "All men are mortal"), in deductive inference, and devoid also of distinctly remembered details of experience in the inferences of induction, but it is highly probable that this is all but exclusively the character of the knowledges and judgments of the lower animals. Language, strictly so called, which some of these animals also have, or signs *purposely used* for communication, is not only required for scientific knowledge, but a second step of generalization is needed, and is made through reflection by which this use of a sign is itself an object of attention, and the sign is recognized in its general relations to what it signifies, and to what it has signified in the past, and will signify in the future. It is highly improbable that such a knowledge of knowledge, or such a *re*cognition, belongs in any considerable, or effective, degree to even the most intelligent of the lower animals, or even to the lowest of the human race. This is what is properly meant by being "rational," or being a "rational animal." It is what I have preferred to call "scientific" knowledge; since the growing vagueness and breadth of application common to all ill-comprehended words (like "Positivism" in recent times) have given to "scientific" the meaning probably attached at first to "rational." This knowledge comes from reflecting on what we know in the common-sense, or semi-instinctive form, or making what we know a field of renewed research, observation, and analysis in the generalization of major premises. The line of distinction between such results of reflection, or between scientific knowledge and the common-sense form of knowledge, is not simply the dividing line between the minds of men and those of other animals; but is that which divides the knowledge produced by outward attention from that which is further produced by reflective attention. The former, throughout a considerable range of the higher intelligent animals, involves veritable judgments of a complex sort. It involves combinations of minor premises leading to conclusions through implicit major premises in the enthymematic reasonings, commonly employed in inferences from signs and likelihoods, as in prognostications of the weather, or in orientations with many animals. This knowledge belongs both to men and to the animals next to men in intelligence, though in unequal degrees.

So far as logicians are correct in regarding an enthymeme as a reasoning, independently of its statement in words; or in regarding as a rational process the passing from such a sign as the human nature of Socrates to the inference that he will die, through the data of experience concerning the mortality of other men—data which are neither distinctly remembered in detail nor generalized explicitly in the formula, "all men are mortal," but are effective only in making mortality a more or less clearly understood part of the human character; that is, making it one of the attributes *suggested* by the name "man," yet not separated from the essential attributes by the contrasts of subject and attributes in real predication—so far, I say, as this can be regarded as a reasoning, or a rational process, so far observation shows that the more intelligent dumb animals reason, or are rational. But this involves great vagueness or want of that precision in the use of signs which the antitheses of essential and accidental attributes and that of proper predication secure. There is little, or no, evidence to show that the animals which learn, to some extent, to comprehend human speech have an analytical comprehension of real general propositions, or of propositions in which both subject and predicate are general terms and differ in meaning. A merely verbal general proposition, declaring only the equivalence of two general names, might be comprehended by such minds, if it could be made of sufficient interest to attract their attention. But this is extremely doubtful, and it would not be as a *proposition*, with its contrasts of essential and added elements of conception that this would be comprehended. It would be, in effect, only repeating in succession two general names of the same class of objects. Such minds could, doubtless, comprehend a single class of objects, or an indefinite number of resembling things by several names; that is, several signs of such a class would recall it to their thoughts, or revive a representative image of it; and they would thus be aware of the equivalence of these signs; but they would not attach precision of meaning and different degrees of generality to them, or regard one name as the name or sign of another name; as when we define a triangle to be a rectilinear figure, and a figure of three sides.

Only one degree of generality is, however, essential to inference from signs, or in enthymematic reasoning. Moreover, language in its relation to thought does not consist exclusively of spoken, or written, or imagined words, but of signs in general, and, essentially, of internal images or successions of images, which are the representative imaginations of objects and their relations; imaginations which severally stand for each and all of the particular objects or relations of a *kind*. Such are the visual imaginations called up by spoken or written concrete general names of visible objects, as "dog" or "tree"; which are vague and feeble as images, but effective as notative, directive, or guiding elements in thought. These are the internal signs of things and events, and are instruments of thought in judgment and reasoning, not only with dumb animals but also with men, in whom they are supplemented, rather than supplanted, by names. But being of feeble intensity, and little under the influence of distinct attention or control of the will, compared to actual perceptions and to the voluntary movements of utterance and gesture, their nature has been but dimly understood even by metaphysicians, who are still divided into two schools in logic—the conceptualists and the nominalists. The "concepts" of the former are really composed of these vague and feeble notative images, or groups of images, to which clearness and distinctness of attention are given by their associations with outward (usually vocal) signs. Hence a second degree of observation and generalization upon these images, as objects in reflective thought, cannot be readily realized independently of what would be the results of such observations, namely, their associations with outward signs. They are probably so feeble, even in the most intelligent dumb animal, that they cannot be associated with outward signs in such a manner as to make these distinctly appear as substitutes, or signs equivalent to them.

So far as images act in governing trains of thought and reasoning, they act as signs; but, with reference to the more vivid outward signs, they are, in the animal mind, merged in the things signified, like stars in the light of the sun. Hence, language, in its narrower sense, as the instrument of reflective thought, appears to depend directly on the intensity of significant, or representative, images; since the power to attend to these and intensify them still further, at the same time that an equivalent outward sign is an object of attention, would appear to depend solely on the relative intensities of the two states, or on the relations of intensity in perception and imagination, or in original and revived impressions. The direct power of attention to intensify a revived impression in imagination does not appear to be different in kind from the power of attention in perception, or in outward impressions generally. But this direct power would be obviously aided by the indirect action of attention when fixed by an outward sign, provided attention could be directed to both at the same time; as a single glance may comprehend in one field of view the moon or the brighter planets and the sun, since the moon or planet is not hidden like the stars, by the glare of day.

As soon, then, as the progress of animal intelligence through an extension of the range in its powers of memory, or in revived impressions, together with a corresponding increase in the vividness of these impressions, has reached a certain point (a progress in itself useful, and therefore likely to be secured in some part of nature, as one among its numerous grounds of selection, or lines of advantage), it becomes possible for such an intelligence to fix its attention on a vivid outward sign, without losing sight of, or dropping out of distinct attention, an image or revived impression; which latter would only serve, in case of its spontaneous revival in imagination, as a sign of the same thing, or the same event. Whether the vivid outward sign be a real object or event, of which the revived image is the counterpart, or whether it be a sign in a stricter meaning of the term—that is, some action, figure, or utterance, associated either naturally or artificially with all similar objects or events, and, consequently, with the revived and representative image of them— whatever the character of this outward sign may be, provided the representative image, or inward sign, still retains, in distinct consciousness, its power as such, then the outward sign may be consciously recognized as a substitute for the inward one, and a consciousness of simultaneous internal and external suggestion, or significance, might be realized; and the contrast of thoughts and things, at least in their power of suggesting that of which they may be coincident signs, could, for the first time, be perceptible. This would plant the germ of the distinctively human form of self-consciousness.

Previously to such a simultaneous consciousness of movements in imagination and movements in the same direction arising from perception, realized through the comparative vividness of the former, all separate and distinct consciousness of the inward sign would be eclipsed, and attention would pass on to the thought suggested by the outward sign. A similar phenomenon is frequently observed with us in successions of inward suggestions, or trains of thought. The attention often skips intermediate steps in a train, or appears to do so. At least, the memory of steps, which appear essential to its rational coherency, has ceased when we revive the train or repeat it voluntarily. This happens even when only a few moments have elapsed between the train and its repetition. Many writers deny that the omitted steps are immediately forgotten in such cases, on account of their feebleness—as we forget immediately the details of a view which we have just seen, and remember only its salient points; and they maintain that the missing steps are absent from consciousness, even in the original and spontaneous movements of the train; or are present only through an unconscious agency, both in the train and its revival. This being a question of memory, reference cannot be made to memory itself for the decision of it. To decide whether a thing is completely forgotten, or has never been experienced, we have no other resource than rational analogy, which, in the present case, appears to favor the theory of oblivion, rather than that of latent mental ties and actions; since oblivion is a *vera causa* sufficient to account for the difference between such revived trains and those in which no steps are missed, or could be rationally supposed to have been present. The theory of "latent mental agency" appears to confound the original spontaneous movement of the train with what appears as its representative in its voluntary revival. This revival, in some cases, really involves new conditions, and is not, therefore, to be rationally interpreted as a precisely true recollection. If repeated often, it will establish direct and strong associations of contiguity between salient steps in the train which were connected at first by feebler though still conscious steps. The complete obliteration of these is analogous, as I have said, to the loss, in primary forms of memory, of details which are present to consciousness in actual first perceptions.

If, as more frequently happens with us, the whole train, with all its steps of suggestion, is recalled in the voluntary revival of it (without any sense of missing steps), the feebler intermediate links, that in other cases are obliterated, would correspond to the feebler, though (in the more advanced animal intelligences) comparatively vivid, mental signs which have in them the germ, as I have said, of the human form of self-consciousness. The growth of this consciousness, its development from this germ, is a more direct process than the production of the germ itself, which is only incidental to previous utilities in the power of memory. Thought, henceforward, may be an object to thought in its distinct contrast, as an inward sign, with the outward and more vivid sign of that which they both suggest, or revive from memory. This contrast is heightened if the outward one is more strictly a sign; that is, is not the perception of an object or event, of which the inward and representative image is a counterpart, but is of a different nature, for instance some movement or gesture or vocal utterance, or some graphic sign, associated by contiguity with the object or event, or, more properly, with its representative image. The "concept" so formed is not a thing complete in itself, but is essentially a cause, or step, in mental trains. The outward sign, the image, or inward sign, and the suggested thought, or image, form a train, like a train which might be wholly within the imagination. This train is present, in all its three constituents, to the first, or immediate, consciousness, in all degrees of intelligence; but in the revival of it, in the inferior degrees of intelligence, the middle term is obliterated, as in the trains of thought above considered. The animal has in mind only an image of the sign, previously present in perception, followed now immediately by an image of what was suggested through the obliterated mental image. But the latter in the higher degrees of intelligence, is distinctly recalled as a middle term. In the revival of past trains, which were first produced through outward signs, the dumb animal has no consciousness of there having been present more than one of the two successive signs, which, together with the suggested image, formed the actual train in its first occurrence. The remembered outward sign is now a thought, or image, immediately suggesting or recalling that which was originally suggested by a feebler intermediate step.

In pure imaginations, not arising by actual connections through memory, the two terms are just the same with animals as in real memory; except that they are not felt to be the representatives of a former real connection. The contrast of the real and true with the imaginary and false is, then, the only general one of which such a mind could be aware in the phenomena of thought. The contrast of thought itself with perception, or with the actual outward sign and suggestion of the thought, is realized only by the revival in memory of the feeble connecting link. This effects a contrast not only between what is real and what is merely imaginary, but also between what is out of the mind and what is within it. The minute difference in the force of memory, on which this link in the chain of attention at first depended, was one of immense consequence to man. This feeble link is the dividing region, interval, or cleft between the two more vivid images; one being more vivid as a direct recollection of an actual outward impression, and the other being more vivid, or salient, from the interest or the motives which gave it the prominence of a thought demanding attention; either as a memory of a past object or event of interest, or the image of something in the immediate future. The disappearance altogether of this feeble link would, as I have said, take from the images connected by it all contrast with any pair of steps in a train, except a consciousness of reality in the connection of these images in a previous experience.[2]

To exemplify this somewhat abstruse analysis, let us examine what, according to it, would be the mental movements in a man, let him be a sportsman—and a domestic animal—let it be his dog—on hearing a name—let it be the name of some game, as "fox." The general character of the phenomena in both would be the same on the actual first hearing of this word. The word would suggest a mental image of the fox, then its movements of escape from its hunters, and the thought would pass on and dwell, through the absorbing interest of it, on the hunter's movements of pursuit, or pass on even to the capture and destruction of the game. This would, doubtless, recall to the minds of the hunter and his hound one or more real and distinctly remembered incidents of the sort. Now if we suppose this train of thought to be revived (as undoubtedly it is capable of being, both in the man and the dog), it will be the same in the man's mind as on its first production; except that the name "fox" will be thought of (as an auditory, or else a vocal, image), instead of being heard; and the visual image of the fox will be recalled by it with all the succeeding parts of the repeated train. But in the dog, either the auditory image of the name will not be recalled, since the vocal image does not exist in his mind to aid the recall (his voluntary vocal powers not being capable of forming it even in the first instance); or if such an auditory image arises, the representative visual or olfactory[3] one will not appear in distinct consciousness. His attention will pass at once from either of these signs, but from one only to the more intense and interesting parts of the train—to the pursuit and capture of the game, or to actually remembered incidents of the kind. Either the first or the immediate sign will remain in oblivion.

Hence the dog's dreams, or trains of thought, when they are revivals of previous trains, or when they rise into prominent consciousness in consequence of having been passed through before, omit or skip over the steps which at first served only as suggesting and connecting signs, following now only the associations of contiguity, established in the first occurrence of the train between its more prominent parts. The suggested thought eclipses by its glare the suggesting one. The interest of an image, or its power to attract attention and increased force, depends in the dog only on its vividness as a memory, of as a future purpose or event, and very little, if at all, on its relations and agency as a *sign*. Images, as well as outward signs, serve, as I have said, in the dumb animals as well as in man in this capacity; but this is not *recognized* by the animal, since those parts of a train which serve only as signs are too feeble to be revived in the repeated train; and new associations of mere contiguity in the prominent parts of it take their places. All that would be recognized in the animal mind by reflection on thought as thought, or independently of its reality as a memory, an anticipation, or a purpose, would be its unreality, or merely imaginary character.

If, on the contrary, a greater intensity, arising from a greater power of simple memory, should revive the feebler parts in repeated trains of thought to the degree of attracting attention to them, and thus bringing them into a more distinct and vivid consciousness, there might arise an interest as to what they are, as to what are their relations, and where they belong, which would be able to inspire and guide an act of distinct reflection. A thought might thus be determined as a representative mental image; and such acts of reflection, inspired also by other motives more powerful than mere inquisitiveness, would by observation, analysis, and generalization (the counterparts of such outward processes in the merely animal mind) bring all such representative images, together with real memories and anticipations, into a single group, or subjective connection. The recognition of them in this connection is the knowledge of them as *my* thoughts, or *our* thoughts, or as phenomena of the mind.

When a thought, or an outward expression, acts in an animal's mind or in a man's, in the capacity of a sign, it carries forward the movements of a train, and directs attention away from itself to what it signifies or suggests; and consciousness is concentrated on the latter. But being sufficiently vivid in itself to engage distinct attention, it determines a new kind of action, and a new faculty of observation, of which the cerebral hemispheres appear to be the organs. From the action of these, in their more essential powers in memory and imagination, the objects or materials of reflection are also derived. Reflection would thus be, not what most metaphysicians appear to regard it, a fundamentally new faculty in man, as elementary and primordial as memory itself, or the power of abstractive attention, or the function of signs and representative images in generalization; but it would be determined in its contrasts with other mental faculties by the nature of its objects. On its subjective side it would he composed of the same mental faculties—namely, memory, attention, abstraction—as those which are employed in the primary use of the senses. It would be engaged upon what these senses have furnished to memory; but would act as independently of any orders of grouping and succession presented by them, as the several senses themselves do of one another. To this extent, reflection is a distinct faculty, and though, perhaps, not peculiar to man, is in him so prominent and marked in its effects on the development of the individual mind, that it may be regarded as his most essential and elementary mental distinction in kind. For differences of degrees in causes may make differences of kinds in effects.

Motives more powerful than mere inquisitiveness about the feebler steps or *mere* thoughts of a revived train, and more efficient in concentrating attention upon them, and upon their functions as signs, or suggesting images, would spring from the social nature of the animal, from the uses of mental communication between the members of a community, and from the *desire* to communicate, which these uses would create. And just as an outward sign associated with a mental image aids by its intensity in fixing attention upon the latter, so the *uses* of such outward signs and the motives connected with their employment would add *extensive* force, or interest, to the energy of attention in the cognition of this inward sign; and hence would aid in the reference of it and its sort to the subject *ego*—a being already known, or distinguished from other beings, as that which wills, desires, and feels. That which wills, desires, and feels is, in the more intelligent domestic animal, known by the proper name, which the animal recognizes and answers to by its actions, and is a consciousness of its individuality. It is not known or recognized by that most generic name "I"; since phenomena common to this individual and to others; or capable of being made common through the communications of language, are not distinctly referred to the individual self by that degree of abstractive attention and precision which an habitual exercise of the faculty of reflection is required to produce. But, in the same manner, the word "world," which includes the conscious subject in its meaning, would fail to suggest anything more to such an intelligence than more concrete terms do—such as what is around, within, near, and distant from consciousness; or it would fail to suggest the *whole* of that which philosophers divide into *ego* and *non-ego*, the outward and inward worlds. A contrast of this whole to its parts, however divided in predication, or the antithesis of subject and attributes, in a divisible unity and its component particulars, would not be suggested to an animal mind by the word "world." The "categories," or forms and conditions of human understanding, though doubtless innate (in the naturalist's sense of the term) or inherited, are only the ways and facilities of the higher exercise of the faculty of reflection. They are, doubtless, ways and facilities that are founded on the ultimate nature of mind; yet, on this very account, are universal, though only potential, in the animal mind generally; just as the forms and conditions of *locomotion* are generally in the bodies of plants; forms and conditions founded on the ultimate natures or laws of motion, which would be exemplified in plants, if they also had the power of changing their positions, and are indeed exemplified in those forms of vegetable life that are transported, such as seeds, or can move and plant themselves, like certain spores.

The world of self-conscious intellectual activity—the world of mind—has, doubtless, its ultimate unconditional laws, everywhere exemplified in the actual phenomena of abstractive and reflective thought, and capable of being generalized in the reflective observations of the philosopher, and applied by him to the explanation of the phenomena of thought wherever manifested in outward expressions, whether in his fellow-men, or in the more intelligent dumb animals. Memory, in the effects of its more powerful and vivid revivals in the more intelligent animals, and especially in the case of large-brained man, presents this new world, in which the same faculties of observation, analysis, and generalization as those employed by intelligent beings in general, ascertain the marks and classes of phenomena strictly mental, and divide them, as a whole class, or *summum genus*, from those of the outward world. The distinction of subject and object becomes thus a classification through observation and analysis, instead of the intuitive distinction it is supposed to be by most metaphysicians. Intuitive to some extent, in one sense of the word, it doubtless is; that is, facilities and predispositions to associations, which are as effective as repeated experiences and observations would be, and which are inherited in the form of instincts, doubtless have much to do in bringing to pass this cognition, as well as many others, which appear to be innate, not only in the lower animals but also in man.

The very different aim of the evolutionist from that of his opponents—the latter seeking to account for the *resemblances* of mental actions in beings supposed to be radically different in their mental constitutions, while the former seeks to account for the *differences* of manifestation in fundamentally similar mental constitutions—gives, in the theory of evolution, a philosophical *rôle* to the word "instinct," and to its contrast with intelligence, much inferior to that which this contrast has had in the discussions of the mental faculties of animals. For the distinction of instinct and intelligence, though not less real and important in the classification of actions in psycho-zoology, and as important even as that of animal and vegetable is in general zoology, or the distinctions of organic and inorganic, living and dead, in the general science of life, is yet, like these, in its applications a vague and ill-defined distinction, and is most profitably studied in the subordinate classes of actions, and in the special contrasts which are summarized by it. Under the naturalist's point of view, the contrasts of dead and living matters, inorganic and organic products, vegetable and animal forms and functions, automatic and sentient movements, instinctive and intelligent motives and actions are severally rough divisions of *series*, which are clearly enough contrasted in their extremities, but ill defined at their points of division. Thus, we have the long series beginning with the processes of growth, nutrition, and waste, and in movements independent of nervous connections, and continued in processes in which sensations are involved, first vaguely, as in the processes of digestion, circulation, and the general stimulative action of the nervous system; then distinctly, as in the stimulative sensations of respiration, winking, swallowing, coughing, and sneezing, more or less under general control or the action of the will. This series is continued, again, into those sensations, impulses, and consequent actions which are wholly controllable, though spontaneously arising; and thence into the motives to action which are wholly dependent on, or involved in, the immediate controlling powers of the will—a series in which the several marks of distinction are clearly enough designated in the abstract, as the colors of the spectrum are by their names, but are not clearly separated in the concrete applications of them.

Again, we have the series of voluntary actions, beginning at the connections between perceptions, emotions, and consequent actions, which are strictly instinctive. These, though inherited, are independent of the effects of higher, and more properly voluntary, actions in the individual's progenitors, as well as in himself. When they are not simple ultimate and universal laws of mental natures, or elementary mental connections, they are combinations produced through their serviceableness to life, or by natural selection and exercise, or in the same general manner in which bodily organs, powers, and functions are produced or altered. Such connections between perceptions, emotions, and consequent actions, derived through natural selection, or even those that are ultimate laws, and determine, in a manner not peculiar to any species, the conditions and uses of serviceable actions—are *instinctive* connections, or powers of *instinct*, in a restricted but perfectly definite use of the word. But following immediately in the series of voluntary actions are, first, the inherited effects of habits, and next, habits properly so called, or effects produced by higher voluntary actions in the individual. *Habits* properly so called, and *dispositions,* which are the inherited effects of habits, are not different in their practical character or modes of action from true instincts; but differ only in their origin and capacity of alteration through the higher forms of volition. The latter, or proper, volitions are connections between the occasions, or external means and conditions of an action, and the production of the action itself through the *motive of the end*, and not through emotions or by any other ties instinctively uniting them. They are joined by the foreseen ulterior effect of the action, or else through a union produced by its influence. The desirableness of what is effected by an action connects its occasions, or present means and conditions, with the action itself, and causes its production through the end felt in imagination. The influence of the end, or ulterior motive in volition, may not be a consciously recognized part of the action, or a distinctly separated step in it, and will actually cease to be the real tie when a series of repeated volitions has established a habit, or a fixed association between them and their occasions, or external conditions. This connection in habits is, as we have said, closely similar to strictly instinctive connections, and is indistinguishable from them independently of questions of origin and means of alterations.

Independently of these questions, the series of voluntary actions starting from the strictly instinctive joins to them natural dispositions, or the inherited effects of habit, and passes on to habits properly so called, thence into those in which the ulterior motives of true volitions are still operative, though not as separate parts of consciousness, and thence on to mere faculties of action, or to those actions in which such a motive is still the sole effective link, though quite faded out of distinct attention, or attended to with a feeble and intermittent consciousness. Thence it comes finally to the distinct recognition in reflective thought of an ulterior motive to an action. The ulterior motive, the end or good to be effected by an action, anticipated in imagination, joins the action to its present means and conditions in actual volitions, or else joins it in imagination with some future occurrence of them in an *intention,* or a predetermination of the will. These ulterior motives, ends, or determinations of an action through foreseen consequences of it, may be *within* the will, in the common and proper meaning of the word, when it is spoken of as free, or unconstrained by an outward force, or necessity; or they may be *without* it, like instinctive tendencies to which the will is said to *consent* or *yield*, as well as in other cases to be *opposed*. The motives within the will, either distinctly or vaguely operative, or completely superseded by *forces* of habit, constitute the individual's character.

To summarize all the steps and contrasts of these series under the general heads of intelligence and instinct would be, from the evolutionist's and naturalist's point of view, only a rough classification, like that of living beings into animals and plants; and any attempts at investigating the distinctions and classes of mental natures by framing elaborate definitions of this summary contrast would be like concentrating all the energies of scientific pursuit in biology, and staking its success on the question whether the sponge be an animal or a plant. This is, in fact, the scholastic method, from which modern science is comparatively, and fortunately, set free; being contented with finding out more and more about beings that are unmistakably animals or plants, and willing to study the nature of the sponge by itself, and defer the classification of it to the end. The more ambitious scholastic method is followed in the science of psycho-zoology by those who seek, in an ultimate definition of this sort, to establish an impassable barrier between the minds of men and those of the lower animals—being actuated apparently by the naive, though generous, motive of rendering the former more respectable, or else of defending a worth in them supposed to be dependent on such a barrier. This aim would be confusing at least, if not a false one, in a strictly scientific inquiry.

Although the cognition of the subject world through the distinction in memory of the phenomena of signification from those of outward perception would be a classification spontaneously arising through inherited facilities and predispositions to associations, which are as effective as repeated experiences would be, it must still be largely aided by the voluntary character of outward signs—vocal, gestural, and graphic—by which all signs are brought under the control of the will, or of that most central, active personality, which is thus connected externally and actively, as well as through the memory, with the inward signs or the representative mental images. These images are brought by this association under stronger and steadier attention; their character, as representative images or signs, is more distinctly seen in reflection, and they are not any longer merely guides in thought, blindly followed. They form, by this association, a little representative world arising to thought at will. Command of language is an important condition of the effective cognition of a sign as such. It is highly probable that the dog not only cannot utter the sound "fox," but cannot revive the sound as heard by him. The word cannot, therefore, be of aid to him in fixing his attention in reflection on the mental image of the fox as seen or smelt by him. But the latter, spontaneously arising, would be sufficient to produce a lively train of thoughts, or a vivid dream. It by no means follows from his deficiencies of vocal and auditory imagination that the dog has not, in some directions, aid from outward signs, and some small degree of reflective power, though this probably falls far short of the clear division of the two worlds realized in the cognition of "*cogito*." Thus, he has at command the outward sign of the chase, incipient movements of his limbs, such as he makes in his dreams; and this may make the mental image of the chase, with its common obstacles and incidents, distinct in his imagination, in spite of the greater interest which carries the thoughts of his dream forward to the end of the pursuit, the capture of the game. He may even make use of this sign, as he in fact does when he indicates to his master by his movements his eagerness for a walk or for the chase.

Command of signs, and, indeed, all the volitional or active powers of an animal, including attention in perception, place it in relation to outward things in marked contrast with its passive relations of sensation and inattentive or passive perception. The distinctness, or prominence, in consciousness given by an animal's attention to its perceptions, and the greater energy given by its intentions or purposes to its outward movements, cannot fail to afford a ground of discrimination between these as causes, both of inward and outward events, and those outward causes which are not directly under such control, but form an independent system, or several distinct systems, of causes. This would give rise to a form of self-consciousness more immediate and simple than the intellectual one, and is apparently realized in dumb animals. They, probably, do not have, or have only in an indistinct and ineffective form, the intellectual cognitions of *cogito* and *sum*; but having reached the cognition of a contrast in subject and object as *causes* both in inward and outward events, they have already acquired a form of subjective consciousness, or a knowledge of the *ego*. That they do not, and cannot, name it, at least by a general name, or understand it by the general name of "I" or *ego*, comes from the absence of the attributes of *ego* which constitute the intellectual self-consciousness. A dog can, nevertheless, understand the application of his own proper name to himself, both in the direct and the indirect reference of our language to his conduct or his wants; and can also understand the application to himself of the general name—"dog." He cannot say, "I am a dog," and probably has but the faintest, if any, understanding of what the proposition would mean if he could utter it; though he probably has as much understanding, at least, as the parrot has in saying, "I am Poll." For there are, in these propositions, two words expressing the abstractest ideas that the human mind can reach. One of them, "I," is the name of one of the two *summa genera*, *ego* and *non-ego*, into which human consciousness is divisible. "I am a dog," and "Camp is a dog," would mean much the same to Camp; just as "I am a child," and "John is a child" are not clearly distinguished by John even after he has acquired considerable command of language. The other word, "am," is a form of the substantive verb expressing existence in general, but further determined to express the *present* existence of the *speaker* or *subject*. These further determinations, in tense, number, and persons, are, however, the most important parts of meaning in the various forms of the substantive verb to the common and barbarous minds, from which we and the philosophical grammarian have received them. The substantive verb is, accordingly, irregular in most languages under the form of a grammatical paradigm. In this form the philosophical grammarian subordinates to the infinitive meaning of a word those determinations which, in the invention of words, were apparently regarded as leading ideas in many other cases as well as in the substantive verb, and were expressed by words with distinct etymologies.

Not only the dog and other intelligent dumb animals, but some of the least advanced among human beings, also, are unable to arrive at a distinct abstraction of what is expressed by "to be," or "to exist." Being is concreted, or determined, to such minds down, at least, to the conception of living or acting; to a conception scarcely above what is implied in the actions of the more intelligent animals, namely, their apprehension of themselves as agents or patients with wills and feelings distinct from those of other animals, and from the forces and interests of outward nature generally. "Your dog is here, or is coming, and at your service," is a familiar expression in the actions of dogs not remarkable for intelligence. A higher degree of abstraction and generalization than the simple steps, which are suffi-cient, as we have seen, for inference in enthymematic reasonings to particular conclusions, would be required in reflection; and a more extensive and persistent exercise of the faculty of reflection, aided by voluntary signs or by language, than any dumb animal attains to, would be needed to arrive at the cognition of *cogito* and *sum*. This is a late acquisition with children; and it would, indeed, be surprising if the mind of a dumb animal should attain to it. But there is little ground in this for believing, with most metaphysicians, that the cognition is absolutely *sui generis*, or an ultimate and underived form of knowledge; or that it is not approached gradually, as well as realized with different degrees of clearness and precision, as the faculty of reflection becomes more and more exercised.

That a dumb animal should not know itself to be a thinking being, is hardly more surprising than that it should not be aware of the circulation of its blood and other physio-logical functions; or that it should not know the anatomy of its frame or that of its nervous system, or the seat of its mental faculties, or the fact that the brain is much smaller in it, in proportion to the size of its body, than in man. Its reflective observation may be as limited in respect to the phenomena of thought as the outward observation of most men is in respect to these results of scientific research. And, on the other hand, the boasted intellec-tual self-consciousness of man is a knowledge of a subject, not through all its attributes and phenomena, but only through enough of them in general to determine and distinguish it from outward objects, and make it serve as the subject of further attributions or predica-tions, as reflective observation makes them known. The abstract forms of this knowledge, the laws of logic and grammar, and the categories of the understanding, which are forms of all scientific knowledge, are all referable to the action of a *purpose* to know, and to fix knowledge by precise generalization; just as the mechanical conditions of flight are refer-able to the purpose to fly and to secure the requisite means. Generalization already exists, however, with particular acts of inquisitiveness in the animal mind; and there is required only the proper degree of attention to signs in order to make it act in accordance with laws which, *if they are universal and necessary laws of the mind*, are equally laws of the animal intelligence, though not actually exemplified in it; just as the laws of locomotion are not actually exemplified in the bodies of plants, but are still potential in them.

The inferior and savage races of men, whose languages do not include any abstract terms like truth, goodness, and sweetness, but only concrete ones, like true, good, and sweet, would hardly be able to form a conception, even a vague and obscure one, of the mystic's research of omniscience in the profundities of self-consciousness. They ought on this account, perhaps, to be regarded as races distinct from that of these philosophers, at least mentally, and to be classed, in spite of their powers of speech and limited vocabularies, with the dumb, but still intelligent, animals. If, however, the theory above propounded be true, this greatest of human qualities, intelligent self-consciousness, understood in its actual and proper limits, would follow as a consequence of a greater brain, a greater, or more powerful and vivid, memory and imagination, bringing to light, as it were, and into distinct consciousness, phenomena of thought which reflective observation refers to the subject, already known in the dumb animal, or distinguished as an active cause from the forces of outward nature, and from the wills of other animals. The degrees of abstraction and the successively higher and higher steps of generalization, the process which, in scientific knowledge, brings not only the particulars of experience under general designations, but, with a conscious purpose brings the less general under the more general, or gives common names not only to each and all resembling objects and relations, but also more general common names to what is denoted by these names, or groups them under higher categories—this process brings together the several forms of self-consciousness. Willing, desiring, feeling, and lastly thinking, also, are seen in thought to belong together, or to the same subject; and by thinking they are brought under a common view and receive a common name, or several common names, to wit, "my mind," "me," "I," "my mental states."

By still further observation, comparison, and analysis on the part of philosophers, this step is seen to be the highest degree of abstraction, since nothing appears to be common to all my mental states, except their belonging together and acting on one another, along with their common independence of other existences in this mutual action. The word "I" is discovered by philosophers to be a word without meaning or determination, or to be as meaningless as the words "thing," "being," "existence," which are subjects stripped of all attributes. "I" is the bare subject of mental phenomena. The word points them out, but does not declare anything of their nature by its meaning, essence, or implied attribution, which is, in fact, no meaning at all. Hence philosophers have placed this term, or name, over against that which is not, or in contrast with all other existences. Common language has no name for the latter, and so philosophers were compelled to call it the *non-ego*, in order to contrast these two highest categories, or *summa genera*, into which they divide all of which we are, or may be, conscious. Grammatical science, however, furnished convenient substitutes for these words. *Ego* and *non-ego* were named "subject" and "object." Yet these terms so applied do not retain any meanings. "Subject" is applicable to denote the *ego*, rather than the *non-ego*, only because it is the positive or more prominent term of the antithesis in its grammatical application, like "active and passive." Sir William Hamilton undertakes, however, to assign them meanings in psychology by representing the *object* as that which *is thought about*, and the *subject* as that which *thinks*, or *acts*, or that in which the thought or action inheres. But this definition is given from the active subject's point of view, and not from the whole scope of the subject-attributes. We act, indeed, in volition and attentive perception on the outer world or *non-ego*; but in sensation and passive perception we are the objects influenced, governed, or acted on by this outer world. Moreover from the point of view of the effects of thinking, both the *object* and *subject* are the subjects of attribution. We attribute qualities to external objects, and, at the same time, to their mental images, which, in their capacity as representative images, or internal signs of objects and relations, are called up and separately attended to in the human consciousness, and are, in turn, referred or attributed to the conscious subject, or to its memory and understanding.

These images, in their *individual* capacity, are not to be distinguished, even in human consciousness, from the object of perception. It is in their specific, or notative, function as signs, and as referring back to memories of like experiences, which they summarize, that they are separately and subjectively cognized. *Individually* they are divisible only into real and unreal, or into remembered and imagined combinations of particular impressions. As inward and mine they are "concepts," or thoughts directing the processes of thought, and are specially related to my will and its motives. The classification of events as inward and outward does not necessarily imply that the scientific process depends on each man's experiences of their connections alone; for the forms of language, and what is indirectly taught in learning a language, guide observation in this matter largely; and so, also, very probably, do inherited aptitudes, ties, or tendencies to combination, which have the same effect in associating the particulars of the individual's experiences as the frequent repetitions of them in himself would have, and are, indeed, by the theory of evolution, the consequences of such repeated experiences in the individual's progenitors. Such a reference of the distinction of subject and object to instinctive tendencies in our minds is not equivalent to the metaphysical doctrine that this distinction is intuitive. For this implies more than is meant by the word "instinctive" from the naturalist's point of view. It implies that the cognition is absolute; independent not only of the individual's experiences, but of all possible previous experience, and has a certainty, reality, and cogency that no amount of experience could give to an empirical classification.

The metaphysical dogmas, for which this formula is given, deserve but a passing scientific consideration. Truths independent of all experience are not known to exist, unless we exclude from what we mean by "experience" that experience which we have in learning the meanings of words and in agreeing to definitions and the conventions of language, on the ground that they depend solely, or may be considered as depending solely, on a lexical authority, from which a kind of necessity comes, independent of reality in the relations and connections of the facts denoted by the words. It is possible that laws exist absolutely universal, binding fate and infinite power as well as speech and the intelligible use of words; but it is not possible that the analytical processes of any finite intellect should discover what particular laws these are. Such an intellect may legislate with absolute freedom in the realm of definition and word-making, provided it limits itself to its autonomy, and does not demand of other intellects that they shall be governed by such laws on account of the universal applications of them in the world of common experience. It is also possible that beliefs, or convictions, may exist, supposed by the mystic to be independent of all ordinary forms of particular experience, "which no amount of experience could produce"; but it is not true that there are any universal or scientific beliefs of this kind. The effects of inherited aptitudes, and of early, long-continued, and constantly repeated experiences in the individual, together with the implications of language itself, in fixing and in giving force and certainty to an idea or a belief, have, probably, not been sufficiently considered by those metaphysicians who claim a preternatural and absolute origin for certain of our cognitions; or else, perhaps, the more dogmatic among these thinkers over-estimate the force and certainty of the beliefs, or mistake the *kind* of necessity they have. The essential importance, the necessity and universality in language, of pronominal words or signs, should not be mistaken for a real *a priori* necessity in the relations expressed by them. Meta-physicians should consider that *ego* and *non-ego*, as real existences, are not individual phenomena, but groups with demonstrative names the least possible determined in meaning, or are the most abstract subjects of the phenomena of experience, though determined, doubtless, in their applications partly by spontaneous, instinctive, or natural and inherited tendencies to their formation.

This view of the origin of the cognition of *cogito* is equally opposed to the schemes of "idealism" and "natural realism," which divide modern schools of philosophy. According to the "idealists," the conscious subject is immediately known, at least in its phenomena, and the phenomena are intuitively known to belong to it; while the existence of anything external to the mind is an inference from the phenomena of self, or a reference of some of them to external causes. Objects are only known mediately "by their effects on *us*." Against this view the "natural realist" appeals effectively to the common-sense, or natural judgment of unsophisticated minds, and is warranted by this judgment in declaring that the object of consciousness is *just as immediately* known as the subject is. But natural realism goes beyond this judgment and holds that both the subject and object are absolutely, immediately, and equally known through their essential attributes in perception. This is more than an unlearned jury are competent to say. For if by immediacy we mean the relation which a particular *unattributed* phenomenon has to consciousness in general, we are warranted in saying that immediately, or without the step of attribution, subject and object are undistinguished in consciousness. Thus, the sensations of sound and color and taste and pleasure and pain, and the emotions of hope and fear and love and hate, *if not yet referred to their causes, or even classified as sensations and emotions*, belong to neither world exclusively. But so far as any man can remember, no such unattributed or unclassified states of consciousness are experienced. He cannot say, however, that they cannot exist, or (what is worse for the theory) or be wrongly attributed or classified. All states of consciousness are, it is true, referred to one or the other, or partly to each of the two worlds; and this attribution is, in part at least, instinctive, yet not independent of all experience, since it comes either from the direct observation of our progenitors, or, possibly, through the natural selection of them; that is, possibly through the survival of those who rightly divided the worlds, and did not often mistake a real danger for a dream or for an imagined peril, nor often mistake a dream of security for real safety. If, however, we mean by immediacy such an instinctive attribution, independent of repeated connections of attributes in their subject through the individual's own experiences, then "natural realism" is most in accordance with our view, with such exceptions as the mistakes and corrections of dreams and hallucinations imply, and excepting the ontological or metaphysical positions that are assumed in it.

If the natural realist is not also an evolutionist (and usually he is not), then his meaning of intuitions must be that they are absolute and underived universal facts of connection in phenomena. He must suppose that distinct phenomena have stamped upon them indelible marks of their ultimate highest class, equivalents for "I" and "not-I," as the individuals of a herd of cattle are branded with the mark of their owner. Such an immutable mark would, however, render the mistakes of insanity, hallucinations, and dreams impossible, or else would refer them (as has actually been supposed[4]) to the mystery of the existence of evil—a convenient disposition of philosophical puzzles. In the doctrine of evolution the meaning of the word "intuition" does not imply immutability in the connections of instinctively combined phenomena, except where such connection is an ultimate law of nature, or is the simplest causal connection, like the laws of motion, or the laws of logic (regarding logic as a science, and not merely as an art). The intuition of space in the blind might be, from this point of view, a different combination of sensibilities from that in other men; and the interpretation of sensations of hearing or sight in hallucinations as being caused by outward objects, when, in reality, they arise from disturbances or abnormal conditions of the nervous system, would not be an interpretation involving violations of ultimate laws, or suspensions in rebellious Nature of relations between cause and effect. Variations in intuitions and instinctive judgments would be as natural and explicable as errors of judgment are in the experiences of the individual man. But the doctrine of natural realism, independently of that of evolution and the implied mutability of instincts, has insurmountable difficulties.

Idealism, on the other hand, appears to contradict not the abnormal, so much as the common, phenomena of consciousness. It appears to be related to the modern sciences of physics and physiology very nearly as natural realism is to scholastic logic and ontology. Dating from the time of Descartes, it appears, in all its forms, to depend on a more exact knowledge of the bodily apparatus and outward physical causes of perception than the ancients possessed. By these researches it appeared that perception, and even sensation, are fully determined or realized in the brain only through other parts of the bodily apparatus, and through outward forces and movements like those of pressure and vibration. That the perception, or sensation, is experienced, or is seated, in the brain, was a natural and proper conclusion from these researches. That the apparent object of perception is not only distant from what thus appeared to be the seat of the perception, but that a long series of usually unknown, or unnoticed, movements intervenes between it and this apparent seat—these facts gave great plausibility to a confused interpretation of the phenomena, namely, that the perception is first realized as a state of the conscious *ego*, and, afterwards, is referred to the outward world through the associations of general experience, as an effect produced upon us by an otherwise unknown outward cause. On similar grounds a similar misinterpretation was made of the phenomena of volition, namely, that a movement in ourselves, originally and intuitively known to be *ours*, produces an effect in the outward world at a distance from us, through the intervention of a series of usually unknown (or only indirectly known) agencies. Remote effects of the outer world on us, and our actions in producing remote effects on it, appeared to be the first or intuitive elements in our knowledge of these phenomena, all the rest being derived or inferential. This was to confound the seat of sensation or perception in the brain with its proper subjectivity, or the reference of it to the subject.

The position in the brain where the last physical condition for the production of a sensation is situated is, no doubt, properly called the place or seat of the sensation, especially as it is through the movements of the brain with other special nervous tracts, and independently of any movements out of the nervous system, that like sensations are, or can be, revived, though these revived ones are generally feebler than those that are set in movement by outward forces. Nevertheless, this physiological seat of a sensation is no part of our direct knowledge of it. *A priori* we cannot assign it any place nor decide that it has, or has not, a place. The place which we do assign it, in case it is outward, is the place determined by a great variety of sensations and active forms of consciousness experienced in the localization of the object to which it is referred. It is only by the association (either spontaneous and instinctive, or acquired) of this sensation with those sensations and actions that are involved in the localization of the object, that we arrive at any notion of its locality. If we do not form any such associations of it with otherwise determined localities, and if it and its kind remain after much experience unlocalized, or only vaguely localized in our bodies, it is then, *but not till then*, referred to the conscious self as a subjective phenomenon. There remains the alternative, of course, in the theory of evolution, that the negative experiences, which would thus determine the subjective character of a phenomenon, may be the experiences of our progenitors, and that our judgment of this character may be, in many cases, an instinctive one, arising from the inherited effects of these former experiences. Otherwise this judgment in the individual mind, and from its own experiences, would appear to be posterior, in point of time, to its acquaintance with the object world, since this judgment would be determined by the *absence* of any uniform connection in the phenomenon with the phenomena of locality. Instead of, being, as the theories of idealism hold, first known as a phenomenon of the subject *ego*, or as an effect upon us of an hypothetical outward world, its first unattributed condition would be, by our view, one of neutrality between the two worlds.

In dissenting, therefore, from both extremes—the theory of idealism and that of natural realism, or assenting to the latter only as qualified by the theory of evolution—I have supposed both theories to be dealing with the two worlds only as worlds of phenomena, without considering the metaphysical bearings and varieties of them with respect to the question of the cognition of non-phenomenal existences, on the grounds of belief in an inconceivable and metaphysical matter or spirit; for, according to the view proposed as a substitute for these extremes, subject and object are only names of the highest classes, and are not the names of inconceivable substrata of phenomena. Ontology or metaphysics would not be likely to throw much original light on the scientific evolution of self-consciousness; but it becomes itself an interesting object of study as a phase of this evolution seen in the light of science. When one comes to examine in detail the supposed cognitions of super-sensible existences, and the faculty of necessary truth which is called "the reason," or else is described in its supposed results as the source of necessary beliefs or convictions, or of natural and valid hypotheses of inconceivable realities, great difficulty is experienced, on account of the abstract character of the beliefs, in distinguishing what is likely to be strictly inherited from what is early and uniformly acquired in the development of the faculty of reflection, and especially from what is imbibed through language, the principal philosophical instrument of this faculty. The languages employed by philosophers are themselves lessons in ontology, and have, in their grammatical structures, implied conceptions and beliefs common to the philosopher and to the barbarian inventors of language, as well as other implications which the former takes pains to avoid. How much besides he ought to avoid, in the correction of conceptions erroneously derived from the forms of language, is a question always important to be considered in metaphysical inquiries.

The conception of *substance*, as a nature not fully involved in the contrast of essential and accidental attributes, and the connection, or co-existence, of them in our experiences, or the conception of it as also implying the real, though latent, co-existence of all attributes in an existence unknown to us, or known only in a non-phenomenal and inconceivable way—this conception needs to be tested by an examination of the possible causes of it as an effect of the forms of language and other familiar associations, which, however natural, may still be misleading. To the minds of the barbarian inventors of language, words had not precise meanings, for definition is not a barbarian accomplishment. Hence, to such minds, definite and precise attributions, as of sweetness to honey and sugar, or light to the day, to the heavenly bodies, or to fire, are strongly in contrast with the vagueness which appears to them inherent in substantive names—inherent not as vagueness, however, but as *something else*. Such names did not clearly distinguish persons and things, for the day and the heavenly bodies were personal, and fire apparently was an animal or a spirit. Removing as much as possible of mere crudeness from such conceptions, predication would yet appear to be a reference of something distinctly known to something essentially unknown, or known only by one or a few attributes needed to distinguish it by a name, as proper names distinguish persons. The meaning of this name, and the conception of it as meaning much more, and as actually referring to unapparent powers of bringing to light attributes previously unknown—powers manifested in an actual effect when a new attribute is added in predication—this vague, ill-defined, and essentially hidden meaning is assimilated in grammar, and thence in philosophy, to an agent putting forth a new manifestation of itself in a real self-assertion.

The contrast of "active and passive" in the forms of verbs illustrates how the barbaric mind mounted into the higher regions of abstraction in language through concrete imaginations. The subject of a proposition, instead of being thought of as that vaguely determined group of phenomena with which the predicate is found to be connected, was thought either to perform an action on an object as expressed through the transitive verb, or to be acted on by the object as expressed through the passive form, or to put forth an action absolute, expressed by the neuter verb, or to assert its past, present, or future existence absolutely, and its possession of certain properties as expressed by the substantive verb, and by the copula and predicate. This personification of the subject of a proposition, which is still manifested in the forms and terminology of grammar, is an assimilation of things to an active, or at least demonstrative, self-consciousness or personality. It had hardly reached the degree of abstraction needed for the clear intellectual self-consciousness of *cogito*. It rather implied that things also think. The invention of substantive names for attributes, that is, abstract names, like goodness or truth—an invention fraught with most important consequences to human knowledge—brought at first more prominently forward the realistic tendencies which philosophers have inherited from the barbarian inventors of language. Abstract names do not seem to have been meant at first to be the direct names of attributes, or collections of attributes, as "goodness" and "humanity," but to be the names of powers (such as make things good, or make men what they are), which appear to be results of the earliest conscious or scientific analysis in the progress of the human mind, but names strongly tainted still by the barbaric conception of words as the names of active beings. Abstract words were not, however, as active or demonstrative as their savage progenitors, the concrete general substantives. They appear rather as artificers, or the agents which build up things, or make them what they are. But, by means of them, concrete general names were deprived of their powers and reduced to subjection. To have direct general names, and to have general powers, seem to be synonymous to savage and semi-barbarous mind.

I have spoken as if all this were a matter of past history, instead of being an actually present state of philosophical thought, and a present condition of some words in the minds of many modern thinkers. The misleading metaphors are, it is true, now recognized as metaphors; but their misleading character is not clearly seen to its full extent. The subjects of propositions are still made to do the work, to bear the impositions, to make known the properties and accidents expressed by their predicates, or to assert their own existence and autonomy, just so far as they are supposed to be the names of anything but the assemblages of known essential qualities or phenomena actually co-existent in our experiences; the qualities which their definitions involve, and to which other attributes are added (but from which they are not evolved) in real predication; or just so far as they are supposed to be the names of unknown and imperceptible entities. Names are directly the designations of things, not of hidden powers, or wills, in things. But it is not necessary to regard them as precisely definable, or as connoting definite groups of qualities or the essential attributes of things, in order that they may fulfill the true functions of words; for they are still only the names of things, not of wills in things, on the one hand, nor of "concepts" or thoughts in us, on the other hand. They are synonyms of "concepts," if we please to extend synonymy so as to include the whole range of the *signs* of things; but both the "concept" and its verbal synonym may be, and generally are, *vague*. For just as in the major premises of syllogisms the subject is, in general, a co-designation of two undivided parts of a class of objects, one known directly to have, or lack, the attributes affirmed or denied in this premise, and the other part, judged by induction to be also possessed, or not possessed of them—a co-designation in which the conclusion of the syllogism is virtually contained, so as to make the syllogism appear to be a *petitio principii* (as it would be but for this implied induction[5])—so in the simple naming of objects the names may be properly regarded as the names of groups of qualities, in which groups the qualities are partly known and partly unknown, predication in real (not verbal) propositions being the conversion of the latter into the former. But in this view of the functions of words, it is necessary, at least, to suppose enough of the known attributes of objects to be involved in the meanings of their names to make the applications of the names distinct and definite. Names, with the capacity they would thus acquire, or have actually had, in spite of metaphysics, of having their meanings modified or changed, are best adapted to the functions of words in promoting the progress of knowledge. From this use of words their essences, both the apparent and the inscrutable, have disappeared altogether, except so far as the actual existence and co-existence of the known attributes of objects are implied by names, or so far as the co-existence of these with previously unknown ones is also implied by the use of names as the subjects of propositions. No inscrutable powers in words or things, nor any immutable connections among the attributes called essential, are thus imposed upon the use of words in science.

Metaphysicians, on the other hand, in nearly all that is left to the peculiar domain of their inquiries, possess their problems and solutions in certain words, such as "substance," "cause," "matter," "mind," still retaining, at least with them, the barbaric characters we have examined. Matter and mind still retain, not only with metaphysicians, but also with the vulgar, designations of unknown inscrutable powers in the outward and inward worlds, or powers which, according to some, are known only to a higher form of intuition through the faculty of "Reason"; or, being really inscrutable and inconceivable by any human faculty, as others hold, they are, nevertheless, regarded as certainly existent, and attested by irresistible natural beliefs. That beliefs in beings, unknown and unknowable, are real beliefs, and are natural (though more so to some minds than to others), seems *a priori* probable on the theory of evolution, without resorting to the effects of early training and the influence of associations in language itself, by which the existence of such beliefs is accounted for by some scientific philosophers. But the authority which the theory of evolution would assign to these beliefs is that of the conceptions which barbarous and vulgar minds have formed of the functions of words, and of the natures which they designate. Inheritance of these conceptions, that is, of aptitudes or tendencies to their formation, and the continued action of the causes so admirably analyzed by Mr. Mill,[6] through which he proposes to account for these beliefs directly, and which have retained, especially in the metaphysical conception of "matter," the barbarian's feelings and notions about real existence as a power to produce phenomena, are sufficient to account for the existence of these beliefs and their cogency, without assigning them any force as authorities.

That some minds have inherited these beliefs, or the tendency to form them, more completely than others, accords with a distinction in the mental characters of philosophers which Professor Masson makes in his work on Recent British Philosophy, and illustrates by the philosophies of Mr. Carlyle, Sir W. Hamilton, and Mr. Mill, namely, the differences arising from the degrees in which the several thinkers were actuated by an "ontological faith," or an "ontological feeling or passion," which, according to Professor Masson, has in the history of the world amounted to "a rage of ontology," and has been the motive of wars and martyrdoms. This passion would appear, according to the theory of evolution, to be a survival of the barbarian's feelings and notions of phenomena as the outward show of hidden powers in things, analogous to his own expressions in language and gesture of his will or interior activity. As he assigned his own name, or else the name "I," to this active inward personality, and not to the group of external characters by which he was known to his fellow-barbarians; and as he also named and addressed them as indwelling spirits, so he seemed to apply his general designations of things. The traces of this way of regarding names and things, surviving in the grammatical inventions and forms of speech, which the barbarian has transmitted to us, include even the sexes of things. The metaphysical meanings of the terms "substance," "matter," "mind," "spirit," and "cause" are other traces. The metaphysical realism of abstract terms appears, in like manner, to be a trace of an original analysis of motives in the powers of things to produce their phenomena, analogous to the barbarian's analysis of motives in his own will or those of his fellows.

According to Professor Masson, Sir W. Hamilton was strongly actuated by "the ontological passion." This would mean, according to our interpretation of it, that he had inherited, or had partly, perhaps, imbibed from his philosophical studies, the barbarian's mode of thought. This appeared in the metaphysical extension which he gave to the doctrine of natural realism, which, with him, was not merely the doctrine of the equal immediacy and the instinctive attribution of subjective and objective phenomena, but included also natural beliefs in the equal and independent, though hidden, existences of the metaphysical substrata of matter and mind. He was, nevertheless, so far influenced by modern scientific modes of thought that he claimed for these natural beliefs not at all the character of cognitions, nor did he claim determinate conception of these existences except their mutual independence. He rejected the metaphysician's invention of a faculty of "reason," cognizant of supersensible realities; and really contradicted himself in claiming, with most modem thinkers, that knowledge of phenomena, is the only possible knowledge, while he held that belief in what could not thus be known had the certainty of knowledge, and was in effect knowledge, though he did not call it knowledge.[7]

Another point in Sir W. Hamilton's philosophy illustrates our theory on a different side. While contending for the equal immediacy of our knowledge of subject and object, he, nevertheless, held that the phenomena of the subject had a superior certainty to those of the object, on the ground that the latter could be doubted (as they were by certain idealists) without logical contradiction, while the former could not be, since to doubt the existence of the subject would be to doubt the doubt, and thus neutralize it. To say nothing of other objections to this as a criterion of subjective certainty, it is obvious that it has no cogency as applied to the metaphysical, or non-phenomenal, existence of the subject. To doubt that a doubt inheres in a non-phenomenal subject, is not to doubt the existence of the doubt itself as a phenomenon, or even as a phenomenon referable to the subject group of phenomena. In regard to the impossibility of doubting the existence of this subject group, which, as including the doubt itself, would thus neutralize it, we ought to distinguish between a doubt of a doubt as a mere phenomenon of consciousness generally, or as unattributed either to subject or object, and the doubt of the validity of the attribution of it to the subject. There can be logical contradiction only in respect to attribution, either explicit or implicit, and so far as the doubt is merely a phenomenon of which nothing is judged or known but its actual existence in consciousness, a doubt of it, though impossible, is yet not so on grounds of' logical contradiction. Its actual presence would be the only proof of its presence, its actual absence the only proof of its absence. But this is equally true of all phenomena in consciousness, generally. If in reflection we examine whether a color of any sort is present, we have inquired, not merely about the bare existence of a phenomenon of which the phenomenon itself could alone assure us, but about its classes, whether it is a color or not, and what sort of a color; and we should attribute it, if present, to the object world, or the object group of phenomena by the very same sort, if not with the same degree, of necessity which determines the attribution of a doubt to the subject-consciousness. If now, having attributed the color or the doubt to its proper world, we should call in question the existence of this world, we should contradict ourselves; and this would be the case equally whether the attribution was made to the outward world, as of the color, or to the inward world, as of the doubt.

There may be different kinds of reflective doubt about either phenomenon. We should not ordinarily be able to question seriously whether the doubt belonged to the class "doubts," its resemblance to others of the class being a relation of phenomena universal and too clear to be dismissed from attention; and the color would call up its class with equal cogency, as well as the class of surfaces or spaces in which it appears always inherent. But we might doubt, nevertheless, seriously and rationally, whether a doubt had arisen from rational considerations in our minds, or from a disease of the nervous system, from hypochondriasis, or low spirits. So also in regard to the color and the forms in which it appears embodied, we may reasonably question whether the appearance has arisen from causes really external, or from disease, as in hallucinations.

There remains one other source of misunderstanding about the comparative certainty of "I think," and of that which I think about. The attributions contained in the latter may be particular, empirical, and unfamiliar, or based on a very limited experience and on *this account* may be uncertain; while the very general and highest attribution of the thought to myself will be most certain. The superior certainty of the clause "I think" over that which I think about disappears, however, as soon as the latter is made an attribution of equal simplicity, generality, and breadth in my experience; as when I say, "I think that there is an outer world," or, "I think that beings beside me exist." "To think that I think," is not more properly the formula of consciousness in general than "To think that a being not-I is thought about." It is not even the complete formula of *self*-consciousness, which, as we have seen, has several forms not necessarily coeval. To think that I will, that I desire, that I feel, is, as we have seen, to refer these several forms of consciousness to the thinking subject; or, more properly, to refer willing, desiring, feeling, and thinking all to the same subject "I"; which is related to the latter attribute more especially, merely because the name "I" is given only in and through the recognition of this attribute in the cognition of *cogito*. To infer the existence of the subject from the single attribute of thinking would be to unfold only in part its existence and nature; though it would note that attribute of the subject through the recognition of which in reflection its name was determined and connected with its other attributes.

The latter, namely, our volitions, desires, and feelings, are in general so obscure in respect to the particular causes which precede them and are ulterior to their immediate determination or production, that introspective observation in reflection can penetrate only a little way, and is commonly quite unable to trace them back to remote causes in our characters, organizations, and circumstances. Hence, the conception of the causes of our own inward volitions, or our desires and intentions, as being of an inscrutable, non-phenomenal nature, would naturally arise. But this conception would probably be made much more prominent in the unreflective barbarian's mind, by his association of it with the obscurity to him of the inward, or personal, causes of outward actions and expressions in others. Darkness is seen where light is looked for and does not appear. Causes are missed where research is made without success. We are conscious of minds in other men and in other animals only through their outward expressions. The inward causes are not apparent or directly known to us as phenomena; and though the inference of their existence is not in all cases, even with men, made through analogy, or from an observation of their connections with similar outward actions and expressions in ourselves, but is grounded, doubtless, in many cases on an instinctive connection between these expressions in others and *feelings*, at least, in ourselves, yet we do not think of them as really inscrutable m their natures, but only as imperceptible to our outward senses. They have their representatives in the phenomena of our imaginations. These would be but vaguely conceived, however, in many cases. Even reverence in the barbarian's mind might prevent him, as an obedient subject, from attempting to fathom or reproduce in his own imagination the thoughts and intentions of his majesty the king. Reverence is not, however, in any case, an unreflective or thoughtless feeling. It would not be like the feelings of the sheep, which, not being able to comprehend through its own experience the savage feelings of the wolf, would only interpret his threatening movements as something fearful, or would connect in an instinctive judgment these outward movements only with anticipated painful consequences. Reverence in the loyal barbarian subject would not go so far as to make his king appear a mere automaton, as the wolf might seem to the sheep. The commands of his king, or of his deity, would be to him rather the voice of a wisdom and authority inscrutable, the outward manifestation of mysterious *power*, the type of metaphysical causation. Accordingly, we find that a capacity for strong, unappropriated feelings of loyalty and reverence, demand-ing an object for their satisfaction, have also descended to those thinkers who have inher-ited "the ontological passion" from their barbarian ancestors. It would, therefore, appear most probable, that the metaphysician's invincible belief in the conception of the will as a mysterious power behind the inward phenomena of volition, and as incapable of analysis into the determinations of character, organization, and circumstances, arises also from inherited feelings about the wills of other men rather than from attentive observation of the phenomena of his own.

Science and scientific studies have led a portion of the human race a long way aside from the guidance of these inherited intellectual instincts, and have also appeared able to conquer them in many minds to which in youth they seemed invincible. Positivists, unlike poets, become—are not born—such thinkers. The conception of the causes of phenomena, with which these studies render them familiar, had small beginnings in the least noble occupations and necessities of life, and in the need of knowing the future and judging of it from present signs. From this grew up gradually a knowledge of natural phenomena, and phenomena of mind also, both in their outward and combined orders or laws and in their intimate and elementary successions, or the "laws of nature." The latter are involved in the relation of effects to their "physical" causes, so called because metaphysicians have discovered that they are not the same sort of powers as those which the invincible instincts look for as ultimate and absolute in nature. But this is not a new or modern meaning of the word "cause." It was always its practical, common-sense, every-day meaning;—in the relations of means to ends; in rational explanations and anticipations of natural events; in the familiar processes and observations of common human life; in short, in the relations of phenomena to phenomena, as apparent causes and effects. This meaning was not well defined, it is true; nor is it now easily made clear, save by examples; yet it is by examples, rather than by a distinct abstraction of what is common to them, that the use of many other words, capable of clear definition, is determined in common language. The relations of invariable succession in phenomena do not, except in ultimate laws where the phenom-ena are simple or elementary, define the relation of phenomenal cause and effect; for, as it has been observed, night follows day, and day follows night invariably, yet neither is the cause of the other. These relations belong to the *genus* of natural successions. The relation of cause and effect is a *species* of this *genus*. It means an *unconditional*, invariable succession; *independence* of other orders of succession, or of all orders not involved in it.

The day illuminates objects; the night obscures them; the sun and fires warm them; the clouds shed rain upon them; the savage animal attacks and hurts others: these facts involve natural orders, in which relations of cause and effect are apparent, and are indi-cated in the antitheses of their terms as the subjects and objects of transitive proposi-tions. But these relations are only indicated; they are not explicitly set forth. Metaphysics undertakes their explication by referring the illumination, obscurity, warmth, rain and hurt to *powers* in the day, the sun and fires, the clouds, and the animal. Modern meta-physics would not go so far as to maintain, in the light of science, that the powers in these examples are inscrutable, or incapable of further analysis. Nevertheless, when the analysis is made, and the vision of objects, for example, is understood to arise from the incidence of the light of the sun on the air and on objects, and thence from reflections on all surfaces of objects, and thence again from diffused reflections falling partly on our eyes, and so on to the full realization of vision in the brain, all according to determinate laws of succession—an analysis which sets forth those *elementary* invariable orders, or *ultimate* and independent laws of succession in phenomena, to which, in their independent combinations, science refers the relations of cause and effect;—when this analysis has been made, then metaphysics interposes, and from its ancient habits of thought ascribes to the elementary antecedent a *power* to produce the elementary consequent. Or when the effect, as in vision, follows from the ultimate properties and elementary laws of great numbers of beings and arrangements—the sun, the medium of light, the air, the illuminated objects, the eye, its nerves and the brain—and follows through a long series of steps, however rapid, from the earliest to the latest essential antecedent, metaphysics still regards the whole process, with the elementary powers involved, as explicated only in its *outward* features. There is still the mystery inherent in the being of each elementary antecedent, of its power to produce its elementary consequent; and these mysterious powers, combined and referred to the most conspicuous essential conditions of the effect (like the existence of the sun and the eye), make in the whole a mystery as great as if science had never inquired into the process.

Metaphysics demands, in the interest of mystery, *why* an elementary antecedent is followed by its elementary consequent. But this question does not arise from that inquisitiveness which inspires scientific research. It is asked to show that it cannot be answered, and hence that all science rests on mystery. It is asked from the feelings that in the barbarian or the child forbid or check inquiry. But, being a question, it is open to answer; or it makes legitimate, at least, the counter-question, When can a question be properly asked? or, What is the purpose of asking a question? Is it not to discover the causes, classes, laws, or rules that determine the existence, properties, or production of a thing or event? And when these are discovered, is there any further occasion for inquiry, except in the interest of feelings which would have checked inquiry at the outset? The feelings of loyalty and reverence, instinctive in our natures, and of the utmost value in the history of our race, as the mediums of co-operation, discipline, and instruction, are instincts more powerful in some minds than in others, and, like all instincts, demand their proper satisfaction. From the will, or our active powers, they demand devotion; from the intellect, submission to authority and mystery. But, like all instincts, they may demand too much; too much for their proper satisfaction, and even for their most energetic and useful service to the race, or to the worth in it of the individual man. But whether it is possible for any one to have too much loyalty, reverence, love, or devotion, is, therefore, a question which the metaphysical spirit and mode of thought suggest. For in the mystic's mind these feelings have set themselves up as absolute excellencies, as money sets itself up in the mind of the miser. And it is clear that, under these absolute forms, it is difficult to deny the demand. It is only in respect to *what is* reverenced, loved, or worshiped, or *what* claims our allegiance, that questions of how much of them is due can be rationally asked.

To demand the submission of the intellect to the mystery of the simplest and most elementary relations of cause and effect in phenomena, or the restraint of its inquisitiveness on reaching an ultimate law of nature, is asking too much, in that it is a superfluous demand. The intellect in itself has no disposition to go any further, and, on the other hand, no impulse to kneel before its completed triumph. The highest generality, or universality, in the elements or connections of elements in phenomena, is the utmost reach both in the power and the desire of the scientific intellect. Explanation cannot go, and does not rationally seek to go, beyond such facts. The invention of *noumena* to account for ultimate and universal properties and relations in phenomena arises from no other necessity than the action of a desire urged beyond the normal promptings of its power. To demand of the scientific intellect that it shall pause in the interest of mystery at the movements of a falling body or at the laws of these movements, is a misappropriation of the quality of mystery. For mystery still has its uses; and, in its useful action, is an ally of inquisitiveness, inciting and guiding it, giving it steadiness and seriousness, opposing only its waywardness and idleness. It fixes attention, even inquisitive attention, on its objects, and in its active form of wonder "is a highly philosophical affection." So also devotion, independently of its intrinsic worth in the mystic's regard, has its uses; and these determine its rational measure, or how much of it is due to any object. In its active forms of usefulness and duty, it is an ally of freedom in action, opposing this freedom only in respect to what would limit it still more, or injuriously and on the whole.

The metaphysical modes of thought and feeling foster, on the other hand, the sentiments of mystery and devotion in their passive forms, and as attitudes of the intellect and will, rather than as their inciting and guiding motives. These attitudes, which are symbolized in the forms of religious worship, were no doubt needed to fix the attention of the barbarian, as they are still required to fix the attention of the child upon serious contemplations and purposes. Obedience and absolute submission are, at one stage of intellectual and moral development, both in a race and in the individual, required as the conditions of discipline for effecting the more directly serviceable and freer action of the mind and character under the guidance of rational loyalty and reverence. The metaphysical modes of thought and feeling retain these early habits in relations in which they have ceased to be serviceable to the race, or to the useful development of the individual, especially when in the mystic's regard obedience has acquired an intrinsic worth, and submission has become a beatitude. The scientific habit of thought, though emancipated from any such outward supports and constraints, is yet not wanting in earnestness of purpose and serious interests, and is not without the motives of devotion and mystery, or their active guidance in the directions of usefulness and duty, and in the investigations of truth. It does not stand in awe before the unknown, as if life itself depended on a mysterious and capricious will in it; for awe is habitual only with the barbarian, and is a useful motive only in that severe instruction which offsets the savage wants, insecurities, and necessities of his life, or constrains the thoughtless by a present fear against evils really greater than what is feared, though less obvious to the imagination.

Nevertheless, the whole nature of the modern civilized man includes both these opposing tendencies in speculation, the metaphysical and scientific; the disposition to regard the phenomena of nature as they appeared naturally and serviceably in the primitive use of language and reflection, and the disposition of the Positivist to a wholly different interpretation of them. This conflict exists, however, only where either disposition invades the proper province of the other; where both strive for supremacy in the search for a clearer knowledge of these phenomena, or where both aim to satisfy the more primitive and instinctive tendencies of the mind. In the forms of ontological and phenomenological, or metaphysical and positive philosophies, this conflict is unavoidable and endless. Deathless warriors, irreconcilable and alternately victorious, according to the nature of the ground, or to advantages of position, continually renew their struggles along the line of development in each individual mind and character. A contrast of tendencies analogous to this, which involves, however, no necessary conflict, is shown in the opposition of science and poetry; one contemplating in understanding and in fixed positive beliefs the phenomena which the other contemplates through firmly established and instinctive tendencies, and through interests, which for want of a better name to note their motive power, or influence in the will, are also sometimes called beliefs. Disputes about the nature of what is called "belief," as to what it is, as well as to what are the true grounds or causes of it, would, if the meanings of the word were better discriminated in common usage, be settled by the lexicographer; for it is really an ambiguous term. Convictions of half-truths, or intimations of truth, coupled with deep feeling, and impressed by the rhythms and alliterations of words, are obviously different from those connections which logic and evidence are calculated to establish in the mind.

The poet inherits in his mental and moral nature, or organic memory, and in his dispositions of feeling and imagination, the instinctive thoughts and feelings which we have supposed habitual and useful in the outward life of the barbarian. In the melody of his verses he revives the habits which were acquired, it is believed, in the development of his race, long before any words were spoken, or were needed to express its imaginations, and when its emotions found utterance in the music of inarticulate tones. The poet's productions are thus, in part, reproductions, refined or combined in the attractive forms of art, of what was felt and thought before language and science existed; or they are restorations of language to a primeval use, and to periods in the history of his race in which his progenitors uttered their feelings, as of gallantry, defiance, joy, grief, exultation, sorrow, fear, anger, or love, and their light, serious, or violent moods, in modulated tones, harsh or musical; or later, in unconscious figures of speech, expressed without reflection or intention of communicating truth. For, as it has been said, it is essential to eloquence to be heard, but poetry is expression to be only overheard. In supposing this noble savage ancestry for the poet, and for those who overhear in him, with a strange delight and interest, a charm of naturalness and of novelty combined by the magic of his art, it is not necessary to conclude that all savage natures are noble, or have in them the germs of the poet's inspiration. It is more probable that most of the races which have remained in a savage state have retained a more primitive condition, in many respects, than that of civilized men, because they lacked some qualities possessed by the noble savage which have advanced him to the civilized state, and because they have been isolated from the effects of such qualities either to improve or exterminate them. The noble savage is not, at any rate, now to be found. Weeding out the more stupid and brutal varieties has, doubtless, been the more effective method of nature in the culture of the nobler qualities of men, at least in that state of nature which was one of warfare.

It is a common misconception of the theory of evolution to suppose that any one of contemporary races, or species derived from a common origin, fully represents the characters of these progenitors, or that they are not all more or less divergent forms of an original race; the ape, for example, as well as the man, from a more remote stock, or the present savage man, as well as the civilized one, from a more recent common origin. Original differences within a race are, indeed, the conditions of such divergences, or separations of a race into several; and original superiorities, though slight at first and accidental, were thus the conditions of the survival of those who possessed them, and of their descendants, and the extinction of others from their struggles in warfare, in gallantry, and for subsistence. The secondary distinctions of sex, or contrasts in the personal attractions, in the forms, movements, aspects, voices, and even in some mental dispositions of men and women, are, on the whole, greatest in the races which have accomplished most, not merely in science and the useful arts, but more especially in the arts of sculpture, painting, music, and poetry. And this in the theory of evolution is not an accidental conjunction, but a connection through a common origin. Love is still the theme of poets, and his words are measured by laws of rhythm, which in a primeval race served in vocal music, with other charms, to allure in the contests of gallantry. There would, doubtless, have arisen from these rivalries a sort of self-attention,[8] or an outward self-consciousness, which, together with the consciousness of themselves as causes distinct from the wills or agencies of other beings, and as having feelings, or passive powers, and desires, or latent volitions, not shared by others, served in the case of the primitive men as bases of reference in their first attention to the phenomena of thought in their minds, when these became sufficiently vivid to engage attention in the revival of trains of images through acts of reflection. The consummate self-consciousness, expressed by "I think," needed for its genesis only the power of attending to the phenomena of thought as signs of other thoughts, or of images revived from memory, with a reference of them to a subject; that is, to a something possessing other attributes, or to a group of co-existent phenomena. The most distinct attention to this being, or subject, of volitions, desires, feelings, outward expressions, and thoughts required a name for the subject, as other names were required for the most distinct attention to the several phenomena themselves.

This view of the origin of self-consciousness is by no means necessarily involved in the much more certain and clearly apparent agency of natural selection in the process of development. For natural selection is not essentially concerned in the *first* production of any form, structure, power, or habit, but only in perpetuating and improving those which have arisen from any cause whatever. Its agency is the same in preserving and increasing a serviceable and heritable feature in any form of life, whether this service be incidental to some other already existing and useful power which is turned to account in some new direction, or be the unique and isolated service of some newly and arbitrarily implanted nature. Whether the powers of memory and abstractive attention, already existing and useful in outward perceptions common to men and others of the more intelligent animals, were capable in their higher degrees and under favorable circumstances (such as the gestural and vocal powers of primeval man afforded them) of being turned to a new service in the power of reflection, aided by language, or were supplemented by a really new, unique, and inexplicable power, in either case, the agency of natural selection would have been the same in preserving, and also in improving, the new faculty (provided this faculty was capable of improvement by degrees, and was not perfect from the first). The origin of that which through service to life has been preserved, is to this process arbitrary, indifferent, accidental (in the logical sense of this word), or non-essential. This origin has no part in the process, and is of importance with reference to it only in determining how much it has to do to complete the work of creation. For if a faculty has small beginnings, and rises to great importance in the development of a race through natural selection, then the process becomes an essential one. But if men were put in possession of the faculties which so pre-eminently distinguish them by a sudden, discontinuous, arbitrary cause or action, or without reference to what they were before, except so far as their former faculties were adapted to the service of the new ones, then selection might only act to preserve or maintain at their highest level faculties so implanted. Even the effects of constant, direct use, habit, or long-continued exercise might be sufficient to account for all improvements in a faculty. The latter means of improvement must, indeed, on either hypothesis, have been very influential in increasing the range of the old powers of memory, attention, and vocal utterance through their new use.

The outward physical aids of reflective thought, in the articulating powers of the voice, do not appear to have been firmly implanted, with the new faculty of self-consciousness, among the instincts of human nature; and this, at first sight, might seem to afford an argument against the acquisition by a natural process of any form of instinct, since vocal language has probably existed as long as any useful or effective exercise of reflection in men. That the faculty which uses the voice in language should be inherited, while its chief instrument is still the result of external training in an art, or that language should be "half instinct and half art," would, indeed, on second thought, be a paradox on any other hypothesis but that of natural selection. For this is an economical process, and effects no more than what is needed. If the instinctive part in language is sufficient to prompt the invention and the exercise of the art,[9] then the inheritance of instinctive powers of articulation would be superfluous, and would not be effected by selection; but would only come in the form of inherited effects of habit—the form in which the different degrees of aptitude for the education of the voice appear to exist in different races of men. Natural selection would not effect anything, indeed, for men which art and intelligence could, and really do, effect—such as clothing their backs in cold climates with hair or fur—since this would be quite superfluous under the furs of other animals with which art has already clothed them. The more instinctive language of gestures appears also to have only indirect relations to real serviceableness, or to the grounds of natural selection, and to depend on the inherited effects of habit, and on universal principles of mental and physiological action.[10]

The language of gestures may, however, have been sufficient for the realization of the faculty of self-consciousness in all that the metaphysician regards as essential to it. The primitive man might, by pointing to himself in a meditative attitude, have expressed in effect to himself and others the "I think," which was to be, in the regard of many of his remote descendants, the distinguishing mark, the outward emblem, of his essential separation from his nearest kindred and progenitors, of his metaphysical distinction from all other animals. This consciousness and expression would more naturally have been a source of proud satisfaction to the primitive men themselves, just as children among us glory most in their first imperfect command of their unfolding powers, or even in accomplishments of a unique and individual character when first acquired. To the civilized man of the present time, there is more to be proud of in the immeasurable consequences of this faculty, and in what was evolved through the continued subsequent exercise of it, especially through its outward artificial instruments in language—consequences not involved in the bare faculty itself. As being the pre-requisite condition of these uses and inventions, it would, if of an ultimate and underived nature, be worthy the distinction, which, in case it is referable to latent natures in pre-existing faculties; must be accorded to them in their higher degrees. And if these faculties are common to all the more intelligent animals, and are, by superior degrees only, made capable of higher functions, or effects of a new and different kind (as longer fins enable a fish to fly), then the main qualitative distinction of the human race is to be sought for in these effects, and chiefly in the invention and use of artificial language.

This invention was, doubtless, at first made by men from social motives, for the purpose of making known to one another, by means of arbitrarily associated and voluntary signs, the wishes, thoughts, or intentions clearly determined upon in their imaginations. Even now, children invent words, or, rather, attribute meanings to the sounds they can command, when they are unable to enunciate the words of the mother tongue which they desire for the purposes of communication. It is, perhaps, improper to speak of this stage of language as determined by conscious invention through a recognized motive, and for a *purpose* (in the subjective sense of this word). It is enough for a purpose (in its objective sense) to be served, or for a service to be done, by such arbitrary associations between internal and external language, or thought and speech, however these ties may, in the first instance, be brought about. The intention and the invention become, however, conscious acts in reflection when the secondary motives to the use of language begin to exert influence, and perhaps before the latter have begun to be reflectively known, or recognized, and while they are still acting as they would in a merely animal mind. These motives are the needs and desires (or, rather, the use and importance), of making our thoughts clearer to ourselves, and not merely of communicating them to others. Uncertainty, or perplexity from failures of memory or understanding, render the mnemonic uses of vivid external and voluntary signs the agents of important services to reflective thought, when these signs are already possessed, to some extent, for the purposes of communication. These two uses of language—the social, and the meditative or mnemonic—carried to only a slight development, would afford the means of recognizing their own values; and the character of the inventions of which languages would be seen to consist. Invention in its true sense, as a reflective process, would then act with more energy in extending the range of language.

Command of language is a much more efficient command of thought in reflective processes than that which is implied in the simplest form of self-consciousness. It involves a command of memory to a certain degree. Already a mental power, usually accounted a simple one, and certainly not involved in "I think," or only in its outward consequences, has been developed in the power of the will over thought. Voluntary memory, or reminiscence, is especially aided by command of language. This is a tentative process, essentially similar to that of a search for a lost or missing external object. Trials are made in it to revive a missing mental image, or train of images, by means of words; and, on the other hand, to revive a missing name by means of mental images, or even by other words. It is not certain that this power is an exclusively human one, as is generally believed, except in respect to the high degree of proficiency attained by men in its use. It does not appear impossible that an intelligent dog may be aided by its attention, purposely directed to spontaneous memories, in recalling a missing fact, such as the locality of a buried bone.

In the earlier developments of language, and while it is still most subject to the caprices and facilities of individual wills (as in the nursery), the character of it as an invention, or system of inventions, is, doubtless, more clearly apparent than it afterwards becomes, when a third function of language rises into prominence. Traditions, by means of language, and customs, fixed by its conservative power, tend, in turn, to give fixity to the conventions of speech; and the customs and associations of language itself begin to prescribe rules for its inventions, or to set limits to their arbitrary adoption. Individual wills lose their power to decree changes in language; and, indeed, at no time are individual wills unlimited agents in this process. Consent given on grounds not always consciously determining it, but common to the many minds which adopt proposals or obey decrees in the inventions of words, is always essential to the establishment or alteration of a language. But as soon as a language has become too extensive to be the possible invention of any single mind, and is mainly a tradition, it must appear to the barbarian's imagination to have a will of its own; or, rather, sounds and meanings must appear naturally bound together, and to be the fixed names and expressions of wills in things. And later, then complex grammatical forms and abstract substantive names have found their way into languages, they must appear like the very laws and properties of nature itself, which nothing but magical powers could alter; though magic, with its power over the will, might still be equal to the miracle. Without this power not even a sovereign's will could oppose the authority of language in its own domain. Even magic had failed when an emperor could not alter the gender of a noun. Education had become the imperial power, and schoolmasters were its prime ministers.

From this point in the development of language, its separations into the *varieties* of dialects, the divergences of these into *species*, or distinct languages, and the affinities of them as grouped by the glossologist into *genera* of languages, present precise parallels to the developments and relations in the organic world which the theory of natural selection supposes. It has been objected[11] to the completeness of these parallels that the process of development in languages is still under the control of men's wills. Though an individual will may have but little influence on it, yet the general consent to a proposed change is still a voluntary action, or is composed of voluntary actions on the part of the many, and hence is essentially different from the choice in natural selection, when acting within its proper province. To this objection it may be replied, that a general consent to a change, or even an assent to the reasons for it, does not really constitute a voluntary act in respect to the whole language itself; since it does not involve in itself any intention on the part of the many to change the language. Moreover, the conscious intention of effecting a change on the part of the individual author, or speaker, is not the agent by which the change is effected; or is only an incidental cause, no more essential to the process than the causes which produce variations are to the process of natural selection in species. Let the causes of variation be what they may—miracles even—yet all the conditions of selection are fulfilled, provided the variations can be developed by selection, or will more readily occur in the selected successors of the forms in which they first appear in useful degrees. These conditions do not include the prime causes of variations, but only the causes which facilitate their action through inheritance, and ultimately make it normal or regular.

So, also, the reasons or motives which in general are not consciously perceived, recognized, or assented to (but none the less determine the consent of the many to changes in language) are the real causes of the selection, or the choice of usages in words. Let the cause of a *proposed* change in language be what it may—an act of free will, a caprice, or inspiration even—provided there is something in the proposition calculated to gain the consent of the many—such as ease of enunciation, the authority of an influential speaker or writer, distinctness from other words already appropriated to other meanings, the influence of vague analogies in relations of sound and sense (accidental at first, but tending to establish fixed roots in etymology or even to create instinctive connections of sound and sense)—such motives or reasons, common to the many, and not their consenting wills, are the causes of choice and change in the usages of speech. Moreover, these motives are not usually recognized by the many, but act instinctively. Hence, there is no intention in the many, either individually or collectively, to change even a single usage—much less a whole language. The laws or constitution of the language, as it exists, appear, even to the reflecting few, to be unchanged; and the proposed change appears to be justified by these laws, as corrections or extensions of previous usages.

The case is parallel to the developments of legal usages, or principles of judicial decisions. The judge cannot rightfully change the laws that govern his judgments; and the just judge does not consciously do so. Nevertheless, legal usages change from age to age. Laws, in their practical effects, are ameliorated by courts as well as by legislatures. No new principles are consciously introduced; but interpretations of old ones (and combinations, under more precise and qualified statements) are made, which disregard old decisions, seemingly by new and better definitions of that which in its nature is unalterable, but really, in their practical effects, by alterations, at least in the proximate grounds of decision; so that nothing is really unalterable in law, except the intention to do justice under universally applicable principles of decision, and the instinctive judgments of so-called natural law.

In like manner, there is nothing unalterable in the traditions of a language, except the instinctive motives to its acquisition and use, and some instinctive connections of sense and sound. *Intention*—so far as it is operative in the many who determine what a language is, or what is proper to any language—is chiefly concerned in *not* changing it; that is, in conforming to what is regarded by them as established usage. That usages come in under the form of good and established ones, while in fact they are new, though good inventions, is not due to the intention of the speakers who adopt them. The intention of those who consciously adopt new forms or meanings in words is to conform to what appears legitimate; or it is to fill out or improve usages in accordance with existing analogies, and not to alter the essential features in a language. But unconsciously they are also governed by tendencies in themselves and others—vague feelings of fitness and other grounds of choice which are outside of the actual traditions of speech; and, though a choice may be made in their minds between an old and a really new usage, it is commonly meant as a truly conservative choice, and from the intention of not altering the language in its essence, or not following what is regarded as a deviation from correct usage. The actual and continuous changes, completely transforming languages, which their history shows, are not, then, due to the intentions of those who speak, or have spoken, them, and cannot, in any sense, be attributed to the agency of their wills, if, as is commonly the case, their intentions are just the reverse. For the same wills cannot act from contradictory intentions, both to conserve and to change a language on the whole.

It becomes an interesting question, therefore, when in general anything can be properly said to be effected by the will of man. Man is an agent in producing many effects, both in nature and in himself, which appear to have no different general character from that of effects produced by other animals, even the lowest in the animal series, or by plants, or even by inorganic forces. Man, by transporting and depositing materials, in making, for example, the shell-mounds of the stone age, or the works of modern architecture and engineering, or in commerce and agriculture, is a geological agent; like the polyps which build the coral reefs, and lay the foundations of islands, or make extensions to mainlands; or like the vegetation from which the coal-beds were deposited; or like winds, rains, rivers, and the currents of the ocean; and his agency is not in any way different in its general character, and with reference to its geological effects from that of unconscious beings. In relation to these effects his agency is, in fact, unconscious, or at least *unintended*. Moreover, in regard to interval effects, his agency in modifying his own mind and character through influences external to himself, under which he comes accidentally, and without intention; many effects upon his emotions and sentiments from impressive incidents, or the general surroundings of the life with which he has become associated through his own agency— these, as unintended effects, are the same in general character as if his own agency had not been concerned in them—as if he had been without choice in his pursuits and surroundings.

Mingled with these unintended effects upon himself, there are, of course, others, either actually or virtually intended, and, therefore, his own effects. If, for example, in conformity with surrounding fashions of dress, he should choose to clothe himself, and should select some one from the existing varieties in these fashions, or should even add, *consciously*, a new feature to them from his individual taste in dress, in each case he would be acting from intention, and the choice would be his own. But so far as he has thus affected the proportions among these varieties, or tends further to affect them by his example, the action is not his own volition, unless we include *within* the will's agency what is properly said to act either *through* or *upon* the will; namely, that which, by an undistinguished influence, guides taste and choice in himself and the others who follow unconsciously his example. Those influences of example and instinctive, or even educated, tastes, which are not raised by distinct attention into conscious motives, would not be allowed by the metaphysician to be parts in the will's action. It would not be *within* but *through* its action that these influences would produce their unintended effects. According to the less definite and precise *physical* theory of the will's action, these effects might be regarded as voluntary; but then the choice would not be different in its character from that effected through other kinds of physical agency. On neither theory, therefore, can unintended effects, or the effects of unrecognized causes acting through the will, be regarded as different in their character from the general results of selection in nature. On the physical theory of the will, man's agency is merged in that of nature generally; but according to the metaphysician's more definite understanding of voluntary actions, which is also that of common usage, *intention* would appear to be the mark by which to determine whether anything is the effect of the will of man, except in an accidental or non-essential manner.

An apparently serious objection to this test arises, however, in reference to another mark of voluntary action, and of the efficacy of the will. The mark *of responsibility* (the subject of moral or legal discipline, the liability to blame or punishment) is justly regarded as the mark of free human agency. But the limits set by this mark are beyond what is actually *intended* in our actions. We are often held responsible, and properly, for more than we intend, or for what we *ought* to have intended. The absence of intention (namely, of the intention of doing differently) renders us liable to blame, when it is involved in the absence of the more general intention of doing right, or of doing what the discipline of responsibility has commanded or implied in its commands. Carelessness, or want of forethought, cannot be said to involve intention in any case, but in many cases it is blameworthy or punishable; since in such cases moral discipline presupposes or presumes intention, or else seeks, as in the case of children, by punishment to turn attention upon moral principles, and upon what is implied in them, whether set forth in instincts, examples, precepts, or commandments. But this extension of the sphere of personal agency and accountability to relations in which effects upon will and character are sought to be produced by moral and legal discipline, its extension beyond what the will itself produces in its direct action, has nothing to do with strictly scientific or theoretical inquiries concerning effects, in which neither the foreseeing nor the obedient will can be an agent or factor, but of which the intellect is rather the recorder, or mere accountant.

If the question concerning the origin of languages were, Who are responsible for their existence and progressive changes, or ought to be credited for improvements, or blamed for deficiencies in them? or if the question were, How men might or should be made better inventors, or apter followers of the best inventions—there would then be some pertinency in insisting on the agency of man in their developments—an agency which, in fact, like his agency in geology, is incidental to his real volitions, and is neither involved in what he intends nor in what he could be made to intend by discipline. So far as human intentions have had anything to do with changes in the traditions of language, they have, as we have said, been exerted in resisting them. Hence the traditions of language, with all the knowledge, histories, arts, and sciences involved and embodied in them, are developments incidental, it is true, to the existence and exercise of self-consciousness, and of free or intelligent wills, yet are developments around and outside of them, so to speak, and were added to them rather than evolved from them. These developments were added through their exercise and serviceableness as powers which stand to the more primitive ones of self-conscious thought and volition in relations similar to those we have seen to exist between the latter and the still more primitive powers of mind in memory and attention.

These relations come, first, from turning an old power to a new account; or making a new use of it, when the power, developed for other uses, acquires the requisite energy (as when the fins of a fish become fitted for flying); or when the revivals of memory become vivid enough to make connecting thoughts in a train distinct and apparent, as mere signs, to a reflective attention. Secondly, the new use increases the old power by its exercise and serviceableness (as flying and its value to life make the fins of the fish still longer), or as the exercise and importance to life of reflective thought make the revivals of memory still more vivid, and enlarge its organ, the brain. Traditions of language, or established artifices of expression, are related to new uses in a power, now in turn become sufficiently energetic, which at first was only the power of associating the sounds of words with thoughts, and thence with their objects, and which was incidental to the distinct recognition of thoughts as signs, or suggestions, of other thoughts. Developed by exercise and its serviceableness to life to the point, not only of making readily and employing temporarily such arbitrary associations, but also of fixing them and transmitting them as a more or less permanent language, or system of signs, this power acquired, or was turned to, a use involving immeasurable consequences and values.

To choose arbitrarily for preservation and transmission one out of many arbitrary associations of sounds with a meaning could not have been a rational or intelligent act of free will, but ought rather to be attributed to chance, lot, or fate; or to *will* in the narrower sense of the word in which one man is said to have more than another, or to be more will-ful, that is, persistent in his caprices. To make by decree any action permanent and regular which in itself is transient or accidental requires *will* it is true, in one sense, or *sticking to a point, merely because it has been assumed*; as some children do in imposing their inven-tions upon their associates. This degree *of arbitrariness* appears necessary to the step in the use of signs which made them traditions of language, permanent enough to be the roots of a continued growth in it—a growth which must, however, have determined more and more the selections of new words, and new uses in old ones, through motives common to the many speakers of a language; such as common fancies, instinctive tendencies, facil-ities, allegiance to authority, and associations in general—the vague as well as distinct ones—which were common to many speakers. These causes would act instinctively, or unconsciously, as well as by design. Tyranny in the growth of language, or the agency of arbitrary wills, persisting in their caprices, must have disappeared at an early date, or must have become insignificant in its effects upon the whole of any established language. Intentional choice would henceforward have the *design* generally of conserving or restoring a supposed good usage; though along with unintended preferences, instinctively followed, it would, doubtless, have the effect of slowly changing the usages of language on the whole. A happy suggestion of change would be adopted, if adopted consciously, with reference to its supposed conformity to the *genius* of the language, or to its will, rather than to the will of an individual dictator; and the influence of a speaker would depend on the supposition that he knew best how to use the language correctly, or was intimate with its genius. But suggestions of change would be more likely to be adopted unconsciously.

History can trace languages back only, of course, to the earliest times of their repre-sentations in phonetic writings or inscriptions; as palaeontology can trace organic species back only to the earliest preservation of them as fossils in the rocks. In neither case do we probably go back to periods in which forms were subject to sudden or capricious varia-tions. Natural selection would, therefore, define the most prominent action of the causes of change in both of them. But just as governments in all their forms depend on the fixed-ness and force of traditions, and as traditions gained this force through the wills of those in the past who established them by arbitrary decrees, and induced in others those habits of respect and obedience which now preserve them, so in language there was, doubtless, a time when *will* was the chief agent in its formation and preservation. But it was Will in its narrower sense, which does not include all that is commonly meant by volitional action. The latter involves, it is true, persistence in some elements—a persistence in memory and thought of consciously recognized motives, principles, purposes, or intentions. Volition is an action through memory, and not merely from a present stimulus, and is accompanied, when free or rational, by the recognition in thought of the motive, the proximate cause of the action, the reasons for it, or the immediate and present tendency to it, which is referred back in turn, but is not analyzed, nor usually capable of being analyzed introspectively into still more remote antecedents in our histories, inherited disposition, characters, and present circumstances. Those causes which are even too feeble to be introspectively recognized are not, of course, the source whence the force or energy of will is derived; but independently of their *directive* agency, this force is indistinguishable from that of pure spontaneity or vital energy. In like manner, the force of water in a system of river-courses is not determined by its beds and banks, but is none the less guided by them. This water-force in the first instance, and from time to time, alters its courses, but normally flows within predetermined courses; as the energy of will flows normally within the directive, but alterable, courses of character and circumstances. The really recognized motives in ordinary volition generally include more than the impulse or satisfaction of adhering to an assumed position, or to a purpose, for the will's sake, as in mere will, or willfulness (which is an overflow, so to speak, of energy, directed only by its own inertia, though often useful in altering character, or the courses of volition, both in the will itself and the wills of others). The habit of conscious persistence, involved in will, but most conspicuous in self-will, was, together with its correlatives, respect and obedience, doubtless serviceable to the rulers of primeval men, the authors of human government; and was, doubtless, developed through this serviceableness before it was turned to new uses in the institution of arbitrary customs and traditions. It thus illustrates anew the general principle shown in the several previous steps of this progress, namely, the turning of an old power to a new account, or making a new use of it, when the power has acquired the requisite energy; and the subsequent further increase of the power through serviceableness and exercise in its new function.

This power in the wills of the political, military, and religious leaders of men must soon, after producing the apotheosis of the more influential among them, have been converted into the sacred force of tradition; that is, into the *fas* or commands of languages themselves; and of other arbitrary customs. Henceforth and throughout all the periods included in the researches of comparative philology in which written remains of languages are to be found, it is probable that no man has consciously committed, or had the power to commit, the sin of intentionally altering their traditions, except for reasons common to many speakers and afforded by the traditions themselves.

NOTES

1. For an intellect complete without appendages of sense or locomotion, see Plato's *Timaeus.*

2. It appears, at first sight, a rash hypothesis to imagine so extensive an action of illusion as I have supposed in the revivals of memory—a self-vouching faculty of which, in general, the testimony cannot be questioned—since each recall asserts for itself in identity with what is recalled by it, either in past outward experiences or in previous revivals of them. But the hypothesis of uniform, or frequent, illusions in individual judgments of memory is not made in contradiction of experiences in general, including those remembered, when reduced to rational consistency. The familiar fact that no memory, even of an immediately past experience, is an adequate reproduction of everything that must have been present in it, in actual

consciousness, and must have received more or less attention, is familiarly verified by repeating the remembered experience. Memory itself thus testifies to its own fallibility. But this is not all. Illusion in an opposite direction, the more than adequate revival of some experiences, so far as vividness and apparently remembered details are concerned, affects our memories of dreams, demonstrably in some, presumably in many. What is commonly called a dream is not what is present to the imagination in sleep, but what is believed, often illusively, to have been present; and is, doubtless, in general, more vivid in memory and furnished with more numerous details, owing to the livelier action of imagination in waking moments. The liveliness of an actual dream is rather in its dominant feeling or interest than in its images.

The order of internal events, or the order of suggestion in actual dreams, is often reversed in the waking memories of them. A dream very long and full of details, as it appears in memory, and taking many words to relate, is sometimes recalled from the suggestions and trains of thought in sleep which are comprised in the impressions of a few moments. Such a dream usually ends in some startling or interesting event, which was a misinterpretation in sleep of some real outward impression, as a loud or unusual noise, or some inward sensation, like one of hunger, thirst, heat, cold, or numbness, which really stood in sleep at the beginning of the misremembered train of thought, instead of constituting its *dénouement* in a remembered series of real incidents. The remembered dream *seems* to have been an isolated series of such incidents, succeeding each other in the natural order of experience; but this appearance may well arise from the absence of any remembered indications of a contrary order; or from the absence, on one hand, of a consciousness in sleep of anything more vivid than the actual dream, and the real feebleness, on the other hand, of the dream itself in respect to everything in it except the salient incident, or the dominant interest, which caused it to be remembered along with the feeble sketch of suggested incidents. Surprise at incongruities in parts of trains often constitutes this interest.

If the waking imagination really fills out this sketch, and avouches the whole without cheek from anything really remembered, the phenomenon would be perfectly accordant with what is known of the dealings of imagination with real experiences, and with what is to be presumed of the comparative feebleness of its powers in sleep. A remembered dream would thus be, in some cases, a twofold illusion—an illusion in sleep arising from misinterpreted sensations, and an illusion in memory concerning what was actually the train of thoughts excited by the mistake, the train being in fact often inverted in such an apparent recollection. Savages and the insane believe their dreams to be real experiences. The civilized and sane man believes them to be true memories of illusions in sleep. A step farther in the application of the general tests of true experience would reduce some dreams to illusive memories of the illusions of sleep.

There does not appear on analysis, made in conformity to the reality of experiences in general, that there is any intrinsic difference between a memory and an imagination, the reality of the former being dependent on extrinsic relations and the outward checks of other memories. Memory, as a whole, vouches for itself, and for all its mutually consistent details, and banishes mere imaginations from its province, not as foreigners, but on account of their lawlessness, or incoherence, with the rest of its subjects, and through the exercise of what is called the judgments of experience, which are in fact mnemonic summaries of experiences (including instinctive tendencies). The imaginations of the insane are in insurrection against this authority of memory in general experience, or against what is familiarly called "reason." When sufficiently vivid, or powerful, and numerous, they usurp the powers of state, or the authority of memory and free intelligent volition. "Reason" is then said to be "dethroned."

The unreality of some dreams would thus appear to be more complete than they are in general discovered to be by mature, sane, and reflective thought, and by indirect observations upon their conditions and phenomena. The supposition of a similar illusion in the phenomena of reflection on the immediately past, or passing, impressions of the mind affords an explanation of a curious phenomenon, not uncommon in waking moments, which is referred to by many writers on psychology, namely, the phenomenon of experiencing in minute detail what appears also to be recalled as a past experience. Some writers have attempted to explain this as a veritable revival, by a passing experience, of a really past and very remote one, either in our progenitors, as some evolutionists suppose; or in a previous life, or in some state of individual existence, otherwise unremembered, as the mystic prefers to believe: a revival affected by an actual coincidence, in many minute particulars, of a present real experience with a really past one. But if a passing real experience could be supposed to be divided, so to speak, or to make a double impression in memory—one the ordinary impression of what is immediately past, and the other a dream-like impression filled out on its immediate revival in reflection with the same details—the supposition would be in accordance with what is really known of some dreams, and would, therefore, be more probable than the above explanations. It is possible to trust individual memories too far, even in respect to what is immediately past, as it is to trust too far a single sense in respect to what is immediately present. Rational consistency, in all experiences, or in experience on the whole, is the ultimate test of reality or truth in our judgments, whether these are "intuitive" or consciously derived.

3. Images in dogs are supposed to depend largely on the sense of smell.

4. Dr. McCosh, *The Intuitions of the Mind Inductively Investigated*, etc.

5. See Mill's *A System of Logic*, vol. 1, book II, chapter iii.

6. See Mill's *An Examination of Sir William Hamilton's Philosophy*, chapter xi.

7. See Mill's *An Examination of Sir William Hamilton's Philosophy*, chapter v.

8. See Darwin's *The Expression of the Emotions in Men and Animals*, Theory of Blushing, chapter xiii.

9. In the origin of the languages of civilized peoples, the distinction between powers of tradition, or *external inheritance*, and proper invention in art becomes a very important one, as will be shown farther on.

10. See Darwin's *The Expression of the Emotions in Man and Animals*.

11. See William Dwight Whitney, "Schleicher and the Physical Theory of Language" (1871), reprinted in his *Oriental and Linguistic Studies*, 2 vols. (New York: Charles Scribner's Sons, 1873), vol. 1, pp. 298–331.

Notes on Nihilism

Written around 1874.

These notes were written by Wright on William James's unpublished paper "Against Nihilism" in the William James Papers at Harvard University's Houghton Library, MS Am 1092.9 (4422). Ralph Barton Perry published a partial and uncorrected version of these notes in *The Thought and Character of William James*, ed. R. B. Perry (Boston: Little, Brown, and Co., 1935), vol. 2, appendix 3, pp. 718–721.

[NOTED IN THE THIRD SECTION OF "AGAINST NIHILISM," AT "*IT IS MEANT*" OF THE SENTENCE STARTING WITH "I HAVE BEEN IN THE HABIT ... "]

This by figure, at least, refers the phenomenon to an assumed intelligent will which as contrasted with it, is posited as non-phenomenal, *i.e.*, noumenal. All phenomena *do* refer to existences besides themselves as individual phenomena,* but these existences are what they *mean* or are *signs of*—and are not what means or intends them; except when they are phenomena of an intelligent will. When the phenomena refer to existences at all determined or determinable, these existences are also phenomena, actual or potential, *i.e.*, present in perception or in conception; the concept being the identical or *ideographic sign* of a perception not present. And the reference of an actual perception to something else—object, matter—is a reference to what it and the accompanying concepts are *signs* of in perceptions not present. The *objectivity* of a phenomenon is its significance. Even the subject becomes an object when any phenomenon is consciously referred to it or is felt to be a sign of it. Not "being meant by", neither "meaning" in an active sense, but being simply and neutrally "a sign of" seems to me to be the substantive reference of a phenomenon in general; and that the active and passive relations are particular ones added to this general neutral one. To be sure, even this is a polar relation—not an equality; since a substance is not conceived as a *sign* of its attributes, but the reverse. A sign as determining must be itself more determined than what it determines. But by "substance" is sometimes meant "essence" or essential attributes; and these may be signs of inseparable accidents. Thus inertia felt by us may signify to us weight, ultimate incompressibility, and indestructibility. In this logical sense "the substance" is a sign of its attributes, or "means" them. In metaphysics "substance" is not a select set of attributes but *all* attributes actual and potential, and the unknown in general as well as the at present unperceived.

* * *

The very individuality of a phenomenon is a determination of it by other phenomena. Its existence as actual, or now existing—self-signifying—that is, without that conception or potential apprehension, going on to or expecting it, which is its existence in thought, or in signs or in the tendency of attention to it as having existence or as being about to exist;—even without this its individual existence is a determination complete in respect to time at least. As individual and actual it is *now*; and "now" is a mutual determination of two series, *ante* and *post*. It may have no relation to space, or such determination in space, as well as time, as an individual thing has; it may have no determination in kind, class or quality, or such as would determine a name or even a thought or any sign of it; still as being actual it is placed between the two series which determine it to be now; and therefore its individuality is not in itself. Neither is it in a common substratum of existence, which negatives all difference and individuality. Common-sense is right, but not skillful in distinctions and dialectics; and what is called Nihilism does not differ from it except in the analysis of being. That which without being present, or in any exact sense existent, is simply signified by what is present, does not gain existence, because the sign is believed in. Its concept or sign is distinguished from the mere suggestion or imagination which has no respect to reality. Belief in the sign has respect to reality; and reality is threefold a past, a present, and a future, one remembered, one perceived, one expected. It is only in the present reality or the present object of belief, that the phenomenon stands for itself; has no fallible representative, is actually itself. And even in the present it is not any kind, class or quality; or instance of a kind, etc.; but is to be so determined only by being a sign of remembered or preconceived phenomena; which as a sign it calls up more or less vaguely as present concepts.

Reality, or that to which logically, or in a process of thought and action, belief has respect, or is relevant, should be distinguished (as it is not by common-sense) from the actuality of a phenomenon, as that beyond which ontologically metaphysics searches for substance. In respect to the quest of metaphysics there is nothing in our knowledge but present phenomena—objective and subjective and mutually related or mutually determining and determined, but ever passing phenomena, ever coming forth and fading out, though not by chance. There is an order in them. This order is partly in the present group and leads continuously on, though more or less unexpected elements continually modify the cognitive order. These are the elements of objective perception. Orderliness is not what needs explanation by a metaphysical cause, but is what affords explanation and prompts to its quest whenever the unexpected occurs. The *Nothing* besides phenomena and their laws, (the laws themselves embodied and exemplified in present specimen phenomena), this doctrine of phenomenalism and nominalism, attaches to the word Nothing a sense which must be understood to relate only to this ontological quest of pure being. The realities of belief are not thereby made present actualities, on the pain of being declared illusory. My expectations are of the real if what I now expect comes to pass or becomes actual; though it has now no existence, or no other existence than having a sign in my present consciousness; that is, a conceived, putative, potential existence in a representative which so far as the individual existence of this as a present phenomenon is concerned, is not different from that of merely imagined unexpected phenomena; seeing that expectation or belief is not dependent on any but a phenomenal difference between what is believed and what is merely imagined; namely, the remembered order of past phenomena.

But after all, Nihilism is rather a discipline than a positive doctrine; an exorcism of the vague; a criticism of questions which by habit have passed beyond the real practical grounds or causes of question. Common-sense is opposed only so far as common-sense is not critical.

[NOTED IN THE THIRD SECTION OF "AGAINST NIHILISM," AT "BUT AS MOMENTS HAVING THIS QUALITY... "]

This quality appears to me to be a merely negative one—simply as *no part* of the phenomena of our activity. Our passivity toward them is not a compulsion by them of our activities, but simply a non-belonging to our activity. Our activity may govern them indirectly, it is true, in all cases where the outward, objective results of our activity affect the conditions of the phenomena. I may cease at will to see, because seeing depends on the positions of my eyes and their openness and these depend on my wishes or motives.

The contrast here indicated is not that of a substance and phenomena, but of subject and object phenomena; in the special relation, moreover, of perception to the *active* phenomena of the self. But perceptions are often or for the most part, two-sided, immediately involving *our* passivities or feelings, and their outward significance. As feelings they are signs of us, ourselves; they mean the subject "we are." As perceptions they mean something not us—not in our particular memories or imaginations—some other phenomena present only by their concept signs, and only vaguely perhaps in these.

[NOTED IN THE THIRD SECTION OF "AGAINST NIHILISM," AT "AN INSTANT CONSCIOUS EXISTENCE" WHICH ENDS A SENTENCE.]

No feeling except perhaps in unreflective consciousness—in an absolutely unremembered consciousness (if any there be)—exists by itself as an instant conscious existence. It passes by its relations—of resemblance, and contiguous association; or by a significance that is grounded on these to other feelings—and this is true quite irrespective of its being a feeling *in* us or a feeling of something else. This *passing* character in a phenomenon, which passes even when continuous or constant in degree, is recognized by all thinkers on both sides. Time is always an element in phenomena, both internal and external, and is the abstract of relations in general. It is the *continuum* of phenomenal existences. It is their "substance" in the logical sense; that is, their universal attribute.

[NOTED IN THE THIRD SECTION OF "AGAINST NIHILISM," AT "ABSOLUTELY SUFFICIENT TO ITSELF" AT THE END OF THE SENTENCE STARTING WITH "SUBSTANCE METAPHYSICALLY CONSIDERED . . . "]

It is nothing without *its relations* of resemblance, contiguous association, significance, and its time; and these when uncompounded of simpler relations belonging to these same highest categories, are self existent in the sense of not being subject to explanation. If derived there is no evidence, nor any conception of their derivation, which does not contradict their nature as the elements of all conceivable explanation.

Charles Sanders Peirce

FRASER'S *The Works of George Berkeley*

North American Review 113 (October 1871): 449–472.

The Works of George Berkeley, D.D., formerly Bishop of Cloyne: including many of his Writings hitherto unpublished. With Prefaces, Annotations, his Life and Letters, and an Account of his Philosophy. By Alexander Campbell Fraser, M.A., Professor of Logic and Metaphysics in the University of Edinburgh. In Four Volumes. Oxford: At the Clarendon Press. 8 vo. 1871.

This new edition of Berkeley's works is much superior to any of the former ones. It contains some writings not in any of the other editions, and the rest are given with a more carefully edited text. The editor has done his work well. The introductions to the several pieces contain analyses of their contents which will be found of the greatest service to the reader. On the other hand, the explanatory notes which disfigure every page seem to us altogether unnecessary and useless.

Berkeley's metaphysical theories have at first sight an air of paradox and levity very unbecoming to a bishop. He denies the existence of matter, our ability to see distance, and the possibility of forming the simplest general conception; while he admits the existence of Platonic ideas; and argues the whole with a cleverness which every reader admits, but which few are convinced by. His disciples seem to think the present moment a favorable one for obtaining for their philosophy a more patient hearing than it has yet got. It is true that we of this day are skeptical and not given to metaphysics, but so, say they, was the generation which Berkeley addressed, and for which his style was chosen; while it is hoped that the spirit of calm and thorough inquiry which is now, for once, almost the fashion, will save the theory from the perverse misrepresentations which formerly assailed it, and lead to a fair examination of the arguments which, in the minds of his sectators, put the truth of it beyond all doubt. But above all it is anticipated that the Berkeleyan treatment of that question of the validity of human knowledge and of the inductive process of science, which is now so much studied, is such as to command the attention of scientific men to the idealistic system. To us these hopes seem vain. The truth is that the minds from whom the spirit of the age emanates have now no interest in the only problems that metaphysics ever pretended to solve. The abstract acknowledgment of God, Freedom, and Immortality, apart from those other religious beliefs (which cannot possibly rest on metaphysical grounds) which alone may animate this, is now seen to have no practical consequence whatever. The world is getting to think of these creatures of metaphysics, as Aristotle of the Platonic ideas: τερετίσματα γάρ ἐστι, καὶ εἰ ἐστιν, οὐδὲν πρὸς τὸν λόγον ἐστίν. The question of the grounds of the validity of induction has, it is true, excited an interest, and may continue to do so (though the argument is now become too difficult for popular apprehension); but whatever interest it has had has been due to a hope that the solution of it would afford the basis for sure and useful maxims concerning the logic of induction—a hope which would be destroyed so soon as it were shown that the question was a purely metaphysical one. This is the prevalent feeling, among advanced minds. It may not be just; but it exists. And its existence is an effectual bar (if there were no other) to the general acceptance of Berkeley's system. The few who do now care for metaphysics are not of that bold order of minds who delight to hold a position so unsheltered by the prejudices of common sense as that of the good bishop.

As a matter of history, however, philosophy must always be interesting. It is the best representative of the mental development of each age. It is so even of ours, if we think what really our philosophy is. Metaphysical history is one of the chief branches of history, and ought to be expounded side by side with the history of society, of government, and of war; for in its relations with these we trace the significance of events for the human mind. The history of philosophy in the British Isles is a subject possessing more unity and entirety within itself than has usually been recognized in it. The influence of Descartes was never so great in England as that of traditional conceptions, and we can trace a continuity between modern and medival thought there, which is wanting in the history of France, and still more, if possible, in that of Germany.

From very early times, it has been the chief intellectual characteristic of the English to wish to effect everything by the plainest and directest means, without unnecessary contrivance. In war, for example, they rely more than any other people in Europe upon sheer hardihood, and rather despise military science. The main peculiarities of their system of law arise from the fact that every evil has been rectified as it became intolerable, without any thoroughgoing measure. The bill for legalizing marriage with a deceased wife's sister is yearly pressed because it supplies a remedy for an inconvenience actually felt; but nobody has proposed a bill to legalize marriage with a deceased husband's brother. In philosophy, this national tendency appears as a strong preference for the simplest theories, and a resistance to any complication of the theory as long as there is the least possibility that the facts can be explained in the simpler way. And, accordingly, British philosophers have always desired to weed out of philosophy all conceptions which could not be made perfectly definite and easily intelligible, and have shown strong nominalistic tendencies since the time of Edward I, or even earlier. Berkeley is an admirable illustration of this national character, as well as of that strange union of nominalism with Platonism, which has repeatedly appeared in history, and has been such a stumbling-block to the historians of philosophy.

The medieval metaphysic is so entirely forgotten, and has so close a historic connection with modern English philosophy, and so much bearing upon the truth of Berkeley's doctrine, that we may perhaps be pardoned a few pages on the nature of the celebrated controversy concerning universals. And first let us set down a few dates. It was at the very end of the eleventh century that the dispute concerning nominalism and realism, which had existed in a vague way before, began to attain extraordinary proportions. During the twelfth century it was the matter of most interest to logicians, when William of Champeaux, Abelard, John of Salisbury, Gilbert de la Porrée, and many others, defended as many different opinions. But there was no historic connection between this controversy and those of scholasticism proper, the scholasticism of Aquinas, Scotus, and Ockam. For about the end of the twelfth century a great revolution of thought took place in Europe. What the influences were which produced it requires new historical researches to say. No doubt, it was partly due to the Crusades. But a great awakening of intelligence did take place at that time. It requires, it is true, some examination to distinguish this particular movement from a general awakening which had begun a century earlier, and had been growing stronger ever since. But now there was an accelerated impulse. Commerce was attaining new importance, and was inventing some of her chief conveniences and safeguards. Law, which had hitherto been utterly barbaric, began to be a profession. The civil law was adopted in Europe, the canon law was digested; the common law took some form. The Church, under Innocent III, was assuming the sublime functions of a moderator over kings. And those orders of mendicant friars were established, two of which did so much for the development of the scholastic philosophy. Art felt the spirit of a new age, and there could hardly be a greater change than from the highly ornate round-arched architecture of the twelfth century to the comparatively simple Gothic of the thirteenth. Indeed, if any one wishes to know what a scholastic commentary is like, and what the tone of thought in it is, he has only to contemplate a Gothic cathedral. The first quality of either is a religious devotion, truly heroic. One feels that the men who did these works did really believe in religion as we believe in nothing. We cannot easily understand how Thomas Aquinas can speculate so much on the nature of angels, and whether ten thousand of them could dance on a needle's point But it was simply because he held them for real. If they are real, why are they not more interesting than the bewildering varieties of insects which naturalists study; or why should the orbits of double stars attract more attention than spiritual intelligences? It will be said that we have no means of knowing anything about them. But that is on a par with censuring the schoolmen for referring questions to the authority of the Bible and of the Church. If they really believed in their religion, as they did, what better could they do? And if they found in these authorities testimony concerning angels, how could they avoid admitting it. Indeed, objections of this sort only make it appear still more clearly how much those were the ages of faith. And if the spirit was not altogether admirable, it is only because faith itself has its faults as a foundation for the intellectual character. The men of that time did fully believe and did think that, for the sake of giving themselves up absolutely to their great task of building or of writing, it was well worth while to resign all the joys of life. Think of the spirit in which Duns Scotus must have worked, who wrote his thirteen volumes in folio, in a style as condensed as the most condensed parts of Aristotle, before the age of thirty-four. Nothing is more striking in either of the great intellectual products of that age, than the complete absence of self-conceit on the part of the artist or philosopher. That anything of value can be added to his sacred and catholic work by its having the smack of individuality about it, is what he has never conceived. His work is not designed to embody *his* ideas, but the universal truth; there will not be one thing in it, however minute, for which you will not find that he has his authority; and whatever originality emerges is of that inborn kind which so saturates a man that he cannot himself perceive it. The individual feels his own worthlessness in comparison with his task, and does not dare to introduce his vanity into the doing of it. Then there is no machine-work, no unthinking repetition about the thing. Every part is worked out for itself as a separate problem, no matter how analogous it may be in general to another part. And no matter how small and hidden a detail may be, it has been conscientiously studied, as though it were intended for the eye of God. Allied to this character is a detestation of antithesis or the studied balancing of one thing against another, and of a too geometrical grouping—a hatred of posing which is as much a moral trait as the others. Finally, there is nothing in which the scholastic philosophy and the Gothic architecture resemble one another more than in the gradually increasing sense of immensity which impresses the mind of the student as he learns to appreciate the real dimensions and cost of each. It is very unfortunate that the thirteenth, fourteenth, and fifteenth centuries should, under the name of Middle Ages, be confounded with others, which they are in every respect as unlike as the Renaissance is from modern times. In the history of logic, the break between the twelfth and thirteenth centuries is so great that only one author of the former age is ever quoted in the latter. If this is to be attributed to the fuller acquaintance with the works of Aristotle, to what, we would ask, is this profounder study itself to be attributed, since it is now known that the knowledge of those works was not imported from the Arabs? The thirteenth century was realistic, but the question concerning universals was not as much agitated as several others. Until about the end of the century, scholasticism was somewhat vague, immature, and unconscious of its own power. Its greatest glory was in the first half of the fourteenth century. Then Duns Scotus,[1] a Briton (for whether Scotch, Irish, or English is disputed), first stated the realistic position consistently, and developed it with great fulness and applied it to all the different questions which depend upon it. His theory of "formalities" was the subtlest, except perhaps Hegel's logic, ever broached, and he was separated from nominalism only by the division of a hair. It is not therefore surprising that the nominalistic position was soon adopted by several writers, especially by the celebrated William of Ockam, who took the lead of this party by the thoroughgoing and masterly way in which he treated the theory and combined it with a then rather recent but now forgotten addition to the doctrine of logical terms. With

Ockam, who died in 1347, scholasticism may be said to have culminated. After him the scholastic philosophy showed a tendency to separate itself from the religious element which alone could dignify it, and sunk first into extreme formalism and fancifulness, and then into the merited contempt of all men; just as the Gothic architecture had a very similar fate, at about the same time, and for much the same reasons.

The current explanations of the realist-nominalists controversy are equally false and unintelligible. They are said to be derived ultimately from Bayle's *Dictionary*; at any rate, they are not based on a study of the authors. "Few, very few, for a hundred years past," says Hallam, with truth, "have broken the repose of the immense works of the schoolmen." Yet it is perfectly possible so to state the matter that no one shall fail to comprehend what the question was, and how there might be two opinions about it. Are universals real? We have only to stop and consider a moment what was meant by the word *real*, when the whole issue soon becomes apparent. Objects are divided into figments, dreams, etc., on the one hand, and realities on the other. The former are those which exist only inasmuch as you or I or some man imagines them; the latter are those which have an existence independent of your mind or mine or that of any number of persons. The real is that which is not whatever we happen to think it, but is unaffected by what we may think of it. The question, therefore, is whether *man*, *horse*, and other names of natural classes, correspond with anything which all men, or all horses, really have in common, independent of our thought, or whether these classes are constituted simply by a likeness in the way in which our minds are affected by individual objects which have in themselves no resemblance or relationship whatsoever. Now that this is a real question which different minds will naturally answer in opposite ways, becomes clear when we think that there are two widely separated points of view, from which *reality*, as just defined, may be regarded. Where is the real, the thing independent of how we think it, to be found? There must be such a thing, for we find our opinions constrained; there is something, therefore, which influences our thoughts, and is not created by them. We have, it is true, nothing immediately present to us but thoughts. Those thoughts, however, have been caused by sensations, and those sensations are constrained by something out of the mind. This thing out of the mind, which directly influences sensation, and through sensation thought, because it *is* out of the mind, is independent of how we think it, and is, in short, the real. Here is one view of reality, a very familiar one. And from this point of view it is clear that the nominalistic answer must be given to the question concerning universals. For, while from this standpoint it may be admitted to be true as a rough statement that one man is like another, the exact sense being that the realities external to the mind produce sensations which may be embraced under one conception, yet it can by no means be admitted that the two real men have really anything in common, for to say that they are both men is only to say that the one mental term or thought-sign "man" stands indifferently for either of the sensible objects caused by the two external realities; so that not even the two sensations have in themselves anything in common, and far less is it to be inferred that the external realities have. This conception of reality is so familiar, that it is unnecessary to dwell upon it; but the other, or realist conception, if less familiar, is even more natural and obvious. All human thought and opinion contains an arbitrary, accidental element, dependent on the limitations in circumstances, power, and bent of the individual; an element of error, in short. But human opinion universally tends in the long run to a definite form, which is the truth. Let any human being have enough information and exert enough thought upon any question, and the result will be that he will arrive at a certain definite conclusion, which is the same that any other mind will reach under sufficiently favorable circumstances. Suppose two men, one deaf, the other blind. One hears a man declare he means to kill another, hears the report of the pistol, and hears the victim cry; the other sees the murder done. Their sensations are affected in the highest degree with their individual peculiarities. The first information that their sensations will give them, their first inferences, will be more nearly alike, but still different; the one having, for example, the idea of a man shouting, the other of a man with a threatening aspect; but their final conclusions, the thought the remotest from sense, will be identical and free from the one-sidedness of their idiosyncrasies. There is, then, to every question a true answer, a final conclusion, to which the opinion of every man is constantly gravitating. He may for a time recede from it, but give him more experience and time for consideration, and he will finally approach it. The individual may not live to reach the truth; there is a residuum of error in every individual's opinions. No matter; it remains that there is a definite opinion to which the mind of man is, on the whole and in the long run, tending. On many questions the final agreement is already reached, on all it will be reached if time enough is given. The arbitrary will or other individual peculiarities of a sufficiently large number of minds may postpone the general agreement in that opinion indefinitely; but it cannot affect what the character of that opinion shall be when it is reached. This final opinion, then, is independent, not indeed of thought in general, but of all that is arbitrary and individual in thought; is quite independent of how you or I, or any number of men think. Everything therefore which will be thought to exist in the final opinion is real, and nothing else. What is the power of external things, to affect the senses? To say that people sleep after taking opium because it has a soporific *power*, is that to say anything in the world but that people sleep after taking opium because they sleep after taking opium? To assert the existence of a power or potency, is it to assert the existence of anything actual? Or to say that a thing has a potential existence, is it to say that it has an actual existence? In other words, is the present existence of a power anything in the world but a regularity in future events relating to a certain thing regarded as an element which is to be taken account of beforehand, in the conception of that thing? If not, to assert that there are external things which can be known only as exerting a power on our sense, is nothing different from asserting that there is a general *drift* in the history of human thought which will lead it to one general agreement, one catholic consent. And any truth more perfect than this destined conclusion, any reality more absolute than what is thought in it, is a fiction of metaphysics. It is obvious how this way of thinking harmonizes with a belief in an infallible Church, and how much more natural it would be in the Middle Ages than in Protestant or positivist times.

This theory of reality is instantly fatal to the idea of a thing in itself—a thing existing independent of all relation to the mind's conception of it. Yet it would by no means forbid, but rather encourage us, to regard the appearances of sense as only signs of the realities. Only, the realities which they represent would not be the unknowable cause of sensation, but *noumena*, or intelligible conceptions which are the last products of the mental action which is set in motion by sensation. The matter of sensation is altogether accidental; precisely the same information, practically, being capable of communication through different senses. And the catholic consent which constitutes the truth is by no means to be limited to men in this earthly life or to the human race, but extends to the whole communion of minds to which we belong, including some probably whose senses are very different from ours, so that in that consent no predication of a sensible quality can enter, except as an admission that so certain sorts of senses are affected. This theory is also highly favorable to a belief in external realities. It will, to be sure, deny that there is any reality which is absolutely incognizable in itself, so that it cannot be taken into the mind. But observing that "the external" means simply that which is independent of what phenomenon is immediately present, that is of how we may think or feel; just as "the real" means that which is independent of how we may think or feel *about it*; it must be granted that there are many objects of true science which are external, because there are many objects of thought which, if they are independent of that thinking whereby they are thought (that is, if they are real), are indisputably independent of all *other* thoughts and feelings.

It is plain that this view of reality is inevitably realistic; because general conceptions enter into all judgments, and therefore into true opinions. Consequently a thing in the general is as real as in the concrete. It is perfectly true that all white things have whiteness in them, for that is only saying, in another form of words, that all white things are white; but since it is true that real things possess whiteness, whiteness is real. It is a real which only exists by virtue of an act of thought knowing it, but that thought is not an arbitrary or accidental one dependent on any idiosyncrasies, but one which will hold in the final opinion.

This theory involves a phenomenalism. But it is the phenomenalism of Kant, and not that of Hume. Indeed, what Kant called his Copernican step was precisely the passage from the nominalistic to the realistic view of reality. It was the essence of his philosophy to regard the real object as determined by the mind. That was nothing else than to consider every conception and intuition which enters necessarily into the experience of an object, and which is not transitory and accidental, as having objective validity. In short, it was to regard the reality as the normal product of mental action, and not as the incognizable cause of it.

This realistic theory is thus a highly practical and common-sense position. Wherever universal agreement prevails, the realist will not be the one to disturb the general belief by idle and fictitious doubts. For according to him it is a consensus or common confession which constitutes reality. What he wants, therefore, is to see questions put to rest. And if a general belief, which is perfectly stable and immovable, can in any way be produced, though it be by the fagot and the rack, to talk of any error in such belief is utterly absurd. The realist will hold that the very same objects which are immediately present in our minds in experience really exist just as they are experienced out of the mind; that is, he will maintain a doctrine of immediate perception. He will not, therefore, sunder existence out of the mind and being in the mind as two wholly improportionable modes. When a thing is in such relation to the individual mind that that mind cognizes it, it is in the mind, and its being so in the mind will not in the least diminish its external existence. For he does not think of the mind as a receptacle, which if a thing is in, it ceases to be out of. To make a distinction between the true conception of a thing and the thing itself is, he will say, only to regard one and the same thing from two different points of view; for the immediate object of thought in a true judgment *is* the reality. The realist will, therefore, believe in the objectivity of all necessary conceptions, space, time, relation, cause, and the like.

No realist or nominalists ever expressed so definitely, perhaps, as is here done, his conception of reality. It is difficult to give a clear notion of an opinion of a past age, without exaggerating its distinctness. But careful examination of the works of the schoolmen will show that the distinction between these two views of the real—one as the fountain of the current of human thought, the other as the unmoving form to which it is flowing—is what really occasions their disagreement on the question concerning universals. The gist of all the nominalists arguments will be found to relate to a *res extra animam*, while the realist defends his position only by assuming that the immediate object of thought in a true judgment is real. The notion that the controversy between realism and nominalism had anything to do with Platonic ideas is a mere product of the imagination, which the slightest examination of the books would suffice to disprove. But to prove that the statement here given of the essence of these positions is historically true and not a fancy sketch, it will be well to add a brief analysis of the opinions of Scotus and Ockam.

Scotus sees several questions confounded together under the usual *utrum universale est a liquid in rebus.* In the first place, there is the question concerning the Platonic forms. But putting Platonism aside as at least incapable of proof, and as a self-contradictory opinion if the archetypes are supposed to be strictly universal, there is the celebrated dispute among Aristotelians as to whether the universal is really in things or only derives its existence from the mind. Universality is a relation of a predicate to the subjects of which it is predicated. That can exist only in the mind, wherein alone the coupling of subject and predicate takes place. But the word *universal* is also used to denote what are named by such terms as *a man* or *a horse*; these are called universals, because a man is not necessarily this man, nor a horse this horse. In such a sense it is plain universals are real; there really is a man and there really is a horse. The whole difficulty is with the actually indeterminate universal, that which not only is not necessarily *this*, but which, being one single object of thought, is predicable of many things. In regard to this it may be asked, first, is it necessary to its existence that it should be in the mind; and, second, does it exist *in re*? There are two ways in which a thing may be in the mind—*habitualiter* and *actualiter*. A notion is in the mind *actualiter* when it is actually conceived; it is in the mind *habitualiter* when it can directly produce a conception. It is by virtue of mental association (we moderns should say), that things are in the mind *habitualiter*. In the Aristotelian philosophy, the intellect is regarded as being to the soul what the eye is to the body. The mind *perceives* likenesses and other relations in the objects of sense, and thus just as sense affords sensible images of things, so the intellect affords intelligible images of them. It is as such a *species intelligibilis* that Scotus supposes that a conception exists which is in the mind *habitualiter,* not *actualiter.* This *species* is in the mind, in the sense of being the immediate object of knowledge, but its existence in the mind is independent of *consciousness.* Now that the *actual* cognition of the universal is necessary to its existence, Scotus denies. The subject of science is universal; and if the existence of universal were dependent upon what we happened to be thinking, science would not relate to anything real. On the other hand, he admits that the universal must be in the mind *habitualiter,* so that if a thing be considered as it is independent of its being cognized, there is no universality in it. For there is *in re extra* no one intelligible object attributed to different things. He holds, therefore, that such natures (i.e. sorts of things) as a *man* and a *horse,* which are real, and are not of themselves necessarily *this* man or *this* horse, though they cannot exist *in re* without being some particular man or horse, are in the *species intelligibilis* always represented positively indeterminate, it being the nature of the mind so to represent things. Accordingly any such nature is to be regarded as something which is of itself neither universal nor singular, but is universal in the mind, singular in things out of the mind. If there were nothing in the different men or horses which was not of itself singular, there would be no real unity except the numerical unity of the singulars; which would involve such absurd consequences as that the only real difference would be a numerical difference, and that there would be no real likenesses among things. If, therefore, it is asked whether the universal is in things, the answer is that the nature which in the mind is universal, and is not in itself singular, exists in things. It is the very same nature which in the mind is universal and *in re* is singular; for if it were not, in knowing anything of a universal we should be knowing nothing of things, but only of our own thoughts, and our opinion would not be converted from true to false by a change in things. This nature is actually indeterminate only so far as it is in the mind. But to say that an object is in the mind is only a metaphorical way of saying that it stands to the intellect in the relation of known to knower. The truth is, therefore, that that real nature which exists *in re,* apart from all action of the intellect, though in itself, apart from its relations, it is singular, yet is actually universal as it exists in relation to the mind. But this universal only differs from the singular in the manner of its being conceived (*formaliter*), but not in the manner of its existence (*realiter*).

Though this is the slightest possible sketch of the realism of Scotus, and leaves a number of important points unnoticed, yet it is sufficient to show the general manner of his thought and how subtle and difficult his doctrine is. That about one and the same nature being in the grade of singularity in existence, and in the grade of universality in the mind, gave rise to an extensive doctrine concerning the various kinds of identity and difference, called the doctrine of the *formalities*; and this is the point against which Ockam directed his attack.

Ockam's nominalism may be said to be the next stage in English opinion. As Scotus's mind is always running on forms, so Ockam's is on logical terms; and all the subtle distinctions which Scotus effects by his *formalitates*, Ockam explains by implied syncate-goremactics (or adverbial expressions, such as *per se*, etc.) in terms. Ockam always thinks of a mental conception as a logical term, which, instead of existing on paper, or in the voice, is in the mind, but is of the same general nature, namely, a *sign*. The conception and the word differ in two respects: first, a word is arbitrarily imposed, while a conception is a natural sign; second, a word signifies whatever it signifies only indirectly, through the conception which signifies the same thing directly. Ockam enunciates his nominalism as follows: "It should be known that *singular* may be taken in two senses. In one sense, it signifies that which is one and not many; and in this sense those who hold that the universal is a quality of mind predicable of many, standing however in this predication, not for itself, but for those many (i.e. the nominalists), have to say that every universal is truly and really singular; because as every word, however general we may agree to consider it, is truly and really singular and one in number, because it is one and not many, so every universal is singular. In another sense, the name *singular* is used to denote whatever is one and not many, is a sign of something which is singular in the first sense, and is not fit to be the sign of many. Whence, using the word *universal* for that which is not one in number—an acceptation many attribute to it—I say that there is no universal; unless perchance you abuse the word and say that *people* is not one in number and is universal. But that would be puerile. It is to be maintained, therefore, that every universal is one singular thing, and therefore there is no universal except by signification, that is, by its being the sign of many." The arguments by which he supports this position present nothing of interest.[2] Against Scotus's doctrine that universals are without the mind in individuals, but are not really distinct from the individuals, but only formally so, he objects that it is impossible there should be any distinction existing out of the mind except between things really distinct. Yet he does not think of denying that an individual consists of matter and form, for these, though inseparable, are really distinct things; though a modern nominalist might ask in what sense things could be said to be distinct independently of any action of the mind, which are so inseparable as matter and form. But as to *relation*, he most emphatically and clearly denies that it exists as anything different from the things related; and this denial he expressly extends to relations of agreement and likeness as well as to those of opposition. While, therefore, he admits the real existence of qualities, he denies that these real qualities are respects in which things agree or differ; but things which agree or differ agree or differ in themselves and in no respect *extra animam*. He allows that things without the mind are similar, but this similarity consists merely in the fact that the mind can abstract one notion from the contemplation of them. A resemblance, therefore, consists solely in the property of the mind by which it naturally imposes one mental sign upon the resembling things. Yet he allows there is something in the things to which this mental sign corresponds.

This is the nominalism of Ockam so far as it can be sketched in a single paragraph, and without entering into the complexities of the Aristotelian psychology nor of the *parva logicalia*. He is not so thoroughgoing as he might be, yet compared with Durandus and other contemporary nominalists he seems very radical and profound. He is truly the *venerabilis inceptor* of a new way of philosophizing which has now broadened, perhaps deepened also, into English empiricism.

England never forgot these teachings. During that Renaissance period when men could think that human knowledge was to be advanced by the use of Cicero's *Commonplaces*, we naturally see little effect from them; but one of the earliest prominent figures in modern philosophy is a man who carried the nominalistic spirit into everything—religion, ethics, psychology, and physics, the *plusquam nominalis*, Thomas Hobbes of Malmesbury. His razor cuts off, not merely substantial forms, but every incorporeal substance. As for universals, he not only denies their real existence, but even that there are any universal conceptions except so far as we conceive names. In every part of his logic, names and speech play an extraordinarily important part. Truth and falsity, he says have no place but among such creatures as use speech, for a true proposition is simply one whose predicate is the name of everything of which the subject is the name. "From hence, also, this may be deduced, that the first truths were arbitrarily made by those that first of all imposed names upon things, or received them from the imposition of others. For it is true (for example), that *man is a living creature*, but it is for this *reason* that it pleased men to impose both those names on the same thing." The difference between true religion and superstition is simply that the state recognizes the former and not the latter.

The nominalistic love of simple theories is seen also in his opinion, that every event is a movement, and that the sensible qualities exist only in sensible beings, and in his doctrine that man is at bottom purely selfish in his actions.

His views concerning matter are worthy of notice, because Berkeley is known to have been a student of Hobbes, as Hobbes confesses himself to have been of Ockam. The following paragraph gives his opinion—

> And as for that matter which is common to all things, and which philosophers, following Aristotle, usually call *materia prima*, that is, *first matter*, it is not a body distinct from all other bodies, nor is it one of them. What then is it? A mere name; yet a name which is not of vain use; for it signifies a conception of body without the consideration of any form or other accident except only magnitude or extension, and aptness to receive form and other accident. So that whensoever we have use of the name *body in general*, if we use that of *materia prima*, we do well. For when a man, not knowing which was first, water or ice, would find out which of the two were the matter of both, he would be fain to suppose some third matter which were neither of these two; so he that would find out what is the matter of all things ought to suppose such as is not the matter of anything that exists. Wherefore *materia prima* is nothing; and therefore they do not attribute to it form or any other accident, besides quantity; whereas all singular things have their forms and accidents certain.
>
> *Materia prima* therefore is body in general, that is, body considered universally, not as having neither form nor any accident, but in which no form nor any other accident but quantity are at all considered, that is, they are not drawn into argumentation. (p. 118)

The next great name in English philosophy is Locke's. His philosophy is nominalistic, but does not regard things from a logical point of view at all. Nominalism, however, appears in psychology as sensationalism; for nominalism arises from taking that view of reality which regards whatever is in thought as caused by something in sense, and whatever is in sense as caused by something without the mind. But everybody knows that this is the character of Locke's philosophy. He believed that every idea springs from sensation and from his (vaguely explained) reflection.

Berkeley is undoubtedly more the offspring of Locke than of any other philosopher. Yet the influence of Hobbes with him is very evident and great; and Malebranche doubtless contributed to his thought. But he was by nature a radical and a nominalist. His whole philosophy rests upon an extreme nominalism of a sensationalistic type. He sets out with the proposition (supposed to have been already proved by Locke), that all the ideas in our minds are simply reproductions of sensations, external and internal. He maintains, moreover, that sensations can only be thus reproduced in such combinations as might have been given in immediate perception. We can conceive a man without a head, because there is nothing in the nature of sense to prevent our seeing such a thing; but we cannot conceive a sound without any pitch, because the two things are necessarily united in perception. On this principle he denies that we can have any abstract general ideas, that is, that universals can exist in the mind; if I think of a man it must be either of a short or a long or a middle-sized man, because if I see a man he must be one or the other of these. In the first draft of the Introduction of the *Principles of Human Knowledge*, which is now for the first time printed, he even goes so far as to censure Ockam for admitting that we can have general terms in our mind; Ockam's opinion being that we have in our minds conceptions, which are singular themselves, but are *signs* of many things.[3] But Berkeley probably knew only of Ockam from hearsay, and perhaps thought he occupied a position like that of Locke. Locke had a very singular opinion on the subject of general conceptions. He says—

> If we nicely reflect upon them, we shall find that general ideas are fictions, and contrivances of the mind, that carry difficulty with them, and do not so easily offer themselves as we are apt to imagine. For example, does it not require some pains and skill to form the general idea of a triangle (which is none of the most abstract, comprehensive, and difficult); for it must be neither oblique nor rectangle, neither equilateral, equicrural, nor scalenon, but all and none of these at once? In effect, is something imperfect that cannot exist, an idea wherein some parts of several different and inconsistent ideas are put together.

To this Berkeley replies—

> Much is here said of the difficulty that abstract ideas carry with them, and the pains and skill requisite in forming them. And it is on all hands agreed that there is need of great toil and labor of the mind to emancipate our thoughts from particular objects, and raise them to those sublime speculations that are conversant about

abstract ideas. From all which the natural consequence should seem to be, that so difficult a thing as the forming of abstract ideas was not necessary to communication, which is so easy and familiar to all sort of men. But we are told, if they seem obvious and easy to grown men, it is only because by constant and familiar use they are made so. Now, I would fain know at what time it is men are employed in surmounting that difficulty. It cannot be when they are grown up, for then it seems they are not conscious of such painstaking; it remains, therefore, to be the business of their childhood. And surely the great and multiplied labor of framing abstract notions will be found a hard task at that tender age. Is it not a hard thing to imagine that a couple of children cannot prate together of their sugar-plums and rattles, and the rest of their little trinkets, till they have first tacked together numberless inconsistencies, and so formed in their minds abstract general ideas, and annexed them to every common name they make use of?

In his private note-book Berkeley has the *following*—

Mem. To bring the killing blow at the last, e.g. in the matter of abstraction to bring Locke's general triangle in the last.

There was certainly an opportunity for a splendid blow here, and he gave it.

From this nominalism he deduces his idealistic doctrine. And he puts it beyond any doubt that, if this principle be admitted, the existence of matter must be denied. Nothing that we can know or even think can exist without the mind, for we can only think reproductions of sensations, and the *esse* of these is *percipi*. To put it another way, we cannot think of a thing as existing unperceived, for we cannot separate in thought what cannot be separated in perception. It is true, I can think of a tree in a park without anybody by to see it; but I cannot think of it without anybody to imagine it; for I am aware that I am imagining it all the time. Syllogistically: trees, mountains, rivers, and all sensible things are perceived; and anything which is perceived is a sensation; now for a sensation to exist without being perceived is impossible; therefore, for any sensible thing to exist out of perception is impossible. Nor can there be anything out of the mind which *resembles* a sensible object, for the conception of likeness cannot be separated from likeness between ideas, because that is the only likeness which can be given in perception. An idea can be nothing but an idea, and it is absurd to say that anything inaudible can resemble a sound, or that anything invisible can resemble a color. But what exists without the mind can neither be heard nor seen; for we perceive only sensations within the mind. It is said that *Matter* exists without the mind. But what is meant by matter? It is acknowledged to be known only as *supporting* the accidents of bodies; and this word 'supporting' in this connection is a word without meaning. Nor is there any necessity for the hypothesis of external bodies. What we observe is that we have ideas. Were there any use in supposing external things it would be to account for this fact. But grant that bodies exist, and no one can say how they can possibly affect the mind; so that instead of removing a difficulty, the hypothesis only makes a new one.

But though Berkeley thinks we know nothing out of the mind, he by no means holds that all our experience is of a merely phantasmagoric character. It is not all a dream; for there are two things which distinguish experience from imagination: one is the superior vividness of experience; the other and most important is its connected character. Its parts hang together in the most intimate and intricate conjunction, in consequence of which we can infer the future from the past. "These two things it is," says Berkeley, in effect, "which constitute reality. I do not, therefore, deny the reality of common experience, although I deny its externality." Here we seem to have a third new conception of reality, different from either of those which we have insisted are characteristic of the nominalist and realist respectively, or if this is to be identified with either of those, it is with the realist view. Is not this something quite unexpected from so extreme a nominalist? To us, at least, it seems that this conception is indeed required to give an air of common sense to Berkeley's theory, but that it is of a totally different complexion from the rest. It seems to be something imported into his philosophy from without. We shall glance at this point again presently. He goes on to say that ideas are perfectly inert and passive. One idea does not make another and there is no power or agency in it. Hence, as there must be some cause of the succession of ideas, it must be *Spirit*. There is no *idea* of a spirit. But I have a consciousness of the operations of my spirit, what he calls a *notion* of my activity in calling up ideas at pleasure, and so have a relative knowledge of myself as an active being. But there is a succession of ideas not dependent on my will, the ideas of perception. Real things do not depend on my thought, but have an existence distinct from being perceived by me; but the *esse* of everything is *percipi*; therefore, *there must be some other mind wherein they exist.* "As sure, therefore, as the sensible world really exists, so sure do there an infinite omnipotent Spirit who contains and supports it." This puts the keystone into the arch of Berkeleyan idealism, and gives a theory of the relation of the mind to external nature which, compared with the Cartesian Divine Assistance, is very satisfactory. It has been well remarked that, if the Cartesian dualism be admitted, no divine *assistance* can enable things to affect the mind or the mind things, but divine power must do the whole work. Berkeley's philosophy, like so many others, has partly originated in an attempt to escape the inconveniences of the Cartesian dualism. God, who has created our spirits, has the power immediately to raise ideas in them; and out of his wisdom and benevolence, he does this with such regularity that these ideas may serve as signs of one another. Hence, the laws of nature. Berkeley does not explain how our wills act on our bodies, but perhaps he would say that to a certain limited extent we can produce ideas in the mind of God as he does in ours. But a material thing being only an idea, exists only so long as it is in some mind. Should every mind cease to think it for a while, for so long it ceases to exist. Its permanent existence is kept up by its being an idea in the mind of God. Here we see how superficially the just-mentioned theory of reality is laid over the body of his thought. If the reality of a thing consists in its harmony with the body of realities, it is a quite needless extravagance to say that it ceases to exist as soon as it is no longer thought of. For the coherence of an idea with experience in general does not depend at all upon its being actually present to the mind all the time. But it is clear that when Berkeley says that reality consists in the connection of experience, he is simply using the word *reality* in a sense of his own. That *an object's independence of our thought about it* is constituted by its connection with experience in general, he has never conceived. On the contrary, that, according to him, is effected by its being in the mind of God. In the usual sense of the word *reality*, therefore, Berkeley's doctrine is that the reality of sensible things resides only in their archetypes in the divine mind. This is Platonistic, but it is not realistic. On the contrary, since it places reality wholly out of the mind in the cause of sensations, and since it denies reality (in the true sense of the word) to sensible things in so far as they are sensible, it is distinctly nominalistic. Historically there have been prominent examples of an alliance between nominalism and Platonism. Abélard and John of Salisbury, the only two defenders of nominalism of the time of the great controversy whose works remain to us, are both Platonists; and Roscellin, the famous author of the *sententia de flatu vocis*, the first man in the Middle Ages who carried attention to nominalism, is said and believed (all his writings are lost) to have been a follower of Scotus Erigena, the great Platonist of the ninth century. The reason of this odd conjunction of doctrines may perhaps be guessed at. The nominalist, by isolating his reality so entirely from mental influence as he has done, has made it something which the mind cannot conceive; he has created the so often talked of "improportion between the mind and the thing in itself." And it is to overcome the various difficulties to which this gives rise, that he supposes this *noumenon*, which, being totally unknown, the imagination can play about as it pleases, to be the emanation of archetypal ideas. The reality thus receives an intelligible nature again, and the peculiar inconveniences of nominalism are to some degree avoided.

It does not seem to us strange that Berkeley's idealistic writings have not been received with much favor. They contain a great deal of argumentation of doubtful soundness, the dazzling character of which puts us more on our guard against it. They appear to be the productions of a most brilliant, original, powerful, but not thoroughly disciplined mind. He is apt to set out with wildly radical propositions, which he qualifies when they lead him to consequences he is not prepared to accept, without seeing how great the importance of his admissions is. He plainly begins his principles of human knowledge with the assumption that we have nothing in our minds but sensations, external and internal, and reproductions of them in the imagination. This goes far beyond Locke; it can be maintained only by the help of that "mental chemistry" started by Hartley. But soon we find him admitting various *notions* which are not *ideas*, or reproductions of sensations, the most striking of which is the notion of a cause, which he leaves himself no way of accounting for experientially. Again, he lays down the principle that we can have no ideas in which the sensations are reproduced in an order or combination different from what could have occurred in experience; and that therefore we have no abstract conceptions. But he very soon grants that we can consider a triangle, without attending to whether it is equilateral, isosceles, or scalene; and does not reflect that such exclusive attention constitutes a species of abstraction. His want of profound study is also shown in his so wholly mistaking, as he does, the function of the hypothesis of matter. He thinks its only purpose is to account for the production of ideas in our minds, so occupied is he with the Cartesian problem. But the real part that material substance has to play is to account for (or formulate) the constant connection between the accidents. In his theory, this office is performed by the wisdom and benevolence of God in exciting ideas with such regularity that we can know what to expect. This makes the unity of accidents a rational unity, the material theory makes it a unity not of a *directly* intellectual origin. The question is, then, which does experience, which does science decide for? Does it appear that in nature all regularities are directly rational, all causes final causes; or does it appear that regularities extend beyond the requirement of a rational purpose, and are brought about by mechanical causes? Now science, as we all know, is generally hostile to the final causes, the operation of which it would restrict within certain spheres, and it finds decidedly an other than directly intellectual regularity in the universe. Accordingly the claim which Mr. Collyns Simon, Professor Fraser, and Mr. Archer Butler make for Berkeleyanism, that it is especially fit to harmonize with scientific thought, is as far as possible from the truth. The sort of science that his idealism would foster would be one which should consist in saying what each natural production was made for. Berkeley's own remarks about natural philosophy show how little he sympathized with physicists. They should all be read; we have only room to quote a detached sentence or two—

> To endeavor to explain the production of colors or sound by figure, motion, magnitude, and the like, must needs be labor in vain. . . . In the business of gravitation or mutual attraction, because it appears in many instances, some are straightway for pronouncing it *universal*; and that to attract and be attracted by every body is an essential quality inherent in all bodies whatever. . . . There is nothing necessary or essential in the case, but it depends entirely on the will of the Governing Spirit, who causes certain bodies to cleave together or tend towards each other according to various laws, whilst he keeps others at a fixed distance; and to some he gives a quite contrary tendency, to fly asunder just as he sees convenient. . . . First, it is plain philosophers amuse themselves in vain, when they inquire for any natural efficient cause, distinct from *mind* or *spirit*. Secondly, considering the whole creation is the workmanship of a *wise and good Agent*, it should seem to become philosophers to employ their thoughts (contrary to what some hold) about the final causes of things; and I must confess I see no reason why pointing out the various ends to which natural things are adapted, and for which they were originally with unspeakable wisdom contrived, should not be thought one good way of accounting for them, and altogether worthy of a philosopher. (Vol. I, p. 466)

After this how can his disciples say *"that the true logic of physics is the first conclusion from his system!"*

As for that argument which is so much used by Berkeley and others, that such and such a thing cannot exist because we cannot so much as frame the idea of such a thing—that matter, for example, is impossible because it is an abstract idea, and we have no abstract ideas—it appears to us to be a mode of reasoning which is to be used with extreme caution.

Are the facts such, that if we could have an idea of the thing in question, we should infer its existence, or are they not? If not, no argument is necessary against its existence, until something is found out to make us suspect it exists. But if we ought to infer that it exists, if we only could frame the idea of it, why should we allow our mental incapacity to prevent us from adopting the proposition which logic requires? If such arguments had prevailed in mathematics (and Berkeley was equally strenuous in advocating them there), and if everything about negative quantities, the square root of *minus*, and infinitesimals, had been excluded from the subject on the ground that we can form no idea of such things, the science would have been simplified no doubt, simplified by never advancing to the more difficult matters. A better rule for avoiding the deceits of language is this: Do things fulfil the same function practically? Then let them be signified by the same word. Do they not? Then let them be distinguished. If I have learned a formula in gibberish which in any way jogs my memory so as to enable me in each single case to act as though I had a general idea, what possible utility is there in distinguishing between such a gibberish and formula and an idea? Why use the term a *general idea* in such a sense as to separate things which, for all experiential purposes, are the same?

The great inconsistency of the Berkeleyan theory, which prevents his nominalistic principles from appearing in their true colors, is that he has not treated mind and matter in the same way. All that he has said against the existence of matter might be said against the existence of mind; and the only thing which prevented his seeing that, was the vagueness of the Lockian *reflection*, or faculty of internal perception. It was not until after he had published his systematic exposition of his doctrine, that this objection ever occurred to him. He alludes to it in one of his dialogues, but his answer to it is very lame. Hume seized upon this point, and, developing it, equally denied the existence of mind and matter, maintaining that only appearances exist. Hume's philosophy is nothing but Berkeley's, with this change made in it, and written by a mind of a more sceptical tendency. The innocent bishop generated Hume; and as no one disputes that Hume gave rise to all modern philosophy of every kind, Berkeley ought to have a far more important place in the history of philosophy than has usually been assigned to him. His doctrine was the half-way station, or necessary resting-place between Locke's and Hume's.

Hume's greatness consists in the fact that he was the man who had the courage to carry out his principles to their utmost consequences, without regard to the character of the conclusions he reached. But neither he nor any other one has set forth nominalism in an absolutely thoroughgoing manner; and it is safe to say that no one ever will, unless it be to reduce it to absurdity.

We ought to say one word about Berkeley's theory of vision. It was undoubtedly an extraordinary piece of reasoning, and might have served for the basis of the modern science. Historically it has not had that fortune, because the modern science has been chiefly created in Germany, where Berkeley is little known and greatly misunderstood. We may fairly say that Berkeley taught the English some of the most essential principles of that hypothesis of sight which is now getting to prevail, more than a century before they were known to the rest of the world. This is much; but what is claimed by some of his advocates is astounding. One writer says that Berkeley's theory has been accepted by the leaders of all schools of thought! Professor Fraser admits that it has attracted no attention in Germany, but thinks the German mind too *a priori* to like Berkeley's reasoning. But Helmholtz, who has done more than any other man to bring the empiricist theory into favor, says: "Our knowledge of the phenomena of vision is not so complete as to allow only one theory and exclude every other. It seems to me that the choice which different *savans* make between different theories of vision has thus far been governed more by their metaphysical inclinations than by any constraining power which the facts have had." The best authorities, however, prefer the empiricist hypothesis; the fundamental proposition of which, as it is of Berkeley's, is that the sensations which we have in seeing are signs of the relations of things whose interpretation has to be discovered inductively. In the enumeration of the signs and of their uses, Berkeley shows considerable power in that sort of investigation, though there is naturally no very close resemblance between his and the modern accounts of the matter. There is no modern physiologist who would not think that Berkeley had greatly exaggerated the part that the muscular sense plays in vision.

Berkeley's theory of vision was an important step in the development of the associationalist psychology. He thought all our conceptions of body and of space were simply reproductions in the imagination of sensations of touch (including the muscular sense). This, if it were true, would be a most surprising case of mental chemistry, that is of a sensation being felt and yet so mixed with others that we cannot by an act of simple attention recognize it. Doubtless this theory had its influence in the production of Hartley's system.

Hume's phenomenalism and Hartley's associationalism were put forth almost contemporaneously about 1750. They contain the fundamental positions of the current English "positivism." From 1750 down to 1830—eighty years—nothing of particular importance was added to the nominalistic doctrine. At the beginning of this period Hume's was toning down his earlier radicalism, and Smith's theory of Moral Sentiments appeared. Later came Priestley's materialism, but there was nothing new in that; and just at the end of the period, Brown's *Lectures on the Human Mind*. The great body of the philosophy of those eighty years is of the Scotch common-sense school. It is a weak sort of realistic reaction, for which there is no adequate explanation within the sphere of the history of philosophy. It would be curious to inquire whether anything in the history of society could account for it. In 1829 appeared James Mill's *Analysis of the Human Mind*, a really great nominalistic book again. This was followed by Stuart Mill's *Logic* in 1843. Since then, the school has produced nothing of the first importance; and it will very likely lose its distinctive character now for a time, by being merged in an empiricism of a less metaphysical and more working kind. Already in Stuart Mill the nominalism is less salient than in the classical writers; though it is quite unmistakable.

Thus we see how large a part of the metaphysical ideas of to-day have come to us by inheritance from very early times, Berkeley being one of the intellectual ancestors whose labors did as much as any one's to enhance the value of the bequest. The realistic philosophy of the last century has now lost all its popularity, except with the most conservative minds. And science as well as philosophy is nominalistic. The doctrine of the correlation of forces, the discoveries of Helmholtz, and the hypotheses of Liebig and of Darwin, have all that character of explaining familiar phenomena apparently of a peculiar kind by extending the operation of simple mechanical principles, which belongs to nominalism. Or if the nominalistic character of these doctrines themselves cannot be detected, it will at least be admitted that they are observed to carry along with them those daughters of nominalism— sensationalism, phenomenalism, individualism, and materialism. That physical science is necessarily connected with doctrines of a debasing moral tendency will be believed by few. But if we hold that such an effect will not be produced by these doctrines on a mind which really understands them, we are accepting this belief, not on experience, which is rather against it, but on the strength of our general faith that what is really true it is good to believe and evil to reject. On the other hand, it is allowable to suppose that science has no essential affinity with the philosophical views with which it seems to be every year more associated. History cannot be held to exclude this supposition; and science as it exists is certainly much less nominalistic than the nominalists think it should be. Whewell represents it quite as well as Mill. Yet a man who enters into the scientific thought of the day and has not materialistic tendencies, is getting to be an impossibility. So long as there is a dispute between nominalism and realism, so long as the position we hold on the question is not determined by any proof *indisputable*, but is more or less a matter of inclination, a man as he gradually comes to feel the profound hostility of the two tendencies will, if he is not less than man, become engaged with one or other and can no more obey both than he can serve God and Mammon. If the two impulses are neutralized within him, the result simply is that he is left without any great intellectual motive. There is, indeed, no reason to suppose the logical question is in its own nature unsusceptible of solution. But that path out of the difficulty lies through the thorniest mazes of a science as dry as mathematics. Now there is a demand for mathematics; it helps to build bridges and drive engines, and therefore it becomes somebody's business to study it severely. But to have a philosophy is a matter of luxury; the only use of that is to make us feel comfortable and easy. It is a study for leisure hours; and we want it supplied in an elegant, an agreeable, an interesting form. The law of natural selection, which is the precise analogue in another realm of the law of supply and demand, has the most immediate effect in fostering the other faculties of the understanding, for the men of mental power succeed in the struggle for life; but the faculty of philosophizing, except in the literary way, is not called for; and therefore a difficult question cannot be expected to reach solution until it takes some practical form. If anybody should have the good luck to find out the solution, nobody else would take the trouble to understand it. But though the question of realism and nominalism has its roots in the technicalities of logic, its branches reach about our life. The question whether the *genus homo* has any existence except as individuals, is the question whether there is anything of any more dignity, worth, and importance than individual happiness, individual aspirations, and individual life. Whether men really have anything in common, so that the *community* is to be considered as an end in itself, and if so, what the relative value of the two factors is, is the most fundamental practical question in regard to every public institution the constitution of which we have it in our power to influence.

NOTES

1. Died 1308.

2. The *entia non sunt multiplicanda praeter necessitatem* is the argument of Durand de St. Pourcain. But any given piece of popular information about scholasticism may be safely assumed to be wrong.

3. The sole difference between Ockam and Hobbes is that the former admits the universal signs in the mind to be natural, while the latter thinks they only follow instituted language. The consequence of this difference is that, while Ockam regards all truth as depending on the mind's naturally imposing the same sign on two things, Hobbes will have it that the first truths were established by convention. But both would doubtless allow that there is something *in re* to which such truths corresponded. But the sense of Berkeley's implication would be that there are no universal thought-signs at all. Whence it would follow that there is no truth and no judgments but propositions spoken or on paper.

Mr. Peirce and the Realists

The Nation 13 (14 December 1871): 386.

Response to Chauncey Wright, Charles Peirce's Berkeley Review (November 1871).

TO THE EDITOR OF THE NATION:

Sir: In your far too flattering notice of my remarks upon mediaeval realism and nominalism, you have attributed to me a degree of originality which is not my due. The common view that realism is a modified Platonism has already been condemned by the most thorough students, such as Prantl and Morin. The realists certainly held (as I have said) that universals really exist in external things. The only feature of the controversy which has appeared to me to need more emphasis than has hitherto been put upon it is that each party had its own peculiar ideas of what it is that is real, the realists assuming that reality belongs to what is present to us in true knowledge of any sort, the nominalists assuming that the absolutely external causes of perception are the only realities. This point of disagreement was never argued out, for the reason that the mental horizon of each party was too limited for it to comprehend what the conception of the other side was. It is a similar narrowness of thought which makes it so hard for many persons to understand one side or the other, at this day.

—Washington, D.C., Dec. 10, 1871.

The Fixation of Belief

Popular Science Monthly 12.11 (November 1877): 1–15.

I.

Few persons care to study logic, because everybody conceives himself to be proficient enough in the art of reasoning already. But I observe that this satisfaction is limited to one's own ratiocination, and does not extend to that of other men.

We come to the full possession of our power of drawing inferences the last of all our faculties, for it is not so much a natural gift as a long and difficult art. The history of its practice would make a grand subject for a book. The mediaeval schoolmen, following the Romans, made logic the earliest of a boy's studies after grammar, as being very easy. So it was, as they understood it. Its fundamental principle, according to them, was, that all knowledge rests on either authority or reason; but that whatever is deduced by reason depends ultimately on a premise derived from authority. Accordingly, as soon as a boy was perfect in the syllogistic procedure, his intellectual kit of tools was held to be complete.

To Roger Bacon, that remarkable mind who in the middle of the thirteenth century was almost a scientific man, the schoolmen's conception of reasoning appeared only an obstacle to truth. He saw that experience alone teaches anything—a proposition which to us seems easy to understand, because a distinct conception of experience has been handed down to us from former generations; which to him also seemed perfectly clear, because its difficulties had not yet unfolded themselves. Of all kinds of experience, the best, he thought, was interior illumination, which teaches many things about Nature which the external senses could never discover, such as the transubstantiation of bread.

Four centuries later, the more celebrated Bacon, in the first book of his *Novum Organum*, gave his clear account of experience as something which must be open to verification and reexamination. But, superior as Lord Bacon's conception is to earlier notions, a modern reader who is not in awe of his grandiloquence is chiefly struck by the inadequacy of his view of scientific procedure. That we have only to make some crude experiments, to draw up briefs of the results in certain blank forms, to go through these by rule, checking off everything disproved and setting down the alternatives, and that thus in a few years physical science would be finished up—what an idea! "He wrote on science like a Lord Chancellor," indeed.

The early scientists, Copernicus, Tycho Brahe, Kepler, Galileo, and Gilbert, had methods more like those of their modern brethren. Kepler undertook to draw a curve through the places of Mars;[1] and his greatest service to science was in impressing on men's minds that this was the thing to be done if they wished to improve astronomy; that they were not to content themselves with inquiring whether one system of epicycles was better than another, but that they were to sit down to the figures and find out what the curve, in truth, was. He accomplished this by his incomparable energy and courage, blundering along in the most inconceivable way (to us), from one irrational hypothesis to another, until, after trying twenty-two of these, he fell, by the mere exhaustion of his invention, upon the orbit which a mind well furnished with the weapons of modern logic would have tried almost at the outset.

In the same way, every work of science great enough to be well remembered for a few generations affords some exemplification of the defective state of the art of reasoning of the time when it was written; and each chief step in science has been a lesson in logic. It was so when Lavoisier and his contemporaries took up the study of chemistry. The old chemist's maxim had been, "*Lege, lege, lege, labora, ora, et relege.*" Lavoisier's method was not to read and pray, not to dream that some long and complicated chemical process would have a certain effect, to put it into practice with dull patience, after its inevitable failure to dream that with some modification it would have another result, and to end by publishing the last dream as a fact: his way was to carry his mind into his laboratory, and to make of his alembics and cucurbits instruments of thought, giving a new conception of reasoning, as something which was to be done with one's eyes open, by manipulating real things instead of words and fancies.

The Darwinian controversy is, in large part, a question of logic. Mr. Darwin proposed to apply the statistical method to biology. The same thing had been done in a widely different branch of science, the theory of gases. Though unable to say what the movements of any particular molecule of gas would be on a certain hypothesis regarding the constitution of this class of bodies, Clausius and Maxwell were yet able, by the application of the doctrine of probabilities, to predict that in the long run such and such a proportion of the molecules would, under given circumstances, acquire such and such velocities; that there would take place, every second, such and such a number of collisions, etc.; and from these propositions were able to deduce certain properties of gases, especially in regard to their heat-relations. In like manner, Darwin, while unable to say what the operation of variation and natural selection in any individual case will be, demonstrates that in the long run they will adapt animals to their circumstances. Whether or not existing animal forms are due to such action, or what position the theory ought to take, forms the subject of a discussion in which questions of fact and questions of logic are curiously interlaced.

II.

The object of reasoning is to find out, from the consideration of what we already know, something else which we do not know. Consequently, reasoning is good if it be such as to give a true conclusion from true premises, and not otherwise. Thus, the question of its validity is purely one of fact and not of thinking. A being the premises and B the conclusion, the question is, whether these facts are really so related that if A is B is. If so, the inference is valid; if not, not. It is not in the least the question whether, when the premises are accepted by the mind, we feel an impulse to accept the conclusion also. It is true that we do generally reason correctly by nature. But that is an accident; the true conclusion would remain true if we had no impulse to accept it; and the false one would remain false, though we could not resist the tendency to believe in it.

We are, doubtless, in the main logical animals, but we are not perfectly so. Most of us, for example, are naturally more sanguine and hopeful than logic would justify. We seem to be so constituted that in the absence of any facts to go upon we are happy and self-satisfied; so that the effect of experience is continually to contract our hopes and aspirations. Yet a lifetime of the application of this corrective does not usually eradicate our sanguine disposition. Where hope is unchecked by any experience, it is likely that our optimism is extravagant. Logicality in regard to practical matters is the most useful quality an animal can possess, and might, therefore, result from the action of natural selection; but outside of these it is probably of more advantage to the animal to have his mind filled with pleasing and encouraging visions, independently of their truth; and thus, upon unpractical subjects, natural selection might occasion a fallacious tendency of thought.

That which determines us, from given premises, to draw one inference rather than another, is some habit of mind, whether it be constitutional or acquired. The habit is good or otherwise, according as it produces true conclusions from true premises or not; and an inference is regarded as valid or not, without reference to the truth or falsity of its conclusion specially, but according as the habit which determines it is such as to produce true conclusions in general or not. The particular habit of mind which governs this or that inference may be formulated in a proposition whose truth depends on the validity of the inferences which the habit determines; and such a formula is called a *guiding principle* of inference. Suppose, for example, that we observe that a rotating disk of copper quickly comes to rest when placed between the poles of a magnet, and we infer that this will happen with every disk of copper. The guiding principle is, that what is true of one piece of copper is true of another. Such a guiding principle with regard to copper would be much safer than with regard to many other substances—brass, for example.

A book might be written to signalize all the most important of these guiding principles of reasoning. It would probably be, we must confess, of no service to a person whose thought is directed wholly to practical subjects, and whose activity moves along thoroughly-beaten paths. The problems which present themselves to such a mind are matters of routine which he has learned once for all to handle in learning his business. But let a man venture into an unfamiliar field, or where his results are not continually checked by experience, and all history shows that the most masculine intellect will ofttimes lose his orientation and waste his efforts in directions which bring him no nearer to his goal, or even carry him entirely astray. He is like a ship in the open sea, with no one on board who understands the rules of navigation. And in such a case some general study of the guiding principles of reasoning would be sure to be found useful.

The subject could hardly be treated, however, without being first limited; since almost any fact may serve as a guiding principle. But it so happens that there exists a division among facts, such that in one class are all those which are absolutely essential as guiding principles, while in the others are all which have any other interest as objects of research. This division is between those which are necessarily taken for granted in asking whether a certain conclusion follows from certain premises, and those which are not implied in that question. A moment's thought will show that a variety of facts are already assumed when the logical question is first asked. It is implied, for instance, that there are such states of mind as doubt and belief—that a passage from one to the other is possible, the object of thought remaining the same, and that this transition is subject to some rules which all minds are alike bound by. As these are facts which we must already know before we can have any clear conception of reasoning at all, it cannot be supposed to be any longer of much interest to inquire into their truth or falsity. On the other hand, it is easy to believe that those rules of reasoning which are deduced from the very idea of the process are the ones which are the most essential; and, indeed, that so long as it conforms to these it will, at least, not lead to false conclusions from true premises. In point of fact, the importance of what may be deduced from the assumptions involved in the logical question turns out to be greater than might be supposed, and this for reasons which it is difficult to exhibit at the outset. The only one which I shall here mention is, that conceptions which are really products of logical reflection, without being readily seen to be so, mingle with our ordinary thoughts, and are frequently the causes of great confusion. This is the case, for example, with the conception of quality. A quality as such is never an object of observation. We can see that a thing is blue or green, but the quality of being blue and the quality of being green are not things which we see; they are products of logical reflection. The truth is, that common-sense, or thought as it first emerges above the level of the narrowly practical, is deeply imbued with that bad logical quality to which the epithet *metaphysical* is commonly applied; and nothing can clear it up but a severe course of logic.

III.

We generally know when we wish to ask a question and when we wish to pronounce a judgment, for there is a dissimilarity between the sensation of doubting and that of believing.

But this is not all which distinguishes doubt from belief. There is a practical difference. Our beliefs guide our desires and shape our actions. The Assassins, or followers of the Old Man of the Mountain, used to rush into death at his least command, because they believed that obedience to him would insure everlasting felicity. Had they doubted this, they would not have acted as they did. So it is with every belief, according to its degree. The feeling of believing is a more or less sure indication of there being established in our nature some habit which will determine our actions. Doubt never has such an effect.

Nor must we overlook a third point of difference. Doubt is an uneasy and dissatisfied state from which we struggle to free ourselves and pass into the state of belief; while the latter is a calm and satisfactory state which we do not wish to avoid, or to change to a belief in anything else.[2] On the contrary, we cling tenaciously, not merely to believing, but to believing just what we do believe.

Thus, both doubt and belief have positive effects upon us, though very different ones. Belief does not make us act at once, but puts us into such a condition that we shall behave in some certain way, when the occasion arises. Doubt has not the least effect of this sort, but stimulates us to action until it is destroyed. This reminds us of the irritation of a nerve and the reflex action produced thereby; while for the analogue of belief, in the nervous system, we must look to what are called nervous associations—for example, to that habit of the nerves in consequence of which the smell of a peach will make the mouth water.

IV.

The irritation of doubt causes a struggle to attain a state of belief. I shall term this struggle *inquiry*, though it must be admitted that this is sometimes not a very apt designation.

The irritation of doubt is the only immediate motive for the struggle to attain belief. It is certainly best for us that our beliefs should be such as may truly guide our actions so as to satisfy our desires; and this reflection will make us reject any belief which does not seem to have been so formed as to insure this result. But it will only do so by creating a doubt in the place of that belief. With the doubt, therefore, the struggle begins, and with the cessation of doubt it ends. Hence, the sole object of inquiry is the settlement of opinion. We may fancy that this is not enough for us, and that we seek, not merely an opinion, but a true opinion. But put this fancy to the test, and it proves groundless; for as soon as a firm belief is reached we are entirely satisfied, whether the belief be true or false. And it is clear that nothing out of the sphere of our knowledge can be our object, for nothing which does not affect the mind can be the motive for a mental effort. The most that can be maintained is, that we seek for a belief that we shall *think* to be true. But we think each one of our beliefs to be true, and, indeed, it is mere tautology to say so.

That the settlement of opinion is the sole end of inquiry is a very important proposition. It sweeps away, at once, various vague and erroneous conceptions of proof. A few of these may be noticed here.

1. Some philosophers have imagined that to start an inquiry it was only necessary to utter a question or set it down upon paper, and have even recommended us to begin our studies with questioning everything! But the mere putting of a proposition into the interrogative form does not stimulate the mind to any struggle after belief. There must be a real and living doubt, and without this all discussion is idle.

2. It is a very common idea that a demonstration must rest on some ultimate and absolutely indubitable propositions. These, according to one school, are first principles of a general nature; according to another, are first sensations. But, in point of fact, an inquiry, to have that completely satisfactory result called demonstration, has only to start with propositions perfectly free from all actual doubt. If the premises are not in fact doubted at all, they cannot be more satisfactory than they are.

3. Some people seem to love to argue a point after all the world is fully convinced of it. But no further advance can be made. When doubt ceases, mental action on the subject comes to an end; and, if it did go on, it would be without a purpose.

V.

If the settlement of opinion is the sole object of inquiry, and if belief is of the nature of a habit, why should we not attain the desired end, by taking any answer to a question which we may fancy, and constantly reiterating it to ourselves, dwelling on all which may conduce to that belief, and learning to turn with contempt and hatred from anything which might disturb it? This simple and direct method is really pursued by many men. I remember once being entreated not to read a certain newspaper lest it might change my opinion upon free-trade. "Lest I might be entrapped by its fallacies and misstatements," was the form of expression. "You are not," my friend said, "a special student of political economy. You might, therefore, easily be deceived by fallacious arguments upon the subject. You might, then, if you read this paper, be led to believe in protection. But you admit that free-trade is the true doctrine; and you do not wish to believe what is not true." I have often known this system to be deliberately adopted. Still oftener, the instinctive dislike of an undecided state of mind, exaggerated into a vague dread of doubt, makes men cling spasmodically to the views they already take. The man feels that, if he only holds to his belief without wavering, it will be entirely satisfactory. Nor can it be denied that a steady and immovable faith yields great peace of mind. It may, indeed, give rise to inconveniences, as if a man should resolutely continue to believe that fire would not burn him, or that he would be eternally damned if he received his *ingesta* otherwise than through a stomach-pump. But then the man who adopts this method will not allow that its inconveniences are greater than its advantages. He will say, "I hold steadfastly to the truth, and the truth is always wholesome." And in many cases it may very well be that the pleasure he derives from his calm faith overbalances any inconveniences resulting from its deceptive character. Thus, if it be true that death is annihilation, then the man who believes that he will certainly go straight to heaven when he dies, provided he have fulfilled certain simple observances in this life, has a cheap pleasure which will not be followed by the least disappointment. A similar consideration seems to have weight with many persons in religious topics, for we frequently hear it said, "Oh, I could not believe so-and-so, because I should be wretched if I did." When an ostrich buries its head in the sand as danger approaches, it very likely takes the happiest course. It hides the danger, and then calmly says there is no danger; and, if it feels perfectly sure there is none, why should it raise its head to see? A man may go through life, systematically keeping out of view all that might cause a change in his opinions, and if he only succeeds—basing his method, as he does, on two fundamental psychological laws—I do not see what can be said against his doing so. It would be an egotistical impertinence to object that his procedure is irrational, for that only amounts to saying that his method of settling belief is not ours. He does not propose to himself to be rational, and, indeed, will often talk with scorn of man's weak and illusive reason. So let him think as he pleases.

But this method of fixing belief, which may be called the method of tenacity, will be unable to hold its ground in practice. The social impulse is against it. The man who adopts it will find that other men think differently from him, and it will be apt to occur to him, in some saner moment, that their opinions are quite as good as his own, and this will shake his confidence in his belief. This conception, that another man's thought or sentiment may be equivalent to one's own, is a distinctly new step, and a highly important one. It arises from an impulse too strong in man to be suppressed, without danger of destroying the human species. Unless we make ourselves hermits, we shall necessarily influence each other's opinions; so that the problem becomes how to fix belief, not in the individual merely, but in the community.

Let the will of the state act, then, instead of that of the individual. Let an institution be created which shall have for its object to keep correct doctrines before the attention of the people, to reiterate them perpetually, and to teach them to the young; having at the same time power to prevent contrary doctrines from being taught, advocated, or expressed. Let all possible causes of a change of mind be removed from men's apprehensions. Let them be kept ignorant, lest they should learn of some reason to think otherwise than they do. Let their passions be enlisted, so that they may regard private and unusual opinions with hatred and horror. Then, let all men who reject the established belief be terrified into silence. Let the people turn out and tar-and-feather such men, or let inquisitions be made into the manner of thinking of suspected persons, and when they are found guilty of forbidden beliefs, let them be subjected to some signal punishment. When complete agreement could not otherwise be reached, a general massacre of all who have not thought in a certain way has proved a very effective means of settling opinion in a country. If the power to do this be wanting, let a list of opinions be drawn up, to which no man of the least independence of thought can assent, and let the faithful be required to accept all these propositions, in order to segregate them as radically as possible from the influence of the rest of the world.

This method has, from the earliest times, been one of the chief means of upholding correct theological and political doctrines, and of preserving their universal or catholic character. In Rome, especially, it has been practised from the days of Numa Pompilius to those of Pius Nonus. This is the most perfect example in history; but wherever there is a priesthood—and no religion has been without one—this method has been more or less made use of. Wherever there is an aristocracy, or a guild, or any association of a class of men whose interests depend or are supposed to depend on certain propositions, there will be inevitably found some traces of this natural product of social feeling. Cruelties always accompany this system; and when it is consistently carried out, they become atrocities of the most horrible kind in the eyes of any rational man. Nor should this occasion surprise, for the officer of a society does not feel justified in surrendering the interests of that society for the sake of mercy, as he might his own private interests. It is natural, therefore, that sympathy and fellowship should thus produce a most ruthless power.

In judging this method of fixing belief, which may be called the method of authority, we must, in the first place, allow its immeasurable mental and moral superiority to the method of tenacity. Its success is proportionately greater; and, in fact, it has over and over again worked the most majestic results. The mere structures of stone which it has caused to be put together—in Siam, for example, in Egypt, and in Europe—have many of them a sublimity hardly more than rivaled by the greatest works of Nature. And, except the geological epochs, there are no periods of time so vast as those which are measured by some of these organized faiths. If we scrutinize the matter closely, we shall find that there has not been one of their creeds which has remained always the same; yet the change is so slow as to be imperceptible during one person's life, so that individual belief remains sensibly fixed. For the mass of mankind, then, there is perhaps no better method than this. If it is their highest impulse to be intellectual slaves, then slaves they ought to remain.

But no institution can undertake to regulate opinions upon every subject. Only the most important ones can be attended to, and on the rest men's minds must be left to the action of natural causes. This imperfection will be no source of weakness so long as men are in such a state of culture that one opinion does not influence another—that is, so long as they cannot put two and two together. But in the most priestridden states some individuals will be found who are raised above that condition. These men possess a wider sort of social feeling; they see that men in other countries and in other ages have held to very different doctrines from those which they themselves have been brought up to believe; and they cannot help seeing that it is the mere accident of their having been taught as they have, and of their having been surrounded with the manners and associations they have, that has caused them to believe as they do and not far differently. And their candor cannot resist the reflection that there is no reason to rate their own views at a higher value than those of other nations and other centuries; and this gives rise to doubts in their minds.

They will further perceive that such doubts as these must exist in their minds with reference to every belief which seems to be determined by the caprice either of themselves or of those who originated the popular opinions. The willful adherence to a belief, and the arbitrary forcing of it upon others, must, therefore, both be given up, and a new method of settling opinions must be adopted, which shall not only produce an impulse to believe, but shall also decide what proposition it is which is to be believed. Let the action of natural preferences be unimpeded, then, and under their influence let men, conversing together and regarding matters in different lights, gradually develop beliefs in harmony with natural causes. This method resembles that by which conceptions of art have been brought to maturity. The most perfect example of it is to be found in the history of meta-physical philosophy. Systems of this sort have not usually rested upon any observed facts, at least not in any great degree. They have been chiefly adopted because their fundamental propositions seemed "agreeable to reason." This is an apt expression; it does not mean that which agrees with experience, but that which we find ourselves inclined to believe. Plato, for example, finds it agreeable to reason that the distances of the celestial spheres from one another should be proportional to the different lengths of strings which produce harmoni-ous chords. Many philosophers have been led to their main conclusions by considerations like this; but this is the lowest and least developed form which the method takes, for it is clear that another man might find Kepler's theory, that the celestial spheres are proportional to the inscribed and circumscribed spheres of the different regular solids, more agreeable to *his* reason. But the shock of opinions will soon lead men to rest on preferences of a far more universal nature. Take, for example, the doctrine that man only acts selfishly—that is, from the consideration that acting in one way will afford him more pleasure than acting in another. This rests on no fact in the world, but it has had a wide acceptance as being the only reasonable theory.

This method is far more intellectual and respectable from the point of view of reason than either of the others which we have noticed. But its failure has been the most mani-fest. It makes of inquiry something similar to the development of taste; but taste, unfor-tunately, is always more or less a matter of fashion, and accordingly metaphysicians have never come to any fixed agreement, but the pendulum has swung backward and forward between a more material and a more spiritual philosophy, from the earliest times to the latest. And so from this, which has been called the *a priori* method, we are driven, in Lord Bacon's phrase, to a true induction. We have examined into this *a priori* method as something which promised to deliver our opinions from their accidental and capricious element. But development, while it is a process which eliminates the effect of some casual circumstances, only magnifies that of others. This method, therefore, does not differ in a very essential way from that of authority. The government may not have lifted its finger to influence my convictions; I may have been left outwardly quite free to choose, we will say, between monogamy and polygamy, and, appealing to my conscience only, I may have concluded that the latter practice is in itself licentious. But when I come to see that the chief obstacle to the spread of Christianity among a people of as high culture as the Hindoos has been a conviction of the immorality of our way of treating women, I cannot help seeing that, though governments do not interfere, sentiments in their development will be very greatly determined by accidental causes. Now, there are some people, among whom I must suppose that my reader is to be found, who, when they see that any belief of theirs is determined by any circumstance extraneous to the facts, will from that moment not merely admit in words that that belief is doubtful, but will experience a real doubt of it, so that it ceases to be a belief.

To satisfy our doubts, therefore, it is necessary that a method should be found by which our beliefs may be caused by nothing human, but by some external permanency—by something upon which our thinking has no effect. Some mystics imagine that they have such a method in a private inspiration from on high. But that is only a form of the method of tenacity, in which the conception of truth as something public is not yet developed. Our external permanency would not be external, in our sense, if it was restricted in its influence to one individual. It must be something which affects, or might affect, every man. And, though these affections are necessarily as various as are individual conditions, yet the method must be such that the ultimate conclusion of every man shall be the same. Such is the method of science. Its fundamental hypothesis, restated in more familiar language, is this: There are real things, whose characters are entirely independent of our opinions about them; those realities affect our senses according to regular laws, and, though our sensations are as different as are our relations to the objects, yet, by taking advantage of the laws of perception, we can ascertain by reasoning how things really are, and any man, if he have sufficient experience and reason enough about it, will be led to the one true conclusion. The new conception here involved is that of reality. It may be asked how I know that there are any realities. If this hypothesis is the sole support of my method of inquiry, my method of inquiry must not be used to support my hypothesis. The reply is this: 1. If investigation cannot be regarded as proving that there are real things, it at least does not lead to a contrary conclusion; but the method and the conception on which it is based remain ever in harmony. No doubts of the method, therefore, necessarily arise from its practice, as is the case with all the others. 2. The feeling which gives rise to any method of fixing belief is a dissatisfaction at two repugnant propositions. But here already is a vague concession that there is some *one* thing to which a proposition should conform. Nobody, therefore, can really doubt that there are realities, or, if he did, doubt would not be a source of dissatisfaction. The hypothesis, therefore, is one which every mind admits. So that the social impulse does not cause me to doubt it. 3. Everybody uses the scientific method about a great many things, and only ceases to use it when he does not know how to apply it. 4. Experience of the method has not led me to doubt it, but, on the contrary, scientific investigation has had the most wonderful triumphs in the way of settling opinion. These afford the explanation of my not doubting the method or the hypothesis which it supposes; and not having any doubt, nor believing that anybody else whom I could influence has, it would be the merest babble for me to say more about it. If there be anybody with a living doubt upon the subject, let him consider it.

To describe the method of scientific investigation is the object of this series of papers. At present I have only room to notice some points of contrast between it and other methods of fixing belief.

This is the only one of the four methods which presents any distinction of a right and a wrong way. If I adopt the method of tenacity and shut myself out from all influences, whatever I think necessary to doing this is necessary according to that method. So with the method of authority: the state may try to put down heresy by means which, from a scientific point of view, seem very ill-calculated to accomplish its purposes; but the only test *on that method* is what the state thinks, so that it cannot pursue the method wrongly. So with the *a priori* method. The very essence of it is to think as one is inclined to think. All metaphysicians will be sure to do that, however they may be inclined to judge each other to be perversely wrong. The Hegelian system recognizes every natural tendency of thought as logical, although it be certain to be abolished by counter-tendencies. Hegel thinks there is a regular system in the succession of these tendencies, in consequence of which, after drifting one way and the other for a long time, opinion will at last go right. And it is true that metaphysicians get the right ideas at last; Hegel's system of Nature represents tolerably the science of that day; and one may be sure that whatever scientific investigation has put out of doubt will presently receive *a priori* demonstration on the part of the metaphysicians. But with the scientific method the case is different. I may start with known and observed facts to proceed to the unknown; and yet the rules which I follow in doing so may not be such as investigation would approve. The test of whether I am truly following the method is not an immediate appeal to my feelings and purposes, but, on the contrary, itself involves the application of the method. Hence it is that bad reasoning as well as good reasoning is possible; and this fact is the foundation of the practical side of logic.

It is not to be supposed that the first three methods of settling opinion present no advantage whatever over the scientific method. On the contrary, each has some peculiar convenience of its own. The *a priori* method is distinguished for its comfortable conclusions. It is the nature of the process to adopt whatever belief we are inclined to, and there are certain flatteries to the vanity of man which we all believe by nature, until we are awakened from our pleasing dream by rough facts. The method of authority will always govern the mass of mankind; and those who wield the various forms of organized force in the state will never be convinced that dangerous reasoning ought not to be suppressed in some way. If liberty of speech is to be untrammeled from the grosser forms of constraint, then uniformity of opinion will be secured by a moral terrorism to which the respectability of society will give its thorough approval. Following the method of authority is the path of peace. Certain non-conformities are permitted; certain others (considered unsafe) are forbidden. These are different in different countries and in different ages; but, wherever you are, let it be known that you seriously hold a tabooed belief, and you may be perfectly sure of being treated with a cruelty less brutal but more refined than hunting you like a wolf. Thus, the greatest intellectual benefactors of mankind have never dared, and dare not now, to utter the whole of their thought; and thus a shade of *prima facie* doubt is cast upon every proposition which is considered essential to the security of society. Singularly enough, the persecution does not all come from without; but a man torments himself and is oftentimes most distressed at finding himself believing propositions which he has been brought up to regard with aversion. The peaceful and sympathetic man will, therefore, find it hard to resist the temptation to submit his opinions to authority. But most of all I admire the method of tenacity for its strength, simplicity, and directness. Men who pursue it are distinguished for their decision of character, which becomes very easy with such a mental rule. They do not waste time in trying to make up their minds what they want, but, fastening like lightning upon whatever alternative comes first, they hold to it to the end, whatever happens, without an instant's irresolution. This is one of the splendid qualities which generally accompany brilliant, unlasting success. It is impossible not to envy the man who can dismiss reason, although we know how it must turn out at last.

Such are the advantages which the other methods of settling opinion have over scientific investigation. A man should consider well of them; and then he should consider that, after all, he wishes his opinions to coincide with the fact, and that there is no reason why the results of those three methods should do so. To bring about this effect is the prerogative of the method of science. Upon such considerations he has to make his choice—a choice which is far more than the adoption of any intellectual opinion, which is one of the ruling decisions of his life, to which, when once made, he is bound to adhere. The force of habit will sometimes cause a man to hold on to old beliefs, after he is in a condition to see that they have no sound basis. But reflection upon the state of the case will overcome these habits, and he ought to allow reflection its full weight. People sometimes shrink from doing this, having an idea that beliefs are wholesome which they cannot help feeling rest on nothing. But let such persons suppose an analogous though different case from their own. Let them ask themselves what they would say to a reformed Mussulman who should hesitate to give up his old notions in regard to the relations of the sexes; or to a reformed Catholic who should still shrink from reading the Bible. Would they not say that these persons ought to consider the matter fully, and clearly understand the new doctrine, and then ought to embrace it, in its entirety? But, above all, let it be considered that what is more wholesome than any particular belief is integrity of belief, and that to avoid looking into the support of any belief from a fear that it may turn out rotten is quite as immoral as it is disadvantageous. The person who confesses that there is such a thing as truth, which is distinguished from falsehood simply by this, that if acted on it will carry us to the point we aim at and not astray, and then, though convinced of this, dares not know the truth and seeks to avoid it, is in a sorry state of mind indeed.

Yes, the other methods do have their merits: a clear logical conscience does cost something—just as any virtue, just as all that we cherish, costs us dear. But we should not desire it to be otherwise. The genius of a man's logical method should be loved and reverenced as his bride, whom he has chosen from all the world. He need not contemn the others; on the contrary, he may honor them deeply, and in doing so he only honors her the more. But she is the one that he has chosen, and he knows that he was right in making that choice. And having made it, he will work and fight for her, and will not complain that there are blows to take, hoping that there may be as many and as hard to give, and will strive to be the worthy knight and champion of her from the blaze of whose splendors he draws his inspiration and his courage.

NOTES

---

1. Not quite so, but as nearly so as can be told in a few words.

2. I am not speaking of secondary effects occasionally produced by the interference of other impulses.

How to Make Our Ideas Clear

Popular Science Monthly 12.1 (January 1878): 286–302.

I.

Whoever has looked into a modern treatise on logic of the common sort, will doubtless remember the two distinctions between *clear* and *obscure* conceptions, and between *distinct* and *confused* conceptions. They have lain in the books now for nigh two centuries, unimproved and unmodified, and are generally reckoned by logicians as among the gems of their doctrine.

A clear idea is defined as one which is so apprehended that it will be recognized wherever it is met with, and so that no other will be mistaken for it. If it fails of this clearness, it is said to be obscure.

This is rather a neat bit of philosophical terminology; yet, since it is clearness that they were defining, I wish the logicians had made their definition a little more plain. Never to fail to recognize an idea, and under no circumstances to mistake another for it, let it come in how recondite a form it may, would indeed imply such prodigious force and clearness of intellect as is seldom met with in this world. On the other hand, merely to have such an acquaintance with the idea as to have become familiar with it, and to have lost all hesitancy in recognizing it in ordinary cases, hardly seems to deserve the name of clearness of apprehension, since after all it only amounts to a subjective feeling of mastery which may be entirely mistaken. I take it, however, that when the logicians speak of "clearness," they mean nothing more than such a familiarity with an idea, since they regard the quality as but a small merit, which needs to be supplemented by another, which they call *distinctness*.

A distinct idea is defined as one which contains nothing which is not clear. This is technical language; by the *contents* of an idea logicians understand whatever is contained in its definition. So that an idea is *distinctly* apprehended, according to them, when we can give a precise definition of it, in abstract terms. Here the professional logicians leave the subject; and I would not have troubled the reader with what they have to say, if it were not such a striking example of how they have been slumbering through ages of intellectual activity, listlessly disregarding the enginery of modern thought, and never dreaming of applying its lessons to the improvement of logic. It is easy to show that the doctrine that familiar use and abstract distinctness make the perfection of apprehension has its only true place in philosophies which have long been extinct; and it is now time to formulate the method of attaining to a more perfect clearness of thought, such as we see and admire in the thinkers of our own time.

When Descartes set about the reconstruction of philosophy, his first step was to (theoretically) permit skepticism and to discard the practice of the schoolmen of looking

to authority as the ultimate source of truth. That done, he sought a more natural fountain of true principles, and professed to find it in the human mind; thus passing, in the
directest way, from the method of authority to that of apriority, as described in my first
paper. Self-consciousness was to furnish us with our fundamental truths, and to decide
what was agreeable to reason. But since, evidently, not all ideas are true, he was led to note,
as the first condition of infallibility, that they must be clear. The distinction between an
idea *seeming* clear and really being so, never occurred to him. Trusting to introspection, as
he did, even for a knowledge of external things, why should he question its testimony in
respect to the contents of our own minds? But then, I suppose, seeing men, who seemed
to be quite clear and positive, holding opposite opinions upon fundamental principles, he
was further led to say that clearness of ideas is not sufficient, but that they need also to be
distinct, i.e., to have nothing unclear about them. What he probably meant by this (for he
did not explain himself with precision) was, that they must sustain the test of dialectical
examination; that they must not only seem clear at the outset, but that discussion must
never be able to bring to light points of obscurity connected with them.

Such was the distinction of Descartes, and one sees that it was precisely on the level
of his philosophy. It was somewhat developed by Leibnitz. This great and singular genius
was as remarkable for what he failed to see as for what he saw. That a piece of mechanism
could not do work perpetually without being fed with power in some form, was a thing
perfectly apparent to him; yet he did not understand that the machinery of the mind can
only transform knowledge, but never originate it, unless it be fed with facts of observation. He thus missed the most essential point of the Cartesian philosophy, which is, that
to accept propositions which seem perfectly evident to us is a thing which, whether it be
logical or illogical, we cannot help doing. Instead of regarding the matter in this way, he
sought to reduce the first principles of science to formulas which cannot be denied without
self-contradiction, and was apparently unaware of the great difference between his position and that of Descartes. So he reverted to the old formalities of logic, and, above all,
abstract definitions played a great part in his philosophy. It was quite natural, therefore,
that on observing that the method of Descartes labored under the difficulty that we may
seem to ourselves to have clear apprehensions of ideas which in truth are very hazy, no
better remedy occurred to him than to require an abstract definition of every important
term. Accordingly, in adopting the distinction of *clear* and *distinct* notions, he described
the latter quality as the clear apprehension of everything contained in the definition; and
the books have ever since copied his words. There is no danger that his chimerical scheme
will ever again be over-valued. Nothing new can ever be learned by analyzing definitions.
Nevertheless, our existing beliefs can be set in order by this process, and order is an essential element of intellectual economy, as of every other. It may be acknowledged, therefore,
that the books are right in making familiarity with a notion the first step toward clearness of apprehension, and the defining of it the second. But in omitting all mention of
any higher perspicuity of thought, they simply mirror a philosophy which was exploded
a hundred years ago. That much-admired "ornament of logic"—the doctrine of clearness

and distinctness—may be pretty enough, but it is high time to relegate to our cabinet of curiosities the antique *bijou*, and to wear about us something better adapted to modern uses.

The very first lesson that we have a right to demand that logic shall teach us is, how to make our ideas clear; and a most important one it is, depreciated only by minds who stand in need of it. To know what we think, to be masters of our own meaning, will make a solid foundation for great and weighty thought. It is most easily learned by those whose ideas are meagre and restricted; and far happier they than such as wallow helplessly in a rich mud of conceptions. A nation, it is true, may, in the course of generations, overcome the disadvantage of an excessive wealth of language and its natural concomitant, a vast, unfathomable deep of ideas. We may see it in history, slowly perfecting its literary forms, sloughing at length its metaphysics, and, by virtue of the untirable patience which is often a compensation, attaining great excellence in every branch of mental acquirement. The page of history is not yet unrolled which is to tell us whether such a people will or will not in the long-run prevail over one whose ideas (like the words of their language) are few, but which possesses a wonderful mastery over those which it has. For an individual, however, there can be no question that a few clear ideas are worth more than many confused ones. A young man would hardly be persuaded to sacrifice the greater part of his thoughts to save the rest; and the muddled head is the least apt to see the necessity of such a sacrifice. Him we can usually only commiserate, as a person with a congenital defect. Time will help him, but intellectual maturity with regard to clearness comes rather late, an unfortunate arrangement of Nature, inasmuch as clearness is of less use to a man settled in life, whose errors have in great measure had their effect, than it would be to one whose path lies before him. It is terrible to see how a single unclear idea, a single formula without meaning, lurking in a young man's head, will sometimes act like an obstruction of inert matter in an artery, hindering the nutrition of the brain, and condemning its victim to pine away in the fullness of his intellectual vigor and in the midst of intellectual plenty. Many a man has cherished for years as his hobby some vague shadow of an idea, too meaningless to be positively false; he has, nevertheless, passionately loved it, has made it his companion by day and by night, and has given to it his strength and his life, leaving all other occupations for its sake, and in short has lived with it and for it, until it has become, as it were, flesh of his flesh and bone of his bone; and then he has waked up some bright morning to find it gone, clean vanished away like the beautiful Melusina of the fable, and the essence of his life gone with it. I have myself known such a man; and who can tell how many histories of circle-squarers, metaphysicians, astrologers, and what not, may not be told in the old German story?

II.

The principles set forth in the first part of these papers lead, at once, to a method of reaching a clearness of thought of a far higher grade than the "distinctness" of the logicians. We have there found that the action of thought is excited by the irritation of doubt, and ceases when belief is attained; so that the production of belief is the sole function of thought. All these words, however, are too strong for my purpose. It is as if I had described the phenomena as they appear under a mental microscope. Doubt and Belief, as the words are commonly employed, relate to religious or other grave discussions. But here I use them to designate the starting of any question, no matter how small or how great, and the resolution of it. If, for instance, in a horse-car, I pull out my purse and find a five-cent nickel and five coppers, I decide, while my hand is going to the purse, in which way I will pay my fare. To call such a question Doubt, and my decision Belief, is certainly to use words very disproportionate to the occasion. To speak of such a doubt as causing an irritation which needs to be appeased, suggests a temper which is uncomfortable to the verge of insanity. Yet, looking at the matter minutely, it must be admitted that, if there is the least hesitation as to whether I shall pay the five coppers or the nickel (as there will be sure to be, unless I act from some previously contracted habit in the matter), though irritation is too strong a word, yet I am excited to such small mental activity as may be necessary to deciding how I shall act. Most frequently doubts arise from some indecision, however momentary, in our action. Sometimes it is not so. I have, for example, to wait in a railway-station, and to pass the time I read the advertisements on the walls, I compare the advantages of different trains and different routes which I never expect to take, merely fancying myself to be in a state of hesitancy, because I am bored with having nothing to trouble me. Feigned hesitancy, whether feigned for mere amusement or with a lofty purpose, plays a great part in the production of scientific inquiry. However the doubt may originate, it stimulates the mind to an activity which may be slight or energetic, calm or turbulent. Images pass rapidly through consciousness, one incessantly melting into another, until at last, when all is over—it may be in a fraction of a second, in an hour, or after long years—we find ourselves decided as to how we should act under such circumstances as those which occasioned our hesitation. In other words, we have attained belief.

In this process we observe two sorts of elements of consciousness, the distinction between which may best be made clear by means of an illustration. In a piece of music there are the separate notes, and there is the air. A single tone may be prolonged for an hour or a day, and it exists as perfectly in each second of that time as in the whole taken together; so that, as long as it is sounding, it might be present to a sense from which everything in the past was as completely absent as the future itself. But it is different with the air, the performance of which occupies a certain time, during the portions of which only portions of it are played. It consists in an orderliness in the succession of sounds which strike the ear at different times; and to perceive it there must be some continuity of consciousness which makes the events of a lapse of time present to us. We certainly only perceive the air by hearing the separate notes; yet we cannot be said to directly hear it, for we hear only what is present at the instant, and an orderliness of succession cannot exist in an instant. These two sorts of objects, what we are *immediately* conscious of and what we are *mediately* conscious of, are found in all consciousness. Some elements (the sensations) are completely present at every instant so long as they last, while others (like thought) are actions having beginning, middle, and end, and consist in a congruence in the succession of sensations which flow through the mind. They cannot be immediately present to us, but must cover some portion of the past or future. Thought is a thread of melody running through the succession of our sensations.

We may add that just as a piece of music may be written in parts, each part having its own air, so various systems of relationship of succession subsist together between the same sensations. These different systems are distinguished by having different motives, ideas, or functions. Thought is only one such system, for its sole motive, idea, and function is to produce belief, and whatever does not concern that purpose belongs to some other system of relations. The action of thinking may incidentally have other results; it may serve to amuse us, for example, and among *dilettanti* it is not rare to find those who have so perverted thought to the purposes of pleasure that it seems to vex them to think that the questions upon which they delight to exercise it may ever get finally settled; and a positive discovery which takes a favorite subject out of the arena of literary debate is met with ill-concealed dislike. This disposition is the very debauchery of thought. But the soul and meaning of thought, abstracted from the other elements which accompany it, though it may be voluntarily thwarted, can never be made to direct itself toward anything but the production of belief. Thought in action has for its only possible motive the attainment of thought at rest; and whatever does not refer to belief is no part of the thought itself.

And what, then, is belief? It is the demi-cadence which closes a musical phrase in the symphony of our intellectual life. We have seen that it has just three properties: First, it is something that we are aware of; second, it appeases the irritation of doubt; and, third, it involves the establishment in our nature of a rule of action, or, say for short, a *habit*. As it appeases the irritation of doubt, which is the motive for thinking, thought relaxes, and comes to rest for a moment when belief is reached. But, since belief is a rule for action, the application of which involves further doubt and further thought, at the same time that it is a stopping-place, it is also a new starting-place for thought. That is why I have permitted myself to call it thought at rest, although thought is essentially an action. The *final* upshot of thinking is the exercise of volition, and of this thought no longer forms a part; but belief is only a stadium of mental action, an effect upon our nature due to thought, which will influence future thinking.

The essence of belief is the establishment of a habit, and different beliefs are distinguished by the different modes of action to which they give rise. If beliefs do not differ in this respect, if they appease the same doubt by producing the same rule of action, then no mere differences in the manner of consciousness of them can make them different beliefs, any more than playing a tune in different keys is playing different tunes. Imaginary distinctions are often drawn between beliefs which differ only in their mode of expression;—the wrangling which ensues is real enough, however. To believe that any objects are arranged as in Fig. 1, and to believe that they are arranged as in Fig. 2, are one and the same belief; yet it is conceivable that a man should assert one proposition and deny the other.

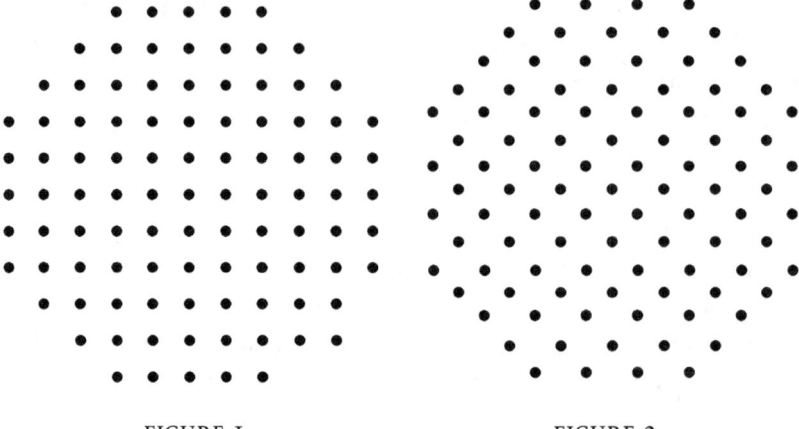

FIGURE 1   FIGURE 2

Such false distinctions do as much harm as the confusion of beliefs really different, and are among the pitfalls of which we ought constantly to beware, especially when we are upon metaphysical ground. One singular deception of this sort, which often occurs, is to mistake the sensation produced by our own unclearness of thought for a character of the object we are thinking. Instead of perceiving that the obscurity is purely subjective, we fancy that we contemplate a quality of the object which is essentially mysterious; and if our conception be afterward presented to us in a clear form we do not recognize it as the same, owing to the absence of the feeling of unintelligibility. So long as this deception lasts, it obviously puts an impassable barrier in the way of perspicuous thinking; so that it equally interests the opponents of rational thought to perpetuate it, and its adherents to guard against it.

Another such deception is to mistake a mere difference in the grammatical construction of two words for a distinction between the ideas they express. In this pedantic age, when the general mob of writers attend so much more to words than to things, this error is common enough. When I just said that thought is an *action*, and that it consists in a *relation*, although a person performs an action but not a relation, which can only be the result of an action, yet there was no inconsistency in what I said, but only a grammatical vagueness.

From all these sophisms we shall be perfectly safe so long as we reflect that the whole function of thought is to produce habits of action; and that whatever there is connected with a thought, but irrelevant to its purpose, is an accretion to it, but no part of it. If there be a unity among our sensations which has no reference to how we shall act on a given occasion, as when we listen to a piece of music, why we do not call that thinking. To develop its meaning, we have, therefore, simply to determine what habits it produces, for what a thing means is simply what habits it involves. Now, the identity of a habit depends on how it might lead us to act, not merely under such circumstances as are likely to arise, but under such as might possibly occur, no matter how improbable they may be. What the habit is depends on *when* and *how* it causes us to act. As for the *when*, every stimulus to action is derived from perception; as for the *how*, every purpose of action is to produce some sensible result. Thus, we come down to what is tangible and practical, as the root of every real distinction of thought, no matter how subtle it may be; and there is no distinction of meaning so fine as to consist in anything but a possible difference of practice.

To see what this principle leads to, consider in the light of it such a doctrine as that of transubstantiation. The Protestant churches generally hold that the elements of the sacrament are flesh and blood only in a tropical sense; they nourish our souls as meat and the juice of it would our bodies. But the Catholics maintain that they are literally just that; although they possess all the sensible qualities of wafer-cakes and diluted wine. But we can have no conception of wine except what may enter into a belief, either—

1. That this, that, or the other, is wine; or,
2. That wine possesses certain properties.

Such beliefs are nothing but self-notifications that we should, upon occasion, act in regard to such things as we believe to be wine according to the qualities which we believe wine to possess. The occasion of such action would be some sensible perception, the motive of it to produce some sensible result. Thus our action has exclusive reference to what affects the senses, our habit has the same bearing as our action, our belief the same as our habit, our conception the same as our belief; and we can consequently mean nothing by wine but what has certain effects, direct or indirect, upon our senses; and to talk of something as having all the sensible characters of wine, yet being in reality blood, is senseless jargon. Now, it is not my object to pursue the theological question; and having used it as a logical example I drop it, without caring to anticipate the theologian's reply. I only desire to point out how impossible it is that we should have an idea in our minds which relates to anything but conceived sensible effects of things. Our idea of anything *is* our idea of its sensible effects; and if we fancy that we have any other we deceive ourselves, and mistake a mere sensation accompanying the thought for a part of the thought itself. It is absurd to say that thought has any meaning unrelated to its only function. It is foolish for Catholics and Protestants to fancy themselves in disagreement about the elements of the sacrament, if they agree in regard to all their sensible effects, here or hereafter.

It appears, then, that the rule for attaining the third grade of clearness of apprehension is as follows: Consider what effects, which might conceivably have practical bearings, we conceive the object of our conception to have. Then, our conception of these effects is the whole of our conception of the object.

III.

Let us illustrate this rule by some examples; and, to begin with the simplest one possible, let us ask what we mean by calling a thing *hard*. Evidently that it will not be scratched by many other substances. The whole conception of this quality, as of every other, lies in its conceived effects. There is absolutely no difference between a hard thing and a soft thing so long as they are not brought to the test. Suppose, then, that a diamond could be crystallized in the midst of a cushion of soft cotton, and should remain there until it was finally burned up. Would it be false to say that that diamond was soft? This seems a foolish question, and would be so, in fact, except in the realm of logic. There such questions are often of the greatest utility as serving to bring logical principles into sharper relief than real discussions ever could. In studying logic we must not put them aside with hasty answers, but must consider them with attentive care, in order to make out the principles involved. We may, in the present case, modify our question, and ask what prevents us from saying that all hard bodies remain perfectly soft until they are touched, when their hardness increases with the pressure until they are scratched. Reflection will show that the reply is this: there would be no *falsity* in such modes of speech. They would involve a modification of our present usage of speech with regard to the words hard and soft, but not of their meanings. For they represent no fact to be different from what it is; only they involve arrangements of facts which would be exceedingly maladroit. This leads us to remark that the question of what would occur under circumstances which do not actually arise is not a question of fact, but only of the most perspicuous arrangement of them. For example, the question of free-will and fate in its simplest form, stripped of verbiage, is something like this: I have done something of which I am ashamed; could I, by an effort of the will, have resisted the temptation, and done otherwise? The philosophical reply is, that this is not a question of fact, but only of the arrangement of facts. Arranging them so as to exhibit what is particularly pertinent to my question—namely, that I ought to blame myself for having done wrong—it is perfectly true to say that, if I had willed to do otherwise than I did, I should have done otherwise. On the other hand, arranging the facts so as to exhibit another important consideration, it is equally true that, when a temptation has once been allowed to work, it will, if it has a certain force, produce its effect, let me struggle how I may. There is no objection to a contradiction in what would result from a false supposition. The *reductio ad absurdum* consists in showing that contradictory results would follow from a hypothesis which is consequently judged to be false. Many questions are involved in the free-will discussion, and I am far from desiring to say that both sides are equally right. On the contrary, I am of opinion that one side denies important facts, and that the other does not. But what I do say is, that the above single question was the origin of the whole doubt; that, had it not been for this question, the controversy would never have arisen; and that this question is perfectly solved in the manner which I have indicated.

Let us next seek a clear idea of Weight. This is another very easy case. To say that a body is heavy means simply that, in the absence of opposing force, it will fall. This (neglecting certain specifications of how it will fall, etc., which exist in the mind of the physicist who uses the word) is evidently the whole conception of weight. It is a fair question whether some particular facts may not *account* for gravity; but what we mean by the force itself is completely involved in its effects.

This leads us to undertake an account of the idea of Force in general. This is the great conception which, developed in the early part of the seventeenth century from the rude idea of a cause, and constantly improved upon since, has shown us how to explain all the changes of motion which bodies experience, and how to think about all physical phenomena; which has given birth to modern science, and changed the face of the globe; and which, aside from its more special uses, has played a principal part in directing the course of modern thought, and in furthering modern social development. It is, therefore, worth some pains to comprehend it. According to our rule, we must begin by asking what is the immediate use of thinking about force; and the answer is, that we thus account for changes of motion. If bodies were left to themselves, without the intervention of forces, every motion would continue unchanged both in velocity and in direction. Furthermore, change of motion never takes place abruptly; if its direction is changed, it is always through a curve without angles; if its velocity alters, it is by degrees. The gradual changes which are constantly taking place are conceived by geometers to be compounded together according to the rules of the parallelogram of forces. If the reader does not already know what this is, he will find it, I hope, to his advantage to endeavor to follow the following explanation; but if mathematics are insupportable to him, pray let him skip three paragraphs rather than that we should part company here.

A *path* is a line whose beginning and end are distinguished. Two paths are considered to be equivalent, which, beginning at the same point, lead to the same point. Thus the two paths, *ABCDE* and *AFGHE*, are equivalent. Paths which do *not* begin at the same point are considered to be equivalent, provided that, on moving either of them without turning

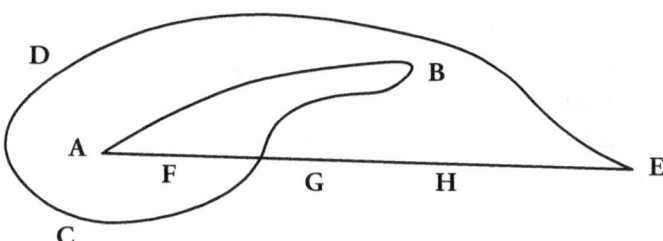

FIGURE 3

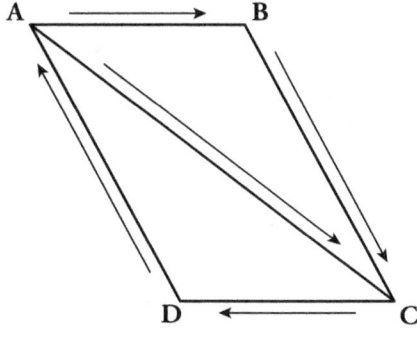

FIGURE 4

it, but keeping it always parallel to its original position, when its beginning coincides with that of the other path, the ends also coincide. Paths are considered as geometrically added together, when one begins where the other ends; thus the path *AE* is conceived to be a sum of *AB*, *BC*, *CD*, and *DE*. In the parallelogram of Fig. 4 the diagonal *AC* is the sum of *AB* and *BC*; or, since *AD* is geometrically equivalent to *BC*, *AC* is the geometrical sum of *AB* and *AD*.

All this is purely conventional. It simply amounts to this: that we choose to call paths having the relations I have described equal or added. But, though it is a convention, it is a convention with a good reason. The rule for geometrical addition may be applied not only to paths, but to any other things which can be represented by paths. Now, as a path is determined by the varying direction and distance of the point which moves over it from the starting-point, it follows that anything which from its beginning to its end is determined by a varying direction and a varying magnitude is capable of being represented by a line. Accordingly, *velocities* may be represented by lines, for they have only directions and rates. The same thing is true of *accelerations*, or changes of velocities. This is evident enough in the case of velocities; and it becomes evident for accelerations if we consider that precisely what velocities are to positions—namely, states of change of them—that accelerations are to velocities.

The so-called "parallelogram of forces" is simply a rule for compounding accelerations. The rule is, to represent the accelerations by paths, and then to geometrically add the paths. The geometers, however, not only use the "parallelogram of forces" to compound different accelerations, but also to resolve one acceleration into a sum of several. Let *AB* (Fig. 5) be the path which represents a certain acceleration—say, such a change in the motion of a body that at the end of one second the body will, under the influence of that change, be in a position different from what it would have had if its motion had continued unchanged such that a path equivalent to *AB* would lead from the latter position to the former. This

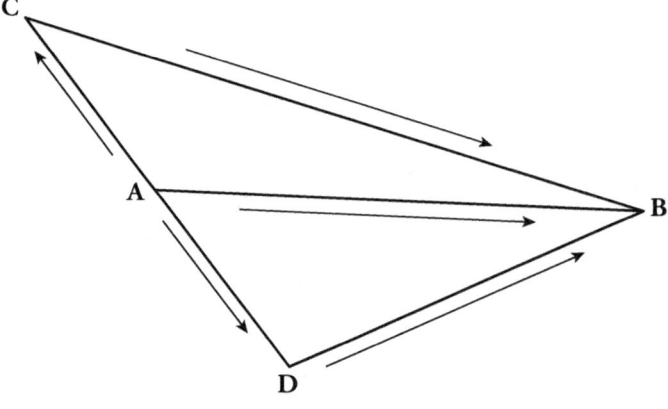

FIGURE 5

acceleration may be considered as the sum of the accelerations represented by *AC* and *CB*. It may also be considered as the sum of the very different accelerations represented by *AD* and *DB*, where *AD* is almost the opposite of *AC*. And it is clear that there is an immense variety of ways in which *AB* might be resolved into the sum of two accelerations.

After this tedious explanation, which I hope, in view of the extraordinary interest of the conception of force, may not have exhausted the reader's patience, we are prepared at last to state the grand fact which this conception embodies. This fact is that if the actual changes of motion which the different particles of bodies experience are each resolved in its appropriate way, each component acceleration is precisely such as is prescribed by a certain law of Nature, according to which bodies in the relative positions which the bodies in question actually have at the moment,[1] always receive certain accelerations, which, being compounded by geometrical addition, give the acceleration which the body actually experiences.

This is the only fact which the idea of force represents, and whoever will take the trouble clearly to apprehend what this fact is, perfectly comprehends what force is. Whether we ought to say that a force *is* an acceleration, or that it *causes* an acceleration, is a mere question of propriety of language, which has no more to do with our real meaning than the difference between the French idiom "*Il fait froid*" and its English equivalent "*It is cold.*" Yet it is surprising to see how this simple affair has muddled men's minds. In how many profound treatises is not force spoken of as a "mysterious entity," which seems to be only a way of confessing that the author despairs of ever getting a clear notion of what the word means! In a recent admired work on "Analytic Mechanics" it is stated that we understand precisely the effect of force, but what force itself is we do not understand! This is simply a self-contradiction. The idea which the word force excites in our minds has no other function than to affect our actions, and these actions can have no reference to force otherwise than through its effects. Consequently, if we know what the effects of force are, we are acquainted with every fact which is implied in saying that a force exists, and there is nothing more to know. The truth is, there is some vague notion afloat that a question may mean something which the mind cannot conceive; and when some hair-splitting philosophers have been confronted with the absurdity of such a view, they have invented an empty distinction between positive and negative conceptions, in the attempt to give their non-idea a form not obviously nonsensical. The nullity of it is sufficiently plain from the considerations given a few pages back; and, apart from those considerations, the quibbling character of the distinction must have struck every mind accustomed to real thinking.

IV.

Let us now approach the subject of logic, and consider a conception which particularly concerns it, that of *reality*. Taking clearness in the sense of familiarity, no idea could be clearer than this. Every child uses it with perfect confidence, never dreaming that he does not understand it. As for clearness in its second grade, however, it would probably puzzle most men, even among those of a reflective turn of mind, to give an abstract definition of the real. Yet such a definition may perhaps be reached by considering the points of difference between reality and its opposite, fiction. A figment is a product of somebody's imagination; it has such characters as his thought impresses upon it. That those characters are independent of how you or I think is an external reality. There are, however, phenomena within our own minds, dependent upon our thought, which are at the same time real in the sense that we really think them. But though their characters depend on how we think, they do not depend on what we think those characters to be. Thus, a dream has a real existence as a mental phenomenon, if somebody has really dreamt it; that he dreamt so and so, does not depend on what anybody thinks was dreamt, but is completely independent of all opinion on the subject. On the other hand, considering, not the fact of dreaming, but the thing dreamt, it retains its peculiarities by virtue of no other fact than that it was dreamt to possess them. Thus we may define the real as that whose characters are independent of what anybody may think them to be.

But, however satisfactory such a definition may be found, it would be a great mistake to suppose that it makes the idea of reality perfectly clear. Here, then, let us apply our rules. According to them, reality, like every other quality, consists in the peculiar sensible effects which things partaking of it produce. The only effect which real things have is to cause belief, for all the sensations which they excite emerge into consciousness in the form of beliefs. The question therefore is, how is true belief (or belief in the real) distinguished from false belief (or belief in fiction). Now, as we have seen in the former paper, the ideas of truth and falsehood, in their full development, appertain exclusively to the scientific method of settling opinion. A person who arbitrarily chooses the propositions which he will adopt can use the word truth only to emphasize the expression of his determination to hold on to his choice. Of course, the method of tenacity never prevailed exclusively; reason is too natural to men for that. But in the literature of the dark ages we find some fine examples of it. When Scotus Erigena is commenting upon a poetical passage in which hellebore is spoken of as having caused the death of Socrates, he does not hesitate to inform the inquiring reader that Helleborus and Socrates were two eminent Greek philosophers, and that the latter having been overcome in argument by the former took the matter to heart and died of it! What sort of an idea of truth could a man have who could adopt and teach, without the qualification of a perhaps, an opinion taken so entirely at random? The real spirit of Socrates, who I hope would have been delighted to have been "overcome in argument," because he would have learned something by it, is in curious contrast with the naive idea of the glossist, for whom discussion would seem to have been simply a struggle. When philosophy began to awake from its long slumber, and before theology completely dominated it, the practice seems to have been for each professor to seize upon any philosophical position he found unoccupied and which seemed a strong one, to intrench himself in it, and to sally forth from time to time to give battle to the others. Thus, even the scanty records we possess of those disputes enable us to make out a dozen or more opinions held by different teachers at one time concerning the question of nominalism and realism. Read the opening part of the "Historia Calamitatum" of Abelard, who was certainly as philo-sophical as any of his contemporaries, and see the spirit of combat which it breathes. For him, the truth is simply his particular stronghold. When the method of authority prevailed, the truth meant little more than the Catholic faith. All the efforts of the scholastic doctors are directed toward harmonizing their faith in Aristotle and their faith in the Church, and one may search their ponderous folios through without finding an argument which goes any further. It is noticeable that where different faiths flourish side by side, renegades are looked upon with contempt even by the party whose belief they adopt; so completely has the idea of loyalty replaced that of truth-seeking. Since the time of Descartes, the defect in the conception of truth has been less apparent. Still, it will sometimes strike a scientific man that the philosophers have been less intent on finding out what the facts are, than on inquiring what belief is most in harmony with their system. It is hard to convince a follower of the *a priori* method by adducing facts; but show him that an opinion he is defending is inconsistent with what he has laid down elsewhere, and he will be very apt to retract it. These minds do not seem to believe that disputation is ever to cease; they seem to think that the opinion which is natural for one man is not so for another, and that belief will, consequently, never be settled. In contenting themselves with fixing their own opinions by a method which would lead another man to a different result, they betray their feeble hold of the conception of what truth is.

On the other hand, all the followers of science are fully persuaded that the processes of investigation, if only pushed far enough, will give one certain solution to every question to which they can be applied. One man may investigate the velocity of light by studying the transits of Venus and the aberration of the stars; another by the oppositions of Mars and the eclipses of Jupiter's satellites; a third by the method of Fizeau; a fourth by that of Foucault; a fifth by the motions of the curves of Lissajous; a sixth, a seventh, an eighth, and a ninth, may follow the different methods of comparing the measures of statical and dynamical electricity. They may at first obtain different results, but, as each perfects his method and his processes, the results will move steadily together toward a destined centre. So with all scientific research. Different minds may set out with the most antagonistic views, but the progress of investigation carries them by a force outside of themselves to one and the same conclusion. This activity of thought by which we are carried, not where we wish, but to a foreordained goal, is like the operation of destiny. No modification of the point of view taken, no selection of other facts for study, no natural bent of mind even, can enable a man to escape the predestinate opinion. This great law is embodied in the conception of truth and reality. The opinion which is fated[2] to be ultimately agreed to by all who inves-tigate, is what we mean by the truth, and the object represented in this opinion is the real. That is the way I would explain reality.

But it may be said that this view is directly opposed to the abstract definition which we have given of reality, inasmuch as it makes the characters of the real depend on what is ultimately thought about them. But the answer to this is that, on the one hand, reality is independent, not necessarily of thought in general, but only of what you or I or any finite number of men may think about it; and that, on the other hand, though the object of the final opinion depends on what that opinion is, yet what that opinion is does not depend on what you or I or any man thinks. Our perversity and that of others may indefinitely postpone the settlement of opinion; it might even conceivably cause an arbitrary proposition to be universally accepted as long as the human race should last. Yet even that would not change the nature of the belief, which alone could be the result of investigation carried sufficiently far; and if, after the extinction of our race, another should arise with faculties and disposition for investigation, that true opinion must be the one which they would ultimately come to. "Truth crushed to earth shall rise again," and the opinion which would finally result from investigation does not depend on how anybody may actually think. But the reality of that which is real does depend on the real fact that investigation is destined to lead, at last, if continued long enough, to a belief in it.

But I may be asked what I have to say to all the minute facts of history, forgotten never to be recovered, to the lost books of the ancients, to the buried secrets.

> Full many a gem of purest ray serene
>   The dark, unfathomed caves of ocean bear;
> Full many a flower is born to blush unseen,
>   And waste its sweetness on the desert air.

Do these things not really exist because they are hopelessly beyond the reach of our knowledge? And then, after the universe is dead (according to the prediction of some scientists), and all life has ceased forever, will not the shock of atoms continue though there will be no mind to know it? To this I reply that, though in no possible state of knowledge can any number be great enough to express the relation between the amount of what rests unknown to the amount of the known, yet it is unphilosophical to suppose that, with regard to any given question (which has any clear meaning), investigation would not bring forth a solution of it, if it were carried far enough. Who would have said, a few years ago, that we could ever know of what substances stars are made whose light may have been longer in reaching us than the human race has existed? Who can be sure of what we shall not know in a few hundred years? Who can guess what would be the result of continuing the pursuit of science for ten thousand years, with the activity of the last hundred? And if it were to go on for a million, or a billion, or any number of years you please, how is it possible to say that there is any question which might not ultimately be solved?

But it may be objected, "Why make so much of these remote considerations, especially when it is your principle that only practical distinctions have a meaning?" Well, I must confess that it makes very little difference whether we say that a stone on the bottom of the ocean, in complete darkness, is brilliant or not—that is to say, that it *probably* makes no difference, remembering always that that stone *may* be fished up to-morrow. But that there are gems at the bottom of the sea, flowers in the untraveled desert, etc., are propositions which, like that about a diamond being hard when it is not pressed, concern much more the arrangement of our language than they do the meaning of our ideas.

It seems to me, however, that we have, by the application of our rule, reached so clear an apprehension of what we mean by reality, and of the fact which the idea rests on, that we should not, perhaps, be making a pretension so presumptuous as it would be singular, if we were to offer a metaphysical theory of existence for universal acceptance among those who employ the scientific method of fixing belief. However, as metaphysics is a subject much more curious than useful, the knowledge of which, like that of a sunken reef, serves chiefly to enable us to keep clear of it, I will not trouble the reader with any more Ontology at this moment. I have already been led much further into that path than I should have desired; and I have given the reader such a dose of mathematics, psychology, and all that is most abstruse, that I fear he may already have left me, and that what I am now writing is for the compositor and proof-reader exclusively. I trusted to the importance of the subject. There is no royal road to logic, and really valuable ideas can only be had at the price of close attention. But I know that in the matter of ideas the public prefer the cheap and nasty; and in my next paper I am going to return to the easily intelligible, and not wander from it again. The reader who has been at the pains of wading through this month's paper, shall be rewarded in the next one by seeing how beautifully what has been developed in this tedious way can be applied to the ascertainment of the rules of scientific reasoning.

We have, hitherto, not crossed the threshold of scientific logic. It is certainly important to know how to make our ideas clear, but they may be ever so clear without being true. How to make them so, we have next to study. How to give birth to those vital and procreative ideas which multiply into a thousand forms and diffuse themselves everywhere, advancing civilization and making the dignity of man, is an art not yet reduced to rules, but of the secret of which the history of science affords some hints.

NOTES

1. Possibly the velocities also have to be taken into account.
2. Fate means merely that which is sure to come true, and can nohow be avoided. It is a superstition to suppose that a certain sort of events are ever fated, and it is another to suppose that the word fate can never be freed from its superstitious taint. We are all fated to die.

William James

TAINE'S *On Intelligence*

The Nation 15.374 (29 August 1872): 139–141.

Review of Hippolyte Taine, *On Intelligence*, trans. T. D. Haye. New York: Holt and Williams, 1871.

"Dieu! ça n'a pas d'actualité," said a French review editor, as he returned an article on the Notion of God which a metaphysical contributor had offered him. Our tardiness in noticing M. Taine's important work might be excused in somewhat similar words. Any time is opportune for metaphysics. Its treatises are continually being read, no matter how long ago they were written. They hardly depend on fashion; and if the present book has met with an unusually prompt success, it is due less to the fact that the pure psychology, of which it partly consists, is beginning to enjoy the honors and penalties of being a positive science—rapid recognition of new contributions on the one hand with their speedy obsolescence on the other—than to the great reputation of the author in other paths of writing. We suppose that many a reader of his translated works feels a certain scepticism as to his competency in a strictly scientific research. He is so eminently an artist, his profession of scientific deduction remains so palpably a mere accompaniment in his works on literature and art, his historical developments are so shallow, his explanations of ethnic peculiarities so plainly trumped up after the facts, that we know more than one of his admirers who would let the whole pretension to scientific rigor in him pass for one of those pleasant foibles in which a bright mind must be allowed to indulge itself if it finds a pleasure therein. But the present treatise is of stricter stuff, and had its author written nothing else, it would give him an honorable name and place in the brotherhood of thinkers, properly so called. It falls asunder roughly into three divisions: one psychological, being an analysis of cognitions into their simplest elements, based largely on the researches of Mill, Bain, and Spencer; one logical, being a theory of reasoning and an account of the manner in which the simpler and more general elements of thought and reality involve and produce the more particular and complex; and an intermediate one, which we may call metaphysical, since it is an attempt to define the quality of the deepest phenomenon, which, lying at the core, may be termed the reality of all the others.

What are M. Taine's opinions on all these matters? The question is easier asked than answered, for the first impression the book makes on a reader is, that one-half of it flatly contradicts the other. In what we have called the psychological portion a nominalism as uncompromising as that of James Mill is professed. "We have, strictly speaking, no general ideas; only tendencies to name and names." Sensations have substitutes in mental images; and these have substitutes in names; but general names cover no peculiar mental modification. A general idea, considered apart, is a nonentity. It has no substantive *quale*, but only a function; it exists but as a *tendency* of certain determinate images to arise. It helps us lighten the baggage of thought, as circular notes enable us to travel without bullion. But the true value of both comes out only when they are converted. In the latter chapters of the book, however, we find a doctrine of reasoning which seems to admit to the fullest possible extent the reality of general qualities as such, and to carry us deep into a world of intelligibles, as they used to be called, of *eternae veritates*, or, as Taine says, of fixed and simple laws which we perceive beneath the flow of transient and complex events.

A more careful examination mitigates, though but partially, the glaringness of the contradiction. One perceives that he means to allow reality only to certain classes of abstractions, and to deny it to others. The latter are distinguished in his mind from the former by their barrenness. They are that prior world of vain substances (we are trying to interpret now, and not to criticise), or causes brought forward as explanations of phenomena, which do but repeat the phenomena under more sounding names—*virtutes dormitivae*, in short; while the abstractions to which he allows validity are all predicative or adjective qualities, as white, straight, heavy. To these he pretends not to ascribe a transcendent existence, independent of particular events; they exist only *in* facts, and are merely a broader kind of facts. To them as *constituents* of phenomena, even though general, reality may be ascribed; while the other class of abstract beings conceived to stand *behind* phenomena as noumenal substances, are mere figments.

Every *real* abstraction is an extract (to use his happy terminology) from a multitude of particular things or events which may differ as to their other details. The British school says the things are "similar" as to this character, but Taine affirms the common character to be literally the "*same*" in all, thus giving it a sort of ontologic status, a real existence differing from that of individuals and events only in possessing superior stability and permanence. The beauty and value of these abstract characters, or generalized extracts, is that they are fertile, for they contain wrapped up in them—sometimes obvious, sometimes latent, and to be discovered only by a keen analytic eye—further properties, other abstractions. Thus the general concept *parallelogram* involves as part of its essence that of two juxtaposed triangles, and we learn from experience that the concept *cold* involves that of diminution of molecular motion and approximation of molecules. An individual fact possessing one general character, perforce possesses also as attributes the further general characters which that one involves. Hence a basis for necessary reasoning; the two triangles, for instance, into which we have analyzed our parallelogram, with their one side in common and the others parallel, possess the further property of being equal-sided each to each; so that having its opposite sides equal is seen to be a necessary attribute of a parallelogram; in like manner, the approximation of molecules involves the further property of diminished mobility; and diminished mobility in a vapor soon involves liquefaction—so we see how cold must necessarily, after a certain point, make vapors liquid.

It is, we repeat, the pregnancy of this class of general qualities that makes M. Taine so partial to them. Whatever they contain they contain universally, because independently of particular circumstances, and necessarily, because analytically involved in them, or as part of their definition. [This latter point, as we shall presently see, marks his deepest divergence from the British empirical school.] The class of abstractions to which he is not thus indulgent differs from the former chiefly in its infecundity. It is that of *substances*, such as matter, the ego, the faculties of the mind, and what may be called the dynamic entities, as power, necessity, cause, force, etc. Here his nominalism stands firm. These are phantoms, products of "metaphysical illusion," void acts, verbal entities, whose appearance of spirituality is but the tumidity of their emptiness. The ego is nothing but the sum of its events. We can extract nothing new by analyzing our idea of it. So to posit a general faculty, as perception, explains nothing of its particular acts, but is a mere barren reduplication of the concrete appearance it professes to explain. So again with force. A particular horse has force enough to draw a given cart, but not force enough to draw a heavier cart. This means that when his muscles are contracted the one cart will be moved, but the other will not be moved. "Here we have a connexion only, that between the muscular contractions and the movement of the cart. A particular force exists when a particular connexion exists; it ceases when this connexion ceases. The force of the muscular contraction is double if the cart moved weighs 10,000 pounds instead of 5,000. In general, if we are given two facts, one antecedent and the other consequent, connected by a constant link, we term the particularity of the antecedent to be always followed by the consequent, *force*, and we measure this force by the magnitude of the consequent. . . . Unfortunately of this particularity which is a relation, we construct by a mental fiction, a substance; we describe it by a substantive name; attribute qualities to it; say it is greater or less; employ it in language as a subject, forgetting that its existence is wholly verbal, that it is in itself nothing more than a character, a property, a particularity of a fact, the particularity of being always followed by another fact, a particularity detached from the fact by abstraction, set apart by fiction, kept in a distinct state by means of a distinct substantive name, till the mind, forgetting its origin, believes it to be independent, and becomes the dupe of an illusion of its own effecting."

We imagine that when M. Taine was a young man with a strong sensibility for facts, and rather for their hard, brutal, concrete aspects than otherwise, with a good deal of iconoclastic passion and conceit, he fell foul of the hypostatized abstractions which abounded in the armory of the then reigning spiritualism of France—"little spiritual beings hidden under the facts as under garments"—as he once called them, and that that youthful animosity has persisted to the present day. But almost as early as this he was vividly and originally impressed by that conception of what we may call the encapsulation of qualities in the universe, of which we have briefly tried above to convey an idea. His thought thus starts from two independent foci to overrun the philosophic field, and where the territories are conterminous, the nominalistic impetus often carries him over the barrier; the old wrath mounts to his eyes, and without being aware of it he tramples down his own grain as if it were his enemies.' Hence a large amount of real confusion and contradiction. Thus, as we have tried to show, his best and deepest reason for rejecting a certain class of abstractions is that they really explain nothing. To explain a thing is to show it to be a case of something else more general already admitted or taken for granted by us. The *reason why* planets keep in their orbits is that they are masses of matter, and *all* such attract each other. To affirm a "centripetal force" *sui generis* we explain nothing, just as, when Adam Smith accounts for the institution of commerce by an inborn tendency in men to exchange, he explains nothing. Nevertheless we find M. Taine constantly forgetting this point of view, and talking as if he found fault with the illicit class of abstractions less for their barrenness than for the isolation and independent entity which their votaries ascribe to them—for their appearing "behind" the phenomenon, not in it. But the abstract characters whose reality he admits must also be taken as independent of the concrete phenomena in which they appear; being "the same" in all, they are independent of each, and require M. Taine to provide a separate plane of being for them to subsist in anterior to their taking on the diverse adventitious particularities which determine their appearance in the diverse concrete shapes. This he often ostensibly denies, but virtually admits in many places, and this admitted, his contempt for the phantoms of metaphysical illusion, the illegitimate children of abstraction, is unjustifiable except on the mere ground of their uselessness. By his own showing in many places they are generated by the same process as that which extracts and isolates the more valid general characters: for instance, force and necessity are "particularities extracted from the events"; in the line of our *subjective* experiences "all the elements present a constant character, which, being continually repeated, seems persistent, *i.e.*, the particularity of being a within, in opposition to the without; and this, later on, will offer to reflection and language, the temptation to isolate it under the name of subject and Ego."

If the character is in the elements, common to all, why is it not as fair to extract it and call it Ego and real, as to do the same by the "character common to all the elements" of a line straight or curved, which we express by its equation and which M. Taine rightly deems so important? This blowing hot and cold is amusingly exemplified on p. 206, where the Ego in the same sentence is defined to be *nothing more* than its series of events placed in succession, and yet *not merely* this series. A questionable shape, indeed! Only our bifocal theory of his speculation can well account for such inconsistencies. Take the notions of power, force, etc. He praises Bain everywhere, yet flies in the face of his teaching as regards activity. Bain admits that our experiences of activity as such contain a peculiar generic *quale* of consciousness which distinguishes them from all merely passive impressions. If this be a true portion of certain sensations, Taine should consent to its extraction and use.

He nevertheless out-Humes Hume in his declaration that all notions of activity are pure nonentities. We can only account for it by supposing his old habit of animosity to M. de Biran to have led him astray.

M. Taine's relation to the English school constantly challenges criticism, showing everywhere superficial adhesion with unconscious deep-lying dissent. The most signal instance of this occurs in his treatment of Mill's "Psychological Theory of an External World," which he quotes with entire approval, and then proceeds to make what he calls an "addition" which is nothing less than a cool and flat contradiction or begging of the whole question again. Mill in his resolution of matter into permanent possibilities of sensation is a thorough-going idealist. The argument either disproves any purely objective form of being, or it does nothing at all. The point of view is wholly subjective. When we say that matter exists independently of our actual sensations, all Mill understands is that we firmly expect other sensations, or are certain of them. After accepting all Mill's premises, for the word *certainty* in the conclusion M. Taine simply substitutes necessity (p. 279), and then naively says he has corrected the theory, and vindicated a noumenal existence. This noumenal existence he afterwards explains to be a mode of motion; thereby falling back on the old theory of primary and secondary qualities, and seeming to forget his previous adoption of the analysis of Spencer and Bain, which explains space away into muscular sensations.

He is too apt to graze the deepest problems without seeming to become aware of them. His account of sensuous perception, for instance, is admirable, considered as mere psycho-physiology, but very unsatisfactory philosophy. Relying on the "law of specific energies" of the organs of sense, he makes hallucination to be the type of the entire process. Perception he defines as "veracious hallucination," and the useful word, "reductive," is introduced to denote the circumstance, usually the contradictory testimony of another sense (or, we may add, the antagonism of past experience), by which an incipient hallucination of one sense is repressed and recognized as subjective. An hallucination of one sense becomes veracious, or in M. Taine's words, "corresponds" to an objective reality when other senses corroborate it; but what warrant he has for postulating this objective against the complex of subjective states, or how out of a conspiracy of hallucinations anything real can be hatched, does not appear. Logically, he should only ascribe to sensible perceptions a harmony, or veracity relatively to each other, but not relatively to the external object. This problem Bain and Mill solve by their idealism, recent German psychologists by their several devices. But M. Taine seems unaware of its existence.

Another of his unsatisfactory evasions of difficulties touches the very core of metaphysics. He simply *assumes* his doctrine that axioms are identical propositions, that general characters contain others *analytically* involved in them, that attributes enter into subjects only as portions of wider sets of attributes, not *per se* or directly—with all that flows from it, as that syntheses of data exist intrinsic and essential, absolute and universal; so that the second one must exist in any possible universe where the first is to be found; and that we may at last reach an universal concept from which the "whole remediless flow of existence" may be proved to spring. The doctrine may be true or false, but the opposite ones of Kant and Mill deserve deeper consideration than the mere contradiction he accords to them.

But with all its shortcomings the book is a valuable one. The early chapters contain the clearest and best account of the psychology of cognition with which we are acquainted, and the best adapted to the general reader. The latter ones are full of ingenious original and permanently valuable suggestions. It is almost a marvel that the hand which wrote the "Voyage aux Pyrénées" should also have produced this book. We are sure that it will play a vital part in the revival of philosophy on an empirical basis which is about to begin in France. And we know no work which advanced students in our own language may better employ to exercise their critical acumen.

Against Nihilism

Written in 1873 or 1874.

This writing is in the William James Papers at Harvard University, bMS Am 1092.9: II Compositions (4422). First published in William James, *Manuscript Essays and Notes* (Cambridge, Mass.: Harvard University Press, 1988), pp. 150–155.

My complaint against Wright's Nihilism after all amounts to this: that he denies this to be a Universe, and makes it out a "Nulliverse."

The assertion that we must admit no kind of existence but plenary existence, and that therefore things only exist once, so to speak, chance to be, de facto, not de jure, contradicts the vague but deep notion of common sense that in each thing, beside its happening to exist as a matter of fact now, there is another kind of being which we may call ideal, and describe by many sayings, as that the thing has a *meaning*, serves a purpose, is a cause, or an end, was intended or predestined, has a "Nature" by virtue of which it is as it is, &c. Now all these attributions connote that the thing operates or is in some way effective or "recognized" where it does not actually and plenarily exist. The criterion of 'reality = effectiveness' here joins hands with common sense. As Peirce's criterion, breadth of relation, only admits as real such elements as enter into the *System*; so that the reality of each thing is measured by a standard extrinsic to its actual existence; so *here*, dynamic connection with other existences becomes the test of substantial reality; or in other words a thing only has being at all as it enters in some way into the being of other things, or constitutes part of a Universe or organism. In other words as to their *being* things are continuous, and so far as this is what people mean when they affirm a substance, substance must be held to exist.

Generally however I suppose more is meant than this, something namely like an other and a primordial *thing* on a plane behind that of the phenomena, & numerically additional to them. All I mean is that unity which comes from the phenomena being continuous with each other. Whether we may add this unit to the sum of phenomenal units I cannot tell. But Renouvier's denial of substance does not seem to me to touch what I affirm so long as he continues to maintain that the "laws" are as real as the phenomena which they unite. The British school say that the laws are nil—*nominis umbra*.

Common people use the larger categories under which things and events are conceived to explain them account for them. He says the categories merely result from the way the things group themselves, are names of modes of grouping, void of positive significance in themselves.

Examples.

1. Some representations are recognized as real or veracious, others as false. We think the former group themselves *so* or together because of a common character; he that the grouping *is* the common character. We that the grouping *means* the reality: He that the reality is but a name for that grouping.

2. "Behind the bare *fact* of resemblance is nothing."

3. He thinks that there is no *Nature* in things. We say that things behave so and so because of their nature or properties. He that they behave so, each time afresh as it were. *If,* (haply,) as before, we say there is a common Nature; if otherwise, that there is no common nature. But the nature is *a posteriori* to the happening, a mere synthetic mark we class it & others by, not *a priori* and determinant of it, as in the popular view.

4. The law of association: "States that have been associated will be reproduced in company," is taken by the vulgar to mean, States will be so reproduced *because* they have been associated. He means no such thing: Their having been associated is at most a token to us to expect them again together but their coming together again is not *due* to their once having done so, but *toto coelo* an absolute & independent fact. To suppose any cause wd. be to posit an *a priori* determining *associability* in each, which is metaphysical.

5. When we rub one body we get heat, another, friction. When we strike one, a clear note, another, a dull one. One receiving a certain blow moves slow, another, being lighter, fast, and so forth, gravity makes a long pendulum go slowly, another rapidly &c. In other words, the transmutations of force are determined in quality, time, amount &c, by the "nature" of the substances and the form of their arrangement [I used to ask if this act of *change* itself were a devourer of force, so that the same amount did not reappear after the change as existed before it. Wright says this need not be supposed] in the popular view. He thinks that the change is but the boundary division, a mere geometrical point, between the distinct phenomena.

And so far from the particularity of the change being due to the pre-existing quality or "Nature" of the substance,[1] what we call the nature of the substance is utterly constituted of the particulars of the change. They existing, it exists, or is posited by us. Were they different we should posit another substance. To assign as cause for the change a substantial nature which the change only when made gives us, is to reason in a circle.

6. He denies that there is any Universe. To most men, even those who should admit that the Universe was a mere system or multitude of representations, the fact that the representations come together, and seem to combine and influence each other leads to the belief in some common ground on which they stand in order to do so. If each representation is totally independent, how does it ever come into collision with any other, how can it be synthesized with another? Space & time at least (if not the ego of apperception) they have in common. And although these are not dynamic or substantial bonds of union, yet they in some sense unite the heterogeneous into a Universe.

7. There is no kind of existence, he says, except actual plenary existence. Potential existence is nothing. What we mean when we talk of it is nothing ontological, but only a logical fact; we expect it, and say it is potential, inasmuch as it will come if our expectation is grounded. But the "grounds" of the expectation, (association or similarity) are no real causes of *it*, such as common sense would suppose under the name, but only forms of thought arbitrarily preceding it, of a being wholly foreign to it, and as we say, having absolutely nothing to do with it.

8. Nihilism denies continuity. Of the two elements of a change it says one does not exist *at all* till the other has ceased *entirely*. Common sense which lets one thing run into another and exists potentially or in substance where its antecedent is allows continuity.

I have been in the habit of indicating the difference between Wright's nominalistic nihilism, so common sense and metaphysics, by saying that the latter admitted a duplication of the phenomenon which the former excluded and by symbolizing this duplication by the formula added to the phenomenon of "*it is meant*." Thus the truth of a perception or conception depends on its *objectivity*—this is equivalent to it is meant that we should *so* perceive or conceive, not otherwise. The goodness or rightness of a state or act can be described by saying they are meant to be, the rationality of a set of thoughts point to something which means them. Now the rudiment of this duplicating element in certain of our experiences which others are devoid of, seems to be found in the peculiarity of certain representations to have coerciveness. We must think them, they are discriminated from the rest, they attract our attention either by a charm which they possess for us (interest) or by a sort of physical cogency (pain) or by a logical propriety which keeps suggesting them, altho' we may try to banish them. The upshot is that we feel peculiarly towards them—as mere moments of our feeling they are exactly like moments belonging to the other set—But as moments having this quality they acquire a different character over and above their intrinsic character as feeling; they are felt in a peculiar way, they stand in a peculiar relation to our general capacity for feeling, a relation difficult analytically to express, but which as familiarly felt is the clearest and simplest of our elementary representations, the relation of reality which implies not only that we feel so & so, but that we *should* feel so, that we are meant to feel so, that there *is* something outside of the feeling itself as an instant conscious existence.

Substance metaphysically considered denotes nothing more than this: "*it is meant*," a *plus* ultra the phenomenon. What this *plus* may be is left undecided—it may be a noumenal world, it may only be the other phenomena with which the present real one is related—it may in a word denote merely the *continuity* of the real world. In any case it is unrecognized by nihilism which maintains that the instant phenomenon is a separate nature absolutely sufficient to itself, and that the peculiarity of coerciveness of various kinds it may possess should be considered merely as one intrinsic mark, incident to its being, enveloped by it not transcending its actuality.

That is the elementary point of divergence. Can anything about a representation be said not to fall within its mere actual quality in consciousness? Has it [2] an objective being which has relations with other beings either of a conscious kind, (other representations) or of a non conscious kind, (things, reality, what is *meant*). Of course if we can say they are objective to it, it becomes objective to them, and can be determined by them, & we may recognize it not only in its actuality and intrinsically, but in objective relation as so determined. The mere distinction of two representations from each other is tantamount to giving to them this objectivity, and nothing but the crassest ignoring of common sense will enable a man to deny that once discriminated they stand (sensibly) in dynamic relations to each other wh. are very variable and of whose variations we are conscious.

If the category of substance only denote that the phenomenon refers outside of itself to *something* else (other phenomena it may *be—vide supra* VII) and is legitimate therefore so far as it does not pretend to double the phenomenon with an ontological backing, but only to assert continuity deny discontinuity for it; why then its legitimacy is tested in the same way in which we test the legitimacy of any *hypothesis*. An hypothesis is vain, metaphysical, mythological which simply repeats the phenomenon under a different name—*virtus dormitiva*, vital force &c—legitimate if it refer it to a class already known in other ways; or declare a property analytically contained from which consequences flow other than those already known; or ascribe it to an entity defined by properties *additional* to the phenomenon in question. All these hypotheses bring the phenomenon into *continuity with something* else. According to the above conception, we may say they confer substantiality upon it. To dispute whether Hamlet is mad is ludicrous if we only mean to say these acts in the play are mad—we know the acts, and to label them mad does not add to our knowledge, unless it enables us to say that their actor wd. be likely to do certain other acts not in the play and specified as characteristic of madmen.

Query? To find the legitimate sphere of the idea of substance, and the justification for the irrepressible metaphysical affirmation.

1. "*It is meant*" this asserts the a priori element.
2. Continuity.

Impossible to say: how pleasant *this* (i.e. saying how pleasant) is. Reference of act beyond itself. At every minute the object of our thought not to be a mere tautology must hypothesis a is b. b must be already known in some other determination *than as* a.

Hodgson's philosophy is absolute in the sense that it is "all embracing" *i.e.* that it admits no *plus ultra* of being beyond what it defines. But it is non-absolute in the sense that its principles are not entities or independent existents. All existents fall within, or are enveloped by its principles. These have it is true no separate being from the concrete existents, but whenever we think of a concrete existent we are forced to perceive time & space portending like a margin beyond it, and this residuary *t. & s.* can never be explained but only assumed & allowed.

NOTES

1. —or to the form of their arrangement—? this and the already recognized-as-present-properties of the "substance" which determines the change are what pre-exist and excuse us for saying the Nature or substance pre exists—inasmuch as they determine an expectancy in us which is gratified.

2. Has its subjectivity objectivity.

Maudsley's *Responsibility in Mental Disease*

Atlantic Monthly 34 (September 1874): 364–365.

Review of Henry Maudsley, *Responsibility in Mental Disease*. London: Henry S. King & Co., 1874.

Dr. Maudsley's work, Responsibility in Mental Disease, is, barring a couple of points which we shall note, admirable as a popular account of the diseases the human mind is heir to, and deserving of its polyglot destiny in the International Scientific Series. Our first cavil is that the accomplished author is somewhat tediously querulous with the "theological" and "metaphysical" way of looking at things, which figure throughout, as if the neck of humanity were still under their foot, and the yearly holocaust of human victims had to be handed in. We can only account for Dr. Maudsley's surliness by supposing it to be based on some harsh personal experiences of his youth. These are known often to leave idiosyncrasies of feeling behind. Our second objection is relative to the main thesis of the book, which we cannot consider the author to have conclusively vindicated. He thinks that American legal decisions, as being more merciful than British ones where possible insanity was involved, have been in advance of the latter; that no act which is a product or offspring of mental disease can be criminal; that a partial "monomania" should shield the wrong-doer from ordinary punishability, even where the crime seems to have no logical connection with the mental disorder; and that "It is truly a strange piece of irony to exact perfect controlling power in a disease the special character of which is to weaken the will and increase the force of passion." We hold that the punishment of the insane is after all a matter of public *policy*, to be decided by many other considerations than the psychological one which Dr. Maudsley has alone considered, namely, whether the subject have flexibility of choice enough to make him properly "accountable" to us for his deeds. This criterion we admit to be ably treated by the doctor; but unable, in this place, to expatiate further on the subject, we may say that Dr. Hammond, in his pamphlet published last year on Insanity in its Relations to Crime, seems to us to have taken a truer, if a less merciful view.

The last chapter in Dr. Maudsley's book, on The Prevention of Insanity, is the most original and valuable. Much has been written of late on the hygiene of the mind, but for a certain depth of intuition and vigor of expression, we remember nothing comparable to this chapter. It is a pity it should not be reprinted as a tract, and dispersed gratis over the land. The first factor in the production of mental disease is the hereditary factor. Second in causative importance comes, according to the author, intemperance. "If the hereditary causes were cut off, and insanity thus stamped out for a time, it would assuredly soon be created anew by intemperance and other excesses." But as men cannot be expected to abandon their excesses at a stroke, it is to the slow education of the race that we must look for relief. "There can be no doubt that in the capability of self-formation which each one has in greater or less degree, there lies a power over himself to prevent insanity. Not many persons need go mad perhaps—at any rate from moral causes—if they only knew the resources of their nature, and knew how to develop them systematically." Accordingly the author sketches his ideal of what should be aimed at. We cannot mar it by short extracts, but will merely say that while Dr. Maudsley's professed criterion of excellence in character is the evolutionist one of "harmony" with the world, he lays immense stress in his conclusions upon inward consistency of thought and action, with self-development as an aim, and indifference to outward fortune as a ruling mood. These conclusions are no doubt true, though it may be doubted whether a rigid and adequate logical bridge to them from the premised harmony with the universe has yet been built. A great Roman emperor said: "O universe, whatever harmonizes with thee is harmonious with me!" The "adjustments" and "correspondences" of the Spenserian philosophy were not in his mind, but the indifference to fortune which Dr. Maudsley preaches, and the *firm* serenity which more than anything else a consciousness of one's consistency will give, were alike features of his moral ideal. Moralists need not be anxious when the most advanced positivism comes to practical conclusions that differ so little from those of the "metaphysically" minded Marcus Aurelius.

TAIT AND STEWART'S *The Unseen Universe*

The Nation 20 (27 May 1875): 366–367.

Review of Peter Guthrie Tait and Balfour Stewart, *The Unseen Universe; or, Physical Speculations on a Future State*. New York: Macmillan, 1875.

In *Nature,* nine or ten months ago, there appeared a communication signed "West," registering, for the sake of establishing priority of date, a discovery which, in the anagrammatic form the author chose to give it at that moment, ran thus:

$$A^8 \ C^3 \ D \ E^{12} \ F^4 \ G \ H^6 \ I^6 \ L^3 \ M^3 \ N^5 \ O^6 \ P \ R^4 \ S^5 \ T^{14} \ U^6 \ V^2 \ W \ X \ Y^2.$$

These letters placed rightly compose a proposition—"Thought conceived to affect the matter of another universe simultaneously with this may explain a future state"—of which this book is the full elucidation and expansion. It seems probable, therefore, that "West" was one of the two reputed authors of the 'Unseen Universe,' and presumably the senior partner. Of him it may be said that he is at all events no sciolist in physics, and the way in which Biblical texts and the most ruthless of modern scientific hypotheses combine to shape and support his conclusions is, in the year of grace 1875, a phenomenon which really gives one an impression of freshness and originality.

His argument runs somewhat as follows: Modern physics postulates, in addition to the gross matter which we can weigh and feel, another form of material existence called the ether, or medium. Some very transcendental speculations have endeavored to explain how such a characteristic property of the gross matter as gravitation might be derived from the pressure of the ether. Furthermore, the qualitative differences which the gross matter presents to our senses and reagents are explicable by various hypotheses as to its quantitative internal molecular arrangement. The "elements" of chemistry may owe their distinction from each other to the different groupings of the homogeneous primordial atoms of which they are built. Now, primordial atoms themselves are supposed by Sir Wm. Thomson to be vortex rings generated out of a perfect fluid filling all space—in other words, eddies in the medium, or portions of it mechanically differentiated. This conception does not, it is true, account for gravitation; hence its originator adopts the additional hypothesis of ultra-mundane corpuscles, which he supposes to be a finer form of vortices. Our present author, who is a determined adherent of development, objects to the hypothesis of the medium being a perfect (frictionless) fluid, because in that case we cannot suppose matter to have been evolved from it, but must needs resort to the hypothesis of creation, which is an appeal to the unconditioned always to be avoided; and moreover, because certain facts connected with the light of the stars suggest the conclusion that the ether is not perfectly transparent, but *absorbs energy*. But with whatever differences of detail, the upshot of all these speculations is that matter and the medium, or the visible and the invisible, are considered materially and dynamically continuous. One arose in time by a coagulation or precipitation occurring in the other, and must needs end in time, if the other be not a perfect (frictionless) fluid, by the undoing of the momentum of rotation it contains. The great law of dissipation of energy, too, which requires us to imagine a constant leakage into the ether of heat vibrations from the visible world—vibrations which will never be restored—leads to the same conclusion. The energy which is leaving our visible world in every direction at the rate of 188,000 miles a second *is not lost*. "It will all be ultimately appropriated by the invisible world, and we may now imagine as a possibility that the separate existence of the visible universe will share the same fate, so that we shall have no huge useless inert mass existing in after ages to remind the passer-by of a form of energy and a species of matter that is long since out of date and functionally effete. Why should not the universe bury its dead out of sight?"

This bold conclusion is the culmination of the author's scientific argument. The use he makes of the ethereal world thus left upon his hands, with all its stored-up energy, is, if possible, more purely speculative still. In the first place, it has a *history* connected with that of the visible world, since by transfer of energy from the latter it is conditioned in time, direction, amount, etc., by the particulars which are now and here occurring. Every event here, then, is recorded by its traces on the invisible world, and these traces may be organized (it is not attempted to define how) into a memory. A possibility is thus afforded for a continuity of being, both conscious and material, between the two worlds, and our faith or fancy may fill out its details in the way that seems most fitting. The author's aim simply is to explode the notion that science *debars* the supposition of such a continuity. He indulges in some further speculations about superhuman intelligences in that world, and concludes that it must contain an *immanent* intelligent agency which once determined the manner of formation of the visible universe from it, and impressed upon the molecules thereof that uniformity which Clerk-Maxwell calls the stamp of the "manufactured" article. This immanent agency is proved by Scripture to be the Second Person of the Trinity as distinguished from the First, who is transcendent.

The points which strike us most in the whole attempt are, first, the urgency of the author's demand for "continuity," or the principle of explaining one conditioned event by another conditioned event, and "pushing back the Great First Cause in time as far as possible," combined with his hopelessness of "driving the Creator out of the field altogether," and resulting in the compromise by which he gives us the Son as indwelling in the world, and merely determinative, not creative, of its molecular events, whilst the Father stays outside in inscrutable majesty, with apparently no function but to keep up logical appearances. Secondly, we are struck by the way in which he immediately resorts to teleology to determine the particular constitution of that unseen world of whose existence his previous arguments have established the probability. In a word, his tactics are in logical form precisely identical with those of the most primitive, "unscientific," and short-winded natural theologian, the only difference being in the scale of his operations. He shows us the same mechanical determinism in the line of events we clearly and familiarly apprehend, and he bounds the penumbra *a parte ante* in the same way by the Absolute Cause, and defines it *a parte post* by faith, guided by teleological reasoning. It *is* only the incomparable superiority of the modern scientific imagination on its *quantitative* side that may seem at first to give our author's speculations a different aspect. And truly enough, if vastness of scale be a real character of the universe, both in space and time, those Hindu-like imaginations which are pleased with the contemplation of monstrous lengths, and are able to feel the difference between sums expressed in units of different orders of infinity, would seem the best fitted to divine its secrets. The German and English imaginations are fast being educated up to this spaciousness, whilst the French mind lags behind both in this point and in its feeling for continuity. Our author, therefore, may enjoy the credit of having attacked the problem of natural theology (and solved it in his way) on a scale not unworthy of the grandeur of the theme's dimensions.

But when he professes to have *mediated* between Science and Religion we cannot grant his claim. He simply gratifies the demands of science for an ever-wider scope, and thus throws upon religion a vaster task for her translating and interpreting powers. But his scientific unseen world is by no means identical with the world "behind the veil" of religion. Christian devoutness has never expressed its trust simply in "another," but always in "another *and a better* world." Our author's belief in the "betterness" of that "other" world which he constructs for us demands from him at the end of his mechanical gyrations, be they never so ingenious and rarefied, the same simple act of teleologic trust, the same faith that the end will crown the work, with which the most narrow-minded old woman so quickly envelops her briefly-recited cosmogony. We for our part not only hold that such an act of trust is licit, but we think, furthermore, that any one *to whom it makes a practical difference* (whether of motive to action or of mental peace) is in duty bound to make it. If "scientific" scruples withhold him from making it, this proves his intellect to have been simply sicklied o'er and paralyzed by scientific pursuits. In the physical realm the "subjective method" of finding truth may be the root of all evil. But the affirmation that this physical world has *also* a moral meaning and a moral plan is one that no argument drawn from purely physical truth can either establish or impugn. It is nevertheless an affirmation which either is or is not true, and which if true may, from the very nature of the case, be intended to command from us only that inward, free, or moral assent, or rather consent, in which the subjective method consists. As we have said, the 'Unseen Universe' does not make this consent essentially easier. It establishes no "continuity" whatever between mechanical reasoning about facts at our feet and teleological reasoning about ultimate things. But it widens the data and horizon which teleology receives from science, in accordance with the sentiment of the day; it will, doubtless, be found suggestive both by men of science and divines; and it deserves to be widely read.

Wundt's *Grundzüge der physiologischen Psychologie*

North American Review 121 (July 1875): 195–201.

Review of Wilhelm Wundt, *Grundzüge der physiologischen Psychologie*. Leipzig: Engelmann, 1874.

On every hand, no less in Germany than in England, there are signs of a serious revival of philosophical inquiry; from a quarter, too, which leads one to indulge the hope that real progress will erelong be made. For it is the men engaged in the physical sciences who are now pressing hard in the direction of metaphysical problems; and although in a certain point of view their education may not specially qualify them for the task, it would be sheer folly not to expect from their trained cunning in experiment, their habits of patience and fairness, and their willingness to advance by small steps at a time, new results of the highest importance.

Nowhere is the new movement more conspicuous than in psychology, which is of course the antechamber to metaphysics. The physiologists of Germany, devoid for the most part of any systematic bias, have, by their studies on the senses and the brain, really inaugurated a new era in this science. Where quasi-scholastic distinction and nomenclature were the only instrument of advance, we now find measurements and objective reactions to help us on our way. And in the main, whilst in France thoroughly, and in England still faintly, the old jealousy between the objective and the subjective methods survives, the one as patronized by religious, the other by materialistic speculation, we find that in Germany the minds of the best investigators on either side are wholly unpreoccupied with any such militant consciousness. The spiritualist Lotze is as hearty a physiologist as the materialist Moleschott; while it is hard to guess from the psychologic contributions of Fechner, Helmholtz, Mach, and Horwicz, what their theologic or antitheologic bias may be, or if they have any at all. This detachment of mind is very healthy, and is in striking contrast with what such writers as Mill, Maudsley, and Huxley show us in England, and McCosh and Porter in this country. But even here we find in Hodgson and Lewes the beginning of a new era of temper, destined surely to be more fruitful than the old regime of unfairness and recrimination.

The Heaven-scaling Titans have had their day in Germany, and the confident systems lie in the dust; for the school-boy performances of a Haeckel and the sensational paradoxes of a Hartmann cannot count as philosophy. A season of headache and apathy, with bald *Empirie*, the mere registration of facts, for a diversion, ensued, as was natural after such a metaphysical debauch. There is something almost dramatic in the way in which the thirsty spirit of man is seen to be regaining its normal appetite again, and with its new desires, indulging in new hopes. Only maturity has brought circumspection, and the old rash notion of scaling the opaque walls of existence by a quick *coup de main*, and ravishing the secret within in an instant, has been given up. The method of patience, starving out, and harassing to death is tried; Nature must submit to a regular *siege*, in which minute advantages gained night and day by the forces that hem her in must sum themselves up at last into her overthrow. There is little of the grand style about these new prism, pendulum, and galvanometer philosophers. They mean business, not chivalry. What generous divination, and that superiority in virtue which was thought by Cicero to give a man the best insight into nature, failed to do, their spying and scraping, their deadly tenacity and almost diabolic cunning, must some day accomplish.

Such as they are, Professor Wundt, the title of whose latest work heads our article, is perhaps their paragon; and his whole career is at the same time a superb illustration of that thoroughness in education for which Germany is so renowned. In that learned land Browning's fable of the Grammarian's Funeral is re-enacted every day. Poor Waitz, for instance, who died a few years ago with his monumental *Anthropologie der Naturvölker* unfinished, began that work merely to educate himself for the study of psychology and the philosophy of religion. Wundt is more fortunate than Waitz, for he has at last reached, at Zurich, the goal he evidently strove for from the first, a University Chair of Philosophy. Still young, his apprenticeship is over and the fruit is to be reaped. But what an apprenticeship! To be Helmholtz's colleague as professor of physiology at Heidelberg; to spend years in a laboratory and to publish numerous elaborate experimental researches; to write a large treatise on Physics, and an admirable handbook of Physiology (both of which have had several editions and been translated into French), besides two volumes of lectures on Psychology, an essay on the law of causation, and various fugitive articles; to study each new subject by giving a year's course of lectures upon it, these are *preparations* on a scale rather fitted to cool than to excite the ardor of an American neophyte in philosophy.

Nevertheless Wundt has now laid them behind him, and in this compactly printed volume he takes, so to speak, an account of stock before embarking on his new career. The work certainly fills a *lacuna*, and circumscribes in a very convenient way all those phenomena of human life which can be studied both by introspection and by objective investigation. The anatomy and physiology of the nervous centres and organs of sense occupy about one third; the natural history of sensations, pleasures, and pains, and perceptions spatial and temporal, follow; and analyses of the aesthetic, volitional, and self-conscious life conclude. The style is extremely concise, dry, and clear, and as the author is as thoroughly at home in the library as in the laboratory, the work is really a cyclopaedia of reference. If, through a large part of it, the reader finds that physiology and psychology lie side by side without combining, it is more the fault of the science than of the author. He has registered no detail without doing his best to reduce and weave it in with the mass. Indeed so uninterrupted is his critical elaboration, that we can think of no book (except perhaps the "Origin of Species") in the course of which the author propounds so many separate opinions.

Their multiplicity forbids our even attempting to give an account of them. But we may single out one or two for notice. Every one has heard of the measurements of the velocity of nervous action which Helmholtz inaugurated. Wundt, after having worked at the subject experimentally for fourteen years, with interruptions, may fairly claim to have brought it for the present to a conclusion. The principle is this: a signal is given to the subject who, immediately on its reception, replies by closing an electric key. The instant of the signal and of the closure are chronographically registered, and the time between them ascertained; and according to the circumstances of the experiment this time undergoes some very interesting variations, whose interpretation by Wundt seems to us particularly felicitous. In a previous chapter on Attention and Consciousness, he has adopted a convenient nomenclature which really is something more than a metaphor. "If we say of all the representations present to the mind at any one time that they are in the *field of vision* of consciousness, we may call that part of them to which the attention is particularly directed the *inward point of sight*. The entrance of a representation into this inner field of vision may be called Perception; its entrance into the focus or point of sight, Apperception." (p. 717.) Now the latter act is often a volitional effort on the part of the subject, a focusing of the attention upon the impression, which adjustment occupies a distinct interval of time. This interval is a part of the time registered in the experiments just referred to. It, *plus* the time occupied in the volitional innervation of the motor nerves which provoke the movement by which the key is closed, are called by Wundt together, the *time of reaction*. It is this interval of psychical activity which is variable according to the experimental conditions. The other subdivisions of the total time, that of transmission from the organ of sense to the brain, that of "perception," and that of transmission to the muscle, are probably invariable. Now the experimental circumstances which shorten the time of reaction are mainly those which define beforehand as to its quality, intensity, or time, the signal given to the observer, so that he may accurately expect it before it comes. The focusing of the attention takes place under these circumstances *in advance*. Where, for instance, we are warned preliminarily by a slight sound that the signal is going to occur, the registered time is reduced to a minimum. The attention, in other words, "is so exactly adjusted to the entrance of the signal into the inner field of vision, that at the very instant of perception, apperception likewise occurs, and with apperception, the volitional mandate." More remarkable still! the time registered may be reduced to zero, that is, the signal may be given and the key closed at objectively the same instant, so that not only the "reaction-time," but also the physiological duration of nerve transmission to and from the brain are abolished. This paradox amounts to saying that the impression is apperceived before it actually occurs, or that expectant attention is equivalent to objective stimulation.[1] And the same phenomenon is made even more strikingly manifest by another set of Wundt's original investigations, which we have not space to describe.

We select these particular researches for notice because they demonstrate as it were mathematically what empiricists are too apt to ignore—the thorough-going participation of the spontaneous mental element in determining even the simplest experiences. The *a posteriori* school, with its anxiety to prove the mind a *product, coûte que coûte,* keeps pointing to mere "experience" as its source. But it never defines what experience is. *My* experience is only what I agree to attend to. Pure sensation is the vague, a semi-chaos, for the *whole* mass of impressions falling on any individual are chaotic, and become orderly only by selective attention and recognition. These acts postulate *interests* on the part of the subject—interests which, as ends or purposes set by his emotional constitution, keep interfering with the pure flow of impressions and their association, and causing the vast majority of mere sensations to be ignored. It is amusing to see how Spencer shrinks from explicit recognition of this law, even when he is forced to take it into his hand, so to speak. Mr. Bain, in principle, admits it, but does not work it out. The only English-writing empiricist who has come near to making any use of it is Mr. Chauncey Wright, in his article on the Evolution of Self-Consciousness in this Review for 1873.

Another section important to English readers is that devoted to touch, vision, and the cognition of space. Wundt's account of vision is unapproached by anything in our language for thoroughness and subtlety. His conclusion as to the nature of our notion of space is in one word this: "It is the resultant of a distinct psychological process, . . . which may be called a *synthesis*, because the evolved product shows properties which are not present in the sensuous material used in its construction." That is to say, our *intuition* of space within the limits in which it exists—a very different thing from our *idea* of space, which has no limits—is that of an undivided *plenum*, a perfectly simple and specific *quale* or affection of consciousness. Whether this new quality of feeling once arisen is *fertile*, that is, whether it be analyzable into different elements from those by whose synthesis it arose, giving us new relations, new propositions concerning them, propositions not *merely* expressive of the *particular* tactile, retinal, and muscular experiences that generated the form of intuition—this is not decided by Wundt, nor do we here affirm it. To prove it would be essentially to reinstate the Kantian philosophy, that is, to vindicate for the mind not only a native wealth in forms of sensibility—every empiricist must admit that!—but the possession of forms with synthetic judgments involved in them.

Wundt's term "synthesis" reminds one of the term "mental chemistry" used by the Mills, or rather admitted into their works, but not used; for both they, Bain, and Spencer are so desperately bent on covering up all tracks of the mind's originality (especially in this field of space, preoccupied by Kant), that they utterly repudiate mental chemistry here, and labor with an energy worthy of a better cause to procure out of mere "association" something never given in any one of the ideas associated, something which after all they have to *escamoter* out of their sleeve as it were, or, in the absurd Spencerian fashion, to call "nascent," and trust that, in that seemingly infantile and innocent guise, you will take no alarm at its intrusion.

We are not at all concerned with the ultimate philosophical bearings of this particular question. Settle the particulars, and philosophy will take its turn. But to be so bribed beforehand by philosophical antipathies as to ignore evidence and shirk conclusions, is a poor business for either psychologist or physiologist.

The notion of mental synthesis or chemistry opens the way to interesting questions. Hitherto most thinkers have admitted that in a state of consciousness the *esse* and the *existere* were one and the same thing, namely, the *sentiri*. In the conscious sphere reality and phenomenon, substance and accident, nature and property, cannot be distinguished as they are in the objective sphere. A thought has only one mode of being at all, namely, as that very thought. *It* cannot become a different thought, nor can it cease to be *thought* without ceasing to *be* altogether. But in the material world, that which we call one and the same thing, a *leaf*, for instance, has relations, and differs according to the point of view. It was green and is now brown. It is a product of chemical forces, a reducing agent, a form of beauty, an effect of luminiferous ether, an affection of my sensorium each in turn, and yet preserves what we call its identity throughout.

Now *when*, in this matter of space, we see feelings of innervation and retinal impressions combining into a novel *quale* of consciousness, what are we to say? Do *they* really exist within the new *quale*, or, in other words, have they, in addition to their simple *sentiri*, another existence, a sort of objective substantiality which may betray itself by producing effects—we being conscious of the effect, but no longer of the original feeling? Or is the process a logical one, the simple feelings being really "perceived" by the mind, but only used as signs to suggest the higher product, that alone being "apperceived," whilst the signs are unnoticed and forgotten? Or, thirdly, have the simple feelings never existed at all as feelings, and has the resultant intuition of space a purely physiological antecedent, in the shape of the *combined* nervous action, whose components, when they were separately excited, corresponded to the retinal and other feelings? These problems lie over the whole field of psychology, and are worthy of explicit discussion.

Wundt does not deal with them at all, except by implication, as above. Neither does he seem ever to have entertained the hypothesis advanced by several English writers recently, that conscious states have no dynamic relations either with each other or with the nervous system. He assumes throughout that feelings as such may combine with each other (as we have just seen in regard to space), and that they may also act as nervous stimuli. We think, for our part, that the Englishmen (only two of whom, Hodgson and Clifford, have deigned to give reasons for their belief) are prematurely dogmatic. Taking a purely naturalistic view of the matter, it seems reasonable to suppose that, unless consciousness served some useful purpose, it would not have been superadded to life. Assuming hypothetically that this is so, there results an important problem for psycho-physicists to find out, namely, *how* consciousness helps an animal, how much complication of machinery may be saved in the nervous centres, for instance, if consciousness accompany their action. Might, for example, an animal which regulated its acts by notions and feelings get along with fewer preformed reflex connections and distinct channels for acquired habits in its nervous system than an animal whose varied behavior under varying circumstances was purely and simply the result of the change of course through the nervous reticulations which a minute alteration of stimulus had caused the nervous action to take? In a word, is consciousness an economical *substitute* for mechanism?

Wundt's book has many shortcomings, but they only prove how confused and rudimentary the science of psycho-physics still is. More workers and critics are wanted in the field, propounders of questions as well as of answers. Whoever they may be, they will find this treatise indispensable for study and reference. All we have cared to do has been to call attention to its importance and to the merits of its singularly acute and learned author.

NOTES

1. The reason why, in these not very frequent cases, we do not notice the signal twice (once as apperceived in advance by our spontaneous attention, and once passively after it has occurred) is probably to be sought in another series of experiments which show that one act of apperception, if it be at all intense, prevents the apperception of other nearly simultaneous impressions. This is by virtue of what Wundt calls the "law of discrete flow" in representations. "Attention demands a certain time to pass from one impression to another. As long as the first impression lasts the entire attention is bent upon it, and cannot, therefore, focus itself in advance, in order to apperceive the second impression at the very instant of its occurrence." The second will then either be apperceived late, or abort, unless indeed it can coalesce in one conception with the first. Of all impressions "perceived," none are remembered for more than a minute, except those which are "apperceived," or brought to the inner focus. In the case related in the text, the *real* impression may either abort (pass unnoticed, unapperceived) or it may coalesce with the imaginary one.

Lewes's *Problems of Life and Mind*

Atlantic Monthly 36 (September 1875): 361–363.

Review of George Henry Lewes, *Problems of Life and Mind, First Series: The Foundations of a Creed, Volume 2.* Boston: J. R. Osgood and Co., 1875.

More problems! Why should we read them if they are not our problems, but only Mr. Lewes's? Of all forms of earthly worry, the metaphysical worry seems the most gratuitous. If it lands us in permanently skeptical conclusions, it is worse than superfluous; and if (as is almost always the case with non-skeptical systems) it simply ends by "indorsing" common-sense, and reinstating us in the possession of our old feelings, motives, and duties, we may fairly ask if it was worth while to go so far round in order simply to return to our starting-point and be put back into the old harness. Is not the primal state of philosophic innocence, since the practical difference is *nil*, as good as the state of reflective enlightenment? And need we, provided we can stay at home and take the world for granted, undergo the fatigues of a campaign with such uncomfortable spirits as the present author, merely for the sake of coming to our own again, with nothing gained but the pride of having accompanied his expedition? So we may ask. But is the pride nothing? Consciousness is the only measure of utility, and even if no philosophy could ever alter a man's motives in life—which is untrue—that it should add to their conscious completeness is enough to make thousands take upon themselves its burden of perplexities. We like the sense of companionship with better and more eager intelligences than our own, and that increment of self-respect which we all experience in passing from an instinctive to a reflective state, and adopting a belief which hitherto we simply underwent.

Mr. Lewes has drunk deep of the waters of skepticism that have of late years been poured out so freely in England, but he has worked his way through them into a constructive activity; arid his work is only one of many harbingers of a reflux in the philosophic tide. All philosophic reflection is essentially skeptical at the start. To common-sense, and in fact to all living thought, matters actually thought of are held to *be* absolutely and objectively as we think them. Every representation *per se*, and while it persists, is of something absolutely *so*. It becomes relative, flickering, insecure, only when reduced, only in the light of *further* consideration which we may bring forward to confront it with. This may be called its *reductive*. Now the reductive of most of our confident beliefs about Being is the reflection that they are *our* beliefs; that we are turbid media; and that a form of being may exist uncontaminated by the touch of the fallacious knowing subject. In the light of this conception, the Being we know droops its head; but until this conception has been formed it knows no fear. The motive of most philosophies has been to find a position from which one could *exorcise the reductive*, and remain securely in possession of a secure belief. Ontologies do this by their conception of "necessary" truth, *i.e.*, a truth with no alternative; with a *praeterea nihil*, and not a *plus ultra possible*; a truth, in other words, whose only reductive would be the impossible, nonentity, or zero.

In such conclusions as these philosophy re-joins hands with common-sense. For above all things common-sense craves for a stable conception of things. We desire to know what to *expect*. Once having settled down into an attitude towards life both as to its details and as a whole, an incalculable disturbance which might arise, disconcert all our judgments, and render our efforts vain, would be in the last degree undesirable. Now as a matter of fact we do live in a world from which as a rule we know what to expect. Whatever items we found together in the past are likely to coexist in the future. Our confidence in this state of things deprives us of all sense of insecurity; if we lay our plans rightly the world will fulfill its part of the contract. Common-sense, or popular philosophy, explains this by what is called the judgment of Substance, that is, by the postulation of a persistent Nature, immutable by time, behind each phenomenal group, which binds that group together and makes it what it is essentially and eternally. Even in regard to that mass of accidents which must be expected to occur in some shape but cannot be accurately prophesied in detail, we set our minds at rest, by saying that the world with all its events has a substantial cause; and when we call this cause God, Love, or Perfection, we feel secure that whatever the future may harbor, it cannot at bottom be inconsistent with the character of this term. So our attitude towards even the unexpected is in a general sense defined.

Now this substantial judgment has been adopted by most dogmatic philosophies. They have explained the collocations of phenomena by an immutable underlying nature or natures, beside or beyond which they have posited either the sphere of the Impossible, if they professed rationalism throughout, or merely a *de facto* Nonentity if they admitted the element of Faith as legitimate. But the skeptical philosophers who have of late predominated in England have denied that the substantial judgment is legitimate at all, and in so doing have seemed among other things to deny the legitimacy of the confidence and repose which it engenders. The habitual concurrence of the same phenomena is not a case of dynamic connection at all, they say. It may happen again—but we have no rational warrant for asserting that it must. The syntheses of data we think necessary are only so to *us*, from habit. The universe may turn inside out to-morrow, for aught we know; our knowledge grasps neither the essential nor the immutable. Instead of a nonentity beyond, there is a darkness, peopled it may be with every nightmare shape. Their total divergence from popular philosophy has many other aspects, but this last thought is their reductive of its tendency to theosophize and of its dogmatic confidence in general.

The originality of Mr. Lewes is that while vigorously hissing the "Substances" of common-sense and metaphysics off the stage, he also scouts the reductive which the school of Mill has used, and maintains the absoluteness and essentiality of our knowledge. The world according to him as according to them is truly enough only the world *as known*, but *for us* there *is* no other world. For grant a moment the existence of such a one: we could never be affected by it; as soon as we were affected, however, we should be knowers of it, in the only sense in which there is any knowledge at all, the sense of subjective determination—and it would have become our world. Now, as such it is a universe and not a heap of sand, or, as has been said, a *nulliverse* like Mill's. Its truths are *aeterna veritates,* essential, exhaustive, immutable. We can settle down upon them and they will keep their promise. The sum of all the properties *is* the substance; the predicates *are* the subject; each property *is* the other viewed in a "different aspect." The same collocations must therefore occur in the future. So far from the notion of cause being illusory, the cause *is* the effect "in another relation," and the effect the procession of the cause. The identification by continuity of what the senses discriminate, and so, according to the reigning empiricism, disunite, is carried so far by Mr. Lewes that in his final chapter he affirms the psychic event which accompanies a tremor in the brain to *be* that tremor "in a different aspect."

His arguments we have not space to expose. One thing is obvious, however: that his results will meet with even greater disfavor from the empirics than from the ontologists in philosophy, and that the pupils of Mill and Bain in particular will find this bold identification of the sensibly diverse too mystical to pass muster. It is in fact the revival of the old Greek puzzle of the One and the Many—how each becomes the other—which they, if we apprehend them aright, have escaped by the simple expedient of suppressing the One. They will join hands too with the ontologists in conjuring up beyond the universe recognized by Mr. Lewes the specter of an hypothetical possible Something, not a Zero— only the ontologists will not join them again in letting this fill the blank form of a logical reductive pure and simple, but will dub it the universe *in se*, or the universe as related to God, if Mr. Lewes still insists on their defining everything as in relation. That Mr. Lewes should say candidly of this thought that *he* is willing to ignore it, cannot restrain them. We may conclude, therefore, that ever-sprouting reflection, or skepticism, just as it preys on all other systems, may also in strict theoretic legitimacy prey upon the ultimate data of Mr. Lewes's Positivism taken as a whole; even though all men should end by admitting that within the bounds of that empirical whole, his views of the necessary continuity between the parts were true. To this reduction by a *plus ultra*, Mr. Lewes can only retort by saying, "Foolishness! So much ontologic thirst is a morbid appetite." But in doing this he simply falls back on the *act of faith* of all positivisms. Weary of the infinitely receding chase after a theoretically warranted Absolute, they return to their starting-point and break off there, like practical men, saying, "Physics, we espouse thee; for better or worse be thou our Absolute!"

Skepticism, or unrest, in short, can always have the last word. After every definition of an object, reflection may arise; infect it with the *cogito*, and so discriminate it from the object *in se*. This is possible *ad infinitum*. That we do not all do it is because at a certain point most of us get tired of the play, resolve to stop, and assuming something for true, pass on to a life of action based on that.

We wish that Mr. Lewes had emphasized this volitional moment in his Positivism. Although the consistent pyrrhonist is the only theoretically unassailable man, it does not follow that he is the right man. Between us and the universe, there are no "rules of the game." The important thing is that our judgments should be right, not that they should observe a logical etiquette. There is a brute, blind element in every thought which still has the vital heat within it and has not yet been reflected on. Our present thought always has it, we cannot escape it, and we for our part think philosophers had best acknowledge it, and avowedly *posit* their universe, staking their persons, so to speak, on the truth of their position. In practical life we despise a man who will risk nothing, even more than one who will heed nothing. May it not be that in the theoretic life the man whose scruples about flawless accuracy of demonstration keep him forever shivering on the brink of Belief is as great an imbecile as the man at the opposite pole, who simply consults his prophetic soul for the answer to everything? What is this but saying that our opinions about the nature of things belong to our moral life?

Mr. Lewes's personal fame will now stand or fall by the *credo* he has published. We do not think the fame should suffer, even though we reserve our assent to important parts of the creed. The book is full of vigor of thought and felicity of style, in spite of its diffuseness and repetition. It will refute many of the objections made by critics to the first volume; and will, we doubt not, be a most important ferment in the philosophic thought of the immediate future.

CHAUNCEY WRIGHT

The Nation 21 (23 September 1875): 194.

The death which we briefly noticed last week reminds us most sadly of the law, that to be an effective great man one needs to have *many* qualities great. If power of analytic intellect pure and simple could suffice, the name of Chauncey Wright would assuredly be as famous as it is now obscure, for he was not merely the great mind of a village—if Cambridge will pardon the expression—but either in London or Berlin he would, with equal ease, have taken the place of master which he held with us. The reason why he is now gone without leaving any work which his friends can consider as a fair expression of his genius, is that his shyness, his want of ambition, and to a certain degree his indolence, were almost as exceptional as his power of thought. Had he, in early life, resolved to concentrate these and make himself a physicist, for example, there is no question but that his would have ranked today among the few first living names. As it was, he preferred general criticism and contemplation, and became something resembling more a philosopher of the antique or Socratic type than a modern *Gelehrter*. His best work has been done in conversation; and in the acts and writings of the many friends he influenced his spirit will, in one way or another, as the years roll on, be more operative than it ever was in direct production. Born at Northampton in 1830, graduating at Harvard in 1852, he left us in the plenitude of his powers. His outward work is limited to various articles in the *North American Review* (one of which Mr. Darwin thought important enough to reprint as a pamphlet in England), a paper or two in the Transactions of the Academy of Arts and Sciences, and a number of critical notices in our own pages—the latest of these being the article entitled "German Darwinism," which we published only two weeks ago. As a writer, he was defective in the shaping faculty—he failed to emphasize the articulations of his argument, to throw a high light, so to speak, on the important points; so that many a casual peruser has probably read on and never noticed the world of searching consequences which lurked involved in some inconspicuously placed word. He spent many years in computing for the *Nautical Almanac* and from time to time accepted some pedagogic work. He gave a course of University lectures on psychology in Harvard College in 1871, and last year he conducted there a course in mathematical physics. As little of a reader as an educated man well can be, he yet astonished every one by his omniscience, for no specialist could talk with Chauncey Wright without receiving some sort of instruction in his specialty. This was due to his irrepressible spontaneous habit of subtle thinking. Every new fact he learned set his whole mental organism in motion, and reflection did not cease till the novel thought was firmly woven with the entire system of his knowledge. Of course in this process new conclusions were constantly evolved, and many a man of science who hoped to surprise him with news of a discovery has been himself surprised by finding it already *constructed* by Wright from data separately acquired in this or that conversation with one or other of the many scholars of Cambridge or Boston, most of whom he personally knew so well.

In philosophy, he was a worker on the path opened by Hume, and a treatise on psychology written by him (could he have been spared and induced to undertake the drudgery) would probably have been the last and most accomplished utterance of what he liked to call the British school. He would have brought the work of Mill and Bain for the present to a conclusion. Of the two motives to which philosophic systems owe their being, the craving for consistency or unity in thought, and the desire for a solid outward warrant for our emotional ends, his mind was dominated only by the former. Never in a human head was contemplation more separated from desire. Schopenhauer, who defined genius as a cognitive faculty manumitted from the service of the will, would have found in him an even stronger example of his definition than he cared to meet. For to Wright's mode of looking at the universe such ideas as pessimism or optimism were alike simply irrelevant. Whereas most men's interest in a thought is proportioned to its possible relation to human destiny, with him it was almost the reverse. When the mere actuality of phenomena will suffice to describe them, he held it pure excess and superstition to speak of a metaphysical whence or whither, of a substance, a meaning, or an end. Just as in cosmogony he preferred Mayer's theory to the nebular hypothesis, and in one of his earliest *North American Review* articles used the happy phrase, "cosmical weather," to describe the irregular dissipation and aggregation of worlds; so, in contemplating the totality of being, he preferred to think of phenomena as the result of a sort of ontologic weather, without inward rationality, an aimless drifting to and fro, from the midst of which relatively stable and so (for us) rational combinations may emerge. The order we observe in things needs *explanation* only on the supposition of a preliminary or potential disorder; and this he pointed out is, as things actually *are* orderly, a gratuitous notion. Anaxagoras, who introduced into philosophy the notion of the νοῦς, also introduced with it that of an antecedent chaos. But if there be no essential chaos, Mr. Wright used to say, an anti-chaotic νοῦς is superfluous. He particularly condemned the idea of substance as a metaphysical idol. When it was objected to him that there must be some principle of oneness in the diversity of phenomena—some *glue* to hold them together and make a universe out of their mutual independence, he would reply that there is no need of a glue to join things unless we apprehend some reason why they should fall asunder. Phenomena *are* grouped—more we cannot say of them. This notion that the actuality of a thing is the absolute totality of its being was perhaps never grasped by any one with such thoroughness as by him.

However different a philosophy one may hold from his, however one may deem that the lack of emotional bias which left him contented with the mere principle of parsimony as a criterion of universal truth was really due to a defect in the active or impulsive part of his mental nature, one must value none the less his formulae. For as yet philosophy has celebrated hardly any stable achievements. The labors of philosophers have, however, been confined to deepening enormously the philosophic *consciousness*, and revealing more and more minutely and fully the import of metaphysical problems. In this preliminary task ontologists and phenomenalists, mechanists and teleologists, must join friendly hands, for each has been indispensable to the work of the other, and the only foe of either is the common foe of both—namely, the practical, conventionally thinking man, to whom, as has been said, nothing has true seriousness but personal interests, and whose dry earnestness in those is only excelled by that of the brute, which takes everything for granted and never laughs.

Mr. Wright belonged to the precious band of genuine philosophers, and among them few can have been as completely disinterested as he. Add to this eminence his tireless amiability, his beautiful modesty, his affectionate nature and freedom from egotism, his childlike simplicity in worldly affairs, and we have the picture of a character of which his friends feel more than ever now the elevation and the rarity.

REMARKS ON SPENCER'S DEFINITION OF MIND AS CORRESPONDENCE

Journal of Speculative Philosophy 12 (January 1878): 1–18.

As a rule it may be said that, at a time when readers are so overwhelmed with work as they are at the present day, all purely critical and destructive writing ought to be reprobated. The half-gods generally refuse to go, in spite of the ablest criticism, until the gods actually *have* arrived; but then, too, criticism is hardly needed. But there are cases in which every rule may be broken. "What!" exclaimed Voltaire, when accused of offering no substitute for the Christianity he attacked, "*je vous délivre d'une bête féroce, et vous me demandez par quoi je la remplace!*" Without comparing Mr. Spencer's definition of Mind either to Christianity or to a "*bête féroce*," it may certainly be said to be very far-reaching in its consequences, and, according to certain standards, noxious; whilst probably a large proportion of those hard-headed readers who subscribe to the *Popular Science Monthly* and *Nature*, and whose sole philosopher Mr. Spencer is, are fascinated by it without being in the least aware what its consequences are.

The defects of the formula are so glaring that I am surprised it should not long ago have been critically overhauled. The reader will readily recollect what it is. In part III of his *Principles of Psychology*, Mr. Spencer, starting from the supposition that the most essential truth concerning mental evolution will be that which allies it to the evolution nearest akin to it, namely, that of Life, finds that the formula *"adjustment of inner to outer relations,"* which was the definition of life, comprehends also "the entire process of mental evolution." In a series of chapters of great apparent thoroughness and minuteness he shows how all the different grades of mental perfection are expressed by the degree of extension of this adjustment, or, as he here calls it, "correspondence," in space, time, speciality, generality, and integration. The polyp's tentacles contract only to immediately present stimuli, and to almost all alike. The mammal will store up food for a day, or even for a season; the bird will start on its migration for a goal hundreds of miles away; the savage will sharpen his arrows to hunt next year's game; while the astronomer will proceed, equipped with all his instruments, to a point thousands of miles distant, there to watch, at a fixed day, hour, and minute, a transit of Venus or an eclipse of the Sun.

The picture drawn is so vast and simple, it includes such a multitude of details in its monotonous frame-work, that it is no wonder that readers of a passive turn of mind are, usually, more impressed by it than by any portion of the book. But on the slightest scrutiny its solidity begins to disappear. In the first place, one asks, what right has one, in a formula embracing professedly the "entire process of mental evolution," to mention only phenomena of cognition, and to omit all sentiments, all esthetic impulses, all religious emotions and personal affections? The ascertainment of outward fact constitutes only one species of mental activity. The genus contains, in addition to purely cognitive judgments, or judgments of the actual—judgments that things do, as a matter of fact, exist so or so—an immense number of emotional judgments: judgments of the ideal, judgments that things *should* exist thus and not so. How much of our mental life is occupied with this matter of a better or a worse? How much of it involves preferences or repugnances on our part? We cannot laugh at a joke, we cannot go to one theater rather than another, take more trouble for the sake of our own child than our neighbor's; we cannot long for vacation, show our best manners to a foreigner, or pay our pew rent, without involving in the premises of our action some element which has nothing whatever to do with simply cognizing the actual, but which, out of alternative possible actuals, selects one and cognizes that as the ideal. In a word, "Mind," as we actually find it, contains all sorts of laws—those of logic, of fancy, of wit, of taste, decorum, beauty, morals, and so forth, as well as of perception of fact. Common sense estimates mental excellence by a combination of all these standards, and yet how few of them correspond to anything that actually *is*—they are laws of the Ideal, dictated by subjective *interests* pure and simple. Thus the greater part of Mind, quantitatively considered, refuses to have anything to do with Mr. Spencer's definition. It is quite true that these ideal judgments are treated by him with great ingenuity and felicity at the close of his work—indeed, his treatment of them there seems to me to be its most admirable portion. But they are there handled as separate items having no connection with that extension of the "correspondence" which is maintained elsewhere to be the all-sufficing law of mental growth.

Most readers would dislike to admit without coercion that a law was adequate which obliged them to erase from literature (if by literature were meant anything worthy of the title of "mental product") all works except treatises on natural science, history, and statistics. Let us examine the reason that Mr. Spencer appears to consider coercive.

It is this: That, since every process grows more and more complicated as it develops, more swarmed over by incidental and derivative conditions which disguise and adulterate its original simplicity, the only way to discover its true and essential form is to trace it back to its earliest beginning. There it will appear in its genuine character pure and undefiled. Religious, esthetic, and ethical judgments, having grown up in the course of evolution, by means that we can very plausibly divine, of course may be stripped off from the main stem of intelligence and leave that undisturbed. With a similar intent Mr. Tylor says: "Whatever throws light on the origin of a conception throws light on its validity." Thus, then, there is no resource but to appeal to the polyp, or whatever shows us the form of evolution just *before* intelligence, and what that, and only what that, contains will be the root and heart of the matter.

But no sooner is the reason for the law thus enunciated than many objections occur to the reader. In the first place, the general principle seems to lead to absurd conclusions. If the embryologic line of appeal can alone teach us the genuine essences of things, if the polyp is to dictate our law of mind to us because he came first, where are we to stop? He must himself be treated in the same way. Back of him lay the not-yet-polyp, and, back of all, the universal mother, fire-mist. To seek there for the reality, of course would reduce all thinking to nonentity, and, although Mr. Spencer would probably not regard this conclusion as a *reductio ad absurdum* of his principle, since it would only be another path to his theory of the Unknowable, less systematic thinkers may hesitate. But, waiving for the moment the question of principle, let us admit that relatively to *our* thought, at any rate, the polyp's thought is pure and undefiled. Does the study of the polyp lead us distinctly to Mr. Spencer's formula of correspondence? To begin with, if that formula be meant to include disinterested scientific curiosity, or "correspondence" in the sense of cognition, with no ulterior selfish end, the polyp gives it no countenance whatever. He is as innocent of scientific as of moral and aesthetic enthusiasm; he is the most narrowly teleological of organisms; reacting, so far as he reacts at all, only for self-preservation.

This leads us to ask what Mr. Spencer exactly means by the word correspondence. Without explanation, the word is wholly indeterminate. Everything corresponds in some way with everything else that co-exists in the same world with it. But, as the formula of correspondence was originally derived from biology, we shall possibly find in our author's treatise on that science an exact definition of what he means by it. On seeking there, we find nowhere a definition, but numbers of synonyms. The inner relations are "adjusted," "conformed," "fitted," "related," to the outer. They must "meet" or "balance" them. There must be "concord" or "harmony" between them. Or, again, the organism must "counteract" the changes in the environment. But these words, too, are wholly indeterminate. The fox is most beautifully "adjusted" to the hounds and huntsmen who pursue him; the limestone "meets" molecule by molecule the acid which corrodes it; the man is exquisitely "conformed" to the *trichina* which invades him, or to the typhus poison which consumes him; and the forests "harmonize" incomparably with the fires that lay them low. Clearly, a further specification is required; and, although Mr. Spencer shrinks strangely from enunciating this specification, he everywhere works his formula so as to imply it in the clearest manner.

Influence on physical well-being or survival is his implied criterion of the rank of mental action. The moth which flies into the candle, instead of away from it, "fails," in Spencer's words (vol. I, p. 409), to "correspond" with its environment; but clearly, in this sense, pure cognitive inference of the existence of heat after a perception of light would not suffice to constitute correspondence; while a moth which, on feeling the light, should merely vaguely fear to approach it, but have no proper image of the heat, would "correspond." So that the Spencerian formula, to mean anything definite at all, must, at least, be re-written as follows: "Right or intelligent mental action consists in the establishment, corresponding to outward relations, of such inward relations and reactions as will favor the survival of the thinker, or, at least, his physical well being."

Such a definition as this is precise, but at the same time it is frankly teleological. It explicitly postulates a distinction between mental action pure and simple, and *right* mental action; and, furthermore, it proposes, as criteria of this latter, certain ideal ends— those of physical prosperity or survival, which are pure *subjective interests* on the animal's part, brought with it upon the scene and corresponding to no relation already there.[1] No mental action is right or intelligent which fails to fit this standard. No correspondence can pass muster till it shows its subservience to these ends. Corresponding itself to no actual outward thing; referring merely to a future which *may* be, but which these interests now say *shall* be; purely ideal, in a word, they judge, dominate, determine all correspondences between the inner and the outer. Which is as much as to say that *mere* correspondence with the outer world is a notion on which it is wholly impossible to base a definition of mental action. Mr. Spencer's occult reason for leaving unexpressed the most important part of the definition he works with probably lies in its apparent implication of subjective spontaneity. The mind, according to his philosophy, should be pure product, absolute derivative from the non-mental. To make it dictate conditions, bring independent interests into the game which may determine what we shall call correspondence, and what not, might, at first sight, appear contrary to the notion of evolution which forbids the introduction at any point of an absolutely new factor. In what sense the existence of survival interest does postulate such a factor we shall hereafter see. I think myself that it is possible to express all its outward results in non-mental terms. But the unedifying look of the thing, its simulation of an independent mental teleology, seems to have frightened Mr. Spencer here, as elsewhere, away from a serious scrutiny of the facts. But let us be indulgent to his timidity, and assume that survival was all the while a "mental reservation" with him, only excluded from his formula by reason of the comforting sound it might have to Philistine ears.

We should then have, as the embodiment of the highest ideal perfection of mental development, a creature of superb cognitive endowments, from whose piercing perceptions no fact was too minute or too remote to escape; whose all-embracing foresight no contingency could find unprepared; whose invincible flexibility of resource no array of outward onslaught could overpower; but in whom all these gifts were swayed by the single passion of love of life, of survival at any price. This determination filling his whole energetic being, consciously realized, intensified by meditation, becomes a fixed idea, would use all the other faculties as its means, and, if they ever flagged, would by its imperious intensity spur them and hound them on to ever fresh exertions and achievements. There can be no doubt that, if such an incarnation of earthly prudence existed, a race of beings in whom this monotonously narrow passion for tribal self-preservation were aided by every cognitive gift, they would soon be kings of all the earth. All known human races would wither before their breath, and be as dust beneath their conquering feet.

But whether any Spencerian would hail with hearty joy their advent is another matter. Certainly Mr. Spencer would not; while the common sense of mankind would stand aghast at the thought of them. Why does common opinion abhor such a being? Why does it crave greater "richness" of nature in its mental ideal? Simply because, to common sense, survival is only one out of many interests—*primus inter pares*, perhaps, but still in the midst of peers. What are these interests? Most men would reply that they are all that makes survival worth securing. The social affections, all the various forms of play, the thrilling intimations of art, the delights of philosophic contemplation, the rest of religious emotion, the joy of moral self-approbation, the charm of fancy and of wit—some or all of these are absolutely required to make the notion of mere existence tolerable; and individuals who, by their special powers, satisfy these desires are protected by their fellows and enabled to survive, though their mental constitution should in other respects be lamentably ill-"adjusted" to the outward world. The story-teller, the musician, the theologian, the actor, or even the mere charming fellow, have never lacked means of support, however helpless they might individually have been to conform with those outward relations which we know as the powers of nature. The reason is very plain. To the individual man, as a social being, the interests of his fellow are a part of his environment. If his powers correspond to the wants of this social environment, he may survive, even though he be ill-adapted to the natural or "outer" environment. But these wants are pure subjective ideals, with nothing outward to correspond to them. So that, as far as the individual is concerned, it becomes necessary to modify Spencer's survival formula still further, by introducing into the term environment a reference, not only to existent things, but also to ideal wants. It would have to run in some such way as this: "Excellence of the individual mind consists in the establishment of inner relations more and more extensively conformed to the outward facts of nature, and to the ideal wants of the individual's fellows, but all of such a character as will promote survival or physical prosperity."

But here, again, common sense will meet us with an objection. Mankind desiderate certain qualities in the individual which are incompatible with his chance of survival being a maximum. Why do we all so eulogize and love the heroic, recklessly generous, and disinterested type of character? These qualities certainly imperil the survival of their possessor. The reason is very plain. Even if headlong courage, pride, and martyr-spirit do ruin the individual, they benefit the community as a whole whenever they are displayed by one of its members against a competing tribe. "It is death to you, but fun for us." Our interest in having the hero as he is, plays indirectly into the hands of our survival, though not of his.

This explicit acknowledgment of the survival interests of the tribe, as accounting for many interests in the individual which seem at first sight either unrelated to survival or at war with it, seems, after all, to bring back unity and simplicity into the Spencerian formula. Why, the Spencerian may ask, may not all the luxuriant foliage of ideal interests—aesthetic, philosophic, theologic, and the rest—which co-exist along with that of survival, be present in the tribe and so form part of the individual's environment, merely by virtue of the fact that they minister in an indirect way to the survival of the tribe as a whole? The disinterested scientific appetite of cognition, the sacred philosophic love of consistency, the craving for luxury and beauty, the passion for amusement, may all find their proper significance as processes of mind, strictly so-called, in the incidental utilitarian discoveries which flow from the energy they set in motion. Conscience, thoroughness, purity, love of truth, susceptibility to discipline, eager delight in fresh impressions, although none of them are traits of Intelligence *in se*, may thus be marks of a general mental energy, without which victory over nature and over other human competitors would be impossible. And, as victory means survival, and survival is the criterion of Intelligent "Correspondence," these qualities, though not expressed in the fundamental law of mind, may yet have been all the while understood by Mr. Spencer to form so many secondary consequences and corollaries of that law.

But here it is decidedly time to take our stand and refuse our aid in propping up Mr. Spencer's definition by any further good-natured translations and supplementary contributions of our own. It is palpable at a glance that a mind whose survival interest could only be adequately secured by such a wasteful array of energy squandered on side issues would be immeasurably inferior to one like that which we supposed a few pages back, in which the monomania of tribal preservation should be the one all-devouring passion.

Surely there is nothing in the essence of intelligence which should oblige it forever to delude itself as to its own ends, and to strive towards a goal successfully only at the cost of consciously appearing to have far other aspirations in view.

A furnace which should produce along with its metal fifty different varieties of ash and slag, a planing-mill whose daily yield in shavings far exceeded that in boards, would rightly be pronounced inferior to one of the usual sort, even though more energy should be displayed in its working, and at moments some of that energy be directly effective. If ministry to survival be the sole criterion of mental excellence, then luxury and amusement, Shakespeare, Beethoven, Plato, and Marcus Aurelius, stellar spectroscopy, diatom markings, and nebular hypotheses are by-products on too wasteful a scale. The slag-heap is too big—it abstracts more energy than it contributes to the ends of the machine; and every serious evolutionist ought resolutely to bend his attention henceforward to the reduction in number and amount of these outlying interests, and the diversion of the energy they absorb into purely prudential channels.

Here, then, is our dilemma: One man may say that the law of mental development is dominated solely by the principle of conservation; another, that richness is the criterion of mental evolution; a third, that pure cognition of the actual is the essence of worthy thinking—but who shall pretend to decide which is right? The umpire would have to bring a standard of his own upon the scene, which would be just as subjective and personal as the standards used by the contestants. And yet some standard there must be, if we are to attempt to define in any way the worth of different mental manifestations.

Is it not already clear to the reader's mind that the whole difficulty in making Mr. Spencer's law work lies in the fact that it is not really a constitutive, but a regulative, law of thought which he is erecting, and that he does not frankly say so? Every law of Mind must be either a law of the *cogitatum* or a law of the *cogitandum*. If it be a law in the sense of an analysis of what we *do* think, then it will include error, nonsense, the worthless as well as the worthy, metaphysics, and mythologies as well as scientific truths which mirror the actual environment. But such a law of the *cogitatum* is already well known. It is no other than the association of ideas according to their several modes; or, rather, it is this association definitively perfected by the inclusion of the teleological factor of interest by Mr. Hodgson in the fifth chapter of his masterly *Time and Space*.

That Mr. Spencer, in the part of his work which we are considering, has no such law as this in view is evident from the fact that he has striven to give an original formulation to such a law in another part of his book, in that chapter, namely, on the associability of relations, in the first volume, where the apperception of times and places, and the suppression of association by similarity, are made to explain the facts in a way whose artificiality has puzzled many a simple reader.

Now, every living man would instantly define right thinking as thinking in correspondence with reality. But Spencer, in saying that right thought is that which conforms to existent outward relations, and this exclusively, undertakes to decide what the reality *is*. In other words, under cover of an apparently formal definition he really smuggles in a material definition of the most far-reaching import. For the Stoic, to whom *vivere convenienter naturae* was also the law of mind, the reality was an archetypal Nature; for the Christian, whose mental law is to discover the will of God, and make one's actions correspond thereto, *that* is the reality. In fact, the philosophic problem which all the ages have been trying to solve in order to make thought in some way correspond with it, and which disbelievers in philosophy call insoluble, is just that: What is the reality? All the thinking, all the conflict of ideals, going on in the world at the present moment is in some way tributary to this quest. To attempt, therefore, with Mr. Spencer, to decide the matter merely incidentally, to forestall discussion by a definition—to carry the position by surprise, in a word—is a proceeding savoring more of piracy than philosophy. No, Spencer's definition of what we ought to think cannot be suffered to lurk in ambush; it must stand out explicitly with the rest, and expect to be challenged and give an account of itself like any other ideal norm of thought.

We have seen how he seems to vacillate in his determination of it. At one time, "scientific" thought, mere passive mirroring of outward nature, purely registrative cognition; at another time, thought in the exclusive service of survival, would seem to be his ideal. Let us consider the latter ideal first, since it has the polyp's authority in its favor: "We must survive—that end must regulate all our thought." The poor man who said to Talleyrand, "*Il faut bien que je vive!*" expressed it very well. But criticise this ideal, or transcend it as Talleyrand did by his cool reply, "*Je n'en vois pas la nécessité*," and it can say nothing more for itself. *A priori* it is a mere brute teleological affirmation on a par with all others. Vainly you should hope to prove it to a person bent on suicide, who has but the one longing—to escape, to cease. Vainly you would argue with a Buddhist or a German pessimist, for they feel the full imperious strength of the desire, but have an equally profound persuasion of its essential wrongness and mendacity. Vainly, too, would you talk to a Christian, or even to any believer in the simple creed that the deepest meaning of the world is moral. For they hold that mere conformity with the outward—worldly success and survival—is not the absolute and exclusive end. In the *failures* to "adjust"—in the rubbish-heap, according to Spencer—lies, for them, the real key to the truth—the sole mission of life being to teach that the outward actual is not the whole of being.

And, now—if, falling back on the scientific ideal, you say that to *know* is the one τέλος of intelligence—not only will the inimitable Turkish cadi in Layard's Nineveh praise God in your face that he seeks not that which he requires not, and ask, "Will much knowledge create thee a double belly?"—not only may I, if it please me, legitimately refuse to stir from my fool's paradise of theosophy and mysticism, in spite of all your calling (since, after all, your true knowledge and my pious feeling have alike nothing to back them save their seeming good to our respective personalities)—not only this, but to the average sense of mankind, whose ideal of mental nature is best expressed by the word "richness," your statistical and cognitive intelligence will seem insufferably narrow, dry, tedious, and unacceptable.

The truth appears to be that every individual man may, if it please him, set up his private categorical imperative of what rightness or excellence in thought shall consist in, and these different ideals, instead of entering upon the scene armed with a warrant—whether derived from the polyp or from a transcendental source—appear only as so many brute affirmations left to fight it out upon the chess-board among themselves. They are, at best, postulates, each of which must depend on the general consensus of experience as a whole to bear out its validity. The formula which proves to have the most massive destiny will be the true one. But this is a point which can only be solved *ambulando*, and not by any *a priori* definition. The attempt to forestall the decision is free to all to make, but all make it at their risk. Our respective hypotheses and postulates help to shape the course of thought, but the only thing which we all agree in assuming is, that thought will be coerced away from them if they are wrong. If Spencer to-day says, "Bow to the actual," whilst Swinburne spurns "compromise with the nature of things," I exclaim, "*Fiat justitia, pereat mundus*," and Mill says, "To hell I will go, rather than 'adjust' myself to an evil God," what umpire can there be between us but the future? The idealists and the empiricists confront each other like Guelphs and Ghibellines, but each alike waits for adoption, as it were, by the course of events.

In other words, we are all fated to be, *a priori*, teleologists whether we will or no. Interests which we bring with us, and simply posit or take our stand upon, are the very flour out of which our mental dough is kneaded. The organism of thought, from the vague dawn of discomfort or ease in the polyp to the intellectual joy of Laplace among his formulas, is teleological through and through. Not a cognition occurs but feeling is there to comment on it, to stamp it as of greater or less worth. Spencer and Plato are *ejusdem farinae*. To attempt to hoodwink teleology out of sight by saying nothing about it, is the vainest of procedures. Spencer merely takes sides with the τέλος he happens to prefer, whether it be that of physical well-being or that of cognitive registration. He represents a particular teleology. Well might teleology (had she a voice) exclaim with Emerson's Brahma:

> "If the red slayer think he slays,
> Or if the slain think he is slain,
>   They know not well the subtle ways
> I keep, and pass, and turn again.

>   *   *   *

>   They reckon ill who leave me out;
> When me they fly, I am the wings;
>   I am the doubter and the doubt," etc.

But now a scientific man, feeling something uncanny in this omnipresence of a teleological factor dictating *how* the mind shall correspond—an interest seemingly tributary to nothing non-mental—may ask us what we meant by saying sometime back that in one sense it is perfectly possible to express the existence of interests in non-mental terms. We meant simply this: That the reactions or outward consequences of the interests could be so expressed. The interest of survival which has hitherto been treated as an ideal *should-be*, presiding from the start and marking out the way in which an animal must react, is, from an outward and physical point of view, nothing more than an objective future implication of the reaction (if it occurs) as an actual fact. If the animal's brain acts fortuitously in the right way, he survives. His young do the same. The reference to survival in no way preceded or conditioned the intelligent act; but the fact of survival was merely bound up with it as an incidental consequence, and may, therefore, be called accidental, rather than instrumental, to the production of intelligence. It is the same with all other interests. They are pleasures and pains incidentally implied in the workings of the nervous mechanism, and, therefore, in their ultimate origin, non-mental; for the idiosyncrasies of our nervous centers are mere "spontaneous variations," like any of those which form the ultimate *data* for Darwin's theory. A brain which functions so as to insure survival may, therefore, be called intelligent in no other sense than a tooth, a limb, or a stomach, which should serve the same end—the sense, namely, of appropriate; as when we say "that is an intelligent device," meaning a device fitted to secure a certain end which we assume. If *nirvana* were the end, instead of survival, then it is true the means would be different, but in both cases alike the end would not precede the means, or even be coeval with them, but depend utterly upon them, and follow them in point of time. The fox's cunning and the hare's speed are thus alike creations of the non-mental. The τέλος they entail is no more an agent in one case than another, since in both alike it is a resultant. Spencer, then, seems justified in not admitting it to appear as an irreducible ultimate factor of Mind, any more than of Body.

This position is perfectly unassailable so long as one describes the phenomena in this manner from without. The τέλος in that case can only be hypothetically, not imperatively, stated: *if* such and such be the end, then such brain functions are the most intelligent, just as such and such digestive functions are the most appropriate. But such and such cannot be declared *as* the end, except by the commenting mind of an outside spectator. The organs themselves, in their working at any instant, cannot but be supposed indifferent as to what product they are destined fatally to bring forth, cannot be imagined whilst fatally producing one result to have at the same time a notion of a different result which should be their truer end, but which they are unable to secure.

Nothing can more strikingly show, it seems to me, the essential difference between the point of view of consciousness and that of outward existence. We can describe the latter only in teleological terms, hypothetically, or else by the addition of a supposed contemplating mind which measures what it sees going on by its private teleological standard, and judges it intelligent. But consciousness itself is not merely intelligent in this sense. It is *intelligent intelligence*. It seems both to supply the means and the standard by which they are measured. It not only *serves* a final purpose, but *brings* a final purpose—posits, declares it. This purpose is not a mere hypothesis—"*if* survival is to occur, then brain must so perform," etc.—but an imperative decree: "Survival *shall* occur, and, therefore, brain *must* so perform!" It seems hopelessly impossible to formulate anything of this sort in non-mental terms, and this is why I must still contend that the phenomena of subjective "interest," as soon as the animal consciously realizes the latter, appears upon the scene as an absolutely new factor, which we can only suppose to be latent thitherto in the physical environment by crediting the physical atoms, etc., each with a consciousness of its own, approving or condemning its motions.

This, then, must be our conclusion: That no law of the *cogitandum*, no normative receipt for excellence in thinking, can be authoritatively promulgated. The only formal canon that we can apply to mind which is unassailable is the barren truism that it must think rightly. We can express this in terms of correspondence by saying that thought must correspond with truth; but whether that truth be actual or ideal is left undecided.

We have seen that the invocation of the polyp to decide for us that it is actual (apart from the fact that he does not decide in that way) is based on a principle which refutes itself if consistently carried out. Spencer's formula has crumbled into utter worthlessness in our hands, and we have nothing to replace it by except our several individual hypotheses, convictions, and beliefs. Far from being vouched for by the past, these are verified only by the future. They are all of them, in some sense, laws of the ideal. They have to keep house together, and the weakest goes to the wall. The survivors constitute the right way of thinking. While the issue is still undecided, we can only call them our prepossessions. But, decided or not, "go in" we each must for one set of interests or another. The question for each of us in the battle of life is, "Can we *come out* with it?" Some of these interests admit to-day of little dispute. Survival, physical well-being, and undistorted cognition of what is, will hold their ground. But it is truly strange to see writers like Messrs. Huxley and Clifford, who show themselves able to call most things in question, unable, when it comes to the interest of cognition, to touch it with their solvent doubt. They assume some mysterious imperative laid upon the mind, declaring that the infinite ascertainment of facts is its supreme duty, which he who evades is a blasphemer and child of shame. And yet these authors can hardly have failed to reflect, at some moment or other, that the disinterested love of information and still more the love of consistency in thought (that true scientific *oestrus*), and the ideal fealty to Truth (with a capital T), are all so many particular forms of aesthetic interest, late in their evolution, arising in conjunction with a vast number of similar aesthetic interests, and bearing with them no *a priori* mark of being worthier than these. If we may doubt one, we may doubt all. How shall I say that knowing fact with Messrs. Huxley and Clifford is a better use to put my mind to than feeling good with Messrs. Moody and Sankey, unless by slowly and painfully finding out that in the long run it works best?

I, for my part, cannot escape the consideration, forced upon me at every turn, that the knower is not simply a mirror floating with no foot-hold anywhere and passively reflecting an order that he comes upon and finds simply existing. The knower is an actor, and co-efficient of the truth on one side, whilst on the other he registers the truth which he helps to create. Mental interests, hypotheses, postulates, so far as they are bases for human action—action which to a great extent transforms the world—help to *make* the truth which they declare. In other words, there belongs to mind, from its birth upward, a spontaneity, a vote. It is in the game, and not a mere looker-on; and its judgments of the *should-be*, its ideals, cannot be peeled off from the body of the *cogitandum* as if they were excrescences or meant, at most, survival. We know so little about the ultimate nature of things, or of ourselves, that it would be sheer folly dogmatically to say that an ideal rational order may not be real. The only objective criterion of reality is coerciveness, in the long run, over thought. Objective facts, Spencer's outward relations, are real only because they coerce sensation. Any interest which should be coercive on the same massive scale would be *eodem jure* real. By its very essence, the reality of a thought is proportionate to the way it grasps us. Its intensity, its seriousness—its interest, in a word—taking these qualities, not at any given instant, but as shown by the total upshot of experience. If judgments of the *should-be* are fated to grasp us in this way, they are what "correspond." The ancients placed the conception of Fate at the bottom of things—deeper than the gods themselves. "The fate of thought," utterly barren and indeterminate as such a formula is, is the only unimpeachable regulative Law of Mind.

NOTES

1. These interests are the real *a priori* element in cognition. By saying that their pleasures and pains have nothing to do with correspondence, I mean simply this: To a large number of terms in the environment there may be inward correlatives of a neutral sort as regards feeling. The "correspondence" is already there. But, now, suppose some to be accented with pleasure, others with pain; that is a fact additional to the correspondence, a fact with no outward correlative. But it immediately orders the correspondences in this way: that the pleasant or interesting items are singled out, dwelt upon, developed into their farther connections, whilst the unpleasant or insipid ones are ignored or suppressed. The future of the Mind's development is thus mapped out in advance by the way in which the lines of pleasure and pain run. The interests precede the outer relations noticed. Take the utter absence of response of a dog or a savage to the greater mass of environing relations. How can you alter it unless you previously *awaken an interest*—*i.e.*, produce a susceptibility to intellectual pleasure in certain modes of cognitive exercise? Interests, then, are an all-essential factor which no writer pretending to give an account of mental evolution has a right to neglect.

The Sentiment of Rationality

Mind o.s. 4.3 (July 1879): 317–346.

I.

What is the task which philosophers set themselves to perform? And why do they philosophize at all? Almost every one will immediately reply: They desire to attain a conception of the frame of things which shall on the whole be more rational than the rather fragmentary and chaotic one which everyone by gift of nature carries about with him under his hat. But suppose this rational conception attained by the philosopher, how is he to recognize it for what it is, and not let it slip through ignorance? The only answer can be that he will recognize its rationality as he recognizes everything else, by certain subjective marks with which it affects him. When he gets the marks he may know that he has got the rationality.

What then are the marks? A strong feeling of ease, peace, rest, is one of them. The transition from a state of puzzle and perplexity to rational comprehension is full of lively relief and pleasure.

But this relief seems to be a negative rather than a positive character. Shall we then say that the feeling of rationality is constituted merely by the absence of any feeling of irrationality? I think there are very good grounds for upholding such a view. All feeling whatever, in the light of certain recent psychological speculations, seems to depend for its physical condition not on simple discharge of nerve-currents, but on their discharge under arrest, impediment or resistance. Just as we feel no particular pleasure when we breathe freely, but a very intense feeling of distress when the respiratory motions are prevented; so any unobstructed tendency to action discharges itself without the production of much cogitative accompaniment, and any perfectly fluent course of thought awakens but little feeling. But when the movement is inhibited or when the thought meets with difficulties, we experience a distress which yields to an opposite feeling of pleasure as fast as the obstacle is overcome. It is only when the distress is upon us that we can be said to strive, to crave, or to aspire. When enjoying plenary freedom to energize either in the way of motion or of thought, we are in a sort of anaesthetic state in which we might say with Walt Whitman, if we cared to say anything about ourselves at such times, "I am sufficient as I am." This feeling of the sufficiency of the present moment, of its absoluteness—this absence of all need to explain it, account for it or justify it—is what I call the Sentiment of Rationality. As soon, in short, as we are enabled from any cause whatever to think of a thing with perfect fluency, that thing seems to us rational.

Why we should constantly gravitate towards the attainment of such fluency cannot here be said. As this is not an ethical but a psychological essay, it is quite sufficient for our purposes to lay it down as an empirical fact that we strive to formulate rationally a tangled mass of fact by a propensity as natural and invincible as that which makes us exchange a hard high stool for an arm-chair or prefer travelling by railroad to riding in a springless cart.

Whatever modes of conceiving the cosmos facilitate this fluency of our thought, produce the sentiment of rationality. Conceived in such modes Being vouches for itself and needs no further philosophic formulation. But so long as mutually obstructive elements are involved in the conception, the pent-up irritated mind recoiling on its present consciousness will criticize it, worry over it, and never cease in its attempts to discover some new mode of formulation which may give it escape from the irrationality of its actual ideas.

Now mental ease and freedom may be obtained in various ways. Nothing is more familiar than the way in which mere custom makes us at home with ideas or circumstances which, when new, filled the mind with curiosity and the need of explanation. There is no more common sight than that of men's mental worry about things incongruous with personal desire, and their thoughtless incurious acceptance of whatever happens to harmonize with their subjective ends. The existence of evil forms a "mystery"—a "problem": there is no "problem of happiness." But, on the other hand, purely theoretic processes may produce the same mental peace which custom and congruity with our native impulses in other cases give; and we have forthwith to discover how it is that so many processes can produce the same result; and how Philosophy, by emulating or using the means of all, may attain to a conception of the world which shall be rational in the maximum degree, or be warranted in the most composite manner against the inroads of mental unrest or discontent.

II.

It will be best to take up first the theoretic way. The facts of the world in their sensible diversity are always before us, but the philosophic need craves that they should be conceived in such a way as to satisfy the sentiment of rationality. The philosophic quest then is the quest of a conception. What now is a *conception*? It is a *teleological instrument*. It is a partial aspect of a thing which *for our purpose* we regard as its essential aspect, as the representative of the entire thing. In comparison with this aspect, whatever other properties and qualities the thing may have, are unimportant accidents which we may without blame ignore. But the essence, the ground of conception, varies with the end we have in view. A substance like oil has as many different essences as it has uses to different individuals. One man conceives it as a combustible, another as a lubricator, another as a food; the chemist thinks of it as a hydro-carbon; the furniture-maker as a darkener of wood; the speculator as a commodity whose market price today is this and tomorrow that. The soap-boiler, the physicist, the clothes-scourer severally ascribe to it other essences in relation to their needs. Ueberweg's doctrine[1] that the essential quality of a thing is the quality of most *worth*, is strictly true; but Ueberweg has failed to note that the worth is wholly relative to the temporary interests of the conceiver. And, even, when his interest is distinctly defined in his own mind, the discrimination of the quality in the object which has the closest connexion with it, is a thing which no rules can teach. The only *a priori* advice that can be given to a man embarking on life with a certain purpose is the somewhat barren counsel: Be sure that in the circumstances that meet you, you attend to the *right* ones for your purpose. To pick out the right ones is the measure of the man. "Millions," says Hartmann, "stare at the phenomenon before a *genialer Kopf* pounces on the concept."[2] The genius is simply he to whom, when he opens his eyes upon the world, the "right" characters are the prominent ones. The fool is he who, with the same purposes as the genius, infallibly gets his attention tangled amid the accidents.

Schopenhauer expresses well this ultimate truth when he says that Intuition (by which in this passage he means the power to distinguish at a glance the essence amid the accidents) "is not only the source of all knowledge, but is knowledge κατ' ἐξοχήν ... is real *insight*.... *Wisdom*, the true view of life, the right look at things, and the judgment that hits the mark, proceed from the mode in which the man conceives the world which lies before him ... He who excels in this talent knows the (Platonic) ideas of the world and of life. Every case he looks at stands for countless cases; more and more he goes on to conceive of each thing in accordance with its true nature, and his acts like his judgments bear the stamp of his insight. Gradually his face too acquires the straight and piercing look, the expression of reason, and at last of wisdom. For the direct sight of essences alone can set its mark upon the face. Abstract knowledge about them has no such effect."[3]

The right conception for the philosopher depends then on his interests. Now the interest which he has above other men is that of reducing the manifold in thought to simple form. We can no more say why the philosopher is more peculiarly sensitive to this delight, than we can explain the passion some persons have for matching colors or for arranging cards in a game of solitaire. All these passions resemble each other in one point; they are all illustrations of what may be called the aesthetic Principle of Ease. Our pleasure at finding that a chaos of facts is at bottom the expression of a single underlying fact is like the relief of the musician at resolving a confused mass of sound into melodic or harmonic order. The simplified result is handled with far less mental effort than the original data; and a philosophic conception of nature is thus in no metaphorical sense a labour-saving contrivance. The passion for parsimony, for economy of means in thought, is thus the philosophic passion *par excellence*, and any character or aspect of the world's phenomena which gathers up their diversity into simplicity will gratify that passion, and in the philosopher's mind stand for that essence of things compared with which all their other determinations may by him be overlooked.

Mere universality or extensiveness is then the one mark the philosopher's conceptions must possess. Unless they appear in an enormous number of cases they will not bring the relief which is his main theoretic need. The knowledge of things by their causes, which is often given as a definition of rational knowledge, is useless to him unless the causes converge to a minimum number whilst still producing the maximum number of effects. The more multiple are the instances he can see to be cases of his fundamental concept, the more flowingly does his mind rove from fact to fact in the world. The phenomenal transitions are no real transitions; each item is the same old friend with a slightly altered dress. This passion for unifying things may gratify itself, as we all know, at truth's expense. Everyone has friends bent on system and everyone has observed how, when their system has once taken definite shape, they become absolutely blind and insensible to the most flagrant facts which cannot be made to fit into it. The ignoring of data is, in fact, the easiest and most popular mode of obtaining unity in one's thought.

But leaving these vulgar excesses let us glance briefly at some more dignified contemporary examples of the hypertrophy of the unifying passion.

Its ideal goal gets permanent expression in the great notion of Substance, the underlying One in which all differences are reconciled. D'Alembert's often quoted lines express the postulate in its most abstract shape: "L'univers pour qui saurait l'embrasser d'un seul point de vue ne serait, s'il est permis de le dire, qu'un fait unique et une grande verité." Accordingly Mr. Spencer, after saying on page 158 of the first volume of his *Psychology*, that "no effort enables us to assimilate Feeling and Motion, they have nothing in common," cannot refrain on page 162 from invoking abruptly an "Unconditional Being common to the two."

The craving for Monism at any cost is the parent of the entire evolutionist movement of our day, so far as it pretends to be more than history. The Philosophy of Evolution tries to show how the world at any given time may be conceived as absolutely identical, except in appearance, with itself at all past times. What it most abhors is the admission of anything which, appearing at a given point, should be judged essentially other than what went before. Notwithstanding the *lacunae* in Mr. Spencer's system; notwithstanding the vagueness of his terms; in spite of the sort of jugglery by which his use of the word "nascent" is made to veil the introduction of new primordial factors like consciousness, as if, like the girl in *Midshipman Easy,* he could excuse the illegitimacy of an infant, by saying it was a very little one—in spite of all this, I say, Mr. Spencer is, and is bound to be, the most popular of all philosophers, because more than any other he seeks to appease our strongest theoretic craving. To undiscriminating minds his system will be a sop; to acute ones a programme full of suggestiveness.

When Lewes asserts in one place that the nerve-process and the feeling which accompanies it are not two things but only two "aspects" of one and the same thing, whilst in other passages he seems to imply that the cognitive feeling and the outward thing cognized (which is always other than the nerve-process accompanying the cognitive act) are again one thing in two aspects (giving us thereby as the ultimate truth One Thing in Three Aspects, very much as Trinitarian Christians affirm it to be One God in Three Persons)—the vagueness of his mode only testifies to the imperiousness of his need of unity.

The crowning feat of unification at any cost is seen in the Hegelian denial of the Principle of Contradiction. One who is willing to allow that A and not-A are one, can be checked by few farther difficulties in Philosophy.

III.

But alongside of the passion for simplification, there exists a sister passion which in some minds—though they perhaps form the minority—is its rival. This is the passion for distinguishing; it is the impulse to be *acquainted* with the parts rather than to comprehend the whole. Loyalty to clearness and integrity of perception, dislike of blurred outlines, of vague identifications, are its characteristics. It loves to recognize particulars in their full completeness, and the more of these it can carry the happier it is. It is the mind of Cuvier *versus* St. Hilaire, of Hume *versus* Spinoza. It prefers any amount of incoherence, abruptness and fragmentariness (so long as the literal details of the separate facts are saved) to a fallacious unity which swamps things rather than explains them.

Clearness *versus* Simplicity is then the theoretic dilemma, and a man's philosophic attitude is determined by the balance in him of these two cravings. When John Mill insists that the ultimate laws of nature cannot possibly be less numerous than the distinguishable qualities of sensation which we possess, he speaks in the name of this aesthetic demand for clearness. When Prof. Bain says:[4]—"There is surely nothing to be dissatisfied with, or to complain of in the circumstance that the elements of our experience are in the last resort two and not one. . . . Instead of our being 'unfortunate' in not being able to know the essence of either matter or mind—in not comprehending their union, our misfortune would rather be to have to know anything different from what we do know,"—he is animated by a like motive. All makers of architectonic systems like that of Kant, all multipliers of original principles, all dislikers of vague monotony, whether it bear the character of Eleatic stagnancy or of Heraclitic change, obey this tendency. *Ultimate kinds* of feeling bound together in harmony by laws, which themselves are *ultimate kinds* of relation, form the theoretic resting-place of such philosophers.

The unconditional demand which this need makes of a philosophy is that its fundamental terms should be representable. Phenomena are analyzable into feelings and relations. Causality is a relation between two feelings. To abstract the relation from the feelings, to unify all things by referring them to a first cause, and to leave this latter relation with no term of feeling before it, is to violate the fundamental habits of our thinking, to baffle the imagination, and to exasperate the minds of certain people much as everyone's eye is exasperated by a magic-lantern picture or a microscopic object out of focus. Sharpen it, we say, or for heaven's sake remove it altogether.

The matter is not at all helped when the word Substance is brought forward and the primordial causality said to obtain between this and the phenomena; for Substance *in se* cannot be directly imaged by feeling, and seems in fact but to be a peculiar form of relation between feelings—the relation of organic union between a group of them and time. Such relations, represented as non-phenomenal entities, become thus the *bête noire* and pet aversion of many thinkers. By being posited as existent they challenge our acquaintance but at the same instant defy it by being defined as noumenal. So far is this reaction against the treatment of relational terms as metempirical entities carried, that the reigning British school seems to deny their function even in their legitimate sphere, namely as phenomenal elements or "laws" cementing the mosaic of our feelings into coherent form. Time, likeness, and unlikeness are the only phenomenal relations our English empiricists can tolerate. One of the earliest and perhaps the most famous expression of the dislike to relations considered abstractedly is the well-known passage from Hume: "When we run over libraries, persuaded of these principles, what havoc must we make! If we take in our hand any volume of divinity or school metaphysic, for instance, let us ask, Does it contain any abstract reasoning concerning quantity or number? No. Does it contain any experimental reasoning concerning matter of fact existence? No. Commit it then to the flames: for it can contain nothing but sophistry and illusion."[5]

Many are the variations which succeeding writers have played on this tune. As we spoke of the excesses of the unifying passion, so we may now say of the craving for clear representability that it leads often to an unwillingness to treat any abstractions whatever as if they were intelligible. Even to talk of space, time, feeling, power, &c., oppresses them with a strange sense of uncanniness. Anything to be real for them must be representable in the form of a *lump*. Its other concrete determinations may be abstracted from, but its *tangible* thinghood must remain. Minds of this order, if they can be brought to psychologize at all, abound in such phrases as "tracts" of consciousness, "areas" of emotion, "molecules" of feeling, "agglutinated portions" of thought, "gangs" of ideas &c., &c.

Those who wish an amusing example of this style of thought should read *Le Cerveau* by the anatomist Luys, surely the very worst book ever written on the much-abused subject of mental physiology. In another work, *Psychologie réaliste*, by P. Sièrebois (Paris 1876), it is maintained that "our ideas exist in us in a molecular condition, and are subject to continual movements. . . . Their mobility is as great as that of the molecules of air or any gas." When we fail to recall a word it is because our ideas are hid in some distant corner of the brain whence they cannot come to the muscles of articulation, or else "they have lost their ordinary fluidity" . . . "These ideal molecules are material portions of the brain which differs from all other matter precisely in this property which it possesses of subdividing itself into very attenuated portions which easily take on the likeness in form and quality of all external objects." In other words, when I utter the word 'rhinoceros' an actual little microscopic rhinoceros gallops towards my mouth.

A work of considerable acuteness, far above the vulgar materialistic level, is that of Czolbe, *Grundzüge einer extensionalen Erkenntnisstheorie* (1875). This author explains our ideas to be extended substances endowed with mutual penetrability. The matter of which they are composed is "elastic like india-rubber." When "concentrated" by "magnetic self-attraction" into the middle of the brain, its "intensity" is such that it becomes conscious. When the attraction ceases, the idea-substance expands and diffuses itself into infinite space and so sinks from consciousness.

Again passing over these *quasi*-pathological excesses, we come to a permanent and, for our purpose, most important fact—the fact that many minds of the highest analytic power will tolerate in Philosophy no unifying terms but elements immanent in phenomena, and taken in their phenomenal and representable sense. Entities whose attributes are not directly given in feeling, phenomenal relations functioning as entities, are alike rejected. Spinozistic Substance, Spencerian Unknowable, are abhorred as unrepresentable things, numerically additional to the representable world. The substance of things for these clear minds can be no more than their common measure. The phenomena bear to it the same relation that the different numbers bear to unity. These contain no other matter than the repeated unit, but they may be classed as prime numbers, odd numbers, even numbers, square numbers, cube numbers, &c., just as truly and naturally as we class concrete things. The molecular motions, of which physicists hope that some day all events and properties will be seen to consist, form such an immanent unity of colossal simplifying power. The "infinitesimal event" of various modern writers, Taine for example, with its two "aspects," inner and outer, reaches still farther in the same direction. Writers of this class, if they deal with Psychology, repudiate the "soul" as a scholastic entity. The phenomenal unity of consciousness must flow from some element immutably present in each and every representation of the individual and binding the whole into one. To unearth and accurately define this phenomenal self becomes one of the fundamental tasks of Psychology.

But the greatest living insister on the principle that unity in our account of things shall not overwhelm clearness, is Charles Renouvier. His masterly exposition of the irreducible categories of thought in his *Essais de Critique générale* ought to be far better known among us than it is. The onslaughts which this eminently clear-headed writer has made and still makes in his weekly journal, the *Critique Philosophique*, on the vanity of the evolutionary principle of simplification, which supposes that you have explained away all distinctions by simply saying "they arise" instead of "they are," form the ablest criticism which the school of Evolution has received. Difference "thus displaced, transported from the *esse* to the *fieri*, is it any the less postulated? And does the *fieri* itself receive the least commencement of explanation when we suppose that everything which occurs, occurs little by little, by insensible degrees, so that, if we look at any one of these degrees, what happens does so as easily and clearly as if it did not happen at all? . . . If we want a continuous production *ex nihilo*, why not say so frankly, and abandon the idea of a 'transition without break' which explains really nothing?"[6]

IV.

Our first conclusion may then be this: No system of philosophy can hope to be universally accepted among men which grossly violates either of the two great aesthetic needs of our logical nature, the need of unity and the need of clearness, or entirely subordinates the one to the other. Doctrines of mere disintegration like that of Hume and his successors, will be as widely unacceptable on the one hand as doctrines of merely engulphing substantialism like those of Schopenhauer, Hartmann and Spencer on the other. Can we for our own guidance briefly sketch out here some of the conditions of most favorable compromise?

In surveying the connexions between data we are immediately struck by the fact that some are more intimate than others. Propositions which express those we call necessary truths; and with them we contrast the laxer collocations and sequences which are known as empirical, habitual or merely fortuitous. The former seem to have an *inward* reasonableness which the latter are deprived of. The link, whatever it be, which binds the two phenomena together, seems to extend from the heart of one into the heart of the next, and to be an essential reason why the facts should always and indefeasibly be as we now know them. "Within the pale we stand." As Lotze says:[7]—"The intellect is not satisfied with merely associated representations. In its constant critical activity thought seeks to refer each representation to the rational ground which conditions the alliance of what is associated and proves that what is grouped *belongs* together. So it separates from each other those impressions which merely coalesce without inward connexions, and it renews (while corroborating them) the bonds of those which, by the inward kinship of their content, have a right to permanent companionship."

On the other hand many writers seem to deny the existence of any such inward kinship or rational bond between things. Hume says: "All our distinct perceptions are distinct existences and the mind never perceives any real connexion among distinct existences."[8]

Hume's followers are less bold in their utterances than their master, but throughout all recent British Nominalism we find the tendency to enthrone mere juxtaposition as lord of all and to make of the Universe what has well been styled a Nulliverse. "For my part," says Prof. Huxley, "I utterly repudiate and, anathematise the intruder [Necessity]. Fact I know; and Law I know; but what is this Necessity, save an empty shadow of the mind's own throwing?"

And similarly J. S. Mill writes: "What is called explaining one law by another is but substituting one mystery for another, and does nothing to render the course of nature less mysterious. We can no more assign a *why* for the more extensive laws than for the partial ones. The explanation may substitute a mystery which has become familiar and has grown to seem not mysterious for one which is still strange. And this is the meaning of explanation in common parlance.... The laws thus explained or resolved are said to be *accounted for*; but the expression is incorrect if taken to mean anything more than what has been stated."[9]

And yet the very pertinacity with which such writers remind us that our explanations are in a strict sense of the word no explanations at all; that our causes never unfold the essential nature of their effects; that we never seize the inward reason why attributes cluster as they do to form things, seems to prove that they possess in their minds some ideal or pattern of what a genuine explanation would be like in case they should meet it. How could they brand our current explanations as spurious, if they had no positive notion whatever of the real thing?

Now have we the real thing? And yet may they be partly right in their denials? Surely both; and I think that the shares of truth may be easily assigned. Our "laws" *are* to a great extent but facts of larger growth, and yet things *are* inwardly and necessarily connected notwithstanding. The entire process of philosophic simplification of the chaos of sense consists of two acts, Identification and Association. Both are principles of union and therefore of theoretic rationality; but the rationality between things associated is outward and custom-bred. Only when things are identified do we pass inwardly and necessarily from one to the other.

The first step towards unifying the chaos is to classify its items. "Every concrete thing," says Prof. Bain, "falls into as many classes as it has attributes."[10] When we pick out a certain attribute to conceive it by, we literally and strictly identify it *in that respect* with the other concretes of the class having that attribute for its essence, concretes which the attribute recalls. When we conceive of sugar as a white thing it is *pro tanto* identical with snow; as a sweet thing it is the same as liquorice; *quâ* hydro-carbon, as starch. The attribute picked out may be *per se* most uninteresting and familiar, but if things superficially very diverse can be found to possess it buried within them and so be assimilated with each other, "the mind feels a peculiar and genuine satisfaction.... The intellect, oppressed with the variety and multiplicity of facts, is joyfully relieved by the simplification and the unity of a great principle."[11]

Who does not feel the charm of thinking that the moon and the apple are, as far as their relation to the earth goes, identical? of knowing respiration and combustion to be one? of understanding that the balloon rises by the same law whereby the stone sinks? of feeling that the warmth in one's palm when one rubs one's sleeve is identical with the motion which the friction checks? of recognizing the difference between beast and fish to be only a higher degree of that between human father and son? of believing our strength when we climb or chop to be no other than the strength of the sun's rays which made the oats grow out of which we got our morning meal?

We shall presently see how the attribute performing this unifying function, becomes associated with some other attribute to form what is called a general law. But at present we must note that many sciences remain in this first and simplest classificatory stage. A classificatory science is merely one the fundamental concepts of which have few associations or none with other concepts. When I say a man, a lizard, and a frog are one in being vertebrates, the identification, delightful as it is in itself, leads me hardly any farther. "The idea that all the parts of a flower are modified leaves, reveals a connecting law, which surprises us into acquiescence. But now try and define the leaf, determine its essential characteristics, so as to include all the forms that we have named. You will find yourself in a difficulty, for all distinctive marks vanish, and you have nothing left, except that a leaf in this wider sense of the term is a lateral appendage of the axis of a plant. Try then to express the proposition 'the parts of a flower are modified leaves' in the language of scientific definition, and it reads, 'the parts of the flower are lateral appendages of the axis.' "[12] Truly a bald result! Yet a dozen years ago there hardly lived a naturalist who was not thrilled with rapture at identifications in "philosophic" anatomy and botany exactly on a par with this. Nothing could more clearly show that the gratification of the sentiment of rationality depends hardly at all on the worth of the attribute which strings things together but almost exclusively on the mere fact of their being strung at all. Theological implications were the utmost which the attributes of archetypal zoology carried with them, but the wretched poverty of these proves how little they had to do with the enthusiasm engendered by archetypal identifications. Take Agassiz's conception of class-characters, order-characters &c., as "thoughts of God." What meagre thoughts! Take Owen's archetype of the vertebrate skeleton as revealing the artistic temperament of the Creator. It is a grotesque figure with neither beauty nor ethical suggestiveness, fitted rather to discredit than honor the Divine Mind. In short the conceptions led no farther than the identification pure and simple. The transformation which Darwin has effected in the classificatory sciences is simply this—that in his theory the class-essence is not a unifying attribute pure and simple, but an attribute with wide associations. When a frog, a man and a lizard are recognized as one, not simply in having the same back-bone, &c., but in being all offspring of one parent, our thought instead of coming to a standstill, is immediately confronted with further problems and, we hope, solutions. Who were that parent's ancestors and cousins? Why was he chosen out of all to found such an enormous line? Why did he himself perish in the struggle to survive? &c.

Association of class-attributes *inter se*, is thus the next great step in the mind's simplifying industry. By it Empirical Laws are founded and sciences, from classificatory, become explanatory. Without it we should be in the position of a judge who could only decide that the cases in his court belonged each to a certain class, but who should be inhibited from passing sentence, or attaching to the class-name any further notion of duty, liability, or penalty. This *coupling* of the class-concept with certain determinate *consequences* associated therewithal, is what is practically important in the laws of nature as in those of society.

When, for example, we have identified prisms, bowls of water, lenses and strata of air as distorting media, the next step is to learn that all distorting media refract light rays towards the perpendicular. Such additional determination makes a law. But this law itself may be as inscrutable as the concrete fact we started from. The entrance of a ray and its swerving towards the perpendicular, may be simply *associated* properties, with, for aught we see, no inwardly necessary bond, coupled together as empirically as the color of a man's eyes with the shape of his nose.

But such an empirical law may have its terms again classified. The essence of the medium may be to retard the light-wave's speed. The essence (in an obliquely-striking wave) of deflection towards the perpendicular may be earlier retardation of that part of the wave-front which enters first, so that the remaining portion swings round it before getting in. Medium and bending towards perpendicular thus coalesce into the one identical fact of retardation. This being granted gives an inward explanation of all above it. But retardation itself remains an empirical coupling of medium and light-movement until we have classified both under a single concept. The explanation reached by the insight that two phenomena are at bottom one and the same phenomenon, is rational in the ideal and ultimate sense of the word. The ultimate identification of the subject and predicate of a mathematical theorem, an identification which we can always reach in our reasonings, is the source of the inward necessity of mathematical demonstration. We see that the top and bottom of a parallelogram must be equal as soon as we have unearthed in the parallelogram the attribute that it consists of two equal, juxtaposed triangles of which its top and bottom form homologous sides—that is, as soon as we have seen that top and bottom have an identical essence, their length, as being such sides, and that their position is an accident. This criterion of identity is that which we all unconsciously use when we discriminate between brute fact and explained fact. There is no other test.

In the contemporary striving of physicists to interpret every event as a case of motion concealed or visible, we have an adumbration of the way in which a common essence may make the sensible heterogeneity of things inwardly rational. The cause is one motion, the effect the same motion transferred to other molecules; in other words, physics aims at the same kind of rationality as mathematics. In the second volume of Lewes's *Problems* we find this anti-Humean view that the effect is the "procession" of the cause, or that they are one thing in two aspects brought prominently forward.[13]

And why, on the other hand, do all our contemporary physical philosophers so vie with each other in the zeal with which they reiterate that in reality nerve-processes and brain-tremors "explain" nothing of our feelings? Why does "the chasm between the two classes of phenomena still remain intellectually impassable"?[14] Simply because, in the words of Spencer which we quoted a few pages back, feeling and motion have nothing whatever in common, no identical essence by which we can conceive both, and so, as Tyndall says, "pass by a process of reasoning from one to the other." The "double-aspect" school postulate the blank form of "One and the Same Fact," appeal to the image of the circle which is both convex and concave, and think that they have by this symbolic identification made the matter seem more rational.

Thus then the connexions of things become strictly rational only when, by successive substitutions of essences for things, and higher for lower essences, we succeed in reaching a point of view from which we can view the things as one. A and B are concretes; *a* and *b* are partial attributes with which for the present case we conceive them to be respectively identical (classify them) and which are coupled by a general law. M is a further attribute which rationally explains the general law as soon as we perceive it to form the essence of both *a* and *b*, as soon as we identify them with each other through it. The softening of asphalt pavements in August is explained first by the empirical law that heat, which is the essence of August, produces melting, which is the essence of the pavement's change, and secondly this law is inwardly rationalized by the conception of both heat and melting being at bottom one and the same fact, namely, increased molecular mobility.

Proximate and ultimate explanations are then essentially the same thing. Classification involves all that is inward in any explanation, and a perfected rationalization of things means only a *completed* classification of them. Every one feels that all explanation whatever, even by reference to the most proximate empirical law, does involve something of the essence of inward rationalization. How else can we understand such words as these from Prof. Huxley? "The fact that it is impossible to comprehend how it is that a physical state gives rise to a mental state, no more lessens the value of our [empirical] explanation of the latter case, than the fact that it is utterly impossible to comprehend how motion is communicated from one body to another weakens the force of the explanation of the motion of one billiard-ball by showing that another has hit it."[15]

To return now to the philosophic problem. It is evident that our idea of the universe cannot assume an inwardly rational shape until each separate phenomenon is conceived as fundamentally identical with every other. But the important fact to notice is that in the steps by which this end is reached the really rationalizing, pregnant moments are the successive steps of conception, the moments of picking out essences. The association of these essences into laws, the empirical coupling, is done by nature for us and is hardly worthy to be called an intellectual act. On the other hand the coalescence-into-one of all items in which the same essence is discerned, in other words the perception that an essence whether ultimate, simple and universal, or proximate and specific, is identical with itself wherever found, is a barren truism. The living question always is, Where *is* it found? To stand before a phenomenon and say *what* it is; in other words to pick out from it the embedded character (or characters) also embedded in the maximum number of *other* phenomena, and so identify it with them—here lie the stress and strain, here the test of the philosopher. So we revert to what we said far back: the genius can do no more than this; in Butler's words—

> "He knows *what's what*, and that's as high
> As metaphysic wit can fly."[16]

V.

We have now to ask ourselves how far this identification may be legitimately carried and what, when perfected, its real worth is. But before passing to these further questions we had best secure our ground by defending our fundamental notion itself from nominalistic attacks. The reigning British school has always denied that the same attribute *is* identical with itself in different individuals. I started above with the assumption that when we look at a subject with a certain purpose, regard it from a certain point of view, some one attribute becomes its essence and identifies it, *pro hac vice*, with a class. To this James Mill replies: "But what is meant by a mode of regarding things? This is mysterious; and is as mysteriously explained, when it is said to be the taking into view the particulars in which individuals agree. For what is there, which it is possible for the mind to take into view, in that in which individuals agree? Every color is an individual color, every size is an individual size, every shape is an individual shape. But things have no individual color in common, no individual shape in common; no individual size in common; that is to say, they have neither shape, color, nor size in common. What, then, is it which they have in common, which the mind can take into view? Those who affirmed that it was something, could by no means tell. They substituted words for things; using vague and mystical phrases, which, when examined, meant nothing";[17] the truth being according to this heroic author, that the only thing that can be possessed in common is a name. Black in the coat and black in the shoe agree only in that both are named black—the fact that on this view the *name* is never the same when used twice being quite overlooked. But the blood of the giants has grown weak in these days, and the nominalistic utterances of our contemporaries are like sweet-bells jangled, sadly out of tune. If they begin with a clear nominalistic note, they are sure to end with a grating rattle which sounds very like *universalia in re*, if not *ante rem*. In M. Taine,[18] who may fairly be included in the British School, they are almost *ante rem*. This *bruit de cloche fêlée* as the doctors say, is pathognomonic of the condition of Ockham's entire modern progeny.

But still we may find expressions like this: "When I say that the sight of any object gives me the *same* sensation or emotion to-day that it did yesterday, or the *same* which it gives to some other person, this is evidently an incorrect application of the word *same*; for the feeling which I had yesterday is gone never to return. . . . Great confusion of ideas is often produced, and many fallacies engendered, in otherwise enlightened understandings, by not being sufficiently alive to the fact (in itself always to be avoided), that they use the same name to express ideas so different as those of identity and undistinguishable resemblance."[19]

What are the exact facts? Take the sensation I got from a cloud yesterday and from the snow to-day. The white of the snow and that of the cloud differ in place, time and associates; they agree in quality, and we may say in origin, being in all probability both produced by the activity of the same brain tract. Nevertheless, John Mill denies our right to call the quality the same. He says that *it* essentially differs in every different occasion of its appearance, and that no two phenomena of which it forms part are really identical even as far as *it* goes. Is it not obvious that to maintain this view he must abandon the phenomenal plane altogether? Phenomenally considered, the white *per se is* identical with itself wherever found in snow or in cloud, to-day or to-morrow. If any nominalist deny the identity I ask him to point out the difference. *Ex hypothesi* the qualities are sensibly indistinguishable, and the only difference he can indicate is that of time and place; but these are not differences in the quality. If our quality be not the same with itself, what meaning has the word "same"? Our adversary though silenced may still grudge assent, but if he analyze carefully the grounds of this reluctance he will, I think, find that it proceeds from a difficulty in believing that the *cause* of the quality can be just the same at different times. In other words he abandons altogether the platform of the sensible phenomenon and ascends into the empyrean, postulating some inner noumenal principle of *quality + time + place + concomitants*. The entire group being never twice alike, of course this ground, or being *in se*, of the quality must each time be distinct and, so to speak, personal. This transcendental view is frankly avowed by Mr. Spencer in his *Psychology*, II., p. 63—(the passage is too complex to quote); but all nominalists must start from it, if they think clearly at all.[20]

We, who are phenomenists, may leave all metaphysical entities which have the power of producing whiteness to their fate, and content ourselves with the irreversible *datum* of perception that the whiteness after it *is* manifested is the same, be it here or be it there. Of all abstractions such entities are the emptiest, being ontological hypostatizations of the mere susceptibility of being distinguished, whilst this susceptibility has its real, nameable, phenomenal ground all the while, in the time, place, and relations affected by the attribute considered.

The truly wise man will take the phenomenon in its entirety and permanently sacrifice no one aspect to another. Time, place, and relations differ, he will freely say; but just as freely admit that the quality is identical with itself through all these differences. Then if, *to satisfy the philosophic interest*, it becomes needful to conceive this identical part as the essence of the several entire phenomena, he will gladly call them one; whilst if some other interest be paramount, the points of difference will become essential and the identity an accident. Realism is eternal and invincible in this phenomenal sense.

We have thus vindicated against all assailants our title to consider the world as a matter susceptible of rational formulation in the deepest, most inward sense, and not as a disintegrated sand-heap; and we are consequently at liberty to ask: (1) Whether the mutual identification of its items meet with any necessary limit; and (2) What, supposing the operation completed, its real worth and import amount to.

VI.

In the first place, when we have rationally explained the connexion of the items A and B by identifying both with their common attribute x, it is obvious that we have really explained only so much of these items as *is* x. To explain the connexion of choke-damp and suffocation by the lack of oxygen is to leave untouched all the other peculiarities both of choke-damp and of suffocation, such as convulsions and agony on the one hand, density and explosibility on the other. In a word, so far as A and B contain l, m, n and o, p, q, respectively in addition to x, they are not explained by x. Each additional particularity makes its distinct appeal to our rational craving. A single explanation of a fact only explains it from a single point of view.[21] The entire fact is not accounted for until each and all of its characters have been identified with their likes elsewhere. To apply this now to universal formulas we see that the explanation of the world by molecular movements explains it only so far as it actually *is* such movements. To invoke the "Unknowable" explains only so much as is unknowable; "Love" only so much as is love; "Thought," so much as is thought; "Strife" so much as is strife. All data whose actual phenomenal quality cannot be identified with the attribute invoked as Universal Principle, remain outside as ultimate, independent *kinds* or *natures*, associated by empirical laws with the fundamental attribute but devoid of truly rational kinship with it. If A and B are to be *thoroughly* rationalized together, *l*, *m*, *n* and *o*, *p*, *q*, must each and all turn out to be so many cases of *x* in disguise. This kind of wholesale identification is being now attempted by physicists when they conceive of all the ancient, separate Forces as so many determinations of one and the same essence, molecular mass, position and velocity.

Suppose for a moment that this idea were carried out for the physical world—the subjective sensations produced by the different molecular energies, color, sound, taste, &c., &c., the relation of likeness and contrast, of time and position, of ease and effort, the emotions of pain and delight, in short, all the mutually irreducible categories of mental life, would still remain over. Certain writers strive in turn to reduce all these to a common measure, the primordial unit of feeling, or infinitesimal mental event which builds them up as bricks build houses. But this case is wholly different from the last. The physical molecule is conceived not only as having a being *in se* apart from representation, but as being essentially of representable kind. With magnified perceptions we should actually see it. The mental molecule, on the other hand, has by its very definition no existence except in being felt, and yet by the same definition never is felt. It is neither a fact in consciousness nor a fact out of consciousness, and falls to the ground as a transcendental absurdity. Nothing could be more inconclusive than the empirical arguments for the existence of this noumenal feeling which Taine and Spencer draw from the sense of hearing.

But let us for an instant waive all this and suppose our feelings reduced to one. We should then have two primordial natures, the molecule of matter and the molecule of mind, coupled by an empirical law. Phenomenally incommensurable, the attempt to reduce them to unity by calling them two "aspects" is vain so long as it is not pointed out who is there *adspicere*; and the *Machtspruch* that they are expressions of one underlying Reality has no rationalizing function so long as that reality is confessed unknowable. Nevertheless the absolute necessity of an identical material substratum for the different species of feeling on the one hand, and the genera feeling and motion on the other, if we are to have any evolutionary *explanation* of things, will lead to ever renewed attempts at an atomistic hylozoism. Already Clifford and Taine, Spencer, Fechner, Zöllner, G. S. Hall, and more besides, have given themselves up to this ideal.

But again let us waive this criticism and admit that even the chasm between feeling and motion may be rationally bridged by the conception of the bilateral atom of being. Let us grant that this atom by successive compoundings with its fellows builds up the universe; is it not still clear that each item in the universe would still be explained only as to its general *quality* and not as to its other particular determinations? The particulars depend on the exact number of primordial atoms existing at the outset and their exact distances from each other. The "universal formula" of Laplace which Du Bois-Reymond has made such striking use of in his lecture *Ueber die Grenzen des Naturerkennens*, cannot possibly get along with fewer than this almost infinite number of data. Their homogeneity does not abate their infinity—each is a separate empirical fact.

And when we now retract our provisional admissions, and deny that feelings incommensurable *inter se* and with motion can be possibly unified, we see at once that the reduction of the phenomenal Chaos to rational form must stop at a certain point. It is a limited process—bounded by the number of elementary attributes which cannot be mutually identified, the specific *qualia* of representation, on the one hand, and, on the other, by the number of entities (atoms or monads or what not) with their complete mathematical determinations, requisite for deducing the fulness of the concrete world. All these irreducible data form a system, no longer phenomenally rational, *inter se*, but bound together by what is for us an empirical law. We merely find the system existing as a matter of fact, and write it down. In short, a plurality of categories and an infinity of primordial entities, determined according to these categories, is the minimum of philosophic baggage, the only possible compromise between the need of clearness and the need of unity. All simplification, beyond this point, is reached either by throwing away the particular concrete determinations of the fact to be explained, or else it is illusory simplification. In the latter case it is made by invoking some sham term, some pseudo-principle, and conglomerating it and the data into one. The principle may be an immanent element but no true universal: Sensation, Thought, Will are principles of this kind; or it may be a transcendent entity like Matter, Spirit, Substance, the Unknowable, the Unconscious, &c.[22] Such attempts do but postulate unification, not effect it; and if taken avowedly to represent a mere claim, may be allowed to stand. But if offered as actual explanations, though they may serve as a sop to the rabble, they can but nauseate those whose philosophic appetite is genuine and entire. If we choose the former mode of simplification and are willing to abstract from the particulars of time, place and combination in the concrete world, we may simplify our elements very much by neglecting the numbers and collocations of our primordial elements and attending to their qualitative categories alone. The system formed by these will then really rationalize the universe so far as its qualities go. Nothing can happen in it incommensurable with these data, and practically this abstract treatment of the world as quality is all that philosophers aim at. They are satisfied when they can see it to be a place in which none but these qualities appear, and in which the same quality appears not only once but identically repeats itself. They are willing to ignore, or leave to special sciences the knowledge of what times, places and concomitants the recurring quality is likely to affect. The *Essais de Critique générale* of Renouvier form, to my mind, by far the ablest answer to the philosophic need thus understood, clearness and unity being there carried each to the farthest point compatible with the other's existence.

VII.

And now comes the question as to the worth of such an achievement. How much better off is the philosopher when he has got his system than he was before it? As a mere phenomenal system it stands between two fires. On the one hand the unbridled craver of unity scorns it, as being incompletely rational, still to a great extent an empirical sand-heap; whilst on the other the practical man despises its empty and abstract barrenness. All it says is that the elements of the world are such and such and that each is identical with itself wherever found; but the question: Where is it found? (which is for the practical man the all-important question about each element) he is left to answer by his own wit. Which, of all the essences, shall here and now be held the essence of this concrete thing, the fundamental philosophy never attempts to decide. We seem thus led to the conclusion that a system of categories is, on the one hand, the only possible philosophy, but is, on the other, a most miserable and inadequate substitute for the fulness of the truth. It is a monstrous abridgment of things which like all abridgments is got by the absolute loss and casting out of real matter. This is why so few human beings truly care for Philosophy. The particular determinations which she ignores are the real matter exciting other aesthetic and practical needs, quite as potent and authoritative as hers. What does the moral enthusiast care for philosophical ethics? Why does the *Æsthetik* of every German philosopher appear to the artist like the abomination of desolation? What these men need is a particular counsel, and no barren, universal truism.

> "Grau, theurer Freund, ist alle Theorie
> Und grün des Lebens goldner Baum."

The entire man, who feels all needs by turns, will take nothing as an equivalent for Life but the fulness of living itself. Since the essences of things are as a matter of fact spread out and disseminated through the whole extent of time and space, it is in their spread-outness and alternation that he will enjoy them. When weary of the concrete clash and dust and pettiness, he will refresh him by an occasional bath in the eternal spring, or fortify himself by a daily look at the immutable Natures. But he will only be a visitor, not a dweller in the region; he will never carry the philosophic yoke upon his shoulders, and when tired of the gray monotony of her problems and insipid spaciousness of her results, will always escape gleefully into the teeming and dramatic richness of the concrete world.

So our study turns back here to its beginning. We started by calling every concept a teleological instrument. No concept can be a valid substitute for a concrete reality except with reference to a particular interest in the conceiver. The interest of theoretic rationality, the relief of identification, is but one of a thousand human purposes. When others rear their heads it must pack up its little bundle and retire till its turn recurs. The exaggerated dignity and value that philosophers have claimed for their solutions is thus greatly reduced. The only virtue their theoretic conception need have is simplicity, and a simple conception is an equivalent for the world only so far as the world is simple; the world meanwhile, whatever simplicity it may harbor, being also a mightily complex affair. Enough simplicity remains, however, and enough urgency in our craving to reach it, to make the theoretic function one of the most invincible and authoritative of human impulses. All ages have their intellectual populace. That of our own day prides itself particularly on its love of Science and Facts and its contempt for all metaphysics. Just weaned from the Sunday-school nurture of its early years, with the taste of the catechism still in its mouth, it is perhaps not surprising that its palate should lack discrimination and fail to recognize how much of ontology is contained in the "Nature," "Force" and "Necessary Law," how much mysticism in the "Awe," "Progress" and "Loyalty to Truth" or whatever the other phrases may be with which it sweetens its rather meagre fare of fragmentary physiology and physics. But its own inconsistency should teach it that the eradication of music, painting and poetry, games of chance and skill, manly sports and all other aesthetic energies from human life, would be an easy task compared with that suppression of Metaphysics which it aspires to accomplish. Metaphysics of some sort there must be. The only alternative is between the good Metaphysics of clear-headed Philosophy and the trashy Metaphysics of vulgar Positivism. Metaphysics, the quest of the last clear elements of things, is but another name for thought which seeks thorough self-consistency; and so long as men must think at all, some will be found willing to forsake all else to follow that ideal.

VIII.

Suppose then the goal attained. Suppose we have at last a Metaphysics in which clearness and unity join friendly hands. Whether it be over a system of interlocked elements, or over a substance, or over such a simple fact as "phenomenon" or "representation," need not trouble us now. For the discussion which follows we will call the result the metaphysical Datum and leave its composite or simple nature uncertain. Whichever it be, and however limited as we have seen be the sphere of its utility, it satisfies, if no other need, at least the need of rationality. But now I ask: Can that which is the ground of rationality in all else be itself properly called rational? It would seem at first sight that in the sense of the word we have hitherto alone considered, it might. One is tempted at any rate to say that, since the craving for rationality in a theoretic or logical sense consists in the identification of one thing with all other outstanding things, a unique datum which left nothing else outstanding would leave no play for further rational demand, and might thus be said to quench that demand or to be rational *in se*. No *otherness* being left to annoy the mind we should sit down at peace.

In other words, just as the theoretic tranquility of the boor results from his spinning no further considerations about his chaotic universe which may prevent him from going about his practical affairs; so any brute datum whatever (provided it were simple and clear) ought to banish mystery from the Universe of the philosopher and confer perfect theoretic peace, inasmuch as there would then be for him absolutely no further considerations to spin.

This in fact is what some persons think. Prof. Bain says: "A difficulty is solved, a mystery unriddled, when it can be shown to resemble something else; to be an example of a fact already known. Mystery is isolation, exception, or it may be apparent contradiction: the resolution of the mystery is found in assimilation, identity, fraternity. When all things are assimilated, so far as assimilation can go, so far as likeness holds, there is an end to explanation; there is an end to what the mind can do, or can intelligently desire.... The path of science as exhibited in modern ages, is towards generality, wider and wider, until we reach the highest, the widest laws of every department of things; there explanation is finished, mystery ends, perfect vision is gained."

But unfortunately this first answer will not hold. Whether for good or evil, it is an empirical fact that the mind is so wedded to the process of seeing an *other* beside every item of its experience, that when the notion of an absolute datum which is all is presented to it, it goes through its usual procedure and remains *pointing* at the void beyond, as if in that lay further matter for contemplation. In short, it spins for itself the further positive consideration of a Nonentity enveloping the Being of its datum; and as that leads to no issue on the further side, back recoils the thought in a circle towards its datum again. But there is no logical identity, no natural bridge between nonentity and this particular datum, and the thought stands oscillating to and fro, wondering "Why was there anything but nonentity? Why just this universal datum and not another? Why any thing at all?" and finds no end, in wandering mazes lost. Indeed, Prof. Bain's words are so untrue that in reflecting men it is just when the attempt to fuse the manifold into a single totality has been most successful, when the conception of the universe as a *fait unique* (in D'Alembert's words) is nearest its perfection, that the craving for further explanation, the ontological Θαυμάζειν arises in its extremest pungency.

As Schopenhauer says, "The uneasiness which keeps the never-resting clock of metaphysics in motion, is the consciousness that the non-existence of this world is just as possible as its existence."[23]

The notion of Nonentity may thus be called the parent of the philosophic craving in its subtlest and profoundest sense. Absolute existence is absolute mystery. Although *selbstständig*, it is not *selbstverständlich*; for its relations with the Nothing remain unmediated to our understanding. One philosopher only, so far as I know, has pretended to throw a logical bridge over this chasm. Hegel, by trying to show that Nonentity and Being as actually determined are linked together by series of successive identities, binds the whole of possible thought into an adamantine unity with no conceivable outlying notion to disturb the free rotary circulation of the mind within its bounds. Since such unchecked motion constitutes the feeling of rationality, he must be held, if he has succeeded, to have eternally and absolutely quenched all its logical demands.

But for those who, like most of us, deem Hegel's heroic effort to have failed, nought remains but to confess that when all has been unified to its supreme degree, (Prof. Bain to the contrary notwithstanding), the notions of a Nonentity, or of a possible Other than the actual, may still haunt our imagination and prey upon the ultimate data of our system. The bottom of Being is left logically opaque to us, a *datum* in the strict sense of the word, something which we simply come upon and find, and about which, (if we wish to act,) we should pause and wonder as little as possible. In this confession lies the lasting truth of Empiricism, and in it Empiricism and imaginative Faith join hands. The logical attitude of both is identical, they both say there is a *plus ultra* beyond all we know, a womb of unimagined other possibility. They only differ in their sentimental temper: Empiricism says, "Into the *plus ultra* you have no right to carry your anthropomorphic affirmations"; Faith says, "You have no right to extend to it your denials." The mere ontologic emotion of wonder, of mystery, has in some minds such a tinge of the rapture of sublimity, that for this aesthetic reason alone, it will be difficult for any philosophic system completely to exorcise it.

In truth, the philosopher's logical tranquility is after all in essence no other than the boor's. Their difference regards only the point at which each refuses to let further considerations upset the absoluteness of the data he assumes. The boor does so immediately, and is therefore liable at any moment to the ravages of many kinds of confusion and doubt. The philosopher does not do so till unity has been reached, and is therefore warranted against the inroads of *those* considerations—but only practically not essentially secure from the blighting breath of the *ultimate* "Why?" Positivism takes a middle ground, and with a certain consciousness of the beyond abruptly refuses by an inhibitory action of the will to think any further, stamps the ground and says "Physics, I espouse thee! for better or worse, be thou my absolute!"

The Absolute is what has not yet been transcended, criticized or made relative. So far from being something quintessential and unattainable as is so often pretended, it is practically the most familiar thing in life. Every thought is absolute to us at the moment of conceiving it or acting upon it. It only becomes relative in the light of further reflection. This may make it flicker and grow pale—the notion of nonentity may blow in from the infinite and extinguish the theoretic rationality of a universal datum. As regards this latter, absoluteness and rationality are in fact convertible terms. And the chief effort of the rationalizing philosopher must be to gain an absoluteness for his datum which shall be *stable* in the maximum degree, or as far as possible removed from exposure to those further considerations by which we saw that the vulgar *Weltanshauung* may so promptly be upset. I shall henceforward call the further considerations which may supervene and make relative or denationalize a mass of thought, the *reductive* of that thought. The *reductive* of absolute being is thus nonentity, or the notion of an *aliter possibile* which it involves. The reductive of an absolute physics is the thought that all material facts are representations in a mind. The reductive of absolute time, space, causality, atoms, &c., are the so-called antinomies which arise as soon as we think fully out the thoughts we have begun. The reductive of absolute knowledge is the constant potentiality of doubt, the notion that the next thought may always correct the present one—resulting in the notion that a noumenal world is there mocking the one we think we know. Whatever we think, some reductive seems in strict theoretic legitimacy always imminently hovering over our thought ready to blight it. Doubleness dismissed at the front door re-enters in the rear and spoils the rationality of the simple datum we flattered ourselves we had attained. Theoretically the task of the philosopher, if he cannot reconcile the datum with the reductive by the way of identification *à la* Hegel, is to exorcise the reductive so that the datum may hold up its head again and know no fear. Prof. Bain would no doubt say that nonentity was a pseud-idea not derived from experience and therefore meaningless, and so exorcise that reductive.[24] The antinomies may be exorcised by the distinction between potentiality and actuality.[25]

The ordinary half educated materialist comforts himself against idealists by the notion that, after all, thought is such an obscure mystical form of existence that it is almost as bad as no existence at all, and need not be seriously taken into account by a sensible man.

If nothing else could be conceived than thoughts or fancies, these would be credited with the maximum of reality. Their reductive is the belief in an objective reality of which they are but copies. When this belief takes the form of the affirmation of a noumenal world contrasted with all possible thought, and therefore playing no other part than that of reductive pure and simple—to discover the formula of exorcism becomes, and has been recognized ever since Kant to be, one of the principal tasks of philosophy rationally understood.

The reductive used by nominalists to discredit the self-identity of the same attribute in different phenomena is the notion of a still higher degree of identity. We easily exorcise this reductive by challenging them to show what the higher degree of sameness can possibly contain which is not already in the lower.

The notion of Nonentity is not only a reductive; it can assume upon occasion an exorcising function. If, for example, a man's ordinary mundane consciousness feels staggered at the improbability of an immaterial thinking-principle being the source of all things, Nonentity comes in and says, "Contrasted with me, (that is, considered simply as *existent*) one principle is as probable as another." If the same mundane consciousness recoils at the notion of providence towards individuals or individual immortality as involving, the one too infinite a subdivision of the divine attention, the other a too infinite accumulation of population in the heavens, Nonentity says, "As compared with me all quantities are one: the wonder is all there when God has found it worth His while to guard or save a single soul."

But if the philosopher fails to find a satisfactory formula of exorcism for his datum, the only thing he can do is to "blink" the reductive at a certain point, assume the Given as his necessary ultimate, and proceed to a life whether of contemplation or of action based on that. There is no doubt that this half wilful act of arrest, this acting on an opaque necessity, is accompanied by a certain pleasure. See the reverence of Carlyle for brute fact: "There is an infinite significance in Fact." "Necessity," says a German philosopher,[26] and he means not rational but simply given necessity, "is the last and highest point that we can reach in a rational conception of the world. . . . It is not only the interest of ultimate and definitive knowledge, but also that of the feelings, to find a last repose and an ideal equilibrium, in an uttermost datum which can simply not be other than it is."

Such is the attitude of ordinary men in their theism, God's fiat being in physics and morals such an uttermost datum. Such also is the attitude of all hard-minded analysts and *Verstandemenschen*. Renouvier and Hodgson, the two foremost contemporary philosophers, promptly say that of experience as a whole no account can be given, but do not seek to soften the abruptness of the confession or reconcile us with our impotence.

Such mediating attempts may be made by more mystical minds. The peace of rationality may be sought through ecstacy when logic fails. To religious persons of every shade of doctrine moments come when the world as it is seems so divinely orderly, and the acceptance of it by the heart so rapturously complete, that intellectual questions vanish, nay the intellect itself is hushed to sleep—as Wordsworth says, "Thought is not, in enjoyment it expires." Ontological emotion so fills the soul that ontological speculation can no longer overlap it and put her girdle of interrogation-marks around existence. Even the least religious of men must have felt with our national ontologic poet, Walt Whitman, when loafing on the grass on some transparent summer morning, that "Swiftly arose and spread over him the peace and knowledge that pass all the argument of the earth." At such moments of energetic living we feel as if there were something diseased and contemptible, yea vile, in theoretic grubbing and brooding. To feel "I *am* the truth" is to abolish the opposition between knowing and being.

Since the heart can thus wall out the ultimate irrationality which the head ascertains, the erection of its procedure into a systematized method would be a philosophic achievement of first-rate importance. As used by mystics hitherto it has lacked universality, being available for few persons and at few times, and even in these being apt to be followed by fits of "reaction" and "dryness"; but it may nevertheless be the forerunner of what will ultimately prove a true method. If all men could permanently say with Jacobi, "In my heart there is light," though they should for ever fail to give an articulate account of it, existence would really be rationalised.[27]

But if men should ever all agree that the mystical method is a subterfuge without logical pertinency, a plaster, but no cure, that the Hegelian method is fallacious, that the idea of Nonentity can therefore neither be exorcised nor identified, Empiricism will be the ultimate philosophy. Existence will be a brute Fact to which as a whole the emotion of ontologic wonder shall rightfully cleave, but remain eternally unsatisfied. This wonderfulness or mysteriousness will then be an essential attribute of the nature of things, and the exhibition and emphasizing of it will always continue to be an ingredient in the philosophic industry of the race. Every generation will produce its Job, its Hamlet, its Faust or its Sartor Resartus.

With this we seem to have exhausted all the possibilities of purely theoretic rationality. But we saw at the outset that when subjectively considered rationality can only be defined as perfectly unimpeded mental function. Impediments which arise in the purely theoretic sphere might perhaps be avoided if the stream of mental action should leave that sphere betimes and pass into the practical. The structural unit of mind is in these days, deemed to be a triad, beginning with a sensible impression, ending with a motion, and having a feeling of greater or less length in the middle. Perhaps the whole difficulty of attaining theoretic rationality is due to the fact that the very quest violates the nature of our intelligence, and that a passage of the mental function into the third stage before the second has come to an end in the *cul de sac* of its contemplation, would revive the energy of motion and keep alive the sense of ease and freedom which is its psychic counterpart. We must therefore inquire what constitutes the feeling of rationality in its *practical* aspect; but that must be done at another time and in another place.[28]

NOTES

1. *Logic,* English tr., p. 139.
2. *Philosophie des Unbewussten,* 2te Auflage, p. 249.
3. *Welt als Wille u. Vorstellung,* II., p. 83.
4. "On Mystery, etc." *Fortnightly Review,* Vol. IV. N.S., page 394.
5. *Essays,* ed. Green and Grose, II., p. 135.
6. *Critique Philosophique,* 12 Juillet, 1877, p. 383.
7. *Microcosmus,* 2nd ed. I., p. 261.
8. *Treatise on Human Nature,* ed. T. H. Green, I., p. 559.
9. *Logic,* 8th Edition, I., p. 549.
10. *Ment. and Mor. Science,* p. 107.
11. Bain, *Logic,* II, p. 120.
12. Helmholtz, *Popular Scientific Lectures,* p. 47.
13. This view is in growing favor with thinkers fed from empirical sources. See Wundt's *Physikalische Axiome* and the important article by A. Riehl, "Causalitat und Identität," in *Vierteljahrssch. f. wiss. Philos.* Bd. I., p. 265. The Humean view is ably urged by Chauncey Wright, *Philosophical Discussions,* N.Y. 1877, p. 406.
14. Tyndall, *Fragments of Science,* 2nd ed., p. 121.
15. "Modern Symposium," *XIXth Century,* Vol. I., 1877.
16. This doctrine is perfectly congruous with the conclusion that identities are the only propositions necessary *a priori*, though of course it does not necessarily lead to that conclusion, since there may be in things elements which are not simple but bilateral or synthetic, like straightness and shortness in a line, convexity and concavity in a curve. Should the empiricists succeed in their attempt to resolve such Siamese-twin elements into habitual juxtapositions, the Principle of Identity would become the only *a priori* truth, and the philosophic problem like all our ordinary problems would become a question as to facts: *What* are these facts which we perceive to exist? Are there any existing facts corresponding to this or that conceived class? Lewes, in the interesting discussion on necessary and contingent truth in the Prolegomena to his *History* and in Chap. XIII of his first *Problem,* seems at first sight to take up an opposite position, in that he maintains our commonly so-called contingent truths to be really necessary. But his treatment of the question most beautifully confirms the doctrine I have advanced in the text. If the proposition "A is B" is ever true, he says it is so necessarily. But he proves the necessity by showing that what we mean by A is its essential attribute x, and what we mean by B is again x. Only *in so far* as A and B are identical is the proposition true. But he admits that a fact sensibly just like A may lack x, and a fact sensibly unlike B may have it. In either case the proposition to be true, must change. The contingency which he banishes from propositions, he thus houses in their terms; making as I do the act of conception, subsumption, classification, intuition, naming, or whatever else one may prefer to call it, the pivot on which thought turns. Before this act there is infinite indeterminateness—A and B may be anything. After the act there is the absolute certainty of

truism—all x's are the same. *In* the act—is A, *x*? *is* B, *x*? or not?—we have the sphere of truth and error, of living experience, in short, of Fact. As Lewes himself says: "The only necessity is that a thing is what it is; the only contingency is that our proposition may not state what the thing is" (*Problems*, Vol. I., p. 395).

17. *Analysis*, Vol. I., p. 249.

18. How can M. Taine fail to have perceived that the entire doctrine of "Substitution" so clearly set forth in the nominalistic beginning of his brilliant book is utterly senseless except on the supposition of realistic principles like those which he so admirably expounds at its close? How *can* the image be a useful substitute for the sensation, the tendency for the image, the name for the tendency, unless sensation, image, tendency and name be *identical* in some respect; in respect namely of function, of the relations they enter into? Were this realistic basis laid at the outset of Taine's *De l'Intelligence*, it would be one of the most consistent instead of one of the most self-contradictory works of our day.

19. J. S. Mill, *Logic*, 8th Ed., I., p. 77.

20. I fear that even after this some persons will remain unconvinced, but then it seems to me the matter has become a dispute about words. If my supposed adversary, when he says that different times and places prevent a quality which appears in them from ever being twice the same, will admit that they do not make it in any conceivable way *different*, I will willingly abandon the words "same" and "identical" to his fury; though I confess it becomes rather inconvenient to have no single positive word left by which to indicate complete absence of difference.

21. In the number of the *Journal of Speculative Philosophy* for April 1879, Prof. John Watson most admirably asserts and expresses the truth which constitutes the back-bone of this article, namely that every manner of conceiving a fact is relative to some interest, and that there are no absolutely essential attributes—every attribute having the right to call itself essential in turn, and the truth consisting of nothing less than all of them together. I avow myself unable to comprehend as yet this author's Hegelian point of view, but his pages 164 to 172 are a most welcome corroboration of what I have striven to advance in the text.

22. The idea of "God" in its popular function is open to neither of these objections, being conceived as a phenomenon standing in causal relation to other phenomena. As such, however, it has no unifying function of a properly *explanatory* kind.

23. *Welt als Wille &c.*, 3 Auflage, I., p. 189.

24. The author of *A Candid Examination of Theism* (Trübner, 1878) exorcises Nonentity by the notion of the all-excluding infinitude of Existence—whether reasonably or not I refrain from deciding. The last chapter of this work (published a year after the present text was written), is on "the final Mystery of Things," and impresses in striking language much that I have said.

25. See Renouvier: *Premier Essai.*

26. Dühring: *Cursus der Philosophie*, Leipzig 1876, p. 35.

27. A curious recent contribution to the construction of a universal mystical method is contained in the *Anaesthetic Revelation* by Benj. P. Blood (Amsterdam, N.Y., 1874). The

author, who is a writer abounding in verbal felicities, thinks we may all grasp the secret of Being if we only intoxicate ourselves often enough with laughing-gas. "There is in the instant of recall from the anaesthetic stupor a moment in which the genius of being is revealed. . . . Patients try to speak of it but invariably fail in a lost mood of introspection. . . . But most will accept this as the central point of the illumination that sanity is not the basic quality of intelligence, . . . but that only in sanity is formal or contrasting thought, while the naked life is realized outside of sanity altogether. It is the instant contrast of this tasteless water of souls with formal thought as we *come to* that leaves the patient in an astonishment that the awful mystery of life is at last but a homely and common thing. . . . To minds of sanguine imagination there will be a sadness in the tenor of the mystery, as if the key-note of the universe were low—for no poetry, no emotion known to the normal sanity of man, can furnish a hint of its primaeval prestige, and its all-but appalling solemnity; but for such as have felt sadly the instability of temporal things there is a comfort of serenity and ancient peace; while for the resolved and imperious spirit there are majesty and supremacy unspeakable." The logical characteristic of this state is said to be "an apodal sufficiency—to which sufficiency a wonder or fear of why it is sufficient cannot pertain and could be attributed only as an impossible disease or lack. . . . The disease of Metaphysics vanishes in the fading of the question and not in the coming of an answer."

28. This article is the first chapter of a psychological work on the motives which lead men to philosophize. It deals with the purely theoretic or logical impulse. Other chapters treat of practical and emotional motives and in the conclusion an attempt is made to use the motives as tests of the soundness of different philosophies.

G. Stanley Hall

PHILOSOPHY IN THE UNITED STATES

Mind o.s. 4 (January 1879): 89–105.

There are nearly 300 non-Catholic colleges in the United States, most of them chartered by the legislatures of their respective states, and conferring the degree of A.B. upon their students at the end of a four years' course, and A.M. three years after graduation. In nearly all these institutions certain studies, aesthetical, logical, historical, most commonly ethical, most rarely psychological, are roughly classed as philosophy and taught during the last year almost invariably by the president. The methods of instruction and examination are so varied that it is impossible in the space at our disposal to report in detail upon the nature and value of the work done in these institutions. More than 200 of them are strictly denominational, and the instruction given in philosophy is rudimentary and mediaeval. More than 60 which in the annual catalogue claim to be non-sectarian are, if not pervaded with the spirit of some distinct religious party, yet strictly evangelical. Indeed there are less than half a dozen colleges or universities in the United States where metaphysical thought is entirely freed from reference to theological formulae. Many teachers of philosophy have no training in their department save such as has been obtained in theological seminaries, and their pupils are made far more familiar with the points of difference in the theology of Parks, Fairchilds, Hodges and the like, than with Plato, Leibnitz or Kant. Many of these colleges were established by funds contributed during periods of religious awakening, and are now sustained with difficulty as denominational outposts by appeals from the pulpit and sectarian press. The nature of the philosophical instruction is determined by the convictions of constituencies and trustees, while professors are to a great extent without independence or initiative in matters of speculative thought. The philosophical character of some institutions is determined by the conditions attached to bequests. A few are under the personal and perhaps daily supervision of the founders themselves, who engage and discharge the members of their faculties as so many day-laborers, and who are likely to be religious enthusiasts or propagandists.

The traditional college-*régime* in the United States was designed to cultivate openness and flexibility of mind by introducing the student hastily to a great variety of studies, so that his own tastes and aptitudes might be consciously developed as guides to ulterior and more technical work. The method of philosophical indoctrination, in striking contrast to this, seeks to prevent the independent personal look at things, and to inoculate the mind with insidious orthodoxies which too often close it for ever to speculative interests. The great open questions of psychology and metaphysics are made to dwindle in number and importance as compared with matters of faith and conduct. Some of the professorlings of philosophy are disciples of disciples of Hopkins, Hickok, Wayland, Upham, Haven. Most have extended their philosophical horizon as far as Reid, Stewart, Hamilton. Many have read Mill's *Examination of Hamilton*, chapters of Herbert Spencer, lectures of Huxley and Tyndall, and epitomes of Kant, Berkeley, Hegel, and Hume. Others, fewer in number, have studied compendious histories of philosophy like Schwegler and Ueberweg, have read Mill's *Logic* and Taine, have dipped into Kant's *Critique*, and have themselves printed essays on Spencer, Leibnitz, Plato, &c., in religious periodicals, have perhaps published compilations on mental or moral science, and are able to aid the sale of small editions of their works by introducing them into their own classes as text-books. Others, fewer yet, to be spoken of later, have had thorough training, and are doing valuable and original work. It is, in any case, plain that there is very small chance that a well-equipped student of philosophy in any of its departments will secure a position as a teacher of the subject. He may find a career as a writer, editor, or instructor in other branches, or he may bring his mind into some sort of platonizing conformity with the milder forms of orthodoxy and teach a philosophy with reservations. That most of the instructors find the limitation of their field of work galling is by no means asserted or implied. Many of them feel no need of a larger and freer intellectual atmosphere. They have never been taught to reason save from dogmatic or scriptural data. Where little science is taught there is a certain dignity attached to their department above all the others, which is as unfavorable to their own advancement as it is to the spirit of persistent inquiry on the part of the students. Summary and original methods of dealing with speculative questions are far more commonly found than philosophical erudition or careful criticism. Yet there is an almost universal complacency in the degree of liberality attained which is in strange and indeed irrational contrast to the feeling with which a philosophy which is entirely emancipated from the theological yoke is regarded. Andover is well pleased, to be thought freer from the rigidity of dogma than Princeton, and Oberlin claims more warmth of feeling and less tyranny of creed than either. While slight differences among the philosophical *idola* of orthodoxy are thus disproportionately magnified, all these institutions unite in impressing upon their students the lesson that there is an abyss of skepticism and materialism into which, as the greatest of all intellectual disasters, those who cease to believe in the Scriptures as interpreted according to the canons of orthodox criticism, are sure to be plunged.

The spirit and aims of philosophical instruction in very many of the smaller colleges have found an admirable exponent in the Boston Monday lectureship of the Rev. Joseph

Cook, whose discourses, now published in several volumes, have had an immense influence upon the semi-theological philosophy of all such centers of learning as we have just characterized. In these forty-minute lectures before immense popular audiences, art, literary criticism, politics, religious history, science and systems of thought are discussed with much display of erudition and with great similitude of candor. Long lists of names and title-pages are read, succinct and often epigrammatic summaries of philosophical and religious systems and tendencies are given; recent discoveries in science are explained or illustrated by diagrams and by illuminated microscopic preparations, until the hearers are convinced that, by a short and easy method now first displayed, the very kernel of truth has been shelled from books and nature by a master-hand. Then, with much liberality of interpretation, scriptural doctrines are compared with these results, all in a conciliatory spirit; but wherever the teachings of science or philosophy are judged to vary from those of Scripture, the supreme authority of the latter is urged with all that intensity of a fervid and magnetic personality which makes dogmatism impressive and often even sublime. The mere brute force of unreasoned individual conviction, which Hegel so wittily characterizes as the animal kingdom of mind, has a peculiar convincing eloquence of its own in religious matters, which, acceptable as it often is to faith, has long been one of the stumbling-blocks in the way of philosophy in America.

Another reason for the backward condition of philosophy in most of these institutions is found in their poverty. A few of them were established by real-estate companies to help the sale of land. By the negligence of the more worthy members of trustee-boards, together with mistaken provisions to fill vacancies, others have fallen under the control of ward-politicians, and professorships are retained or declared vacant by a scarcely better than popular suffrage. Still others are under the immediate control of state-legislatures, which have it in their power to reduce or even to withhold the annual appropriation. Nearly all of them are poorly endowed, and some are entirely without funds save those accruing from tuition-fees; and thus, so numerous are they, so sharp is the competition for patronage, and so quick and sagacious is parental jealousy of any instruction which shall unsettle early and home-bred religious convictions, that it is not surprising that there is little philosophical or even intellectual independence to be found in these institutions. Again the faculty or *corps* of professors generally consists of from three to ten men, or occasionally ladies, who must instruct in mathematics, natural and physical science, ancient and two or three modern languages, political and literary history, oratory, theme-writing, &c., and who are thus obliged to spend from three to six hours per day in the class-room. Thus fatigue, coupled with the dissipation of teaching miscellaneous subjects, generally renders original thought and research impossible even where otherwise it might have led to valuable results.

While thus business conspires with Bethel to bring mental science into general disfavor, the average American college is in no position to lead or even to resist popular opinion and sentiment, supposing it inclined to do so. The shrewd practical money-making man, even in one of the learned professions, can make little use of philosophy; indeed it is liable to weaken his executive powers and make him introspective and theoretical. The popular philistinism which we have heard impressed as a weighty philosophical motto in the exhortation, "Look outward not inward, forward not backward, and keep at work," and which seems no more rational than the superstitious aversion to science in the Middle Ages, has been strangely efficacious against philosophical endeavor here. Hence all branches of mental science have come to be widely regarded as the special appanage of a theological curriculum, where despite the limitations above described a little speculation is a trifle less dangerous than for a practical business man.

The above, however, we hasten to say, is the darker side of the picture and is truer in general of Western than of Eastern colleges. The most vigorous and original philosophical instruction is almost everywhere given in ethics, though like nearly all other subjects it is taught from text-books. Those most commonly used are Alexander's *Moral Philosophy*, Hopkins's *Law of Love and Love as a Law*, Wayland's and Fairchild's *Moral Science*. Calderwood's and Peabody's treatises have lately been introduced into three of the larger institutions. Portions of Cicero's *De Officiis* we also find in three catalogues as part of the required course in ethics. The work with text-books is commonly supplemented by lectures where ethical principles are applied to law, trade, art, conduct, &c., in a more or less hortatory manner. The grounds of moral obligation are commonly deduced from Revelation, supplemented by the intuitions of conscience, which are variously interpreted. The practical questions of daily life are often discussed in the class-room with the professor with great freedom, detail and interest. Current social or political topics are sometimes introduced, and formal debates by students appointed beforehand by the professor, and followed by his comments, may occasionally take the place of regular recitations and lectures. In one large institution each member of the class in ethics is required to write a thesis during the senior year, to be read before the class on one of such topics as the following, which we copy from a printed list—"Is it right to do evil that good may come?" "Is falsehood ever justifiable, and if so, when?" "The moral character of Hamlet." "My favorite virtues and why?" "How far is Plato's Republic truly moral?" "Discussion of the conflict of duties, e.g., in Jephthah, Orestes." "The Utilitarianism of J. S. Mill." "How far may patriotism justify the motto, *My country right or wrong*." "The moral difficulties in the way of civil service reform." That the subjects thus attempted are far too vast and general for thorough discussion by the students who essay them cannot be denied, but it is possible that definite and permanent centers of interest in the infinite questions of ethics may often be thus established in the most immature minds. On the whole the average student completes his course in moral science with the conviction that there is a hard and fast line between certain definite acts and habits which are always and everywhere, wrong, and others which are right; that above all motives, circumstances, insights, the absolute imperative of conscience must determine the content as well as the form of actions. The psychological nature and origin of conscience are questions which have excited very little interest.

The theory of the syllogism is taught in nearly all the colleges from elementary textbooks, of which Fowler's *Deductive Logic* and Jevons's smaller treatise, which have lately come into quite general use, are the best. As a rule but little time is devoted to work in this department, and the methods of induction are often entirely ignored.

Mental philosophy is usually taught during perhaps half the senior year from such text-books as Bowen's abridgement of Hamilton's *Metaphysics*; *The Human Intellect*, by President Porter of Yale College, which has been epitomized in a smaller volume; Haven's, Upham's and Wayland's *Mental Philosophy*; Everett's *Science of Thought*; Hickok's *Rational and Empirical Psychology*. Schwegler's *Outline of the History of Philosophy*, of which Seeley's translation is far superior to that of Stirling, is coming into use in the larger institutions. Locke's *Essay*, portions of Berkeley, of Kant's *Critique of Pure Reason*, and even Mill, Hamilton, Spencer's *Psychology*, Bain, and Taine, are also occasionally introduced.

Æsthetics, so called, is taught in many colleges from various text-books, such as Day, Bascom, Kames's *Elements of Criticism*, and compendiums of art-history. An immense range of topics, from landscape-gardening and household-furniture to painting, poetry, and even music, are summarily treated, and more or less arbitrary psychological principles are laid down as fundamental canons of taste. The work done in this department we regard as not merely worthless, but as positively harmful. No attempt is made to explain the ulterior causes or the nature of feelings of pleasure and pain; and without museums, galleries, or even photographs, little can be learned of the history or principles of art.

Butler's *Analogy*, Natural Theology, the Evidence of Christianity, Pedagogics, and the Catechism, are taught in a few institutions as a part of the philosophical discipline. The question of the order in which the above studies should be pursued, was lately brought forward in a general convention of college officers, but has attracted little attention. In at least four of the larger theological seminaries, courses of lectures on the history of philosophical speculation are given by the professor of systematic divinity. In very many of the higher schools and colleges for female education, especially if they are under evangelical control, instruction is given in mental science. In the annual catalogues of the very smallest and poorest of these colleges, we have seen one teacher dubbed professor of mental, moral and physical science, and in another of natural and intellectual philosophy. Literature, history, mathematics, and more often political economy, may be found as part of the work of the instructor in philosophy.

The serious and introspective frame of mind which religious freedom and especially pietism tends to develop; the enterprise and individuality which are characteristic of American life, and which have shown themselves in all sorts of independent speculation; the principle of self-government, which in the absence of historical precedents and tradition inclines men to seek for the first principles of political and ethical science, have combined to invest semi-philosophical themes with great interest even for men of defective education. From the pulpit and even in the adult Sunday-school class or the debating society, in the club-essay and the religious press, metaphysical discussions are often heard or read, and not infrequently awaken the liveliest discussions. Yet, on the other hand, dogmatism and the practical spirit have combined thus far quite too effectually to restrain those who might otherwise have devoted themselves to the vocation of thinking deeply, fearlessly and freely on the ultimate questions of life and conduct. If "philosophers in America are as rare as snakes in Norway," it is because the country is yet too young. The minds of business and working men, whether skeptical or orthodox, have short, plain, and rigid methods of dealing with matters of pure reason or of faith, and are not always tolerant of those who adopt other and more 'unsettling' ones. If, however, we may find in Hegel's *Phenomenology* a program of the future, the hard common sense which subdues nature and organizes the objective world into conformity with man's physical needs will, at length, when it has done its work, pause in retrospect, and finally be reflected as conscious self-knowledge which is the beginning of philosophical wisdom. As a nation we are not old enough to develop, and yet too curious and receptive to despair of, a philosophy.

As we pass either from the smaller to the larger or from the Western to the Eastern institutions, we find in general a much better condition of things. The older Edwards, the influence of whose writings is still very great upon the religious philosophy of New England and the Middle States, did much to rationalize Calvinism and to inspire confidence in the verdicts of reason. In his great work on the freedom of the Will, he taught that the essence of right and wrong lies in the nature of acts and motives and not in their cause, that spontaneity and not self-determination is the characteristic of a free act. Subjectively, virtue is the love of being in general. Adam's sin was not imputed to his descendants, but its effects were naturally transmitted as the withdrawal of higher spiritual influences. The new birth is not the advent of a new but the new activity of an old principle. The disciples of Edwards—Dr. Dwight, C. G. Finney, E. A. Parks, Horace Bushnell, Moses Stuart, and many others—have modified and widely extended his opinions.

Deserving of special mention are Mark Hopkins and L. L. Hickok. The latter, lately professor of philosophy in Union College, N.Y., has written text-books entitled *Rational Psychology, Moral Science, Empirical Psychology, Rational Cosmology, Creator and Creation*, &c., some of which are made the basis of instruction in Amherst College. On the ground of a modified Kantianism he attempts to reconcile an original interpretation of post-Kantian idealism with orthodox theology. His subtle mysticism has found many admirers. Mark Hopkins, long president of Williams College, though laying claim to no great scholarship even in his own department, brings with singular independence and individuality the skill of nearly half a century of paedagogic experience, and a most impressive force and sweetness of character, to enforce in a direct Socratic way the lesson that philanthropy is the substance of both religion and morals. His influence, not only on many generations of students, but wherever his lectures and text-books have been read, has been considerable.

At Yale College, philosophy is taught mainly by President Porter on the basis of his compendious text-book above named, but with auxiliary lectures, books of reference, &c. Although a clergyman of the congregationalist denomination, he has devoted a life of study largely to philosophy, and is a vigorous expositor of the Scotch-Kantian speculation as opposed to Darwinism and materialism.[1]

The influence of W. E. Channing, Theodore Parker, R. W. Emerson, and the considerable body of Unitarian writers, has been most wholesome in stimulating and liberalizing speculative thought, especially at Harvard University where the most extended course of philosophic study is now offered. The amount of work *required* of all students is much less than at Yale, and instead of the topical method, by which sensation, representation, reason, &c., are followed separately through ancient and modern systems, the historical method is adopted. Jevons's *Logic* and Locke's *Essay*, each two hours per week, are prescribed for all students during the junior year. But in addition to this, five optional courses are offered in the last annual catalogue as follows: (1) Cartesianism, Descartes, Malebranche, Berkeley, Hume; (2) Spinoza, Leibnitz and Kant, Bouillier's *Histoire de la philosophie Cartésienne*, Kant's *Critique of Pure Reason*, Schwegler's *History of Modern Philosophy*, Lectures on French and German Philosophy; (3) German Philosophy of the present day—Schopenhauer's *Die Welt als Wille und Vorstellung*, Hartmann's *Philosophie des Unbewussten*; (4) Psychology— Taine's *On Intelligence*, Recitations and Lectures; (5) Ethics—Grote's *Treatise on the Moral Ideals*, Cicero's *De Officiis*, Lectures. Each of these courses occupies three hours per week through the year, and all, especially the first two, are largely attended. The fourth course has been organized only two years, and is conducted by the assistant professor of physiology. It was admitted not without some opposition into the department of philosophy, and is up to the present time the only course in the country where students can be made familiar with the methods and results of recent German researches in physiological psychology: the philosophical stand-point of Dr. James is essentially that of the modified new-Kantianism of Renouvier. Professor Bowen, who has been for many years at the head of the philosophical department, has recently published his lectures on the History of Modern Philosophy in the form of a text-book, a review of which has already appeared in *Mind*. He is a very lucid expositor, especially of Kant and Schopenhauer, and a vigorous antagonist of materialism and infidelity: his philosophical stand-point is essentially theistic and his method eclectic. Assistant professor Palmer, who has for some years taught the first course, and more recently Kant's *Critique*, is purely objective, impersonal and historical in his expositions, which are remarkably acute and thorough. Professor C. C. Everett, of the theological department, lectures on the history of German philosophy from a modified Hegelian stand-point. How independent and original his interpretations have been may best be seen in his *Science of Thought*. John Fiske, formerly lecturer on philosophy in the university, and widely known by his *Outlines of Cosmic Philosophy* as the American expositor of Herbert Spencer, was the first to elaborate the doctrine that the development of sympathy and philanthropy was due to the prolongation of the period of human infancy. Following Mr. Spencer's sociological researches, he has more recently turned his attention to historical subjects. Chauncey Wright, whose philosophical papers have lately been edited by Professor Norton, was a man of great philosophical acumen, whose untimely death was most unfortunate for philosophy in Cambridge. It is impossible, even after a careful study of his writings, either to epitomize his views or to account for his influence upon those who came in contact with him. The latter was no doubt largely due to the uniform sweetness of his disposition, to his unusual powers of ready conversational exposition and illustration, and to the extent and variety of his mental acquisitions. His most considerable essay, on the "Origin of Self-Consciousness," unfolds the view that when a subjective sequence of mental terms or states can be held along with, though distinct from, an objective sequence, involving thus at least four terms in all, self-consciousness may be first said to exist. How this comes to pass and how thence the higher faculties are developed, is unfolded with most characteristic analytic subtlety. With an almost Coleridgean power of abstract ratiocination, favored by his mathematical profession, he combined the tastes of a student of nature. His correspondence with Mr. Darwin, more lately printed among his letters, shows how carefully he had pondered the details of the theory of natural selection, the expression of emotion, &c. It can scarcely be doubted, however, by those who attempt to shell out the kernel of his speculations, that vagueness and even ambiguity most seriously impair the value of his work. Finally, no account of philosophy in Cambridge would be complete which failed to mention the name of J. E. Cabot, a member of the visiting board of the University in philosophy, and widely known for the extent of his learning and the breadth of his sympathies and opinions.

President Le Conte of the University of California, most favorably known for his acute contributions to the phenomena and theory of binocular vision, has for some years instructed his classes from the text-books of Bain, Spencer, Carpenter, &c. It is also hoped that the new University of Baltimore will soon establish a chair of physiological psychology and another of the history of philosophy. A special professorship of the former department is more or less definitely contemplated by several of the larger institutions.

Outside of schools and colleges, philosophical interests have taken on the whole a wide range. Trendelenburg, Schleiermacher, Krause, Schelling, Fichte, Herbart and Lotze have all found more or less careful students and even disciples among men of partial leisure in the various professions, who have spent the last year or two of student-life in Germany. Above all these, however, stand first the influence of Hegel, which since 1867 has been represented by the quarterly *Journal of Speculative Philosophy*, edited by Wm. T. Harris of St. Louis, and secondly that of Herbert Spencer and other English evolutionists, which has been greatly extended by the *Popular Science Monthly*, edited by Dr. E. L. Youmans of New York. Mr. Harris is a pronounced Hegelian, adopting in the main the interpretation of Rosenkranz. As superintendent of the public schools of his city, he has had but little time for original contributions to his *Journal*, but all English students who wish to understand Hegel's *Logic*, particularly the third part, should not fail to read Mr. Harris's compendious articles as part of the necessary propaedeutic. He has gathered about him a circle of young men who have been led by his influence to interest themselves in German speculations, and whose contributions are found in nearly every number of the *Journal*. Unfortunately it has never quite paid its expenses, and the editor himself has year after year made up the deficit from his own purse. Yet the quality of the original articles has steadily improved, and the influence of the *Journal* seems on the whole to be increasing in the country. From the first a large portion of each number has been given to translations from Greek, French, and especially German philosophers. Important chapters of Fichte, Kant, Trendelenburg, Rosenkranz, and especially of Hegel's *Aesthetics, Phenomenology, Logic*, &c., have appeared here for the first time in English. Many convenient epitomes of more extended works by the above and other writers have also been published. The editor has from the first carefully studied the bearings of philosophical speculation upon methods of education, and the high character of the schools under his care and the wide interest felt among teachers in his annual reports, bear witness to the discretion with which abstract principles have been utilized as practical suggestions. German paedagogical methods have also been introduced to the notice of teachers in the pages of the *Journal*. Among its earlier more prominent contributors Mr. Kroeger has lately turned his attention to translating Fichte, Mr. Schneider to Shakespearian criticism, and Mr. Davidson to Aristotle, whose *Metaphysica* he is now translating with new interpretations in Athens.

The appearance of such a journal in America, and above all in a great center of western trade, supported by enthusiastic self-trained thinkers who had the hardihood to attempt to translate into Anglo-Saxon the ponderous nomenclature of the absolute idealism of the *Wissenschaftslehre* and the Hegelian *Logic*, has been often spoken of as surprising and even anomalous. The explanation, however, may not be far to seek. There is perhaps no spot in America where during the last quarter of a century illustrations of the powers of the human mind over nature have been so numerous and so impressive as in St. Louis. In a city so young and so large, the geographical and commercial center between west, east, and south, the inference that in a more than poetic sense thought is creative and man is the maker of the world, is not merely congenial, but to a certain degree spontaneous and irresistible. Again there is such a pleasing sense of liberty in the perpetual recurrence of dialectic alternatives, and yet of security, inspired by the regularity with which the beats and clicks of the triadic engine are heard, and above all there is such a largeness and scope in the formula of Hegel, as if the Universe itself might be 'done' once for all by reading a few thousand pages, that it is no wonder his sun should rise upon the new as it sets in the old world. Where every thing is an open question it is pleasing to feel that "all progress is advancement in the consciousness of freedom." But this is not all. No one can spend a week among the philosophical coteries of St. Louis without feeling—still more perhaps than by reading the *Journal*—that these causes, aided by the influences of reaction from a severely practical and business life, have awakened the faculty of philosophy to a most hopeful and inquiring receptivity. There seems scarcely a doubt that, should Mr. Harris decide to open his *Journal* to psychological as well as to metaphysical discussions, and in preference to the aesthetical selections which have been so often weary and unprofitable, it would soon become not only self-supporting but remunerative.

One of the most acute of the so-called "right wing" Hegelians is Professor Howison of the Massachusetts Technological School in Boston. His course of lectures on the history of philosophy is extended and thorough, though attended largely by ladies. He has lately delivered a course of public lectures in the Lowell Institute on the Logic of Grammar mainly in the spirit of Aristotle and Trendelenburg.

In Germany it is said that Hegelianism has been an excellent *Vorfrucht* to prepare the philosophical soil for the theories of evolution. It limbers and exercises without fevering the mind, making a safe and easy transition from the orthodox to the scientific standpoint. Even its adversaries often admit that as a mental discipline at a certain stage of philosophical culture it is unsurpassed. However this may be, it is certain that the theories of Herbert Spencer, G. H. Lewes and other English evolutionists, which have exerted such an immense influence in the United States during the last decade, are not indebted to Hegelianism, but are represented almost entirely by scientific men not especially interested in the history of speculation. If the worst side of the American college is the philosophical, its best is the scientific department. The value and thoroughness of the work done here is probably too little appreciated abroad. While in some of the smaller colleges it is poor enough, in many others the professors have had a thorough European training and lack only leisure and library and laboratory opportunities for valuable and original work. With comparatively few exceptions, all the most competent teachers of natural or physical science either tacitly accept or openly advocate the fundamental principles of evolution. Even the most orthodox institutions are often no exceptions to this rule. One of the largest of these long and vainly sought for a professor of zoology who would consent to pledge himself beforehand to say nothing in favor of Darwinism. In eight or nine out of more than thirty of those institutions which the writer has visited, instructors in this department are allowed to teach the principles of Huxley and Haeckel, if they wish, unmolested. It must be said, however, that very often the adoption of the formulae of the development-theory is so premature as seriously to interfere with the patient mastery of scientific details, or, through the students' impatience with other methods, to lower the standard of work and attainment in other departments. In a country of such remarkably rapid development as our own, where the ploughboy is never allowed to forget that he may become a millionaire or even President if he wills it earnestly enough, the catchwords of evolution often excite an enthusiasm which is inversely as the power to comprehend its scope and importance. Many of the more semi-popular aspects of Herbert Spencer's philosophy have been admirably presented by Mr. John Fiske in courses of lectures in Harvard University, in Boston, New York, and in several of the Western cities. In the periodical, especially the religious, press, criticisms almost without number have been published. Professor Bowne of the new Boston University has elaborated his strictures of Herbert Spencer into a small volume which is one of the most subtle and forcible criticisms of the *First Principles* and the *Psychology* that have ever proceeded from an essentially evangelical standpoint.

About a year ago Mr. C. S. Peirce, assistant in the United States Coast Survey, began in the *Popular Science Monthly* a series of papers entitled "Illustrations of the Logic of Science," which is still progressing. The author is a distinguished mathematician, and this discussion, in which he long ago interested himself, promises to be one of the most important of American contributions to philosophy. Thought, he premises, is excited by the irritation of doubt, and ceases when belief is attained. Feigned hesitancy, whether for amusement or otherwise, stimulates mental action. The production of belief is thus the sole function of thought. It involves moreover the establishment in our nature of a rule of action or a habit. Beliefs are distinguished by the different modes of action to which they give rise. There is no distinction of meaning so fine as to consist in anything but a possible difference of practice. Our idea of anything is our idea of its sensible effects. To attain the highest degree of clearness we must consider what effects that may have practical bearings we conceive the object of our concern to have. Our conception of these effects is then the whole of our conception of the object. In calling a thing hard, *e.g.*, we say that it will not be scratched by many substances. We may indeed say that all hard bodies remain soft till they are touched. There is no falsity in such a *mode of speech*. The question of what would occur under circumstances which do not actually arise is not a question of facts, but only of the most perspicuous arrangement of them. (*Cf.* Helmholtz, *Physiol. Optik*, ss. 431–443.) If we know the *effects* of force, we are acquainted with every fact which is implied in saying that force exists, and there is nothing more to know. All the effects of force may be correctly formulated under the rule for compounding accelerations. Processes of investigation, if pushed far enough, will give one certain solution for every question to which they can be applied. The general problem of Probabilities, which is simply the problem of Logic, is from a given state of facts to determine the universal probability of a possible fact. The probability of mode of argument is the proportion of cases in which it carries truth with it. But it springs from an inference which is repeated indefinitely. The number of probable inferences which a man draws in his whole life is a finite one, and he cannot be certain that the mean result will accord with probabilities at all. A gambler, an insurance company, a civilization, although the value of their expectations at any given moment, according to the doctrine of chance, is large, are yet sure to break down at some time. The fact of death makes the number of our risks and impressions finite, and therefore their mean result uncertain. Yet the idea of probability assumes that this number is indefinitely great. Hence Mr. Peirce infers that logicality inexorably requires that our interests should not be limited. They must not stop at our fate but must embrace the community. Logic is thus rooted in the social principle. He who would not sacrifice his own soul to save the world is illogical in all his impressions collectively. Interest in an indefinite community, recognition of the possibility of this interest being made supreme, and hope in the unlimited continuance of intellectual activity are the indispensable requirements of Logic. After laying down three fundamental rules for the calculation of chances, which are all he is willing to recognize, and deducing from his definition of the probability of a consequence rules for the addition and multiplication of probabilities, he comes to the discussion of what Mr. Venn distinguishes as the conceptualistic in opposition to the materialistic view. The former, as expounded by De Morgan, regards probability as the degree of belief which ought to attach to a proposition; while, according to the latter, it is the proportion of times in which an occurrence of one kind is *in fact* accompanied by an occurrence of another kind. He concludes that the conceptualistic view though answering well enough in some cases is quite inadequate. The problem proposed by the conceptualists he understands to be this—Given a synthetic conclusion; required to know out of all possible states of things how many will accord to any assigned extent with this conclusion. This he regards as only an absurd attempt to reduce synthetic to analytic reason, and believes that no definite solution is possible. As all knowledge comes from synthetic inference which can by no means be reduced to deduction, it is inferred that all human certainty consists merely in our knowing that the processes by which our knowledge has been derived are such as must generally lead to true conclusions. In discussing the order of nature, Mr. Peirce concludes that although this universe ought to be presumed too vast to have any character, yet the spirit of science is hostile to any religion except one like that of M. Vacherot, who worships a supreme and perfect ideal whose non-existence he finds as essential to the conception of it as Descartes found its existence to be. Any plurality of objects have some character in common which is peculiar to them and not shared by anything else. A chance-world is simply the actual world as it would look to a polyp at the vanishing point of intelligence. If we do not limit ourselves to such characters as have *for us* importance, interest or obvious-ness, then any pair of objects resemble one another in just as many particulars as any other pair. The division of synthetic inferences into induction and hypothesis, the discussion of Mill's doctrine of the uniformity of nature, and of the assumption of De Morgan's Formal Logic, are very suggestive and interesting; but we have no space for further quotations and must refer the reader to the original papers.

Perhaps the most general characteristic of American intellectual life is its hetero-geneity. Not only has each religious sect or denomination its own revered and authori-tative founders or reformers, its own newspapers and literature, and often its own set of duties and associations, beyond the limit of which the thoughts and interests of its more uneducated members rarely pass, but also many semi-philosophical sects have a more or less numerous representation. Swedenborgianism has many churches and expositors, the best of the latter being Mr. Parsons and Mr. Henry James, father of the well known novelist. The sort of life produced under the influence of this system is broadly sympa-thetic, charitable, intelligent, and in every way admirable. Its disciples in America have succeeded in making it in the best sense of the word a practical system. Again, the later speculations of Comte in the *Politique Positive* have found a number of admirers in New York and elsewhere. The voluminous works of S. P. Andrews best illustrate the incoher-ency and assumption of this rather insignificant coterie. What might be called its right wing contents itself with the discussion of revolutionary social and economic theories, particularly of the relation of labor and capital, while its left shades off by insensible gradations into all the vagaries of spiritualism. The general sect of spiritualists is very large and has produced a vast and dismal body of literature. Most physiologists and psychologists are now convinced that here is one of the most interesting fields for scien-tific observation, such as will never be made by spiritualists themselves, but no serious study of the phenomena has as yet been attempted.

On the whole, in view of the intellectual conditions of the United States, it is not to be wondered at that minds of a philosophical cast are often found to be eclectic and perhaps hypercritical. Probably in no other country is a man of high culture tempted by so many and varied considerations to criticize or instruct rather than to add to the sum of the world's intellectual possessions by doing original work.

The influence of German modes of thought in America is very great and is probably increasing: Du Bois Reymond observed in a public address some years ago that no two countries could learn so much from each other. Scores of American students may be found in nearly all the larger German universities. Most of even the smaller colleges have one or two professors who have spent from one to three or four years in study in that country, whose very language is a philosophical discipline. The market for German books in the United States is in several departments of learning larger than in Germany itself, though this is partly, of course, to be accounted for by the number of German residents. The Hegelianism of St. Louis was not only first imported but has always been to some extent supported by native Germans.

It has been urged that a nation, like ours, which inherits a ready-made language and a rich literature which it has not itself developed, is apt to be superficial in thought and shallow in sentiment. But it is surely forgotten that this is a heritage to which every generation is born. Besides, language knows no political or geographical distinction, and even the best literature is no longer national. And may we not, at least, modestly claim that enough philosophical thinking has been done to show that we are not behind in power of mental assimilation?

Protestantism in America has its well-developed grammar of dissent, and has been in the past an invaluable philosophical discipline. The American, perhaps, even more than the English, Sunday might almost be called a philosophical institution. A day of rest, of family life and introspection, it not only gives seriousness and poise to character and brings the saving fore-, after-, and over-thought into the midst of a hurrying objective and material life, to which its wider sympathies and interests and new activities are a wholesome alternative, but it teaches self-control, self-knowledge, self-respect, as the highest results of every intellectual motive and aspiration. In its most developed forms, especially among the Unitarians, Protestantism has more or less completely rationalized not only the dogmas of theology but their scriptural data, and now inculcates mainly the practical lessons of personal morality and the duty of discriminative intellectual, political and aesthetical activity.

Finally we shall venture to call patriotism a philosophical sentiment in America. It is very deeply rooted and persistent even in those who take the most gloomy view of the present aspect of our political life, who insist that the Constitution needs careful and radical revision, and who are not disposed to over-rate the magnitude of events in our national history thus far. It is philanthropic, full of faith in human nature and in the future. And if, according to a leading canon of the new psychology, the active part of our nature is the essential element in cognition and all possible truth is practical, then may we not rationally hope that even those materialisms of faith and of business which we now deplore, are yet laying the foundations for a maturity of philosophical insight deep enough at some time to intellectualize and thus harmonize all the diverse strands in our national life?

NOTES

1. Dr. Porter has also published a brief historical sketch of philosophy in the United States, with an exhaustive bibliography, in Ueberweg's *History of Philosophy* (translated by Professor G. S. Morris of Michigan University) Vol. II., pp. 422, ff.

Part Two

Law and Pragmatism

Law and Pragmatism

AN INTRODUCTION

Brian Butler

THERE IS NO DISPUTING THE CENTRAL IMPORTANCE OF THE METAPHYSICAL CLUB FOR American philosophy. Even so, the importance of the philosophers in the club was probably eclipsed for many decades by the tremendous influence of its lawyers: Joseph Bangs Warner, Nicholas St. John Green, and Oliver Wendell Homes Jr. The following words written by Oliver Wendell Holmes Jr. in the first paragraph of *The Common Law* published in 1881 may be the most famous statement in American legal history: "The life of the law has not been logic; it has been experience. The felt necessities of the time, the prevalent moral and political theories, intuitions of public policy, avowed or unconscious, even the prejudices which judges share with their fellow-men, have had a good deal more to do than the syllogism in determining the rules by which men should be governed."[1] The somewhat parallel cliché that is oft-heard about Holmes says that he was not a good legal mind but just the greatest judge, and yet most influential legal theorist in American history.

The ideals found in Holmes's writings are developed in the writings of Green and Warner as well. Indeed, if we take Peirce's word for it, Green's influential advocacy of Bain entitled Green to the status of "grandfather of pragmatism." At the very least, as Philip Wiener puts it "We owe to these lawyers—so far as the history of American social thought goes—the first major steps in the extension of scientific thinking to one of the most difficult of social disciplines, the clarification of the nature and sources of positive law."[2] Indeed, the lawyers of the Metaphysical Club have profoundly affected American jurisprudence. As opposed to the formalist ideals exemplified by Christopher Columbus Langdell, the positivist jurisprudence of John Austin, or the natural law theory of William Blackstone, the pragmatist doctrines propounded by Green, Holmes, and Warner offered a more pluralist, and functionalist view of law, a view that still challenges legal orthodoxy today.

Many of the ideas that are exemplified in the legal thought of the members of the Metaphysical Club were adopted from earlier sources. For instance, the historicizing of legal concepts in order to problematize current practice can be traced to various traditions.

Further, sociological traditions in jurisprudence are found before the members of the Metaphysical Club utilized them in a more thoroughly pragmatic conception of law. But the pragmatic conception of law offered by Green, Holmes, and Warner combines a historical and sociological approach with Bain's conception of belief as "that upon which a man is prepared to act" and evolutionary thought. Here, as among the philosophers of the Metaphysical Club, the context of action and future aims determines the use of the other strategies. For instance, a "legal realist" might use history in order to show the absolute arbitrariness of legal terminology. For the members of the Metaphysical Club, on the other hand, historical analysis of a concept will identify its progression in light of how it has been used, but for the overriding aim of finding out how to make it more predictable and useful in the future.

Of the lawyers of the Metaphysical Club, the oldest member was Nicolas St. John Green. He was born on March 30, 1830, in Dover, New Hampshire. His father was James D. Green, Harvard class of 1817, who became a Unitarian minister of the East Cambridge church, and later the mayor of Cambridge. Green received his Harvard AB in 1851. He then studied law with Harvard law professor Joseph Story and became junior partner to Boston lawyer Benjamin Franklin Butler. He earned his law degree from Harvard in 1861. With the outbreak of the Civil War, Green enlisted and served as a paymaster. After the war, Green opened his own practice and was appointed as an instructor in mental philosophy at Harvard, where he taught logic, metaphysics, psychology, and political economy. The publication of noteworthy articles in *The American Law Review* led Harvard to appoint Green as lecturer in the Law School in 1870. In 1873 Green accepted a professorship of law in Boston University's new law school, and he also served as its acting dean during 1874–76. Green died on September 8, 1876, in Cambridge, Massachusetts.

In the preface of the first volume of *Criminal Law Reports*, Green states that law must be investigated both historically and theoretically in order to truly understand it. An illustration of the fertility of historical analysis is provided in Green's "Proximate and Remote Cause." The concept of cause in law is standard philosophical grist, and Green's take on it reads as sophisticated as any current analysis. Green shows, possibly more clearly than anything in Holmes's writings, that legal cause is a term not related to any physics, philosophy, or metaphysics, but is a term of policy. His investigation aims at understanding the evolving meaning of proximate cause.

The investigation leads from Aristotle and Scholasticism through Bacon to modern ideas of proximate cause. According to Green, proximate cause originally meant necessary cause. After the theories of Bacon and Descartes and the events of the Reformation, that original meaning fell into neglect. In place of the earlier idea of proximate cause another false path was offered; this was the metaphor of the "chain of causation." This idea is a trap because it "raises in the mind an idea of one determinate cause, followed by another determinate cause, created by the first, and that followed by a third, created by the second, and so on."[3] A single linear causal line is a nice and tidy image, yet it is much too simplistic: "The true cause is the whole set of antecedents taken together."[4]

And because these antecedents are multiple, ultimately legal cause or "proximate cause" is a concept that is so pluralistic that its content depends upon the purpose we have. Green concludes that what is to be taken as a cause in law therefore cannot be answered by "philosophy" or "metaphysics," but only through a choice of public policy. What is legally described as cause depends upon the purposes we have and the policies we adopt. This principle is also illustrated in Green's "Insanity in Criminal Law," a review of I. Ray's treatise on the criminal law of insanity. After distinguishing the personal nature of psychological treatment outside of criminal law, Green points out that law is social, "made for the protection of society." So, not only is the law to treat insanity globally, but the use of insanity as a concept in law is predicated upon prevention of like actions by other members of society. In other words, in criminal law, the concept of insanity cannot be understood outside of the law's interest in influencing social behavior. Green points out the difficulty of concepts implicated by insanity such as will, intent, and mind (the latter being described as a "metaphysical abstraction"). The vagaries of such concepts proves difficult for use in law, but there is a simple way to understand criminal insanity. Green summarizes the use of the concept of insanity in criminal law as follows: "[I]n this way, and in no other, can insanity be said to be a defense to a criminal prosecution. It is an attempt to show that if an intent with the requisite knowledge might be a fair inference from a portion of the facts, still such an inference cannot be drawn from the whole body of facts admissible in evidence."[5]

If Green showed hostility toward the metaphysical abstractions inherent in the idea of insanity, his attitude toward such traditional justifications of law as natural law and religious tradition is even more dismissive. His review of J. P. Bishop's *Commentaries on the Law of Married Women*, published in the *American Law Review,* shows sarcasm and wit attached to a scathing critique of the traditional explanations for the discounted position of married women in law. Green fixes upon a justification offered by Bishop for the legal position that the wife is treated as having no will of her own within marriage and then, in various ways, puts this justification to severe test. Bishop claims that this legal law is founded on the scriptural view that husband and wife are of one flesh and it is the position of the husband to command and the wife to obey. Because of this, Bishop claims that the law of marriage therefore "shaketh hand with Divinitie." Green takes up on this idea and turn of phrase and finds evidence from the same treatise, less consciously adduced by Bishop, that the law of marriage also "shaketh hand" with "Paganism," the "Romish Church," as well as misguided ideas of "Chivalrie" when, for example, women are to be burned alive instead of being mangled publicly due to deference to issues of "decency due to the sex." Green's historical research leads him to conclude, "The whole common law of husband and wife is founded upon the institution of slavery,—of capture and purchase." In summary, "The law of the status of women is the last vestige of slavery."[6]

This analysis is quite damning, and convincing. An aside of particular note in the article is the analysis of the dysfunctional results created by domestic abuse laws. Green notes that if the wife is given the legal right to have her husband prosecuted for abuse, and the prosecution is successful, the result will be a fine or imprisonment. If the punishment is a

fine, it punishes the wife as well. If, on the other hand, the conviction results in imprisonment, this hurts the wife's financial situation during the sentence, and leaves the situation
ambiguous after her husband's release.

If historical analysis can show how various factors have colluded in a manner that
has created an unjustifiable set of marriage laws, an analysis of legal history can also show
that mistakes in historical analysis can have legal consequences. In "The Three Degrees
of Negligence," Green claims that a mistake in the historical explication of the concept
of negligence in Roman law transplanted into American law an unintelligible division of
negligence into three categories. While this mistake is not necessarily culpable because, as
he puts it, "[l]aw is always in a state of change: like the river of Heraclitus, it is not twice
the same. When nine thousand extracts, thus made from such sources, were incorporated
under different titles into one work as a system of law, no matter what care may have been
used in compilation, it might well be a matter of surprise is there should not be found
texts seemingly or really in conflict one with another."[7] This mistake has diverted attention from the real important question; which is what policies the concept of negligence
should be founded upon.

The most famous of the Metaphysical Club lawyers was Oliver Wendell Holmes Jr.
Holmes was born on March 8, 1841, in Boston, the son of Amelia Jackson and Oliver
Wendell Holmes Sr., the latter a professor of anatomy at the Harvard Medical School and
a well-known poet and writer. Holmes began his studies at Harvard College in 1857, graduated in 1861, and joined the Twentieth Massachusetts regiment. After a distinguished
military record and serious wounds, he entered Harvard Law School in 1864 and graduated in 1866. He engaged in the private practice of law in Boston from 1867 until 1882,
while editing *The American Law Review* and lecturing occasionally at Harvard Law School.
Holmes was appointed to the Massachusetts Supreme Judicial Court in 1882 and became
chief justice in 1899. He was appointed by Theodore Roosevelt as Associate Judge of the
United States Supreme Court in 1902. Holmes retired in 1932, and died on March 6,
1935, in Washington, D.C.

Holmes was a prolific writer. In addition to highly influential legal opinions and dissents,
Holmes wrote central works in American legal thought including *The Common Law* (1881) and
"The Path of the Law" (1897). His earlier writings sound many of the themes he is rightfully
famous for. In "Codes, and the Arrangement of the Law," Holmes starts with a quite memorable and representative line: "It is the merit of the common law that it decides the case first
and determines the principle afterwards."[8] Here is shown a firm commitment to experience
over principle, and common-law or case-based law over code. The experimental process of law
is emphasized. Cases are decided incrementally, and are later reconciled and modified through
necessity more than through abstraction and generalizations. Further, because each decision
is created by unique situations, decided by trained legal practitioners, and "resisted at every
step" by other legal practitioners, case law "embodies the work of many minds." Here, while
"philosophical" abstraction might have its place, because it is a practical tool, "compromises
with practical convenience are highly proper." Code, on the other hand, displays flaws that

are rarely found in applying the common law. Holmes says, "New cases will arise which will elude the most carefully constructed formula."[9] Looking only to the code, a court will either decide the case wrongly; or the court may infer a rule. But in the latter case the code does not eliminate the need for common law.

More interesting, possibly, than the discussion of the relative merits of common law and code is the attention Holmes gives to Austin's question as to what is law. Holmes critiques Austin's positivistic definition of law through the questioning of the definition's central concept: sovereignty. For Holmes, sovereignty is a question of "fact and degree" and therefore cannot supply the clarity desired by Austin. Further, Holmes claims that a source-based definition of law ignores the more important factors of "the definiteness of its expression and the certainty of its being enforced."[10] Here we see the beginning development of the famous "bad-man theory of law." The only aspect of law that is really determinate is not pedigree or natural law, but "such rules as the courts enforce."[11] And the rules are only of interest because of their worldly effects.

Holmes's conception of law is significantly elaborated in an 1872 review of a *Law Magazine and Review* article by Frederick Pollock about Austin's definition of law. Once again, from a lawyer's point of view the only question worth asking is, "How will the judges act?"[12] And to answer this question, "Any motive for their action . . . is worthy of consideration."[13] Here Holmes offers a radically decentered and pluralist notion of law in the place of Austin's sovereign-centered view. In fact, "there might be law without sovereignty,"[14] other bodies might generate law, and custom might be law regardless of a tacit consent of the court. Here the only determinate test of law, once again, is how a judge will act. This, quite obviously, is a judge-centered picture of law, a picture of law based upon its effects in the world.

The pluralism and external bias Holmes shows in the above articles are even more clearly shown in "Primitive Notions in Modern Law." Here, though, the historicist Holmes is accentuated. The basic theory underlying the article is that civil liability, the theme of the previous article, was originally attached to the object that did the damage, and acted as a form of retaliation, and only later evolved into a regime of compensation attached to the concept of negligence. This theory is combined with an illuminating claim as to the evolution of legal doctrine. Holmes claims that "it will be found that the various considerations of policy which are not infrequently supposed to have established these doctrines, have, in fact, been invented at a later period to account for what was already there."[15] There is not enough room here to outline the historical evidence offered in the article—it is sufficient to say that Holmes marshals an encyclopedic amount. But the historical data are devastating to any claim that legal history follows a straight path and utilizes an essential stock of conceptual forms. A legal realist or Critical Legal Studies scholar might find the analysis strong enough to warrant a rejection of the modern tools of tort. Holmes, on the other hand, offers a conclusion that is both more measured and more optimistic. He writes: "Practical conclusions can only be drawn with caution from the opinions advanced in this article. Taking it as true that the various rules which have been mentioned did not originate in the different principles of policy to which they have been commonly ascribed, but that the principles of policy were thought out in the effort to account for the rules, it does not follow that the principles are unsound, or that the rules do not work well in practice. If truth were not often suggested by error, or old implements could not be adjusted to new uses, human progress would be slow. But, nevertheless, enough has been said to justify scrutiny and revision."[16] Here, very explicitly, Holmes's pragmatism wins out over skepticism.

The above essays help clarify what Holmes means when he writes in Lecture 1 of *The Common Law* that "the life of law has not been logic; it has been experience." The lecture recapitulates many of the themes developed in the above lectures. Law is described as inexplicably bound to its pluralist sources, is diverse history, its institutional situations. This is why Holmes claims that to understand law we cannot just look to academic logic in the hope for an axiomatized system. Instead, "We must alternately consult history and existing theories of legislation."[17] This is significant, and Holmes emphasizes it by claiming that one can err both by considering concepts to be natural just because they feel so at the moment and by privileging the idiosyncrasies highlighted through historical scholarship.

Toward the end of Lecture I, he summarizes his findings with a memorable description of law's evolutionary development. Holmes writes that law's evolution is logical, but logical in the sense that a cat's clavicle is logical. That is, "just as the clavicle in the cat tells of the existence of some earlier creature to which the collar-bone was useful, precedents survive in the law long after the use they once served."[18] This highlights why a logical historical and evolutionary logic of development does not necessarily imply a consistent and systematic logic in current law. An example of this type of development is offered by the moral terminology in law. For Holmes, in contrast to legal positivism, there is no strict separation between law and morality. But what is the case is that moral terminology in law should not be used to infer that the terminology is used in the same way, and with the same content. The law "by the very necessity of its nature, is continually transmuting those moral standards into external and objective ones"[19] and the earlier moral terms often have a cat's clavicle–like relationship to the law's external standards.

Holmes's ultimate conclusion in the readings is that law is essentially legislative. It is best thought of as the "unconscious result of instinctive preferences and inarticulate convictions"[20] and that these are all founded upon "views of public policy." This conclusion is powerful both in its positive claim, that judges are legislators who often make their decisions based upon expediency, historical precedent, legal practice and history, etc., as well as in its negative claim, that law is not a separate dimension or governmental branch with an essentially different function than the legislative. When stated so clearly, it is easy to see that the implications of Holmes's early writings have not been digested even now. His theory is a powerful combination of historical scholarship and analytic analysis. He often works within the legal tradition, but just as often he critiques law from an outsider's stance. He may have been too centered upon the judge as the arbiter of what is or is not law, but his pluralistic and forward-looking, even experimental conception of law as legislative and policy driven has had a huge impact upon current theories of law.

The youngest attorney member was Joseph Bangs Warner. He was born on August 5, 1848, in Boston, Massachusetts. After receiving his bachelors degree from Harvard in 1869, Warner attended Peirce's lectures while earning the law degree from Harvard. Warner taught history at Harvard during 1872–73, and worked with Holmes on his version of *Kent's Commentaries on American Law*, and gave lectures for the Law School in 1886–87. Warner practiced law in Boston until 1916. His other relationship with the Metaphysical Club came in 1891, when he agreed to be Josiah Royce's lawyer during a dispute with Frank Abbot over the publication of recriminatory attacks on each other's philosophical abilities. His son, Langdon Warner (1881–1955) was a prominent historian and advocate of Asian traditions of art. Warner died on January 1, 1923, in Boston.

Warner's most significant writing is his review of Holmes's *The Common Law* in the *American Law Review*. This review reiterates many of the themes developed in the essays by Green and Holmes. Warner first remarks upon the breadth of the historical knowledge that is shown within the analysis, and highlights the quest to root out unacknowledged reasons and subconscious influences. Further, Warner notes that Holmes "has an eye for the growth of an idea which belongs to an historian of institutions."[21] But here the pragmatic sensibility comes into the review—a fear is raised that such a facile use of history may be used in such an ingenious way as to become "over-ingenious." Warner, though, finds that common sense, an awareness of the real complications of life, the acceptance of spontaneity and "the living power of man interfering to make things as he wants them,"[22] trump the possibility that Holmes's analysis would be hampered by a distorting attachment to theory and logic.

In Warner's article are also offered the familiar Holmesian claims that law is better off acknowledging its legislative aspects and evolving toward more external, "objective" standards. The ultimate conclusion is that the historical analysis of law serves an eminently practical aim; the clarification of legal terms used in the daily practice of law. As law is a practical profession based upon intellectual activity, theoretical investigation of its most central concepts through a combination of historical, evolutionary, and forward-looking tools all in reference to what should be acted upon most effectively becomes eminently pragmatic.

Many contemporary legal practitioners and theorists are self-described legal pragmatists. But the theories offered by the lawyers of the Metaphysical Club have influenced other legal theorists as well. For instance, the legal realists. Legal realists are clearly indebted to Holmes, but they use many of the tools developed above in service of a more destructive agenda. For instance, whereas Holmes might question the idea that law is a separate and unique domain, he never doubts that the common law has a useful place in society. Legal realists, and even moreso their contemporary counterparts, scholars of Critical Legal Studies, have thought that the conclusion entailed is much more severe. Another contemporary line in legal thought—often considered the most influential—the law and economics movement, puts great weight upon the idea that law is essentially legislative in nature. But the law and economics movement relies less upon history and often returns to a formalist style of reasoning relying upon analysis of given concepts rather than experimental evidence, therefore distorting the findings of the early legal pragmatists. What remains the same, however, is that it is exceedingly difficult to identify any legal scholarship today, as well as any legal practitioner, that has not been profoundly affected by the legal theorists of the Metaphysical Club.

NOTES

1. Holmes, *The Common Law* (Boston: Little, Brown, 1881), 1.

2. Philip P. Wiener, *Evolution and the Founders of Pragmatism* (Cambridge: Harvard University Press, 1949), 152.

3. Green, "Proximate and Remote Cause," *American Law Review* 4 (January 1870): 211.

4. Ibid.

5. Green, "Review of I. Ray, *A Treatise on the Medical Jurisprudence of Insanity*, 5th ed.," *American Law Review* 5 (July 1871): 709.

6. Green, "Review of J. P. Bishop, *Commentaries on the Law of Married Women under the Statutes of the Several States and at Common Law and in Equity*," *American Law Review* 6 (October 1872): 72.

7. Green, "The Three Degrees of Negligence," *American Law Review* 8 (July 1874): 663.

8. Holmes, "Codes, and the Arrangement of Law," *American Law Review* 5 (October 1870): 1.

9. Ibid., 2.

10. Ibid., 4.

11. Ibid., 5.

12. Holmes, "Notice of Pollock on Austin's Definition of Law," *American Law Review* 6 (July 1872): 724.

13. Ibid.

14. Ibid., 723.

15. Holmes, "Primitive Notions in Modern Law," *American Law Review* 10 (April 1876): 423.

16. Ibid., 437–38.

17. Holmes, *The Common Law*, 1.

18. Ibid., 35.

19. Ibid., 38.

20. Ibid., 36.

21. Warner, "Holmes's Common Law," *American Law Review* 2 (May 1881): 332.

22. Ibid., 333.

Nicholas St. John Green

PROXIMATE AND REMOTE CAUSE

American Law Review 4 (January 1870): 201, 203–204, 210–216 (selections).

In jure non remota causa, sed proxima, spectatur, is the first of Lord Bacon's "Maxims of the Law."

An unsuccessful search for this maxim has been made in the civil law. It does not appear to have been used in the English law prior to Lord Bacon's time. As he plainly intimates that some of the maxims were original with him, this was probably one of that number.

• • •

Taking that view of causes which Lord Bacon did, what is more natural than that, when framing maxims which, according to his own account, were the commencement of the application of his system of philosophy to that particular science, he should commence by asserting that doctrine which he regarded as the cornerstone of all philosophy; that in law, as in every thing else, proximate and not remote causes were the proper objects of inquiry? He expresses the groundwork of his philosophy in a single sentence. He places the maxim in its proper position as the first, the introduction to the others. There is significance in the first words, *"In jure."* He had, in other places, taught that the neglect of the remote and the search for the proximate cause was the key to all science. Now, when treating of a particular science, he re-asserts it in regard to that science.

The maxim then, as used by Bacon, is but the assertion of the general principle of philosophical inquiry. He uses the word cause in the broad signification which it has in the writings of Aristotle and his commentators the schoolmen, that is, as nearly synonymous with the word reason.

The examples cited by him, by way of illustration, prove this. They show that the law deals with definite reasons, and is not led into uncertain speculation. They are no authority for the maxim as now commonly used.

But is not the maxim capable of a more exact application? What is the precise thing which is a proximate cause to be searched out, and what is the precise thing which is a remote cause to be neglected in true philosophical reasoning?

* * *

If the schoolmen took an incomplete view of causation, so also did Bacon. If the incomplete view which they did take was, in fact, erroneous, that error was common to both. They differed not so much as to what causation is, as they did as to the manner of its investigation. The schoolmen assumed their causes. The theologians at the present day, writing upon the same subjects, do the same. Bacon searched for his causes by a system of enumeration of instances and exclusion of foreign causes. Neither method is of practical use. It is impossible to find the art of making gold by blind experiment. It is equally impossible to find it by an enumeration of instances of yellowness, of weight and of ductility. When Bacon gave it as his opinion that it was easier to make silver than to make gold, because silver was the simpler metal, he reasoned like a schoolman, but like a schoolman who had not yet attained to subtlety.

We have seen that Bacon adopts Aristotle's classification of causes, which was also the classification of the schoolmen. This is the formal, the final, the material, and the efficient. But this is a grouping together of different things because they have the same name. There is no real, and nothing but a fanciful, similarity between them. The efficient cause alone is the cause, which produces effects. Causation is the law of cause in relation to effect. Nothing more imperils the correctness of a train of reasoning than the use of metaphor. By its over free use the subject of causation has been much obscured. The phrase "chain of causation," which is a phrase in frequent use when this maxim is under discussion, embodies a dangerous metaphor. It raises in the mind an idea of one determinate cause, followed by another determinate cause, created by the first, and that followed by a third, created by the second, and so on; one succeeding another till the effect is reached. The causes are pictured as following one upon the other in time, as the links of a chain follow one upon the other in space. There is nothing in nature which corresponds to this. Such an idea is a pure fabrication of the mind.

There is but one view of causation which can be of practical service. To every event there are certain antecedents, never a single antecedent, but always a set of antecedents, which being given the effect is sure to follow, unless some new thing intervenes to frustrate such result. It is not any one of this set of antecedents taken by itself which is the cause. No one by itself would produce the effect. The true cause is the whole set of antecedents taken together. Sometimes also it becomes necessary to take into account, as a part of the set of antecedents, the fact that nothing intervened to prevent the antecedents from being followed by the effect. But when a cause is to be investigated for any practical purpose, the antecedent which is within the scope of that purpose is singled out and called the cause, to the neglect of the antecedents which are of no importance to the matter in hand. These last antecedents, if mentioned at all in the inquiry, are called conditions. Suppose a man to have been drowned. What was the cause of his death? There must have been a man, and there must have been water, and there must have been a coming together of the man and the water under certain circumstances. The fact of there being a man, and the fact of there being water, and each and every attending circumstance, without the presence of which circumstance the death would not have taken place, together with the fact that there was nothing intervening to prevent, constitute the true cause.

What one of the various circumstances necessary to the death we shall single out as the cause, to the neglect of the other circumstances, depends upon the question for what purpose we are investigating the death. For each different purpose with which we investigate we shall find a different circumstance, which we shall then intelligibly and properly call the cause. The man may have committed suicide; we say he himself was the cause of his death. He may have been pushed into the water by another: we say that the other person was the cause. The drowned man may have been blind, and have fallen in while his attendant was wrongfully absent: we say the negligence of his attendant was the cause. Suppose him to have been drowned at a ford which was unexpectedly swollen by rain: we may properly say that the height of the water was the cause of his death. A medical man may say that the cause of his death was suffocation by water entering the lungs. A comparative anatomist may say that the cause of is death was the fact that he had lungs instead of gills like a fish. The illustration might be carried to an indefinite extent. From every point of view from which we look at the facts, a new cause appears. In as many different ways as we view an effect, so many different causes, as the word is generally used, can we find for it. The true, the entire, cause is none of these separate causes taken singly, but all of them taken together. These separate causes are not causes which stand to each other in the relation of proximate and remote, in any intelligible sense in which those words can be used. There is no chain of causation consisting of determinate links ranged in order of proximity to the effect. They are rather mutually interwoven with themselves and the effect, as the meshes of a net are interwoven. As the existence of each adjoining mesh of the net is necessary for the existence of any particular mesh, so the presence of each and every surrounding circumstance, which, taken by itself, we may call a cause, is necessary for the production of the effect.

In this view of causation there is nothing mysterious. Common people conduct their affairs by it, and die without having found it beyond their comprehension. When the law has to do with abstract theological belief, it will be time to speculate as to what abstract mystery there may be in causation; but as long as its concern is confined to practical matters it is useless to inquire for mysteries which exist in no other sense than the sense in which every thing is a mystery.

In physical science there is a search for what may with some propriety, perhaps, be called the proximate cause. It is a search for the conditions immediately antecedent to and concomitant with the effect. For instance, it is observed that the limbs of the body apparently move in obedience to the will. The assumption is made that they do actually so move, and the inquiry is for the cause of the movement. The will and the movement are the limits of the investigation. The cause is to be found between those limits. When the inquirer examines the bones and the muscles, and the attachments of the muscles to the bones, he sees a mechanism obviously adapted to produce this effect by the contraction of certain of the muscles. Examining further he finds a connection with the brain and other nervous centres by nervous filaments with which all muscles are provided, which appear to be under the control of the will. From this, in connection with other considerations, he infers that the nervous filaments are the media through which a stimulus is conveyed, and that this is a part of the immediate cause of the voluntary movement. It may be called a part of the proximate cause, since it is invariably present, and the nearest to the effect of any thing which we at present know. But this only raises another question, as to how the will acts upon the nervous filaments. If this should be ascertained to be by the action of the brain, the inquiry would then be in what manner does the brain act. There would also still be the further inquiry as to how the muscles are stimulated to contraction, and the still further one as to how they in fact contract. The inquiry for the cause thus draws closer and closer to the effect without ever finding a true proximate cause. The word proximate therefore, in such an inquiry as this, is not an absolute but a relative term. It signifies the nearest known cause considered in relation to the effect, and in contrast to some more distant cause.

In the law there is no such investigation as this. The law, in the application of this maxim, is not concerned with philosophical or logical views of causation. When the maxim is applied, the whole body of facts has been ascertained by testimony. The facts are the subject of inquiry for a single purpose. That purpose is to determine the rights and liabilities of the respective parties to the proceedings. Those facts alone are viewed as causes and effects which have a direct bearing upon those rights and liabilities. The question is, sometimes, whether a cause is proximate to the effect; sometimes, the question is whether an effect shall be referred to a certain cause as its proximate result; sometimes, it is to which of several causes the effect shall be so referred. These, though different views of the same thing, are often distinct subjects of inquiry. The inquiry is often one of difficulty. The difficulty is not owing to any great ambiguity in the meaning of the word cause. That word is used in its popular signification. One difficulty is, that philosophy and metaphysics are sometimes brought into a discussion to which they do not belong. Another is, that cause and effect are often viewed as parts of a "chain of causation," and the discussion thus becomes meaningless. The chief difficulty, however, is that the term proximate and the term remote have no clear, distinct, and definable significations. Sometimes, causes are decided to be proximate which are remote in time; sometimes those are decided to be proximate which are remote in space. The division is neither scientific not logical. It is not the scholastic division, though it often has many of its characteristics. Above all, it is not a fixed and constant division. It varies in different classes of actions. The same cause and effect which would be considered proximate in one class of actions, the attendant circumstances being unchanged, would be considered remote in others. The meaning of the terms, proximate and remote, is contracted or enlarged, according to what is the subject-matter of the inquiry.

The maxim, when applied in actions of contract, is essentially a rule of construction. It is the same thing to say a thing comes within a contract as it is to say the contract embraces the thing. It is the same thing to say the loss is a proximate consequence of a peril insured against, as it is to say that the parties intended that such a loss should be covered by the policy. The different forms of expression are one in meaning.

A policy of insurance is a contract of a fixed form. By use its terms have obtained a settled meaning. Its subject-matter is extensive. It is a contract made in the interest of trade. Large amounts of property are covered by policies containing the same stipulations. The contract is one of indemnity. In determining the question, whether a peril insured against was the proximate or the remote cause of a loss; or, what is the same question, whether a loss of that general description was intended by the parties to be covered by the policy, the peculiar nature of a policy of insurance, and the class of interests it covers, are taken in to account. The particular intent of the parties is subservient to the public bearing of the question. The terms proximate and remote, in their application to questions of insurance, thus receive in some respects a more enlarged, and in some a more restricted, signification than they have when they are used in giving a construction to other contracts. But the maxim is as well applicable as a rule of construction for all contracts.

In actions for negligence, a defendant is held liable for the natural and probably consequences of his misconduct. In this class of actions his misconduct is called the proximate cause of those results which a prudent foresight might have avoided. It is called the remote cause of other results.

In determining the amount of damages in an action of contract, the breach of contact is called the proximate cause of such damages as may reasonably be supposed to have contemplated by the parties. If there are other damages, of those it is called the remote cause.

There is not settled rule for the application of the maxim in determining the damages in actions of tort. In such actions, the damages, which are called proximate, often vary in proportion to the misconduct, recklessness, or wantonness of the defendant.

Our anticipation of the future is founded upon our experience of the past. The experience of the past is the experience of the successions of causes and effects which always surround us. We can estimate, with a reasonable degree of certainty, the probabilities of the future occurrence of many of these successions. About successions of this kind men make contracts. Large classes of such successions can be grouped together, and the order and frequency of their happening can be predicted from past experience with something which approaches to mathematical precision. With events of this kind, underwriters deal. Experience also teaches us that various effects, which we can foresee with a greater or less degree of certainty, will or may follow from our own acts. The law makes us responsible for those effects of our voluntary acts which might reasonably have been foreseen, or which are of a kind analogous to effects which might thus have been foreseen. There is generally no other way of determining whether certain events, or whether events analogous to them in kind, were or might haven been anticipated or foreseen, than by an appeal to experience. By applying this maxim, we make that appeal. We determine whether given causes and effects are proximate or remote, in the legal sense of those words, from our own experience of the succession of cause and effect.

The use of the maxim is liable to lead to error by withdrawing the attention from the true subject of inquiry. We cannot add clearness to our reasoning by talking about proximate and remote causes and effects, when we mean only the degree of certainty or uncertainty with which the connection between cause and effect might have been anticipated. But this is an inconvenience which must be submitted to by those who attempt to make a practical application of the maxim.

Insanity in Criminal Law

American Law Review 5 (July 1871): 704–709.

A Medico-Legal Treatise on Malpractice and Medical Evidence, comprising the Elements of Medical Jurisprudence. By John J. Elwell, M.D., member of the Cleveland bar; one of the editors of new edition of Bouvier's Law Dictionary: Professor in Ohio State and Union Law College, and Western Reserve Medical College, &e., &c. Third Edition, revised and enlarged. New York: Baker, Voorhis, & Company. 1871.

A Treatise on Medical Jurisprudence of Insanity. By I. Ray, M.D. Fifth Edition, with additions. Boston: Little, Brown, & Company. 1871.

Mr. Elwell, in the introduction to his work, says: "Frequent, important, and troublesome as are the cases of alleged malpractice by medical men, there is yet no work treating upon the subject; and medical and legal inquiries after information upon the question are obliged to seek it in the vast range of elementary works upon medicine and law, and in the unlimited field of reports, constituting the larger part of every lawyer's library. The author trusts that in the first part of this work he has supplied this *desideratum*—at least, to a considerable extent."

The first two hundred and sixty pages of the book are accordingly devoted to the subject of malpractice. Chapter I. treats of the "General principles of law applicable to medical men." It is probably intended particularly for the instruction of medical men and not of lawyers, as the principles of law are not clearly stated, and as the cases cited are cited without method or selection. A lawyer in need of such information can get more and better from a section of "Story on Bailments," than he can from this entire chapter. Chapters II. and III. "are designed more particularly for the legal profession. Their truth is well understood by all intelligent medical men." The second is upon "The inherent elementary difficulties connected with the practice of medicine and surgery"; and the third is upon "What definite knowledge is possible and essential for the physician and surgeon." They point out to the attorney that by bringing unfounded actions for malpractice he renders the profession of surgery a dangerous one, and hinders competent physicians from undertaking surgical operations in time of need, through fear that if the result of such an operation be unsatisfactory to the patient, the physician will be subjected to a groundless action. There is truth in this. We have known a couple of pettifogging actions for alleged malpractice to have the effect of rendering every respectable physician in the county rightfully averse to undertake any surgical operation outside the families he regularly attended.

Our author then treats of "malpractice from amputation," and of "malpractice in fractures and dislocations." He gives "A digest of Professor F. II. Hamilton's reports of cases of deformities after fractures," which we advise every attorney to read before commencing an action against a surgeon for malpractice. He gives throughout the book many English and American adjudged cases, quoted, perhaps, with unnecessary fullness, but as nothing appears to have been inserted for the mere purpose of increasing the bulk of the book, we are not disposed to find faith; on the contrary, with this exception, them appear so many traces of a successful endeavor to avoid prolixity that we are disposed to give him thanks. He has labored to give the purchaser a book worth its price; a thing the legal profession are latterly unused to. The twelfth chapter is upon the responsibility of druggists. Then follow four chapters upon "Criminal Malpractice," including abortion. There are eight chapters upon insanity. This subject is treated with some fulness, and in a very sensible manner. "Poisoning," "Infanticide," "Wounds," and "Rape," are also treated of; and the book closes with a chapter upon "Coroner's Office and Inquests."

In this last chapter the author lays down a doctrine which we cannot let pass without protest. It is this: "the guilty or suspected person may himself be put upon the stand, if he does not object, when he may be subjected to the severest cross-examination possible." Is it not the duty of the coroner to inform him of his right to object? "No technicalities trammel the coroner, and if he understands his business and his powers, and is ingenious enough, he may extort from a witness a confession of his guilt or complicity." This is "Crowner's 'quest law.' " Is the coroner's inquest as well as parliament superior to every thing? To a lawyer the author appears to have a large knowledge of medicine and surgery; to the physician and surgeon he may appear to have a large knowledge of law.

Notwithstanding the faults of the book it is as good as, and in some respects batter than, could be expected. A really first-rate book upon the subject it would be hard to write. The person qualified to do it must be a thorough lawyer, surgeon, physician, chemist, and must have given special attention to the subject of insanity. The proverb tells the fate of him who rides two horses; what must become of him who attempts to ride five?

It is difficult to see how "medical jurisprudence," so called, ever came to be considered a branch of the law. There are times, it is true, when some knowledge of medicine is useful to a lawyer. So there are times when a knowledge of mechanics and of the anatomy and diseases of the horse would be useful; but we have never had a mechanical or a veterinary jurisprudence. We do not mean to say that books upon medical jurisprudence may not be useful; but we do mean to protest against the rank which that misleading title asserts for them as books of science, and to caution the reader against placing reliance either upon their law, medicine, or surgery. The only way to obtain thorough knowledge upon any point, either of science or of art, is to seek it from original sources. Any lawyer who rests content with the smattering of knowledge to be got from any medical jurisprudence may have the pleasant feeling that he is astonishing the bystanders by his show of learning; but must also have at heart the unpleasant feeling that he is a humbug.

As to Dr. Ray's book on Insanity, it has been before the public for thirty-three years, and has passed through five editions. It has as many merits and as few defects as such a book can have, and is invaluable to a lawyer who wishes to establish the insanity of his client. It is an arsenal and magazine full to the covers of arms and of ammunition.

An objection to Dr. Ray's book is, that the author looks at all questions of insanity from a medical and not from a legal point of view. It is perhaps creditable to his humanity that he does. Insanity may be the same thing from which ever point it is viewed; but the question of its treatment is different. The physician deal with a single individual considered as his patient, and has nothing to do with the community or the interests of the community. If he has an insane patient, his whole attention is given to this particular cure without looking beyond. He can promise reward as well as threaten punishment. If in his opinion the expectation of reward for future good conduct will have a more beneficial effect upon the character of his patient than the threat of punishment, he is right in refraining from punishment.

But law is made for the protection of society. It is for the community, and not for the individual; except as through the individual it may affect the community, and promote the safety of society at large. The defendant in a criminal case is not a patient whose moral and physical health is the sole object of solicitude. The object of legal punishment is to prevent not only the defendant, but all other persons, from violating the law.

Again, there are distinctions in the law which is unknown in medicine. In medicine there may be effective and ideational, impulsive and moral, partial and general insanity, &c. But in law the insanity which will acquit a prisoner is one thing; that which will set aside a testamentary disposition of property is another; that which will justify the placing a person under guardianship another; and that which authorizes the confinement of his person still another. But this is unsatisfactory to Dr. Ray, who says: "That a person, whom the law prevents from managing his own property, by reason of his mental impairment, should, in respect to criminal acts, be considered as possessing all the elements of responsibility, and placed on the same footing with men of the soundest and strongest minds, is a proposition so strange and startling, that few, uninfluenced by professional biases, can yield to it unhesitating assent, or look upon it in any other light than as belonging to that class of doctrines which, while they may be the perfection of reason to the initiated, appear to be the height of absurdity to every one else." p. 16. It certainly is the "height of absurdity" to maintain that spend-thrifts may murder at discretion.

Insanity in its relation to the law is a subject very difficult to discuss. The principal words used convey to no two persons the same, or to any person more than a vague, meaning.

What is insanity? There is no rule by which it can be measured, so that one can say this is, and this is not, insanity. Definitions of it are but restatements of the same thing in different words. Generally, too, in speaking of insanity one speaks of the "will"; but the word *will* is perhaps the vaguest and most complex of any in the language, and is peculiarly inapt as here used. It is said that the action of an insane man are not controlled by his will; but a man's actions are always controlled by his will, unless he is constrained by outward force, or is in convulsions. The opinions, moreover, which persons have upon the amenability of an insane person to punishment, if the case in question is one of the debatable ones, will differ according to their views of the object of punishment, and of the grounds upon which it is justifiable. Between Owen, who thought no man should be punished, and the advocate of unsparing punishment, there are infinite shades of difference.

Insanity cannot be known till we know what sanity is; nor can the laws which govern the modes of mind called insanity be known till we have a well-established psychology. The mind itself is a metaphysical abstraction; it does not exist as an entity. No man knows the nature of it. Mental action, as far as at present known, is dependent upon nervous structure. By Henry Maudsley, who is at present the highest authority upon the subject we are discussing, sanity is considered to be a stability, and insanity an instability, or rather, a deterioration, of nervous structure—instability of nervous structure constituting an insane temperament. In this view of the matter, sanity and insanity are but matters of degree. Between the highest and finest intellect and the lowest maniac there are many gradations of infinitely complex modes of mental action. It must be impossible to draw any line upon one side of which shall lie the sane, and upon the other the insane.

It is a meaningless phrase to say that the acts of an insane person are not under the control of his will. If he did not will he could not act. He wills to do the thing he does do. His motives for doing the act remaining the same, he could not will otherwise. A boy has a fit of passion. He objects to punishment upon the ground that he could not help it. True, he could not; but, nevertheless, he is punished in order that the fear of punishment may in the future be an additional motive of restraint, and that by the help of this additional motive he may be enabled to help it in the future. This is the end of all human punishment—not to revenge past, but to prevent future wrong. Now many who are insane can be restrained by fear of punishment. Punishment of some kind, not corporal punishment, but restraint, or "the deprivation of some customary indulgence or privilege," is a recognized made of treating the insane in hospitals. When the inmates who are not in close confinement see one of their number sent to his room because he has done some act of violence, it is a check of some permanence upon the passions of all of them. They are all furnished with an additional motive for good behavior. There are many insane persons who are in no confinement at all. If these know that an insane person has been punished for a deed of violence, may not that knowledge prove a check upon at least some of them? May it not furnish some of them with an additional motive for refraining from similar deeds of violence? But it can well be urged that humanity would be shocked by the punishment of the insane, and that the community would be more harmed by thus blunting the kindly feelings of men than it would be by allowing all the insane to go free. Such questions as these are questions rather for the legislator than the judge. The judge should administer the law as he finds it. The law does not punish all the insane, neither does it permit every one whom a physician may call insane to escape. It is governed by general principles which, if properly administered, give protection to all. What errors there are, are perhaps in the administration of the law rather than in the law itself.

It may be laid down as a general, and might be laid down as a universal rule, had not the Supreme Court of Massachusetts endeavored to make an unfounded distinction in regard to statute offences—that an intent, or, to state it with greater accuracy, either an intent or negligence, is a necessary ingredient of every crime. This intent or negligence appears to be what Blackstone and other writers on criminal law mean when they use the very indefinite and inappropriate term, "will." Blackstone says (Book IV. p. 20 et seq.: "All the several pleas and excuses which protect the committer of a forbidden act from the punishment which is otherwise annexed thereto may be reduced to this single consideration, the want or defect of *will*. An involuntary act, as it has no claim to merit, so neither can it induce any guilt; the concurrence of the will, when it has its choice either to do or to avoid the fact in question, being the only thing that renders human actions either praiseworthy or culpable. Indeed, to make a complete crime cognizable by human laws, there must be both a will and an act.... And as a vicious will without a vicious act is no civil crime, so, on the other hand, an unwarrantable act without a vicious will is no crime at all.... Now there are three cases in which the will does not join with the act: 1. Where there is a defect of the understanding.... 2. Where there is understanding and will sufficient residing in the party but not called forth and exerted at the time of the action done; which is the case of offences committed by chance or ignorance.... 3. Where the action is constrained by some outward force and violence." Under the first division he brings the cases of infants, of idiots, and of lunatics.

But it is not true to state as Blackstone states, and as other writers have often carelessly expressed it, that infancy, idiocy, or lunacy "are *pleas* and *excuses* which protect the committer of a forbidden act from the punishment which is otherwise annexed thereto." Neither of these things is a substantive defense. The evidence is admitted under the general issue. It is evidence to contradict the inference which the jury might otherwise draw from the evidence of the prosecution. It is incumbent upon the prosecution to prove every ingredient of the alleged crime. For the sake of illustration take a case where an intent is necessary to constitute the crime, omitting cases like those of manslaughter, in which a reckless negligence may supply the place of an intent; for it is immaterial which class of cases we consider, because, if an intent is a necessary ingredient of the offence, the prosecutor must prove the intent; and if negligence is a necessary ingredient, it is incumbent upon him to prove the negligence. Where an intent is necessary to constitute the crime, the prosecutor must prove not only the defendant's acts and their consequence, that is, the result following from those acts—in other words, *corpus delicti*—but he must also prove that those acts were done with the intent that that consequence should follow. But no direct evidence of intent is possible. An intention of the mind is an idea; it cannot be perceived by the senses; it can only be inferred from acts. If it is proved that the defendant said he intended to commit the crime, still his speech is but an act, and the intent is matter of inference depending upon the truth of his admission. All the proof then that the prosecutor can give is proof of the defendant's acts, and from those acts the jury are generally justified in inferring an intent of the defendant that the consequence of those acts, that the *corpus delicti*, should follow. Because experience shows that men act for the purpose of producing that effect which naturally follows their acts, the jury infers that the acts were done in order that the consequence might follow. If the defendant's manner of associating his ideas is so deranged that for that reason he does not foresee the usual and probable consequences of his acts there has never been a question, even at law, as to his insanity.

But it is not enough that the simple consequence, or *corpus delicti*, should have been intended or foreseen (which is an equivalent expression), it must have been foreseen with a certain amount of knowledge of the defendant's duty and of the relation of the *corpus delicti* to that duty. This appears to be what is meant by those who have made the possession of "a mind capable of distinguishing between right and wrong" the test of accountability. The foreseeing the consequence, and the knowledge of the duty, and the relation which that consequence bears to the duty, are distinct things. But, as it is rarely, if ever—except in questions of insanity, idiocy, or infancy—that any question arises as to the defendant's knowledge of his duty and of the relation of the *corpus delicti* to that duty, in discussing the general question of responsibility the latter are either entirely ignored and the intent only dwelt upon, or if recognized at all, are recognized but obscurely, as in the phrase "criminal intent," or in the phrase "guilty knowledge." This knowledge of duty, &c., as well as the intent (both together making the criminal intent), is, nothing to the contrary appearing, found by the jury as a necessary inference. If there are any facts not put in evidence by the prosecutor which show that either the defendant had not this intent or this knowledge, it becomes necessary that he should introduce them as his own evidence. Such is the defense of insanity; and in this way, and in no other, can insanity be said to be a defense to a criminal prosecution. It is an attempt to show that if an intent with the requisite knowledge might be a fair inference from a portion of the facts, still such an inference cannot be drawn from the whole body of facts admissible in evidence.

We have said the defendant must have a certain amount of knowledge; but when the question is asked, "How much knowledge must he have?" it cannot be definitely answered. Perhaps it might be said he must have at least as much knowledge as a child seven years old. But if this is so, the difficulty is but narrowed; it is not removed. It is the same difficulty as that of drawing a line between the sane and the insane. It is the difficulty which is continually recurring in law, and which pervades all matters of human investigation. All things in nature, all things external, all ideas, all sensations, all emotions, shade into each other by imperceptible degrees. No absolute lines calm be drawn. Things are separated from one another by a debatable ground. The difficulty is inherent in the nature of man. Human power can make but an approach to precision. It is the ancient puzzle of the

Sophists concerning the heap of sand. One throws down a little sand. It is not a heap. He adds sand grain by grain till at length it becomes one. When did it become a heap? Was it by the addition of the fiftieth or of the one hundred and fiftieth grain? The question cannot be answered satisfactorily; there must be a margin of doubt. But certainly as far as human wisdom can provide, the question is answered; and that too in favor of humanity, by giving the defendant the benefit of that doubt.

If the defendant committed the acts with a criminal intent, as that intent has been above explained, than he is guilty. If the law as thus interpreted does not sufficiently protect persons of weak or of unsound intellect, then writers upon medical jurisprudence must seek the remedy from the legislator, for it is useless to rail at the judge. The judge is in duty bound to go to this extent; and without a violation of his duty he can go no further.

The Power of the Will over Conduct

Criminal Law Reports, Volume 1 (New York: Hurd and Houghton, 1874), p. 390.

There is always a tendency to act out an idea. This fact is very observable in young children, who endeavor to give an account of anything they have seen or done. Some persons cannot think over what they have said or what they intend to say upon a future occasion without muttering and talking to themselves. Any one who thinks a verse of poetry or a sentence of prose can feel a tendency in his tongue and lips to pronounce the words. In the waking state this tendency to act out an idea is restrained by the will and by a power of control acquired by habit, but in dreams it is much more manifest; then a train of ideas sometimes result in somnambulism. This tendency is something distinct from, and something often acting in opposition to the will. It acts with a strength proportioned to the vividness of the idea. When one mentally reviews a scene which at the time excited his indignation, he again becomes angry. He is in the presence of no one with whom he should be angry, but, he truly says, he is "indignant at the idea."

We have no direct power of banishing a painful idea from the mind. The more painful it is and the more we wish it away, the more persistent it becomes. Our will in freeing us from a painful idea can act but imperfectly and indirectly. What power it has in this respect, is in enabling us to endeavor to direct our thoughts into another channel.

An idea may be so vivid and persistent that the will is powerless. The most common case of this is the case of fear. Any one who has observed animals and children must have remarked instances of it. Men and animals are rendered frantic by fear. The manner in which a panic spreads through a multitude is enough to show that the tendency, in spite of reason or the will, to act out an idea, is not an exception but a universal rule

A person standing upon a precipice, when the idea of falling occurs to him, feels a tendency to act out the idea and throw himself down, which it requires a struggle to resist. From this tendency such a position is perilous to one unaccustomed to it, and suffering from feebleness of body or from disordered nerves. A woman while being delivered of a bastard child, alone by herself, with nothing to distract her thought, if the idea of killing it enters her mind, may be impelled from very horror to act out the idea, as a bird is fascinated by a snake.

The infection of certain ways of committing crime and suicide is a matter of common remark. In this way, no doubt, harm is done by the general publication of the detail of crime. A minute detail excites an undue interest in morbid and susceptible minds, and a series of crimes of a like kind, or of suicides committed in the same manner, is the result. The New England clergyman who felt called upon to preach against suicide, and to dwell upon the awful situation of the hanging sinner, was rewarded by the sight of his sexton's body suspended in the bell rope.

The Maxim that a Man is Presumed to Intend the Natural Consequences of His Acts

Criminal Law Reports, Volume 2 (New York: Hurd and Houghton, 1875), pp. 244–246.

That "a man must be held to intend the natural consequences of his acts," is at the present day regarded as a presumption of fact; a presumption which a jury can or should draw, instead of an irrefutable conclusion of law. Formerly regarded as a presumption of law, it has been the fruitful source of all constructive crimes. By this supposed rule of law, the Duke of Norfolk was convicted and attainted. "The duke's purpose to marry the Queen of Scotland, who had formerly laid claim to the crown of England, and signifying it by letters, and all this done without the consent of the Queen of England, was held an overt act to depose the Queen of England, and to compass her death; for if the Queen of Scots claimed the crown of England, he that married her must be presumed to claim it also in her right, which was not consistent with the safety of the Queen of England, and her title to the crown; and although this extending of treason (as to this point of marriage) by illation and consequence was hard, yet the duke was convict and attaint of treason generally upon this indictment." 1 Hale's P. C. 120. Or, as it is stated by Mr. Amos, "It was adjudged that, as he sought to marry the Queen of Scots (which appeared by the *overt act* of *love-letters*), and as she claimed the crown of England, and as upon marrying her he would naturally assert her right, and as, therefore, he must seek to depose Queen Elizabeth, and as it must be presumed that on deposing her he would kill her; *argal,* the duke compassed and imagined the death of the queen." Amos, Ruins of Time exemplified in Sir Matthew Hale's Pleas of the Crown, p. 79.

King Edward 4, hunting one day in the park of Thomas Burdet, killed a white buck which was a great favorite, and Burdet, much vexed, wished the buck, horns and all, in the belly of the man that counseled the king to kill it. But it appeared no man had counseled the king to kill it. He had counseled himself to kill it; therefore Burdet had wished the buck, horns and all, in the king's belly; but if the deer, horns, bones and all, were in the king's belly, it would kill him, therefore Thomas Burdet had wished the king's death; but the natural consequence of a wish is an act, therefore Burdet compassed the death of the king, and was guilty of treason. And upon such reasoning he was tried, condemned, and executed.

Mr. James Fitzjames Stephen, one of the latest and ablest writers upon criminal law, treats the maxim that "The law presumes that a man intends the natural consequences of his actions," not as a presumption of law against which no evidence can be received, but as in all cases a presumption of fact for the jury. He says, "Though it is impossible to lay down any rule as to the point at which the burden of proof shifts to the prisoner, in terms sufficiently general to cover every case, a certain number of partial rules have been laid down as to particular cases of common occurrence, which in practice are very useful. The commonest of all is the rule that the fact of the possession of stolen goods shortly after the theft throws on the possessor the burden of accounting for it. A broader rule of the same sort is often expressed by the phrase, 'the law presumes that a man intends the natural consequences of his actions.' This might, perhaps, be more accurately, though less graphically, expressed thus: Proof that a man's body has gone through a set of motions usually caused by a certain state of mind raises a presumption that they were so caused in the particular case at issue. This is more accurate than the commoner and easier phrase, because it recognizes the fact that every action consists as such of inward feelings and outward motions, the motions forming the evidence of the feelings. If a man's body goes through the motions which make up the process of loading a pistol and firing it at another person's heart, it lies on him, if he is indicted for shooting with intent to murder, to show that he did not mean to commit murder; or, if he actually did kill, that he was actuated by some state of mind not described by the law as malice..."

"This rule is sometimes insisted on as if it were a mere parry to a quibble. 'I did not mean any harm,' says the prisoner. 'In my own mind,' says the judge, 'I do not care whether you did or not, but as against you I have a right to say you must have meant to do what you really did.' Legal fictions are always matter of regret. Even if they are practically convenient, they have a strong tendency to make men indifferent to truth; and if the intention of prisoners really were irrelevant, it would be better to throw the law into a different shape, and to enact specifically that persons who do acts, of which the natural consequence is to kill, &c., shall be punished, instead of introducing the question of intent at all. I think, however, that in the present case the common argument is sounder than it is supposed to be by those who use it. For what is the meaning of intent?

It means the end contemplated at the moment of action, and by reference to which the visible parts of the action are combined. This intent is seldom permanent for any very considerable time, and often varies from moment to moment, especially in people who are either weak or wicked. A man meditating a crime may be, and probably often is, in twenty minds (to use the common and most expressive phrase) about it up to the very moment of execution. How, then, can it be known which particular intent was present at that moment? Perhaps he himself was not then distinctly conscious of it, and probably his subsequent recollection would be treacherous. The way in which, in fact, he did move is the only trustworthy evidence on the subject, and consequently is the evidence to which alone (in all common cases), the jury ought to direct their attention." General View of the Criminal Law of England, p. 304.

But whatever may be the case with respect to common-law offences (a subject which it is not necessary now to consider), the settled rule of law is that wherever an intent is made an ingredient of a statute crime, the intent is a fact to be proved to and found by the jury, and not an inference of law.

* * *

In considering cases on this subject, it is necessary to bear in mind that before the common law rule was changed by statute, in cases where an intent to injure or to defraud was an ingredient of an offence, it was necessary to allege an intent to injure or to defraud *a particular person.* Under indictments in this form, it was held that after a general intent to injure or to defraud had been found, then on the principle that every one intends the consequences of his acts, the intent to defraud should be found to be an intent to defraud *the person named in the indictment,* if such person could have been defrauded by the act of the prisoner. *But the question of the general intent to defraud always was a question of fact for the jury on all the evidence.*

Reasonable Doubt

Criminal Law Reports, Volume 2 (New York: Hurd and Houghton, 1875), p. 437.

Belief considered by itself without reference to the thing believed in and as a feeling, is a feeling of satisfaction—it is an easy and pleasant feeling.

Doubt is a feeling of dissatisfaction, an uneasy and unpleasant feeling. When one believes, then he is satisfied and wishes for no further proof; when he doubts, he is dissatisfied and wants more information. As every one knows for himself better than he can be told by another whether a pin pricks him or not, so he knows whether he doubts or not.

Any attempt at explanation which may be made may confuse but cannot enlighten him. A reasonable doubt is a doubt which is felt by a reasonable man.

Jurors are selected because they are reasonable men. The whole machinery of selection has this end in view—to select reasonable men.

A reasonable doubt is the doubt which a juryman feels when he is not satisfied as to the truth of the fact to be established by evidence on the part of the prosecution. If he feels uneasy as to the truth of the fact in saying guilty, he has a reasonable doubt.

Oliver Wendell Holmes, Jr.

CODES, AND THE ARRANGEMENT OF LAW

American Law Review 5 (October 1870): 1–13.

It is the merit of the common law that it decides the case first and determines the principle afterwards. Looking at the forms of logic it might be inferred that when you have a minor premise and a conclusion, there must be a major, which you are also prepared then and there to assert. But in fact lawyers, like other men, frequently see well enough how they ought to decide on a given state of facts without being very clear as to the *ratio decidendi*. In cases of first impression Lord Mansfield's often-quoted advice to the business man who was suddenly appointed judge, that he should state his conclusions and not give his reasons, as his judgment would probably be right and the reasons certainly wrong, is not without its application to more educated courts. It is only after a series of determinations on the same subject-matter, that it becomes necessary to "reconcile the cases," as it is called, that is, by a true induction to state the principle which has until then been obscurely felt. And this statement is often modified more than once by new decisions before the abstracted general rule takes its final shape. A well settled legal doctrine embodies the work of many minds, and has been tested in form as well as substance by trained critics whose practical interest it is to resist it at every step. These are advantages the want of which cannot be supplied by any faculty of generalization, however brilliant, and it is noticeable that those books on which an ideal code might best be modeled avowedly when possible lay down the law in the very words of the court. When, then, it is said to be one of the advantages of a code that principles are clearly enunciated and not left to be extricated from cases, either the definiteness of well settled law is underrated, or it is intended to anticipate the growing process we have described, and to develop by legislation doctrines of which the germs may be found in isolated decisions. We need not dwell on the latter alternative, as its possible importance is obviously small.

Suppose that a code were made and expressed in language sanctioned by the assent of courts, or tested by the scrutiny of a committee of lawyers. New cases will arise which will elude the most carefully constructed formula. The common law, proceeding, as we have pointed out, by a series of successive approximations—by a continual reconciliation of cases—is prepared for this, and simply modifies the form of its rule. But what will the court do with a code? If the code is truly law, the court is confined to a verbal construction of the rule as expressed, and must decide the case wrong.[1] If the court, on the other hand, is at liberty to decide *ex ratione legis*—that is, if it may take into account that the code is only intended to declare the judicial rule, and has done so defectively, and may then go on and supply the defect—the code is not law, but a mere text-book recommended by the government as containing all at present known on the subject.

Another mistake, as we cannot but think, is that a code is to be short. This probably springs from the thoroughly exploded notion that it is to make every man his own lawyer, and would hardly be worth mentioning did not the makers of both the New York and Canada Civil Codes seem to entertain it. A code will not get rid of lawyers, and should be written for them much more than for the laity. It should therefore contain the whole body of the law in an authentic form. When the ablest text writers in the competition of the open market exhaust volumes on subdivisions, what inspiration is there in government patronage to produce a different result?

We are inclined to believe that the most considerable advantage which might be reaped from a code is this: that being executed at the expense of government and not at the risk of the writer, and the whole work being under the control of one head, it will make a philosophically arranged *corpus juris* possible. If such a code were achieved, its component treatises would not have to be loaded with matter belonging elsewhere, as is necessarily the case with text-books written to sell. Take up a book on sales, or one on bills and notes, or a more general treatise on contracts, or one on the domestic relations, or one on real property, and in each you find chapters devoted to the discussion of the incapacities of infants and married women. A code would treat the subject once and in the right place. Even this argument does not go much further than to show the advantage of a connected publication of the whole body of the law. But the task, if executed *in extensor*, is perhaps beyond the powers of one man, and if more than one were employed upon it, the proper subordination would be more likely to be secured in a government work. We are speaking now of more serious labors than the little rudimentary text-books in short sentences, which their authors by a happy artifice have called codes instead of manuals. Indeed we are not aware that any of the existing attempts are remarkable for arrangement. The importance of it, if it could be obtained, cannot be overrated. In the first place it points out at once the leading analogy between groups. Of course cross-divisions will be possible on other principles than the one adopted, and text-books arranged by these subordinate analogies, like Mr. Joshua Williams's two volumes, are instructive and valuable. The perfect lawyer is he who commands all the ties between a given case and all others. But few lawyers are perfect, and all have to learn their business. A well-arranged body of the law would not only train the mind of the student to a sound legal habit of thought, but would remove obstacles from his path which he now only overcomes after years of experience and reflection.

As to what the method of arrangement should be, of course there is room for infinite argument. Our own impression is pretty strong that it should be based on *duties* and not on *rights*, and we suspect the fact that the custom has been the other way to be at the bottom of some difficulties which have been felt. Duties precede rights logically and chronologically. Even those laws which in form create a right directly, in fact either tacitly impose a duty on the rest of the world, as, in the case of patents, to abstain from selling the patented article, or confer an immunity from a duty previously or generally imposed, like taxation. The logical priority of the duty in such instances is clear when we consider that in its absence any man might make and sell what he pleased and abstain from paying for ever, without assistance from law. Another illustration is, that, while there are in some cases legal duties without corresponding rights, we never see a legal right without either a corresponding duty or a compulsion stronger than duty. It is to be understood that these are the principles of the general scheme only. From what point of view the several topics should be treated in detail is a mere question of convenience. And this suggests a further remark. Law is not a science, but is essentially empirical. Hence, although the general arrangement should be philosophical, even at the expense of disturbing prejudices, compromises with practical convenience are highly proper. There are certain legal units which must be preserved although they lie on both sides of a great natural dividing line; *e.g.*, contract. Some subjects have acquired a unity in practice that it might be unprofitable to analyze, *e.g.*, *dominium* or ownership. Other conceptions again, although complex, if we break them up into the ideas out of which modern law is built, lie, historically speaking, at its foundation, and have acquired cohesion from their very antiquity; *e.g.*, parts of the *jus personarum*. We shall refer to some of these examples again.

We proceed to illustrate our views of arrangement a little more in detail, although, of course, only in a fragmentary way.

A word in the first place as to the subject-matter. What is law? We doubt whether Austin did not exaggerate the importance of the distinctions he drew. A law, we understand him to say, is a command (of a definite political superior, enforced by a sanction), which obliges (intelligent human beings) to acts or forbearances of a class. This as a definition of what lawyers call law is doubtless accurate enough. But it seems to be of practical rather than philosophical value. If names are to mark substantial distinctions, one hesitates to admit that only a definite body of political superiors can make what is properly called a law. In the first place, who has the sovereign power, and whether such a power exists at all, are questions of fact and of degree. But waiving this, by whom a duty is imposed must be of less importance than the definiteness of its expression and the certainty of its being enforced. In the nature of things, which is most truly a law, the rule that if I am invited to a dinner party in London I must appear in evening dress under the penalty of not being asked to similar entertainments if I disobey; or the statute against usury in New York, which juries do not decline to carry out simply because they are never asked to do so? If it be said that an indefinite body cannot directly signify a command, it is to be remembered that the rules of judge-made law are never authentically promulgated as rules, but are left to be inferred from cases. Certainly some social requirements are to be inferred as easily from social penalties explained by common discourse. The difference which might be insisted on with most effect is in the definiteness of the sanction, and the sanction of some laws improperly so called according to Austin is quite as definite as the uncertain chance of a jury's inflicting an uncertain amount of damages. A sovereign or political superior secures obedience to his commands by his courts. But how is this material, except as enhancing the likelihood that they will be obeyed? Courts, however, give rise to lawyers, whose only concern is with such rules as the courts enforce. Rules not enforced by them, although equally imperative, are the study of no profession. It is on this account that the province of jurisprudence has to be so carefully determined. The further difficulty which might be suggested, of fixing the line when the desires of indefinite bodies become so certain in form and sanction as to come within the category of laws (philosophically speaking), is no greater than that which a court encounters in deciding whether a custom has been established.

The importance of these considerations, in spite of the fact that lawyers have little to do professionally with results falling outside of Austin's division, lies in their application to international law. This is a subject which lawyers do practically study, while according to Austin it is not law at all, but a branch of positive morality. But if, as we have tried to show, his definition can only be supported on grounds of practical convenience, and if they fail in this case, the ancient name may properly be retained. Is not that law which is certain in form and in sanction? Here are rules of conduct so definite as to be written in text-books; and sanctioned in many cases by the certainty that a breach will be followed by war; why does it so much matter that they are not prescribed by a sovereign to a political inferior? If on these grounds it is admitted not to be an anomaly to include international law in the law-student's curriculum, we are content to stand by the lines as now drawn, and to omit ethics until the coming of a second Grotius.

Our first division then contains duties of sovereign powers to each other. For although the doctrines of this branch are copied in great measure from municipal law, convenience requires that they receive a separate treatment.

The second division would probably be duties without corresponding rights, or duties to the sovereign. Here belongs, for instance, the duty to pay taxes, often mentioned as an implied contract, a phrase to which we shall refer again. Another example is the law of treason. Perhaps under this head, also, should come the great body of criminal law, as administered in this country. For, not only is the sovereign the formal plaintiff, and for an offence against the sovereign well-being, but the private person injured has not any voice, in theory, as to whether the public prosecuting officer shall or shall not push a case to trail. How can a man be said to have a right to his life, in a legal sense, when he can in no wise affect or dispense with the duty on which the alleged right depends? Whether this part of the law falls on one side of the line or the other, however, it connects the second division with the third, which contains duties from all the world to all the world. Under this would clearly come assault and battery, libel, slander, false imprisonment, and the like, considered as causes of actions *civiliter.*

To the fourth division belong duties of all the world to persons in certain particular positions or relations. Here we should first consider the situation known as absolute ownership of a specific thing. Property in this restricted sense, or title, as the word is often used by English lawyers, although not an ultimate legal conceptions, is one of those practical units to which we have referred, and which should be discussed in one place. Although this division is devoted to duties of all the world, it would probably even be found convenient to deal here with the restrictions on the use of property by its owner, (*sic utere tuo,* etc.), rather than to place them in separate division of duties of persons in particular positions or relations. *Dominium,* ownership, or property, are phrases expressing the aggregate of rights corresponding to the duties of all the world to persons in a certain situation. Laying out of the case special doctrines like tenure, or the prerogative of the sovereign in cases of treasure trove and the like, which only complicate the subject, and duration, which is not material to our purposes, the primitive elements are possession, which is a fact or situation outside of the law, and a duty imposed on the rest of the world to respect it. This duty is absolute only toward the earliest of immediately successive possessors, or his representative. We say earliest, for, without raising any harder question, if the possessor be not the earliest or his representative, but a disseizer, for instance, or a finder, there is one person as against whom his possession is not protected. And possession is not called ownership unless it is protected against all. The words "immediately successive" are inserted to meet the case of abandonment. The common law as to animals *feræ naturæ,* illustrates the fact that the essential elements of ownership are what we have stated. The so-called right of user in the owner is not derived from the law. Any man, unless restrained, may use any thing he can lay his hands on, in any way he can devise. But the analysis is not yet complete. The law adds to the primary constituents the possibility of substitution in the objects of the duties in question. When this is accomplished by delivery, there occurs only a repetition of the previous case; that is, we have a protected possession as before, though the possessor is changed. But the same result may be obtained while the possession remains with a third person *e.g.,* by conveyance or descent. The rest of the world will owe a duty to the purchaser or heir in this case, in most respects the same as that owed to the actual possessor before. This gives to title a more extensive signification than protected possession, and makes of it that metaphysical entity which a lawyer gets to regard as a positive thing, changing hands from time to time, like coin or other tangibles. It would be possible indeed to postpone title by conveyance, etc., without possession, to the subdivision next to be suggested, but perhaps with more inconvenience than advantage. The text-books commonly treat, under the head of sale, title by delivery, in which case sale is analogous to gift, title by conveyance, and title by contract which turns into a conveyance on the occurrence of some event. While on the subject of successions it might be desirable to point out the extent of the conception. Thus agency resembles conveyance and descent in so far that in each case there is an aggregate of rights and duties analogous to a *persona* which remains unchanged in spite of the substitution of successive natural persons as the object of such duties, and as entitled to such rights. When the agent assumes a part of his principal's *persona,* the latter is not necessarily excluded from it to a corresponding degree, as is the case between grantor and grantee, or decedent and executor or heir, but this does not seem to affect the resemblance, any more than the fact that the duty is still in form owed only to the principal. It is to be observed that the various means of succeeding to the position of object of the duties explained, or as it is commonly expressed, of transferring title, are considered in the text-books from the point of view of right. The same is equally true of the learning of estates, involving the duration of such position, and the occupation of it by one or more. These two subjects, moreover, constitute much the most considerable part of the law of property. But as we have said already, the side of the shield contemplated is unimportant, if it is not suffered to become a source of delusion.

Without pausing to discuss the exact place of duties to judges, and other law arising out of what might be called a status independent of a relation (*e.g.*, the law of contempt), which, on practical considerations, might belong elsewhere, we come to a class of relations which belong in the general division we are now considering, and which, like ownership of a specific thing, are correlative to a duty from all the world, but which, unlike it, are peculiarly burdensome on a particular individual. Here we are in the midst of very difficult questions, as to which we can only offer a few suggestions *de bene*. If we are right, this subdivision should include or refer to easements, contracts, and some other obligations, and status so far as involving a personal relation, domestic or other, if this be a proper title at all. To explain. It is pretty decidedly to be inferred from *Lumley v. Gye*, 2 El. & Bl. 216, that an action would lie against a stranger to a contract for forcibly and maliciously preventing its performance, with intent to cause a loss to the plaintiff, the contractor, which the defendant knew would follow his act. If this be so, it would seem that the distinction between *jura in rem*, in the sense of rights against all the world, and obligations, which are also called *jura in personam*, and supposed to be rights against a particular individual only, is not absolute as Austin supposed it, but that the latter are simply a class of *jura in rem*, which are more likely to be infringed by a certain person, (*i.e.*, the party obliged) than by the rest of the world, and the parties to which are subject to more extensive liabilities than others. Other reasons for this belief will appear shortly. Assuming it to be well founded, it will nevertheless be observed that if contract were approached from the side of duty, the duties of strangers only would fall on this side of the dividing line, and those of parties would be considered in a new division, duties of persons in particular relations. But the right may be thought of as a single right, more or less qualified, against A., B., C., and all the rest of the alphabet, that A. shall do a particular thing. Whether on this ground both classes of duties should be kept together, in one division or the other, with a cross reference to point out that a distinction exists, is a question of detail.

An easement, like a contract, is a right as against all the world,[2] but imposes a particular burden on the servient owner. But it may be said, the duties imposed on the parties to contracts are often positive, whereas, as Austin lays it down in a different connection, that of a servient owner is always negative. If there be any ground for a legal distinction between duties to do and to forbear, it is sufficient to observe that some easements impose positive duties, *e.g.*, to repair fences. There is perhaps one minor difference which should be adverted to. Easements being rights of qualified enjoyment or possession of a particular thing, are more nearly connected with the complex conception property, which we have just explained. Again, the duty of a servient owner is without doubt generally negative, and that of a party to an ordinary contract is generally positive. In contracts, therefore, the duty of the party obliged is all in all, and that of third persons is so rarely called in question, that it is hardly supposed to exist. Hence there is a fair question to which we have just alluded, whether contracts should not be kept for a fifth division. It is true again that although an easement may be created as well by way of covenant as by grant (a fact which marks in an interesting way the relationship we are insisting upon), and is presumably binding on a *bonâ fide* purchaser, without notice, other executory (true) contracts touching a specific thing would not have this effect. At law, such a contract (*e.g.*, to sell) would not bind a subsequent purchaser, even with notice, but the remedy would have to be sought in equity. But it is immaterial, for the purposes of classification, whether equity or law gives the remedy, so long as a remedy is given. That equity would afford one in the latter case, is another evidence that contracts impose duties on all the world.

As a matter of speculation our inference from *Lumley v. Gye* does not want reason or analogy. It is proper to say, however, that the doctrine that a party to a contract may be sued upon it for non-performance, although caused by *vis major*, looks the other way, and as the subject is not yet exhausted it may be held that the only remedy in the case we supposed is by action against the contractor, leaving him to his remedy over if he has one. Should this ever be so determined, it would perhaps justify the absolute distinction drawn between *jura in rem* and *obligationes* in existing schemes, and would certainly throw the latter into the fifth division we have spoken of.

But at all events it remains the law that if the contracting party may be called the plaintiff's servant, the master has an action *per quod servitium amisit*, although his only right to those services in our times arises out of contract. Were the contrary determination reached in the case of an ordinary contract, it would afford a reason beside those usually given for retaining the *jus personarum* or law of status, so far as involving a personal relation, as a distinct title. It is not material to our point whether the action is given to the master by the Statute of Laborers or whether it arises from the fact that the duties incident to a well recognized status were settled before a contract was ever heard of; as would seem to be shown by the fact that an action by a parent for enticing away his daughter has been sustained on the ground of loss of service, although there was no pregnancy and of course no actual contract of service.[3] So long as anomalous duties exist it may be well to keep the ancient classification and put them under a separate head, either where they are provisionally placed above or in the fifth division. At the same time it is very clear that many of the component elements of a status or *persona*, *e.g.*, the capacity of an infant to contract, his liability for crime, the immunities and disabilities of a slave, and the like, might as well be noted under strictly legal divisions such as we have suggested. Mr. Maine has noticed the transition from status to contract as a mark of progressive societies. To consider the relations of master and servant, and husband and wife, as originating in contract, is an innovation which may be a step towards treating them as dependent on contract throughout, and so toward the disappearance of the conception of status from the law. As things are now, we venture to say that more than one intelligent student reading Kent's chapters on master and servant, and on principal and agent, has wondered why they were separated by half a volume, and where the one subject ended and other began.

We go back a little to make on or two more suggestions. There are several titles now in use which we believe it would be well to give up, and others which required explanation. Thus Austin, if we remember rightly, has shown the absurdity of the phrase incorporeal hereditaments. Bailment seems to us objectionable for other reasons. At the time the term was originated, delivery, like the conveyance of the legal title to land at the present day, so far passed the property to the bailee that a sale and delivery by him was good as against his principal.[4] This may have been that special property in the bailee which has left its impress on later law. It may be conjectured and would rather seem from the abridgments that, in those early days at least, there were few cases turning on other points than that of title in which the delivery of a chattel was the essential fact. But in modern times under bailments are collected matters not only of title but contract, and of a kind which would be equally possible in the nature of things if there were no delivery or bailment at all. Not to mention the unsuccessful attempt to get in telegraphs, we find thrust into this omnium gatherum the duty of innkeepers, which certainly never depended either on delivery or contract, but on the custom of the realm which compelled them to receive all travelers (with unimportant exceptions), and to be responsible for the safety of their goods and chattels *infra hospitia*. It is said in Calye's case that "although the guest doth not deliver his goods to the inn holder to keep, nor acquaint him with them, yet if they be carried away or stolen the innkeeper shall be charged." We must add with regard to the usual subdivisions taken from the civil law that very generally where we find that law retaining its original form in the body of our own, it seems to us to be a source of anomalies and confusion.

As an instance of a subdivision requiring explanation, we have already mentioned implied contracts. Under this head we find included both contracts which are truly express, and cases which are not contracts at all. If A. requests B., his grocer, to send him home a barrel of flour, and says nothing more, and B. does as requested, there is a true contract on A.'s part to pay for it. It is called implied, and is so if that only means that A. does not put his promise into words or state the terms of it, but leaves B. to infer both from his acts. But that distinction is unimportant, for A.'s acts are intended to lead to the inference drawn, and therefore express a promise as well as words would have done. On the other hand, under the same head of implied contracts are often included another totally distinct class of cases which in fact are not contracts, but which are analogous to the *obligationes quasi ex contractu* of the civil law. Thus in some states, the law recognizes as a duty to be enforced by action the duty to pay taxes, which has been already alluded to as one of those called by the name in question. But the law is confined to certain definite forms of action, and cannot proceed on a simple statement of the actual facts to enforce performance or award damages for non-performance. The forms of action available for the recovery of money are or are supposed to be based upon a contract. Hence the law by a fiction supplies such elements as are wanting to make this duty into one. But a legal fiction does not change the nature of things. And a fiction which is only invented to conceal the fact that the common law does not afford a remedy in a case where one must be hand, and which would be needless with another system of pleading and practice, like that of equity, cannot be allowed to affect a classification on the principles proposed.

We return to our main subject. A duty, strictly so called, is only created by commands which may be broken at the expense of incurring a penalty. That which the law directly compels, although it may onerously affect an individual, cannot be said to impose a duty upon him. The law addresses itself to the thing to be done, not to the person affected, and does not punish his failure to co-operate. In the classification of principal rights—that is, of the great body of jurisprudence, this distinction is less important than the considerations which induce us to neglect it. Thus, on account of the practical cohesion of the conception property, we bring together under it not only the true duty to respect possession which is enforced by the action of trover, but likewise the *quasi* duty, the performance of which is compelled by the officers of the law when they give possession to the successful plaintiff in a real action. So again we do not distinguish between nuisances which the sheriff is ordered to abate, and those which the court persuades the defendant to put an end to by inflicting damages. When we come to what Austin calls sanctioning rights, these reasons cease. In a classification by duties we cannot but doubt whether they would find an independent place. Take the case of a successful plaintiff in trover. He has undoubtedly a right to his damages, which he may discharge or assign. But when the law seizes and sells the defendant's goods to satisfy the judgment, can the latter be said to be performing a duty? It would seem to be more proper that the sanctions should follow the duties to which they are attached. Having decided on this, we should put in the same class (with proper cross-references) equitable remedies like decrees for specific performance; although these may fairly be said to impose duties, sanctioned by liability to process for contempt.

The place for pleading and practice presents some difficulties. In the time of the common-law forms of action the question was partly solved by placing rights under the remedies by which they were enforced. This, however imperfect, was a legal arrangement; for the distinctions between the different remedies were legal distinctions, and embodied a kind of philosophy of the law. If forms of action and the distinctions between law and equity are to wholly pass away, and the courts are by and by to enforce duties on a plain statement of the facts out of which they arise, the little of pleading that remains beside the name will come in with sanctions under the duty to which it applies. In an intermediate condition, such as most of the United States is now in, pleading retains an arbitrary element, which makes it more convenient to treat it separately. Practice does not seem to be a part of the law in any other sense than parliamentary law, or the by-laws of certain corporations. If it goes in the *corpus juris* it is for the practical convenience of lawyers, and it will, of course, have a separate place.

NOTES

1. But see *post* pp. 114, 115.

2. This is not likely to be denied, and is very clearly implied by *Saxby* v. *Manchester, Sheffield, &c., Railway Co., L. R.* 4 C. P. 198.

3. *Evans* v. *Walton*, L. R. 2 C. P. 615.

4. Y. B. 21 H. 7, 89; See 2 E. 4, 4.

Notice of Pollock on Austin's Definition of Law

American Law Review 6 (July 1872): 723–725.

The Law Magazine and Review. New Series. No. 8, April 1, 1872. London: Butterworth's.

In the third article of this interesting number, Mr. Frederick Pollock discusses Austin's definition of law. As his results more or less coincide with opinions which were expressed more at length at the beginning of a course of lectures on jurisprudence, delivered at Harvard College while his article was going through the press, it may be interesting to briefly state some of the points developed by the lecturer, as we hope to present them more at length at some future time.

The general opinion that Austin's definition was not satisfactory from a philosophical point of view has been already expressed in our pages. According to him, law, properly so called, is defined as a command of a definite political superior, or sovereign, which obliges political inferiors or subjects to acts or forbearances of a class, by the imposition of a penalty in case of disobedience; and all sovereign commands which purport to do that are laws. Now it is admitted by every one that who is the sovereign is a question of fact equivalent to the question who has the sum of the political powers of a state in his hands. That is to say, sovereignty is a form of power, and the will of the sovereign is law, because he has power to compel obedience or to punish disobedience, and for no other reason. The limits within which his will is law, then, are those within which he has, or is believed to have, power to compel or punish. It was shown by many instances that this power of the sovereign was limited not only without, by the liability to war (which it was shown might be a true sanction), but within, as by conflicting principles of sovereignty (the territorial and the tribal), by organizations of persons not sharing in the sovereign power, and by unorganized public opinion. It was shown that there might be law without sovereignty, and that where there is a sovereign, properly so called, other bodies not sovereign, and even opinion, might generate law in a philosophical sense against the will of the sovereign. For it is to be remembered that in most states there has been a large number, and in many a numerical majority of males, who have had no share in the political power; while at the same time their physical power, and consequently their desires, were not to be ignored, and in some cases were not to be disobeyed.

In the lectures referred to, it was doubted whether law, in the more limited meaning which lawyers give to the word, possessed any other common attribute than of being enforced by the procedure of the courts, and therefore of practical importance to lawyers. It was shown that the rules enforced in that way did not always depend on the courts for their efficacy in governing conduct, and that it was a mere fiction to say that, either philosophically or legally, they necessarily emanated from the will of the sovereign as *law.*

Austin said, following Heineccius (*Recitations,* § 72), that custom only became law by the tacit consent of the sovereign manifested by its adoption by the courts; and that before its adoption it was only a motive for decision, as a doctrine of political economy, or the political aspirations of the judge, or his gout, or the blandishments of the emperor's wife might have been. But it is clear that in many cases custom and mercantile usage have had as much compulsory power as law could have, in spite of prohibitory statutes; and as to their being only motives for decision until adopted, what more is the decision which adopts them as to any future decision? What more indeed is a statute; and in what other sense law, than that we believe that the motive which we think that it offers to the judges will prevail, and will induce them to decide a certain case in a certain way, and so shape our conduct on that anticipation? A precedent may not be followed; a statute may be emptied of its contents by construction, or may be repealed without a saving clause after we have acted on it; but we expect the reverse, and if our expectations come true, we say that we have been subject to law in the matter in hand. It must be remembered, as is clear from numerous instances of judicial interpretation of statutes in England and of constitutions in this country, that in a civilized state it is not the will of the sovereign that makes lawyers' law, even when that is its source, but what a body of subjects namely, the judges, by whom it is enforced, *say* is his will. The judges have other motives for decision, outside their own arbitrary will, beside the commands of their sovereign. And whether those other motives are, or are not, equally compulsory, is immaterial, if they are sufficiently likely to prevail to afford a ground for prediction. The only question for the lawyer is how will the judges act? Any motive for their action, be it constitution, statute, custom, or precedent, which can be relied upon as likely in the generality of cases to prevail, is worthy of consideration as one of the sources of law, in a treatise on jurisprudence. Singular motives, like the blandishments of the emperor's wife, are not a ground of prediction, and are therefore not considered.

Passing to the sufficiency of Austin's definition for determining what sovereign commands are to be called law, it was thought, in the lectures referred to, that the specific penalty or sanction which Austin seemed to tacitly assume as the final test, could not always be relied on.

The notion of duty involves something more than a tax on a certain course of conduct. A protective tariff on iron does not create a duty not to bring it into the country. The word imports the existence of an absolute wish on the part of the power imposing it to bring about a certain course of conduct, and to prevent the contrary. A legal duty cannot be said to exist if the law intends to allow the person supposed to be subject to it an option at a certain price. The test of a legal duty is the absolute nature of the command. If a statute subjects a person to a penal action in case of certain conduct on his part, but such conduct is protected and treated as lawful in all the other connections in which it may come before the court, an option is in fact allowed. A very striking illustration will be found in the well known case of the *Creole*, 2 Wall. Jr. 485, where a statute providing that certain vessels should be "obliged" to employ a pilot or "forfeit and pay" a sum spoken of as "a penalty," was held to leave the employment optional, subject to a tax—whether rightly or not is immaterial. The imposition of a penalty is therefore only evidence tending to show that an absolute command was intended (a rule of construction). But an absolute command does not exist—penalty or no penalty—unless a breach of it is deprived of the protection of the law, which is shown by a number of consequences not accurately determinable in a general definition, such as the invalidity of contracts to do the forbidden act;—the rule *in pari delicto potior est conditio defendentis*—the denial of relief when the illegal act is part of the plaintiff's case, &c.

A fortiori in those cases where there is no penalty directly attached to a given act, the existence of a legal duty to abstain from or to perform it, must be determined by these collateral consequences. Liability to pay the fair price or value of an enjoyment, or to be compelled to restore or give up property belonging to another, is not a penalty; and this is the extent of the ordinary liability to a civil action at common law. In a case of this sort, where there are no collateral consequences attached, (which is perhaps the fact with regard to some contracts, to pay money, for instance), it is hard to say that there is a duty in strictness, and the rule is inserted in law books for the empirical reason above referred to, that it is applied by the courts and must therefore be known by professional men.

As liability to a civil action is not a penalty or sanction of itself creating a duty, so, on the other hand, it does not necessarily imply culpability, or a breach of duty, as Austin thought, who looked at the law too much as a criminal lawyer. The object of the law is to accomplish an external result. When it can best accomplish that result by operating on men's wills, or when it is secure of what it desires in the absence of willfulness or negligence, then it may very properly make willfulness or negligence the gist of the action— one of the necessary elements of liability. But in other instances it may be thought that this is too narrow a limit; it may be thought that titles should be protected against even innocent conversion; that persons should be indemnified, at all events, for injuries from extra-hazardous sources, in which case negligence is not an element. Public policy must determine where the line is to be drawn. The rule of the common law, requiring the owner of cattle to keep them on his land at his peril, has been very properly abandoned in some of the western states, where the enclosure of their vast prairies is necessarily for a long time out of the question.

Primitive Notions in Modern Law

American Law Review 10 (April 1876): 422–439.

In a former investigation in these pages,[1] we endeavored to show, that, more generally than has been supposed, civil liability depends not on culpability as a state of the defendant's consciousness—that is to say, upon the particular defendant's having failed to do the best that he know how to do—but upon his having failed to come up to a more or less accurately determined standard in his overt acts or omissions. If a person is proved to have done acts which the court thinks it perfectly clear ought to make him liable, it lays down a rule of law, that on those facts he is liable. If the acts proved are at the other extreme, the court rules that they are not the foundation of a claim. In many instances, at least, when the question of negligence is left to the jury, the meaning is not, that they are to consider whether the person concerned has culpably failed to advert to consequences of his acts or omissions which he had the intelligence to have perceived, and might have perceived; but the meaning is, that the case falls in the doubtful region between the two extremes, and that, as the court has no clear standard in its own mind, it adopts as its standard what the jury thinks would have been the conduct of a prudent man under the circumstances, and adjudicates that the person concerned was bound at his peril to conform to that. The function of the fact found by the jury is the same as that of other facts of which the court satisfies itself as it sees fit, such as the existence of a statute or a custom, namely, to suggest a rule of law.[2]

To lay the foundation for the discussion to which we have referred, we were led to glance incidentally at the historical origin of liability in some cases which Austin, following the jurists of the mature period of Roman law, had interpreted on grounds of culpability; and to point out that it sprung from the much more primitive notion, that liability attached directly to the thing doing the damage. This suggestion will be found to have occurred to earlier writers who will be quoted. But we shall endeavor in this article to explain that primitive notion more at length, to show its influence on the body of modern law, and to trace the development from it of a large number of doctrines which in their actual form seem most remote from each other or from any common source; a task which we believe has not been attempted before. If we are successful, it will be found that the various considerations of policy which are not infrequently supposed to have established these doctrines, have, in fact, been invented at a later period to account for what was already there—a process familiar to all students of legal history.

To begin with a few examples. A man builds a house upon his land, which falls, and does damage to his neighbor's person or property, for which the latter recovers compensation. Why? It is, says the analytical jurist, because he has been negligent in building or maintaining it; and one who is negligent is culpable, and one who culpably does damage ought to pay for it; or, if the reader prefers, the reason may be stated in terms suggested above.

A man has an animal of known ferocious habits, which escapes, and does his neighbor damage. He can prove that the animal escaped through no negligence of his; but again he is held liable. And this time he is told, that, although he was not negligent in guarding it, he was guilty of remote heedlessness, or negligence, to use the generic word, in having such a creature at all. Or, to put the proposition in what we believe to be its true form, that although, in general, the law lets accidents rest as they fall, yet, in the case of certain extra-hazardous things, it is deemed policy to make the owner answer for all the harm they do.

A man's servant, while driving his master's cart, carelessly runs another down; and the master asks why he should be liable for the illegal act of another. Thu answer, from Ulpian and Austin alike, is, because of his remote negligence in employing an improper person. If this is perceived to be inadequate, as the liability is unaffected by the greatest care in choosing the servant, it is perhaps laid down that there ought to be a remedy against some one who can pay the damages, or perhaps that such wrongful acts as by ordinary human laws are likely to happen in the course of the service are imputable to the service.

Let us turn to a case where a limit has been set to liability which had previously been unlimited. In 1851, Congress passed a law by which the owners of ships in all the more common cases of maritime loss can surrender the vessel and her freight then pending to the losers; and thereupon it is provided that further proceedings against the owners shall cease. The legislators to whom we owe this act argued, that, if a merchant embark a portion of his property upon a hazardous venture, it is reasonable that his stake should be confined to what he puts at risk—a principle similar to that on which corporations have been so largely created in America within the last fifty years.

It has been a rule of criminal pleading, down into the present century, that an indictment for homicide must set forth the value of the instrument causing the death, in order that the king or his grantee might claim forfeiture of the *deodand*, as Blackstone says, "as an accursed thing."

Here is a medley of rules gathered from the four corners of the law, each with its more or less adequate reason, and each certainly showing no trace of connection with any other, yet all of which, with many others, as we shall presently show, may plausibly be referred for their origin to the primitive notion which we have mentioned.

Turning first to the Roman law, we read in the Pandects, "*Si quadrupes pauperiem fecisse dicetur, action ex lege duodecim tabularum descendit; quæ lex voluit, aut dari [id] quod nocuit, id est, id animal, quod noxiam commisit; aut estimationem noxiæ offerre.*"[3] That is, in case of damage done by a quadruped, the law of the Twelve Tables (451 B.C.) required the surrender of the animal that did the damage, or payment. It will be observed, with reference to what is to follow, that this is not stated as a limit of liability, but that, on the contrary, the payment is only an alternative in case of a failure to surrender the quadruped.

Paulus tells us that the equity of the law was made to cover other animals as well as quadrupeds.[4]

We learn from Gaitis and other sources, that the same principle was applied from the beginning to the torts of children or slaves.[5] They might be surrendered in like manner; although, in Justinian's time, the milder manners which then prevailed had put an end to the surrender of sons or daughters.[6]

It seems, too, that what came to be regarded as the benefit of surrender was extended to inanimate objects, such as a house; and as Gaius, explaining it on such grounds of policy as occurred to him, had said that it was unjust that the fault of children or slaves should be a source of loss to their parents or owners beyond their own bodies, Ulpian reasoned, that *a fortiori* was this true of things devoid of life, and therefore incapable of fault.[7]

If Gaius was mistaken in his reason for the limit of the liability in question, it is equally certain that the liability itself stood on no ground of fault. Such, indeed, was the assumption on which the reasoning of Gaius proceeded. But the decisive fact is, that all these *noxales actiones*, as they were called, *caput sequuntur*. That is to say, the notion was brought, not against the person who owned the slave, animal, or thing, when the damage was done—who of course, if any one, was the person in fault, for not preventing the injury—but against him who was owner at the time of action brought.[8] And, in curious contrast with the principle as inverted to meet the modern explanation of public policy, if the animal was *feræ naturæ*—that is, in the very case of the most ferocious animals—the owner ceased to be liable the moment it escaped, *quia desinit dominus esse ubi fera evasit.*[9]

On the other hand, probably, in the first form of the principle, the offending thing only was liable, notwithstanding the owner's fault, except where it was merely a tool in his hands.[10] Gaius and Ulpian, as we have seen, showed an inclination to cut the *noxæ deditio* down to a privilege of the owner in case of misdeeds committed without his knowledge; but Ulpian is obliged to admit, that by the ancient law, according to Celsus, the action was noxal where a slave was guilty even with the privity of his master.[11]

All this, as we have said, can only be explained by the notion that liability attaches directly to the thing that does the damage. To show how strongly this was held, it is instructive to add, that, although Ulpian says the action is gone if the animal dies *ante litem contestatam*,[12] there is some ground for believing that the guilty object itself was not always released even by death. Livy relates that the Samnites, having agreed to surrender Brutulus Papius, who had caused a breach of truce with the Romans, sent his lifeless body, he having avoided disgrace and punishment by suicide. The matter-of-course way in which he speaks of it will be particularly noticed: "*Fetiales Romam, ut censuerunt, missi, et corpus Brutuli exanime: ipse morte voluntaria ignominiæ se ac supplicio subtraxit. Placuit cum corpore bona quoque ejus dedi.*"[13] With this should be compared an unfortunately defective passage in Gaius, iv. § 81, which also seems to point to the surrender of dead bodies. We give the reading of Huschke: "*Licere enim etiam si fato is fuerit mortuus, mortuum dare; nam quamquam diximus, non etiam permissum reis esse, et mortuos homines dedere, tamen et si quis cum dederit, qui fato suo vita excesserit, æquo liberatur.*"

These passages seem already to carry us back even farther than those first quoted. But it must be remembered that Roman law was considerably developed even in the time of the Twelve Tables. We shall get more light by considering the still older and more primitive customs of Greece.

In Plutarch's Solon, Draco is said to have ordered that process should be carried on even against inanimate things. Pausnias tells us expressly, that they sit in judgment upon such things in the Prytaneum:[14] and although, in his time, this scorned to need explanation and comment, æschines mentions it as a familiar matter, and evidently without thinking it at all extraordinary, that "we banish beyond our borders stocks and stones and steel, voiceless and mindless things, if they chance to kill a man; and, if a man commits suicide, bury the hand that struck the blow afar from its body,"—only to point an antithesis to the honors heaped upon Demosthenes, whom he charged with greater crimes.[15] Plutarch also tells us that a dog that had bit a man was to be delivered up bound to a log four cubits long[16] and we read in Plato's Laws, xi. 14, that, if a slave does damage to which the injured party did not contribute as a joint cause, the owner of the slave is either to remedy the mischief, or hand over the slave.

The laws of Greece and Rome were kindred systems; but the principle we are discussing was not confined to them. We find it among the Jews in the well-known passage from Exodus, xxi. 28: "If an ox gore a man or a woman that they die, than the ox shall be surely stoned, and his flesh shall not be eaten; but the owner of the ox shall be quit."

And in a body of customs probably independent of both Roman and Hebrew influences, in the old text of the *Lex Salica*, it is provided, that, if a man is slain by a domestic animal, the owner shall pay half his composition, and for the other half surrender the animal.[17]

The provisions of the early English ordinances should be read in connection with these last. Thus, in the Kentish laws of Hlothhære and Eadric,[18] we find, "If any one's *esne* [slave] slay a freeman, whoever it be, let the owner pay with a hundred shillings, *give up the slayer*," &c., and several other similar provisions. In like manner, in the laws of Alfred,[19] "If a neat wound a man, let the neat be delivered up or compounded for"; and, "If, at their common work, one man slay another unwillfully, let the tree be given to the kindred, and let them have it off the land within thirty days; or let him take possession of it who owns the wood."[20] According to a note in Fitzherbert's *Natura Brevium*, it was the law in Edward III's time, that "if my dog kills your sheep, and I, freshly after the fact, tender you the dog, you are without remedy."

In the derivative case of deodand, to which we alluded at the outset, it did not matter that the forfeited instrument belonged to an innocent person. "When a man killeth another with the sword of *John at Stile*, the sword shall be forfeit as deodand, and yet no default is in the owner."[21]

By this time, the universality of the notion we are discussing must have struck the reader as surprising. In the earlier investigation to which we have referred above, we were led to compare the passages cited from the Roman law for the limited purpose of showing that Austin's explanation of the ground of liability in certain cases was not sustained by history, and to lay a foundation for the analysis there attempted. But we are now carried on to the question, What was the meaning of the state of mind which we find thus reflected in the institutions of so many independent tribes and nations? At this point, anthropology comes in to aid the researches of jurisprudence.

There is a passage in Mr. Tylor's great work on Primitive Culture which is full of instruction upon the subject: "First and foremost among the causes which transfigure into myths the facts of daily experience, is the belief in the animation of all nature, rising it its highest pitch to personification. This, no occasional or hypothetical action of the mind, is inextricably bound in with that primitive mental state whore man recognizes in every detail of his world the operation of personal life and will . . .

"Let us put this doctrine of universal vitality to a test of direct evidence, lest readers new to the subject should suppose it a modern philosophical fiction, or think that if the lower races really express such a notion, they may do so only as a poetical way of talking. Even in civilized countries it makes its appearance as the child's early theory of the outer world, nor can we fail to see how this comes to pass. The first beings that children learn to understand something of are human beings, and especially their own selves; and the first explanation of all events will be the human explanation, as though chairs and sticks and wooden horses were actuated by the same sort of personal will as nurses and children and kittens. Thus infants take their first step in mythology by contriving, like Cosette with her doll, '*se figurer que quelque chose est quelqu'un*'; and the way in which this child-like theory has to be unlearnt in the course of education shows how primitive it is. Even among full-grown civilized Europeans, as Mr. Grote appositely remarks, 'the force of momentary passion will often suffice to supersede the acquired habit, and even an intelligent man may be impelled in a moment of agonizing pain to kick or beat the lifeless object from which he has suffered.' In such matters, the savage mind well represents the childish stage. The wild native of Brazil would bite the stone he stumbled over, or the arrow that had wounded him. Such a mental condition may be traced along the course of history, not merely in impulsive habit, but in formally enacted law. The rude Kukis of Southern Asia were very scrupulous in carrying out their simple law of vengeance, life for life; if a tiger killed a Kuki, his family were in disgrace till they had retaliated by killing and eating this tiger, or another; but further, if a man was killed by a fall from a tree, his relatives would take their revenge by cutting the tree down, and scattering it in chips. A modern king of Cochin-China, when one of his ships sailed badly, used to put it in the pillory as he would any other criminal. In classical times, the stories of Xerxes flogging the Hellespont and Cyrus draining the Gyndes occur as cases in point, but one of the regular Athenian legal proceedings is a yet more striking relic. A court of justice was held at the Prytaneum, to try any inanimate object, such as an axe or a piece of wood or stone, which had caused the death of any one without proved human agency, and this wood or stone, if condemned, was in solemn form cast beyond the border. The spirit of this remarkable procedure reappears in the old English law (repealed in the present reign), whereby not only a beast that kills a man, but a cart-wheel that runs over him, or a tree that falls on him and kills him, is deodand, or given to God, i.e., forfeited and sold for the poor: as Bracton says, '*Omnia quæ movent ad mortem sunt deodanda.*' "[22]

Without insisting too much upon the theory of a definitely held belief, we may say that it is the universal tendency of the human mind (which psychology might perhaps have demonstrated unaided) to hold a material object, which is the proximate cause of loss, in some sense unanswerable for it. The untrained intelligence only imperfectly performs the analysis by which jurists carry responsibility back to the beginning of a chain of causation. But, as Mr. Bain remarks,[23] without clothing inanimate objects in personality, we cannot feel proper anger towards them. It will be noticed that the most important cases which occur under the various laws from which we have quoted are living things, principally animals and slaves; and that the tree is specially alluded to, not only in the passage just given from Mr. Tylor, but in the laws of Alfred and those of the Saxons and others to be hereafter referred to. If a man was run over, the Roman lawyers did not surrender the wagon which crushed him, but the ox which drew the wagon.[24] The more undeveloped the institutions, however, the closer should we expect to find the liability to the immediate visible and tangible cause of the damage.

We assume here, and shall try to prove farther on, that the original object of the various procedures we arc considering was vengeance, not compensation. They belong, therefore, to an earlier stage of society than an action for damages. They afterwards became at once a means of indemnity and a limit of liability. The unlimited personal liability of the owner of animals or slaves, in cases where he was not the active cause of the mischief, on the ground that he had the power of control, appears still later, and seemingly as a further development from the same primitive root.

We ask the reader's attention to the order of progress. We see that in a body of customs more ancient than the laws of Rome, and, in some respects, more primitive than the ordinances of Moses, this responsibility was so vividly conceived, that it was enforced by a judicial process expressly directed against the object animate or inanimate. The Twelve Tables made the owner of the offending thing defendant, instead of the thing itself, but did not in any way change the ground of his liability or affect its limit. It was simply a way of allowing him to intervene *pro interesse suo*,[25] The liability was not based upon his fault, nor its limit upon his innocence. Nearly two centuries later than the Twelve Tables, personal liability for damage was enlarged by the Aquilian law, and still more by the scope given to that plebiscite by interpretation. The master became personally liable for certain wrongs committed by his slave with his knowledge, where previously only a noxal action lay.[26] If a pack-mule threw off his burden upon a passer-by because he had been improperly overloaded, or a dog which might have been restrained escaped from his master and bit any one, the noxal action gave way to an action under the new law to enforce a general personal liability.[27] The distinction is made between negligent wrongs and accidents.[28] We may see that the law is becoming more refined by the increased attention to the actual culpability of the person charged. The prætor, in imposing a new liability upon occupants of houses for damage done by throwing things from them into the street, saves the benefit of the *noxæ deditio* to a master whose slave has acted without his knowledge.[29] By and by, ship-owners and inn-keepers are made liable *quasi ex maleficio* for torts on board ship or in the tavern, although, of course, committed without their knowledge. But, after what has been said, it is not surprising to find that the jurists, who regarded the *noxæ deditio* as a privilege intended to limit liability where there was no fault, explained the new liability on the ground that the inn or ship owner was to a certain degree guilty of negligence in having employed the services of bad men.[30] The true reason was one of policy.[31] But through that door the doctrine of agency passed into the law; and to this day, as we have seen, the reason offered by the Roman jurists in a particular case is made to justify the extended responsibility of a principal for his agent, as well as of a master for his servant.

It would seem that a similar development may be noticed from the early Salic law in the later Germanic folk-laws. The earlier liability for slaves and animals seems to have been mainly confined to surrender; the later to have become personal, as at Rome. It is true the Salic law ordains, that, in certain cases, the master shall restore what his slave has stolen, or its value;[32] but the later laws impose a general personal liability on the master to make good damage done by his slave,[33] and one nearly as extensive on the possessor or owner of animals.[34]

In Exodus xxi. 29, a personal liability is imposed on the owner in case he knew of the vicious propensities of the animal, side by side with the provision referred to above.

We have still to examine the most striking transformation of ancient doctrine which occurs in modern law. It is only fair to admit at the outset that the opinions to be expressed are partly conjectural; and, as such, they are submitted to the judgment of the reader. Some time before his attention had been called to the provisions of the Roman law which have been discussed, and still longer before he had soon the works of MM. Tissot and Tylor which have just been cited, the writer was forced to the conclusion, from a study of the law as it is to-day, that the root of the maritime law was the personification of the ship.[35] A ship is the most living of all inanimate things. Servants sometimes say "she" of a clock; but all men give a gender to vessels, which are not the least alive to those who know most about them. We might expect, therefore, that in this case, if anywhere, there was room for the operation of that way of thinking which we have already described, and which is shown by manifold instances to be by no means extinct at the present day. With the aid of the hypothesis that the ship was considered by the old *prudhommes* of the sea somewhat in the light of a person, the arbitrary seeming peculiarities of the maritime law at once become consistent and logical consequences.

For instance: A collision takes place between two vessels, X. and Z., through the fault of Z. alone. Z. is under a demise at the time, and the lessee has his own master in charge. The owner and lessor of Z is free from any personal liability on elementary principles; yet there is a lien on his vessel for the amount of the damage done, and she may be arrested and sold for it in any admiralty court whose process will reach her. If a collision had happened between two wagons under similar circumstances, no one would think of urging such a claim.[36]

But, again, suppose the vessel, instead of being under lease, is in charge of a pilot, whose employment is made compulsory by the laws of the port to which she has sailed.

The Supreme Court of the United States holds the ship liable in this case also. In England, a contrary result would probably have been reached, even apart from exonerating statutes[37] for there the maritime law has shown a tendency to assimilate common-law doctrines, perhaps under the influence of a court of appeal largely composed of common lawyers: and, if the ship cannot be condemned except where the person in charge is the servant of the owner, it is clear that this is right. It is also clear, that, upon ordinary principles, one who could not impose a personal liability on the owner, could not bind a particular chattel to answer for a tort of which it had been the instrument. But the Supreme Court has long recognized that the master may bind the ship when he could not bind the owners personally, because not their agent.

If, now, we seek for the reason of these anomalies, the usual answer would be, that whether it was so by the maritime law as settled from time immemorial. Ingenuity might devise a ground of policy, that, whether just or not, the early tribunals naturally preferred to allow the person wronged to seize the property most available for his satisfaction, rather than send him to a foreign jurisdiction. We shall refer to this again; but we have already indicated what seems to us the probable explanation. If we should say to an uneducated man to-day, "She did it, and she ought to pay for it," it may be doubted whether he would see the fallacy, or be ready to explain that the ship was only property, and that "the ship has to pay for it"[38] was simply a dramatic way of saying that somebody's property was to be sold, and the proceeds applied to pay for a wrong not committed by the owner. Moreover, by the maritime law of the middle ages, the ship was not only the source, but the limit, of liability.[39] The rule already prevailed, which has been adopted by English statutes and our own act of 1851, that the owner was discharged from responsibility for the wrongful acts of the master appointed by himself upon surrendering his interest in the vessel, and the freight which she had earned. By the doctrines of agency, he would be personally liable for the whole damage. The ground for the modern legislation has been alluded to already. If that were the original ground of the early rule, of course it would have no connection with what has gone before. If the explanation offered here be accepted, the connection is obvious; and it is difficult to believe that such a connection did not exist. There is no historical evidence that this mode of dealing with the ship was suggested by the noxal action. It would seem that it might have been; although the Roman lawyers thought that an action only lay, in cases of collision, under the Aquilian law, against persons actually negligent in handling the ship.[40] It may have come from universal habits of mind. There is some evidence that ships were originally forfeited, at least in practice, when persons were drowned from them by reason of their motion.[41]

Let us take now another principle, for which, as usual, there is a plausible explanation of policy. Freight is the mother of wages; for, we are told, "*if the ship perished*, . . . *if the mariners were to have their wages in such cases, they would not use their endeavors, nor hazard their lives, for the safety of the ship.*"[42] On the other hand, there is the exception, that in case of shipwreck, *so long as any portion of the ship was saved*, the lien of the mariners remained—perhaps to encourage so deserving a class of men. If we consider that the sailors were regarded as employed by the ship, we shall understand very readily both the rule and the exception. If the debtor perished, there was an end of the matter. If a part came ashore, that might be proceeded against. The italicized words show the reference to the life of the ship, even in the modern form of the rule. It is interesting to remark, that, in the Judgments of the Sea—which, according to Sir Travers Twiss,[43] is the most ancient extant source of modern maritime law, except the decisions of Trani—the statement is, that the mariners will lose their wages when the ship is lost. *Ans perdront lurs loers quant la nef est perdue*.[44] So, in his edition of the Customs of the Sea—which, he tells us, is the oldest Part of the Consulate,[45]—we read, that, "whoever the freighter may be who runs away or dies, the ship is bound to pay the mariners," &c.[46]

It will be observed that the general reasoning of this article applies more clearly to torts than to voluntary dealings; and therefore a few words must be said, in this connection, about the other usual maritime liens.

"By custom, the ship is bound to the merchandise, and the merchandise to the ship." The ship is bound by the contract of affreightment as well as by her torts, although under demise at the time. In such cases also, according to the Supreme Court, the master may bind the vessel when he cannot bind the general owners.[47] With regard to the usual maritime contracts, it may be urged, no doubt with force, that, in an enlightened sense, the dealing must be on the security of the ship or merchandise in many cases, and therefore that it is policy to give this security in all cases; that this element is calculable, and that ship-owners must take it into account when they let their vessels. Moreover, the party asserting a maritime lien *ex contractu* has generally improved the condition of the thing upon which the lien is claimed; and we do not forget that the Roman law gave a tacit privilege on this ground.[48] But it may at least be suspected that the same metaphysical confusion which naturally arose as to the ship's torts affected the way of thinking as to her contracts. The whole manner of dealing with vessels obviously took the form which prevailed in the cases first mentioned. Pardessus says[49] that the lien for freight prevails even against the owner of stolen goods, as the master deals "less with the person than with the thing." In many cases of contract, as well as tort, the vessel was not only the security for the debt, but the limit of the owner's liability.[50]

Whether this confusion rose to the height of a doctrine in the early low of contract, it is beyond the scope of this article to inquire. Some things which seem to point that way are better explained otherwise. But it is not amiss to mention Livy's story, that Postumius, after the disgraceful peace of the Caudine Forks had been concluded *per sponsionem*, proposed to the Romans that the persons who had actually made the contract should be given up in satisfaction of it; saying that nothing but their bodies were due, the Roman people not having sanctioned the agreement, and replying to the tribunes who denied that this could be done: "*Nam quod deditione nostra negant exsolvi religione populum, id istos magis ne dedantur, quam quia ita se res habeat, dicere, quis adeo juris fetialium expers est, qui ignoret?*" They were accordingly surrendered in these words, which seem to show an attempt to bring the case within the *noxæ deditio*: "*Quandoque hisce homines injussu populi*

Romani Quiritium fœdus ictum iri spoponderunt, atque ob eam rem noxam nocuerunt; ob eam rem, quo populus Romanus scelere impio sit solutus, hosce homines vobis dedo.[51] Cicero narrates a similar surrender of Mancinus by the *pater-patratus* to the Numantines, who, however, like the Samnites in the former case, refused to receive him.[52] We may also recall in this connection the well-known law of the Twelve Tables, by which, in case of the existence of several creditors of an insolvent debtor, they might divide his body among them;[53] for although the right of a single creditor to reduce his debtor to slavery, and in modern times the peculiar effect ascribed to taking the body of a defendant on execution, may well be judicial reproductions of self-help by private war, this particular provision does not seem quite accounted for, unless the obligation of the debt was conceived very literally to inhere in or bind the body of the debtor, with a *vinculum juris.*

Undoubtedly it might be argued, that not only this, but most of the cases which have been stated, are derived from an extra-legal seizure of the offending thing as security for reparation. Such an argument has been advanced with regard to the noxal actions of Rome.[54] The latter explanation, like that offered here, would show that modern views of responsibility had not yet been attained, as the owner of the thing might very well not be the person in fault. But a consideration of the earliest instances will show, as might have been expected, that vengeance, not compensation, and vengeance on the offending thing, was the original object. The ox in Exodus was to be stoned. The axe in the Athenian law was to be banished. The tree in Mr. Tylor's instance was to be chopped to pieces. The deodand was an accursed thing. The personification of even inanimate objects, as in the Athenian procedure, finds it explanation in passion, not in self-interest. The limit of liability when a guilty patty was before the court is ill accounted for, except upon the view here advocated; and we may add, that, if the first step had been one of self-help, we should rather have expected to find that the legal proceedings began with the other party, as in the case of replevin, which has been so lucidly explained by Sir Henry Maine.[55]

It should be said, in closing, that practical conclusions can only be drawn with caution from the opinions advanced in this article. Taking it as true that the various rules which have been mentioned did not originate in the different principles of policy, to which they have been commonly ascribed, but that the principles of policy were thought out in the effort to account for the rules, it does not follow that the principles are unsound, or that the rules do not work well in practice. If truth were not often suggested by error, or old implements could not be adjusted to new uses, human progress would be slow. But, nevertheless, enough has been said to justify scrutiny and revision. The limitation of liability to the value of ship and pending freight has been adopted, as we have seen, by the most enlightened legislatures. On the other hand, the rule that freight is the mother of wages has been put to an end by statutes both in England and America. The considerations here advanced would perhaps have had some weight if they had been before the court in a case of compulsory pilotage like the *China,*[56] and, as it seems, are not without their bearing on the *Lottawanna,*[57] recently discussed in these pages. The question moved in that case was, whether, under our law, material men have a lien for repairs and supplies furnished to a vessel in her home port. It will be remembered that the question generally comes up as between them and subsequent *bona fide* purchasers; and the effect which the lien, if sustained, would have upon the rights of the latter, must manifestly be taken into account in considering whether it is consistent with the general system of our laws. Continental precedents are appealed to for the purpose of showing the general doctrine of the maritime law. But, if the lien originated in the same way as the other liens adverted to above, the value of the precedents, merely as such, is impaired. On the other hand, if we consider the grounds of policy on which the lien has been maintained in modern times, we shall find that they have been applied equally by European law to liens upon houses and other things on which labor has been spent. But, with regard to houses and the like, we should encounter a conflicting principle in this country in the policy of our registry laws, which is inconsistent with the allowance of an unrecorded lien. We submit that the same policy has been universally accepted by our legislation with regard to ships. The statutes which have given a lien require recording as a condition. There is no very clear ground for preferring domestic material men to other artisans in this respect; for it will be remembered that a domestic material man is nearly always, and, if the home port were determined by admiralty districts instead of by States, would always be, one who lives in the same district with the owner of the ship, and who, therefore, is not cut off from the ordinary personal remedies with which other persons have to content themselves. The State courts also are as accessible to him as to others. It is otherwise in the case of work done on a vessel not in the home port, to which the foregoing reasoning does not apply; and the extraordinary remedy may well be allowed where the vessel which is in need, and the person who supplies the need, would otherwise be helpless.

NOTES

---

1. "The Theory of Torts," 7 Am. Law Rev. 652. See also Kent's Comm. (12th ed.) ii. 561, n. 1.

2. This view seems to have been adopted by the Supreme Court in a subsequent case. *R.R. Co. v. Stout*, 17 Wall. 657, 663. Negligence is only one example of the principle which was discussed. Some cases of what is called constructive fraud will furnish another. For although fraud, of all things, seems to require the presence of an actual intent, yet if the acts go to a certain height, especially where the situation of the parties is such as to put one at the mercy of the other, the courts lay it down as a matter of law that such acts are constructively a fraud; which is only a roundabout way of saying that those overt acts are a ground of liability irrespective of the party's honesty. So, in slander and libel, the distinction between malice in law and malice in fact seems to give the result, that the usual ground of liability in such actions is simply doing certain overt acts; viz., making the false statements complained of, irrespective of intent; and that an actual wish or intent to injure is not taken into consideration, except to rebut privilege; to rebut privilege, again, only signifying, to show that words

ordinarily actionable, apart from intent, were not used under such circumstances of duty or otherwise as would excuse their use.

3. D. 9, 1, 1, pr.; Just. Inst. 4, 9; XII Tab. viii. 6.

4. D. 9, 1, 4.

5. Gaii Inst. iv. 75, 76; D. 9, 4, 2, § 1; *si servus furtum faxit noxiam ve noxit.* XII Tab. xii. 2.

6. Just. Inst. iv. 8, § 7.

7. D. 89, 2, 7, §§ 1, 2.

8. D. 9, 1, 1, § 12.

9. D. 9, 1, 1, § 10; Inst. 4, 9, pr. Compare *May v. Burdett,* 9 Q. B. 101, 113.

10. Which would be the case, for instance, where a man willfully turned his cattle into the grain of another. D. 19, 5, 14 § 8; Plin. Nat. Hist. xviii. 3.

11. *In lege antiqua si servus sciente domino furtum fecit, vel aliam noxiam commisit, servi nomine actio est noxalis, nec dominus suo nomine tenetur.* D. 9, 4, 2.

12. D. 9, 1, 1, § 13.

13. Livy, viii. 39; cf. Zonaras, vii. 26; Niebuhr ed., vol. 43, p. 97. τὴν αἰτίαν τοῦ πολέμου Ῥουτύλῳ ἀνδρὶ δυνατῷ παρ' αὐτοῖς ἐπιγράφοντες · οὐ τὸ ὀστῦ, ἐπεὶ φθύσας ἐκεῖνος διεχειρίσατο ἑαυτόν, διέῤῥιψαν.

14. I. 28 (11).

15. ΚΑΤΑ ΚΤΗΣΙΦ. 244, 245.

16. *Ubi supra.*

17. C. xxxvi. (ed. Merkel). Provisions for the surrender of slaves will be found in the *Pactus pro tenore pacis, Child. et Chloth.* c. 5, the *Decretio Chlotharii,* c. 5, Edict of Hilperic, c. 5, which may be compared with c. 40 of the Salic Law (ed. Merkel) and the observations of Sohm in his treatise on the Procedure of the Salic Law, §§ 20, 27.

18. Thorpe's Ancient Laws, i. pp. 27, 29.

19. C. 24, Thorpe, i. p. 79.

20. Ib. c. 18, Thorpe, i. p. 71.

21. Doct. and Stud. D. 2, c. 51; cf. Bracton, 122; Fleta, i. c. 25, § 9; Britton, 6*b*, 15*b*. Note, as to *motion,* Y. B. 30 & 31 Ed. I. p. 525; 1 Blackst. Comm. 301, and below in this article.

22. Primitive Culture, i. Am. ed. p. 285 *et seq.* Earlier writers have made similar observations. Thus M. Tissot, in his Droit Penal, i. p. 20 (1860), said that there were four epochs to be distinguished in procedure such as we have been describing. The earliest was that in which the *animal, or even the inanimate object, was regarded as endowed with life (animée), and treated seriously as being so.* Later, the animal was only proceeded against symbolically, to impress the popular imagination; then it was abandoned by way of indemnity; finally, protected in the interests of public morals. Tissot, however, from lack of historical perspective, did not sufficiently distinguish between the law of the Twelve Tables and that of Justinian; nor did he seem to recognize the descent of his second and third stages from his first. He did not realize that the earlier institutions were not arbitrarily introduced as a matter of policy, or that the decemvirs were incapable of the comparatively civilized reasoning of Ulpian.

23. Mental and Moral Science, Book 3, c. 8, p. 261.

24. D. 9, 1, 1, § 9. But cf. 1 Hale P. C. 420.

25. Gaius tells us, Inst. iv. § 77, that a noxal action may change to a direct, and, conversely, a direct action to a noxal. If a *paterfamilias* commits a tort, and then is adopted or becomes a slave, a noxal action now lies against his master in place of the direct one against himself as the wrong-doer.

26. D. 9, 4, 2 § 1.

27. D. 9, 1, 1, §§ 4, 5.

28. Gaius iii. § 211; Just. Inst. iv. 3, § 8; cf. XII Tab. viii. 5; Ortolan, Instituts, i. p. 115.

29. D. 9, 8, 1, pr.

30. Gaius, in D. 44, 7, 5, § 6; Just. Inst. 4, 5, § 8.

31. Cf. D. 4, 9, 1, § 1; ib. 7, § 4.

32. C. xii. (ed. Merkel.)

33. Lex Angl. et Wer. xvi.; Karol. M. Capit. Minora, A.D. 803, cap. 5, § 12: "*Nemini liceat servum suum propter damnum a se dimittere; sed juxta qualitatem culpæ dominus ejus pro ipso servo respondeat aut componat,*" &c. Cf. the liability in case of *knowledge*, under the Lex Saxonum, Tit. xi. and Tit. ii § 5. Also Hludowici I. Imp. Constit. ad Theodonis villam A.D. 821, and Hludowici II. Imp. Constit. A.D. 856, cited in Lehuërou, Inst. Caroling. pp. 224, 228.

34. Lex Anglor. et Werin. Tit. xi.; Lex Alamann. Tit. xcix. 22, 23; Lex Saxon. Tit. xiii. (Compare the modified personal liability in case of *accident* from a tree, &c., ib. tit. xii., Leg. Alamann. Tit. xcix. 24, with the laws of Alfred, &c., previously cited.)

35. This will be found expressed in several notes to Kent's Comm. (12th ed.), iii. 138, n. 1; 218, n. 1; 176, n. 1; 188, n. 1; 232, n. 1 (c).

36. Kent (12th ed.), iii. 232, n. 1 (c).

37. Kent (12th ed.), iii. 176, n. 1.

38. Black Book of the Admiralty, iii. 103.

39. 3 Kent, 218.

40. D. 9, 2, 29, § 37.

41. Black Book of Admiralty, i. 242. Declaration of the Commons, Rot. Parl. 51 Ed. III. n. 73; cf. Bracton, 122; 1 Hale, P.C. 423.

42. Kent, iii. 188.

43. Black Book of the Admiralty, ii. Introduction, pp. xliv., xlvii.

44. Black Book, ii. 213. Pardessus, in a note on this passage (Lois Marit. i. 825, n. 8), thinks that the rules requiring the sailors to look to what was saved for their wages was introduced in the middle ages to interest them in the preservation of the ship. The decisions of Trani have nothing on the subject.

45. Black Book, iii. pp. lix., lxxiv.

46. Ib. 263. It should be added, however, that in the same book it is laid down that, if the vessel is detained in port by the local authorities, the master is not bound to give the mariner wages, "for he has earned no freight." Cf. ib. 345.

47. Kent (12th ed.), iii. 218, ib. 138, n. 1.

48. D. 20, 4, 5, & 6.

49. Droit Comm., n. 961.

50. Grotius de J. B. & P. ii. 11, § 13; Emerigon, Contr. à la Grosse, c. iv. sect. 11; Pardessus, Lois Maritimes, iv. 520; Black Book, iii. 245.

51. Livy, Lib. ix., cap. 5, 8, 9, 10; cf. Zonaras, vii. 26, ed. Niebuhr, vol. 43, pp. 98, 99.

52. De Orator. i. 40, and elsewhere. It is to be noticed that Florus, in his account, says *deditione Mancini expiavit*. Epitome, ii. 18; cf. Livy, 9, 1. Both stories seem to suggest that the object of the surrender was expiation as much as they do that it was satisfaction of a contract. Zonaras *sup.* says, Postumius and Calvinus εἰς ἑαυτοὺς τὴν αἰτίαν ἀναδεχομένων, and cf. the passage cited earlier in this article. But cf. Wordsworth's Fragments and Specimens of Early Latin, note to XII Tab. xii. 2, p. 538.

53. Aul. Gell. Noctes Attici, 20, 1; Quintil. Inst. Orat. 3, 6, 84; Tertull. Apol. c. 4.

54. Colquhoun's Roman Civil Law, iii. § 2196.

55. Early Hist. of Inst., Lect. 9, p. 268.

56. 7 Wall. 53.

57. 21 Wall. 558.

The Common Law

The Common Law (Boston: Little, Brown, 1881), chap. 1, pp. 1–5, 34–38.

The object of this book is to present a general view of the Common Law. To accomplish the task, other tools are needed besides logic. It is something to show that the consistency of a system requires a particular result, but it is not all. The life of the law has not been logic: it has been experience. The felt necessities of the time, the prevalent moral and political theories, intuitions of public policy, avowed or unconscious, even the prejudices which judges share with their fellow-men, have had a good deal more to do than the syllogism in determining the rules by which men should be governed. The law embodies the story of a nation's development through many centuries, and it cannot be dealt with as if it contained only the axioms and corollaries of a book of mathematics. In order to know what it is, we must know what it has been, and what it tends to become. We must alternately consult history and existing theories of legislation. But the most difficult labor will be to understand the combination of the two into new products at every stage. The substance of the law at any given time pretty nearly corresponds, so far as it goes, with what is then understood to be convenient; but its form and machinery, and the degree to which it is able to work out desired results, depend very much upon its past.

In Massachusetts today, while, on the one hand, there are a great many rules which are quite sufficiently accounted for by their manifest good sense, on the other, there are some which can only be understood by reference to the infancy of procedure among the German tribes, or to the social condition of Rome under the

Decemvirs.

I shall use the history of our law so far as it is necessary to explain a conception or to interpret a rule, but no further. In doing so there are two errors equally to be avoided both by writer and reader. One is that of supposing, because an idea seems very familiar and natural to us, that it has always been so. Many things which we take for granted have had to be laboriously fought out or thought out in past times. The other mistake is the opposite one of asking too much of history. We start with man full grown. It may be assumed that the earliest barbarian whose practices are to be considered, had a good many of the same feelings and passions as ourselves.

The first subject to be discussed is the general theory of liability civil and criminal. The Common Law has changed a good deal since the beginning of our series of reports, and the search after a theory which may now be said to prevail is very much a study of tendencies. I believe that it will be instructive to go back to the early forms of liability, and to start from them.

It is commonly known that the early forms of legal procedure were grounded in vengeance. Modern writers have thought that the Roman law started from the blood feud, and all the authorities agree that the German law begun in that way. The feud led to the composition, at first optional, then compulsory, by which the feud was bought off. The gradual encroachment of the composition may be traced in the Anglo-Saxon laws,[1] and the feud was pretty well broken up, though not extinguished, by the time of William the Conqueror. The killings and house-burnings of an earlier day became the appeals of mayhem and arson. The appeals *de pace et plagis* and of mayhem became, or rather were in substance, the action of trespass which is still familiar to lawyers.[2] But as the compensation recovered in the appeal was the alternative of vengeance, we might expect to find its scope limited to the scope of vengeance. Vengeance imports a feeling of blame, and an opinion, however distorted by passion, that a wrong has been done. It can hardly go very far beyond the case of a harm intentionally inflicted: even a dog distinguishes between being stumbled over and being kicked.

Whether for this cause or another, the early English appeals for personal violence seem to have been confined to intentional wrongs. Glanvill[3] mentions mêlées, blows, and wounds—all forms of intentional violence. In the fuller description of such appeals given by Bracton[4] it is made quite clear that they were based on intentional assaults. The appeal *de pace et plagis* laid an intentional assault, described the nature of the arms used, and the length and depth of the wound. The appellor also had to show that he immediately raised the hue and cry. So when Bracton speaks of the lesser offences, which were not sued by way of appeal, he instances only intentional wrongs, such as blows with the fist, flogging, wounding, insults, and so forth.[5] The cause of action in the cases of trespass reported in the earlier Year Books and in the Abbreviatio Placitorum is always an intentional wrong. It was only at a later day, and after argument, that trespass was extended so as to embrace harms which were foreseen, but which were not the intended consequence of the defendant's act.[6] Thence again it extended to unforeseen injuries.[7]

It will be seen that this order of development is not quite consistent with an opinion which has been held, that it was a characteristic of early law not to penetrate beyond the external visible fact, the *damnum corpore corpori datum*. It has been thought that an inquiry into the internal condition of the defendant, his culpability or innocence, implies a refinement of juridical conception equally foreign to Rome before the Lex Aquilia, and to England when trespass took its shape. I do not know any very satisfactory evidence that a man was generally held liable either in Rome[8] or England for the accidental consequences even of his own act. But whatever may have been the early law, the foregoing account shows the starting-point of the system with which we have to deal. Our system of private liability for the consequences of a man's own acts, that is, for his trespasses, started from the notion of actual intent and actual personal culpability.

The original principles of liability for harm inflicted by another person or thing have been less carefully considered hitherto than those which governed trespass, and I shall therefore devote the rest of this Lecture to discussing them. I shall try to show that this liability also had its root in the passion of revenge, and to point out the changes by which it reached its present form. But I shall not confine myself strictly to what is needful for that purpose, because it is not only most interesting to trace the transformation throughout its whole extent, but the story will also afford an instructive example of the mode in which the law has grown, without a break, from barbarism to civilization. Furthermore, it will throw much light upon some important and peculiar doctrines which cannot be returned to later.

A very common phenomenon, and one very familiar to the student of history, is this. The customs, beliefs, or needs of a primitive time establish a rule or a formula. In the course of centuries the custom, belief, or necessity disappears, but the rule remains. The reason which gave rise to the rule has been forgotten, and ingenious minds set themselves to inquire how it is to be accounted for. Some ground of policy is thought of, which seems to explain it and to reconcile it with the present state of things; and then the rule adapts itself to the new reasons which have been found for it, and enters on a new career. The old form receives a new content, and in time even the form modifies itself to fit the meaning which it has received. The subject under consideration illustrates this course of events very clearly.

* * *

We have now followed the development of the chief forms of liability in modern law for anything other than the immediate and manifest consequences of a man's own acts. We have seen the parallel course of events in the two parents—the Roman law and the German customs—and in the offspring of those two on English soil with regard to servants, animals, and inanimate things. We have seen a single germ multiplying and branching into products as different from each other as the flower from the root. It hardly remains to ask what that germ was. We have seen that it was the desire of retaliation against the offending thing itself. Undoubtedly, it might be argued that many of the rules stated were derived from a seizure of the offending thing as security for reparation, at first, perhaps, outside the law.[9] That explanation, as well as the one offered here, would show that modern views of responsibility had not yet been attained, as the owner of the thing might very well not have been the person in fault. But such has not been the view of those most competent to judge. A consideration of the earliest instances will show, as might have been expected, that vengeance, not compensation, and vengeance on the offending thing, was the original object. The ox in Exodus was to be stoned. The axe in the Athenian law was to be banished. The tree, in Mr. Tylor's instance, was to be chopped to pieces. The slave under all the systems was to be surrendered to the relatives of the slain man, that they might do with him what they liked.[10] The deodand was an accursed thing. The original limitation of liability to surrender, when the owner was before the court, could not be accounted for if it was his liability, and not that of his property, which was in question. Even where, as in some of the cases, expiation seems to be intended rather than vengeance, the object is equally remote from an extrajudicial distress.

The foregoing history, apart from the purposes for which it has been given, well illustrates the paradox of form and substance in the development of law. In form its growth is logical. The official theory is that each new decision follows syllogistically from existing precedents. But just as the clavicle in the cat only tells of the existence of some earlier creature to which a collar-bone was useful, precedents survive in the law long after the use they once served is at an end and the reason for them has been forgotten. The result of following them must often be failure and confusion from the merely logical point of view.

On the other hand, in substance the growth of the law is legislative. And this in a deeper sense than that what the courts declare to have always been the law is in fact new. It is legislative in its grounds. The very considerations which judges most rarely mention, and always with an apology, are the secret root from which the law draws all the juices of life. I mean, of course, considerations of what is expedient for the community concerned. Every important principle which is developed by litigation is in fact and at bottom the result of more or less definitely understood views of public policy; most generally, to be sure, under our practice and traditions, the unconscious result of instinctive preferences and inarticulate convictions, but none the less traceable to views of public policy in the last analysis. And as the law is administered by able and experienced men, who know too much to sacrifice good sense to a syllogism, it will be found that, when ancient rules maintain themselves in the way that has been and will be shown in this book, new reasons more fitted to the time have been found for them, and that they gradually receive a new content, and at last a new form, from the grounds to which they have been transplanted.

But hitherto this process has been largely unconscious. It is important, on that account, to bring to mind what the actual course of events has been. If it were only to insist on a more conscious recognition of the legislative function of the courts, as just explained, it would be useful, as we shall see more clearly further on.[11]

What has been said will explain the failure of all theories which consider the law only from its formal side; whether they attempt to deduce the *corpus* from *a priori* postulates, or fall into the humbler error of supposing the science of the law to reside in the *elegantia juris*, or logical cohesion of part with part. The truth is, that the law always approaching, and never reaching, consistency. It is forever adopting new principles from life at one end, and it always retains old ones from history at the other, which have not yet been absorbed or sloughed off. It will become entirely consistent only when it ceases to grow.

The study upon which we have been engaged is necessary both for the knowledge and for the revision of the law.

However much we may codify the law into a series of seemingly self-sufficient propositions, those propositions will be but a phase in a continuous growth. To understand their scope fully, to know how they will be dealt with by judges trained in the past which the law embodies, we must ourselves know something of that past. The history of what the law has been is necessary to the knowledge of what the law is.

Again, the process which I have described has involved the attempt to follow precedents, as well as to give a good reason for them. When we find that in large and important branches of the law the various grounds of policy on which the various rules have been justified are later inventions to account for what are in fact survivals from more primitive times, we have a right to reconsider the popular reasons, and, taking a broader view of the field, to decide anew whether those reasons are satisfactory. They may be, notwithstanding the manner of their appearance. If truth were not often suggested by error, if old implements could not be adjusted to new uses, human progress would be slow. But scrutiny and revision are justified.

But none of the foregoing considerations, nor the purpose of showing the materials for anthropology contained in the history of the law, are the immediate object here. My aim and purpose have been to show that the various forms of liability known to modern law spring from the common ground of revenge. In the sphere of contract the fact will hardly be material outside the cases which have been stated in this Lecture. But in the criminal law and the law of torts it is of the first importance. It shows that they have started from a moral basis, from the thought that some one was to blame.

It remains to be proved that, while the terminology of morals is still retained, and while the law does still and always, in a certain sense, measure legal liability by moral standards, it nevertheless, by the very necessity of its nature, is continually transmuting those moral standards into external or objective ones, from which the actual guilt of the party concerned is wholly eliminated.

NOTES

1. E. g. Ine, c. 74; Alfred, c. 42; Ethelred, IV. 4, § 1.

2. Bract., fol. 144, 145; Fleta, I. c. 40, 41; Co. Lit. 126 *b*; Hawkins, P. C, Bk. 2, ch. 23, § 15.

3. Lib. I. c. 2, *ad fin.*

4. Bract., fol. 144 *a*, "*assultu præmeditato.*"

5. Fol. 155; cf. 103 *b*.

6. Y. B. 6 Ed. IV. 7, pl. 18.

7. Ibid., and 21 H. VII. 27, pl. 5.

8. D. 47. 9. 9.

9. Colquhoun, Roman Civil Law, § 2196.

10. Lex Salica (Merkel), LXXVII.; Ed. Hilperich., § 5.

11. See Lecture III., *ad fin*.

Joseph Bangs Warner

Holmes's Common Law

American Law Review 2 (May 1881): 331–338.

Review of Oliver Wendell Holmes Jr., *The Common Law*. Boston: Little Brown, 1881.

The habitual readers of *The American Law Review* can need no introduction to Mr. Holmes. It was through its pages that he first gave to the public those essays on the historical development of the law which were parts of a scheme now accomplished in this book. We have here the entire work, the material already published being used, though worked over, and a still greater amount of new material being added. It is not therefore without some foretaste of its quality that the profession to which such work chiefly appeals receives Mr. Holmes's first completed volume, but any expectations which the published articles might warrant are far more than fulfilled in the book.

It is a book of large proportions, from whichever side approached.

The thing which first strikes the reader, and impresses him to the last, is the author's extraordinary research. Merely to glance at the references in the foot-notes is to look over a track which starts in the dimness of archaic customs, and has traversed some portion, greater or smaller, of Jewish, Greek, Roman, Salic, Anglo-German, Anglo-Norman, mediaeval and modern English law, with by-paths into Greek and Roman classics, Icelandic sagas, German philosophy, and modern legal and historical literature. To appreciate the comprehension of the work one must consider also how small is the material appearing in direct quotation or reference compared with the mass which must be examined and used, positively or negatively, before any conclusion can be ventured.

The book treats, as the previous articles indicate, of the historical development of several of the cardinal principles of the common law, and defines and analyzes some of its leading doctrines. It would be hard to give a layman an adequate notion of the difficulties in the way of tracing the development of a legal doctrine, and probably harder still, if he did realize them, to persuade him of its possibility. Lawyers have become familiar with the business of catching and pinning such a doctrine as it exists today; of picking the elements from a mass of specialized decisions, and working disconnected, discordant, and apparently conflicting rules into a reasonable principle. That it is possible to do it at all in a system of law which lies at the seeming mercy of every judge, is a wonder which familiarity never entirely removes. But how is the complication complicated when the problem is to trace a doctrine back and find the reason which no one has ever given, to detect in the decisions of courts the subconscious influences which turned them this way or that, to show the effect of ancient habits upon judges who never heard of them, to discover the lurking analogies which bridge whole centuries and prolong the life of some unsuspected idea, and thus work back into a dead system of law in the midst of a civilization little more than conjectural!

Mr. Holmes has the genius fit for this legal embryology. He has the historical imagination, which, the power of getting and holding the material being assumed, is the great requisite. With Mr. Holmes, however, it is not a graphic or pictorial imagination. He has allowed himself too little of this. It would be a relief were there more. But he has the eye for the growth of an idea which belongs to an historian of institutions. He undoes the present, turns familiar thoughts wrong side out, puts himself in the midst of the old order of things, and then makes those unexpected and apparently haphazard connections which establish the continuity, and prove, as it were, the intangible apostolic succession. Widely scattered considerations are made to converge, and chance corroboration seems to spring up on every hand.

Now the great danger in such business, and one proportioned to the skill of the writer, is that the theorizer shall become enamored of his theories and account for too much. It is a fascinating employment for ingenuity to be over-ingenious. The historian who hits upon a happy explanation is not always inclined to recognize the multitude of other elements which may have entered into the results he is handling. We confess that in reading Mr. Holmes's articles, as they have appeared in *The America Law Review*, we have sometimes suspected such over refinement. Elaborate historical explanations of ideas which have their sufficient source in the constant traits of human nature are not only superfluous but irritating. It is possible for a keen man to look too deep. When a legal doctrine finds an obvious and sufficient explanation in the straightforward reasons which are given for it, may we not rest content? But, though beginning Mr. Holmes's book with some expectation of finding traces of an over-fine theorizing, we have read it with a growing admiration of his moderation and good sense, and increasing confidence in his judgment. He has suggested more than one theory about which we may feel doubts, and may even end skeptics; but we shall find that Mr. Holmes has himself suggested the most formidable difficulties and has softened nothing. However dexterous the argument and ingenious the interpretation of authorities, we never fool that we are lifted off the ground of common sense. On the contrary, we find ourselves in the hands of one whose sensitiveness to difficulties and objections is of the keenest, and who concludes only with caution.

Mr. Holmes recognizes fully that the course of the common law has been determined by the complications of life, and has always refused to grow in the shapes cut by logic. He has, above all, made ample allowance at every step for the spontaneity of mankind, and admits that common sense and the exigencies of life arc the great controlling agencies, however tenaciously old ideas may cling to the rules of law. One of the most instructive things in the book is the clear way in which it sets out the complicated influences which work the law into shape, and its practical common-sense recognition of the fact that, however conservative and continuous our system has been, it has yet felt at every stage the living power of man interfering to make things as he wants them.

We are not sure, indeed, that Mr. Holmes does not go even further that most lawyers would follow him in his belief in the constant adaptation of law to the needs of the community. "The substance of the law at any given time," he says, "pretty nearly corresponds, so far as it goes, with what is then understood to be convenient." It is true that most of the popular dissatisfaction with the law (which has always been pretty emphatic) is rather with its administration than its substance. The law's delay, its excessive cost, the frequent miscarriages of justice, the uncertain and arbitrary awards of juries—these are the burden of endless complaints and the familiar target of sarcasm. The substance of the law is safer from rough criticism because it is very little understood, but it is always treated as mysterious and unintelligible to a degree which indicates a pretty wide separation between it and the common affairs of life. We think that most lawyers would hardly say that the law can be trusted to meet the changing needs of society with great promptness. Considerations of convenience and policy must in the end prevail, and in new questions get at once a tolerably fair hearing, but it cannot be denied that time dead hand of the old law lies with no light pressure upon the courts.

> "Once git smell'o musk into a draw,
>   An' it clings hold like precedents in law,"

says Hosea Biglow. While there remains this proverbial reluctance to overrule old decisions, and almost the only escape is through the ingenious shifts which patch the new, in gradually increasing pieces, on to the old, we must admit that the law is someway behind the demands of society. Whether this conservatism is not of more value than a greater ease of change could be, is a different question. We are now only considering the statement that the law keeps up, not denying that it may be safer for it to lag.

One timing is probable, which is that the adaptability of the law is decidedly increasing. The legislative function of courts has hitherto been much disguised. Judges trained in the peculiar conservatism of our system, venerating the old law and professing only to discover and apply it, have gone out of their way to conceal even from themselves their work in making new law. Courts have seldom made avowed use of their legislative power, and have kept up a fictitious and unsubstantial deference to precedents when they did use it; advocates have hesitated openly to appeal to it. Such unconsciousness and such pretence are sure to weaken under the matter-of-fact scrutiny of modern thought. The very book we are discussing brings into unaccustomed clearness the legislative office of the courts. Let this become very prominent, and let the traditional conservative temper of the judges be affected by some of the newer fashions of thought, and our system of judge-made law may be severely strained.

Of the particular results of Mr. Holmes's studies in the evolution of the law little can be said here. Each is a *tour de force*, bold, brilliant, impossible until done. Perhaps the most dramatic (though not the most subtle) is that of the first chapter, which is on "Early Forms of Liability." Starting with vengeance as the admitted basis of primitive legal procedure, the author shows that it ran against all offending things—men, slaves, animals, and even, lifeless objects. Objects both animate and inanimate which had been the agents or instruments of violence were surrendered to the injured man or his representatives, to work their will upon, or condemned to solemn public destruction.

That the owner of an offending slave or animal might keep his property by paying money in place of it to the sufferer was a subsequent innovation, and from this descends the modern rules of liability of masters for the acts of their servants, and owners for their animals. This is a bald statement of a course of argument which is enriched with a learned exposition of the authorities in various systems of law, abounds in happy illustration and keen observation. The treatment of the old tendency to personify inanimate things, with its corroboration in familiar traits of human nature, and its survival in the modern admiralty law, which treats the ship as a responsible person, is especially skilful.

One is inclined, however, to ask whether the practice of surrendering and destroying animals, trees, or weapons which had caused death had not primarily a religious significance rather than any relation to purposes of vengeance. This seems the most obvious meaning of many of the instances named, and quite clearly that of the verse in Exodus (xxi. 28), on which considerable stress is laid—"If an ox gore a man or a woman, that they die: then the ox shall be surely stoned, and his flesh shall not be eaten; but the owner of the ox shall be quit." With this verse should be read that which immediately follows it in the original, that it may be seen how far beyond any primitive notion of vengeance the law had grown, and how nearly a clear conception of the modern ground of liability had been gained—"But if the ox were wont to push with his horn in time past, and it hath been testified to his owner, and he hath not kept him in, but that he hath killed a man or a woman; the ox shall be stoned, and his owner also shall be put to death."

Contrasted with the early legal procedure which was directed toward the flagrant crimes of violence is the modern refined notion of legal liability, which Mr. Holmes discusses, with much incidental matter, in the three succeeding chapters. His main conclusion—and one emphasized at every convenient point throughout the book—is that the law has now for almost all purposes, finally fixed upon external standards of conduct as the measure of liability, discarding all, excepting perhaps a conventional reference to actual intent or the state of the defendant's mind. We think this a just conclusion, and one of far more significance than may appear when it is stated as a naked generalization. It is necessary to follow Mr. Holmes's discussion to understand the importance of reaching a clear notion upon this fundamental matter. It goes deeper into the substance of the law, and has more effect upon its practical treatment of actual cases, than can be made apparent in any short compass. If consistently adopted it cuts out some of its most embarrassing and unmanageable features. It brings a unity into that quasi-philosophical region of the law where it is much needed. The principle itself may be considered as but a manifestation of the tendency in modern ethics toward objective grounds, and away from intuitive anti metaphysical theories of morals.

The general rule of liability for negligence being made definite—that conduct must be up to the prudence and caution of an average man—Mr. Holmes claims that the province of the jury can be more and more curtailed. The findings of juries upon specific cases of facts settle the question for such facts. They are or are not within the rule prescribed by law; they are or are not up to standard. As to these facts, therefore, the answer is final, and may be solidified into a rule of law which can be applied by the courts, there being nothing for the jury to settle but the question whether or not the actual facts exist in the case at bar. Thus, as experience increases, the need of a jury for anything but settling upon the special facts gradually shrinks.

If we get the whole force of this argument, we do not think it can carry the law far towards independence of juries. It might accomplish the result for cases where there was an exact repetition of facts, provided there were any provision for noting and fixing the findings of juries, and the habit of doing so. But exact repetitions are too rare to be of any account, and the variation of a single fact opens the whole, and entitles the defendant to have his case judged as new. The application of the standard is not the application of an abstract rule of law. It is the answering of a hypothetical question of fact—"Would a man of average prudence have done so?" In every case, therefore, there is the actual question, "What was done?" and the hypothetical question as just put. Of course, as experience goes forward, some of the grosser forms of negligence or the clearer cases of absence of negligence may get such plain recognition that courts will venture to pass upon them, But upon the whole we do not see why much should be expected in this direction.

But, whatever one may think upon this incidental point, the value of the discussion of the rival theories of liability as given in Mr. Holmes's book remains; and his treatment of it cannot soon be equaled in thoroughness, learning, and acumen.

What has been said should serve to show that this book is by no means solely historical in purpose. A good part of it is devoted entirely to an analysis of the existing principles of the law. The treatment of the doctrines of possession, of the elements of contracts, of void and voidable contracts, and of ownership and covenants in real estate, is extraordinarily acute, learned, and suggestive. We do not know where else there is to be found an extended analysis of the principles of our case law equal to this. Direct analysis is everywhere supplemented with the results of historical research. The study of contract liability shading off, in some of its forms, from liability in tort, and in others touching proprietary rights, is especially fertile in instructive suggestions.

In the chapter on the history of contract we have a theory of consideration which one would almost call audacious, it is so bold a piece of historical conjecture. But if one is inclined to put a slight value upon it because he finds his doubts and objections irrepressible (for it is confessedly something of a hazard), and is tempted to call it useless, let him, after reading it, take up Professor Langdell's chapter which treats of debt and consideration, and read it with Mr. Holmes's theories, illustrations, and suggestions in mind. It is not necessary to say that Professor Langdell is probably the greatest analyst of this particular branch of the law that has ever written. Yet we shall be surprised if the reader does not find a new and unexpected light thrown upon these pages by the historical treatment which Mr. Holmes has given the same topics. The study of the genesis of an idea adds an entirely new interest, and gives an almost inexplicable case of comprehension when the direct analysis of the idea is undertaken. We shall not stop hero to account for the fact, but do insist upon it as a very real advantage, which we appeal to any careful reader to corroborate.

We feel that such work as Mr. Holmes's must meet at the outset a very blunt challenge, and must be prepared to answer the question, Of what use is it all? The book is addressed to a hard-worked body of men, engaged in a very practical though an intellectual employment. It is upon a subject which is, or should always be, treated as, in a high and just sense, practical. We think the question, therefore, by no means a brutal one, and feel sure that Mr. Holmes would be quick to admit its justice.

As for the answer, we feel no hesitation in saying that it is deeply useful and practical.

No one can think much upon the law, or practice it intelligently, without finding that much of his most troublesome perplexity comes from an uneasy doubt about some of its fundamental principles. Not even in the simplest actual case can he be sure that this uncertainty will not rise up and confuse his reasoning, and it always remains an uncomfortable reminder of contradictions and doubts unsettled. Moreover, all practitioners suffer from the demoralizing consequences of using their legal knowledge for special purposes, hurriedly, one-sidedly, incompletely, and with much want of mental candor.

To correct these evils, and all the mischiefs of a narrow and superficial study; to clear one's mind upon the great underlying foundations on which the law is raised; to get even a little of the idea of the development and growth of the conceptions which one handles daily, and to learn to dissect them with skill—surely these are in no overwrought sense practical aims. To these things, as well as to an increase of positive knowledge by an enormous store of valuable learning, Mr. Holmes's book is a great contribution.

We think it but just to say, that in many parts the style could be made easier. The author has adopted the conciseness of the scholar, and has compressed to such a closeness that unpacking is made needlessly difficult. The reasoning in some cases is so very elliptical that it becomes almost obscure. He has sternly refused to let himself go where we feel sure he might go easily and pleasantly and to the great relief of his readers.

We cannot close without expressing again our admiration of a book which is so ingenious and so temperate; so rich in learning, thought, argument, and brilliant intuitions.

Part Three

Varieties of Idealism

Varieties of Idealism

AN INTRODUCTION

James A. Good

AMERICAN IDEALISM HAS A LONG BUT LARGELY NEGLECTED HISTORY. BECAUSE THE purpose of this introduction is historical rather than philosophical, I shall eschew the centuries-long debate about the precise definition of idealism wherein detractors have depicted its proponents as fixated by the realm of pure thought to the neglect of empirical existence. The view common to the American idealists of the late nineteenth century holds that the way we experience the world is never entirely independent of our beliefs and interests. To some degree, in some way, the human mind actively participates in the construction of human experience and what we call knowledge.

Philosophers who sought to develop pluralistic versions of idealism dominated the second phase of the Metaphysical Club. With the participation of Borden Parker Bowne and George Holmes Howison, their meetings may be considered the birthplace of both Boston and California personalism. The specter of American Transcendentalism must have loomed large in their meetings, although only James Elliot Cabot might be viewed as a disciple of that school. Common themes among the participants were a rejection of positivism, materialism, and reductive naturalism, manifesting in a Romantic naturalism bordering on supernaturalism. Highly critical of Herbert Spencer's social Darwinism, each of these thinkers believed that Darwinian biology was consistent with human freedom and spirituality. With Charles Darwin, they rejected the concept of fixed species, and more fundamentally, they rejected substance metaphysics in favor of process metaphysics, emphasizing the reality of particular things not as static atemporal entities but as constellations of temporal relations.

These idealists maintained a foot in the future and one in the past. They sought ways to assert a Darwinian naturalism, viewing individuals as engaged in a struggle against antagonistic forces, without surrendering nineteenth-century spiritual and ethical values. They rejected the fixed forms of pre-Darwinian biology by embracing various types of process metaphysics, and they asserted the value of the individual during the emergence of twentieth-century mass society. They embraced metaphysical and epistemic relativism, while asserting communal conceptions of truth, and values such as universal education. In many ways, the pluralistic idealism that characterized the second phase of the Metaphysical Club was a vital link between the earlier romantic transcendentalism and the emerging movement of scientific pragmatism.

JOHN FISKE

Fiske was born in Hartford, Connecticut, March 30, 1842, the only child of Edmund Brewster Green and Mary Fiske Bound. Fiske displayed astonishing intelligence as a child, graduating from Harvard College in 1863 and from Harvard Law School in 1865. Although he was admitted to the Suffolk bar in 1864, Fiske never practiced law. Even before his graduation from Harvard, Fiske began publishing frequent articles in American and British periodicals. From 1869 to 1871, Fiske lectured at Harvard on philosophy and history, and worked as assistant librarian from 1872 to 1879. He was elected a member of the board of overseers in 1879, and was reelected to that position in 1885. Also in 1879, Fiske began a career as a renowned lecturer on American history, speaking at University College London in 1879, at the Royal Institution of Great Britain in 1880, and Washington University, St. Louis, Missouri, in 1881. In 1884, Fiske accepted a professorship of American history at Washington University, but always maintained his residence in Cambridge, Massachusetts. By the end of his career, Fiske had delivered hundreds of lectures in cities throughout the United States and Great Britain. He died on July 4, 1901, in East Gloucester, Massachusetts.

Fiske is remembered today primarily as a historian. Historians who specialize in the early national period recall Fiske's rather romantic thesis in *The Critical Period of American History, 1783–1789* (1888), declaring that at the Constitutional Convention the Founding Fathers courageously rescued the new nation from the failures of the Articles of Confederation government. His views on science and philosophy are no less provocative. Fiske's study of human progress fueled his interest in evolution and led to publications that popularized the biological theory of Darwin, whom he deeply admired. Influenced by Herbert Spencer's philosophical interpretation of Darwinian biology, Fiske published extensively on that topic. He was a proponent of nineteenth-century studies of brain size as a measure of human intelligence, then championed by many scientists including Darwin's cousin Francis Galton and the French neurologist Paul Broca. Based on these studies, Fiske was convinced of the racial superiority of the "Anglo-Saxon race," despite an unflagging commitment to the abolition of slavery on moral grounds.

In his best-remembered philosophical work, *Outlines of Cosmic Philosophy* (1874), Fiske argued that there is no conflict between religion and science when the two are properly understood. All of reality is in constant change, with organisms struggling to survive through adaptation to a hostile environment. Life is somehow "foreshadowed in simple chemical activity." Mind has emerged as an immaterial process, more complex and efficient than material process. Similarly, human society evolves from the homogeneous family to the heterogeneous nation, again through adaptation to opposing forces. The infinite God and the universe are inscrutable to finite creatures who can only know things as they manifest in consciousness. The Cosmos is the phenomenal world of our experience, "the realm of the knowable," and is also known only in consciousness, rendering all knowledge relative. The relativity of knowledge, however, compels us to postulate the existence of an Absolute Reality that transcends, both spatially and temporally, finite consciousness. We learn about this reality through both science and rational reflection. Fiske's cosmic philosophy aroused considerable debate within the Metaphysical Club.

CHARLES CARROLL EVERETT

Charles Carroll Everett was born in Brunswick, Maine, on June 19, 1829, the son of Ebenezer Everett, a lawyer and the first cousin of the orator and statesman Edward Everett, and Joanna Bachelder Prince Everett. The precocious Everett graduated from Bowdoin College in 1850. After graduation, he studied at the Bowdoin Medical College, but soon turned to a religious vocation. He then traveled to the University of Berlin to study under Hegel's successor, Georg Andreas Gabler, during 1851–52. From 1853 to 1857 Everett taught modern languages at Bowdoin, but was denied tenure because he was a Unitarian. Undaunted by this setback, he then entered Harvard Divinity School and graduated in 1859. Everett was called to the pulpit of the Independent Congregational (Unitarian) Church in Bangor, Maine, where he served for ten years. In 1869, he published his first book, *The Science of Thought: A System of Logic,* a treatise on the principles of human thought. That book attracted the attention of Harvard University, which promptly appointed him as the first Bussey Professor of Theology.

The faculty of Harvard Divinity School had been engaged in bruising battles against the transcendentalist controversy prior to the Civil War and, after the war, another battle over Darwinian biology. Within a few years after the Civil War, however, new professors replaced the entire faculty and were able to redirect the course of the school. Many believed that the appointment of Everett, which occurred the same year that Charles Eliot took over the presidency of Harvard University and began to modernize the institution, rescued the beleaguered Divinity School from its doldrums.[1] When he became dean of the Divinity School in 1878, Everett set down a broad philosophical plan to define the school's purpose and curriculum. His two regular courses in theology were "The Psychological Elements of Religious Faith" and "Theism and the Christian Faith." Everett participated in the philosophy clubs in the 1870s, demonstrating his links with the Harvard philosophers, and the catalogue listed his courses with those in philosophy.

Everett's major works testify to the broad range of his interests: *Religions before Christianity* (1883), *Fichte's Science of Knowledge* (1884), *Essays on Poetry, Comedy, and Duty* (1888), *Ethics for Young People* (1891), and *The Gospel of Paul* (1893). A collection of his writings, *Essays, Theological and Literary,* was published (1901) after his death.

Everett's type of idealism was a significant concession to transcendentalism's doctrine of intuitive knowledge and its spiritualization of nature. Moreover, his metaphysics made room for evolution, as long as it was interpreted teleologically. Many scholars claim that Everett "was an exponent of Fichtean and Hegelian idealism," but beyond the fact that he published a study of Fichte's epistemology in the Griggs Philosophical Classics series, there is little evidence of Fichtean influence on Everett's thought. Everett concluded *Fichte's Science of Knowledge* with a Hegelian critique of Fichte. He argued that Fichte could not bridge the gap between the finite and the infinite, the individual and the absolute, because his conception of reality was mechanistic. Everett claimed that Hegel's organicism, according to which the finite is an integral component of the infinite, held the key to the irresolvable dichotomy at the heart of Fichte's philosophy. "Hegel, by identifying thought and being, broke down the barrier that repressed the speculation of Fichte, and life took the place of mechanism."[2] Hegel's organic conception of reality was at the core of Everett's *Science of Thought*.

Everett's philosophical work, including the *Science of Thought*, had one overriding purpose, which was to establish scientifically the truths of religion. Everett did not, however, use the term *scientific* in the sense that arose during the late nineteenth century and dominated the twentieth. Everett's science of thought, for example, was not based upon laboratory experimentation; the development of a science of thought was a matter of systematizing the truths of logic under general principles. His study of world religions was also an effort to formulate scientifically the general principles of all religion. This does not mean that Everett was opposed to empirical observation. On the contrary, for Everett, the primary shortcoming of previous logic was that it ignored the way thought actually functioned within the world. His idealism was certainly indebted to Hegel and Gabler, but he made room for religious faith to a degree that would have troubled Hegel.

JAMES ELLIOT CABOT

Cabot, a Boston native, was born on June 18, 1821. He graduated from Harvard College at age nineteen, and spent the next three years in Europe. At the University of Berlin, Cabot heard F. W. J. Schelling lecture on what became his "Essay on Freedom." While traveling, Cabot also began reading the American Transcendentalist periodical *The Dial,* with a particular interest in Ralph Waldo Emerson's recently published *Essays* (1841). Cabot anonymously submitted a brief essay on "Immanuel Kant," which appeared in the last issue of *The Dial* (April 1844). Cabot met Emerson the following year, and the two remained close friends for the next thirty years. Indeed, Cabot assumed the duties of editorial assistant to Emerson in 1875.

Upon Emerson's death in 1882, Cabot was named Emerson's literary executor and official biographer, organizing Emerson's writings into twelve volumes titled the *Collected Work of Ralph Waldo Emerson.* Cabot's *A Memoir of Ralph Waldo Emerson* (1887) appeared as the thirteenth and fourteenth volumes of that set. Cabot's lengthy memoir is his best-known literary achievement. Cabot relied heavily on firsthand documentary sources to fashion a narrative of Emerson's life with little interpretation. The memoir provided scholars access to numerous unpublished essays, letters, and journal entries that are now more widely available in anthologies. For many decades, the memoir stood as an impartial chronology of biographical information supplemented and corroborated with extensive primary source material.

Cabot was a founder of *The Atlantic Monthly*, he collaborated with Theodore Parker as editor of *The Massachusetts Quarterly Review*, and he assisted Louis Agassiz, the acclaimed Harvard naturalist, in composing the results of his exploration of Lake Superior. He died on January 16, 1903, in Brookline, Massachusetts.

THOMAS DAVIDSON

Thomas Davidson was born on October 25, 1840, near Aberdeen, Scotland. He won a scholarship to King's College at the University of Aberdeen. After graduating with honors in 1860, he taught Latin and Greek for six years in Scotland and England. Emigrating to America, he first studied with New England transcendentalists in Boston in 1867, and then joined the St. Louis Hegelians from 1868 to 1875, before returning to Boston.

In addition to fellow philosophers William James and John Dewey,[3] Davidson had a profound influence on people as diverse as Joseph Pulitzer and Princess Carolyn of Sayn-Wittgenstein, mistress of Franz Liszt. He was a particularly close personal friend of two of the authors in the present volume, George Holmes Howison and William Torrey Harris, with whom he studied in St. Louis. In the late 1880s Davidson lectured at Bronson Alcott's Concord Summer School of philosophy. Given Davidson's ability to organize intellectuals into clubs and discussion groups, it is no surprise that he revived the Metaphysical Club in the mid-1870s. In 1883 he went on to found "The Fellowship of the New Life" in London, which he renounced when members such as Edward Carpenter, Havelock Ellis, Ramsay McDonald, and George Bernard Shaw transformed it into the more politically oriented Fabian Society. Davidson was always focused on the spiritual growth of individuals rather than political solutions to social problems and especially suspicious of any solution tainted by socialism. After extensive travels and studies throughout Europe from 1877 to 1888, Davidson founded his own school of philosophical and literary studies, first at Farmington, Connecticut, but finally established "The Glenmore Summer School for the Culture Sciences" on Mt. Hurricane near Keene, New York, which operated from 1890 to 1900.

Davidson envisioned Glenmore as an educational experiment in the whole person in intellect, affections, and will. He described the culture sciences as the study of "man's spiritual nature." His description of the school itemizes two main themes: "(1) scientific, (2) practical. The former it will seek to reach by means of lectures on the general outlines of the history and theory of various culture sciences. . . . The latter it will endeavor to realize by encouraging its members to conduct their lives in accordance with the highest ascertainable ethical laws . . . to discipline themselves in simplicity, kindness, thoughtfulness, regularity, and promptness."[4] In addition to the literary topics that had become the focus of the Concord Summer School, the programs at Glenmore focused on formal philosophy (for example, an 1890 class centered on the philosophy of T. H. Green) and wide-ranging social and political problems such as church-state relations. Glenmore attracted a diverse and distinguished group of intellectuals. Among others, William James, John Dewey, Josiah Royce, Hugo Münsterberg, and William T. Harris gave lectures. As late as 1904, four years after Davidson's death, James delivered five lectures at Glenmore that were later published as his *Essays in Radical Empiricism.*

Davidson labeled his mature philosophy "apeirotheism," a theory of gods infinite in number. Charles Bakewell accurately described apeirotheism as a "form of pluralistic idealism . . . coupled with a stern ethical rigorism."[5] Davidson's theory was heavily indebted to the pluralism of Aristotle and Leibniz. Aristotle's "soul" is the rational, living aspect of a living substance and cannot exist apart from the body because it is not a substance, but rather an essence; Nous is rational thought and understanding. Davidson argued that Aristotle's Nous identified God with rational thought, and that God could not exist apart from the world just as the Aristotelean soul could not exist apart from the body, thereby grounding an immanent Emersonian World Soul in a sophisticated Aristotelian metaphysics. Davidson's apeirotheism can also be described as a panpsychistic monadology, a theory that reality consists of an infinite number of mental or spiritual substances, each with an Aristotelian telos. Human psyches are unique however, because they possess autonomy, which provides the potential to become divine through proper moral association with other human psyches. Davidson rejected pantheism because God is left "scattered through the universe . . . so that the total Absolute exists only in the sum of things taken together."[6] Rather, Davidson argued, God exists everywhere, as well as fully in each monad. Reality is a *Göttergemeinschaft,* a society of gods; metaphysical, social, and spiritual unity is moral rather than ontological.

Apeirotheism was utterly democratic and perfectionistic because it entailed that each individual has the potential to be a God, although restrictive social relations have thwarted the development of most people's potential. For Davidson, because we contain the divine within us, our unfettered natural instincts would impel us to act morally. As individuals became increasingly aware of the divine within themselves, so they became increasingly moral. William James believed that this individualistic religion made Davidson "indifferent . . . to socialisms and general administrative panaceas." According to James, Davidson taught that "[l]ife must be flexible. You ask for a free man and these Utopias give you an interchangeable part, with a fixed number, in a rule-bound social organism."[7] Apeirotheism called for the release of each individual's potential divinity through self-cultivation and the nurturing of others rather than through changes in one's material conditions. Davidson was convinced that this release would lead to the only true reform of human society.

During the last ten years of his life, Davidson spent his winters in the Lower East Side of New York City. He continued to give public lectures, and he founded the Breadwinners' College to enlarge educational opportunities for the working class. His publications shifted away from abstract philosophical issues to the history of education, ethics, and issues of social justice. Although Davidson would have denied it, his writings on education were, in essence, Hegelian histories of the self-development of *Geist*, which is humanity. Davidson considered the Breadwinner's College to be his greatest achievement, but his efforts were cut short by his death in 1900.

BORDEN PARKER BOWNE

Born in Atlantic Highlands, New Jersey, on January 14, 1847, Bowne was a product of his Christian upbringing. His father, Joseph Bowne, was a Methodist minister, justice of the peace, and a farmer. His mother, Margaret Parker, was descended from Quakers, and his parents retained their commitments to a personal relationship with God and to simplicity. Staunch abolitionists, both parents bequeathed to their son a strong belief in the dignity of all persons and demonstrated the courage to assert their convictions.

Bowne graduated as valedictorian from the University of the City of New York in 1871s and promptly joined the New York East Conference of the Methodist church. He was ordained as a Methodist deacon in 1872 and assigned to the Methodist Episcopal church at Whitestone, Long Island. Within a year he seized an opportunity to pursue advanced theological and philosophical studies in Paris, Halle, and Göttingen (1873–75), where he published his first book, *The Philosophy of Herbert Spencer* (1874). Soon after his return to the States, Bowne accepted a position as assistant editor of the *The Independent* while completing a Master of Arts degree at New York University. Refusing offers from Yale University and the newly founded University of Chicago, Bowne accepted a call from the Boston University philosophy department in 1877. From 1888 until his death in 1910, Bowne served as the first Dean of the Graduate School at Boston University. Throughout his long career, Bowne was a prodigious scholar, publishing seventeen books and 132 scholarly articles. He died in Boston on April 1, 1910.

Bowne referred to his philosophical system as a Kantianized Berkelianism, then as transcendental empiricism, and finally as personalism. While participating in the Metaphysical Club, Bowne held to a blend of Kantian transcendental idealism, including the categories of understanding, and George Berkeley's theistic idealism. He held that human experience transcended the senses and adamantly defended human freedom against determinism on the grounds that freedom was a necessary condition for knowledge.

There can be little doubt that other members of the Metaphysical Club—particularly Davidson, Howison, and James—contributed to the development of Bowne's pluralistic personalism, which emerged full blown many years later in *Personalism* (1908). Prior to that work, Bowne had already defended an early version of process metaphysics in *Metaphysics* (1882). Similar to Alfred North Whitehead's conception of God, Bowne's God was neither substance nor the ground of being, but the personal ground of the process of reality. The idea of the person was the central principle from which we could derive usable metaphysical descriptions and understand our place within reality. Reality must somehow be compatible, he averred, with our personal mode of existence. Bowne never deviated from this religious viewpoint, focusing much of his writing on the moral implications of his metaphysical commitments. In *The Philosophy of Theism* (1887), Bowne defended the personhood of God. Under the influence of the higher criticism of the Bible, however, he rejected the doctrine of scriptural infallibility.

FRANCIS ELLINGWOOD ABBOT

Abbot was born in Boston, Massachusetts, to Unitarian parents on November 6, 1836. He graduated first in his class from Harvard University in 1859 and then graduated from Meadville Theological School in 1863. Although Abbot served Unitarian churches in Dover, New Hampshire, and Toledo, Ohio, his criticisms of Christianity made him increasingly controversial. In 1868 the highest court of New Hampshire ruled that he was insufficiently Christian to serve his congregation.[8] Abbot's troubles arose from his espousal of Free Thinking, according to which liberal Christians should enjoy complete intellectual freedom and should not be required to base their religious views on the authority of Christ.

Abbot published three articles that made him the first American philosopher to endorse Darwin's theory of evolution. "The Philosophy of Space and Time" and "The Conditioned and the Unconditioned" both appeared in the *North American Review* in 1864, and "Theism and Christianity" appeared in *The Christian Examiner* in 1865. In these articles, he praised the concepts of natural law and evolutionary adaptation as the foundations of all truth and as proofs of the unity of all existence. The so-called truths of philosophy and theology, according to Abbot, must conform to natural science.

While in Toledo, Abbot founded the *Index* in 1870, a weekly periodical that promoted the radical religious and social philosophy of his Free Religious Association. Convinced that Christian superstition and dogmatism had enslaved American thought, Abbot moved the *Index* to Boston in 1873 where he called for the organization of Liberal Leagues across the nation dedicated to the separation of church and state. In 1876, these organizations met in Philadelphia where they formed the National Liberal League with Abbot as its permanent president. In 1880 Abbot embarked on doctoral studies in philosophy at Harvard University, receiving a PhD the following year. Failing to obtain an academic appointment, he taught at a local academy in Cambridge from 1881 to 1892.

Abbot's theological views were most fully developed after his participation in the Metaphysical Club, in his books *Scientific Theism* (1885) and *The Way Out of Agnosticism* (1890). Much like Davidson, he argued that universal education would elevate the unity and fellowship of all humankind. Society had a duty to develop every individual through moral education, and every individual had a duty to promote morality. In his metaphysical reflections, Abbot argued for the objective reality of the relations between objects. He argued that the scientific method provides the tools to obtain all knowledge in a view he called scientific realism. He described the universe as a natural process of self-evolution in time and space, or as the creative life of God. After completing his two-volume *The Syllogistic Philosophy*, he died on October 23, 1903, in Beverly, Massachusetts.

GEORGE HOLMES HOWISON

Howison, one of Davidson's dearest friends, was born in Maryland on November 29, 1834, and grew up in Ohio. He graduated from Marietta College in 1852 and Lane Theological Seminary in Cincinnati in 1855. He opted to pursue a teaching career rather than preach from a pulpit. After serving as an itinerant high school teacher in Ohio for four years, Howison relocated to Salem, Massachusetts, where he married another schoolteacher, Lois Thompson Caswell, in 1863. The newlyweds moved to St. Louis in 1864, where Howison accepted a position as professor of mathematics at Washington University, ultimately teaching both political economy and Latin as well. Howison became an active member of the St. Louis Philosophical Society. Harris and Brokmeyer nurtured a nascent interest in the writings of Kant and Hegel, which provided the underpinning of Howison's own form of personalistic idealism. When Emerson and Alcott lectured in St. Louis, Howison was also influenced by their versions of American Transcendentalism.

Although he was only in St. Louis for seven years, Howison earned a reputation as a dynamic lecturer and completed his first book, *A Treatise on Analytic Geometry*, in 1869. In 1871, he moved to Boston to be closer to the center of intellectual activity, where he was fortunate to receive an appointment at Massachusetts Institute of Technology as professor of logic and philosophy of science. Howison's professional success seemed assured as he enjoyed participating both in the Harvard Philosophical Club and the Metaphysical Club. When his position at MIT was abruptly eliminated in 1878 due to financial exigency, Howison spent 1879 through 1884 in a variety of pursuits, including a one-year appointment at Harvard Divinity School and one year at the University of Michigan; studying in Europe with Rudolf Lotze, Jules Michelet, and Friedrich Paulsen; lecturing at the Concord School of Philosophy; and a year of private tutoring in Boston. In 1885 he accepted the Mills Chair of Mental and Moral Philosophy and Civil Polity at the University of California, Berkeley. Howison died there on December 31, 1916.

At Berkeley, Howison experienced the greatest success of his long career in higher education. In addition to continuing success in the classroom, Howison built the philosophy department, served on the editorial boards of *Psychological Review, Kantstudien*, and the *Hibbert Journal*. He also established the Philosophical Union, which, in the spirit of the St. Louis Philosophical Society, drew intellectuals from the broader San Francisco community into philosophical study. The Union focused on a philosophical topic for a year, ending each year with lectures from a celebrated philosopher and the publication of the years' work. Josiah Royce spoke on the conception of God in 1896. William James introduced pragmatism in a lecture in 1898, and the following year Dewey spoke on "Psychology and Philosophic Method."

While publishing many essays and reviews, Howison worked on his single important philosophical book, *The Limits of Evolution and Other Essays*, which appeared in 1901. Much like Davidson, he developed a pluralistic, personal idealism. Howison was dubious of Hegel's ability to account for the reality and agency of the individual, and thus drew on

Aristotle and Leibniz to develop his own version of personal idealism. Similar to Bowne, in Howison's personal idealism what is real is dependent on the community of minds in the universe. The primary problem with pantheism, according to Howison, is that it contradicts freedom and immortality by absorbing the individual into God. Without freedom, the ability to choose right from wrong, man has no moral responsibility; without immortality, he has no hope, nothing to strive for. Howison embraced pluralism—the reality, freedom, and immortality of the individual—because he believed monistic theories such as pantheism deny the dignity of man.

In "Is Modern Science Pantheistic?" Howison's central concern was that the scientific theories of biological evolution and the conservation of energy might be taken by uncritical minds to imply pantheism. Evolution teaches that those species that are best fitted to the whole tend to survive; it is the whole environment that selects species for survival. The conservation of energy seems to reduce the multiplicity of particulars to cosmic motion that is ultimately unchanging and eternal. One might conclude that both theories, particularly when taken in conjunction, subordinate the reality of the individual to the whole. But Howison concluded that concern about the pantheistic implications of these theories is unwarranted. Since science must be based on empirical observation of particular events, a general theory such as pantheism is inherently beyond its ken. Where it comes to matters of theology, Howison avowed, science must be agnostic.

NOTES

1. Consult George Williams Huntston, ed., *The Harvard Divinity School: Its Place in Harvard University and in American Culture* (Boston: Beacon Press, 1954).

2. Charles Carroll Everett, *Fichte's Science of Knowledge: A Critical Exposition* (Chicago: S. C. Griggs, 1884), 285.

3. Michael DeArmey, "Thomas Davidson's Apeirotheism and Its Influence on William James and John Dewey," *Journal of the History of Ideas* 48 (Oct.–Dec. 1987): 691–708. James A. Good, "The Value of Thomas Davidson," *Transactions of the Charles S. Peirce Society* 40, no. 2 (Spring 2004), 289–318.

4. Quoted in William Knight, ed., *Memorials of Thomas Davidson: The Wandering Scholar* (Boston: Ginn, 1907), 60.

5. Charles M. Bakewell, "Thomas Davidson," in *Dictionary of American Biography*, ed. Dumas Malone (New York: Charles Scribner's Sons, 1932), 96.

6. Davidson, "Noism," *The Index* (April 29, 1886): 522–25, at 525.

7. James, "Professor William James's Reminiscences," in *Memorials of Thomas Davidson*, 115.

8. *Hale v. Everett*, 53 N.H. 9 (1868).

John Fiske

Cosmic Theism

Outlines of Cosmic Philosophy (Boston: Houghton Mifflin, 1874), vol. 2, pp. 411–431.

The conclusions reached in the foregoing chapter were purely negative, and would therefore be very unsatisfactory if we were obliged to rest in them as final. Upon the religious side of philosophy as well as upon its scientific side, the mind needs some fundamental theorem with reference to which it may occupy a positive attitude. According to the theory of life and intelligence expounded in previous chapters, mere skepticism can discharge but a provisional and temporary function. To the frivolously-minded the mere negation of belief may be in no wise distressing; but to the earnest inquirer the state of skepticism is accompanied by pain, which, here as elsewhere, is only subserving its proper function when it stimulates him to renewed search after a positive result. In the present transcendental inquiry it may indeed at first sight seem impossible to arrive at any positive result whatever, without ignoring the relativity of knowledge and proving recreant to the rigorous requirements of the objective method. Nevertheless, as was hinted at the close of the preceding chapter, this is not the case. Although the construction of a theology, or science of Deity, is a task which exceeds the powers of human intelligence, there is nevertheless one supremely important theorem in which science and religion find their permanent reconciliation, and by the assertion of which the mind is brought into a positive attitude of faith with reference to the Inscrutable Power manifested in the universe. The outcome of the present argument is not Atheism or Positivism, but a phase of Theism which is higher and purer, because relatively truer, than the anthropomorphic phase defended by theologians.

This all-important theorem in which science and religion are reconciled, is neither more nor less than the theorem which alone gives complete expression to the truth that all knowledge is relative. In the first chapter of this work it was elaborately proved that as soon as we attempt to frame any hypothesis whatever concerning the Absolute, or that which exists out of relation to our consciousness, we are instantly checkmated by alternative impossibilities of thought, and when we seek to learn why this is so, we are taught by a psychologic analysis that, from the very organization of our minds, and by reason of the very process by which intelligence has been evolved, we can form no cognition into which there do not enter the elements of likeness, difference, and relation—so that the Absolute, as presenting none of these elements, is utterly and for ever unknowable. Translating this conclusion into more familiar language, we found it to mean, *first*, "that the Deity, in so far as absolute and infinite, is inscrutable by us, and that every hypothesis of ours concerning its nature and attributes can serve only to illustrate our mental impotence,"—and, *secondly*, "that the Universe in itself is likewise inscrutable; that the vast synthesis of forces without us, which in manifold contact with us is from infancy till the close of life continually arousing us to perceptive activity, can never be known by us as it exists objectively, but only as it affects our consciousness."[1]

These are the closely-allied conclusions which were reached in our opening discussion. But since such abstruse theorems need to be taken one by one into the mind, and allowed one after the other to dwell there for a while, in order to be duly comprehended, it did not then seem desirable to encumber the exposition with any reference to the third statement in which these two are made to unite; nor, indeed, would it have been possible to illustrate adequately this third statement until we had defined our position in relation to the questions of phenomenality, of causation and deanthropomorphization, of the persistence of force, and of the evolution of the phenomenal world. But now, having obtained definite conclusions upon these points, we are at last enabled to present the case as a whole. Having seen that in certain senses the Deity and the Cosmos are alike inscrutable, let us now see if there is any sense in which it may be legitimately said that the Unknowable contained in our first theorem is identical with the Unknowable contained in our second theorem.

Upon what grounds did we assert the unknowableness of Deity? We were driven to the conclusion that Deity is unknowable, because that which exists independently of intelligence and out of relation to it, which presents neither *likeness*, *difference*, nor *relation*, cannot be cognized. Now by precisely the same process, we were driven to the conclusion that the Cosmos is unknowable, only in so far as it is absolute. It is only as existing independently of our intelligence and out of relation to it, that we can predicate unknowableness of the Cosmos. As manifested to our intelligence, the Cosmos is the world of phenomena—the realm of the knowable. We know stars and planets, we know the surface of our earth, we know life and mind in their various manifestations, individual and social. But, as we have seen, this vast aggregate of phenomena exists as such only in relation to our intelligence. Its *esse* is *percipi*. To this extent we have gone with Berkeley. But underlying this aggregate of phenomena, to whose extension we know no limit in space or time, we have found ourselves compelled to postulate an Absolute Reality—a Something whose existence does not depend on the presence of a percipient mind, which existed before the genesis of intelligence, and would continue to exist though all intelligence were to vanish from the scene. Without making such a postulate, we concluded that it would be impossible to frame any theory whatever, either of subjective or of objective phenomena. Thus the theorem of the relativity of knowledge, when fully expressed, asserts that there exists a Something, of which all phenomena, as presented in consciousness, are manifestations, but concerning which we can know nothing save through its manifestations.

Let us now take a step further, and turning to the conclusions reached in the first chapter of Part II., let us inquire *what is the Force of which we there asserted the persistence?* "It is not," says Mr. Spencer, "the force we are immediately conscious of in our own muscular efforts; for this does not persist. As soon as an outstretched limb is relaxed, the sense of tension disappears. True, we assert that in the stone thrown or in the weight lifted, is exhibited the effect of this muscular tension; and that the force which has ceased to be present in our consciousness, exists elsewhere. But it does not exist elsewhere under any form cognizable by us. It was proved that though, on raising an object from the ground, we are obliged to think of its downward pull as equal and opposite to our upward pull; and though it is impossible to represent these pulls as equal without representing them as like in kind; yet, since their likeness in kind would imply in the object a sensation of muscular tension, which cannot be ascribed to it, we are compelled to admit that force as it exists out of our consciousness, is not force as we know it. Hence the force of which we assert persistence is that Absolute Force of which we are indefinitely conscious as the necessary correlate of the force we know. Thus by the persistence of force, we really mean the persistence of some Power which transcends our knowledge and conception. The manifestations, as occurring either in ourselves or outside of us, do not persist; but that which persists is the Unknown Cause of these manifestations. In other words, asserting the persistence of force is but another mode of asserting an Unconditioned Reality, without beginning or end." Thus as "a subjective analysis proved that while, by the very conditions of thought, we are prevented from knowing anything beyond relative being; yet that, by these very same conditions of thought, an indefinite consciousness of Absolute Being is necessitated—so here, by objective analysis, we similarly find that the axiomatic truths of physical science unavoidably postulate Absolute Being as their common basis."[2]

Combining, therefore, these mutually harmonious results, and stating the theorem of the persistence of force in terms of the theorem of the relativity of knowledge, we obtain the following formula—*There exists a* POWER, *to which no limit in time or space is conceivable, of which all phenomena, as presented in consciousness, are manifestations, but which we can know only through these manifestations.* Here is a formula legitimately obtained by the employment of scientific methods, as the last result of a subjective analysis on the one hand, and of an objective analysis on the other hand. Yet this formula, which presents itself as the final outcome of a purely scientific inquiry, expresses also the fundamental truth of Theism— the truth by which religious feeling is justified. The existence of God—the supreme truth asserted alike by Christianity and by inferior historic religions—is asserted with equal emphasis by that Cosmic Philosophy which seeks its data in science alone. Thus, as Mr. Lewes long ago observed, the remark of Comte, that the heavens declare no other glory than the glory of Hipparchos and Newton, and such others as have aided in detecting the order of sequence among celestial phenomena, seems as irrational to the scientific inquirer as it seems impious to the religious mind. The Cosmist may assert, as consistently as the

Anthropomorphist, that "the undevout astronomer is mad." Though science must destroy mythology, it can never destroy religion; and to the astronomer of the future, as well as to the Psalmist of old, the heavens will declare the glory of God.

Before proceeding further to expound this theorem, in which science and religion find their reconciliation, it is desirable to turn aside for a moment and contrast the views here expounded with the views maintained by Comte concerning the true object of the religious feeling. We shall thus the better elucidate our own position, while once more pointing out the world-wide difference between our philosophy and Positivism. Let us examine the conception of Deity formed by the thinker to whom the heavens manifested no other glory than that of Hipparchos and Newton and their compeers.

Comte recognized, though vaguely, the truth that while the human race in the course of its philosophic evolution must outgrow theology, it can never outgrow religion. He justly maintained that, while the conception of a presiding quasi-human Will must eventually be discarded as an inadequate subjective symbol, there will nevertheless remain to the last the powerful sentiment of devotion which has hitherto attached itself to that anthropomorphic conception, but must finally attach itself to some other conception. Throughout future time, while science is supreme, no less than in that past time when mythology was supreme, there must be a religion, and this religion must have an object. So far the position taken by Comte appears to be defensible enough. But now when we come to consider the object of the religious sentiment in Comte's scheme, we must pronounce his position not only irreconcilable with sound philosophy, but hopelessly retrograde as compared even with the current anthropomorphism. Seeing only the negative side of the theorem of relativity, and thus failing explicitly to recognize the existence of that Absolute Power of which the web of phenomena is but the visible garment, he was obliged to search for his Deity in the realm of the finite and the knowable. Working under these conditions, the result at which he finally arrived appears to have been legitimately evolved from the conception of the aims and scope of philosophy which he had framed in early life, at the very outset of his speculations. The thinker who from the beginning consistently occupied the anthropocentric point of view, who regarded philosophy, not as a unified theory of the Cosmos, but as a unified theory of Man, who depreciated the development theory and the study of sidereal astronomy as interfering with his anthropocentric notions, and to whom the starry heavens declared no glory save that of finite men, arrived ultimately at the deification of Humanity. Comte "refers the obligations of duty, as well as all sentiments of devotion, to a concrete object, at once ideal and real; the Human Race, conceived as a continuous whole, including the past, the present, and the future." "It may not be consonant to usage," observes Mr. Mill, "to call this a religion; but the term, so applied, has a meaning, and one which is not adequately expressed by any other word. Candid persons of all creeds may be willing to admit, that if a person has an ideal object, his attachment and sense of duty towards which are able to control and discipline all his other sentiments and propensities, and prescribe to him a rule of life, that person has a religion. . . . Many indeed may be unable to believe that this object is capable of gathering around it feelings sufficiently strong: but this is exactly the point on which a doubt can hardly remain in an intelligent reader of Comte; and we join with him in contemning, as equally irrational and mean, the conception of human nature as incapable of giving its love and devoting its existence to any object which cannot afford in exchange an eternity of personal enjoyment."[3] With the general tenor of this passage I heartily agree. I have no sympathy with those critics who maintain that the idea of Humanity is an unworthy idea, incapable of calling forth to a high degree our sentiments of devotion and reverence. No doubt, as the Comtists tell us, the majestic grandeur of which that idea is susceptible can be realized only after long and profound contemplation. And we may perhaps admit, with Mr. Mill, that "ascending into the unknown recesses of the past, embracing the manifold present, and descending into the indefinite and unforeseeable future, forming a collective Existence without assignable beginning or end, it appeals to that feeling of the Infinite which is deeply rooted in human nature." We may still further admit that all morality may be summed up in the disinterested service of the human race—such being, as already shown (Part II. chap. xxii.), the fundamental principle of the ethical philosophy which is based on the Doctrine of Evolution. And it is, moreover, easy to sympathize with the feeling which led Comte formally to consecrate the memories of the illustrious dead, whose labors have made us what we are; that "communion of saints, unseen yet not unreal," as Carlyle nobly expresses it, "whose heroic sufferings rise up melodiously together unto Heaven, out of all times and out of all lands, as a sacred *Miserere*; their heroic actions also, as a boundless everlasting Psalm of triumph." This intense feeling of the community of the human race, this "enthusiasm of Humanity," as the author of "Ecce Homo" calls it, forms a very considerable part of Christianity when stripped of its mythology, and is one of the characteristics which chiefly serve to difference the world-religion of Jesus and Paul from the ethnic religious of antiquity.

Nevertheless, after freely acknowledging all these points of excellence in the Comtean conception, it must still be maintained that Comte's assignment of Humanity as the direct object of religious worship was a retrograde step, when viewed in contrast, not only with the cosmic conception of Deity already clearly foreshadowed by Goethe, but even with the anthropomorphic conception as held by contemporary liberal theologians. A fatal criticism—omitted, and apparently overlooked by Mr. Mill, in his account of the Comtean religion—remains to be made upon it. I do not refer to the difficulty of ascribing godhood to a product of evolution, neither is it necessary to insist upon the marvelous shading-off of collective apehood into Deity which must puzzle the Comtist who stops to confront his theory with the conclusions now virtually established concerning man's origin; though beneath the cavil and sarcasm which cannot be kept from showing itself upon the surface of such objections, there lies just scientific ground of complaint against the Comtean hypothesis. The criticism to which I refer is one the force of which must be acknowledged even by those who have not yet learned to estimate the resistless weight of the evidence by which the development theory is supported. However grand Humanity may be as an object of contemplation, it is still finite, concrete, and knowable. It has had a beginning; in all probability it is destined to have an end. We can no longer, since the Copernican revolution, regard it as the chief and central phenomenon of the universe. We know it but as a local assemblage of concrete phenomena, manifested on the surface of a planet that is itself a lesser member of a single group among innumerable groups of worlds. It is no less significant than amusing that toward the last Comte would fain have banished from astronomy not only the study of the stars, but even the study of those planets in our own system which do not considerably perturb the motions of the earth. He wished to exclude from science everything which does not conspicuously affect human interests, and everything which by its magnitude dwarfs the conception of Humanity. Far sounder would his views have been had he now and then permitted his thoughts to range to the uttermost imaginable limits of the sidereal universe, and brought himself duly to realize how by the comparison Humanity quite loses its apparent infinitude. Or had he more carefully analyzed the process of human thinking itself, the study of which he stigmatized as "metaphysical" and profitless, he might perhaps have seen that the world of phenomena speaks to us, everywhere and at all times, if we only choose to listen, of an Infinite and Unknowable Reality, whereas the conception of Humanity is but the conception of a Finite and Knowable Phenomenon. Here we touch the bottom of his error. This great Being, says the Comtist, this collective Humanity, is our supreme Being—"the only one we can know, *therefore* the only one we can worship." On the other hand, the Cosmist asserts, what we know is not what we worship; what we know is matter of science; it is only when science fails, and intelligence is baffled, and the Infinite confronts us, that we cease to analyze and begin to worship. "What men have worshipped, from the earliest times, has been not the Known, but the Unknown. Even the primeval savage, who worshipped plants and animals, worshipped them only in so far as their modes of action were mysterious to him—only in so far as they constituted a part of the weird uninterpreted world by which he was surrounded. As soon as he had generalized the dynamic phenomena presented by the plant or the animal, that is, as soon as it became an object of knowledge, it ceased to be an object of worship. As soon as the grander phenomena of sunrise and sunset, storm and eclipse, had been partially generalized, they were no longer directly worshipped, but unseen agents were imagined as controlling the phenomena by their arbitrary volitions, and these agents, as being mysterious, were worshipped. So when polytheism began to give place to monotheism, the process was still the same. The visible and tangible world was regarded as the aggregate of things which might be understood; but above and beneath all this was the mysterious aspect of things—the Dynamis, the Demiurgus, the Cause of all, the Ruler of all—and this mighty Something was worshipped. Though theology has all along wrestled with the insoluble problems presented by this supreme Mystery, and, by insisting on divers tangible propositions concerning it, has implicitly asserted that it can be at least partially known; the fact remains that only by being unknown has it continued to be the object of the religious sentiment. Could the theologian have carried his point and constructed a "science of Deity"; could the divine nature have been all expressed in definite formulas, as we express the genesis of vegetation or the revolutions of the planets, worship would have disappeared altogether. Worship is ever the dark side of the shield, of which knowledge is the bright side. It is because science can never explain the universe, it is because the enlarging periphery of knowledge does but reveal from day to day a greater number of points at which we meet the unknowable lying beyond, that religion can never become obsolete. Though we have come to recognize the most refined symbols by which men have sought to render Deity intelligible as inadequate and misleading symbols; though we sacrifice the symbol of personality, because personality implies limitation, and to speak of an infinite personality is to cheat oneself with a phrase that is empty of meaning; yet our recognition of Deity is only the more emphatic. Thus "the object of religious sentiment will ever continue to be that which it has ever been." The God of the scientific philosopher is still, and must ever be, the God of the Christian, though freed from the illegitimate formulas by the aid of which theology has sought to render Deity comprehensible. What is this wondrous Dynamis which manifests itself to our consciousness in harmonious activity throughout the length and breadth and depth of the universe, which guides the stars for countless ages in paths that never err, and which animates the molecules of the dew-drop that gleams for a brief hour on the shaven lawn— whose workings are so resistless that we have naught to do but reverently obey them, yet so infallible that we can place our unshaken trust in them, yesterday, today, and for ever? When, summing up all activity in one most comprehensive epithet, we call it Force, we are but using a scientific symbol, expressing an affection of our consciousness, which is yet powerless to express the ineffable Reality. To us, therefore, as to the Israelite of old, the very name of Jehovah is that which is not to be spoken. Push our scientific research as far as we may, pursuing generalization until all phenomena, past, present, and future, are embraced within a single formula;—we shall never fathom this ultimate mystery, we shall be no nearer the comprehension of this omnipresent Energy. Here science must ever reverently pause, acknowledging the presence of the mystery of mysteries. Here religion must ever hold sway, reminding us that from birth until death we are dependent on a Power to whose eternal decrees we must submit, to whose dispensations we must resign ourselves, and upon whose constancy we may implicitly rely.

Thus we begin to realize, more vividly than theology could have taught us to realize, the utter absurdity of atheism. Thus is exhibited the prodigious silliness of Lalande, who informed mankind that he had swept the heavens with his telescope and found no God there—as if God were an optical phenomenon! Thus, too, we see the poverty of that anthropomorphism which represents the infinite Deity as acting through calculation and contrivance, just as finite intelligence acts under the limitations imposed by its environment. And thus, finally, we perceive the hopeless error of the Positivist, who would give us a finite knowable, like Humanity, for an object of religious contemplation. The reasoning which demonstrates the relativity of knowledge, demonstrates also the failure of all such attempts to bind up religion in scientific formulas.

The anthropomorphic theist, habitually thinking of God as surrounded and limited by an environment or "objective datum," will urge that the doctrine here expounded is neither more nor less than Pantheism, or the identification of God with the totality of existence. So plausible does this objection appear, at first sight, that those who urge it cannot fairly be accused either of dullness of apprehension or of a desire to misrepresent. Nevertheless it needs but to look sharply into the matter, to see that the doctrine here expounded is utterly opposed to Pantheism. Though the word "pantheism" has been almost as undiscriminatingly bandied about among theological disputants as the word "atheism," it has still a well-defined metaphysical meaning which renders it inapplicable to a religious doctrine based upon the relativity of knowledge. In the pantheistic hypothesis the distinction between absolute and phenomenal existence is ignored, and the world of phenomena is practically identified with Deity. Of this method of treating the problem the final outcome is to be seen in the metaphysics of Hegel, in which the process of evolution, vaguely apprehended, is described absolutely, as a process of change in the Deity, and in which God, as identified with the totality of phenomenal existence, is regarded as continually progressing from a state of comparative imperfection to a state of comparative perfection. Or, in other words—to reduce the case to the shape in which it was presented in the first chapter of this work—the Universe, as identified with God, is regarded as self-evolved. Such a hypothesis, equally with that of the anthropomorphic theist, implicitly limits Deity with an "objective datum," and renders it finite; for, as Mr. Mansel has observed in another connection, "how can the Infinite become that which it was not from the first?" Obviously for the change an ulterior Cause is needed; and thus the pantheistic hypothesis resolves itself into the affirmation of a limited Knowable conditioned by an unlimited Unknowable—but it is the former, and not the latter, which it deifies.

Hence to the query suggested at the beginning of this chapter, whether the Deity can be identified with the Cosmos, we must return a very different answer from that returned by the Pantheist. The "open secret," in so far as secret, is God—in so far as open, is the World; but in thus regarding the ever-changing universe of phenomena as the multiform revelation of an Omnipresent Power, we can in nowise identify the Power with its manifestations. To do so would reduce the entire argument to nonsense. From first to last it has been implied that, while the universe is the manifestation of Deity, yet is Deity something more than the universe.

The doctrine which we have here expounded is, therefore, neither more nor less than Theism, in its most consistent and unqualified form. It is quite true that the word "theism," as ordinarily employed, connotes the ascription of an anthropomorphic personality to the Deity. But in this connotation there has been nothing like fixedness or uniformity. On the other hand the term has become less and less anthropomorphic in its connotations, from age to age, and in the sense in which it is here employed the deanthropomorphizing process is but carried one step farther. There was a time when theism seemed to require that God should be invested with a quasi-human body, just as it now seems to require that God should be invested with quasi-human intelligence and volition. But for us to concede the justice of the latter restriction would be as unphilosophical as it would have been for the early monotheists to concede the justice of the former. Just as the early Christians persisted in calling themselves theists while asserting that God dwells in a temple not made with hands, so may the modern philosopher persist in calling himself a theist while rejecting the arguments by which Voltaire and Paley have sought to limit and localize the Deity. Following out the parallel, we might characterize the doctrine here expounded as the "higher theism," in contrast with the "lower theism" taught in the current doctrine. Or in conformity with the nomenclature which has already done us such good service, we may still better characterize it as Cosmic Theism, in contrast with the Anthropomorphic Theism of those theologians who limit the Deity by an "objective datum."

This happy expression of Mr. Martineau's lays bare the anthropomorphic hypothesis to the very core, and when thoroughly considered, lets us into the secret of that superficial appearance of antagonism between Science and Religion which has disturbed so many theologians and misled so many scientific inquirers. Though as an act of lip-homage anthropomorphism asserts the infinitude and omnipotence of God, yet in reality it limits and localizes Him. Though it overtly acknowledges that "in Him we live and move and have our being," yet it tacitly belies this acknowledgment by the implication, which runs through all its reasonings, that God is a person localized in some unknown part of space, and that the universe is a "datum objective to God" in somewhat the same sense that a steam-engine is an "objective datum" to the engineer who works it. I do not say that such a conception would be avowed by any theologian: as thus overtly stated, it would no doubt be generally met with an emphatic disclaimer. Nevertheless this conception, whether avowed or disclaimed, lies at the bottom of all the arguments which theologians urge either against the theory of evolution or against any other theory which extends what is called "the domain of natural law." Take away this conception, and not only do their specific arguments lose all significance, but their entire position becomes meaningless: there ceases to be any reason for their opposing instead of welcoming the new theory. For if "extending the domain of natural law" be equivalent to "extending our knowledge of Divine action," what objection can the theologian logically make to this? Manifestly his hostile attitude is wholly prescribed by his belief, whether tacit or avowed, that the sphere of natural law and the sphere of Divine action are two different spheres, so that whatever is added to the former is taken from the latter. It is assumed that the universe is a sort of lifeless machine, which under ordinary circumstances works along without immediate Divine superintendence, in accordance with what are called natural laws, very much as the steam-engine works when once set going, in accordance with the harmoniously cooperating properties of its material structure. Only by occasional interposition, it is assumed, does God manifest his existence—by originating organic life, or creating new species out of dust or out of nothing, or by causing prodigies to be performed within historic times for the edification of gaping multitudes. So deep-seated is this assumption—so vitally implicated is it with all the habits of thought which theology nurtures—that we sometimes hear it explicitly maintained that when natural law can be shown to be coextensive with the whole of nature, then our belief in God will *ipso facto* be extinguished.

Such a position is no doubt as irreligious as it is unscientific; but it is not difficult to see how it has come to be so commonly maintained. Not only is it often apparently justified by the unphilosophical language of scientific men—especially of those shallow writers known as "materialists"—who speak of "natural law" as if it were something different from "Divine action"; but it is also the logical offspring of that primitive fetishism from which all our theology is descended. For as physical generalization began to diminish the sphere of action of the innumerable quasi-human agencies by which fetishism sought to account for natural phenomena, there could hardly fail to arise a belief in some sort of opposition between invariable law and quasi-human agency. On the one hand you have a set of facts that occur in fixed sequences, and so are not the result of anthropomorphic volition; on the other hand you have a set of facts that seem to occur according to no determinable order, and so are the result of anthropomorphic volition. The fetishistic thinker could not, of course, formulate the case in this abstract and generalized way; but there can be no doubt that a crudely felt antithesis of the kind here indicated must have been nearly coeval with the beginnings of physical generalization. Now the gradual summing up and blending together of all the primeval quasi-human agencies into one grand quasi-human Agency, could not at once do away with this antithesis. On the contrary, the antithesis would naturally remain as the generalized opposition between the realm of "invariable law" and the realm of "Divine originality." It would be superfluous to recount the various metaphysical shapes which this conception has assumed, in some of which Nature has even been personified as an intelligent and volitional agency, distinct from God, and working through law while God works through miracle. The result has been that, as scientific generalization has steadily extended the region of "natural law," the region which theology has assigned to "Divine action" has steadily diminished, until theological arguments have become insensibly pervaded by the curious assumption that the greater part of the universe is godless. For it is naively asked, if plants and animals have been naturally originated, if the world as a whole has been evolved and not created, and if human actions conform to law, what is there left for God to do?[4] If not formally repudiated, is he not thrust back into the past eternity, as an unknowable source of things, which is postulated for form's sake, but might as well, for all practical purposes, be omitted?

The reply is that the difficulty is one which theology has created for itself. It is not science, but theology, which has thrust back Divine action to some nameless point in the past eternity and left nothing for God to do in the present world. For the whole difficulty lies in the assumption of the material universe as a "datum objective to God," and in the consequent distinction between "Divine action" and "natural law,"—a distinction for which science is in nowise responsible. The tendency of modern scientific inquiry, whether working in the region of psychology or in that of transcendental physics, is to abolish this distinction, and to regard "natural law" as merely a synonym of "Divine action." And since Berkeley's time the conception of the material universe as a "datum objective to God" is one which can hardly be maintained on scientific grounds. It is scientific inquiry, working quite independently of theology, which has led us to the conclusion that all the dynamic phenomena of Nature constitute but the multiform revelation of an Omnipresent Power that is not identifiable with Nature. And in this conclusion there is no room left for the difficulty which baffles contemporary theology. The scientific inquirer may retort upon the theologian—Once really adopt the conception of an ever-present God, without whom not a sparrow falls to the ground, and it becomes self-evident that the law of gravitation is but an expression of a particular mode of Divine action. And what is thus true of one law is true of all laws. The Anthropomorphist is naturally alarmed by the continual detection of new uniformities, and the discovery of order where before there seemed to be disorder; because his conception of Divine action has been historically derived from the superficial contrast between the seemingly irregular action of will and the more obviously regular action of less complex phenomena. The Cosmist, on the other hand, in whose mind Divine action is identified with orderly action, and to whom a really irregular phenomenon would seem like the manifestation of some order-hating Ahriman, foresees in every possible extension of knowledge a fresh confirmation of his faith in God, and thus recognizes no antagonism between our duty as inquirers and our duty as worshippers. He will admit no such inherent and incurable viciousness in the constitution of things as is postulated by the anthropomorphic hypothesis. To him no part of the world is godless. He does not rest content with the conception of "an absentee God, sitting idle, ever since the first Sabbath, at the outside of his universe, and 'seeing it go'; "for he has learned, with Carlyle, "that this fair universe, were it in the meanest province thereof, is in very deed the star-domed City of God; that through every star, through every grass-blade, and most through every living soul, the glory of a present God still beams."[5]

From the anthropomorphic point of view it will quite naturally be urged in objection, that this apparently desirable result is reached through the degradation of Deity from an "intelligent personality" into a "blind force," and is therefore in reality an undesirable and perhaps even quasi-atheistic result. To the theologian the stripping-off the anthropomorphic vestments with which men have sought to render the Infinite representable in imagination, always means the leaving of nothing but "blind force" as a residuum. Trained upon the subjective method, and habitually applying to all propositions the test of metaphysical congruity only, he naturally regards the possibilities of human thought as fairly representative of the possibilities of existence. Accordingly since human intelligence is the highest mode of Being which we know—being in the nature of things the highest mode, since it is the mode in which we ourselves exist, and which we must therefore necessarily employ as a norm by which to estimate all other modes—the theologian infers that any higher mode of Being is not only inconceivable but impossible. And so, when a vast extension of our knowledge of nature shows (or seems to show) that the workings of quasi-human intelligence form but an inadequate and misleading symbol of the workings of Divine Power, it naturally seems to the theologian that we are giving up an "intelligent personality" for a "blind force."

Here, however, as before, the difficulty is one which theology has created for itself. It is not science, but theology, which conjures up a host of phantom terrors by the gratuitous use of the question-begging epithet "blind force." The use of this, and of the kindred epithet "brute matter," implies that matter and force are real existences—independent "data objective to" consciousness. Such a view, however, as already shown, cannot be maintained. To the scientific inquirer, the terms "matter" and "force" are mere symbols which stand *tant bien que mal* for certain generalized modes of Divine manifestation: they are no more real existences than the *x* and *y* of the algebraist are real existences. The question as to identifying Deity with Force is, therefore, simply ruled out. The question which really presents itself is quite different. Theologically phrased, the question is whether the creature is to be taken as a measure of the Creator. Scientifically phrased, the question is whether the highest form of Being as yet suggested to one petty race of creatures by its ephemeral experience of what is going on in one tiny corner of the universe, is necessarily to be taken as the equivalent of that absolutely highest form of Being in which all the possibilities of existence are alike comprehended. It is the same question which confronted us in our opening chapter, and which returned to confront us in sundry other chapters of our Prolegomena. Already we have more than once answered it, in a general way, by showing that "the possibilities of thought are not coextensive with the possibilities of things." We have now to give it a more special answer, by inquiring into the possibility of a mode of existence not limited by the conditions which limit conscious existence within the narrow domain of our terrestrial experience. In other words, we have to inquire into the relations between Matter and Spirit; and the inquiry, besides throwing light on questions which must have arisen in the course of our exposition of the evolution of life and intelligence, will also furnish us with the means for emphasizing the theistic conclusions obtained in the present chapter.

NOTES

1. See vol. 1, p. 15.

2. *First Principles*, pp. 189, 190.

3. Mill, *Auguste Comte and Positivism*, p. 122.

4. "Illos omnes Deum aut saltem Dei providentiam tollere putant, qui res et miracula per causas naturales explicant aut intelligere student." Spinoza, *Tractatus Theologico-Politicus*, vi. *Opera*. iii. 86. Οὐ γὰρ ἠνείχοντο τοὺς φυσικοὺς καὶ μετεωρολέσχας τότε καλουμένους, ὡς εἰς αἰτίας ἀλόγους καὶ δυνάμεις ἀπρονοήτους καὶ κατηναγκασμένα πάθη διατρίβοντας τὸ θεῖον." Plutarch, *Nikias*, cap. 23. The complaint, it will be seen, is the same in modern that it was in ancient times. Compare Plutarch, *Perikles*, cap. 6; Cicero, *Tusc. Disp.* i. 13, *Opera*, ed. Nobbe, tom. viii, p. 299.

5. *Sartor Resartus*, bk. ii. chap. vii.; bk. iii. chap. viii.

Charles Carroll Everett

THE KNOWN AND THE UNKNOWABLE IN RELIGION

The Unitarian Review and Religious Magazine 3 (May 1875): 445–456.

We have a homelike feeling shut in as we are by the incrustation of habit, otherwise I do not know how we could escape the constant sense of wonder and awe at the mystery of the universe. The Englishman on his little island forgets that his island is not a continent. He almost forgets that it is not the world. So we, on our little island of the known, forget the mighty ocean of the unknown and the unknowable that stretches about us. Yet no one can always escape the consciousness of this. Many have some special riddle, some one point, where they feel the impotence of their knowledge, feel how little science or philosophy or theology can do towards solving the question that haunts them. We speak of immortality as explaining the mystery of life, but it simply postpones an explanation, simply gives the possibility of such an explanation. And then of the teeming life about us, of the life of flower, of forest, of beast, of the life of the geologic epochs, of monster and reptile, of all this, the doctrine of immortality, at least as it is ordinarily held, says nothing. Theodore Parker understood as well as any other the meaning of suffering and the blessing of it. He understood it so well that it furnished the ground of his wonder. The form in which the mystery of the universe seems to have met him is this: How to understand the suffering of the lower animals and their cruelty towards one another. Human suffering, human cruelty, he could understand, but the suffering of the beast without apparent end or compensation, he could not understand. Robertson understood as well as any other the great law of duty and the healthfulness of retribution for sin. But as always the darkest mystery lies closest to what is best understood, so the great form in which the world's riddle presented itself to him was this: Why should our heaviest sufferings come commonly not from our faults, but from our mistakes? Why should error cause more suffering than sin? I knew one man to whom the great riddle of the world appeared to put itself in this form: Why should we be encouraged and impelled to cultivate and beautify the earth, to work early and late to raise flower and fruit, while insects were at the same time sent forth to oppose us, meeting us, at every point, with some special warfare of destruction, fitted each by its special instinct and construction to undo all our work. I say this was the form in which the riddle seemed to present itself to him, though doubtless this presentation was only the symbol of the blighted hopes and baffled struggles of life.

And, after all, these special examples that I have referred to are only varied forms of one mystery, that of suffering and sorrow, a mystery that every man must face sooner or later. We may have an answer ready to the questions that arise in regard to the general suffering and sorrow of life. We may have our theory at our tongues' end. We may say there must be sorrow, for through it alone come the highest spiritual gains; but when the form of sorrow enters our own door, that form, in the shadow of which the beauty and brightness of life seem to wither and fade away, when the iron hand of suffering seizes our own frame with a grasp against which we vainly struggle, then the mystery which we had thought vanquished and vanished comes back with new vastness and power. Then, if not before, the question presses, "Could not an omnipotent and all-wise Creator have established a different relation of things; or are there in the moral and spiritual world, as in the arithmetical and geometrical world, relations which even omnipotence must recognize, which even it cannot set aside?"

And this in its turn is only one form of the great mystery of the universe. God is infinite and man is finite; how then can the finite comprehend the infinite. If his ways are not as our ways, his thoughts are not as our thoughts, do not our most common words lose their meaning, lose all meaning, when applied to him?

Thus we are like dwellers in the cottage of a lighthouse, upon some solitary island. We look each from his little window and see mystery in that one direction. But when we ascend the tower and look about us we unite those scattered views, and see that we are surrounded by the mighty ocean of the unknown and unknowable. We feel the presence of that infinite and incomprehensible power which is in all things and through all things, which is under and overall.

It is singular that, while theology has been growing more and more comprehensible, suiting itself to the tenderest capacities, while what we call orthodox theology is growing more and more simple and rational, and liberal theology is priding itself upon be coming wholly simple and rational, all at once this sense of mys tery should come back and flood the whole, like an ocean exulting over broken and buried dykes. In this age of rationalism, Herbert Spencer, who represents the extreme of rationalism, who is looked upon by many as the leader of the liberal movement in England and America, affirms that the religious sense is nothing but the sense of mystery, that religion is only the recognition of the incomprehensibility which is at the heart of all things, and the awe in the presence of this mystery. And this form of speech is continually meeting us. It is a formula adopted by many of the leading thinkers of the time.

It is certain that in many forms of religion this sense of mystery is very prominent. In parts of the Hindoo literature it stands out to the exclusion of everything besides. In the book of Job, in the creeds and worship of the mediaeval church, we feel its power. Indeed there is perhaps no deep religious literature that does not sooner or later give utterance to it. Tertullian uttered the principle of this form of thought when he cried, "It is credible because it is foolish. It is certain because it is impossible." He knew that human thought could not comprehend the infinite. He knew that when the divine truth appeared to him it would stretch before him vast and immeasurable. So when among the familiar facts of life, among the familiar truths of thought, there arose one shadowy and huge, not to be defined, not to be taken in by the gaze of the grandest soul, he felt that it was for that very reason divine, and he worshiped before it. Balboa and his brave followers, after their dreary and toilsome pilgrimage through the wilderness of the Isthmus, reached a height from which an ocean different from the one that they had left behind them burst upon their gaze. They shouted, in glad surprise, "The sea! the sea!" and their leader, rearing the cross, poured out their common thanksgiving to God. How did they know that it was the sea? Did they discern the navies of the world floating upon it? Did they see the rich shores of India skirting its farthest edge? Did they see the capitals of the world drawing tribute from it? Did they see all this, and did they by these marks know that it was the ocean? Nothing of all this they saw; only a hazy stretch of water with no boundary line. They believed that it was the ocean because they could not see across it. In such a spirit cried that reverent soul of whom I spoke. "It is credible because it is impossible."

Mystery, then, has its place in religion, but, according to Herbert Spencer, religion is all mystery. This involves two statements. The first is that the only element common to all religions is the sense of mystery; the second is that in this recognition lie all the truth and power of religion.

The highest flight of religious ecstasy, then, has been the recognition of the insoluble mystery; the fullest praise to God, in fact, as well as in theory, has been to say to him, "We know nothing of thee or of thy attributes." Strangely must one have listened to the utterances of religious souls through all the history of the world, to gain from them an impression like this. The prayers and hymns, in which the very life of the purest and noblest souls has uttered itself, have indeed recognized a mystery, but they have been filled with a sense of something that was not mystery. Moreover, the mystery in the presence of which these souls have bowed themselves was not the cold abstraction of mystery. It was not simply the Unknowable. The mystery grew out of and gathered about that which was known. Men did not begin with the mystery, and seek to bridge it over with fine words. They began with what was known, with what was simple and clear as the facts of daily life; but this stretched, as they gazed upon it, till it assumed measureless proportions; and what was simple as a child's thought overawed them with its infinite vastness. So the waves of the ocean ripple up the beach, and the child may run races with them, or may dig his little wells for them to fill; but he who launches on the ocean finds it stretching before him and beneath him and about him with a vastness that the imagination cannot grasp.

To the religious thinker the mystery was always a mystery of something. With Paul it was love that furnished the mystery. He bade us know the love of Christ which passeth knowledge. He knew what love was well enough; he had sung its praises as no one else had done. It was only the measurelessness of the love that he could not comprehend. Sometimes it has been the collision of two mighty principles that caused the mystery, each of which was clear enough, and each of which was felt to be supreme by its own right; but the reign of each seemed to dethrone the other, and the awed soul could simply yield its allegiance to each, and watch the strife in which it could be neither neutral nor partisan. Sometimes the mystery has arisen from the conflict of truth with prejudice and mistake that claimed the sanctity of truth. But, whatever has been the source of the mystery, knowledge, positive faith, has been its center. The strains that uttered the sense of mystery have formed only a deep undertone to the songs that chanted the real faith and aspiration of the soul.

Herbert Spencer says, with a certain truth, that it is as religion is developed that the sense of mystery becomes more strong. A better statement would be that it is as the simple natural religious faith is beginning to spend itself, is beginning to pass into speculation, that this sense becomes marked. At the birth of a religion, at the moment when it is most religious, then it is most full of confidence, and sees the horizon most clear about it. Even when the reflective stage of which I spoke begins, this simple confidence, in most cases, still is prominent. David was full of trust in the Lord who was his shepherd, who cared for him as he cared for his flocks. Job, coming later, was filled with the awe of the Unknown and the Unknowable; yet even Job cried with a confident earnestness that the sweetest strains of our modern song strive to echo for us, "I know that my Redeemer liveth." I do not remember that Jesus, with whom religion entered upon a new life, ever spoke of the Unknowable. He lived like a child in the sunlight of a father's smile. With Paul the reflective stage had already begun; yet he could say, with a careful thoughtfulness that added weight to his words, "Now I know in part." Even when the simplicity of religion became overlaid with questioning, the old confidence was not lost. Augustine did much to draw about the Christian spirit the mists of speculation, to torment it with insoluble riddles. Yet, when bewildered by the mysteries of infinitude he had exclaimed, "Who art thou, then, my God?" he could answer, "What but the Lord God, . . . most highest, most good, most potent, most omnipotent; most merciful, yet most just."

The same is true of other religions. The Hindoo religion began with hymns full of confidence in themselves and in their object. The later hymns first began to utter the voice of questioning and of awe before the Unknown. It was centuries later that the Unknowable was put in the place of God; and to be incomprehensible was felt to be the *proprium* of divinity, so that it was defined when it was called the undefinable. This was the transformation of religion into philosophy. It was not the development of religion: it was its decay. But the religious heart of the nation could not rest with this. Religion again affirmed itself—a religion that had its darkness and its terror and its mystery, but which had also its faith and its promise.

Thus in all forms of religion the central and essential thing has been something other than mystery. The element that is the common bond between all religions is not negative, but positive. Men have believed that there was a power about them or above them—a power distinct from and mightier than the ordinary forces of nature, to which they could trust. Sometimes, as with the poor fetich-worshiper, it dwelt in the stocks and stones of earth; sometimes, as with the polytheist, it was broken up into shining points; sometimes, as with the monotheist, it was gathered about one luminous center; sometimes, as with the Hebrew, it was a power "that made for righteousness"; sometimes, as with John, it was love, or, as with Jesus, it was spirit. One nation has called it by one name and another by another; one has perceived it more dimly, another more clearly; one has attached one limitation to it, another has attached another; sometimes it has reflected more and sometimes less of our human imperfections, as the deep midnight heaven reflects the glare of a city's lamps—but all have united in this, that there was something that one could trust to. Out from all limitations and contradictions appeared this fact of a power of helpfulness. So the tenderness and sympathy of Buddha shone out from the black despair that formed the background of his teaching. So the love of Jesus shone out from the dark mystery of the mediaeval creeds. Men may pray to a mystery, but they cannot praise it; they may bring offerings to it, but they cannot trust it; they may seek in ways chosen at random to soothe it, or win its favor, but they cannot love it: and take out of religion praise and trust and love, and not only its best beauty, but its best reality, will be gone.

But though the element common to all religions is knowledge rather than ignorance, the known rather than the unknowable, perhaps the other part of the statement of Herbert Spencer is true. Perhaps all this has been a mistake, and all the truth there has been in religion has been that minor part, namely, the sense of awe in the presence of mystery. Here it may be helpful to notice the sense in which the phrase that speaks of the unknowable is used by those who would make religion consist wholly in the recognition of this. To state the proposition in its most simple and general terms, it is this: Take away all that we know from any object and we should not know what was left. To state the proposition in a phrase that would be better recognized by those who use it, we are familiar with relations, but of that which is behind and within relations, we know nothing. We do not know what anything is in itself. We use the word "force," but the thought we attach to it involves contradictions. The word stands for something that is unknown by us. We do not even know our own souls. Spirit is as unknowable as matter. I think that if all this were fairly understood, the phrase that speaks of religion as having to do merely with the Unknowable would lose for many much of its terror. If it were understood that God is unknowable in the sense that our own souls are unknowable, I think that many would be content to leave the matter so.

Here we meet a fact that may throw still more light upon our theme. Herbert Spencer, and those who agree with him, show that the words "matter" and "force," and kindred terms, stand simply for the Unknowable, and yet they continue to use them. The reason for this is that the course of things is the same as it would be if the words stood for something known. They are thus relatively, though not actually, true. Your watch may be wholly wrong, and yet relatively right. You cannot tell the time by it, but you can measure off by it the hours and minutes as they pass. After, then, all this demonstration that science as well as religion ends in a mystery, science keeps on its old course as if nothing had happened. It uses its old words. It talks about time and space, and force and motion, as if the words had a meaning and a true one. Religion alone is expected to be bound by the new order. If it ventures to use its old words it is reproved for its presumption.

But why, I would ask, may not religion, as well as science, use its words, recognizing the relative truth that is in them? Few thinking men, however strong their religious faith, have, I think, used the terms of religion, accepting them as true in their gross literalness. Here is the source of the contradiction which Herbert Spencer has pointed out between the professions both of knowledge and ignorance on the part of religious thinkers. The knowledge was relative, but yet practically real. God's ways are not as our ways. Our love is but a symbol of his love, our righteousness of his righteousness, our spirituality of his nature. But though the words are relative, they are relatively true. The course of things is the same as if they were true. If there is "a power not ourselves that makes for righteousness," if without us, and yet more clearly within us, it upholds the right and marks the evil with its condemnation, why should we not call it holy? If it confers upon us all the blessings of, life, and when these outward goods are lost, it bestows, often, a still greater blessing, why should we not call it good? If it chooses the best ways to reach its chosen ends, if under its guidance all things fit together to form a perfect whole, why should we not call it wise? If the soul feels it nearer to it than itself, if it finds in it a tender and sublime companionship, if there flows from it a helpful sympathy in sorrow, and in gladness a blessing sweeter than the joy, why should it not ascribe to it the attribute of love? And when it has used in regard to it the words "holiness," "wisdom," and "love," why need it hesitate to use in regard to it the word "spirit"?[1] We use these words because they are the best we have, and the truest because they are the best. When we speak of God under these terms, we speak with far more truth than when we speak of him simply as a power, or even as an unknowable power. If we know that the terms of spirit represent him more nearly than the terms of matter, then we speak of him most truly when we speak of him in the terms of spirit. When we look through these symbols we are looking towards him; when we approach him through these we are drawing near him. One who is lost in some vast cavern may wander hopelessly till he sees in one direction a gray glimmering that shows him in what direction he must turn to reach the outer light. This gray glimmering is not the daylight, but it points towards the daylight; and the wanderer who follows it, pressing in the direction where the darkness is least dense, is pressing towards the light. According to the very terms of the system which remands religion to the realm of the Unknowable, we may then have a practical working knowledge of religious truth, just as we have of scientific truth.

But I further claim for this knowledge that it is something more than merely a working formula. This may be illustrated, first, by the fact that there is absolutely no mystery without some knowledge. We could not even speak of the Unknowable unless we had some knowledge of that of which we speak. The unknown is absolutely nothing till it is seen in connection with the known, just as the known is worth little till it is seen against the great background of the unknown. "Science," cries the ancient philosopher, "is born of wonder." "Nay," answers the modern, "wonder is born of science," and both are right. I have spoken of the mystery of the ocean, but I think that one does not get the fullest sense of this mystery and this sublimity when one is far out at sea, floating upon the ocean, shut in only by the circle of the horizon. For myself, I have felt the vastness and the infinitude of the ocean, much more while standing upon the shore and looking out upon its pathless waste, and seeing the waves roll up, one after another, the sloping beach, or beat with the might of their gigantic strength against some rocky barrier, than I have when sailing on mid-ocean: for it is where land and water meet that we feel the sublimity of the land, which would bind the ocean, and the sublimity of the ocean which will not be bound! Thus it is in religion and in thought. The point of sublimity, nay, the point of real knowledge, is the point where the known and the unknown, the plain and the incomprehensible, touch one another.

There is, I repeat, no mystery without knowledge; and the more pressing the mystery the sharper and clearer must be the knowledge out of which it springs. The brute recognizes no mystery because its knowledge is insufficient. A single illustration will make this clear. I will suppose that none of you have ever heard the word "asymptote." When you hear the word for the first time it suggests no mystery, because it suggests no meaning. I explain the word to you. I tell you that an asymptote is a line which is continually approaching a curved line, but that however long the lines might be drawn they would never meet. With this explanation you begin to see something of the mystery that the word involves. But still the mystery does not press upon you, for my words in regard to it sound foolish, and you attach little meaning to them. But if you study mathematics for yourself, if you study the mathematical formula for this line, if you see it proved by absolute demonstration that the one line is always approaching the other but can never reach it, then you will feel the full power of the mystery, because you have at last reached some full and definite knowledge.

Our knowledge, then, though partial, must be real. This will appear more clearly, if in the next place we examine more closely the sense in which our knowledge is denied. We know, it is said, things only in their relations, and not as they are in themselves. But things exist only in relations; out of these they are nothing. If we know them out of these relations we should know them falsely. We know of soul only that it thinks and feels. Its very being is to think and feel; apart from thinking and feeling it is nothing. If we know of anything only its relations to ourselves, we know so much about it really and truly. An object really is, even in the slightest and weakest manifestations of itself, just as the ocean is in every little wave that ripples and breaks at your feet. When you see these you see the ocean; when you touch them you touch the ocean. You are asked what you know of your dearest friend in himself; you know his smile, his form, his voice, his love, his nobleness, but these, you are told, are attributes only. But you know that your friend is in those words and tones and looks and acts that are so dear to you. They are all manifestations and revelations of him.

You do not know God in himself. Thank him that you have no necessity to do this, for the universe is full of his manifestation of himself.

The simple fact that throws light on these mixed questions and may solve our doubts is this, that *God is in the known as much and as truly as he is in the unknown.* If we could fairly take this thought into our minds we should have the truth of religion. If we could take it into our hearts, we should have the reality of religion.

Since all things proceed from God all things must be full of him and must bear some revelation of him. His presence is in the world about us and the heavens over us, in the past behind us, and in the future before us. The little flower that opens at our feet comes forth from this unseen power that we call God, and brings its revelation. The magnificent order of the universe, the majestic regularity of the earth and the heavens, are simply manifestations and revelations of him. Some see God mainly in this order and regularity. When they trace out a law they feel that they have discovered the footsteps of God. Others see him in the uncomprehended and incomprehensible. The grand truth is that God is in both. The mother's love that watched over your childhood was a revelation of God. It was his love that looked through her eyes and sheltered you in her arms. The love of Christ was a revelation of God. Jesus was no stranger and foreigner. He also came forth from the great power which is within and behind and above all things. Can you comprehend the height and the depth, the length and the breadth of the love of God, which was manifested in Jesus Christ, that which Paul tells us passes knowledge. Its height is as high as heaven, its depth is as deep as sin, its length is as long as eternity, its breadth as broad as humanity. Thus Jesus loved. His love stooped to the lowest sinners, it stooped to those who mocked and crucified him. It lifted them up with its last prayer to God. This was the love of God, for without God Jesus was nothing.

But is there not evil as well as good in the universe, and does not this also manifest God? Did not Judas as well as Jesus come forth from him?

You go through the galleries of a sculptor. You see works in every degree and stage of completion. Here is a block of marble where you can see, just hinted at, some form of man. Here is one where the form has half emerged. Here, one that as yet is only pitted and disfigured by the master's blows. Here, at last, you reach the perfect triumph of his skill. It stands light, graceful, beautiful, instinct with a life higher than human. Do you doubt in which work the master displays himself? Such an artist's gallery is the world. Now the spirit is buried in the sensual, now half revealed through it. Here it stands in its unveiled splendor. Do you doubt which best displays the spirit and power of Him who is all in all? He is in all, but you cannot find him in all. You do not know the method of his art. You do not understand the blows, sharp and terrible often, that are needed to evolve beauty out of the formless. But though you know not the method of his art, you recognize its end, and you recognize the master in this end.

But God does not manifest himself outside of us alone, but within us also. His life is in us, and in him we live. Our spirit somehow answers to his spirit. The deeps of our being answer to the deeps of his, as the waters of the sheltered bay feel the drawings of the tidal flow of the ocean.

Such is the relation between mystery and knowledge, the known and the unknowable, in religion. We need them both.

We need the sense of mystery to humble our spirits, and to awaken them by its mighty challenge. We need the simplicity of religion to be the light and comfort and strength of our lives; and with all the mystery let us never forget the limitation of the mystery. There is a sense in which love is always love, and right is always right, and reason always reason. There is a vast formula of love that will take in the love of God as well as the love of the child. We may not comprehend this love, but we can recognize it, and know something of what it is. The child lies in its mother's arms. It cannot comprehend the source and strength and compass of her love. Yet it recognizes that love. It rests in it, and is content. In like manner may we rest peaceful and content, while we know that love that passeth knowledge.

NOTES

1. Mr. Fiske, in his valuable work entitled *Outlines of Cosmic Philosophy*, says, "Provided we bear in mind the symbolic character of our words, we may say that 'God is Spirit' " (vol. ii., p. 449). This is an important concession. I do not see, however, why reasoning similar to that by which this result was reached would not justify, with a like qualification, a like use of terms expressive of the highest spiritual activity.

James Elliot Cabot

SOME CONSIDERATIONS ON THE NOTION OF SPACE

The Journal of Speculative Philosophy 12 (July 1878): pp. 225–236.

All bodies are extended, or exist in Space—that is, they are outside of us, and outside of each other; and this *outness* we imagine indefinitely prolonged in all directions—as indefinite *room* for others. Yet, although Extension is the most general character of bodies, when we ask ourselves what it is, we find only negative predicates; it is pure indifference to every one of the sensible qualities; they may all be changed without touching the extension of the body; and we can at last only define this extension as the *otherness*, the mutual externality, of the parts.

How, then, do we get any knowledge of it; or to what possible impressions does it correspond?

It is natural to us to say that we *see* the place, distance, direction, and extent of bodies—that the separateness of the letters on this page, for example, is visible, just as the black color of the ink and the whiteness of the paper are visible. This was the prevalent opinion before Berkeley, and many psychologists seem to be returning to it.[1] Evidently, however, this is a figurative way of speaking; for it is not meant, I suppose, that Extension is an affection of the optic nerve; in other words, that it is a color. If this *is* meant, then we are entitle to ask, What color? Some one, I forget who, has suggested that Space is of a bluish tint; Mr. Riehl considers it to be a consciousness of black and white, or of light and shade. If these hypotheses are to be taken in earnest, they require us to suppose the existence, as a physical fact, of an indefinite *substratum* as a ground-work upon which all particular colors are spread out, and as the condition of their being perceived. This, I think, is too much like the old notion of a Substance without attributes, existing merely as the subject of attributes, to find favor with scientific men.

No visual impression of any kind can be the condition of our perception of Space, for blind persons in whose experience this condition is wanting have this perception. Indeed, if

Space be a sensation, it is one that is common evidently to several of our senses—probably in some measure to all. Many animals hunt principally by scent, and blind persons discriminate position and distance with great accuracy by hearing alone. M. Delboeuf[2] considers our association of Space with sight and touch to be merely a matter of habit, connected with the superior development of particular organs in the human race, and thinks that we can easily imagine a nose or an ear that should *see* Extension as truly as our eyes *see* it. A nose or an ear differentiated to the same extent with our eyes, viz., having upon the sensitive surface one spot of intenser sensibility, provided with a refracting medium capable of presenting a wide field of sound or scent, and with a movable tube permitting the field to be freely explored in all directions—would, we can hardly doubt, be able to discriminate positions in Space, if not as well, yet as really, and in substantially the same way, with our eyes or hands. On the other hand, an eye reduced to the same conditions with our nose or ear would possess as little power of discrimination.

Is Space, then, an occult quality in bodies, which modifies our apprehension of them without our being able to identify it with any nervous affection, or in any way to demonstrate its presence apart from the inferences to which it gives rise? Science is jealous of occult qualities, and rightly, for it is an hypothesis very hard to control. No doubt we have a sense of Extension—just as we have a sense of right and wrong; but to allege this sense only states the problem, without any attempt to solve it.

On reflection, it is evident, I think, that no simple feeling of any kind can be conceived as giving us by itself the impression of Extent; we cannot suppose it constituting a surface, or consisting of parts arranged above or below, or on the right or left hand of each other. Our feelings are by their very nature internal; occupy no room, and exist, as Hume said, *nowhere* but only in being felt. Nor can any assemblage of these zeroes give us what they do not themselves contain.

Evidently the extension of a body is not a quality, like weight, color, odor, etc., belonging to each part of it independently of the rest, but resides wholly in the relative position of the parts, of whatever nature they may happen to be. Hence it is that the particular character of the impressions makes no difference in their extent. Seen Extension is the very same thing with that which is felt, heard, or smelt, and in all these cases it is equally distinct from the sensations with which it is associated. A sound or a smell is localized, not as definitely perhaps, yet as really, as a color or a touch; and in all alike the situation is a fact of a different order from the nervous affection. Assuming, then, that Extension is not a sensible quality, but a relation which may subsist among impressions of any quality, or, at any rate, of various qualities, the next question is how we become aware of it. The only grounds of relation between our various sensations are resemblance, and sequence in Time. Affections of the same organ are more or less like each other: every taste is a taste, every sound a sound, and even black and white are alike colors, however they differ within this limit. Affections of different organs are neither like nor unlike; and, finally, all our sensations are related in the time of their occurrence, as being either before, after, or simultaneous with some other.

Such being the materials with which Experience has to work, it is natural to look to successiveness in time as the experience originally corresponding to the outward fact of a diversity of parts; and, on the other hand, to the similarity of like sensations as giving us the impression of continuity or juxtaposition.

Accordingly, many psychologists have traced the notion of Extension to the compound impression of a series of feelings so closely associated with a single feeling as to become identified with it—*e.g.*, if I move my hand back and forth with different degrees of rapidity, I get a series of impressions (of points successively touched, varying pressures upon the tissues, successive muscular efforts, etc.), succeeding each other at different rates, and thus conveying the impression of mere distance or extent. Then, if the motion be interrupted by contact with a resisting object (as, where different parts of the same thing are successively touched, or the hand is passed across a smooth, hard surface)—or, if the consciousness of it is interrupted by the consciousness of accompanying muscular effort, the amount of which remains the same whatever the rate of movement may be—the diversity of successive feelings is changed, by association with the feeling that remains the same, into the complex image of a diversity of parts in one object. The order of the impressions is, in the first place, detached from their particular sequence, and then, by a further step, it is apprehended as a diversity which is, also, from another point of view, identity, and these are associated together as one fact.

To this theory, in the form in which it was propounded by Dr. Thos. Brown, Sir Wm. Hamilton objected that the diverseness or remoteness here spoken of is remoteness in Time, not in Space; and he might have added—perhaps he did—if it were to become obliterated, the result would be, not that we should become conscious of objects in Space, but that we should cease to be conscious of events in Time.

Mr. J. S. Mill, in his *An Examination of William Hamilton's Philosophy*, rejects this criticism rather roughly, with the *argumentum baculinum* that, whatever our notion of length in Space may be, it is, as a matter of fact, constructed by the mind's laws, out of the notion of length in Time. What those laws of the mind are, that can give us the notion of a *synchronous succession*, he does not explain, but it is safe to say that this is not the notion of Space. The obliviscence of Duration is a phenomenon that is familiar to us in all our habitual actions, and we find nothing of the kind in it. Any set of complicated movements often repeated comes to seem like one; a practiced player upon the piano-forte, *e.g.*, comes to regard the successive adjustment of his hands, etc., as a single act; but there is no appearance here of a construction of Space.

Whatever plausibility belongs to any of the various attempts that have been made to evolve Extension from purely intensive feelings, with the help of the consciousness of movement, is due to the fact that, in assuming this consciousness, they assume the whole of their case. The movement must start from some point, and this point is already spatial. Now, if we may look upon our sensations as things existing outside of us at particular distances in definite directions, there is no further difficulty in the matter. But just this is our question: How they can have any *place* except in our consciousness—or how we come to imagine that they have any other? It seems impossible that a purely sentient being, having no knowledge of Extension, should ever arrive at such a notion.

Let us suppose the case of such a being, and, in order to cut off the associations with Extension that so obstinately cling to our visual sensations, let us further suppose that he is blind, but that his sense of hearing is so developed as to present to him a wide auditory field in which he can discriminate particular sounds with great accuracy. Now, let us bring him into a concert-room where a large orchestra is playing, and seat him in the middle of the front row. He will at once single out (let us say) the violoncello, and he will be more or less dimly aware of the first and second violins on either side, and of the other instruments further off. Judging from analogy, we should say that he will probably, after a while, turn his ear first in one direction and then in another, so as to bring various instruments successively before him—just as we see a baby turn its eyes from one bright spot on the ceiling to another. In short, he will act just as if he knew that they are co-existing things at certain distances and in certain directions from him and from each other. But to conclude that he *has* such a knowledge seems to me an important step, and a step entirely in the air, for it is supposing him to reason in contradiction to his premises. He has every reason to believe that he has created the violoncello, and that he will successively create the violins and the other pieces, and annihilate them the next moment—just as he creates a sweet taste by putting a lump of sugar upon his tongue, and destroys it by tasting something else. All these facts are parts of him—of that series of feelings which he is—and it is utterly inconceivable that any association or combination of them, or such further facts as that certain of them occur now successively, and now all at once, should ever lead him to the contrary opinion, or to the belief that different parts of one object can be present at once, and yet be distinct from each other. How should similar sensations be distinguished except as present or not present? Shall we say that he has an innate capacity for distinguishing them as signs of different objects, which accordingly may exist even when they are not perceived? No doubt we are conscious of such a faculty in ourselves; but this consciousness no more explains this faculty than the *virtus dormitiva* explains the action of opium in putting us to sleep; it is only another statement of the fact. Evidently there is something that needs explanation in the claim to perceive as existing all at once something which is in reality successive. The only object that he knows of is the sensation he actually feels; the only *place* is place in a sequence of feelings, and this is indivisible and admits of no discrimination, and no relation of different things of the same kind, except between that which exists and that which does not exist. The presence of several feelings at once must mean the coincidence of affections of different organs; such as a smell, a taste, and the feeling of a smooth surface occurring at the same time with the sound to which he is listening. But these do not form parts of one whole, nor, whether they occur all at once or successively, is there any Space between them.

Of course our blind man will be free to admit the existence of certain general conditions, normally accompanying his particular sensations—that is to say, certain preliminary feelings generally announce to him that he is in a position to evoke a sweet taste, or the sound of the violoncello, etc. But the assertion that these conditions are *external* to him, and continue to exist whether they are felt or not; that, besides their quality as sensations, they have another quality as signs, in virtue of which they are *somewhere* all the time, ready to evoke similar sensations; or are capable observing as fixed points, in relation to which the position of other sensations can be fixed, must seem to him a most violent paradox, and it would not be mitigated, so far as I can see, by the universal prevalence of such an opinion, or by any degree of regularity in the order of phenomena. How should he ever come to suppose that they are anything else than just what they appear to be?

In order to admit such a conclusion he must first have come, not merely to distrust his senses, but to the implicit assumption that their informations are of no value whatever; that their value lies in what they prove, not in what they are—in short, he must have begun to think, instead of merely to feel.

To think is to apprehend the universal relations of our particular and personal experiences; to discover what they signify, or what hypothesis they oblige us to adopt. If it be asked why we put ourselves to this trouble, why, instead of contentedly dwelling in our sensations, we at once go beyond them, try to account for them, and make them intelligible, the only answer is that we cannot help it; that such is our nature. A being like that above supposed, who makes no assumption as to the meaning of his impressions, draws no inferences from them, but just takes them as they are, is the abnormal man, the idiot. The normal man, at the first awakening of consciousness, finds himself with this presumption in his mind: that every one of his sensations is a sign, or has *some* necessary relation to the rest of the universe.

The first *naïve* expression of this discovery is given in the sense of Space—the indefinite *otherness*, the externality and mutual externality of all objects of perception. This is the first aspect of the conception of reality, and by contrast the negation of the reality of the present sensation.

It is impossible to antedate this experience, or to derive it from any simpler *data*. We can analyze it into its implied elements, but then we must not mistake these for facts of Experience, for we have no such experience.

In discussions of Space, as this notion presents itself to common-sense, we are apt to leave out of view this fundamental negation of immediate feeling, upon which it rests, and to take up the matter further on, where this indefinite otherness of the real world has become so familiar, and the presumption of it so instinctive that we are only vaguely conscious of it as a general background underlying all our perceptions. At the same time, it is so intimately associated with each one of them, and above all, of course, with the most familiar—viz., those of sight and touch—that we not unnaturally imagine it as something positive, and suppose that we *see* or *feel* Extension as if it were a general color or surface, distinct from all particular colors and surfaces, instead of being, as it is, not indeed the negation of color or resistance, but the negation of any reality in the sensible qualities taken by themselves.

But this vague image of the general relatedness of objects—if we treat it as if it were derived from experience, by merely leaving out of view the special qualities of our sensations, as visual, tactual, etc., and retaining their positions—dissolves as soon as we endeavor to realize it to our minds in a particular case; for it is, in truth, the picture of a relation without related terms. Our sensations, when we have abstracted from them their special qualities, are simply nothing at all, and cannot be brought into relations with each other or with anything else; and we have to fill out their empty forms with an occult quality of *localization*, which really signifies only the exigencies of our theory.

This is the position of the *local-sign* theory, proposed by Lotze and adopted, with some modifications, by Helmholtz and by Wundt.[3] In this theory, Experience appears (though sometimes under protest) as a *logical* function, a process of interpretation and inference, and not as the simple reflex of a physical process. But, as it is still supposed that all knowledge of matters of fact or of sensible things must be derived immediately from Sensation, the question at once occurs, What is the sensation that informs us of the difference between (say) one edge of a sheet of white paper and the other edge? There is no difference in the sensations. The different positions of the retinal images? This is not a sensation, any more than the width of the sheet is a sensation; it is a physical fact, and our question is how this quantitative fact is derived from nervous affections, which admit of no differences except of quality and degree.

The local-sign theory has no answer to give to this question; it can only urge that there *must have been* a quality in our sensations, or in some of them, which informed us of the position of their objects—else we could never have come to distinguish one part of our body from the others. Lotze[4] conjectures that every impression that can be localized may consist of a fixed association of two elements: a physical process which gives rise to the consciousness of a particular quality (a color, a feeling of warmth, etc.), and a parallel process of unknown nature, perhaps connected with innervation feelings, which is the same for all kinds of impressions, but different for different parts of the body. We cannot tell, says Wundt, precisely in what these differences consist, because we only make use of them for the sake of localization; and apparently have forgotten what they were before we so used them. To such straits are scientific men reduced in their anxiety to avoid metaphysics.

It would be more scientific, I think, to state the fact just as we find it—viz., to say that these differences, so far as we know, do not *exist* until we use them; that the relation of Extension and its terms come into being together, in our perception of external objects; and that we have no knowledge of either of them apart from the other. A single object, alone in the universe, would be nowhere, and it would be unextended, until we conceived it as divided into parts, standing in relations to each other.

In short, our case is that we have no discernment of things as they are by themselves, directly corresponding to our nervous affections, but only of phenomena—*i.e.*, of things determined and made what they are by the relations which the mind discovers in them; things as they must be thought, not things as they are felt. The object seen is not the impression on the retina, nor anything corresponding to it—for nothing can correspond to one affection of my nervous system except another affection of it—but such a thing "as must be present in order to produce, under the normal conditions of observation, these retinal images."[5] Or, rather, not *these*, for that is impossible, but images requiring the same interpretation. Accordingly, whatever presents the evidence requiring that interpretation presents the object, whether it is there or not. No reader, probably, sees in this page a blank space (or two blank spaces) "big enough to contain eleven full moons"; but the reason why everybody does not see it is that most persons see what is to them convincing proof that the page is full of letters, and, accordingly, supply the letters where they are wanting. A practiced observer, who has turned his attention to these matters, sees the *lacuna*; but, if he supposes that by any study or any perfection of apparatus he will ever come to see things "just as they are," without any interference of the mind, he is the victim of misplaced confidence in a metaphysical theory. He will only substitute new hypotheses for the old.

To wind up these somewhat cursory remarks: The notion of Space, like all our notions, and like the whole content of our experience, is the workmanship of the mind operating with *data* of which, because they lie below consciousness, we know nothing directly. If we call these *data* sensations, then it is clear that there is no sensation of Space as an objective fact, because there is no sensation of any object—because Sensation is its own object, and has no other. "There is something there," means something *else* than my sensation. If we say (as we may) that to be conscious of a feeling is to be conscious that it has relation to *something* beyond itself, then there is no objection to the position that we have a feeling, or a sense, of Space, which needs only to be clearly set before the mind and to have its implications made explicit, in order to become the notion of Space; only that, as it differs from those organic feelings which we commonly call sensations precisely in this, that it *can* be made more explicit—in other words, that we can discriminate those operations of the mind for which it stands—it becomes superfluous and misleading to insist on the fact that it is *also* a sensation. Superfluous because any of our experiences may take the form of sensations, if we dwell only on the personal impressions they make upon us; and misleading because saying this seems to say that they are nothing more—as if we were to say of a man that he is an animal.

If, finally, it be asked, as it has been lately asked, whether the notion of Space, then, is a purely mental creation, or whether it corresponds to something independent of the mind, the answer is that this depends upon what we mean by the mind.

If we mean a consciousness of feelings, past and present, connected by the thread of memory, evidently such a sequence cannot create a system of necessary relations between its various parts—still less be conscious of them as all present at once. To such a consciousness spatial existence must appear as something altogether strange and incomprehensible—an ultimate fact, not to be reconciled with the other facts of experience. The feelings of an infant when first it begins to dawn upon him that there is something outside of himself we may conjecture to be of this sort. But there is no reason why we should endeavor to perpetuate this infantile state of mind.

If we mean Self-consciousness—the mind returning upon itself and its impressions, and qualifying these as true or false, real or unreal, through their rational interpretation as signs of something ulterior (which is our actual state)—we may say that Space is the creation of the mind, just as we may say that the sense or the notion of right or wrong is the creation of the mind—since nothing is right or wrong until somebody sees it to be so—without meaning that it is anything unreal, or admitting the possibility of a state of things in which these distinctions would not hold good.

NOTES

1. E.g., Stumpf: *Über den psychologischen Ursprung der Raumvorstellung.* Leipzig, 1873. Riehl: *Vierteljahrsschrift für wissenschaftliche Philosophie*, 1877, 2tes H., p. 215.

2. *Psychologie comme science naturelle.* See, also, Rév. Philos., 1876, p. 745.

3. *Grundzüge der physiologischen Psychologie*, 478 f.

4. *Mikrokosmus* I, 357.

5. Helmholtz: *Populäre wissenschaftliche Vorträge*, 2tes H., p. 91.

Thomas Davidson

Individuality

Sketches and Reminiscences of the Radical Club of Chestnut Street, ed. Mary Elizabeth Fiske Sargent (Boston: J. R. Osgood, 1880), pp. 334–338.

This summary of Davidson's paper, for which no original is extant, is dateable to 21 October 1878. Sergeant's preface explains, "The volume has been made up from the recollections of friends, from notes and reports made of the meetings" but no dates for meetings are provided. The magazine *The Christian Union* (New York) for 30 October 1878 published this religious news on p. 357–8:

The Boston "Chestnut St. Club"—which is a very informal organization—takes its name from the fact that its meetings are held in the parlors of the house on Chestnut Street long the residence of the late Rev. John T. Sargent. Mr. Sargent died last year, and Mrs. Sargent, who is a residual legatee of her husband's intellectual and spiritual assets, still opens her doors to the resort of the old illustrious company. The very few of its members who are in any way identified with Christian churches are Unitarians of the distinctively liberal wing. At its meeting Monday a week ago the guests were received by the Rev. Dr. Bartol, who congratulated them that the club does not hibernate but estivates, as it were, and is now ready for the new season. The Club has been defined as a meeting of the unintelligible to discuss the unknowable. The title was substantiated in part by the character of the present meeting, the feature of which was a paper by Mr. Thomas Davidson, on Individuality. Mr. Davidson went back to the Greek philosophers, to begin with, and ended with an exposition of his own sense "of the necessity of contradiction in our ideas of unity and multiplicity." The discussion which followed his essay, participated in by Dr. Bartol, Prof. Benjamin Peirce, of Harvard College, Prof. Felix Adler, the Rev. D. A. Wasson and Col. Higginson, wandered off into such depths of metaphysical abstruseness that Mr. Davidson was obliged to say at the close that he doubted if he could make himself clearer where he had not been understood. The purpose of his essay, he explained, "had been to show that all existence implies an absolute identity of contraries, and that we must reject the law of formal logic which says that A is A, and that A is not not A. The trouble in modern thought is that it asserts the impossibility of conceiving the unity of contradictions." To what amazing heights is not the Boston intellect capable of soaring!

Mr. Davidson traced the progress of philosophical thought from its beginning with the Greek philosophers, and concluded with a statement of his own views on the doctrine of individuality, and the necessity of contradiction in our ideas of unity and multiplicity. "Individual," in its radical meaning, is much like "atom" as it is used by modern physicists. The fundamental question of all, which embraces the whole subject of philosophy, is, "What is the nature of individuality?" All early attempts at philosophy were to find a rational explanation of the external universe. Thought first rested upon the conception of a universal physical element; then Pythagoras introduced the idea of abstract form or number. First there was the idea of unity; Pythagoras introduced that of multiplicity, though he really assumed it in his very argument. Thus we get the primitive forms of the antithetic identity and multiplicity which runs through all philosophy. Heraclitus developed the Ionic school, and the Eleatics the Pythagorean. Among the followers of the former are the Stoics and the whole school of Hegel. Neither Heraclitus nor the Eleatics arrived at permanent individuality. The one assumed absolute matter and denied absolute form; the other assumed absolute form and denied absolute matter; but both matter and form are predicates of individuals, though neither is alone.

Mr. Davidson traced the progress of philosophy in its quest for a tenable individuality through Anaxagoras, Socrates, the Sophists, Plato, and Aristotle, showing that each had a logical place in the development of thought—the succession being, first, a positing of formless matter; second, of matterless form, or number; third, conditioned matter; fourth, conditioned ideas. But none of these accounts for things as they are. A *deus ex machina* is always needed, and, being the ground of all real existence, is, of course, all real existence—a pantheism with which no human mind was ever satisfied. After Plato had brought philosophy to the conditioned idea, came Aristotle, and tried to account for all being. His great service to philosophy was, that he saw the law that the true individual is always subject, and never can be predicate; but he failed to find a permanent real individuality. In the Middle Ages the contest between Platonism and Aristotelianism came into the Church with success to the latter; and to this day the

Roman Catholic Church holds the doctrines of Aristotle.

In the later part of his paper Mr. Davidson elaborated his theory of individuality. Individualism implies unity and multiplicity and the absolute identity of the two. If God's creating man in his own image means anything, it is that he gave as his substantial essence something which should at once be one and many, and one in the very same sense in which it is many. In consciousness we have the only thing which corresponds to the conception of unity with multiplicity. The unity is in the subject or *ego*, and the multiplicity is in the objective world which is necessary to our thought of personal identity, and the two are identified in thought. The entire unity of consciousness is in every thought, and every separate thought presupposes the entire unity of consciousness. This identification of individuality with triune consciousness makes both atheism and pantheism impossible.

In the Middle Ages, freedom—that is, individuality—was nearly quenched by the doctrine of the omnipotence of God and the nothingness of the human creature. Since the Reformation the case has been nearly reversed. The present cry for freedom, which takes the form of atheism, license, and universal suffrage, is just as one-sided and leads to results as little desirable as the theory of entire subjection which prevailed in mediaeval Europe. Only with freedom in subjection and subjection in freedom is perfect individuality possible.

Professor Peirce followed. "We would like to know more of the connection between the old Greek and the Chaldaic philosophers," he said. "From the tablets lately discovered in Nineveh it seems that the final result of their philosophy was, that there were two beings—the idea and chaos. Power and motion then came in, and the universe was developed. Moses probably got his accounts from the Chaldees, and added the idea of a deity." Professor Peirce doubted if the human mind could reason with regard to the Infinite. From our observations of the stars we find that the universe is finite. If we go back to chaos and have nothing but that, there would be a stable equilibrium. If it was disturbed by force, it would come to rest again. In the beginning there must have been a force in which all change was differentiated. Chaos must have had a plan of the universe put upon it from without. The tendency of modern science is to come to a point where there shall be no final action. Then the force in the universe must be a finite force. But the power in the universe could not have had a beginning, and it must have been in the world at its beginning. If anything is true in physics this is; and this power is infinite. Man cannot reason about it: we may call that power bad, or anything else—you have God in every part of the universe.

Professor Felix Adler stated that the mind demands a first cause; but immediately, finding that everything which conditions is conditioned, it demands the cause of the first cause, and so we have no first cause at all. Both these demands of the mind—for first cause and its cause—should be recognized. If God was the cause of the world and was eternal, then the world was eternal—a contradiction. The doctrine of the trinity is only a fair, alluring fantasy. It covers the abyss of the infinite, and is simply a bridge of flowers, which does not bear substantial footsteps.

Mr. Wasson followed with an earnest protest against individualism, and the sophistry that there is no universal truth. In that doctrine there is nothing which has power to say "Thou shalt." We have ten thousand million "I wills," and out of them comes our democracy. Until we get a "Thou shalt" into politics, we have no commonwealth.

Mr. Higginson was not in favor of insisting upon the importance of authority at the present time. He shrinks from communism and the principle of absolute obedience to an absolute authority. It points directly to the time when the people will rise, and take all the railroads and trains, perhaps, and work them in the interest of that absolute power. The only ways in which we can get that absolute power are through a hereditary monarchy, through the Roman Catholic Church, or through the commune. He believes the only safe way is not to rebel against universal suffrage or individualism. He believes it best to have as little government as possible; and the laws here are respected because we make them ourselves.

Mr. Wasson again urged the necessity of a "Thou shalt," saying that behind this lies the "ought"; and Mr. Higginson replied that the representative teacher of that doctrine, Carlyle, had always stopped short of telling how far the "ought" went. For a practical way of learning what it is—apart from the three arbitrary ways above mentioned—we are left to the clumsy method of educating the race. That is the best way of finding the "ought."

Professor Hyatt doubted the conclusion that may be reached regarding the nature of thought. At present he thinks we can predicate nothing beyond the statement that matter is infinite. Nothing is proved about form or thought, and the world is disputing whether they exist at all.

At the close Mr. Davidson spoke briefly. The purpose of his essay had been to show that all existence implies an absolute balance of contraries; that Being itself, as Being, as thinkable, is necessarily triune—an object implying a subject and a relation of entire real unity and ideal difference between the two. He expressed satisfaction at finding that those who understood him agreed with him.

Borden Parker Bowne

The Cosmic Philosophy

Methodist Quarterly Review 58 (October 1876): 655–678.

Review of John Fiske, *Outlines of Cosmic Philosophy, Volume 2*. Boston: Houghton Mifflin, 1874.

Mr. Fiske has been before the public for some time as the disciple and interpreter of Mr. Spencer, and needs, therefore, no introduction. The work before us is, in brief, a popular exposition of the Spencerian philosophy. Nor could Mr. Spencer wish for a more sympathetic interpreter. Mr. Fiske has reproduced the evolution philosophy, and that, too, with all the freshness of originality. The style leaves nothing to be desired. The obscurity, if there be any, is in the thought, and not in the expression. Our plan is to give some general hints whereby the reader may judge of the Spencerian philosophy in general, and of Mr. Fiske's work in particular. This philosophy, as based upon sensational psychology, is open to all the objections against sensationalism. Hume proved, once for all, that a sensational philosophy must end in utter skepticism. The disciples have not disproved the master's conclusion; they have ignored it, a procedure which is creditable to neither their consistency nor their insight. We will not delay, however, upon these general considerations, but proceed at once to the more specific features of the doctrine.

The student of the Spencerian philosophy is met with a puzzle at the outset in the theory of the unknowable. This theory was originally intended to reconcile science and religion by forbidding both to speculate concerning the ultimate cause of things. It is commonly understood as meaning that we can make no positive affirmations whatever concerning the ground of the universe. "It is forever inscrutable," and all our affirmations concerning it land us in insoluble contradictions. This is the common conception of the doctrine, and the greater part of Mr. Spencer's and Mr. Fiske's language supports this view. The difficulty is, that both of these philosophers have written great works concerning this ultimate ground, and have made diverse positive affirmations about it; in all of which, too, they seem to have unlimited faith. Throughout their systems this unknowable appears as a mechanical cause working according to mechanical laws, and having sundry attributes and not having sundry others. Now, it is plain that if we are to take the word unknowable in its strict sense, we should forever hold our peace after having laid down this know-nothing theory; for if it be strictly unknowable, then all theories, scientific as well as religious, are without objective validity. To set them up is a waste of time; but to claim for one greater authority than the other is a wanton impertinence. Now, as these philosophers have written books in favor of their views of things, and inasmuch as these views include sundry theories concerning the ground of things and its modes of activity, we must conclude that by unknowable they do not mean unknowable. Mr. Fiske has a passage (vol. ii, p. 469) which seems to give up the literal meaning of the word. Our notions are not false, but symbolic. But here a new difficulty arises. If a symbol is not false, it must represent, at least approximately, the true nature of the thing. If this is the theory, the unknowable becomes a mere commonplace, and the reconciliation between science and religion which it was intended to bring about vanishes. For, now that we admit that our religious and scientific symbols may approximate the truth, the question arises, Which of these symbols best represents the objective fact of the universe? That is, the old quarrel between science and religion breaks out as fiercely as ever. There is another theory, which we merely mention, namely, that when they say, We know nothing of the nature of things, the we is the we editorial, and means the opponents of the doctrine. Many passages could be brought in support of this view, as the unknowable is not unfrequently used as a sort of *Medusa's* head to petrify antagonists. We merely mention this theory, without pretending to support it. The real dilemma is this: if the ground of things be strictly unknowable, we must all keep still—scientist and theologian alike. If it is not unknowable, why, then, it is not unknowable, and every one must be allowed to bring forward his views and support them by evidence. So much for the unknowable in general. A word remains to be said concerning its value in a scientific system.

The problem of science is to find a comprehensive ground for a definite body of phenomena, and the unknowable is postulated as such a ground. But it needs no argument to show that an indefinite nnknowability is worthless for this purpose. As long as x in mathematics is brought into no definite relations to known quantities, it may stand for anything, and is nothing. But as soon as this indefinite is put into a determinate equation it acquires a fixed value. In the same way, when we attempt to solve the equation expressing the relation between the absolute and the known body of phenomena, we must either give that absolute a definite value, or throw away the equation. We must either postulate it as a definite cause with definite attributes and definite ways of working, or we must not postulate it at all. What these attributes are can be settled only by a careful study of the facts; but it is clear that there are certain conditions to be fulfilled, and a first cause which will not fulfill them must be dismissed without further ado; first, as a logical impostor, and, second, as philosophically and scientifically worthless. The Positivist doctrine, which refuses to admit anything behind phenomena, is intelligible and consistent. The opposite view, which insists upon a definite cause with assignable attributes or ways of working, is also intelligible and consistent. But the Spencerian theory, which is not content to stop with phenomena, but affirms a cause = x, is neither intelligible nor consistent; and neither Mr. Spencer nor Mr. Fiske have succeeded in being true to the theory. Here, again, our previous conclusion emerges that the term unknowable is not to be taken in a strict sense; that is, it degenerates into the philosophic commonplace that we do not know everything.

But what is it to know? This question is vital to the whole discussion, and its answer describes the element of truth in the nescience doctrine. The problem of knowledge is not to tell how being is made, or to give a recipe for creation. It is rather to comprehend the manifold of existence under the various categories of thought. If anyone demands how the essence of being is constituted, we cheerfully admit that we do not know. If creation were our business it might be an important question, but otherwise not. To know in the only sense possible to men is, first, to be sure that a thing exists; and, second, that it falls under certain categories, or has certain definite attributes or ways of working. Assuming, for example, that the soul exists, our knowledge thereof would consist, not in an insight into its substance, but in our certainty: first, that it exists; and, second, that it has certain definite modes of activity. In this way we gain all our knowledge. Going out from the facts of experience, we are forced to assume, first, that a thing exists; and, second, that it has certain properties. This constitutes our knowledge of the thing. Plainly, a knowledge of the first cause in this sense must be possible, because phenomena force us to assume its existence, and to attribute to it definite properties. What these properties may be, must be determined from a study of the facts; but when the facts force us to assume such a first cause, and force us to attribute to it certain definite properties, then we know that first cause in precisely the same sense in which we know anything. This theory of knowledge leaves "the mystery of being" just where it was; and in so far the know-nothing is right, but no further. How being is made, or how action is possible, we do not know. The fact that things exist and that interaction is possible, is the great and omnipresent mystery. But to say we cannot tell how being is made is one thing; to say that we know nothing about it when it is made is quite another. Is knowledge in this sense possible? If so, we are content.

Mr. Fiske's main objection against such knowledge of the ground of phenomena is the contradictions into which reason falls whenever it ascribes any attributes whatever to the absolute. He reaches this conclusion in the regular way, namely, by analyzing the idea of the absolute, of the infinite, and of first cause. It is somewhat disheartening to find this sophism reproduced with so much confidence, resting, as it does, purely upon the etymology of the words, and not upon an analysis of their psychological content. The etymological absolute cannot co-exist with the relative, for the word means cut off and separate. No more can the etymological infinite co-exist with the finite, for etymologically the infinite is the all; and it is absurd enough to suppose that there should be something outside of the all. Hence the first cause, which we must conceive of as absolute and infinite, cannot be conceived as co-existing with the finite and relative without insoluble contradiction. Mr. Fiske makes his task still easier by defining the absolute as that "which exists out of all relations," (vol. i, p. 9); and, of course, an absolute which never comes into any relations with anything could never come into knowledge. How the absolute thus defined could be the cause and support of phenomena, as Mr. Fiske assumes it is, does not appear. In this way Mr. Fiske routs all theistic philosophies. Unluckily, however, etymologizing is not philosophizing; and the etymological absolute and the etymological infinite are not identical with the real absolute and the real infinite. Upon a study of nature we find that its manifold of forces and things are all conditioned and limited. We are carried, then, by the laws of our thinking, to affirm an unconditional and unlimited being. This being is *not unconditioned in the sense of being out of relation*, but as being the source of the conditions and limitations of things to which it stands in causal relation. It is not infinite in the sense of being the all, but as limiting finite things without being in turn determined by them. This is the true content of the notion of the absolute and the infinite. The absolute is not unrelated, but unrestricted by anything external to itself; the infinite is not the all, but the independent something upon which the finite depends. If the know-nothing claims that absolute and infinite are not proper terms for the being thus described, we have no objection; we only insist that the true content of these notions be kept in mind by whoever attempts to reason upon them. Grammatical exegesis is good in its place, but it cannot do the work of psychological analysis.

One need not be told that Mr. Fiske is far from faithful to his own logic. After having objected to theism because it involves the contradictory notions of the absolute, infinite, and first cause, and after having shown that the absolute cannot come into relation, he tells us, "The cosmic philosophy is found upon the recognition of an absolute power, manifested in and through the world of phenomena."—Vol. i, p. 263. When the theist said "theistic philosophy is founded upon a recognition of an absolute power (God) manifested in and through the world of phenomena," Mr. Fiske protested with all his might,"The absolute exists out of all relations"; "it can be known only by ceasing to be the absolute"; it cannot come into relation without losing its absoluteness. And yet, when, instead of theistic philosophy, we read cosmic philosophy—that is, Mr. Fiske's philosophy—the refractory and recalcitrant absolute kindly consents to be known, to enter into relations, to manifest itself in space and time—the very thing which, by the way, Mr. Fiske says it cannot do, at least for theistic philosophers. We have failed to find any satisfactory explanation of this peculiar partiality of the absolute for the cosmic philosophy.

Again, in treating of theism, Mr. Fiske, following in the wake of Mr. Spencer, objects to it as teaching a self-existent God. The idea is declared to be viciously unthinkable, and any system involving it is found to be untenable. But here, again, the same peculiar partiality of the absolute for the cosmic philosophers appears. The fundamental reality which they postulate as the support of phenomena, turns out to be self-existent, infinite, absolute, and first cause—the very notions which were declared to be fatal to theism. The explanation is, doubtless, that the absolute is not subject to the law of non-contradiction, and if it chooses to do for the cosmists what it will not do for the theists, why the latter must grin and bear it. Of course, Mr. Fiske is serious, but his use of the absolute is strikingly like the heathen

Chinese's use of the right bower. Perhaps, however, Mr. Fiske is like that old Church father whose faith was so strong that the contradictions of a doctrine were the strongest reasons for belief. It is certain that the pride of sinful reason could not be more effectually mortified than by an acceptance of the cosmist's creed on this point.

Another strong support of the know-nothing doctrine is the theory of relativity. The insufficiency of this doctrine as a theory of knowledge, so far as it is anything but the baldest truism, has been abundantly shown, and by no one better than by Professor Martin.[1] We pass over this discussion, therefore, and content ourselves with pointing out the utter irrelevancy of the doctrine. For it is plain that whatever discredit this doctrine casts upon our faculties, it must be impartially distributed over them all. Such discredit, therefore, belongs as much to scientific as to religious theories. Considering, therefore, the prophecies of peace on the philosophic earth, and of good-will between scientists and theologians when once this doctrine should be recognized, it is quite disheartening to find only another instance of the mountain's being in labor and bringing forth a mouse. For universal skepticism is none—a doctrine which discredits all our beliefs and notions, leaves them all in the same relative position, and really discredits none of them. A skepticism which builds upon the more immediate intuitions, and then proceeds to discredit those which lie at a greater distance from direct certainty, is the only dangerous one. For example: A skepticism which should go out from our mathematical and mechanical notions, and claim to deduce from them the moral and religions sentiments, would be absolutely fatal if it could make out its thesis. But a skepticism which discredits all alike is harmless. If the theologian can show that religious ideas have as much evidence as scientific ones, he is perfectly content to allow the skeptic to vapor as he pleases about the uncertainty of human knowledge. The healthy trust of the mind in itself, and daily contact with reality, will speedily cure these eruptions. It is too evident to need any proof that peace between science and religion can never be secured in this way, for either this doctrine reduces us all to silence, or else it allows all to speak. In the former case all theories, scientific as well as religious, are subjective delusions; in the latter case the doctrine gives us no means of deciding between rival theories. Even granting that all our notions concerning the first cause are but symbolisms, if we are to think at all, we must think in terms of those symbolisms; and the question arises whether religious or scientific symbolisms better represent the fact—shall we think of it as a mechanical cause, or as a free creator? as a blind force, or as a conscious person? Thus the problem emerges at the end of the discussion in just the same form as at the beginning, while, as in the case of the sheared pig, the amount of serviceable wool secured from the transaction is far from atoning for the discomfort of the attending outcry. This conclusion can be escaped only by saying that all our ideas are utterly false, in which case the notions of evolution and of mechanical science, as well as those of philosophy and religion, must vanish into delusion and dream, and all theorizing must cease. When Mr. Fiske claims that certain mechanical conceptions of the primal activity are the only tenable ones, and seeks thereby to deprive the theistic argument of its force, it is simply a monstrous inconsistency.

The determined skeptic may say, in criticism of our theory of knowledge, that although certain conclusions may be necessary for us, it does not follow that they are true in themselves. Our thinking comes necessarily to certain ways of regarding the cause of things, but we can never prove that those ways are objectively real. The subjective necessity does not prove objective fact. It is admitted that the laws of our thought make the conclusion necessary, but no proof can ever be given; that this conclusion represents objective fact. To refute this objection is impossible. If there be any objective necessity it can only appear in knowledge as a subjective necessity. But we may test its value by applying it. The mathematician says, "The radii of the same circle are all equal"; or "a straight line is the shortest distance between two points"; or "if equals be added to equals the sums will be equal." The relativist says, "How do you know that?" The other replies, "I cannot think them otherwise." The answer is, of course, "Ah, yes! but it is only a subjective necessity which forces you to think so; it may well be that in fact your mathematics have no objective validity." This skepticism is always possible, but the mathematician is not at all dismayed, nor do mathematics run any very serious risks from such attacks. Now the skepticism which objects to our affirmations about the first cause or any other cause on the ground of their subjectivity, has just as much value and no more; it is forever irrefutable and forever barren. It is merely gratuitous skepticism; it can offer no reasons, and so long it is a mere impertinence which busy and earnest men may justly ignore. The natural healthy trust of the mind in itself will never allow one to trouble himself long with such doubts as these. We must, therefore, regard the theory of the unknowable as a worthless piece of philosophic lumber. The psychologist rejects it as resting upon a false theory of knowledge; the scientist rejects it as coming into no intelligible relations to phenomena, and therefore useless in scientific explanations; the theologian rejects it as worthless in religion, and finally Mr. Fiske and Mr. Spencer themselves reject it by the most expressed contradictions of the theory. The only mode of escape is the one to which we have several times referred, namely, to say that the word unknowable is not to be taken in its strict sense, in which ease the theory loses all meaning and importance.

It is interesting to know that the theory is rapidly falling into discredit even among scientists. A writer in the *Fortnightly Review* declares, in a review of Mr. Fiske, that it is high time to save the evolution doctrine from its best friends, adding that this ontological abstraction of the unknowable which cannot be brought into intelligible relation to our physical theories is of no use to anyone. Mr. Lewes, also, has felt called upon to repudiate Mr. Spencer's physics and metaphysics. This is an advance, and is prophetic of further progress. Hitherto, owing to the scientific language of this philosophy, every attack upon it was apt to be resented as an outbreak of theological hostility. It is gratifying, therefore, to find a growing recognition of the fact that a system does not become science by merely calling itself scientific.

We pass now to the scientific part of Mr. Fiske's system with the full understanding that the theories therein advanced shall not be allowed to take advantage of the doctrine of the unknowable to cover up weak logic, but shall be subject to the same rules of evidence and conceivability as every other system. We have seen that any discredit which Mr. Fiske's metaphysics may have thrown upon the knowing mind, must be impartially distributed all around; and, therefore, scientific, philosophic, and religious doctrines remain all in the same relative position which they had at first. We have gained, therefore, nothing from the doctrine of the unknowable except another and unusually sad instance of wasted effort. We have now to inquire whether Mr. Fiske's mechanical theory of the universe agrees better with the facts and the laws of our thinking than does the theistic theory.

We mention, in passing, a huge gap which Mr. Spencer left in his system at this point, and which Mr. Fiske has not filled up. Their unknowable in both works is left, like the gods of Epicurus, without any thing to do beyond gorgonizing opponents. This scientific exposition is based almost entirely upon the atomic conception of matter. Their deduction of the universe demands only a manifold of atoms. This granted, they are ready for unlimited deduction. These atoms, interacting according to the known laws of mechanics, must, it is proved, build up the actual universe. All phenomena are proved, with painful elaborateness, to be but special cases of molecular mechanics. Now, in all this the unknowable one plays no part; and it is plain that it is useless, unless it can be shown that the atoms necessitate the assumption of a primal unity. But this is a proof which we are unable to find in either Mr. Spencer's or Mr. Fiske's writings. Both have, indeed, pronounced the atomic conception inconceivable; but, then, they have pronounced every other conception equally inconceivable; and as we must form some conception, it may as well be the atomic as any other if scientific facts seem to render it necessary. Moreover, if we should strike out from their works the arguments based upon this conception, there would be next to nothing remaining. His scientific argument, therefore, demands only the assumption of a primitive plurality and not a primitive unity. Both Mr. Fiske and Mr. Spencer have taken it very easy in this matter. It does not follow because *noumena* are inaccessible to our intelligence that they are, therefore, one. Oxygen, hydrogen, carbon, might well be unknowable in their essence without being identical in essence. Arguments might possibly be found to necessitate such an assumption, but neither Mr. Fiske nor Mr. Spencer have given them. Admitting the justice of their metaphysics, we reach a plurality of unknowables and not an unknowable one. This they have simply assumed. It might possibly be said that the correlation of the forces proves the unity of the ground of phenomena; but no one will say so who knows what the doctrine means.

Mr. Fiske reproduces Spencer's doctrine of evolution, and adopts his famous definition, as follows: "Evolution is an integration of matter and concomitant dissipation of motion during which the matter passes from an indefinite incoherent homogeneity to a definite coherent heterogeneity, and during which the retained motion undergoes a parallel transformation." Of this definition much might be said. The word in definite must not be taken strictly for that which is strictly indefinite—that is, without definite attributes or powers—is incapable of anything. First of all, then, we must assume a definite agent or agents, with definite laws in place of the indefinite homogeneous. The homogeneous, too, must not be strictly homogeneous, for, remembering that this homogeneous represents the all, it is clear that strict homogeneity would make change impossible. Next, we replace the indefinite homogeneous by a definite heterogeneous in order to make change conceivable. The formula then reads: Evolution is a change from a definite heterogeneous to another definite heterogeneous. Moreover, it is difficult to tell precisely what is meant by this indefinite homogeneous. One would expect the unknowable to play some part in it; but the most of the argument upon it assumes it to be the original nebula of material atoms with all their definite powers and relations, which is far enough from being an indefinite homogeneous, or even a homogeneous of any kind. Finally, Mr. Spencer's formula is a description, and not an explanation. It is not, by any means, self-evident that things must take the course here described. It is necessary, therefore, to prove that this original homogeneity must originate the present orderly system. This Mr. Spencer attempts to do by establishing the three principles of the "instability of the homogeneous," the "multiplication of effects," and the "integration of correspondences." Three very formidable looking principles which certainly ought to be able to accomplish something.

It has been a frequent boast of Mr. Spencer's admirers that his critics have not ventured to grapple with these principles, and they have further remarked that so long as these doctrines stood, Spencerism was invulnerable. Mr. Fiske, too, has great faith in them, though he refers the reader to Mr. Spencer for their full development and proof. Let us see, then, what these doctrines may have to say for themselves. And, first, we examine the alleged instability of the homogeneous. The doctrine is, that the homogeneous being unstable, must fall into heterogeneous forms, and some of these heterogeneities will be worlds, and solar systems, and forms of life, and these will go on improving until things look as if they had had an intelligent maker. The doctrine looks amazingly like the old doctrine of chance; but has this principle itself any warrant? Remember, this homogeneous is to be considered mechanically; and now suppose the original force perfectly homogeneous, what will follow? If homogeneous, it must be in equilibrium, and change could never result. The mathematician knows this, and proves that if the world be merely a mechanical system, it must have been in motion with a certain direction and velocity from all eternity, because no interaction of any system of material bodies can affect the sum of their motion measured in any direction whatever. The examples given by Mr. Spencer and Mr. Fiske consist invariably of seeming homogeneities in the presence of heterogeneous forces, and the resulting action is offered as an illustration of the instability of the homogeneous—

In the impossibility of balancing an accurately made pair of scales, in the equal impossibility of keeping a tank of water free from currents, in the rusting of iron, and in the uneven cooling of heated metals, is exemplified the principle that the state of homogeneity is an unstable state. Universally the tendency of things amid the conflict of unlike forces is toward heterogeneity. (vol. I, p. 353)

This is as good as anything that either Mr. Spencer or Mr. Fiske has upon the subject. "Things amid the conflict of unlike forces" are universally adduced as illustrations of the homogeneous! The rusted iron is a composite effect depending on the interaction of iron and nascent oxygen; the two together being far enough from homogeneous. If instead of oxygen one should put nitrogen in contact with the iron, the homogeneity would not be diminished, and yet it would be stable enough. The light bearing either is assumed to be homogeneous, but it shows no signs of instability. Even our own atmosphere is sufficiently homogeneous to allow the principle a fair chance to work, but it does not evolve anything to speak of.

Mr. Spencer, however, is not content with an induction of this principle. It is not sufficient to point out that mortar gets lumpy, that iron rusts, and that jelly is very apt to candy; it must be rationally deduced from some ulterior principle. And here the hopeless helplessness of the doctrine appears. The principle upon which the instability of the homogeneous rests is the persistence of force. Force is forever at work producing changes, and hence the instability of the homogeneous. But it is plain that instability in general, both of the homogeneous and of the heterogeneous, ought to result from such a principle. Force is ever weaving, and force is ever unweaving; hence all things pass. But how in the face of this notion Mr. Spencer can erect the stability of the heterogeneous into a principle is one of the many mysteries which he has bequeathed to the philosophic world. One can easily understand how necessary the assumption is to fit out the new philosophy; but where it finds its warrant in any mechanical system is more than we can tell. Mr. Spencer offers it as a fact, however, and points out that it is exemplified in the paths of the planets, none of which are circles (homogeneous) but rather ellipses (heterogeneous). We are not quite sure of the principle by which the ellipse is determined to be heterogeneous and the circle homogeneous; but the pretended stability of the elliptical orbit lies in the fact that a curve may go through any number of variations and still be an ellipse, while the circle cannot change at all without ceasing to be a circle. The orbits of the planets are never the same ellipses from one hour to another; but since the ever-changing orbit remains an ellipse, the common name is made to cover the variability, and the result is held up as an example of the stability of the heterogeneous! Finally, the other principle of the integration of correspondences is the direct contradiction of the instability of the homogeneous. The aim of that principle is to get like with like, that is, to produce the homogeneous—a procedure against which the instability of the homogeneous must resolutely set its face. Hence, the three great creative principles are at war with one another, and no one can be true without destroying the rest. It is possible enough that here, as elsewhere, wisdom is justified only of her children, and that some peculiar insight is vouchsafed to the disciples of this school which is denied to the outside world. There seems to be no other way of explaining the enthusiasm which they seem to feel.

In fact, this whole attempt to make the order of the world mechanically intelligible is an unpardonable sin against the first principles of the mechanical theory. The notion of a mechanical system is not very clearly defined, but this certainly belongs to it: any given event flows with necessity from its antecedents. Hence, if at any point whatever in the flow of things we make a cross section, we find the actual balance and disposition of things which must in time bring forth the present order. If now, with Mr. Spencer and Mr. Fiske, we view nature mechanically, there never was a time when the present order was not given, or when any other order was possible. It is plain, therefore, that a mechanical system does not really explain the order of the universe, but assumes it at the start. The fundamental fact of such a system is an orderly ongoing of the universe, and all that appears in the course of that ongoing must be regarded, not as explained by science, but as the several phases of the first fact thus assumed. The seeming indeterminateness of lower forms, instead of explaining the harmony and order of the higher ones, is only a preliminary stage through which the universal unfolding has passed in its onward march. The elements are assumed in definite relations, with definite powers and definite direction, so that no other order than the present is possible. By and by, the implicit assumption becomes the explicit fact, and then the whole is held up as a miracle of constructive reasoning. Teleology is forthwith warned off, and word goes round that intelligence is no longer needed to explain the harmony and order of the universe. If it could be shown that the physical order is sufficient unto itself, and that everything can be explained by reference to it, then, and only then, would teleology be finally overthrown. In that case, however, nothing would be explained; everything would be assumed. The error of Mr. Spencer in attempting a mechanical explanation of the universe lies in the assumption that the elements were once a chaos, without definite law, order, or relation. Science, however, knows of no such time. The present forms of things have not always existed, but science knows of no time when the present order of law and of definite relation did not exist; and science knows of no point in the physical flow of things which was not determined by its antecedents. As science, therefore, it knows nothing of a first moment or of a chaos. If, however, an indefinite and chaotic condition of things were thinkable, the chances are infinity to one against any production of harmony or order therefrom. A font of type, knocked into pi, and shaken, would sooner produce a reasonable discourse, than a chaotic mass of atoms would build up the harmony of creation. Mr. Spencer has completely missed the true conception of mechanical science, and his objections to teleology on the authority of his speculations are the weakest possible. The same is to be said of Mr. Fiske's attempt to play off the Darwinian theory against teleology. A mechanical science which understands itself does not go behind phenomena, but rather below them; and if the aim is to dispense with a God, it does not talk of a first moment or of a primal chaos—neither of which are thinkable—but rather of a self-centered world-order, of which the changes of things are the several phases. Such atheistic science recognizes that it explains nothing, but assumes everything. When, however, the teleologist objects that that order must be explained, the just reply is, Every system must assume something to start with, and why may not a primal order be that first fact? "What better right has chaos to existence than harmony? It is the everlasting wonder of the world that it should be so, but then it is so. This reply, which is the strongest one that atheistic science can make, renders the ordinary teleological argument worthless. It points out that nature is driven from behind and not led from before, and that, therefore, final causes are rendered needless by the demonstrable sufficiency of the physical causes to explain phenomena. To meet this argument teleology must reconstruct its argument and choose another standpoint. It must show that this world-order is not independent; and it must show that the very notion of science involves the doctrine of final cause. This, however, is not the place for this discussion. It is plain that Mr. Spencer's and Mr. Fiske's attempt to do away with final causes involves a pitiable lack of insight into the conditions of the problem. From this stand-point their formula of evolution reduces to this: Evolution is evolution.

Nevertheless, Mr. Spencer and Mr. Fiske both claim that this doctrine is not atheism; for although all phenomena, mental and physical alike, can be expressed in terms of matter and motion, and although the seeming intelligence of the universe is but a necessary result of simple mechanical laws, still the fundamental reality is neither matter nor spirit, but a something above both. To be sure, both philosophers habitually speak of this reality in terms of matter and motion; but both are equally emphatic in denying that it can be identified with matter and motion. Mr. Fiske declares that if he had to choose between saying that God is a force and God is a spirit, he would prefer the former expression. However, there is no need of choice, for the fundamental reality is above both matter and spirit. We cannot, indeed, conceive of it; but, then, it lies in the very notion of the unknowable to be unconceivable; and to say that there can be nothing higher than spirit and intelligence, is to confound the inconceivable with the impossible. This is the gist of their argument upon this point. Mr. Spencer further illustrates it by reference to the impiety of the pious, and dressing up an old satire of Xenophanes. The position is, nevertheless, untenable, for whatever we think of must be thought of in either terms of matter or spirit; there is no room in thought for this third something which is neither. Very good, says Mr. Fiske; but do you not see that you are erecting the limits of thought into the limits of being? You are asserting that a thing is impossible because you cannot think it. I occupy a much more modest position, and I find it entirely possible that there may be orders upon orders of being above either material or spiritual existence. It is quite possible, says Mr. Spencer, that there may be forms of being as far above intelligence as intelligence is above mechanism. We answer, we are not concerned about the limits of possibility at all. If they choose to solace themselves with dreams of possible orders of being, we have no objection; but when such an assumption appears as a factor in a philosophical system, we do mean to have it proved, and an appeal to possibility is no proof. The possible is not necessarily real. Remember, we are trying to explain a definite body of material and mental phenomena, and not to invent hypotheses. A spiritual cause will furnish such an explanation; but what help do we get from postulating this third something which is neither material nor spiritual, conscious nor unconscious? It merely doubles our difficulties and removes none. Besides, the notion is nothing new in philosophy. Spinoza adopted it, Schelling adopted it, and neither succeeded in making anything out of it. It was pure assumption to start with, and pure assertion to end with; of no value to science, and impossible in thought. We rule it out, therefore, as both useless and unprovable, and return to see what objections Mr. Fiske has to offer concerning the cause of things as a living intelligence.

Although Mr. Fiske claims to have shown that intelligence is needed to produce the harmony of the universe, he, nevertheless, says that this problem of an intelligent God is incapable of demonstrative solution either way—

I believe that it is beyond the power of science to prove that the Divine Power immanent in the cosmos, either does or does not work by anthropomorphic methods.
We cannot expect, therefore, to obtain a result which, like a mathematical theorem,
shall stand firm through mere weight of logic; or which, like a theorem in physics,
can be subjected to a crucial test.—Vol. ii, p. 378.

It would seem at first sight as if the explanation of the universe by mechanical causes
would render the assumption of intelligence needless; possibly, however, Mr. Fiske has
doubts concerning the thoroughness of his mechanical explanation, and orders up the
following reinforcements—

> Here we are upon the brink of the abyss into which the anthropomorphic hypotheses
> must precipitate us, if instead of passively acquiescing in it as a vague authoritative
> formula, we analyze it with the scientific appliances at our command. To those who
> have acquired some mastery of the physical truths upon which our cosmic philoso-
> phy is based, the doctrine not only ceases to be intellectually consoling, but becomes
> a source of ungovernable disturbance. For to represent the Deity as a person who
> thinks, contrives, and legislates, is simply to represent him as a product of evolution.
> The definition of intelligence being the continuous adjustment of specialized inner
> relations to specialized outer relations, it, follows that to represent the Deity is intel-
> ligent, is to surround Deity with an environment, and thus to destroy its infinity
> and its self-existence. The eternal Power, whereof the web of phenomena is but the
> visible garment, becomes degraded into a mere strand in the web of phenomena,
> and the cosmos is exchange for the loss of the infinite find inscrutable God, receives
> an anomalous sovereign of mythologic pedigree. (vol. ii, p. 398)

As the result, Mr. Fiske says—

Our choice is no longer between an intelligent Deity and none at all: it lies between
a limited Deity and one that is without limit. For, as the foregoing discussion has plainly
shown, and as it must appear in every similar discussion of the subject in terms of the
doctrine of evolution, an anthropomorphic God cannot be conceived as an infinite God.
Personality and infinity are terms expressive of ideas which are mutually incompatible. The
pseudo idea, "infinite person," is neither more nor less unthinkable than circular triangle.
(vol. ii, p. 401)

We doubt if Mr. Fiske would have been quite so dogmatic if he had been a little surer
of his position. The extra emphasis seems to flow from an uneasy, half-consciousness that
the positions are armed chiefly with Quaker guns. Merely noting, by the way, that the
fundamental reality appears in this quotation as self-existent, an impossible idea according to Mr. Fiske, the objections urged are two: God cannot be intelligent, first, because
intelligence is the "continuous adjustment of specialized inner relations to specialized outer
relations"; and, second, because intelligence is only thinkable as a product of evolution. It
is quite a favorite method with the philosophers of the new school to define their terms

in their own interests; thus Mr. Spencer, in arguing against Mr. Martineau, that mind cannot be the cause of things, quietly defines mind as "a series of states of consciousness," and calls upon Mr. Martineau to show how a series of sensations could account for the universe. Mr. Fiske also appears with a definition framed in the interests of his philosophy, and having defined intelligence as "the continuous adjustment of specialized inner relations to specialized outer relations," there is no more to be said upon the subject. Still, victory by definition is so cheap as to arouse suspicion. A philosopher of the old school might object that by an intelligent being he means one capable of conscious thought, knowledge, and action; and for aught we see, this definition would be full as consonant with experience as the other about inner and outer relations. Moreover, Mr. Fiske's definition does not cover the greater part of our intellectual life. It applies, if at all, only to sense perception; but gives no account of the abstract and creative action of the mind, in which there is no trace of adjustment to outer relations. Besides, the definition itself needs explanation. What is meant by "inner relations?" There is really no place for true inwardness in the mechanical scheme. The expression means nothing, unless it means a knowing subject, and then the definition runs, "Intelligence is the continuous adjustment of the knowing subject to the various objects which surround it." This adjustment, however, appears to be only the subject's knowledge of objects, for any other adjustment presupposes conscious intelligence; that is the subject's conscious adjustment of himself to his surroundings would imply a previous knowledge of those surroundings. The definition, then, becomes "Intelligence is a continuous knowing," a very safe proposition, but not a very valuable one. The philosopher of the old school might further point out that although our intelligence is developed, it does not lie in the notion of intelligence that it must be developed. An eternal intelligence is, metaphysically, as possible as an eternal non-intelligence. As to the objection that intelligence and consciousness are incompatible with infinity, we may remark that the denial of those modes of being to the fundamental reality is even more fatal to its infinity. Intelligence and consciousness are higher modes of being than unintelligence and unconsciousness; and to deny them to the infinite is to limit it both qualitatively and quantitatively. Mr. Fiske declares that the infinite must have all power, include all modes of being, and yet it cannot fulfill the conditions of conscious intelligence. But Mr. Fiske's argument on this point is mainly a quibble, based upon a false notion of the infinite. The really weighty objections against the personality of the infinite are not those which he gives.

This question concerning the personality and the intelligence of the first cause has been so twisted and inverted by modern philosophers that it has passed into a philosophical dogma that the notion is self-destructive. It may, therefore, be worthwhile to leave Mr. Fiske for the moment, and inquire whether this traditional philosophic dogma is anything but a prejudice. The question is whether this infinite power back of phenomena exists for itself? whether its activity is attended with consciousness? In affirming personality of that power we merely mean to give an affirmative answer to these questions. The objections thereto, we conceive, are mainly logical rather than psychological. First, it is said that consciousness involves the distinction of subject and object. The destruction of either factor is fatal to consciousness. The reply is, that though the subject may not be thought, except in distinction from an object, it can certainly be experienced without any such distinction. The developed self-consciousness of the mature man acquires form and fullness through this distinction, but it rests as a fact upon an immediate feeling of self. There has never been any successful attempt to deduce this immediate feeling itself from any interaction of a subject and object. It is an ultimate and primal fact of our soul life. It is, too, just as strong in the child as in the developed man. The child knows nothing of ego and non-ego, of subject and object; but he certainly has as lively a feeling of himself as could be desired. The conscious antithesis, then, of subject and object, is not necessary in order to experience one's self. Besides, logically, the notion of self must have a positive content if the notion of not-self is to have any meaning whatever. To make each the mere negation of the other is to reduce both to zero.

It is further urged, that though our consciousness is not caused by the outer world, it is, nevertheless, occasioned by it. The, soul may well contain in it the laws of its development, so that upon proper occasion it shall develop only in certain directions; yet this development depends both for its impulse and for its continuance upon the co-working of an external world. Externality is, therefore, absolutely necessary for the production of consciousness; hence it is concluded that the first cause, for whom there is no objective world, cannot be conscious. The reply is, first, that the continuance of our intellectual life does not depend on external impulse. When once the stream of association is formed, and the constructive powers of the mind are awakened, there is thenceforth no further need of external impulse to maintain the stream of conscious life at its full. In the second place, while our consciousness has a beginning, it does not lie in the notion of consciousness that it should have a beginning. To the question, "What originally started the stream of thought in the eternal mind? we reply, It never was started. Of course, the objector's hands go up at this, but before he breaks out we beg leave to call one or two points to his attention. Credit is very unequally divided between scientists and theologians. The metaphysical difficulties involved in scientific statements are generally overlooked or taken on trust; while the moment statements are made on the other side, which involve no greater difficulties, these objections are brought out in a mass. Every system of the world must begin with something of which it is impossible to give any further account than that it is. The necessary assumption of every materialistic or mechanical system is an eternal motion either in the world substance or among the physical elements. The theistic system, on the contrary, postulates as its primal fact, back of which it cannot go, an eternal mind, whose consciousness and whose thoughts, like itself, are from everlasting. Now it is plain that the metaphysical objections against the latter doctrine are at least no greater than those against that of an eternal mechanical motion; and we object, therefore, to bringing them forward as fatal in one case, while everything is taken on trust in the other. The objections against it are merely the incomprehensibility of all ultimate facts, or they consist in transferring to the infinite the limitations of our finite minds. The objection that consciousness implies finiteness is a mere quibble based upon the mistaken notion that the real infinite must be the all. It is, in brief, a striking proof of the inverted position of our philosophy that it is necessary to prove that the conditions of self-knowledge, and of knowledge in general, are not lacking to the infinite power which we are told contains the fullness of being and transcends all limitations. Indeed, we must say with Lotze,[2] that full personality is possible only to the infinite. We ourselves are more passive than active. But a small part of the powers that work within us are our own. We are the theater upon which mysterious forces appear. We have but the scantiest insight into our own nature. In so far we are machines rather than persons. Pure personality exists only where the nature is transparent to self; where all the powers are under absolute control; where the spirit remains ever by itself, and where past and present are equally transparent. Such personality is not ours; it can belong only to the infinite, of whose full personality ours is but the faint and imperfect image.

Returning to Mr. Fiske, his solution of the materialistic question demands attention. He fairly labors in repelling the charge of materialism to find words to express himself; we must, therefore, believe that Mr. Fiske does not mean to be a materialist. In attempting to determine, however, what Mr. Fiske's doctrine is, the chronic difficulties of his exposition still beset us. We understand that his formula of evolution is intended to cover the whole field of mind as well as of physics, and according to that formula the development of mind is only a special case of the "redistribution of matter and motion." Mental phenomena appear only in connection with material phenomena, and both disappear together. The mental action is a function of nervous organization, and disappears along with it. This is undoubtedly the doctrine of a good part of Mr. Fiske's exposition, and this is what common people mean by materialism. The name is indifferent so long as the matter be understood. If the redistribution of matter and motion includes and accounts for all phenomena, then the world will continue to regard this system as materialistic in spite of Mr. Fiske's protest. On the other hand Mr. Fiske's views, like those of Mr. Spencer, appear to have undergone an evolution in the course of the discussion, and we find toward the close of his work the most emphatic denial of the possibility of expressing mental phenomena in terms of material ones.[3] In a recent work, "The Unseen World," Mr. Fiske has the following emphatic passages—

> Modern discovery, so far from bridging over the chasm between mind and matter, tends rather to exhibit the distance between them as absolute. . . . But what has been less commonly remarked, is the fact that when the thought and the molecular movement thus occur simultaneously, in no scientific sense is the thought the product of the molecular movement. . . . To be sure, the thought is always there when summoned, but it stands outside the dynamic circuit as something utterly alien from and incomparable with the events which summon it. (pp. 41, 42)

We think Mr. Fiske quite correct in these statements; indeed, we doubt if the relation of the mind to the brain has ever been so clearly expressed. But who does not see that the original evolution formula has hopelessly broken down? The mind refuses in any way to be brought into line with matter, and the whole mental world lies outside of the redistribution of matter and motion; and the dreaded dualism of mind and matter remains an impassable gulf. An attempt is made to bridge it by an appeal to the unknowable—that is, by an appeal to *x*, which is, in fact, an abandonment of the problem. Besides, the attempt to find a common cause for these incommensurable sets of phenomena is a sin against the first principles of empiricism. The great rule of empirical induction is, that like effects indicate like causes. The converse of this proposition is, that irreducible difference in the effects indicates difference in the causes, and the attempt to unite them in one is a failure. It may be possible to other philosophies, but never to empiricism.

Of the numberless other points that have puzzled us we will mention only one. In the chapter on Causation, Mr. Fiske expressly teaches that causation is nothing but unconditional and invariable sequence. The notion that the antecedent exercises any controlling force whatever upon the consequent is distinctly repudiated. We have really labored to imagine what need there is of a fundamental reality in such a scheme. For as every phenomenon is really independent of every other—a self-creation, in fact—there is no need to assume a fundamental reality for its support. Besides, if we assume such a fundamental reality, it can contribute nothing to the production of the phenomenon, being itself only one more powerless antecedent. Plainly, if we are to abide by this notion of causation, we can get along as well without this new antecedent as with it; and inasmuch as the sum of phenomena has no real causal connection with this reality, their existence can never be any reason for postulating it. The same difficulty returns when we read the chapter on freedom of the will. There Mr. Fiske finds himself called upon in the name of causation to reject the notion of freedom. There would seem to be some warrant for this, if a compelling external force controlled all volitions; but surely there need be no difficulty with the doctrine of freedom if every phenomenon, as well those of volition as of the outer world, is strictly independent of external control. We have never been able to see what possesses empirical philosophers, after denying the reality of interaction, to lug in the notion when they treat of mental phenomena. Upon their principles, there is no more reason for assuming uniformity in either the outer or inner world, than there is for assuming non-uniformity. There can be no *a priori* reasoning upon the subject; and if experience point to freedom of the will, they can consistently urge nothing against it. The solution of this mystery, as well as of many others in Mr. Fiske's exposition, must be left to posterity. Possibly, however, posterity will never hear of the work; and in that case the secret will probably be buried with its author.

Thus we have touched upon the principal peculiarities of the cosmic philosophy. It goes without saying that its sensational psychology cannot stand the strain which the system makes upon it. Pure sensationalism undermines the possibility of science and system, and its legitimate outcome is nihilism. Whenever, therefore, any one attempts to build up a system on such principles, it is inevitable that he should contradict his own theory at every step. The cosmic philosophers are no exception to this rule, and their contradictions are more numerous and glaring than others in proportion as their system is more ambitious. But this lies in the nature of the case, as we said at the beginning, and we may therefore pass the point in silence. The peculiarities of the system we find unsatisfactory enough.

They are expressed throughout in an ambiguous language which gives one a high idea of the advantages of a judicious looseness of statement; but when forced to speak one tongue, they either destroy themselves, or sink to commonplaces. We have no doubt that Mr. Spencer and Mr. Fiske really think that they have furnished a higher and truer conception of the world than that given by theistic philosophy; but unfortunately the theology of the unknowable contains so many affronts to reason, and still worse, its logic is so partial or amphibious, that we doubt if the new doctrine will much advance the interests of either religion or science.

NOTES

1. See *Methodist Quarterly Review*, July, 1875.
2. *Mikrokosmus*, vol. iii, S. 573 ff.
3. Vol. ii, part iii, chap. iv.

REALISM, IDEALISM, AND PHENOMENALISM

Metaphysics: A Study in First Principles (New York: Harper & Brothers, 1882), pp. 450–487.

In the progress of our studies, our thoughts about things have undergone various transformations; but it has not occurred to us to doubt that things exist in some form in external reality. Possibly the thing may be only a form of divine energizing; possibly it may be such a hard and fast reality as common-sense assumes; but in either case it has an objective existence. But the results of the last chapter cannot fail to shake this natural faith. We came to the conclusion that the outer world is revealed to us only through sensation, and that if this order of sensation were maintained in us apart from any action of the world, the world might fall away without our missing it. Moreover, our thought of the outer world is made up entirely of subjective elements. The sense-elements of knowledge are universally admitted to be only objectified affections of the soul; while the rational elements of knowledge, as lying outside of any possible sense-experience, are entirely contributed by the mind itself. The mind must build the world out of its own states and ideas. The sensationalist allows it only sensations as the material for its world-construction. The intuitionist adds a certain outfit of apriori ideas; but neither school escapes the need of constructing the objective world out of subjective elements. But if the content of the thought be thus subjective, may not the thing also be only a mental product? In addition, we must remember that perception comes under the general head of interaction, and that our world-vision must be an effect in us. But what shall assure us that the external cause of this effect is anything like the effect? Analysis has shown us that all that we receive from the outer world is certain sensations, against which the mind reacts by constructing in itself a world-vision. All that we theoretically need, then, is an objective ground of our sensations; and this objective ground turns out to be not the object as perceived, but the all-enfolding God. Thus the world of perception threatens to disappear from reality and become only an effect in us. This brings us to consider the nature of the object in perception. Has it an ontological, or only a phenomenal reality?

This question as to the reality of the object in perception must be carefully distinguished from this other question, Is there an objective reality? The common conception of idealism is that it does nothing but raise the latter question; and a good part of realistic polemics is based on the confusion. Thus many realists have thought to overthrow idealism by pointing out that in our sense-experience we find ourselves coerced and resisted by something not ourselves. This fact would be conclusive if the aim were to prove the existence of something besides ourselves; but this no one doubts. Berkeley affirmed an objective and spiritual ground of our sensations as an absolute necessity of thought. He questioned only the external existence of the object in perception, and reduced it to an effect in us. But this question cannot be decided by appealing to the fact that we are conditioned in our sense-experience and objective effort. The idealist who understands his own system is as far as the realist from claiming that all existence is a mode of his own imagination. Everyone knows that in sensation he is conditioned by something not himself. If asked how we know it, the answer is that no one knows how he knows it, but everyone knows that he knows it. There will always be at the foundation of our mental life propositions which cannot be mediated or deduced. Acceptance or rejection alone is possible. Hence the question how we know a thing has meaning only when the knowledge is mediate and inferential; to immediate knowledge it has no application. In like manner, the demand for proof has application only to derived knowledge. If there be anything of which we are immediately certain, proof is both impossible and superfluous. The necessity in the present case is indeed only a necessity of fact, but it is none the less cogent. There is no contradiction in solipsism, but it is none the less impossible. No one can regard himself as the universe. What we cannot help doing must be done; and we cannot help admitting that we are conditioned by something not ourselves. Both idealist and realist are forced to admit an objective ground of our sensations; and both are equally far from regarding them as arbitrary fancies of our own. Hence, instead of the question, Is there reality? the idealist rather asks, "What is the real and what its true nature? In opposition to technical realism, he questions whether the object in perception is of such a kind as to be capable of real existence.

Again, the dispute between the idealist and the realist in no way concerns the phenomenal world. For both alike phenomena have an external cause; and the same phenomena may exist for both and in the same order. Even the Berkeleian idealist regards the order of phenomena as constant, and views given phenomena as the permanent sign of the possibility of other phenomena. Berkeley himself insisted upon this point so strongly and so frequently that it is inconceivable that any presumably rational beings could have thought it relevant to urge him to knock his head against a post, or to thrust his hand into a fire. Our entire sense-experience can be consistently and sufficiently expressed in terms of sensation, actual or expected; and all that is needed for the guidance of conduct is to know that the combinations and sequences of sensation have a fixed order. With this knowledge the most pronounced idealist is practically as wise as the most fanatical realist. The question is not as to the nature and laws of phenomena, but concerns solely their interpretation. From this standpoint it is plain that the senses themselves can never settle the question; for the debate lies beyond their realm. It is also plain that the idealist is not to be charged with distrusting the senses. He admits as unquestionable all that the senses give; but he denies that they give as much as the realist assumes. All that the senses can give is coexistent or sequent orders of sensation. To our sensibility a thing is only a clump of sense-qualities. The realist declares that a law of thought forces him to assume something more. The idealist allows the claim, but adds that the nature and position of that something more form the point in dispute. The idealist believes in reality as much as the realist himself. They differ not on the fact of reality, but on its nature and location. The decision between them cannot be reached by appeals to the senses, but only by consistent thinking. We pass to the discussion.

Three views are possible concerning the object in perception. We may regard it (1) as a thing in the common meaning of the term; (2) as a phenomenon of an objective fact of some kind; and (3) as only an effect in us. In the first case, we have the common realism; in the second, we have phenomenalism or objective idealism; in the third, we have subjective idealism. We consider the last view first.

At first glance subjective idealism appears to be the simplest and best-founded theory. The demand for a sufficient reason is fully met by providing an objective and spiritual ground as the cause of our sensations, and by referring to the constructive action of the mind whereby the object is built up in thought. These two factors suffice to explain all the facts. An effect is observed and referred to its adequate causes; and what more can we ask of any theory? This view is certainly possible. Our world-vision, considered simply as a fact in our minds, not only does not need anything more for its explanation, but it must be explained in this way, even by the most realistic thinkers. We are forced to this admission by the fact that every theory of perception must bring the process under the law of interaction, and that the outer world at most only contributes certain unpicturable affections of ourselves, which have to be built into form by the mind before perception is reached. The view, too, is not only possible, but it admits of no psychological or metaphysical disproof. Some have sought to disprove it by referring to the distinction of subject and object. The subject and object, it is said, are given in necessary antithesis, and consciousness vouches equally for both. But this mistakes a mental form for an ontological fact. There can, indeed, be no thought or proper consciousness without the distinction of subject and object; but this does not imply that the object is a proper thing and ontologically diverse from the subject. We have the same form of objectivity in dreams, but certainly the objects in dreams are not metaphysical realities. Much of the argument against idealism, based on this distinction and the necessary correlation of subject and object, is of so crude a kind as to suggest that the writers conceive the subject to be the body and the objects to be other bodies, and then seek to prove that the surrounding bodies are as real as our own. It has also been urged that we find ourselves resisted and coerced in our objective experience, and that thus the reality of the object is assured. This would be relevant if the question were to prove that there is some reality beyond the individual self; but it has no bearing upon the reality of the object in perception, unless we once more identify the subject with the organism, and the object with surrounding bodies. Kant attempts a disproof of subjective idealism in the second edition of the "Critique," but even his argument rests mainly upon confounding our general conditionedness in external experience with the reality of the perceived object. The lack of logical connection is plain. The ground of our presentations is external. We cannot have them at will nor dismiss them at our pleasure. We are, then, conditioned in this respect; but it does not follow that our presentations are anything more than effects in us. Kant further argues, in expounding the analogies of experience, that the possibility of physics depends on the principle that substance is real and permanent. In all changes of phenomena substance must be assumed permanent, and the quantity thereof in nature can be neither increased nor diminished. Hence, Kant concludes that subjective idealism, by denying substance, wrecks science, and hence must be false. But this argument is doubly a failure. It is directed against the idealist as empiricist and not as metaphysician. The psychology and theory of knowledge of many idealists, notably in the case of Berkeley, have been very imperfect and often mistaken; but this fact does not affect their metaphysics. And, after all Kant's argument, it turns out that this permanent and indestructible substance is, even in his own system, only a mental function, and not a fact of reality. For him, things are only syntheses of sense-qualities under the form of permanence; they are in no sense proper substances. It is possible for the subjective idealist to adopt Kant's general theory of knowledge and retain his own metaphysical conclusion. Indeed, they agree so nearly in their metaphysics that Kant's attempt to disprove idealism has very generally been regarded as a grave inconsequence. Finally, Kant's charge that idealism would make science impossible is especially unfortunate; for it would overturn science in no other sense than Kant's own system does. If Kant's theory be true, at least nine tenths of our theoretical science is illusion. The entire universe of forces and substances, of atoms and ethers, disappears. These things become only the way in which the mind represents to itself the inscrutable ground of cosmic movement and manifestation. They are mental products, and have only a mental existence. Berkeley himself would scarcely take us further. Both views admit of practical science, and conflict only with theoretical science. If there be an infinite spirit, which embraces all finite spirits and furnishes them with sense-experiences in a fixed and orderly way, it is still a most useful and necessary work to study the orders of coexistence and sequence in our experiences. Knowing this order, we shall be practically as wise as the wisest, and shall be in a position to reap the best possible results of practical science. We might have the greatest enthusiasm for the working methods of science, and first detect traces of lukewarmness when it should be proposed to regard the devices of method as ontological facts.

Do we, then, accept subjective idealism? Not yet. We have only pointed out that it cannot be psychologically or metaphysically disproved. No consideration of the process of perception, or of the apparent immediateness and self-sufficiency of our knowledge, will avail to disprove the doctrine. If, then, the only aim were to explain our world-vision as a fact in us, we should have no reason for affirming any objective reality besides the infinite. But this world-vision is not only an effect, it also claims to be a revelation of facts beyond ourselves, and this claim must be considered. Possibly we shall find in the content of the facts thus revealed some ground for viewing them as real.

The fact mentioned in the opening paragraph of the chapter, that the content of our thought of the world is made up of subjective elements, is in itself indecisive, as this must be so in any case. No matter how real the world may be, it can be known to us only through thought, and this thought must be a subjective product. Some idealists have thoughtlessly urged this necessity as an argument for idealism; but its legitimate outcome is solitary egoism, for our thought of persons, other than ourselves, is as purely a subjective product as our thought of things other than ourselves. But no philosopher is allowed to disgrace philosophy by making it farcical. Hence every speculator is under obligations to good taste and good faith to accept as an undoubted fact the coexistence of others like himself. To question this is to reduce philosophy to a low and disingenuous farce, and to justify the contempt of every earnest mind. We say disingenuous because every such speculator forthwith seeks to induce others to accept his views, although by hypothesis they are only fancies of his own. Of course this admission of personality does not imply the admission of substantial corporeality, but only of the thinking and feeling self. Here, then, is one class of things of such a kind as to assure us of their objectivity.

But brave as are these words about disingenuous farces, they do not serve to repress the question as to the real ground of our faith in the existence of other persons like ourselves. We have seen that the infinite mediates all interaction of the finite, and hence that all affections of ourselves are immediately from the infinite. God is the cause of causes and the true objective ground of our changing states. But if these states were given in their present order, we should as certainly construct a world of persons as we do a world of things. If the world of persons should drop away, we should never miss them, but should continue to have the same apparent personal interaction and communion which we have at present. If, then, God had any interest in deceiving us, he could as easily impose upon us an unreal world of persons as an unreal world of things, and in neither case would there be any psychological or metaphysical method of detecting the deceit. What, then, is the real ground for admitting the existence of persons? We may refer the belief to instinct; but this is only to decline the question while seeming to answer it. Besides, if we allowed the answer, the question would renew itself in the further inquiry, What ground have we for trusting our instincts? The true reason can be found neither in psychology nor in metaphysics, but only in ethics. Our belief rests ultimately upon the conviction that it would be morally unbecoming on the part of God to subject us to any such measureless and systematic deceit. We conclude, then, (1) that the infinite is more certainly known than the objective finite;

(2) that perception is essentially a revelation by the infinite to the finite; and (3) that faith in the revelation must be based on an ethical faith in the revelator. Hence, although our thoughts of persons other than ourselves are purely subjective products, and although the existence of such persons is by no means necessary to explain our mental state, we still regard such persons as really existing, not, however, because of the psychologic necessity of the admission, but because of the ethical absurdity of the denial. And for the validity of all objective knowledge of the finite we are shut up either to faith in God or to a blind and irrational instinct.

It seems, then, that we are clear of idealism; for if we trust our faculties when they reveal a world of persons like ourselves, why should we not trust them when they reveal a world of things? How can we throw doubt upon one result without also throwing doubt upon the other? We have broken through the claim that objects do not exist because our perception of them is only an effect in us. In one case we have found ourselves compelled to affirm that the objects have real existence. Hence, the questions just asked would be conclusive against an idealism based simply upon the process of perception, and not upon the nature of the product. In that case any discrimination against one class of objects would be purely arbitrary, and the system could be held only by volition. It is of no use to say that persons are not objects of perception such as things are; for, so far as the knowing process is concerned, both stand on the same ground. Neither persons nor things are perceived by the senses; but upon occasion of certain subjective affections we posit persons or things as their objective ground. Hence the idealist must change his line of argument. It is not enough to show that our objects are thought-constructions; for they must be this in any case. He must rather show that the affirmation of things, in the common-sense of the term, is not only not necessary but is inconsistent, or that the so-called material world is seen upon reflection and analysis to be incapable of existence apart from thought. That is, the idealist must base his conclusion upon an analysis of the product of perception rather than upon the process. We assume, then, with common-sense, that the world of things does not depend on our thinking, but is in itself a fact of some sort, and ask only what kind of a fact it is. Is it such a fact as it seems to be, or something quite different? Meanwhile the debate with the subjective idealist will lie over.

Allowing the world to be in itself a fact of some kind, two views are possible concerning its nature. The realist's position is this: The system of the world is a complex of substantial things which are endowed with various forces, and which are the real and constant factor in the changes of phenomena. As such they exist apart from any thought, and when we perceive them we add nothing, but recognize what they are. This is the view of common-sense, and if analysis detected no difficulties and inconsistencies in it, it must be allowed to stand. The idealist, on the other hand, thinks as follows: We think under the law of substance and attribute, or of thing and quality. Both thought and language are impossible without nouns as the independent base of the sentence. Accordingly, we tend to give a substantive form to every object of thought. So we speak of gravitation, electricity, magnetism, etc., as agents or things; and it is not until we reflect that we perceive that they are forms of agency only. Indeed, every constant phenomenon tends to be viewed as a thing. Now the world owes its substantial existence entirely to this tendency. This substantive character is merely the form under which certain objective activities of the infinite appear to us. The idealist, then, proposes to replace the nouns of realism by certain constant forms of activity on the part of the infinite. Change in things he views as a change in these forms. Progress he views as a higher form of this activity. There are no fixed points of being in the material world; but everywhere there are law and order. The continuity of the system expresses simply the constancy of the divine action. The uniformity of the system expresses the steadiness of the divine purpose. In short, the world, considered in itself, is an order of divine energizing, which, when viewed under the forms of space and time, of causality and substance, appears as a world of things. In distinction from subjective idealism, this view may be called objective idealism. The former does not allow the world to be an objective fact, but only a series of presentations in us; the latter allows it to be an objective fact, but holds that it cannot exist as it appears apart from mind.

The realistic view is, of course, more harmonious with spontaneous thought than the idealistic view, but it properly has no advantage, except for the imagination. It is more easily pictured than idealism, but both views are equally compatible with phenomena and with objective science. We have seen that even subjective idealism is compatible with science, so far as the latter deals with phenomena and eschews metaphysics, while objective idealism allows all the facts even of scientific metaphysics to stand, and seeks only to go deeper. It allows the atom and its laws, and suggests only that the atom, though the basis of physical science, may itself be phenomenal of some basal fact. Thus all the principles of physical science remain undisturbed, although they may be referred to something behind them, and which is the reality in them. But, even if the principles of objective science were disturbed, it would not follow that idealism is false, for there is no warrant for making the possibility of physics the final test of truth. The imagination will find more assurance of the uniformity of nature in the hard reality of the physical elements than in the purpose and nature of the infinite; but, in any case, this is a fancy. We have seen that the finite, of whatever kind, comes into existence, and remains there, only because of the demands of the system. This is as true of the material elements as of anything else. Hence, we have no ontological assurance of the uniformity of nature in any respect. For all that we know, the most unimaginable revolution may take place at any moment, and in the most unimaginable way. For knowledge on this point, we must have either a revelation from the infinite or a perfect intuition of its nature and tendency. Hence the uniformity of nature can never have any foundation better than the constancy of the purpose and nature of the infinite. Both views, then, are possible. To decide between them, we must analyze the nature of the object known. In general, this was the course taken by Berkeley. The chief part of his polemic against matter consisted in showing that matter, as then conceived, could not exist apart from mind. On the basis of Locke's philosophy, this was very easy work; for, according to Locke, material substance was only a complex of simple sensations, and hence, in logic, it was capable of existing only in sensibility. Again, matter was then conceived as pure passivity and inertness. Berkeley pointed out that matter, as thus conceived, would account for nothing, and could only be an idea. It is in this analysis of the object that Berkeley is at his best, and it is here that the strength of his argument lies. It must be allowed that no empirical philosophy can escape his conclusion.

In analyzing the object, we point out, in the first place, that the sense-qualities of things are generally regarded as having only subjective existence. Spontaneous commonsense regards heat, color, etc., as immediate qualities of the object; but this view has long been abandoned. Nor do we rest this conclusion on the fact that every such quality is primarily a reaction of our sensibility against external action. This is the case with all knowledge, and does not exclude the possibility that the subjective quality may also be a quality of the thing. Nor does the complicated mechanism of nerves and vibrations exclude the same possibility. These, again, might be the machinery whereby we become aware of the true qualities of things. We have an illustration of this possibility in the communication of thought by language. The airy waves and nervous vibrations have nothing in common with the thought from which they proceed, and yet they result in the reproduction of that thought. The real ground of the doctrine lies (1) in the general teachings of physics, which leave no place for sense-qualities, except as effects in sensitive beings; and (2) in the fact that these qualities are without significance when conceived as existing apart from sensibility. How a thing tastes when it is tasted, or feels when it is felt, is revealed in our sensations; but how it tastes when it is not tasted, or feels when it is not felt, is a problem without any meaning. A toothache which no one feels is just as possible as a sight which no one sees. Tastes and odors, sights and sounds, have no assignable meaning apart from a sensitive subject. All that can be said of the object is, that it is such as to be capable of producing these sensations in us under the proper circumstances. When the thing is seen, it will produce in us a sensation of color. When it is felt, it will produce in us certain tactile sensations. When it is tasted, it will produce certain sensations of taste. What it must be to do this is partly revealed by physical science. The body which is to appear with a certain color must be able to set the ether in vibration in a certain definite way. The body which is to produce sensations of taste must cause certain chemical or electric changes in the proper organs. The sensations themselves, however, are purely and only subjective. In itself, the world is neither light nor dark, neither sounding nor silent, neither sweet nor bitter, neither hard nor soft, but such that it produces these phenomena in us under the proper conditions. All that the realist can mean by affirming that these qualities are there apart from our experience is, that they are there for everyone who fulfils the conditions; and this universality he mistakes for objectivity. Light, sound, odor, etc., in the proper psychological significance, are contributed to the world by the mind; and, apart from the mind, the world cannot exist as luminous, resonant, odorous. If, then, the object be only a complex of sense-qualities, as the sensationalists maintain, Berkeley's subjective idealism is a demonstrable necessity.

So much the realist admits. The secondary qualities of matter he hands over to subjectivity. They are only effects in us, and have no claim to reproduce their cause. The familiar fact of color-blindness shows that the same object may have different apparent colors. Hence sense-qualities are not only effects; they are also contingent upon the state of our nerves. But there is a universal element in perception. In the so-called primary qualities of matter we come upon something which is independent of our thought and organization. Here, then, the realist makes another stand, but without success. These primary qualities are those which are based upon the relation of things to space, such as extension, form, space-filling, etc. These qualities, the realist holds, are recognized, not constituted, by the mind. But, in our discussion of space, we found that space, and all its sub-categories of size, extension, and distance, have only a subjective existence. They are the form which non-spatial realities take on in intuition. The realist's claim that there is a universal element in perception may be allowed, without in any way admitting that that element is independent of thought. We have seen that relations in general are incapable of objective existence; that they exist, and can exist, only in the relating act of thought. Hence the world, as a great system of relations—that is, as the object of science and of all rational study—cannot possibly exist apart from thought. It has its character of spatiality and inter-relatedness only in the mind and in the movement of thought. What was said of the world as luminous, etc., must be repeated of the world as a system of relations; it cannot exist apart from mind. When the realist attempts to escape this by saying that the mind recognizes relations, but does not make them, all that he can maintain is, that there is a universal element in the relations. Those relations do not exist for the thought of one alone, but for the thought of all. They are, then, not individual, but belong to reason itself. This we not only allow, but we also steadfastly affirm. But the realist curiously confuses universality in thought with independence of thought, and thinks to secure the former only by affirming the latter. The difference, however, is very great. All relations, as such, are products of thinking, and exist only in the act of thought.

It only remains that the realist take his stand on the substantiality of the physical world. Whatever it may not be, it at least is real and substantial. In this element of substantiality the realist puts the great difference between himself and the idealist. For the latter, things are only phenomena, while for the former they are also things in themselves. For the latter, the only existence in things apart from thought is the system of activities on the part of the infinite; for the former, things have real existence apart from any thought. Herein the realist fancies that he has a great practical advantage over the idealist; but the advantage is, in fact, only a relief to the imagination. In particular, he fancies that he has a better explanation of the permanent possibility of sensation which is found in sense experience. When certain conditions are fulfilled, certain phenomena are present to us. By varying the conditions we vary the phenomena, and by restoring the conditions we restore the phenomena. Hence, under given conditions, there is what Mill called a permanent possibility of sensation, but which would better be called a permanent possibility of phenomena. But it is hard to see in what this possibility is better explained by the impersonal thing than by the constant activity of the infinite, especially as, without an activity of the infinite, the impersonal thing would never affect us at all. Permanence and universality are, at least, as well accounted for by the idealist as by the realist. Indeed, the latter has to make just as many demands upon the infinite as the former, while the thing which he posits in addition is only a new element of perplexity.

Finally, we must recall what we found in our discussion of change. We were there concerned to see how we could possibly reconcile change and identity. We are accustomed to speak of things with changing states, and apply the notion without any question of its validity. But when we inquired as to its use, we found to our surprise that it applies only to the personal. The impersonal is simply and solely process and law. Permanence and proper existence can be found only in spirit. These conclusions must be applied here. The question of the substantiality of the physical world reduces to the question of the substantiality of the physical elements. If these are impersonal, they can only be flowing processes of the infinite. On the other hand, there is no warrant for attributing to them personality of any kind. The fancy to which we yielded in discussing materialism, that the elements may be alive and have a true subjectivity, is utterly groundless. The only thing which leads to it is the purpose to explain mentality by materiality, and this makes it necessary to include mentality in the notion of materiality. For the rest, the notion is a gratuitous embarrassment in every respect. In discussing matter and force, we saw the difficulties which attend the atomic theory of matter viewed as an ontological fact, and we decided for the view that the elements are not properly things, but only constant forms of the action of the infinite according to fixed laws. In addition, the discussion of interaction has shown that the impersonal finite can lay no claim to existence. For, as impersonal, it is without subjectivity; and as finite, its objective action is mediated by the infinite, that is, it is done by the infinite. It has, then, no longer any reason for existence; and there is no longer any ground for affirming its existence. It does nothing, and is nothing but a form of thought based upon the activity of something not itself. This view we reproduce as our final verdict. Matter and material things have no ontological, but only a phenomenal, existence. Their necessary dependence and lack of all subjectivity make it impossible to view them as capable of other than phenomenal existence. This world-view, then, contains the following factors: (1) The Infinite energizes under the forms of space and time; (2) the system of energizing according to certain laws and principles, which system appears in thought as the external universe; and (3) finite spirits, who are in relation to this system, and in whose intuition the system takes on the forms of perception. This view is not well described as idealism, because it makes the world more than an idea. If the word had not been appropriated to denote positivistic doctrines, phenomenalism would be a much better title. This word sufficiently implies the objective nature of the world-process, while at the same time it implies that, apart from mind, the phenomena would not exist. Perhaps, with all its disadvantages, there is less risk of misunderstanding in using phenomenalism than in using idealism. If it be asked how there can be an energizing which neither has an object nor which gives itself an object, the answer must be that the energizing according to a law and plan is the object. We may get some hint of what this may mean from the scholastic doctrine of preservation as continuous creation. Such creation could be nothing more than a movement of the divine activity according to the idea of the thing.

But here subjective idealism cannot fail to suggest itself once more. When we were considering the nature of perception, we could find no reason for making things subjective which would not also make persons subjective; and, as solipsism is too ghastly an absurdity for any patience, we had to admit the existence of other persons. But, so far as the process of perception is concerned, things have as sound a claim to objective existence as persons. We had, then, to assume that things are what they seem, until analysis and reflection should compel us to change our conceptions. But, on going to work in this way, it soon became apparent that the outer world is altogether other than it appears. At last it became clear that the cosmos can be nothing other than a mode of divine energizing which has the forms of perception only in mind. And since this is so, why not go one step further, and declare the cosmos to be only a series of presentations which the infinite produces in the finite? We have now found a reason for affirming pure subjectivity of things which does not apply to persons. Persons are capable of proper existence; but things, in the common sense of the term, are not. Why not, then, regard the infinite spirit and finite spirits as comprising all existence, and make the cosmos merely a series of presentations in finite spirits which have no existence whatever apart from their being perceived? What possible advantage can there be in lumbering up our system with anything more?

These questions also can be answered only by reflection upon the nature of the presentations. It may be that we shall find them such as to compel the admission that our thought of the world is not its only reality. But, first, an exposition of the theory is necessary.

If it were possible for one to play upon another's mind so as to produce a dream-world in the other's thought, that dream-world would have its objective cause, but in itself it would be only an effect in the subject's mind. On this theory of idealism the world of perception would be such a subjective effect, and the creation of the world by God would mean the creation of the thought of a world in finite minds. But for God himself there would be no world-process, no world-activity, no world-development, and no world-history. There would be only God and finite spirits; and then God, who embraces all finite spirits in his own existence, would produce in them a consistent and harmonious world-vision. His objective activity would be exhausted in furnishing spirits with this vision, and the world would exist for God only as a rule of the process.

Berkeley never attained to any consistency in his thought, but a good part of what he said reduces to this view. Still he was very far from realizing all its implications. First, it is plain that on this theory the object of perception is strictly individual; it may, indeed, be repeated in others' minds in similar form, but in itself, as an effect in us, it cannot carry us beyond itself. There is, too, not the least necessity for any two persons having the same presentations. It would be entirely possible that one person should have the presentations which we label Boston, and that his neighbor should have at the same time the presentations which we label London. There would be no more need that adjacent persons should see the same objects than that persons who sleep in the same bed should dream the same dreams. Idealists have sought to escape this difficulty by saying that all persons have the same presentations under the same circumstances; but, unluckily, the theory gives no hint of what may be meant by the same circumstances for persons other than myself. If I leave my room, I may say that I should have certain presentations if I returned. This statement is not affected by the consideration that the room itself is a presentation, for I may still say that along with the presentation of my room goes also the presentation of the objects in my room. But all this fails to carry me a single step towards the conclusion that my neighbor has the same presentations. Assuming the uniformity of the divine procedure, I may be sure that if he had the presentation of my room he would also have the presentation of the objects in the room; but the fact that I have the presentation of the room is no ground whatever why he should have it. Everything having vanished into presentations, there is no longer any objective standard of reference. We no longer see the same thing, but have similar presentations; and that we have similar presentations, we learn only in an extremely indirect way. In the nature of the presentation itself there is nothing to warrant us in thinking that it is shared by anyone else whatever. If the world as it appears, though phenomenal, were phenomenal of a world-process or cosmic movement apart from, our thought, these difficulties could be escaped. Phenomena would then represent the thought-side of the process, and would have a universal element. Difference of relation to the process would explain difference of phenomena, and position could be defined by reference to the phenomena. But when this is not the case, the object is strictly individual.

These obvious conclusions from the theory the subjective idealists have not always been disposed to admit. Thus Berkeley, at times, goes so far as to affirm a universality of the object in perception. The object which exists for one exists for all, though on what he bases his conclusion does not clearly appear. It seems to be, however, the objectivity of the intuition which leads him to this result. Thus, he insists that we know the object to be independent of our mind, and of finite minds in general; and he even makes this manifest independence of the object an argument for the divine existence. For, as the object is independent of finite minds, and yet cannot exist apart from mind, it follows that there must be an infinite and omnipresent mind in which the material world exists. Here the world acquires an objective and independent existence, so far as the finite mind is concerned. It is not merely a series of presentations in finite minds, but these presentations are revelations to those minds of a world existing apart from them. We do not, then, have similar presentations only, but we see the same world.

The view thus reached abandons the extreme form of subjective idealism. Instead of insisting that we cannot transcend ourselves, and that our ideas are only effects in us, it declares the universality and independence of the object, so far as the finite is concerned. Thus the question is transferred from psychology to metaphysics, and the claim is set up that this universal and independent object cannot exist apart from mind, and hence that it exists in the infinite mind. This view is not very different from Malebranche's doctrine of the vision of all things in God. But Berkeley is very unclear as to the relation of this world to God. At times he allowed the world to exist eternally in the divine thought, and declared creation to be only the manifestation of this eternal thought to finite minds; but still he failed to tell in what the reality of the world consists. To explain the difficulty, we may adopt the Leibnitzian notion of many possible worlds, conceptions of which fill the divine imagination. In such a case there would be no reason for calling one of these systems real rather than another; and there would be no distinction between imagination and reality. All alike would be equally real and equally imaginary. Now Berkeley, in declaring the world to be real for God, gives no ground for distinguishing this real world from another like it which should only be conceived or imagined. If there be no distinction, then the world is not real for God, except as any conception is real for the mind that forms it. For God himself the world is only a thought, and not a reality; in his relation to finite minds it is only a rule for producing ideas. Beyond this the world has no existence. Yet this is the view which Berkeley was not always willing to accept. The only way out of the difficulty is that taken by Leibnitz. For him the world was not merely a divine thought, but a divine act also. As God is will as well as thought, so the world is his act as well as his conception. Without this assumption the world has only a conceptual reality.

But these difficulties result entirely from trying to give the world a reality beyond our presentations. Any movement in this direction must be away from subjective idealism. But may we not leave Berkeley to shift for himself, and return to the view that the world-vision is purely an effect in us, and also purely individual? We are not in a common world, but only seem to be; and this seeming is due to the fact that the infinite produces consistent and harmonious ideas in different minds. But here, too, we meet with difficulties. First of all, our ability permanently to modify phenomena seems to point to something beyond our presentations. Again, the phenomenal world not only suggests a reality beyond our thoughts, but also a history. The world which appears not only seems now to exist, but also to have existed. The fossils and strata of geology, and the general wear and tear of things, point to a continuous and independent process. These things would be quite out of place in a system of pure presentations, unless the aim were to deceive us. Finally, perception claims to be a revelation of things and processes without us; but on this theory of subjective idealism it is a pure fiction. There is no world-process, no cosmic movement, no going-forth of creative power, no manifestation of omnipotence, but only a magic-lantern show which, after all, shows nothing. The mountains were never brought forth; the foundations of the earth were never laid. We lift up our eyes to the heavens, and instead of a revelation of might and magnificence, we have a presentation; and this we falsely interpret. God is doing nothing in time but furnishing finite spirits with ideas which, for the most part, are illusory. Now it is impossible to avoid a feeling of dissatisfaction with this view as at once poverty-stricken and unworthy. At the same time, it is entirely possible and admits of no disproof. If God have any interest in deceiving us in regard to external knowledge, we have no psychological or metaphysical means of defense against the fraud. Our only ground of assurance is the ethical conviction that such a tissue of deceit and magic would be disgraceful and outrageous. If we further ask what this conviction is based upon, the answer must be that there is nothing deeper than itself. If this fail, there is nothing left. We hold, then, that the world-process, the cosmic movement, is not in our thought alone; and that the presentations which we have concerning it are real revelations, and not individual phantoms. The world is not merely God's thought, it is also his act. It is founded in the divine will as well as in the divine intelligence. But the ground of this conviction is found less in the psychologic necessity of the admission than in the ethical and aesthetic absurdity of the denial. Thus it appears once more that all objective knowledge of the finite must rest on an ethical trust in the infinite.

Combining the result thus reached with the outcome of previous reflection, we come to the conclusion that the world in itself apart from mind is simply a form of the divine energizing, and has its complete existence only in thought. But since we have shaken off the subjective idealist by appealing to the divine veracity, what shall hinder the realist from using the same argument against ourselves? The disciple of the senses finds both views about equally unsubstantial, and declares that both alike reduce the world to a delusion. If, then, the general truthfulness of the system tells against one view, it must tell with equal force against the other. The answer to this must be that our faculties compel one conclusion and not the other. Our form of idealism is not based upon distrust of our faculties, but upon trust in them. It is held because reason itself leads up to it, and because reason itself shows the common realism to be inconsistent. Some further exposition is needed to clear up remaining misunderstandings.

In reply to the charge of reducing the world to a delusion, the objective idealist calls upon the realist to master the distinction between subjectivity and delusion. Light and sound are subjective, but they are not, therefore, delusions. In our sensibility they have their full reality and value. If, then, the physical universe has its proper significance and reality only in thought, it does not on that account become a delusion, but may still be a strict universal. The idealist further points out that the realist's objections rest on unfounded assumptions. He assumes that the physical system is perfect in itself apart from thought and sensibility, and that the mind has only the function of a copyist. Not even the divine thought and sensibility are constitutive, but only cognizant of what could exist as well without them. Both of these assumptions the idealist denies. He holds that the mind is no copyist simply, that the sentient, emotional, and rational life has a value of its own, and is constitutive as well as cognizant. It is in this life only that the system acquires any significance and truly comes to itself. The realist makes the value of mentality to consist in a copying of the external; while the idealist reverses this view, and makes the value and significance of the outer to consist entirely in its relation to the mental life. What right, he asks, has the realist to charge the mind with falsehood if, instead of a tiresome monotone of vibration, it gives us the world of light and sound with its richness of color and harmony? And what greater right has he to abuse the mind, if it translate the ineffable and unpicturable activities of the infinite into a world of things instinct with the divine thought and life, and alike expressive of both? It cannot be too often repeated that mind itself is a part of the general system; and therefore it cannot be surprising if the system have its complete existence only in mind. Plainly, if the mind is not meant to be a copyist, all ground for charging it with failure and falsehood falls away. Only that is a failure which does not perform its proper function. Only that is false which wanders from its proper path. Every theory has to allow that to a large extent the mind makes the world it sees. Our sensibility clothes the world with light and color and harmony. In itself the physical system cannot attain unto these forms. The sensitive mind must come before the system can put on these forms of value and significance. The idealist but extends the same thought further. As the system cannot rise to the forms of sense until sensibility is attained, no more can it rise to the forms of rationality until reason is reached. It is thought which gives the system its rational character, and weaves the network of law and relation in which and by which the system has its existence. But in saying this, the idealist is careful to add that this thought in which the system has its existence is not this or that man's thought only, but thought in general. It is the universal reason of the infinite in which the system primarily exists. The infinite, as well as the finite, has thought and reason. In a previous paragraph we pointed out that it is not enough to consider the system as a divine thought alone, but that it must also be viewed as a divine act. Now we point out on the other hand that it is not enough to consider it as a divine act, but that it must be a divine thought as well. And so the final claim of the idealist is that the world cannot exist in will alone nor in thought alone, but in will and thought together. Will gives the reality of the world-process and thought gives the form, and neither has any significance apart from the other.

Still it will be urged that the mind is in some sense a copyist. It has to reproduce in thought the external fact; and what is this but to copy it? And if it fail to reproduce this fact, what can we say but that it distorts it? We are often enough mistaken in our perceptions, and what are such delusions but distortions or a failure to copy the fact as it is? These questions take us back to the Introduction. We there pointed out that thought can never transcend itself so as to grasp objects other than through the conceptions we form of them. From this it was concluded that it is absurd to speak of a knowledge of things apart from thought, and that the true aim of knowledge is not to reach what is true apart from thought, but to reach the universal in thought. In no case, then, can we rationally talk of the mind as copying the fact; for this would imply that the fact could exist for the mind apart from the conception, and that the latter might be formed on the model of the former. The aim, then, of perception is not to copy objectivity, but to get the universal in intuition; and sense-delusions are not failures to copy reality, but to reach the universal. If the world-process is to be known, it must have a fixed thought-equivalent; and a perfect intelligence would be one which should fully possess this equivalent. Such an intelligence would grasp all phases of the world-process, not only from the absolute, but also from every relative standpoint. It would, then, be aware of all possible sides and phases of being and of all possible relations. All its perceptions and judgments would represent a universal, and any departure from them by other minds would be an error. The aim of perception is to reach such universals, and not to copy something existing apart from all thought. We aim to conceive reality as this being would conceive it from our standpoint. The standard of truth is not absolute being, but perfect knowledge; and error consists not in the parallax of our thought with being, but in its parallax with absolute thought. For us God is such a perfect intelligence; and hence we may say that in perception the aim is not to copy the

364 VARIETIES OF IDEALISM

thing, but to rethink the divine thought and reproduce the divine intuition. There is nothing in rational idealism to warrant the assumption that the thought-side of the world-process is an arbitrary one, or that the process may be conceived in any and every way. Such a view would declare thought essentially unrelated to the process, and could only end in pure idealism. It is, then, entirely compatible with our view to hold that the thought-side is fixed and universal. Our sensibility may be differently affected according to our relations to the process; and it is quite possible that new senses should reveal new qualities. But these qualities would only be modes of our sensibility, and would represent no fixed nature of the object, but only the way in which it affects our feeling. But this admission is compatible with the claim that, so far as we think the process under the categories of reason, we may attain to strict universality. The decision of this question depends upon our faith or unfaith in the mind's power to reach the universal. Here we content ourselves with pointing out that idealism is compatible with the strict universality of thought and intuition; indeed, it is the only doctrine which is thus compatible.

But what we have said of the inability of thought to transcend itself can hardly fail to leave the impression that there is an opaque mystery of being in some outlying realm of existence from which thought is forever shut out. And we seem to have left the divine thought also in the same state of exclusion. This difficulty arises from separating God as knower from God as doer. The basal fact of the universe is a self-conscious agent. As agent, he maintains a series of activities; and as knower, he gives these activities the form of the world. As agent, he is not independent of himself as knower; and as knower, he is not independent of himself as agent. The divine agency has the forms of intuition only in the divine knowing; and the divine knowing has an object only through the divine agency. Without either of these elements God would not be God. He must be the indivisible synthesis of knowing and doing. As reason, he is real only through the act; and as actor, he is real only through the reason. The reason gives law to the act, and the act realizes the reason. In the ontology we forbade all attempts to analyze the notion of cause into being and power, as if these could be separated; so here we must forbid all attempts to separate between God as agent and God as knower. He is the absolute unity which is at once reason and will, knower and known. With regard to the world-process, it has its reality in the divine will, and its form in the divine thought; so that it could not exist apart from either. Here we come again on the old antithesis of matter and form. These are absolutely inseparable. Will gives the matter, and thought gives the form. The various stages and states of the world-process have a definite representative in thought; and our thoughts and perceptions, so far as valid, are to be viewed as sections of the universal thought-aspect of reality and its processes. The world, then, is no individual fiction, but is a proper universal. It exists not in finite thought alone, but in the infinite thought and the infinite volition. This constitutes its reality and universality, and distinguishes what we have called objective idealism, or proper phenomenalism, from the subjective idealism of the empiricists. A common conception of idealism is that it teaches only a gigantic and continuous sense-delusion like that of insane persons who fill space with phantoms. And just as the sane see that space to be empty which to the madman teems with demons, so the mind, percipient of reality, would find none of those things in space which we seem to find. The complete difference of our view is apparent. For us space is as real as the phenomena in it, and these in turn are as real as the space in which they appear. Both alike are subjective; but both alike are universal, in that they are phases of the thought-side of reality and are valid for all intelligence from the particular standpoint.

By the world-process, in the preceding paragraphs, we mean only that process which underlies the so-called material world or the physical system. And when we say that this process has its reality in the divine will and its form in the divine thought, and that these two factors are inseparable, we mean to teach no theory of a double-faced substance after the fashion of Spinoza, but only that in the infinite knowing and willing must go together. The finite spirit must be excluded entirely from the cosmic process, as being no part or phase of it. In one sense the finite mind belongs to the system, and in another sense it does not. When by the system we mean the totality of the infinite's activity and manifestation, of course the finite mind is a part of it. But when by the system is meant only that part of the infinite's activity which underlies the physical manifestation, then the finite mind is no part of the system, but is in interaction with it. Nor can we allow that the physical side of the system has any tendency whatever to pass into or produce the spiritual side as found in finite minds. No doubt it would seem simpler here to speak of a single process which is on one side thought and on the other side act; but such a view identifies the world with absolute being, and leaves no place for the finite spirit. It was at this point that German idealism passed into materialism. All finite life and consciousness were viewed as phases of the one process which, in its ceaseless on-going, brings alike to life and death; and this was simply materialism expressed in uncommon words. We must hold in opposition that there is nothing in the physical process which tends in the slightest degree to pass into the mental by any logical or dynamic necessity; and hence that the spiritual orders of creation are something superinduced upon the physical. To the charge that this is dualism, we reply that the opposite view rests upon a false conception of unity. Unity does not consist in playing the entire oratorio on a single string; but in the accord and common law of many. The unity of a life does not consist in perpetually doing only the same thing, but in subjecting all the activities to a common plan. So the unity of nature, or of creation, consists in no way in the deduction of everything from a common process, but in subjecting everything to a common plan. The unity of the system consists, first, in the metaphysical unity of the basal reality, and in the unity of plan which governs all creative activity and manifestation. Doubtless the entire system might be deduced from its plan, supposing we knew it; but this does not imply that there may not be new beginnings all along the line of the process, which were not dynamically implied in any previous state of the system, but which were logically implied in the basal plan of the whole. And if we are to escape materialism, we must admit a double process in the infinite—the physical process, and a second process whereby the finite spirit is put into relation to that process, and is thus enabled to enter into the divine thought and activity as shown in what we call the world.

In estimating the argument of this chapter we must remember that it is rooted in our ontology, and cannot be adequately criticized from a purely psychological standpoint. It has, doubtless, been a surprise to the reader to find the common order of thought so completely inverted as it is in our claim that the infinite is the most certain factor in objective knowledge, and that knowledge of the objective finite must rest upon ethical grounds for its ultimate assurance. This seems preposterous in any case, and especially so at a time when atheism has received a new lease of life. Hence a theory of perception into which God enters as the chief factor must be a very doubtful speculation. In reply to these scruples we must recall the general course of the whole discussion. In the earlier part of the work we undertook an analysis of our basal notions in order to see how we must think them in order to make them self-consistent and adequate to the function assigned them in our thought-system. This analysis was quite independent of the question whether reality exists or not; it aimed only to tell how we must think of things supposing they should exist. In this inquiry we were led to the discovery that a plurality of things cannot be ultimate, but that they must exist in dependence upon some basal and unitary world-ground as their conditioning source. From this time on, we held that the ground of the world is one; and that the many, if the many exist, can only be in some sense a function of this unitary ground. We had already found that this being must be conceived as an agent, and on further inquiry we discovered that thought cannot rest in any other conception than that this agent is personal, free, and intelligent. Any other view was seen to be suicidal in its results; and theism appeared as the absolute postulate of all knowledge, science, and philosophy. These results were reached by a simple analysis of thought itself, and are independent of all external perception. Thereafter God was to us at least as certain as any objective fact whatever. We then came to study the process of perception, and we found that, unless we were to content ourselves with a superficial description of our mental states, our psychology must be subordinated to our metaphysics. In particular, we found ourselves compelled to bring the process under the general head of interaction, and make our perceptions effects in us. But what should assure us that they were more? In any case the infinite appears as the real objective ground of our sensations; and we have seen that if these sensations were given, the world of finite persons and things might fall away without our missing them. Hence we had to say that God is the most certain fact of objective knowledge, and that knowledge of the objective finite must rest for its assurance on an ethical trust in God. Formal truth is self-sufficient. The testimony of consciousness to our own states cannot be impugned. The necessity of affirming the infinite can be demonstrated. The necessity of viewing the infinite as free and intelligent, and hence as personal, is likewise demonstrable if we are to escape skepticism of reason itself. But the finite, as other than a phenomenal fact, must be received by faith. Cosmic knowledge, as distinct from a knowledge of our own presentations, is not self-sufficing, but rests on an ethical basis. This is a curious reversal of current views, but there is no help for it. Thus trust in God appears as the factor without which no tenable theory of truly objective perception can be constructed. Psychology alone does not even touch the problem, but merely tells us what we believe, without saying why. References to instinct explain nothing, and simply postpone the question. Metaphysics but makes the problem and its difficulties clear. Only ethics can solve it. By judiciously ignoring the difficulty, by ad-captandum appeals to common-sense, and, above all, by begging the question, such a solution may be made to seem both unnecessary and absurd; but such a procedure is not compatible with either clear thought or mental integrity.

Having thus secured some ground for trust in objective and universal knowledge, it next remained to inquire what kind of a world our faculties give. The phenomenal world needs no description, and to spontaneous thought seems to be a self-sufficing fact. Reflection, however, served to show that this fact could not be final. Much of it had to be handed over to subjectivity as simply our way of looking at the world-process. But these subjective elements did not, because subjective, appear to be delusions. On the contrary, it seemed possible to regard them as universal though subjective, or as representing the universal thought-side of the cosmos and its processes. Our final conclusion was that if the world be other than a presentation, it can only be a mode of divine energizing which has its reality in the divine will, and its form in the divine thought. In that case, in so far as we have any knowledge of it, we rethink the divine thought and reproduce the divine intuition.

But if this view is to be maintained, another assumption must be made. Sensations are the raw material of knowledge, the incitements which lead the mind to a construction of its objects. But sensations seem to be arbitrarily connected with the physical system. There is no assignable reason why a sensation should attend one form of physical movement or action rather than any other whatever. Besides, there is nothing in sensation itself which favors one kind of cause rather than another. But if the resulting knowledge is to have any universal validity, or is to reveal to us the world-process as it exists in the absolute thought, then these sensations must be so adjusted on the one side to that process, and on the other to the nature of the finite mind, that the resulting construction must lie parallel to the absolute thought of the system. Without this assumption of an exact adjustment of heterogeneous elements, our cosmic knowledge loses all claim to universality. But, complex as this assumption seems, it must be made by every system which rejects pure presentationism. If not made, then similar sensations do not point to similarity of cause and relation, and unlike causes have like effects. In that case every possibility of objective knowledge falls away, and scientific reasoning about the cosmos and its forms is at an end. It is very common to hear the physicist declaring that we know directly nothing but phenomena, and that these phenomena are totally unlike the things which underlie them. But it is equally common to hear him speaking with great confidence of things which are not and never can be phenomenal. Yet if the phenomena are quite unlike the things, what shall warrant us in concluding from them to things? Plainly such conclusions are absurd without the implicit assumption that the subjective phenomenal elements are accurately adjusted to the objective noumenal realities. If we admit nothing but our own thought-process, we are egoists. If we find this view absurd, and admit other thought-processes than our own, then, in order to make personal communion possible and trustworthy, we have to affirm an exact adjustment between these processes and the mechanism of communication. Finally, if we admit a world-process, we have also to affirm an exact adjustment of sensation to the world-process on the one hand and to the thought-process on the other. We do not, however, make complexity by this theory; we only recognize the complexity which really exists. This general assumption is only a special case of that part of the doctrine of the pre-established harmony which we have seen is a necessary factor of every system which understands its own meaning. For all interaction there must be an exact quantitative and qualitative adjustment of each to each, or chaos will be the result.

The idealism which we have expounded is essentially that of Kant, although we differ from Kant in his denial of noumenal knowledge. The general method is that of Herbart, who developed the realistic side of the Kantian philosophy. But the most pretentious form of idealism has not been mentioned. This is the absolute idealism of the later German speculators. Kant's philosophy could not stay where it stopped, but either the realistic or the idealistic factor must be given up. Kant himself certainly thought it possible to retain both, but he combined them so unfortunately that while one cannot become a Kantian without being a realist, one cannot remain a Kantian and retain realism. His basal distinction of phenomena and noumena implies both elements. But, unluckily, his denial of objective significance to the categories left the noumena without any ground of existence. Causation, reality, substance, interaction, are categories, and have only a subjective validity. But since we pass to the outer world only by the bridge of causality, there can be no reason for affirming things apart from the mind when this bridge is broken down. The mind is self-determining, and produces its objects from itself. At this parting of the ways the development of Kant's philosophy took a double direction. Herbart and his followers developed the realistic side; and Fichte, Schelling, and Hegel developed the idealistic side. If we take Kant's doctrine of the categories in earnest, the mind is all, and must develop its own objects. Accordingly Fichte set out to show how and why the mind furnishes itself with objects. He showed how the ego must posit itself, and how, in order to do this, it must limit itself that is, must give itself objects. In this self-position and self-limitation Fichte finds the origin of the objective world. This world is not something ontologically diverse from the ego, but only a mode of limitation whereby the ego comes to self-consciousness. But if we take terms in their common meaning, this implies that any individual mind creates its objects entirely from itself and without any incitement from without; indeed, a good many of Fichte's critics understood him to mean that he was the absolute creator of his own universe. Kant's doctrine could lead to nothing but this; but this view was too absurd for any patience. Hence Fichte declared that by the ego he did not mean the individual and empirical ego, but the transcendental ego. But what this ego might be he was not at pains to state very clearly. For the most part, he seems to have meant by it the universal reason, and this is a pure abstraction from the mental operations of thinking beings, who are the only realities. Fichte is as inconsequent as Kant. After having made a great show of logic in denying any external ground of our sensations, he saves himself from pure egoism by the fiction of a transcendental ego which is the reality in all individual and finite egos; and this fiction is reached in defiance of all logic.

But the development did not stop with Fichte. It went on dropping element after element of reality until in the Hegelian school thought was identified with being, and the attempt was made to deduce the universe from the bare notion of existence. In the obvious meaning of the term this doctrine is absurd; and hence to make the proposed identification we must take the words out of their proper signification. When we declare that thought is being, we cannot mean by thought a simple conception, for this would be the extremest nonsense. In that case our thoughts would be things. Or if we prefer to say that pure thinking is being, we must mean by pure thinking something more than the process of comparing, judging, and inferring, which we commonly call thinking; for this is not being, but only a movement in the mind. Besides, both thought and thinking, as thus used, imply a thinker as their subject and the ground of their possibility. Sometimes pure thought is identified with the system of categories, and these again are identified with being. The ground of this procedure is the fact that if there is to be any knowledge of being, the categories of thought must also be categories of being. But this fact does not justify the identification; for it only says that thought must be able to know being or to grasp its content. The categories as conceived are thoughts only and not existences. The ineffable difference between thought and thing remains untranscended and unexplained. There is not the slightest attempt to show how that which exists as conception in our minds can take its place in the world as real. We have simply an analysis of the content of reason or of formal truth, and no proper identification of thought and reality. But this formal truth is lumped together in the general term reason, and reason is hypostasized into the supreme and only reality. There is throughout a failure to name the thinking subject, apart from which neither truth nor reason has any significance. The concrete and living person disappears, and in its place is put the abstraction of an idea or a system of ideas. The treatment is logical rather than psychological or metaphysical; and the utmost result is to show a kind of connection among our fundamental ideas. Reality is not constructed, but reason is analyzed.

But supposing that the mystery of being cannot be deduced, it is still possible that the various forms of existence can be evolved from thought. If the categories of thought are categories of being, it is possible that an analysis of these categories would reveal what must be true in being. How the content of reason is enabled to be real rather than conceptual may be passed by as an insoluble problem, but it would be a great thing to show that the actual system is a necessary part of that content. This also the absolute idealists sought to do. We have referred to this attempt in discussing the various apriori cosmologies. We there found that the utmost that could be reached by an analysis of thought would be a formal outline of a possible system, but no insight whatever into the actual system. We further found that even the categories themselves admit of no deduction or construction by thought, but have rather to be accepted by thought as something given. Being, change, cause, space, time, etc., are data of thought, not constructions by thought. They are as impenetrable in their possibility and connection as they are necessary in their affirmation. The sensitive and emotional side of our nature is equally inaccessible to a thought-construction. Here thought but recognizes and gives form to a content which it could never generate of itself. Both the categories of thought and the content of the sensibility are data of the rational process, and are by no means its products. The understanding supplies the name and the logical form of these elements, but for the meaning we have always to fall back upon an immediate experience or intuition. Thus the absolute idealism fails in both of its aims. It neither secures any intelligible identification of thought with being, nor does it deduce the actual features of the system as necessary implications of reason. Finally, the doctrine could only result in a static pantheism, like that of the Eleatics. The consequences and implications of reason are as changeless and eternal as reason itself. With rational truths time has naught to do, but all alike coexist forever. Such a system excludes all movement and progress; and the appearance of movement can only be reckoned a delusion. That this system should ever have given itself out as a system of development is a most extraordinary inconsequence.

But insufficient as we find the doctrine of the absolute idealists, we must admit that the problem at which they wrought demands a solution. Thought cannot transcend itself. It can deal with reality only through ideas. All our scientific effort is but an attempt to bring certain ideas awakened in us by experience into a rational order; and when we have brought these ideas into such connection that we see how one set must give rise to another set, or how one order of phenomena must be followed by another order of phenomena, we have done all that we can ever hope to do. But all the while we are doing nothing but systematizing our own conceptions. In the Introduction we referred to two orders of mental movement, one of experience and one of reason. The work of science consists solely in transforming the order of experience into the order of reason, or in replacing the factual and opaque conjunctions of experience by the rational and transparent conjunctions of thought. Thought seeks thought everywhere. For the reflective mind, nature is not the complex of external things, but the reason in things. Even when we recognize a system independent of ourselves, our aim is still to think the thought expressed in it. And since thought can never transcend thinking, there must arise, first, an unwillingness to admit anything beyond itself, and, second, a desire to generate all its objects in its own self-enclosed movement. Thus the finite mind comes into difficulties. On the one hand, it cannot view itself as the independent generator of its objects; and, on the other hand, it cannot admit any existence which is essentially unrelated to thought. The only solution of the problem lies in the theistic conception. First, we must hold that the system of things is essentially a thought-system. It is, however, not merely a thought, but a thought realized in act. As such it is real; and as such, it is transparent to thought. Our actual thinking may not grasp it; but, as an expression of thought, it is ever open to the penetration of intelligence. It may be unknown; it cannot be essentially unknowable. Second, we must hold that in the absolute person knowing and being are coextensive. In the divine knowing all is transparent, as in the divine doing all is real. In no other conception can the mind find relief from an untenable idealism on the one hand, or from a suicidal doctrine of the unknowable on the other, or rather from a dreary and endless oscillation between them.

Francis Ellingwood Abbot

THE GOD OF SCIENCE

Scientific Theism (Boston: Little, Brown, and Co., 1885), pp. 202–218.

§ 84. The immanent relational constitution of the universe *per se* is, then, not that of an infinite machine, which is a self-destructive concept, but that of an infinite self-created and self-evolving organism, which is the only concept capable of effecting an absolute reconciliation of the Many and the One. The immanent life-principle of this cosmical organism is endocosmic and monistic teleology, the omnipresent and eternal teleological activity of the infinite creative understanding or Infinite Self-conscious Intellect; for the free creation of ends and means (relational systems both subjective and objective) has been shown to be at once the essential *Method of all Being* and the essential *Method of all Thought*, and therefore, through this unity of method, the absolute *Ground of the Identity of Being and Thought* (§ 46). The absolute end of Being-in-itself, therefore, is the absolute "full-filling" of Thought-in-itself—that is, creation of the Real out of the Ideal; and the absolute realization of this end is the Eternal Teleological Process of the Self-Evolution of Nature in Space and Time—in a word, the Infinite Creative Life of God.

§ 84. This is the meaning of the principle that the universe is an organism, and not a machine—a principle which is the logically necessary result of the thorough philosophizing of the scientific method. It shows that the whole universe of Being is instinct with an infinitely intelligible and infinitely intelligent Energy, working actively, in every point of Space and every moment of Time, according to the intelligible principle of Ends and Means—ends that are cosmical in their reach and scope, means that are cosmical in their dignity and effectiveness. It shows that this "Infinite and Eternal Energy from which all things proceed" effectively reveals itself in Nature to the human understanding—is in no sense "Unknowable," but essentially knowable *per se*, and actually known to the precise extent to which science has discovered the immanent relational constitution, or organic

371

idea, of Nature itself. It shows that Nature is not *a "manifestation" which does not manifest*, but rather the veritable, natural, and infinitely intelligible self-revelation of the noumenal in the phenomenal, of the absolute in the relative, of the infinite in the finite, of the eternal in the temporal. It shows that there is a fundamental spiritual identity between man and the universe in point of essential nature; that free creativeness is the supreme characteristic of intellect, whether finite or infinite, and effectuates itself in the actual creation of ends and means, as subjective or ideal relational systems; that free executiveness, or will, is the necessary concomitant of intellect, whether finite or infinite, and effectuates itself in the realization of these ends and means in Nature, as objective or real relational systems. This is the profound truth underlying the crude conception of primitive religions that "God created man in his own image." Anthropomorphism and anthropopathism are no absolute errors, but contain elements of truth which philosophy will earnestly seek to find, and reverently cherish when found. Infinite Wisdom and Infinite Will are characteristic attributes of God which stand luminously revealed in the organic or teleological conception of the universe *per se*. But teleology has not yet yielded its richest fruit.

§ 86. In our study of the concept of the organism (§ 78), we found that every organism has a twofold end—the Indwelling or Immanent End and the Outgoing or Exient End. Nature provides for the realization of this exient end of the finite organism, so far as it is her own immanent end as the infinite organism, by implanting in every finite organism of the higher orders the love of its own kind, the desire of offspring, the divine passion of maternal and paternal affection, the deep and indestructible yearning to repeat itself in that whose life is a renewal and continuation of its own—in that which is at once both itself and not itself. Now, if the universe of Being is indeed an organism, nay, the one supreme and infinite organism, this exient end, it would seem, must needs be defeated; for there is nothing beyond itself to which it can go out, and it cannot reproduce itself in another infinite. But it is not, for all that, lost. This exient principle of the universal organism, this self-abnegating and sublimest and most exquisitely beautiful element in the organic idea, constitutes that attribute in the character of God which is the rational foundation of religious trust and hope and love. For, far from vanishing or expiring in impotency, it reappears with redoubled power; it diffuses itself internally throughout the infinite organism itself, as a deepened energy and enhancement of the immanent end; it manifests itself as that Natural Providence of Law and Love in One which is the support of every instructed, steadfast, and religious mind; it returns, so to speak, into the bosom of the universe as illimitable love of itself—as ineffable satisfaction in its own fulness, beauty, and perfection, and as boundless tenderness for the spiritual offspring, veritable "children of God," who "live and move and have their being" in itself alone. What is this but infinite beatitude, infinite benignity, infinite love—the All-Embracing Fatherhood-and-Motherhood of God?

§ 87. If such is the form in which the principle of exiency must show itself in the infinite organism, no less sublime and glorious is the form taken by the principle of immanency.

"The absolute end of Being-in-itself is the absolute 'full-filling' of Thought-in-itself—that is, the creation of the Real out of the Ideal": this we saw at the opening of this last chapter. Now the Ideal appears as the subjective relational system freely created by the creative under-standing; and the Real appears as the objective relational system effectuated in Nature by the subordinate realizing activity of the executive will. The blindly executive will, however, is nothing but the objectively creative potency of the understanding itself: Thought is Force, and Force is Substance. The absolute "full-filling" of Thought-in-itself, therefore, or the embodiment of the Ideal in the Real, is the eternal self-legislation of Thought-in-itself into Thought-in-Being—of the subjective relational system into the objective relational system of the Real Universe. The ground of this realization can only be the inherent and uncre-ated fitness of the Absolute Ideal to Be—that is, to become the Absolute Real; and the perception of this absolute fitness of the Ideal to become the Real—a profoundly ethical perception—is the ground of the Eternal Creative Act. Here, then, the infinite organism manifests itself essentially as Moral Being—as a universe whose absolute foundation is Moral Law, of such absolutely self-inherent sanctity that the creative understanding itself obeys it and the whole fabric of creation embodies and enforces it; and the moral nature of man, derived from this moral nature of the universe itself, is the august revelation of the infinite purity, rectitude, and holiness of God. The unspeakable sublimity of the moral nature of man is, therefore, testimony to the immeasurably vaster sublimity of the moral nature of the universe itself; for, as the atom is to infinite Space, so is the grandest virtue of man to the infinite holiness of God.

§ 88. I do not forget the problem of evil: alas, who that is human can forget that? But neither do I forget that evil is simply the pressure of our own finitude, and that even the Infinite Love and Compassion could not relieve us of that without accomplishing the inherently impossible, to which omnipotence itself cannot extend; for, just as omni-science, rationally conceived, is the knowledge of all that is knowable, but not of the unknowable (the non-existent or nonsensical), so omnipotence, rationally conceived, is power to do all that is doable, but not to do the inherently undoable—that which involves self-contradiction or violates the necessary nature of things. Derivative being cannot, in the nature of things, either be or become infinite; and nothing short of infinitude could bring to us release from all evil. Evil is no end in itself; it cannot exist in the universe as an infinite whole, but only in the mutual relation of its parts, as the inevitable shad-ow-side of all finite reality. If it could be avoided—if the finite real could possibly exist at all without the finitude which weighs upon it and is the source of all its woes—then might we justly blame the universe for the evil that is simply inevitable. Is it not enough to lay this "spectre of the mind" to know that, without this finitude, finite being could not be; that finite being is better than non-being; and that, between these two grim but sole possibilities, Infinite Goodness and Love itself would choose the former? If that is not precisely optimism, neither is it pessimism; and it is theodicy enough to satisfy at least one not easily satisfied mind.

§ 89. Let us now review the general course of thought which we have been pursuing in these investigations, and gather together in a brief summary the large elements of that noumenal conception of the universe which naturally flows from the philosophized scientific method.

1. Because the universe is in some small measure actually known in human science, it must be in itself both absolutely self-existent and infinitely intelligible; that is, it must be a noumenon because it is a phenomenon.

2. Because it is infinitely intelligible, it must be likewise infinitely intelligent.

3. Because it is at the same time both infinitely intelligible and infinitely intelligent, it must be an infinite subject-object or self-conscious intellect.

4. Because it is an infinitely intelligible object, it must possess throughout an immanent relational constitution.

5. Because it possesses an infinitely intelligible relational constitution, it must be an absolutely perfect system.

6. Because it is an absolutely perfect system, it cannot be an infinite machine, but must be an infinite organism.

7. Because it is an infinite organism, its life-principle must be an infinite immanent Power, acting everywhere and always by organic means for organic ends, and subordinating every event to its own infinite life—in other words, it must be infinite Will directed by infinite Wisdom.

8. Because it is an infinite organism, its exient organic end disappears as such, but reappears as infinite Love of itself and infinite Love of the finite.

9. Because it is an infinite organism, its immanent organic end appears as the eternal realization of the Ideal, and therefore as infinite Holiness.

10. Because, as an infinite organism, it thus manifests infinite Wisdom, Power, and Goodness, or thought, feeling, and will in their infinite fulness, and because these three constitute the essential manifestations of personality, it must be conceived as Infinite Person, Absolute Spirit, Creative Source and Eternal Home of the derivative finite personalities which depend upon it, but are no less real than itself.

§ 90. Such appears to me to be the conception of the universe which flows naturally, logically, inevitably, from the philosophized scientific method; and such, therefore, appears to me to be the Idea of God which is the legitimate outcome of modem science. In truth, it is the scientific and strictly *a posteriori* proof of God's existence, attributes, and character, based solely upon the *data of universal human experience of universal Nature*, as organized into the living process of the scientific method, and upon the strictly legitimate philosophizing of that method. New England Transcendentalism[1] denies on a priori grounds the possibility of any such proof; but the proof itself now lies before the world, and the world will judge its conclusiveness.

§ 91. The further question, whether this idea of God is Pantheism, is a question of the proper definition of the word, and of far less significance. A score of years ago I named and promulgated this essential idea as Scientific Theism, and I still judge that to be the most appropriate designation of it. If all forms of Monism are necessarily deemed Pantheism, on the ground that Pantheism must include all systems of thought which rest on the principle of one sole substance, then Scientific Theism must be conceded to be Pantheism; for it certainly holds that the All is God and God the All—that the Dualism which posits Spirit and Matter as two incomprehensibly related substances, eternally alien to each other and mutually hostile in their essential nature, is a defective intellectual synthesis of the facts, and therefore greatly inferior to the Monism which posits the absolute unity of substance and absolute unity of relational constitution in one organic universe *per se*, and which conceives God, the Infinite Subject, as eternally thinking, objectifying, and revealing himself in Nature, the Infinite Object. Dualism is inevitably driven to Deism, with its clumsy makeshift of creation *ex nihilo*; and Deism is the only form of the mechanical theory of evolution which does not flatly contradict the mechanical concept. Abundant reasons have already been given why the "monistic" mechanical theory should be rejected; but whatever cogency they may have tells with equal force against Dualism itself, except in the one point of teleology.

§ 92. If, on the other hand, Pantheism is the denial of all real personality, whether finite or infinite, then, most emphatically, Scientific Theism is *not* Pantheism, but its diametrical opposite. Teleology is the very essence of purely spiritual personality; it presupposes thought, feeling, and will; it is the decisive battle-ground between the personal and impersonal conceptions of the universe. There is no such thing as unconscious teleology; if it is not conscious in the finite organism, as of course it is not in the organic structure as distinguished from the organic consciousness and action, then it must be conscious in the infinite organism which creates the finite. Ends and means are inconceivable and impossible, except as ideal or subjective relational systems which the creative understanding absolutely produces, and which the will reproduces in Nature as real or objective relational systems; hence the recognition of Teleology in Nature is necessarily the recognition of purely spiritual Personality in God. Yet Teleology, say what one will, cannot be escaped by any device in the comprehension of Nature; it is either openly confessed in, or else surreptitiously introduced into, all philosophical systems of evolution, as has been instanced above in the systems of Haeckel and Spencer. Teleology conjoined with Dualism, however, yields only the most awkward and artificial form of the mechanical theory—that of Deism, or the theory of an external creator, creation *ex nihilo*, and meaningless "second causes"; while Teleology conjoined with Monism yields the organic theory of evolution or Scientific

Theism, which includes only so much of Pantheism as is really true and has appeared in every deeply religious philosophy since the very birth of human thought.

§ 93. For every deeply religious philosophy must hold fast, at the same time, the two great principles of the Transcendence and the Immanence of God; and that of his Immanence, thought down to its foundation, is Monism. If God is not conceived as transcendent, he is confounded with matter, as in Hylozoism, Materialism, or Material Pantheism. But, if he is not conceived as immanent, he is banished from his own universe as a Creator *ex nihilo* and mere Infinite Mechanic. Scientific Theism conceives him as immanent in the universe so far as it is known, and transcendent in the universe so far as it remains unknown—immanent, that is, in the world of human experience, and transcendent in the world which lies beyond human experience. This is the only legitimate or philosophical meaning of the word transcendent; for God is still conceived as immanent alone, and in no sense transcendent, in the infinite universe *per se*. Hence the merely subjective distinction of the Transcendence and Immanence of God perfectly corresponds with that of the "Known" and the "Unknown," as absolutely one in Real Being; God is "Known" as the Immanent, and "Unknown" as the Transcendent; but he is absolutely knowable as both the Immanent and the Transcendent. It is really denial of him to confound him with the "Unknowable" or Unintelligible—that is, the Non-Existent. Scientific Theism does not insult and outrage the human mind by calling upon it to worship what it cannot possibly understand—an unreal quantity, a surd, a square root of *minus* one, an "Unknowable Reality" which is only a synonym for Impossible Reality or Absolute Unreality; for that is the quintessence of superstition. But it gives an idea of God which not only satisfies the demands of the human intellect, but no less those of the human heart.

§ 94. In vain will the soul of man strive to worship, to venerate, to love, that which has no intelligible being: the clear idea must precede the vivid and deep and strong emotion, just as necessarily as the fountain-head must precede the beautiful river with its glory of smiling banks. So long as man is finite, so long indeed will the Mysterious, the Transcendent, the Unknown abide, as the infinite Beyond to which the finite cannot reach; and the presence of this ever-abiding Mystery perpetually excites those sentiments of sublimity and awe which are indeed the unfailing concomitant of all true worship. But every sentiment of true worship is absolutely extinguished in the intelligent mind where no clear idea is presented—where no luminous thought shoots its radiance into the fathomless abyss of Being, but where all is black with impenetrable darkness. If the glorious thought of a universe in which God is at once the Self-Manifesting and the Self-Manifested, the Self-Revealing and the Self-Revealed—a universe in which the adoring Kepler might well exclaim in awe unspeakable, "O God, I think Thy thoughts after Thee!"—a universe which is the eternally objectified Divine Idea, illumining the human intellect, inspiring the human conscience, warming the human heart—if, I say, this glorious thought begotten of science has no power to stir the depths of the human soul and lift it up to the sublimest heights of worship and self-consecration to the service of the Most High, then religion is dead indeed, and the light of the universe is gone out forever. But, if this thought of God, the reflected glory of its divine source, has, as in truth it has, such a divine force and energy in itself as to soothe the woes of life, and dull the pangs of sorrow, and minister new strength to the soul faltering in the path of painful duty, then religion is not dead, but sleeping, and will yet rise from its bier at the commanding word of Science.

§ 95. Ralph Waldo Emerson, whose great memory hovers like a benediction over the heads of this mighty and happy people, uttered, in one of the latest, if not the very latest, of his public addresses (and it was my signal privilege to listen to it), this dignified lament over one of the immediate, yet I believe transient, effects of the spread of the scientific spirit in our day:

> In consequence of this revolution in opinion, it appears, for the time, as the misfortune of the period that the cultivated mind has not the happiness and dignity of the religious sentiment. We are born too late for the old and too early for the new faith. I see in those classes and those persons in whom I am accustomed to look for tendency and progress, for what is most positive and most rich in human nature, and who contain the activity of to-day and the assurance of to-morrow—I see in them character, but skepticism; a clear enough perception of the inadequacy of the popular religious statement to the wants of their heart and intellect, and explicit declarations of this fact. They have insight and truthfulness; they will not mask their convictions; they hate cant; but more than this I do not readily find. The gracious motions of the soul—piety, adoration—I do not find. Scorn of hypocrisy, pride of personal character, elegance of taste and of manners and of pursuit, a boundless ambition of the intellect, willingness to sacrifice personal interests for the integrity of the character—all these they have; but that religious submission and abandonment which give man a new element and being, and make him sublime—it is not in churches, it is not in houses. I see movement, I hear aspirations, but I see not how the great God prepares to satisfy the heart in the new order of things.[2]

§ 96. The great seer saw not deeply enough into the recesses of this new scientific spirit; the great prophet of New England Transcendentalism read not deeply enough that mighty *striving after truth* which is born of the scientific method, and in turn bears fruit in the bewildering scientific discoveries of this new time. He saw not the slow and obscure beginnings of a new form of faith, sprung not from the "ecstatic intuition" of Transcendentalism, but from a closer contact of the human intellect with the real universe than was ever possible before—heralded, not by the earthquake and the wind of the great discoveries themselves, but by the "still, small voice" of their creator, the Scientific Method, which only those can hear who are patient enough to ponder, to meditate, and to muse. If I have rightly divined the inner character, spirit, and tendency of this philosophy fated to be, it will not only "satisfy the heart in the new order of things," but also (condition antecedent to this heart-satisfaction[3]) satisfy the head as well. For the head has been too long sacrificed to the heart in religion; and the result today is the satisfaction of neither. Scientific Theism is more than a philosophy: it is a religion, it is a gospel, it is the Faith of the Future, founded on knowledge rather than on blind belief—a faith in which head and heart will be no more arrayed against each other in irreconcilable feud, as the world beholds them now, but will kneel in worship side by side at the same altar, dedicated, not to the "Unknown God," still less to the "Unknowable God," but to the Known God whose revealing prophet is Science.

For the idea of God which science is slowly, nay, unconsciously, creating is that of no metaphysical abstraction spun out of the cobwebs of idealistic speculation, but rather that of the immanent, organific, and supremely spiritual Infinite Life, revealing itself visibly in Nature, and, above all, invisibly in Nature's sublimest product—human nature and the human soul. Scientific Theism utters in intelligible speech the very heart, the Infinite Heart, of the universe itself, and speaks with resistless persuasion to the heart of all who can comprehend it. He who can firmly grasp the torch of this self-luminous Knowledge of God possesses an "Inner Light" beside which all other lights are wandering wills-o'-the-wisp, and knows himself to be in absolute security, come what may, so long as he walks the paths of destiny by the clear and steady radiance it sheds, and lifts up his soul in secret loyalty and adoration to Him from whose infinite being all human knowledge itself is a shining ray. With all reverence and tenderness for the illustrious dead be it spoken: I *do* "see how the great God prepares to satisfy the heart in the new order of things." For Scientific Theism is the Philosophy of Free Religion and the Religion of Free Philosophy.

NOTES

1. "It is my belief that reason in its original capacity and function has no knowledge of spiritual truth, not even of the first and fundamental truth of religion, the being of God. . . . I deny the ability of the human intellect to construct that ladder, whose foot being grounded in irrefragable axiom, and its steps all laid in dialectic continuity, the topmost round thereof shall lift the climbing intellect into vision of the Godhead. Between the last truth which the human intellect can reach by legitimate induction and the being of God there will ever lie—'deserts of vast eternity.' Not by that process did any soul yet arrive at that transcendent truth; not from beneath, but from above—not by intellectual escalade, but by heavenly condescension—comes the idea of God, even by the condescending Word," etc. (F. H. Hedge, *Reason in Religion*, p. 208, Boston, 1865.) Dr. Hedge's distrust and fear of the understanding, or "human intellect," which is shared by most of the Transcendentalists, arises from defective comprehension of the spirit, tendency, and immanent philosophical creativeness of the scientific method.

2. Ralph Waldo Emerson, *Lectures and Biographical Sketches*, ed. James Elliot Cabot (Boston: Houghton Mifflin, 1883), pp. 201–211.

3. Dante (*Paradiso*, XXVIII. 106–111) beautifully expresses this thought that the *vision* of Divine Truth must precede the *love* of it, and constitute the foundation of beatitude:

> "E dei saver che tutti hanno diletto,
>   Quanto la sua veduta si profonda
>   Nel Vero, in che si queta ogn' intelletto.
>
> Quinci si può veder come si fonda
>
>   L'esser beato nell' atto che vede,
>   Non in quel ch'ama, che poscia seconda."

George Holmes Howison

Is Modern Science Pantheistic?

Journal of Speculative Philosophy 19 (October 1885): 363–384.

In turning over the foregoing question for several months, I have become more and more impressed with the conviction that any satisfactory answer to it depends upon a clear apprehension of the meaning of its terms. What *is* pantheism? And what features are there in modern science that can give color to the supposition that pantheism is its proper result? Or, if such a supposition is well founded, why should the result be regarded as undesirable? If science establishes, or clearly tends to establish, the pantheistic view of the universe, why should this awaken alarm? What hostility to the vital interests of human nature can there be in such a view? Can there be a possible antagonism between the truth and the real interests of man?

The question before us probably does not convey to most minds the depth and intensity of interest which is so manifestly conveyed by the question of Immortality recently discussed—at least not on its surface. Yet a consideration of it in the detail of the subsidiary questions that have just been mentioned will not only secure the clearness requisite to an intelligent answer, but will bring the real depth of its interest into view, and will show this to be no less profound, while it is far more comprehensive than that of the former problem. It is for this reason that I venture to offer the reflections that have passed in my own mind in the endeavor to clear up the detailed questions that the general problem involves. In the hope of contributing something toward that definite apprehension of its bearings which is indispensable to any real and permanent effect of its discussion, I will proceed to consider those questions in their proper succession.

I. WHAT PANTHEISM IS

Of the several questions that I have specified, perhaps none is surrounded with such vagueness and obscurity as the first—What is pantheism? The generally recognized defenders of religion, the theologians who speak with the hoary authority and with the weight of presumptive evidence that the traditional and, indeed, historic bodies of organized and instituted religion naturally impart, are in the habit of drawing a sharp *verbal* distinction between theism and pantheism, as they also do between theism and deism; but when the independent and unbiased thinker, anxious for clearness and precision, inquires after the *real* distinction intended by these names, he hardly finds it in any sense that awakened thought will recognize as at once intelligible and reasonable. We constantly hear that theism is contradicted by both deism and pantheism; by the one through its assertion of the divine personality at the expense of the divine revelation and providence; by the other through its assertion of the divine omnipresence at the expense of the separateness of the divine personality from the world. We hear constantly, too, that theism, to be such, must teach that there is a being who is *truly* God, or that the First Principle of the universe is a Holy Person, who has revealed his nature and his will to his intelligent creatures, and who superintends their lives and destinies with an incessant providence that aims, by an all-pervading interference in the events of the world, to secure their obedience to his will as the sole sufficient condition of their blessedness. All this, however, is but an abstract and very vague formula, after all. Of the *quomodo* for reconciling the contradiction whose extremes are represented by the deism and the pantheism which it condemns it has nothing to say. *How* the divine personality is to be thought so as to comport with the divine omnipresence, or *how* the omnipresent providence of God is to be reconciled with his distinctness from the world, the general proclamation of orthodox theism has no power to show. And, when we pass from the general formula to the desired details, we are too often then made aware that the professedly theistic doctrine is hampered up with a mass of particulars which are, in truth, profoundly at variance with its own principle; that confusion or contradiction reigns where clearness ought to be; that merely anthropomorphic and mechanical conceptions usurp the place of the required divine and spiritual realities. We discover, for instance, that, in the mechanical interpretation of theism, every doctrine is construed as deism that refuses its assent to a discontinuous and special providence, or to an inconstant, limited, and contra-natural revelation; and that, on the other hand, every theory is condemned as pantheism that denies the separation of God from the world, and asserts instead his omnipresent immanence in it. And we even find that, in the hands of such interpreters, theism is identified with the belief in mechanical and artificial theories of the *quomodo* of atonement, or, as such writers are fond of calling it, of "the plan of salvation." Into the rightful place of the sublime fact of the all-pervading providence and all-transforming grace that makes eternally for righteousness are set hypothetical explanatory schemes of expiation by sacrifice, of appeasal by the suffering of the innocent, of ransom by blood, of federal covenant and imputation, of salvation by faith alone; and the theories of the divine nature and administration which omit these details, or refuse to take them literally, are stamped as deism or as pantheism, even though the omission or refusal be dictated by a perception of the incompatibility of the rejected schemes with the fundamental principles of ethics, and, therefore, with the very nature of divine revelation. And thus, in the end, by mere confusion of thought and by inability to rise above conceptions couched in the limited forms of space and of time, the original theistic formula—which, in its abstract setting off of theism against deism and pantheism, is quite unobjectionable, and indeed, so far as it goes, entirely correct—is brought into contradiction with its own essential idea.

Still, it must never be forgotten that these ill-grounded efforts at the completer definition of theism are made in behalf of a real distinction. We shall not fail to find it true, I think, that there *is* a view of the world for which deism may be a very proper name, and another view which may most appropriately be called pantheism; that these are radically distinct from theism, defined as the doctrine of a personal Creator who reveals himself by omnipresent immanence in the world, to the end of transforming it, through the agencies of moral freedom, into his own image, and of establishing a realm of self-determining persons, who freely and immortally do his will. Nor, as I believe, shall we fail to find that the doctrines named deism and pantheism are *historic* doctrines; that they are not merely conceivable abstractions, but have been advocated by actual men, of a very real persuasion and a very discernible influence. Nor can I doubt that these two doctrines, in their deviations from the theistic theory, will be recognized by our sound judgment as *defects*, and consequently be reckoned as injurious opinions. Only it must be understood that the sole ground of this judgment is to be our untrammelled rational conviction; and that if we were to find this conviction on the side of deism or of pantheism, we ought none of us to hesitate to take the one or the other as the sounder and more commendable view.

In asking, now, what pantheism exactly is, we may avail ourselves of a useful clue, for a beginning, in the apparent meaning of the name itself. The derivation of this from the two Greek words *pan*, all, and *theos*, God, would seem to make it mean either (1) that the All is God, or else (2) that God is all—that God alone really exists. The name, then, hints at two very distinct doctrines: it signifies either (1) that the mere total of particular existences is God; in other words, that the universe, as we commonly call it, is itself the only absolute and real being; or (2) that God, the absolute Being, is the only real being—all finite existence is merely his transitory form of appearance, and is thus, in truth, illusion. We might convey the one or the other of these diverse doctrines by the name, according as we should pronounce it *pan*-theism or pan-*the*ism. In either way, the word may be made to cover an absolute identification of God and the universe. In the former way, God is merged in the universe; in the latter, the universe is merged in God.

And, in fact, pantheism, as an historic theory, has actually presented itself in these two forms. The doctrine has come forward in a considerable variety of expressions or schemes of exposition, such as those of Heraclitus, Parmenides, and the Stoics, in ancient times, not to speak of the vast systems lying at the basis of the Hindu religions; or those of Bruno and Vanini, Schelling (in his early period), Oken, Schopenhauer, and Hartmann, in our modern era. But various as are these schemes, they may all be recognized as falling into one or the other of the two comprehensive forms which we have just seen to be suggested by the common name. These two forms may evidently be styled, respectively, the atheistic and the acosmic form of pantheism, as the one puts the sensible universe in the place of God, and thus annuls his being, while the other annuls the reality of the cosmos, or world of finite existences, by reducing the latter to mere modes of the being of the one and only Universal Substance. Both forms are manifestly open to the criticism visited upon pantheism by the standard defenders of theism—namely, that it contradicts the essence of the divine nature by sacrificing the distinctness of the divine personality to a passion for the divine omnipresence; the sacrifice of the distinctness, at any rate, is obvious, even if the incompatibility of such a loss of distinct being with the true nature of a godhead be not at first so evident; though that this loss *is* incompatible with a real divinity will, I think, presently appear. And both forms of pantheism are, in the last analysis, atheisms; the one obviously, the other implicitly so. The one may be more exactly named a physical or theoretical atheism, as it dispenses with the distinct existence of God in his function of Creator; the other may properly be called a moral or practical atheism, as, in destroying the freedom and the immortality of the individual, it dispenses with God in his function of Redeemer. Under either form, the First Principle is emptied of attributes that are vital to deity: in the first the *entire* proper and distinct being of God disappears; in the second, all those attributes are lost that present God in his adorable characters of justice and love, and in the ultimate terms of his omniscience and omnipotence. Perfect omniscience and omnipotence are only to be realized in the complete control of *free* beings, and the creation in them of the divine image by *moral* instead of physical influences.

II. THE RELATION OF PANTHEISM TO MATERIALISM AND IDEALISM

It will aid us in a correct apprehension of pantheism if we appreciate its relations to other anti-theistic forms of philosophy, particularly to materialism, and to what is known as subjective idealism. It will become clear that it forms a higher synthesis of thought than either of these. Its conception of the world may be read out either in materialistic or ideal-istic terms; and this is true whether we take it in its atheistic or its acosmic form. Yet, on a first inspection, this hardly seems to be the case. On the contrary, one is at first quite inclined to identify its first form with materialism outright, and to recognize in its second form a species of exaggerated spiritualism; and hence to contrast the two forms as the mate-rialistic and the idealistic. Further reflection does not entirely do away with this mistake, for the apparent identity of atheistic pantheism with materialism is very decided; and the only correction in our first judgment that we next feel impelled to make, is to recognize the double character of acosmic pantheism. The one and only Universal Substance, in order to include an exhaustive summary of all the phenomena of experience, must be taken, no doubt, as both extending and being conscious. But is the Universal Substance an extended being that thinks? or is it a thinking being that apprehends itself under a peculiar mode of consciousness called extension? In other words, is the thinking of the one Eternal Substance grounded in and mediated by its extended being? or has its extension existence only in and through its thinking? Which attribute is primary and essential, and makes the other its derivative and function? Under the conception of the sole existence of the Absolute, the

question is inevitable, irresistible, and irreducible. It thus becomes plain that, to say nothing of a third hypothesis of the mutually independent parallelism of the two attributes,
acosmic pantheism may carry materialism as unquestionably as it carries idealism, though
not, indeed, so naturally or coherently. And sharper inquiry at last makes it equally clear
that atheistic pantheism will carry idealism as consistently as it carries materialism, if
doubtless less naturally. For, although in the sum-total of the particular existences there
must be recognized a gradation from such existences as are unconscious up to those that
are completely conscious, and although it would be the more natural and obvious view to
read the series as a development genetically upward from atoms to minds, still the incomprehensibility of the transit from the unconscious to the conscious cannot fail to suggest
the counter-hypothesis, and the whole series may be conceived as originating ideally in the
perceptive constitution and experience of the conscious members of it. There is, however, a
marked distinction between the two orders of idealism given, respectively, by the acosmic
pantheism and by the atheistic: the former, grounded in the consciousness of the Universal
Substance, has naturally a universal and, in so far, an *objective* character; the latter has
no warrant except the thought in a particular consciousness, and no valid means of raising this warrant even into a common or general character, much less into universality;
it is accordingly particular and *subjective*. Pantheism, then, in both its forms, is not only
a more comprehensive view of the world than either materialism or any one-sided idealism, whether abstractly universal or only subjective, inasmuch as it makes either of them
possible; but it is also a deeper and more organic view, because it does bring in, at least in
a symbolic fashion, the notion of a universal in some vague sense or other. This advantage,
however, it does not secure with any fulness except in the acosmic form. Indeed, the atheistic form is so closely akin to the less organic theories of materialism and subjective idealism that we may almost say we do not come to pantheism proper until we pass out of the
atheistic sort and find ourselves in the acosmic. An additional gain afforded by pantheism,
and eminently by acosmic pantheism, is the conception of the intimate union of the First
Principle with the world of particular phenomena; the creative cause is stated as spontaneously manifesting its own nature in the creation; it abides immanently in the latter, and
is no longer conceived as separated from it and therefore itself specifically limited in space
and in time, as it is conceived in the cruder dualistic and mechanical view of things, with
which human efforts at theological theory so naturally begin.

III. THE CONTRAST BETWEEN PANTHEISM AND DEISM

At this point we strike the eminent merit of pantheism, as contrasted with deism. By
the latter name it has been tacitly agreed to designate that falling short of theism which
stands counter to pantheism. As the latter is defective by confounding God and the
world in an indistinguishable identity, so deism comes short by setting God in an
isolated and irreducible separation from the world. Deism thus falls partly under the
same condemnation of materiality which a rational judgment pronounces upon sensuous

theism, with its physically anthropomorphic conceptions of the Creator, dwelling in his peculiar quarter of space called Heaven, and its mechanical theory of his communication with the world by way of "miracle" alone—by way, that is, independent, and even subversive, of the ordered process of means and end in nature.[1] But while thus suffering from mechanical limitations in thought, deism must still be allowed its relative merit, too. That merit is the criticism which it makes upon the mechanical method of physically anthropomorphic theism. If, in the interest of distinguishing the Creator from the creation, God is to be thought as capable of existing without a world, and as *separated* from the creation, then, as deism justly says, it is purely arbitrary to declare the separation overcome by means of mechanical miracle. Consistency, and, in so far, rationality, would rather require that the separation be kept up; and the folly of the anthropomorphic dualism is made to display itself in the deistic inference, which it cannot consistently refute, that the divine revelation and providence, without which the practical religion indispensable to the reality of theism cannot have being, are, by the separateness of the divine existence, rendered impossible.

IV. THE PERMANENT INSIGHT CONTAINED IN PANTHEISM

In approaching, then, the question, Why should pantheism be regarded as a doctrine to avoid? we must be careful not to neglect the fact that it plays a valuable and, indeed, an indispensable part in the formation of a genuine theological theory. It is the transitional thought by which we ascend out of the idolatrous anthropomorphism of sensuous theism into that complete and rational theism which has its central illumination in the realized truth of the divine omnipresence. In the immanence of God in the world it finds the true basis—the rational theory—of the divine perpetual providence; in his indwelling in the creature, as "the Light which lighteth every man that cometh into the world," it finds a like basis and theory for the universal and perpetual divine revelation. Indeed, in this realized and now fully uttered omnipresence of God, and in God's active indwelling in the inmost spirit of man, it lays the rational foundation for the Perpetual Incarnation, the doctrine of the Divine Humanity; and, when Christianity sets the doctrine of the Triune God in the very centre of practical religion, pantheism prepares the way to vindicate it as the genuine interpreter of a rational theism. That the Eternal eternally generates himself in our higher human nature; that this Son of Man is truly and literally the Son of God, and the Son only begotten: that, by the discipline of life in worlds of imperfection, men, and through them the whole creation, ascend by devout faith (or fidelity) toward this Son, and, by his life, immortally unto God in the Holy Spirit—this, the epitome and essence of Christian theism, first becomes apprehended as a rationally natural truth in the insight which pantheism brings with it, that God is not separate from the world but immediately present in it, and that the distinction between the Creator and the creature, between the human soul and its redeeming God, can never be truly stated as a distinction in place and time, as a separation in space and by a period. And it is not until the pantheistic insight has been realized in our minds, whether by name or no it matters not, that we discover clearly that this fundamental religious truth, which none of us, upon reflection, would think of denying, and which in some sense we may rightly say we have always known, is effectually violated by our ordinary anthropomorphic conceptions.

V. THE PERMANENT DEFECT OF PANTHEISM

But, while this permanent insight of pantheism must be carried up into all genuine theistic thought, it remains also true that it falls seriously short of the theological conception demanded by the highest practical religion. For the possibility of religion as a practical power in human life—the very conception of theism as an operative force in the spirit—depends not merely on the omnipresent existence and work of God, but upon the freedom (that is, the unqualified reality) and the immortality of man. Indeed, if the space permitted, it might clearly be shown, not only that man cannot be properly man apart from freedom, immortality, and God, but that God cannot be properly God apart from man and man's immortality and freedom; in other words, that the self-existent, free perfection of the Godhead, by virtue of its own nature, demands for its own fulfilment the establishment and the control of a world that is God's own image; the *divine* creation must completely reflect the divine nature, and must therefore be a world of moral freedom, self-regulating and eternal. But this demand of a genuine theism pantheism cannot meet. Its theory, whether in the atheistic or in the acosmic form, lies in the very contradiction of human freedom and immortality. Indeed, we may say, summarily, that the distinction between theism and pantheism, even in the loftiest form of the latter, lies just in this—that theism, in asserting God, asserts human freedom and immortality; but that pantheism, while apparently asserting God to the extreme, denies his moral essence by denying the immortality and the freedom of man.

VI. WHY PANTHEISM IS A DOCTRINE TO BE DEPRECATED

And now we see why pantheism is at war with the permanent interests of human nature. Those interests are wholly identified with the vindication of freedom and immortal life; and this not on the ground of the mere immediate desire we have for freedom and permanent existence, which would, indeed, be shallow and even unworthy of a rational being, but on the profound and never-to-be-shaken foundation laid by reason in its highest form of conscience. For, when this highest form of reason is thoroughly interpreted, we know that the value of freedom and immortality lies in their indispensableness to our discipline and growth in divine life. To no theory of the world can man, then, give a willing and cordial adhesion, if it strikes at the heart of his individual reality and contradicts those hopes of ceaseless moral growth that alone make life worth living. Not in its statement of the Godhead as the all and in all, taken by itself, but in its necessarily consequent denial of the reality of man—of his freedom and immortal growth in goodness—is it that pantheism betrays its insufficiency to meet the needs of the genuine human heart. It is true, to be sure, that this opposition between the doctrine of the One Sole Reality and our natural longings for permanent existence, or our natural bias in favor of freedom, and responsibility, in itself settles nothing as to the truth or falsity of the doctrine. It might be that the system of nature—it might be that the Author of nature—is not in sympathy or accord with "the bliss for which we sigh." But so long as human nature is what it is, so long as we remain prepossessed in favor of our freedom and yearn for a life that may put death itself beneath our feet, so long will our nature reluctate, and even revolt, at the prospect of having to accept the pantheistic view; so long shall we inevitably draw back from that vast and shadowy Being who, for us and for our highest hopes, must be verily the Shadow of Death. Nay, we must go farther, and say that, even should the science of external nature prove pantheism true, this would only array the interests of science against the interests of man—the interests that man can never displace from their supreme seat in *his* world, except by abdicating his inmost nature and putting his conscience to an open shame. The pantheistic voice of science would only proclaim a deadlock in the system and substance of truth itself, and herald an implacable conflict between the law of nature and the law written indelibly in the human spirit. The heart on which the vision of a possible moral perfection has once arisen, and in whose recesses the still and solemn voice of duty has resounded with majestic sweetness, can never be reconciled to the decree, though this issue never so authentically from nature, that bids it count responsible freedom an illusion, and surrender existence on that mere threshold of moral development which the bound of our present life affords. Such a defeat of its most sacred hopes the conscience can neither acquiesce in nor tolerate. Nor can it be appeased or deluded by the pretext that annihilation may be devoutly accepted as self-sacrifice in behalf of an infinite "fulness of life" for the universe—a life in which the individual conscience is to have no share. In defense of this pantheistic piety, quoting the patriarch of many tribulations, in his impassioned cry, "Though He slay me, yet will I trust in Him!" is as vain as it is profane. This is only to repeat the fallacious paradox of those grim and obsolete sectarians who held that the test of a state of grace was "willingness to be damned for the glory of God." The spirit that truly desires righteousness longs with an unerring instinct for immortality as the indispensable condition of entire righteousness, and, when invited to approve its own immolation for the furtherance of the divine glory, will righteously answer as a noble matron, applying for admission to the Church, once answered the inquisitorial session of her Calvinistic society: "I am assuredly *not* willing to be damned for the glory of God; were I so, I should not be *here!*"

VII. THE PROFOUND INTEREST OF THE PANTHEISTIC PROBLEM

This is what makes the question of pantheism, as a possible outcome of science, of such vital concern. Science is thus made to appear as the possible utterer of the doom of our most precious hopes, the quencher of those aspirations which have hitherto been the soul of man's grandest as well as of his sublimest endeavors, the destroyer of those beliefs which are the real foundation of the triumphs of civilization—of all that gives majesty and glory to history. To present universal nature as the ocean in which man and his moral hopes are to be swallowed up is to transform the universe for man into a system of radical and irremediable *evil*, and thus to make genuine religion an impossibility; and not only genuine religion, but also all political union and order, which stands, among the affairs and institutions of this world of sense, as the outcome and the image of the religious vision. Belief in the radical and sovereign goodness of the universe and its Author and Sustainer is the very essence of religious faith and of political fealty. It is impossible that either faith or fealty can continue in minds that have once come to the realizing conviction that the whole of which we form a part, and the originating Principle of that whole, are hostile, or even indifferent, not merely to the permanent existence of man, but to his aspirations after the fulness of moral life. A professed God who either cannot or will not bring to fulfilment the longing after infinite moral growth that has once arisen in his creature, is not, for such a creature, and cannot be, true God at all:

"The wish that of the living whole

> No life may fail beyond the grave—
> Derives it not from what we have

The likest God within the soul?

· · ·

"And he, shall he?—

"Man, the last work, who seemed so fair,

> Such splendid purpose in his eyes,
> Who rolled the psalm to wintry skies,

Who built him fanes of fruitless prayer—
"Who trusted God was love indeed,

> And love Creation's final law,
> Though Nature, red in tooth and claw

With ravine, shrieked against his creed—
"Who loved, who suffered countless ills,

> Who battled for the True, the Just—
> Be blown about the desert dust,

Or sealed within the iron hills?
"No more?—A monster, then, a dream,

> A discord! Dragons of the prime,
> That tare each other in their slime,

Were mellow music, matched with him!"

It is this profound feeling, which Tennyson has thus so faithfully expressed, that gives, to the question before us in these days its anxious import. Let us not fail to realize that pantheism means, not simply the all-pervasive interblending and interpenetration of God and the creation, but the sole reality of God, and the obliteration of freedom, of moral life and of immortality for man.

VIII. WHY SHOULD MODERN SCIENCE GIVE ALARM OF PANTHEISM?

It is urgent, then, to inquire if there is anything in the nature of modern science that really gives color to the pantheistic view. It is obvious enough that there are not wanting philosophers, or even schools of philosophy, who read pantheism in science as science appears to them. But the real question is: Is such a reading the authentic account of the teachings of science itself? Here we must not mistake the utterances of men of science for the unadulterated teachings of science; for, on this borderland of science and philosophy, it need not be surprising if men familiar with only that method of investigation which science pursues, and not at home in the complex and varied history of philosophical speculation, should sometimes, or even often, be inclined to a hasty inference when the borderland is reached, and, overlooking the fact that their science and its method have necessary limits, take that view in philosophy which the illegitimate extension of their method would indicate. Disregarding, then, the mere opinions of certain cultivators of science, we are here to ask the directer, more searching and more pertinent question, What is there—if, indeed, there be anything—in the nature of science itself, as science is now known—what are the elements in it and in its method, that might be taken to point toward a pantheistic interpretation of the universe and its Source?

And to this it must in all candor be answered that, both in the method of modern science and in the two commanding principles that have legitimately resulted from that method, there is that which unquestionably *suggests* the pantheistic view. Nothing less than the most cautious discrimination, founded on a precise and comprehensive knowledge of the course of philosophical inquiry, can detect the exact reach, the limits, and the real significance of this suggestion, or expose the illegitimacy of following it without reserve. The trait to which I am now referring in the *method* of science is its rigorously experimental and observational character; indeed, its strictly empirical or tentative character. And the two commanding *results*, which now in turn play an organizing part in the subsidiary method of all the sciences, are (1) the principle of the conservation of energy, and (2) the principle of evolution manifesting itself in the concomitant phenomenon of natural selection—the struggle of each species with its environment for existence, and the survival of the fittest. The apparent implications of this method and of these two principles accordingly deserve, and must receive, our most careful present attention.

How, then, does the experimental, or, more accurately, the empirical, method of science suggest the doctrine of pantheism? By limiting our serious belief to the evidence of experience—exclusively to the evidence of the senses. The method of science demands that nothing shall receive the high credence accorded to science, except it is attested by the evidence of unquestionable presentation in sensible experience. All the refinements of scientific method—the cautions of repeated observation, the probing subtleties of experiment, the niceties in the use of instruments of precision, the principle of reduction to mean or average, the allowance for the "personal equation," the final casting out of the largest mean of possible errors in experiment or observation, by such methods, for instance, as that of least squares—all these refinements are for the single purpose of making it certain that our basis of evidence shall be confined to what has actually been present in the world of sense; we are to know beyond question that such and such conjunctions of events have *actually* been present to the senses, and precisely *what* it is that thus remains indisputable fact of sense, after all possible additions or misconstructions of our mere thought or imagination have been cancelled out. Such conjunctions in unquestionable sense-experience, isolated and purified from foreign admixture by carefully contrived experiment, we are then to raise by generalization into a tentative expectation of their continued recurrence in the future—*tentative* expectation, we say, because the rigor of the empirical method warns us that the act of generalization is a step beyond the evidence of experience, and must not be reckoned any part of science, except as it continues to be verified in subsequent experience of the particular event. Thus natural science climbs its slow and cautious way along the path of what it calls the laws of nature; but it gives this name only in the sense that there has been a constancy in the conjunctions of past experience, a verification of the tentative generalization suggested by this, and a consequent continuance of the same tentative expectancy, which, however, waits for renewed verification, and refrains from committing itself unreservedly to the absolute invariability of the law to which it refers. Unconditional universality, not to say necessity, of its ascertained conjunctions, natural science neither claims nor admits.

Now, to a science which thus accepts the testimony of experience with this undoubting and instinctive confidence that never stops to inquire what the real grounds of the possibility of experience itself may be, or whence experience can possibly derive this infallibility of evidence, but assumes, on the contrary, that the latter is underived and immediate—to such a science it must seem that we have, and can have, no verifiable assurance of any existence but the Whole—the mere aggregate of sense-presented particulars hitherto actual or yet to become so. Thus the very method of natural science tends to obliterate the feeling of the transcendent, or at least to destroy its credit at the bar of disciplined judgment, and in this way to bring the votary of natural investigation to regard the Sum of Things as the only reality.

On this view, the outcome of the scientific method might seem to be restricted to that form of pantheism which I have named the atheistic. Most obviously, the inference would be to materialism, the lowest and most natural form of such pantheism; yet subtler reasoning, recognizing that in the last resort experience must be consciousness, sees in the subjective idealism which states the Sum of Things as the aggregate of the perceptions of its conscious members, the truer fulfilment of the method that presupposes the sole and immediate validity of experience. But beyond even this juster idealistic construction of atheistic pantheism—beyond *either* form of atheistic pantheism, in fact—the mere method of natural science would appear to involve consequences which, even granting the legitimacy of belief in the transcendent, would render the transcendent God the sole reality—that is, would bring us to acosmic pantheism. For the empirical method, so far from vindicating either the freedom of the personal will or the immortality of the soul, withholds belief from both, as elements that can never come within the bounds of possible experience; so that the habit of regarding nothing but the empirically attested as part of science dismisses these two essential conditions of man's reality beyond the pale of true knowledge, and into the discredited limbo of unsupported assumptions.

It is, however, not until we pass from the bare method of natural science to its two great modern consequences, and take in their revolutionary effect as subsidiaries of method in every field of natural inquiry, that we feel the full force of the pantheistic strain which pulls with such a tension in many modern scientific minds. It is in the principle of the conservation of energy, and in that of evolution, particularly as viewed under its aspect of natural selection, that we encounter the full force of the pantheistic drift. And it seems, at the first encounter, irresistible. That all the changes in the universe of objective experience are resolvable into motions, either molar or molecular; that, in spite of the incalculable variety of these changes of motion, the sum-total of movement and the average direction of the motions is constant and unchangeable; that an unvarying correlation of all the various modes of motion exists, so that each is convertible into its correlate at a constant numerical rate, and so that each, having passed the entire circuit of correlated forms, returns again into its own form undiminished in amount: all this seems to point unmistakably to a primal energy—a ground-form of moving activity—one and unchangeable in itself, immanent in but not transcendent of its sum of correlated forms, while each instance of each form is only a transient and evanescent mode of the single reality. Nor, apparently, is this inference weakened by the later scholium upon the principle of the conservation of energy, known as the principle of the dissipation of energy. On the contrary, the pantheistic significance of the former principle seems to be greatly deepened by this. Instead of a constant whole of moving activity, exhibited in a system of correlated modes of motion, we now have a vaster correlation between the sum of actual energies and a vague but prodigious mass of potential energy—the "waste-heap," as the physicist Balfour Stewart has pertinently named it, of the power of the universe. Into this vast "waste-heap" all the active energies in the world of sense seem to be continually vanishing, and to be destined at last to vanish utterly: we shift, under the light of this principle of dissipation, from a primal energy, immanent, but not transcendent, to one immanent in the sum of correlated actual motions, and also transcendent of them. Very impressive is the view that here arises of a dread Source of Being that engulfs all beings; it is Brahm again, issuing forth through its triad Brahma, Vishnu, and Siva—creation, preservation, and annihilation—to return at last into its own void, gathering with it the sum of all its transitory modes. And let us not forget that the conceptions out of which this image of the One and All is spontaneously formed are the ascertained and settled results of the science of nature in its exactest empirical form.

When to this powerful impression of the principle of conservation, as modified by that of dissipation, we now add the proper effect of the principle of evolution, the pantheistic inference appears to gather an overpowering weight, in no way to be evaded. As registered in the terms of a rigorous empirical method, evolution presents the picture of a cosmic Whole, constituted of varying members descended from its own primitive form by differentiations so slight and gradual as not to suggest difference of origin or distinction in kind, but, on the contrary, to indicate clearly their kinship and community of origin. Still, these differentiations among the members, and the consequent differences in their adaptation to the Whole, involve a difference in their power to persist amid the mutual competition which their common presence in the Whole implies. In this silent and unconscious competition of tendencies to persist, which is called, by a somewhat exaggerated metaphor, the struggle for existence, the members of the least adaptation to the Whole must perish earliest, and only those of the highest adaptation will finally survive. So, by an exaggeration akin to that of the former metaphor, we may name the resulting persistence of the members most suited to the Whole the survival of the fittest; and as it is the Whole that determines the standard of adaptation, we may also, by figuratively personifying the Whole, call the process of antagonistic interaction through which the survivors persist a process of natural selection. Here, now, the points of determinative import for inference are these: that the "survival" is only of the *fittest to the Whole*; that it is the Whole alone that "selects"; that no "survival," as verified to the strictly empirical method, can be taken as permanent, but that even the latest must be reckoned as certified only to date, with a reservation, at best, of "tentative expectancy" for hope of continuance; that "natural selection," as empirically verified, is a process of cancellation, a selection only to death; and that the Whole alone has the possibility of final survival. The "tentative expectation" founded on the entire sweep of the observed facts, and not extended beyond it, would be that the latest observed survivor, man, is destined, like his predecessors, to pass away, supplanted by some new variation of the Whole, of a higher fitness to it. And so on, endlessly.

This clear pointing, by an empirically established and empirically construed doctrine of evolution, toward the One-and-All that swallows all, seems to gain further clearness still when the principles of conservation and of evolution are considered, as they must be, in their inseparable connection. They work in and through each other. Conservation and correlation of energy, and their "rider" of dissipation, are in the secret of the mechanism of the process of natural selection, with its deaths and its survivals; evolution is the field, and its resulting forms of existence, more and more complex, are the outcome of the operations of the correlated, conserved, and dissipated energies; and, in its principle of struggle and survival, evolution works in its turn in the very process of the correlation, dissipation, and conservation of energy. It therefore seems but natural to identify the potential energy—the "waste-heap" of power—of correlation with the Whole of natural selection. And thus we appear to reach, by a cumulative argument, the One and Only in which all shall be absorbed.

If we now add to these several indications, both of the method and of the two organic results of modern science, the further weighty discredit that the principles of conservation and evolution appear to cast upon the belief in freedom and immortality, the pantheistic tone in modern science will sound out to the full. This discredit comes, for human free-agency, from the closer nexus that the correlation of forces seems plainly to establish between every possible human action and the antecedent or environing chain of events in nature out of which the web of its motives must be woven; and from the pitch and proclivity that must be transmitted, according to the principle of evolution, by the heredity inseparable from the process of descent. For immortality, the discredit comes, by way of the principle of evolution, through its indication, under the restrictions of the empirical method, of the transitoriness of all survivals, and through its necessary failure to supply any evidence whatever of even a *possible* survival beyond the sensible world, with which empirical evolution has alone to do; while, by way of the principle of the conservation and dissipation of energy, the discredit comes from the doom that manifestly seems to await all forms of actual energy, taken in connection with the general discredit of everything unattested by the senses, which the persistent culture of empiricism begets.

In short, while the empirical method ignores, and must ignore, any supersensible principle of existence whatever, thus tending to the identification of the Absolute with the Sum of Things, evolution and the principle of conservation have familiarized the modern mind with the continuity, the unity, and the uniformity of nature in an overwhelming degree. In the absence of the conviction, upon independent grounds, that the Principle of existence is personal and rational, the sciences of nature can hardly fail, even upon a somewhat considerate and scrutinizing view, to convey the impression that the Source of things is a vast and shadowy Whole, which sweeps onward to an unknown destination, "regardless," as one of the leaders of modern science has said, "of consequences," and unconcerned as to the fate of man's world of effort and hope, apparently so circumscribed and insignificant in comparison.

IX. MODERN SCIENCE IS, STRICTLY, NON-PANTHEISTIC

But now that we come to the closer question, whether this impression is really warranted, we stand in need of exact discrimination. With such discrimination we shall find that, decided as the inference to pantheism from the methods and principles just discussed seems to be, it is, after all, illegitimate.

Our first caution here must be to remember that it is not science in its entire compass that is concerned in the question we are discussing. It is only "modern science," popularly so called—that is, science taken to mean only the science of nature; and not only so, but further restricted to signify only what may fitly enough be described as the *natural* science of nature; that is, so much of the possible knowledge of nature as can be reached through the channels of the senses; so much, in short, as will yield itself to a method strictly observational and empirical.

Hence, the real question is, whether empirical science, confined to nature as its proper object, can legitimately assert the theory of pantheism. And with regard now, first, to the argument drawn with such apparent force from the mere method of natural science, it should be plain to a more scrutinizing reflection that shifting from the legitimate *disregard* of a supersensible principle, which is the right of the empirical method, to the deliberate assumption that there *is* no such principle, because there is and can be no sensible evidence of it, is an abuse of the method in question—an unwarrantable extension of its province to decisions lying by its own terms beyond its ken. This shifting is made upon the assumption that there can be no science founded on any other than empirical evidence. That there is, and can be, no science deserving the name, except that which follows the empirical method of mere *natural* science, is a claim which men of science are prone to make, but which the profoundest thinkers the world has known—such minds as Plato, or Aristotle, or Hegel—have certainly pronounced a claim unfounded, and, indeed, a sheer assumption, contradicted by evidence the clearest, if oftentimes abstruse. When, instead of blindly following experience, we raise the question of the real nature and the sources of experience itself, and push it in earnest, it then appears that the very possibility of the experience that seems so rigorously to exclude supersensible principles, and particularly the rational personality of the First Principle, is itself dependent for its existence on such Principle and principles; that, in fact, these enter intellectually into its very constitution. But, in any case, this question of the nature of experience, of the limits of possible knowledge, and whether these last are identical with the limits of possible experience, is one in the taking up of which we abandon the field of nature and enter the very different field of the theory of cognition. In this, the pursuer of natural science, as such, has not a word to say. Here his method is altogether insufficient and unavailing; if the problem can be solved at all, it can only be by methods that transcend the bounds of merely empirical evidence.

So, again, in the inferences to pantheism from the conservation of energy and the principle of evolution. Strong as the evidence seems, it arises in both cases from violating the strict principles of the natural scientific method. All inferences to a whole of potential energy, or to a whole determinant of the survivals in a struggle for existence, are really inferences—passings beyond the region of the experimental and sensible *facts* into the empirically unknown, empirically unattested, empirically unwarranted region of supersensible *principles*. The exact scientific truth about all such inferences, and the supposed realities which they establish, is, that they are unwarranted by natural science; and that this refusal of warrant is only the expression by natural science of its incompetency to enter upon such questions.

Natural science may therefore be said to be silent on this question of pantheism; as indeed it is, and from the nature of the case must be, upon all theories of the supersensible whatever—whether theistic, deistic, or atheistic. Natural science has no proper concern with them. Science may well enough be said to be non-pantheistic, but so also is it non-theistic, non-deistic, non-atheistic. Its position, however, is not for that reason anti-pantheistic any more than it is anti-theistic, or anti-deistic, or anti-atheistic. It is rather *agnostic*, in the sense, that is, of declining to affect knowledge in the premises, because these are beyond its method and province. In short, its agnosticism is simply its *neutrality*, and does not in the least imply that agnosticism is the final view of things. The investigation of the final view, the search for the First Principle, science leaves to methods far other than her own of docile sense-experience—methods that philosophy is now prepared to vindicate as higher and far more trustworthy. Yet, when once the supersensible Principle is reached in some other way—the way of philosophy, as distinguished from that of natural science—science will then furnish the most abundant confirmations, the strongest corroborations; the more abundant and the stronger in proportion as the First Principle presented by philosophy ascends, evolution-wise, from materialism, through pantheism, to rational theism. For science *accords* most perfectly with the latter, although she is, in herself, wholly unable to attain the vision of it. But it must be a theism that subsumes into its conceptions of God and man all the irrefutable insights of materialism, of deism, and, eminently, of pantheism; of which, as I will hope this paper has shown, there are those of the greatest pertinence and reality, if also of the most undeniable insufficiency.

NOTES

1. I must be understood here as reflecting only upon the popular thaumaturgical conceptions of the supernatural. The genuine doctrine of miracle has, to my mind, a speculative truth at its basis, profound and irrefragable; the truth, namely, that the causal organization of nature—the system of ever-ascending evolution from cause to differing effect—can never be accounted for in terms of the mere sensible antecedents, but requires the omnipresent activity of an immanent but supersensible, transcendent, rationally personal cause; and that the system of nature is therefore a Perpetual Miracle. The natural order flowing from this Miracle is, however, immutable and irreversible, and irreconcilable with the possibility of "miracle" in the vulgar sense.

INDEX OF NAMES

INDEX OF SUBJECTS

www.ingramcontent.com/pod-product-compliance
Lightning Source LLC
Chambersburg PA
CBHW082107290526
45822CB00023B/498